Evolutionary Anthropology

Evolutionary Anthropology

An Introduction to Physical Anthropology and Archaeology

Edward Staski

New Mexico State University

Jonathan Marks

Yale University

Harcourt Brace Jovanovich College Publishers

Fort Worth   Philadelphia   San Diego   New York   Orlando   Austin   San Antonio
Toronto   Montreal   London   Sydney   Tokyo

Publisher	Ted Buchholz
Acquisitions Editor	Christopher P. Klein
Developmental Editor	Stacy Schoolfield
Senior Project Editor	Charlie Dierker
Production Manager	Ken Dunaway
Manager of Art & Design	Guy Jacobs
Text Design	Duo Design Group
Cover Design	Patty Ryan
Photo Research	Molly Shepard
Cover	Tufa formations at sunset, Mono Lake, Calif.

This book is dedicated to Pauline Darcy-Staski and Jennifer Staski, and to Renée and Richard Marks.

Library of Congress Cataloging-in-Publication Data

Staski, Edward.
    Evolutionary anthropology: an introduction to physical
anthropology and archaeology / Edward Staski, Jonathan Marks.
       p.   cm.
    Includes bibliographical references and index.
    1. Physical anthropology.   2. Archaeology.   3. Human Evolution
I. Marks, Jonathan M.   II. Title
GN50.8.S72   1991
573—dc20

ISBN: 0-03-23732-7

Address for Editorial Correspondence
Harcourt Brace Jovanovich, Publishers, 301 Commerce Street, Suite 3700, Fort Worth, TX 76102

Address for Orders
Harcourt Brace Jovanovich, Publishers, 6277 Sea Harbor Drive, Orlando, FL 32887
1-800-782-4479, or 1-800-433-0001 (in Florida)

Printed in the United States of America

2 3 4 5   039   9 8 7 6 5 4 3 2 1

Photo credits appear following the index.

Preface

Evolutionary Anthropology introduces students to evolution in its two most common spheres, as studied within the discipline of anthropology. The two spheres are *biological* and *cultural*—how we as a species have come to be as we are (biological evolution) and how we as members of society have come to be as we are (cultural evolution). Biological evolution concerns physical changes that have brought our bodies to their recognizably human form. Cultural evolution refers to behavioral and organizational changes that have shaped the contemporary state of our lives.

The key variable in any sphere of evolution is time. The processes or mechanisms of evolution and their results can be studied either through time or at a specific point in time. The text discusses both approaches: *diachronic* (through time) and *synchronic* (at one time). Comparisons are used extensively to examine different species and societies that exist now and existed in the past.

Intellectual history is also a theme of this text. We want to examine not only what contemporary scientists think about biological and cultural evolution, but also what earlier scientists thought and why that thinking has changed. Instead of using tables and lists of data for students to memorize, we present frameworks for understanding the data. Data are used primarily to illustrate theories and ideas of contemporary anthropologists.

Section One of *Evolutionary Anthropology* includes Chapters One, Two, Three, and Four. This section begins with an introduction to the discipline of anthropology. Because human behavior is to a large extent symbolic, we discuss the nature of symbols. We introduce the four subfields of anthropology: biological anthropology, archaeology, cultural anthropology, and anthropological linguistics.

We discuss the nature of science, and of anthropological science in particular. Science is a cultural product, a world view derived from eighteenth-century European society. It is important that we understand the way in which science developed if we are to understand the way it currently operates—what science is, what scientists do, and what they can ultimately promise and deliver. We review the general ways in which one carries out field research in a modern scientific manner. We then trace the development of theory concerning human origins and behaviors from the seventeenth century, which witnessed fundamental changes in the way people thought about human nature, the relations of animal species to one another, the history of the world, and the way the natural world could be comprehended by the human mind. We then summarize the modern theories of biological and cultural evolution.

The second section incorporates Chapters Five and Six, with an emphasis on synchronic approaches to the study of biological evolutionary products. We do this by looking at the diversity of living primates, those animal species most closely related to our own, and by looking at the different ways in which primates behave. We recognize some of the important implications this information has in understanding our own evolution.

The third section of this text consists of Chapters Seven, Eight, and Nine. This section examines synchronic approaches to understanding how biological evolution works. The principles of heredity are presented, and the genetic relationships of humans to other primates are examined. The biological diversity that exists among contemporary human populations, how it has been studied in the past, and how it can most profitably be studied in the future are also discussed.

In the fourth section (Chapters Ten, Eleven, and Twelve) we take a diachronic approach to biological and cultural evolution, considering not *how things happen* but *what has happened*. We introduce the principles of studying the past, the ways it differs from studying contemporary phenomena, and the advantages and liabilities it presents. We then apply this to the study of the 65 million years of primate evolution. We next turn to the 2.5 million years during which our genus *Homo* has existed, examining both the anatomical and technological aspects of its emergence and continuity.

The fifth section (Chapters Thirteen, Fourteen, and Fifteen) continues the diachronic analysis, focusing on three major watersheds in human prehistory and history. Theories and data concerning the rise of domestication and then the evolution of complex society are reviewed. Discussions of the European Middle Ages and the Industrial Revolution, relatively recent periods in human culture history follow. We note that both domestication and complexity arose independently in several parts of the world, while industrialism was unique to western Europe. Treating this most recent series of events is rare in anthropology texts, though necessary if a total history is to be presented.

The concluding section of the book (Chapters Sixteen, Seventeen, and Eighteen) brings us back to synchronic studies, the study of contemporary societies. First, we discuss the archaeology of living people, the study of relationships between human behavior and material culture that are occurring now. Then, we consider the related roles of biology and culture in creating and shaping human lives. We face the ancient issue of "nature vs. nurture" and show it to be an uninformed question, given the complexity of biological and cultural interdependence. Finally, we conclude with the importance of anthropological knowledge, the role anthropologists can play in applying their expertise to the resolution of real human issues.

We would like to thank the various colleagues, friends, and students who took time to read and comment on portions of this text: Jacqueline Beidl, Laura Bishop, Timothy Bromage, Amos Deinard, Andrew Hill, Daria Lucas, Sally McBrearty, Fred Plog, Alison Richard, Alfred Rosenberger, Scott Rushforth, Michael Schiffer, David Sprague, Karen B. Strier, Wenda Trevathan, and Steadman Upham. We also want to thank our colleagues who reviewed this text. Their constructive comments and suggestions helped us throughout the development of *Evolutionary Anthropology:* Robert Bailey, University of California, Los Angeles; David Begun, Smithsonian Institute; Richard Davis, Bryn Mawr College; Steven Falconer, Arizona State University; Kathleen Fine, Fort Lewis College; Nicholas Fintzelberg, San Diego Mesa College; Paul A. Garber, University of Illinois, Urbana Champaign; Michael S. Gibbons, University of Massachusetts, Boston; David Glassman, Southwest Texas State University; Francis Harrold, University of Texas at Arlington; H. Leedom Lefferts, Drew University; Lawrence Martin, State University of New York; Stony Brook; Don Lenkit, Modesto Junior College; Donald H. Morris, Arizona State University; Charles Norris, William Rainey Harper College; and David Weaver, Wake Forest University.

We would also like to thank the various people at Harcourt Brace Jovanovich for making this all possible, especially Stacy Schoolfield.

Finally, we would like to recognize a shared intellectual heritage. We each received our Ph.Ds from the University of Arizona, Department of Anthropology. In recognition of the department's seventy-fifth year, we would like to express our gratitude to those who inspired us and many others through the years.

Table of Contents

Understanding Our Place in Nature

Introducing Anthropology

Introducing Anthropology

anthropology
The study of humans; their biology and behavior; their beliefs and views; their antecedents, relatives, and present conditions.

What Is Anthropology?

This is a book about **anthropology**, the study of our species. More precisely, we define anthropology as the social science that tries to explain the totality of human beings and human experience, both biological and nonbiological (or cultural), in all times and from all places. Clearly, this is a vast field of research and learning (Figure 1–1). Indeed, although the focus of anthropology is our own species, *Homo sapiens*, anthropology does not stop there. *Homo sapiens* does not exist in isolation but rather as part of a stream of life history, and therefore the study of our species includes the study of the ancestors of our species and of the close relatives of our species.

HUMAN BIOLOGY AND BEHAVIOR

Anthropology investigates human biology and behavior in its manifold forms and antecedents. Like all modern sciences, anthropology studies variation and focuses on contrasts in order to understand its subject. Just as a biologist may study different forms of life in order to understand the principles of life or as a chemist may study the properties of different compounds in order to understand the ways in which elements combine, an anthropologist studies the forms and behaviors of different groups of people and of the different species of **primates** in order to understand who we are and how we came to be.

primates
A group of closely related mammals. Humans belong to this group.

As an academic discipline, anthropology is unique for the breadth of its study. It is often characterized as **holistic** because it concerns all human beings in a number of diverse ways. There is more, however. Traditionally, academic curricula are divided into four categories: the physical sciences, the natural sciences, the social sciences, and the humanities. Anthropology encompasses parts of each of these, using approaches derived from all. For example, in the study of fossil humans and past cultures, the principles of geology (a physical science) must be applied. Many archaeological investigations also draw from disciplines such as history (primarily part of the humanities) and geography (a social science). And in the study of human evolution, the principles of evolutionary biology (a natural science) must be mastered and applied.

holistic
Broad in scope, emphasizing the functional interactions among parts of systems; the opposite of *atomistic*.

In addition to being partly a "hard science," anthropology is also the study of human behavior, which makes it a social science, overlapping subjects such as economics and psychology. And finally, because human behavior, as we shall see, is largely mediated by symbols, much of anthrpology involves *interpretation*, which makes it overlap the humanities.

This fusion of "hard" and "soft" science in anthropology creates its central tension: tension between the scientific and humanistic approaches to its subject matter. Is the goal of anthropology to *explain* human behavior or to *interpret* human behavior? Anthropologists are divided in their attempts to answer that question. Nevertheless, this tension has the effect of generating complementary approaches, some of which are analytical and scientific, and others of which are **hermeneutic** and humanistic.

DEVELOPMENT OF CULTURE

Why is this tension—or even confusion—embedded within the primary goals of anthropology at all? Because the key biological adaptation of the human species, unique among all the extant flora and fauna of the earth, is the development of **culture**. Culture is the historical accumulation of **symbolic** knowledge possessed by a society. We discuss this at greater length below, but for now, let us focus on the word *symbolic*.

Symbolism is an **arbitrary** association between two things in the mind of an observer. These two things might be a sound and an image, for example. The sounds that compose the articulated word *water* might conjure an image of a waterfall, or the idea of general wetness, or that of a thirst quenched (Figure 1–2). Yet the association between the sound and the image is arbitrary, for the image could as easily have been evoked by the articulated words *aqua* or *mayim*—if the person listening were a native speaker of Latin or Hebrew rather than English. There is nothing intrinsically watery about the word *water*—it is simply the combination of sounds *that our society recognizes* to be symbolic of that wet stuff. Thus, the association is arbitrary—to another society, it most likely would be another combination of sounds. This is the basis of human thought and expresses itself in virtually all aspects of our lives.

Art is a distinctively human form of communication. Its sole purpose is to evoke thoughts symbolically. And art, as pictorial symbols of ideas, pervades every sphere of our behavior—from the economic (check the artwork on a dollar bill), to the political (think of the flag), to the social and technological, to the purely recreational (Figure 1–3).

The Subdisciplines of Anthropology

Traditionally, American anthropology has been divided into four subfields. **Physical** or **biological anthropology** has as its central foci the place of humans among the living and extinct species of the earth and biological variation among contemporary humans. **Archaeology** has as its focus the material remains of human behavior, in large measure the remains of past cultures. **Cultural anthropology** is the study of contemporary societies: how the behavior, symbol systems, and modes of thought of people in different societies vary. **Linguistic anthropology** studies the most quintessential human symbol system—language.

hermeneutic

Inferring or finding meanings, especially hidden ones.

culture

The historical accumulation of symbolic knowledge possessed by a society.

symbol

An arbitrary association between two things in the mind of an observer.

arbitrary

Based on choice or custom rather than on physical or natural law.

physical anthropology, biological anthropology

Study of the place of the human species in nature; biological variation among humans and between humans and their relatives and ancestors.

archaeology

Study of the material remains of cultures and their patterns, particularly as they relate to patterns of human behavior.

cultural anthropology

Study of the differences and similarities among contemporary human societies; often divided into ethnography (detailed studies of specific groups) and ethnology (analyses of features common to many groups).

linguistic anthropology

Study of human communication, in primarily mental and social aspects.

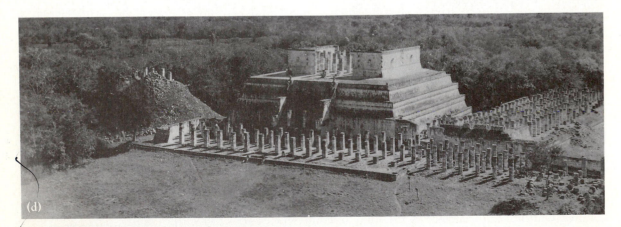

Figure 1-1. The diverse subject matter of anthropology.

Anthropologists study (a) aspects of modern industrial society; (b) non-Western, nonindustrial societies, such as this family in Rwanda; (c) nonhuman primates, such as this macaque; (d) ancient societies, such as this Mesoamerican city.

Figure 1-2. Diverse images associated symbolically with water.
(a) Tranquility, a lake; (b) thirst; (c) danger, a flood; (d) purity, a baptism.

Figure 1–3. Familiar examples of art, a uniquely human medium of communication.

Ideas, feelings, and aesthetics are transmitted or stimulated symbolically this way.

Generally, cultural anthropologists and linguistic anthropologists approach their subject matter more humanistically, while physical anthropologists and archaeologists approach theirs more scientifically. This is because a primary goal of the first two subfields is to understand how people approach the world and why they say and do things the way that they do. Their subject matter is, consequently, to a large extent records of things said and done. The subject matter of physical anthropology and archaeology, on the other hand, tends to be more concrete and, therefore, more amenable to scientific study. While the focus of this book is on the scientific side of anthropology, it is important to appreciate the complexity of our species by understanding how anthropology is both humanistic and scientific.

The humanistic side of anthropological research argues that if we want to understand human behavior, we have to learn to interpret other people's symbol systems. But interpreting symbols is not science. On the other hand, humans think symbolically, and that is in large measure what being human, and being a part of a culture, is all about. Therefore, the argument runs, in order to understand other cultures, we cannot be scientists because the interpretation of cultures is not amenable to scientific study. It is by nature humanistic. One can learn about American culture by reading Tom Wolfe, or by watching "Dallas," or by analyzing the rules and passions of football—but experiments and statistics will not help an outsider understand what it means to be part of American society. And this humanistic focus in anthropology emphasizes meaning. To learn about a culture, one must understand its symbols; one must learn what they mean to the people.

Cultural and Linguistic Anthropology: The Symbolic Nature of Human Behavior

All animals communicate. One bee must tell another where the nectar is. One bird must tell another not to come into its territory. This kind of communication involves **signs**—stereotypical sounds or motions that indicate very limited and highly specific information (Figure 1–4).

LANGUAGE

Human communication is considerably different from the communication systems of other species. It can be used to refer to things that do not exist or that existed in the past. It can be used to evoke emotional states, to insult, or to praise. It reinforces the identity of local populations—ethnic groups and other subcultures. It enables humans to build on one another's ideas. All humans have and need a language system. And most significantly, language is highly symbolic and based on shared rules (like other aspects of culture), thus encapsulating in large measure what it means to be a human.

The symbolic nature of language illustrates another aspect of human behavior—that much of it is unconscious and simply taken for granted. Yet language is structured according to very precise rules. These rules are highly arbitrary and extend through four levels.

Phonological Rules   The first arbitrary level concerns which sounds are meaningful. The human body is capable of producing many sounds, but in any language, only a subset is used—the rest are meaningless. For example, to Spanish speakers, the word *perro* is pronounced with a trilled *r* and means "dog". The word *pero* is pronounced with a rolled *r* and means "but." To American English speakers, who do not use the trilled *r,* the two words sound slightly different but are perceived as merely slightly different pronunciations of the same set of sounds. Usually, an English speaker cannot even duplicate the sound of the trilled *r.* Why? Because the difference between a trilled *r* and a rolled *r* is not meaningful in English. It *is* in Spanish.

This is, of course, a direct parallel to the stereotypical speaker of Japanese who may have difficulty distinguishing the *r* and *l* sounds in English. And yet these are but two minor examples of how languages differ in their concepts of which sounds are meaningful and which are not. Many South African languages use clicks. Many languages make use of the guttural *ch* sound, as in pronouncing the Jewish holiday Chanukah. French uses nasal sounds; the possible examples are innumerable. Further, there are rules about how certain sounds can be used. For example, the *ng* sound in English can be used in the middle or at the end of a word, but it

sign

An indication of an object that is highly specific, not arbitrary, as smoke indicates fire; contrasting with symbol, in which the connection between the indicator and its referent is arbitrary.

Figure 1-4

Bees communicate, but not symbolically.

phonology

The study of the sounds in human speech.

cannot start a word. There is no good reason why not—that sound can start a word in Swahili.

These rules are at the level of **phonological** information. There exists, at this level, a set of unconscious rules for distinguishing which sounds are meaningful in a language and which are not—a set of rules that speakers know but of which they are not consciously aware.

Morphological Rules   All meaningful sounds are combined into words or parts of words, which are themselves assigned meanings. Thus, the series of sounds that comprise the word *book* is assigned to mean something—namely, a book. Or, the *s* sound at the end of a word may mean something—namely, more than one of them. These, again, are arbitrary and unconscious rules, and they exist at a second level of arbitrariness. We call this the level of **morphological** information.

morphology

The study of meanings of words or parts of words.

grammar

The way in which a language organizes words to express thoughts in a recognizable and appropriate manner; syntax.

Grammatical Rules   Groups of words can express thoughts, but in order to do so, they must be combined in special ways. These rules may be a bit more conscious, as we often have to confront them formally in English class. Nevertheless, the **grammatical** structure of languages varies greatly. In English, we can say, "John ate broccoli," but not "John broccoli ate". This is because proper English dictates an order of words that proceeds subject–verb–object, not subject–object–verb. On the other hand, sentences in Latin and many other languages could be ordered subject–object–verb. These rules exist at a third level of arbitrariness—the level of grammatical information.

social

reflecting interactions among individuals.

Social Context   Finally, a level of **social** information is superimposed upon any utterance. The tone, the inflection of the words, the facial expression, and the nature of the interpersonal relationships present—can all convey meaningful information to members of the culture. When comedian Steve Martin said the sentence, "Well, excuse me" on "Saturday Night Live," it was amusing to those listening because of the irony he conveyed. Yet the amusement would not be enjoyed by someone who had a knowledge of only the phonological, morphological, and grammatical information of that statement. Indeed, the meaning of "Well, excuse me" can have very different (and sometimes unamusing) meanings, depending on the context. Now imagine living in another culture and struggling to learn the language so that you could communicate competently—then having to face up to such social realities as irony, inferring the opposite meaning of an utterance by virtue of only the way it is spoken!

CULTURE

Not only language, but all aspects of human behavior are permeated with arbitrary rules. These rules are not created each generation but are passed down with only slight variations from generation to generation. How to dress, those with whom you can pursue a sexual relationship, the kinds of foods you should or should not eat, where you can live, how you can support yourself —all these are aspects of culture, and all are mediated by sets of rules like those of language. To understand a culture, one must understand its rules—one must get inside the heads of the people following them.

Interpreting rules across human groups and understanding the variation in expression of human behavior across the world is the province of cultural anthropology. Understanding the most pervasive rules, the linguistic ones, which in some measure create the categories perceived as significant by people, is the province of linguistic anthropology. Both these endeavors involve getting inside people's heads and understanding how they think about the world—or how they *think* they think about the world. It is thus often highly interpretative and humanistic.

It is not known when the various cultural rules evolved, but it is clear that they are in some fundamental way a product of our biological heritage. The name of our species, *Homo sapiens*, (literally, "wise person") might profitably be interpreted as "person wise enough to make, to follow, and to understand the complex rules of culture." The specific rules vary, but following a set of rules is what it means to be a part of a culture, and thereby an integral part of what it means to be human.

Alternative approaches in anthropology involve analyzing material (as opposed to mental) data and trying to explain human phenomena in a more objective or scientific fashion. In general, this is the approach taken by physical, or biological, anthropology and by archaeology.

Physical Anthropology and Archaeology

Physical anthropology is the study of the evolution of our species. It is, therefore, the study of our origin, our similarities and differences from other species, our relationships to other species, and the biological variation that currently exists within our species.

Archaeology is the study of the relationships between patterns of material culture and patterns of human behavior. Material culture consists of all the objects humans manufacture or otherwise manipulate. Many archaeologists study the past because material culture is often preserved, but it is not necessary to do so in order to be an archaeologist (see Table 1–1).

Table 1–1:

Major Branches of Archaeology and Physical Anthropology

Archaeology	Physical Anthropology
Prehistoric archaeology	Paleoanthropology
Historical archaeology	Human biology and variation
Ethnoarchaeology	Primate evolution
Modern material cultures	Primate behavior

evolution

Modification and divergence
through time.

As scientific subdisciplines of anthropology, physical anthropology and archaeology share a focus on **evolution**—descent and the emergence of diversity. Physical anthropology focuses on our biological evolution, asking questions about the roots of the human species. Archaeology focuses on cultural evolution, asking how human societies have emerged and changed through time.

This text focuses on evolution, the unifying scientific principle. Evolution means change. Our species has evolved from ape to human within the last few million years. The societies of our more recent ancestors have evolved from an economic system based on gathering and hunting and a social system in which all people had roughly equal status and lived principally in small groups composed of relatives, to our modern industrial though impersonal societies over the last several thousand years.

The nature of these changes and how they have occurred is the subject of *Evolutionary Anthropology*. As we will see elsewhere, particularly in Chapter 2, evolution is one of many possible ways of interpreting human history, but it is the only one compatible with the standards of modern scholarship and science. Thus, in order to understand who we are and how we came to be, we have to understand how change occurs, and has occurred, in both biological and cultural systems. These processes have often been confused and need to be teased apart in order to understand who and what we are. The intellectual history of the study of human biological and cultural evolution, how we have come to the current understanding of the subject, is discussed in Chapter 3.

EVOLUTIONARY PROCESSES AND PRODUCTS

evolutionary process

Mechanism by which evolution
occurs.

Anthropologists study both **evolutionary processes** and **evolutionary products**. Evolutionary processes are the mechanisms by which change occurs. These are discussed in Chapter 4.

evolutionary product

Results of the action of evolution.

Evolutionary products can be analyzed in two principal ways: by studying and comparing related lineages or societies at the same time (a **synchronic** study) or by studying specific lineages or societies changing through time (a **diachronic** study). In Chapters 5 through 9, we examine our evolutionary history synchronically, and in Chapters 10 through 15 we examine the evolution of our species diachronically.

synchronic

Analysis of things occurring at
one time.

The Relation between Biological and Cultural Evolution

diachronic

Analysis of things occurring
through time.

Our form and behavior is the result of our evolution. Our form, our appearance, is the result of genetic evolution, though considerable leeway at all times is provided by variation in the environment. Our behavior, similarly, is the product of cultural evolution, though there is room for individual choice. Yet our prior biological history constrains the range of possible morphologies that the environment can elicit, just as our prior cultural history constrains the kinds of decisions we have available to us.

Biological and cultural evolution are processes that have often been confused, even by anthropologists. The reasons they have been confused are that they are both operating on humans and are both concerned with change. They consist, however, of different sets of processes and are related to each other only by **analogy**.

Evolution, either biological or cultural, is simply descent and diversity with modification. Thus, it involves time (descent), space (diversity), and change (modification). Biological evolution is the change in appearance, or more fundamentally, genetic makeup, in groups of organisms. Cultural evolution is the change in behaviors and ideas in societies. These may overlap in certain ways, but they proceed by intrinsically different laws, and while both are critical for our understanding of the human species, it is most useful to keep them analytically separate.

BIOLOGICAL ADAPTATION

Much of evolution is concerned with **adaptation**—how an organism relates to its environment. All animal species adapt principally through biological evolution. Humans do as well, to some extent. There are groups of humans who, relative to the members of other groups, retain heat more efficiently, for example. Others radiate heat more efficiently, and others are more or less resistant to certain diseases. Some groups require more or less sunlight to activate their vitamin D than do other groups. Human groups can so distinguish themselves in numerous ways. Yet, all are unique in the extent to which they are not limited by their biology.

analogy

The reasoning that if two things are similar in a certain way, then they are also similar in other ways.

adaptation

(1) the process of maintaining a relationship between an organism or species and its environment; (2) a specific feature of an organism or species that enables it to function efficiently in its environment.

Figure 1-5

The development of artificial illumination permits a human society to function at night, for humans ordinarily cannot see very well in the dark.

technology

All the ways in which a group of people provide themselves with resources and produce energy from the environment.

CULTURAL ADAPTATION

Technology enables humans lacking particular biological adaptations to function as or more efficiently than people better biologically adapted. Thus, warm clothing, vitamin D-supplemented milk, and vaccines are all ways in which culture has enabled poorly adapted populations to adapt in powerful, nonbiological ways (Figure 1–5).

Culture is, in this sense, the great equalizer. It makes any human group as adequate as any other in a given environment. More than that, it makes humans the equals or superiors of any other species in a given environment. While a human is no physical match for a leopard, a human with a spear or gun may well be.

Technology is thus the primary adaptive component of culture. The emergence of technology is first apparent in the material record as chipped stone tools, manufactured over 2 million years ago. While it is possible that humans used antlers, bones, or sticks as tools before then, these are not detectable as tools in the material record. Such materials would not be preserved over long periods of time. Thus, we can say that technology has been a part of our lineage for *at least* a little more than 2 million years.

The crude pebble tools of our ancestors are not terribly impressive by our standards (Figure 1–6), and it is difficult to imagine that they made a great difference to the general adaptation of the species that used them. In the past few tens of thousands of years, however, the descendants of those species became fully dependent on the technological descendants of those tools. The survival of the organisms became, at some time, intimately involved with the development and use of the technology. Our ancestors made the crucial evolutionary step when technology provided an efficient, highly responsive, and easily altered manner of coping with the environment. It is that technology which has provided humans with the capability of thriving on every continent, in varied climates, with varied diets, and with different animals and plants surrounding them. Human evolutionary history over the past few millennia has been primarily cultural evolution—the many ways in which humans have exploited the resources available, coped technologically with their surroundings, and built on and reacted to previous cultural developments.

Figure 1-6

Both stone tools and high-powered rifles can be useful in subsistence. Our ancestors' success in using stone tools ultimately resulted in the development of more complex technologies.

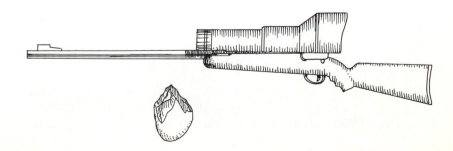

Human history unfolds as first principally biological evolution, then principally cultural evolution. It is important to remember, however, that cultural evolution was proceeding in our biological ancestors. Hundreds of thousands of years ago, before our species had evolved, culture started to be nearly as important as biology as an adaptive mechanism. By 30,000 or 40,000 years ago, it had become our primary means of adaptation, and with the emergence of animal and plant domestication, only several thousand years ago, it has become virtually a new environment in itself and the most obvious cause of diversity in appearance from group to group. Nevertheless, biological evolution is still occurring, as genetic changes in response to environmental stresses continue. What is different now is the relative significance of the adaptations to human survival. Presently, cultural adaptations are vastly more important than are biological adaptations. In all human societies, the most prevalent and most efficient way of dealing with the environment is through technology—through culture.

Culture: The Human Adaptation

Culture is the historical accumulation of symbolic knowledge possessed by a group of people, a **society**. A culture's symbols, including those of its language, are developed over time.

SYMBOLS

A symbol can be a powerful and often unconscious stimulus of behaviors or emotional states. Consider the effect of desecrating the American flag, as opposed to any other country's flag, on Americans (Figure 1–7). Obviously, a citizen of another country would be expected to have a similar reaction, but in this case, only when *that* country's flag is desecrated. Why? Because different flags have different symbolic associations for different groups of people.

Consider the behavior of humans who cry after seeing a movie like *E.T.* or a musical like *Les Misérables* (Figure 1–8). This is again a peculiarly human characteristic. Storytelling is present in all human societies but absent in all other species, and its purpose is to evoke emotional states and ideas symbolically, usually through language, but even more effectively through images or movements.

Symbols vary from group to group, but all human groups have and use them. Shared symbols bind people together not simply because they share a language, but because they share the same behaviors and elicited feelings.

CULTURAL HISTORY

A second significant aspect of culture is that it is cumulative. A culture has a history on which it has built. In the same way that any species at any time is partly a make-over of its ancestors, a culture at any time is partly a make-over of its antecedents. Just as we are physically made-over

Figure 1-7

The burning of an American flag is such a powerful symbol that many Americans would like to restrict other citizens' freedom of expression and make it illegal.

society

A group, or population, of interacting individuals, and the ways in which they interact.

Figure 1-8
Although *Les Misérables* relates events that never occurred in "real life," it evokes powerful emotions in humans as literature and theater. Here, Eponine, who has harbored unrequited love for Marius, dies in his arms as the rebelling students look on.

apes, we are culturally made-over gatherer-hunters and nonindustrial agriculturalists.

Thus, a culture at any time is in some sense a result of and a response to earlier times. We can build on the ideas of our predecessors—we can do as they did, or we can improve on their work by learning from their mistakes (though unfortunately, we often do not). Sometimes we simply keep our forebears' ideas with us, such as blessing someone who has sneezed, eating three meals a day rather than two or four, or giving children their father's last name.

Economy and Technology Many such conservative elements of culture exist. By contrast, the most dynamic aspects are in the areas of economy and technology, where technology can change in response to the perceived needs of the society. How a society interacts with its environment and extracts the necessities of life from it are obviously of fundamental importance for the survival of the people involved and the maintenance of their quality of life. But the solutions to problems always arise from preexisting technology. Thus, the aspect of culture involved in helping people cope, the technological aspect, is a cumulative one. The people of one generation do not start afresh—they start with the technology, the solutions, and the problems they were left by the previous generation. As we will see later on, one generation's solutions invariably cause a later generation's problems. The important point, however, is that every generation has a starting point bequeathed to it by its history. Culture is a cumulative phenomenon.

SOCIETY AND CULTURE

In addition to being symbolic and cumulative, culture has a third element of interest: It is the property of a society, not of any particular individual.

That is, an individual person does not have a culture, any more than that person can have a death rate or a goal-line defense. These things are properties of a collectivity, not of any individual person. Certainly a person has knowledge and can make contributions to cultural change, but what any person knows is only a tiny portion of the culture.

The vocabulary of the English language, for example, is far more vast than any single person can entirely command. Yet even though no single person could do it, society has produced the *Oxford English Dictionary*. While our society can produce televisions from ore, rubber, and a few other raw materials, that achievement is far beyond the capabilities of any individual (Figure 1–9). It requires refineries, precision manufacturing, metallurgy, polymer chemistry, glass blowing, and engineering, to name only a few of the resources and skills that would have to be mastered. Imagine yourself alone, with nothing but your good sense and raw materials—would you be able to build the institutions, both social and material, of the complex, modern world? No—an individual does not have that capacity. To return to the example of the television, even if you could construct one, you would have nothing to watch unless you also built a transmitter! Society is the unit of reference for culture and cultural evolution.

Thus, although televisions and every other object and institution we take for granted are obviously a part of our culture, the ability to construct them belongs to our society, not to any individual member of it. That is why it is incorrect to consider culture as information shared by

Figure 1-9

A television is not the product of any single mind but of the cumulative knowledge of society; many industries must be present before a television can be built and used.

people, although sometimes even anthropologists do. Some cultural information, the rules and knowledge discussed earlier, is shared among individuals. But probably little, if any, is shared by *all* the members of a society. The information on how to build a television from raw materials is shared by no one, yet it is a property possessed by the collectivity, the society. The knowledge that any individual has is a small subset of the cultural knowledge possessed by the society.

THREE ASPECTS OF CULTURE

Every human society has a culture. Cultures differ from one another as a result of divergence, borrowing and mixing, and descent through time, processes that we call cultural evolution. A general principle of cultural evolution is that culture is composed of three interrelated aspects—they are often thought of as subsystems of the overall cultural system. These three aspects are: 1) the *technological,* consisting of all the tools and techniques employed by a society to adapt to the physical and social environments; 2) the *societal,* consisting of all the relations within and among groups of people and the rules governing these relations; and 3) the **ideological,** consisting of the ideas and beliefs of the members of a society.

ideology

The ideas, beliefs, and attitudes of a group of people.

According to many anthropologists, the technological aspect plays a primary role in driving cultural evolution, being the most responsive to environmental stresses and being the most responsible for shaping the societal and ideological subsystems. Further, the societal is often seen as having a secondary role, while the part played by the ideological is tertiary, or least influential in shaping cultural evolutionary change. This view, called **cultural materialism**, traces its modern form to the works of Leslie White and Marvin Harris, two major figures in the anthropology of the latter half of the twentieth century. While controversial in its extreme forms, this perspective has been a useful guide for anthropologists and particularly for archaeologists, for whom technology is usually the most accessible part of a cultural system. And, after all, technology influences survival directly, and one has to survive before one can develop a kinship system or religion.

cultural materialism

The viewpoint that takes technology as the independent variable or as the aspect of culture that changes first and thereby influences other cultural subsystems disproportionately.

Technology does not shape everything in a culture. Both the societal and ideological subsystems can be influential at times, even on the nature of technology itself. Nevertheless, the broad sweep of cultural evolution suggests that technology has a primary role in influencing other aspects of cultural systems.

CULTURAL RELATIVISM

As we will see in Chapter 3, one of the long-standing themes of science has been the (false) notion of a **Great Chain of Being**, a single line on which all creatures could be ranked. This was undermined in the eighteenth and nineteenth centuries with the recognition that species formed clusters of descent from ancestral species. What one encounters, therefore, is not species that are *higher or lower* than one another, but species

Great Chain of Being

The belief that groups of organisms or cultures can be arranged along a single line from lowest to highest or worst to best.

that are *more or less closely related* to one another. Thus, some species may be more similar to humans than others, but all species are equal in any reasonably objective way one chooses to judge them.

Concurrently, social changes initiated in the United States, England, and France legalized the proposition that no *individual humans* were higher or lower than others. The aristocracy were no longer higher than the peasants, for example—all would enjoy equal rights under the law. Thus, some citizens may be wealthier than others, but all people are equal.

Somewhat more tenaciously, the idea of ranking different *cultures* linearly hung on until well into the twentieth century. This idea, of course, was useful to people who wished to subjugate other societies—if some societies were "lower," then domination by a "higher" society would be natural and destined. But what if, on the other hand, there were no higher or lower societies, but merely *different* ones? In that case, domination would be unjustified. In addition, the eradication of other societies would lead to the loss of considerable information about the scope of human behavior.

The doctrine of **cultural relativism**, promoted by Franz Boas and his students (Chapter 3), holds that (like species and like individual people) no culture is higher or lower than any other. Cultures differ, and they differ for various reasons, but they cannot be ranked on any scale of better or worse. They vary in nearly all conceivable ways, and that variation is to a large extent arbitrary. For example, beyond the necessity of keeping warm, there are many ways in which one could dress. But the style in which one chooses to dress is determined very rigidly by the cul-

cultural relativism
The view that cultures are different but not overall better or worse than one another.

Figure 1-10

Simply within our own culture, young middle-class Americans vary greatly in their styles of dress through time. Across classes and cultures and times, dress styles vary tremendously, although they all serve ostensibly the same function.

Issues in Anthropology 1–1

The Application of Cultural Relativism

The concept of cultural relativism carries some subtle but important implications for thinking about, and interacting with, other societies. We know, for example, that the Nazis in World War II committed atrocities of astounding proportions against civilians. We know this was a culmination of the ideology or philosophy that they or their leaders held. Can't we simply agree that our culture is "better" than theirs?

While it may be difficult to accept at face value, especially for those who fought in World War II, lost relatives, or simply grew up with the wartime propaganda, it is nevertheless important not to lose one's professionalism even when dealing with emotionally charged issues. We were certainly "better" than Nazi Germany if our standard is the value placed on individual human lives. By that criterion we rank above them, but why should that be the only criterion?

There are many nations and cultures out there, and many variables or criteria by which to rank them. In terms of the criterion above, we might well rank 1939 America above 1939 Germany. Yet the same criterion that we would use to rank ourselves in 1939 above the !Kung San of the Kalahari Desert—namely, technology—would put us below the Germans. So, the use of a single scale to rank cultures is arbitrary and subjective. But in the global perspective of diplomacy, two other points are significant.

First, we must remember that World War II was not fought because we disagreed with Nazi ideologies. If we went to war against everyone with whom we disagreed, there would soon be no other nations left, and we would destroy each other. We entered World War II for several reasons, most significantly the (accurate) perception of an immediate, physical threat to our society by the Axis powers.

Second, to suggest that the United States is blessed with a high degree of moral rectitude often strikes the citizens of other nations as smug and hypocritical. Civilian targets suffered greatly by the American presence in Vietnam, and elsewhere in southeast Asia; and the non-military American presence in nations such as the Shah's Iran and various South American countries has long condoned or abetted highly immoral and repugnant

ture, the time, and the place (Figure 1–10). In other words, dressing styles are highly arbitrary, highly variable, and highly specific. Thus, cultures differ in time and space but cannot be judged better or worse. Some cultures may be technologically superior to others, but all cultures are equal overall.

Cultural relativism, very importantly, does not say that society dictates no values and that, therefore, anyone can do anything they want. All societies have beliefs, standards, and values that, when broached, define people as deviants. The fact that there are people who ordinarily wear nothing but a string and a flap of cloth does not mean that it is acceptable for people in our society to do that. Cultural relativism says that the fact that there are people who do something in one society has no bearing on what is or should be considered acceptable in another society. Thus, the behavior and beliefs of the Yanomamo of South America,

regimes. If we abhor the displacement of Palestinians, how do we account for our own displacement of Native Americans? If we abhor apartheid in South Africa, how do we account for racism in America?

We must distinguish between opposing a belief because we consider it unjust and are generally opposed to injustice and opposing it because we think that it is wrong and that our society is better. One major difference between these viewpoints is that the first implies the recognition of problems at home and the second does not. It is all too easy to look at another culture and see a more glaring injustice being committed than we are accustomed to experiencing in America; we could also easily decide that the more glaring problem needs our intervention and rectification and that the problems in our own society do not. It is always in a political administration's interest to focus attention on social injustice in other nations—keeping the attention of its own citizens diverted from domestic injustices.

This is not to suggest that we condone injustice wherever we encounter it abroad, but rather, that we consider carefully our reasons for opposing it and what they may imply. Is our society really more just than, say, South Africa's? And if so, is our society no longer in need of improvement? Does the greater subtlety of the barriers to advancement of the underprivileged in America make those barriers much more tolerable? In other words, we live in a society with injustice and oppression: how confident are we in judging that the injustice and oppression in another society is worse than ours, and thereby more deserving of our energies?

Cultural relativism is, first a methodological construct in studying people, which is what anthropologists try to do. To accomplish that end, we know that world views must be studied, analyzed, and approached on their own terms. The application of this understanding to the complex problems of global politics tells us that world views cannot reasonably be approached from the standpoint that one set of beliefs is unconditionally superior to another. Politically, such a standpoint leads straight to confrontation; internationally, to the perception of imperialism and hypocrisy; and intellectually, to a loss of information about what human groups do and what they are capable of doing.

the Dinka of Africa, or the Eskimo of Greenland are not relevant to the values and standards we accept in our own society.

More importantly, the reverse is also true—the standards of our society are irrelevant to those in other societies. Our culture is not better or higher than another, merely different (Box 1–1). It is simpler in some ways (kinship and language systems, for example) and more complex in others (our technological and economic systems). These cultural differences are the results of our different histories and adaptations and must be appreciated as variation, not betterment.

There are, of course, ways in which we think we can discern **progress** in cultural change. Our lifetimes are longer than our ancestors', and we have eradicated polio. Isn't this progress? Doesn't this mean that our culture is better than the culture of our ancestors'? Again, no. As we will see, cultural change is a tradeoff—improvement in one thing leads to

progress

General improvement through time.

retrogression in something else. This is because culture is a system, composed of interacting elements, and a change in one thing creates changes in others, often changes that can not be foreseen. When they are noticed, they become problems that need to be dealt with, and dealing with them causes new problems.

Thus, we are left with the proposition of cultural relativism—like the relationships of species to one another and the relative rights of individual citizens, cultures are neither better nor worse than one another.

It is beneficial to any member of one society to study the culture of another society, to see how other people live and think. This is what much of anthropology is about. Such study may be the source of new ideas and opinions for the student or at the very least will provide the foundation for an appreciation of the breadth of the human experience. Nevertheless, being a part of one culture means functioning within the specific rules of that culture. In other words, the rules may be arbitrary, but they are ours.

Summary

This book is concerned with anthropology, a social science that studies the totality of human beings and human experience. Many anthropologists study culture and language from a humanistic perspective, and their work is very important. In contrast, however, this text explores human biological and cultural evolution from a materialistic and scientific standpoint. We focus on physical (or biological) anthropology and archaeology.

Technology is widely regarded as the primary driving force behind cultural evolutionary change. This is the doctrine of cultural materialism. Evolutionary studies also teach us that no culture is better or worse than any other, even though they may exhibit simpler or more complex technologies and vary greatly in many other ways. This is the doctrine of cultural relativism. Like differences among species and individuals, we have learned to accept cultures as merely different from one another as different societies cope with their diverse environments.

1. How do the four subfields of anthropology relate to one another?

2. Why do you think the viewpoint of cultural materialism has been a particularly useful paradigm in archaeology?

3. Could the principle of cultural relativism be applied usefully in the area of international relations? In other words, how can you balance the idea of (for example) universal human rights against the ideas of preserving cultural diversity and against the charge of Euro-American imperialism?

For Further Reading

Binford, L. R. (1983). *In pursuit of the past: Decoding the archaeological record.* New York: Thames and Hudson.

Boas, F. (1928). *Anthropology and modern life.* New York: W. W. Norton.

Tattersall, I., Delson, E., & Van Couvering, J. (1988). *The encyclopedia of human evolution and prehistory.* New York: Garland.

Thomas, D. H. (1989). *Archaeology.* Fort Worth: Holt, Rinehart and Winston.

White, L. A. (1949). *The science of culture.* New York: Farrar, Straus, and Giroux.

Anthropology as Science

Anthropology as Science

Science as a Branch of Scholarship

It is important to distinguish science from nonscience and pseudoscience. We regard all pseudoscience as work that is lacking in scholarship, regardless of its subject. In contrast, both science and nonscience can be scholarly in nature. The first part of this chapter defines science and scientific work. The second half of this chapter describes some of the scientific methods of archaeology and physical anthropology.

SCHOLARSHIP AND SCIENCE: FOUR CRITERIA

Before something can be regarded as scientific, it must be scholarly. Of many scholarly endeavors, however, only some are scientific. Literary criticism can be considered scholarship, for example, but it is not science. Indeed, all of the humanities—the nonsciences—are bound to the sciences in this manner. There are four general criteria for defining **scholarship:** insight, mastery of the subject, definitive evidence, and logic.

Insight   The first criterion for scholarship is insight—all scholarship tells us something new about its subject. Whether the scholar is the philosopher St. Thomas Aquinas, the economist John Maynard Keynes, or the biochemist Arthur Kornberg, all scholarship has some element of originality to it. Consequently, some element of originality applies to all science as well.

Mastery of the Subject Manner   The second criterion for scholarship is a mastery of the subject matter. No great strides in scholarship have ever been taken by people who didn't know what they were doing. Some advances have been made by accident, of course, but the only way one can capitalize on a fortuitous circumstance is to know enough about it to utilize it. Thus, scholarship is associated with commitment and long-term study—**dilettantism** has no place. Associated with knowledge of the subject matter is a thorough knowledge of previous work in the area. To write a scholarly work about George Bernard Shaw, one obviously must be familiar not only with the playwright's works but also with how previous generations of scholars have analyzed them. In science, this quality often distinguishes a scholar from a technician.

Evidence   The third criterion for scholarship involves the relationship of the evidence to the conclusions. A clear indication of the absence of scholarship, as in pseudoscience, is the false, misleading, or incomplete presentation of evidence. Such work tends to start with a conclusion and then find whatever evidence that can be invoked to bol-

scholarship
Useful contribution to a body of learning, which subsumes insight, knowledge, open-mindedness, and logical reasoning.

dilettante
One who contributes to a scholarly field without the requisite mastery of the subject.

ster it—no matter how better explained those data might be in other ways. Some situations require this kind of reasoning—this is the way lawyers make their cases, for example—although this strategy is fundamentally different from the way scholars, especially scientists, think. A lawyer begins with a conclusion ("My client is innocent") and then seeks to prove it by any means possible. Scholarship, in contrast, strives to *find* a conclusion. While this manner of reasoning (beginning with a conclusion and trying to prove it correct) is appropriate in the courtroom, it is not scholarly reasoning and is inappropriate when transferred to that arena.

Perhaps the clearest example of this nonscholarly way of thinking can be found among the modern biblical creationists, who set out to prove the inerrancy of the Bible, collect evidence to support it, and then—not surprisingly—conclude that the Bible is inerrant. Many popular books have been written in support of the idea that Noah's Ark has been located on Mount Ararat in the Near East, for example, and that wood has been retrieved from it (Figure 2–1). To some, this may be held as a source of evidence for the infallibility of the Bible.

Usually withheld, however, is the information that the wood retrieved from Mount Ararat was radiocarbon-dated by several laborato-

Figure 2–1
The wood on Mount Ararat is most likely from a medieval monastery, not from a vast boat that had pairs of every earthly species on board 5,000 years ago.

ries to the seventh century A.D. This is not compatible with the idea that the wood is from Noah's Ark, but it is compatible with the idea that it came from a medieval monastery built on the mountaintop. Also withheld is the information that Mount Ararat has only been called that since the Middle Ages. One need only refer to Genesis 8:4 to see that the ark wasn't reported to have landed on Mount Ararat at all, but on "the mountains of Ararat." As evidence for biblical infallibility, then, this proof is nonscholarly.

Logic   The fourth criterion of scholarship is logic. Scholarly reasoning is logical, following formal rules derived from Aristotle and René Descartes. These rules are now such an ingrained part of our academic training that we can often take them for granted. Thus, we can easily recognize the absurdity in Woody Allen's syllogism: All men are mortal; Socrates was a man; therefore, all men are Socrates. Here, the premises, or assumptions, are true, but the conclusion does not follow.

While scholarship, and by inclusion science, involves logical reasoning, the presence of logic does not guarantee scholarship. Not only must the reasoning be sound, but the premises must hold as well. The faultier the premises, the less scholarly the work. Thus, simply because a train of thought is logical, it is not necessarily either scientific or scholarly. Some of the most bizarre pseudoscience is quite logical internally, but it is based on faulty assumptions.

For example, the mystic Edgar Cayce would recall his past life on Atlantis while under hypnotic trance. Acceptance of this apparently sincere belief as evidence for reincarnation is predicated on two assumptions, however. The first is that hypnosis brings out the truth and the recollection of true archaic memories. In fact, hypnosis makes subjects highly suggestible, and they often "remember" what the hypnotist wants or expects—regardless of whether the event actually happened. The second assumption is that the Atlantis of myth was a real place, when in fact, the only references to it made in ancient times are found in two of Plato's dialogues (*Timaeus* and *Critias*), which did not even purport to be true (only illustrative) and which differ in their details. Indeed, no archaeological or geological evidence suggests that a technologically advanced people lived on an island continent that sank thousands of years ago. What has been claimed as evidence can be better explained in other ways. And the "technologically advanced" part of the story is not even Plato's—it comes from Francis Bacon's novel about Atlantis, written in the seventeenth century.

Atlantis has no greater claim to historical reality than does Shangri-La or the Metropolis of Superman. Thus, one can claim to be a reincarnation of one of Atlantis's inhabitants with no more logical validity than one can claim to be a reincarnation of Lex Luthor, Perry White, or Lois Lane.

THE SCIENCES AND HUMANITIES

What tends to set the scientific and humanistic disciplines apart, distinguishing science from nonscience (or humanities from nonhumanities), is their approach to evidence. Often, the same evidence can be interpreted in many ways, which can yield many answers. In the humanities, a scholarly work is often a work of advocacy, the presentation of a particular view of things—one creative way of interpreting the facts. In contrast, a scientific work generally seeks to analyze data thoroughly and with as much objectivity as possible. Both the sciences and the humanities, however, need to present the issues and information bearing on the subject comprehensively—this differentiates both of them from pseudoscience (see above).

Modern *scientific* explanations deal fundamentally with questions of "how" and not with questions of "why." This is an important distinction and one that is often glossed, even by scientists, who often phrase things sloppily. To phrase a question beginning with "why" is to imply a purpose or reason for the phenomenon. To explain *why* Aunt Tillie was run over by a bus would imply a reason for it, like a reason for the cue ball's being in motion and knocking the 7 ball into the pocket. That reason, of course, was the intent of the billiards player. But must there be a reason for the bus to have run Aunt Tillie down at this time, in this place? In theory, one could offer an explanation in terms of the driver's sobriety, Aunt Tillie's senses and reflexes, the maintenance of the bus, the distractions in the street, the climatic conditions, and so on. But this would be a description of only the circumstances—it would not tell us *why* Aunt Tillie was run over. She could have been run over yesterday but wasn't. Why did it happen today?

To science, such a question is unapproachable. Perhaps there was a reason, perhaps there was not a reason—the resolution is impossible for science to deal with. One may recall Kurt Vonnegut's response in *Slaughterhouse-Five* to the question, "Why me?" It was, "Why anybody?" Science does not deal with this kind of issue. Thus, science usually is limited to a form of explanation by processes or mechanisms, not reasons for specific events or phenomena.

This does not, however, invalidate the search for reason—which is often carried out with great insight in the humanities. As we have seen, this is one major criterion that distinguishes scientific from humanistic endeavors—the discovery of reasons involves principally *interpretation*, and it is difficult to distinguish good interpretation from bad interpretation, for interpretation by its nature is highly subjective. Therefore, the most acceptable reason is often simply the most cleverly argued reason. Freudian psychoanalysis, for example, which explains human behavior by recourse to unconscious desires and images, is not usually regarded as scientific, although it is certainly clever and may be valid.

Science in Culture

Science is a way of thought, a world view, which emerged in its modern form during the eighteenth century—a period in European history that has come to be known as the Enlightenment (Chapter 3). It was part of a philosophical movement that had a radical goal—the *accurate* description and explanation of the universe. All cultures everywhere attempt to describe and explain things, such as the rain, the rising of the sun, Aunt Tillie's being run over by a bus, why good things happen to bad people, and vice versa. But what set the scientific movement apart and continues to do so was its goal of giving the most accurate answers possible.

The most accurate answers depend upon the state of knowledge at any given time (chemistry before Lavoisier or physics before Einstein was less accurate, but not necessarily less scientific), so it follows that science is a cultural endeavor. What stands as good science in one time and place may not stand as good science in another time and place. But all science shares a goal—in the words of immunologist Peter Medawar, the distinction between the possible and the actual. In other words, all science at all times tries to discover and distinguish what *is* from the many things that *might be*.

Thus, two phases of science are always operating; one creative, and one critical. The creative phase of science turns out the possible explanations for things, and the critical phase pares them down and subjects them to scrutiny to determine whether they are, in fact, the best explanations available.

Assumptions of Science

All scientists proceed from a few basic assumptions, assumptions we all tend to take for granted as they are our cultural inheritance from the Enlightenment. Foremost among these assumptions is that the universe can be understood—that things can be explained and that questions do have answers. We may not know the explanations, but if we study, we will ultimately find them.

Isaac Newton, for example, was led (according to legend) to his formalization of the theory of gravity by asking himself, "What made this apple fall?" The answer to his question could have been, "Nothing made this apple fall." If that had been the answer, then the science of physics would not exist—only the assumption that *something* made the apple fall laid the foundation for modern physics. Similarly, Charles Darwin laid the foundation for modern biology by asking, "What makes some species more similar to one another than to other species?" If the answer had been, "Nothing," then there would be no biology. But as far as we can tell, *something* makes some species more or less similar to one another. That something, Darwin later came to understand, is their recency of common ancestry. The question he posed had an answer, indeed, many possible answers.

The second assumption that all scientists proceed from is that things are as they appear. If, for example, we are merely being tricked into believing that apples fall by a false appearance, then Newton's explanation for falling objects is of little use. If this seems absurd, consider the anti-Darwinian explanation for biology seriously proposed by some nineteenth-century theologians—that species have not evolved but only *appear* to have evolved!

Thus, science not only tries to answer questions about the universe but tries to answer questions about a *specific* universe the one that we encounter. Of course, some questions are unanswerable as posed—they need to be put in a different way to be answerable. And sometimes appearances can be deceiving. For example, the question "Why does the sun move through the sky every day?" has no answer, for the sun does not literally move through the sky—the earth rotates. Often, revolutions in science have been brought about by thinkers who posed the same old problems in new ways, which in turn led to new answers. Copernicus, who reformulated that very question with a new approach to the relative movements of the sun and earth, was one of those thinkers (see Chapter 3).

Kinds of Science

There are two fundamentally different kinds of scientific endeavor: synchronic and diachronic studies. Synchronic studies are concerned with things that occur at a single point in time. Diachronic studies have as a primary subject things that happen through time, sometimes beginning in the distant past.

SYNCHRONIC STUDIES

A synchronic study usually involves directly observable phenomena—things that can be seen and documented as they happen—because most synchronic studies concern the present. This type of study often has the property of being **replicable**—the scientist hopes that the experiment will come out the same way tomorrow as it did today and that the subject under study will behave in a similar fashion under similar circumstances. If it does, then we can make a **generalization** about those things we have studied and a prediction about those we have not.

DIACHRONIC STUDIES

Diachronic studies, on the other hand, have as their primary subjects things that happen through time, sometimes beginning in the distant past. These studies, which subsume history, much of archaeology, and paleontology, require different methods and modes of analysis than synchronic studies. Obviously, the behavior of a living chimpanzee (which can be the subject of a synchronic study) can be observed in much more direct ways (Figure 2–2) than the behavior of a *Proconsul africanus*, which lived about 15 million years ago (Chapter 11).

replicate

To generate the same conclusions as a prior study, either using the same method with new data or the same data with new analyses. This can help distinguish a "fluke" result from a valid one, but replication does not guarantee correctness.

generalization

A broad statement about the relationship between two variables.

But diachronic studies have certain advantages as well. Often, natural processes occur at slow rates, and limiting ourselves to one point in time might never lead to our observing or understanding these processes. By studying them through time, we may be able to see their regularities and effects more clearly. For example, one can interview and give questionnaires to living people and find out a great deal about them. Still, archaeological evidence of the changes people have experienced through time tells us many additional things—things that we could learn in no other way and that those people may not even have been aware of.

In general, then, synchronic studies rely more on experiment, on replication of results, and on direct observation, while diachronic studies rely more on **inference** and on the explanation of past events. But diachronic studies approach the past directly, while synchronic studies approach it only indirectly.

inference

A statement based on logical reasoning from a body of data.

What Does It Mean to Be Scientific?

Modern science has a number of defining attributes that allow us to distinguish it from other modes of thought, such as humanities or religion. Four principal criteria help to define modern science: It is empirical, self-correcting, probabilistic, and parsimonious. These are emphasized to different degrees by different philosophers of science, but all are important, and the absence of any one of them helps to distinguish a work of modern science from anything else.

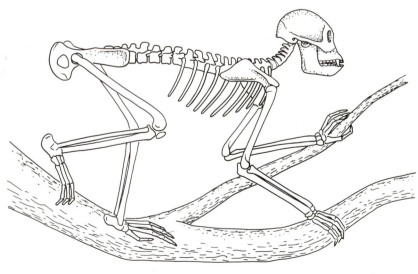

Figure 2-2
The behavior of chimpanzees can be observed; the behavior of *Proconsul* cannot.

SCIENCE IS EMPIRICAL

Science is **empirical**; the data on which it is based can consist of any number of things, including answers to questionnaires, photographs, X-ray films, manuscripts, pot sherds, and so on—but the absence of data is always the absence of science. There are two general kinds of data: 1) observation, or reporting; and 2) experiment, a planned and controlled activity.

Collecting Data   The earliest science was simply the recording of data and the observation of regularities, which led early agriculturalists (or even earlier peoples) to the development of the oldest science, astronomy. The reasoning they used, starting from many specific observations and subsequently moving to general conclusions, is known as **induction**.

The world, however, is full of things to observe, and scientists have since tended to look for specific things while having particular ideas in mind. These ideas are what guide scientists, and tell them what to look for. The guidelines are crucial, given that there are so many things to see out there.

Modern science is, therefore, not simply the haphazard accumulation of data. Rather, it begins with the perception of a problem and follows with the construction of a way to obtain a solution to it. This form of thinking is called **deduction**.

Developing Hypotheses   The other half of the process of data collection, then, involves deciding which data to collect—which experiment to perform, which behaviors to observe, and which questions to ask an informant, to name but a few possibilities. These decisions are spelled out in a document called a research design and are based on elaborating **hypotheses** and projecting the consequences of those hypotheses.

Deduction is a mental activity. The scientist says, "If X is true, then I should find A, B, and C." If the scientist collects the data and instead finds D, E, and F, and if the reasoning has been sound, then the scientist knows that X is not true. If X is not true, what *might be* true? The scientist must frame and test another hypothesis to find out.

Science advances by the construction of alternative hypotheses and the refutation of them via empirical data. Data are collected to illuminate hypotheses, and reciprocally, hypotheses are constructed to account for data. This leads to the collection of more data. The construction of hypotheses tells us what might be true, and the collection of data tells us what is *likely* to be true. These are two parts of the activity of science which work together, a process summarized by philosopher Karl Popper as "conjecture and refutation" and by Peter Medawar as "proposal and disposal." The relation between hypothesis and data, or deduction and induction, is like that of thought and act. The former tells you what to do—doing it produces another round of thought.

empirical

Grounded in tangible or reproducible data.

induction

Reasoning from the specific (a mass of data) to the general (their patterns and explanations for them).

deduction

Reasoning from the general (an idea about the patterns of data to be encountered) to the specific (the data that indicate whether the reasoning was valid or not).

hypothesis

A statement of relationship between two variables, which can be falsified by the collection of a body of data.

explanation

An account of why the specific results were obtained, relying on proximate causes and material forces.

Explanation   In addition to collecting data and conceiving hypotheses, a third kind of activity is required in science—**explanation**. This can be outside the cycle of hypotheses and data but is, nevertheless, intimately involved in both. But not any kind of explanation will do. In modern science, we deal with proximate causes (not ultimate causes) and material forces (not mystical forces).

A *proximate cause* is a mechanism directly responsible for a given condition, a literal answer to the question "What are the general rules that govern this particular phenomenon?" An answer to that question (such as "The planets are revolving around the sun because of their gravitational attraction, which is a property of matter") leads to another question: "Where did those rules come from?" Very often, major scientific breakthroughs involve recognizing highly specific things or events as instances of a broader, generalized mechanism or law. The generalization, then, becomes a direct explanation of the specific instance—a proximate cause. What is the cause of an apple falling? The answer is the gravitational attraction between two masses. And what causes mass to be attractive? The answer to that is an *ultimate cause*.

Ultimate causes are usually beyond the purview of modern science. When Newton discovered the regularities behind gravitational attraction, he discovered a proximate cause. Yet he couldn't address the cause of those proximate causes scientifically. Who caused the cause? God, reasoned Newton. This form of explanation actually goes back to Aristotle, who saw God as a first cause of all things. Newton, however, had a role which cannot be underestimated because, in essence, he displaced God.

Where previously God had been invoked as the direct, or proximate, cause of apples falling downward and planets staying in orbit, Newton showed that God didn't need to be involved at all in the behavior of specific apples or specific planets, for the behavior of those objects was an intrinsic property of their matter. "Where did those properties come from?" is an altogether different question, one whose answer concerns ultimate causes, and is presently outside the scope of science.

Darwin was even more explicit than Newton in his distinction between proximate and ultimate causes. What is the cause of human bipedalism? A restructuring of the back, pelvis, leg, and foot. What is the cause of that restructuring? Natural selection. And the cause of natural selection? Darwin ended the first edition of *The Origin of Species* with the observation that such great biological diversity as we now see originated from life "having been originally breathed into a few forms or into one." No one doubted that he was removing God from the act of individually creating every species, as Newton had done for every falling body. Yet where did those original life-forms come from? That was an ultimate cause and not relevant to the scientific arguments of *The Origin of Species,* which was about proximate causes of differences among species. In a later edition of the book, Darwin added "by the Creator" to the end of that thought about the origin of life in order to make his acceptance of the explanation for the ultimate cause more explicit.

Modern science also does not take recourse in forces that cannot be objectively perceived. Explanations are made in terms of forces and processes that can be measured, recorded, bottled up, or otherwise documented. Thus, while the paleontologist Robert Broom (Chapter 11) believed that good and bad angels carried out the business of evolution, this is not acceptable as an explanation in modern science. Telekinesis and the powers of ESP have likewise never been documented objectively and so fail as scientific explanations.

To be scientific does not mean to be atheistic, which means to deny the existence of supernatural beings. To perform science, however, means to be agnostic, which means to deny that supernatural beings, whether or not they exist, have any place in an acceptable scientific explanation. In other words, supernatural beings may exist, but they are beyond science, which explains natural phenomena by recourse to natural forces.

Why are natural explanations preferable? Because a supernatural force is capricious—it cannot be measured or studied directly. It is not a regularity and, therefore, cannot be used reliably to predict future phenomena. In other words, if angels, rather than gravity, make apples fall, then how do we know that the angels will make the next apple fall and not float in the air? Yet the natural explanation, gravity, has proven to be adequate to explain the falling of apples without any necessary recourse to supernatural beings or powers. While such beings may exist, natural forces have been continuously supplanting them as adequate and accurate explanations over the course of the past few hundred years, and it seems reasonable to expect that they will continue to do so.

SCIENCE IS SELF-CORRECTING

In its goal to come closer and closer to an empirically accurate description and explanation of things, today's science is constantly superseding the work of previous generations—meaning that science is *self-correcting*. This is a major difference between science and many other endeavors. In the humanities, we regard the Sphinx, Homer's *Iliad,* and Michaelangelo's Sistine Chapel ceiling as great works—great when they were executed, and great now. Yet the science of dynastic Egypt, ancient Greece, and Renaissance Italy is now quaint and archaic. Today's art stands beside yesterday's art, but today's science supplants yesterday's science. Our taste in art may vary through time, but our knowledge of the world has improved (Figure 2–3).

This improvement, this approximation of our goal to understand the universe, occurs because, in addition to the new store of information accumulated, at any given time the mistakes made by a previous generation of scientists are being corrected by a new generation of scientists. In

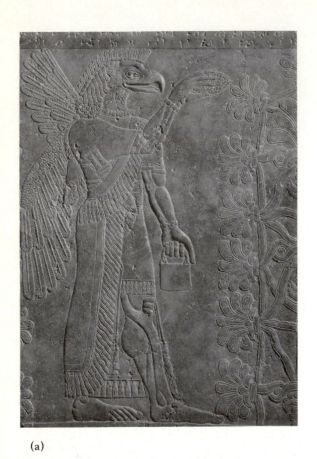

(a)

(b)

(e)

(c)

(d)

Figure 2-3
Science (our attempt to know the world)
is continually improving, while art forms
vary according to time, place, and taste.
(a) Ninth-century B.C. Assyrian bas-
relief; (b) *Adoration of the Magi* by Luca
Signorelli (A.D. fifteenth century); (c)
male figure from the Ivory coast (A.D.
nineteenth century); (d) *Night Cafe* by
Vincent van Gogh (A.D. nineteenth
century); (e) *Deer Drinking* by Winslow
Homer (A.D. nineteenth century); (f)
First Steps by Pablo Picasso (A.D.
twentieth century).

(f)

paleoanthropology, for instance, some fossils found in the Piltdown gravels in England in 1912 suggested that human ancestors had large brains and ape-like teeth. Subsequent finds in Africa, however, soon suggested the opposite—ape-like brains and human-like teeth for our ancestors. This led to a closer examination of the Piltdown fossils, which were shown in 1953 to be deliberately fraudulent.

Thus, by the processes of hypothesizing, collecting data, and critically scrutinizing, paleoanthropology in 1953 was considerably better than it was in 1912. Yet painting was not—styles were different, but not better. Nonscience is not self-correcting, as science is.

SCIENCE IS PROBABILISTIC

probability

The chances of a certain phenomenon occurring or being valid, out of a larger universe of possibilities.

Science is **probabilistic**. Scientists are interested in the most likely explanations for things. For this reason, theologians are always more secure in their positions than scientists are. A scientist knows what is likely but also what might be wrong; a theologian knows what is "true."

Three reasons explain this insecurity in scientific statements. The first is that scientific conclusions are contingent upon the state of knowledge at any time. When greater knowledge is accumulated, conclusions may have to be revised. The second reason is that many processes in science are probabilistic. For example, the processes of meiosis dictate that sperm bearing X-chromosomes and Y-chromosomes will be produced in equal numbers. For this reason, the chances of an egg being fertilized by one or the other are equal, and male and female children are produced in equal numbers. Because this is a statistical process, a scientist cannot make a definite prediction about the sex of any future child. However, science does allow us to calculate that the chances of having five boys in a row is only 1 in 32. The third reason is that there are exceptions to every generalization, and if 99 percent of the cases can be explained, a scientist has been eminently successful. The remaining 1 percent are interesting and deserving of further study but constitute the proverbial "exceptions that prove the rule."

SCIENCE IS PARSIMONIOUS

parsimony

Simplicity; the property of an explanation to make use of the fewest number of steps, variables, or processes.

Finally, one of the major operating assumptions of science is the principle of **parsimony**. This is also known as Occam's (or Ockham's) Razor, after William of Occam (or Ockham), who formulated it. The principle is simple—indeed, it is literally simplicity. The principle of parsimony says that when choosing among alternative explanations, the one with fewer assumptions—the simpler one—and the one that explains the most is the better choice.

For example, in the primate fossil record, we find two broad groups of animals capable of habitual bipedalism—hominines (genus *Homo*) and australopithecines (see Chapter 11). We can either say that these were not closely related to each other because bipedalism evolved twice in separate primate lineages, or we can say that these are closely related because bipedalism evolved only once in a common ancestor of the two groups. We choose the latter alternative.

Of course, the principle of parsimony is not always correct. It is a rule of thumb, a first approximation. At the other end of the spectrum we have H. L. Mencken's wisecrack, "To every complex problem, there is a simple solution—and it's wrong." Thus, the lack of a tail in hominoids (apes and humans) and Manx cats does not associate them as being close relatives. Instead, we look at all the other data we can find, and we conclude that the most likely explanation is that the tail was lost twice in separate lineages, once in the Manx cat lineage and once in the hominoid lineage.

Scientific Methods

To be a scientist requires more than following the general guidelines of performing science, discussed above. It also requires following the specific methods of a chosen scientific discipline. The study of human origins and behavior entails the use of many methods, some borrowed from other fields. Fundamentally, the choice of which particular method to use is determined by considering the nature of the research questions one wishes to address, along with the given parameters of a project. Research questions are developed in a document critical to all scientific undertakings—the *research design*.

RESEARCH DESIGN

The research design is exactly what it seems to be—a plan or design for carrying out a scientific investigation. The simplicity of this definition, along with the commonsense awareness of the importance of having such a document, might lead one to believe that research designs have been prepared for all scientific undertakings. Unfortunately, this is not always the case. There are several problems with undertaking a scientific investigation without the use of a research design.

First, without a research design, an investigator does not know what to expect on beginning a project. Without background research, or with haphazard background research, the investigator is really not in a position to anticipate the nature of the upcoming data collection adequately. A research design involves the documentation and evaluation of previous studies on the topic and setting of interest. In this way, the investigator becomes prepared for many sorts of contingencies.

Second, without a research design, there is no explicit list of questions for the investigator to address. If one does not know what to ask, it is unlikely that one can come up with any good answers! Indeed, with only vague ideas about expectations, it is possible that an investigator may not recognize the answers when confronting them. Formal research questions are designed so that they can be answered with the available

Figure 2-4
Scientists generally do not like surprises; they like to know what to expect.

methods. A failure to state them explicitly in a research design creates the possibility that one may ask questions that cannot be answered, which would be a waste of everyone's time and effort.

Third, the absence of a research design makes it difficult (if not impossible) to predict the possible results of a project. But prediction is critical in scientific work. If one does not know what to expect, then all results are equally surprising. And to be surprised means *not to know what is happening*—which is the *opposite* of the goal of science.

Consequently, scientists are rarely thrilled by finding something they did not anticipate, especially if its existence could radically change the course of a project. Small changes in research strategy will always be necessary, and a good research design allows for them. Yet one of the important purposes of a research design is to minimize the chances of a major surprise (Figure 2–4).

The point is that, without a research design, many materials and data will be lost. Many important questions will not be addressed, and a project will probably have little scientific value. Research designs are prepared by all good scientists.

FIELDWORK

As mentioned above, a major task in science is the gathering of empirical evidence that can be used to assess the various hypotheses that have been posed. In much of physical anthropology (particularly in paleoanthropology) and archaeology, this task involves recovering materials (fossils and artifacts, for example) in a controlled fashion so that information about the materials (location, condition, and association to other materials) is not lost. This information is part of the data a scientist must generate in order to address research questions. (Data generation is covered in a later section of this chapter.)

When paleoanthropologists or archaeologists recover materials, we say that they are doing *fieldwork* The scientist is "in the field," literally meaning at a location where the desired materials can be found. These locations can be quite isolated, and life in the field can be difficult (Figure 2–5). Not all fieldwork has this character, however, and not all work is done in the field. Some physical anthropologists gather materials

Figure 2-5
The site of Fort Cummings, in southwest New Mexico, is fairly isolated. The nearest town, Deming, is nearly 20 miles distant.

Figure 2-6
The interval tower on the Roman wall in York, England, is revealed in the middle of the downtown area.

and generate data in modern laboratories. And some archaeologists labor in the centers of large, bustling cities, about as far away from any genuine field as one can get (Figure 2–6).

Still, fieldwork has been traditionally and commonly a time in which most anthropologists face exotic and primitive conditions, within which they must conduct the highest possible order of careful, scientific research. Indeed, the conditions often create the greatest challenges, and the managerial skills needed to direct a field exercise properly are often the most difficult to master. It is imperative that students acquire a sound background in fieldwork, through experience, not only to learn the necessary methods of the discipline but also to direct a field exercise properly when given the chance to do so.

Effective Field Methods   Though *excavation* has been the mainstay of paleoanthropological and archaeological research, it is preceded and often superseded by other kinds of fieldwork. There are four reasons for this.

First, excavation takes a lot of time if done competently, and many projects require more efficient procedures if materials and potential data are to be rescued from modernization or vandalism (Chapter 18). Second, excavation is very expensive, and often it is simply not possible for scientists to raise the capital necessary for proper research. Third, and most importantly, excavation is a form of destruction—a scientific procedure that nevertheless erases the paleoanthropological and archaeological records. Researchers try to recover all the materials they need and record all the information as it is revealed. But this is an impossible, ideal goal. No matter how careful the fieldworker, no matter how thorough the research design, some material and information will be lost forever. Thus, excavation inevitably leads to the elimination of potential data. As a way of rectifying this situation, anthropologists have devised a number of nondestructive field methods, including reconnaissance and survey, which we discuss below.

Some materials and data are destroyed by excavation because field techniques are not perfect—they are still being improved. Thus, many researchers, if they choose to excavate at all, regularly excavate only a sample of a site, preserving some for future investigators. **Sampling** is the selection of a recognized subset of a population so that it can be studied. A **population**, in turn, consists of all the materials of interest, which cannot all be studied due to the existence of time and cost constraints. Sampling strategies allow the subset to be selected so that it is reasonably representative of the population, and thus reflective of its nature. And sampling is used not only when sites are being excavated—reconnaissance and survey strategies also depend on sampling.

The fourth reason for seeking alternatives to excavation is related to the scale of investigation. Recently, more and more researchers have been approaching the material record at the regional scale—large areas or

sampling

Choosing a subset of all the possible data; this may be based on specific criteria or be random.

population

In general, the entire collection of things of interest.

regions of the landscape can be investigated as single, though diverse, units. Excavation lends itself to the investigation of single *sites*, which are important units of study. Additionally, the results of a series of excavations at sites within a region can be combined to reach a regional view. It nevertheless remains that other methods offer more direct approaches to regional understanding. And this regional understanding is critical to addressing some of the most important and interesting research questions.

Research relating to the emergence of our species, demographic changes subsequent to that emergence, trade and exchange among human populations, and the development of several sociocultural conditions that have had profound impacts on our lives (including the rise of domestication and complex society) is most effectively undertaken with a regional perspective. And all these topics, which we consider in some detail throughout this book, are related to one another by their reliance on evolutionary theory. Indeed, if one wishes to study evolution, the ruling paradigm in anthropology and related sciences, one needs to work at the regional scale. Evolution is itself a regional phenomenon.

Reconnaissance   One method by which extensive disturbance of the subsurface is avoided is **reconnaissance**. It is often the first of several steps in fieldwork because it can cover a relatively large region with little effort—it is the least intensive undertaking in the field. Information from a reconnaissance can guide the paleoanthropologist or archaeologist to more specific locations, where more intensive fieldwork (survey, for example) could be undertaken most profitably.

Reconnaissance can be done in several ways. The type of reconnaissance chosen depends on the type of material being sought. Usually, a combination of approaches is used. One approach does not even require that the researcher go into the field—it involves assessing relevant documents, maps, and even reports of previous field research. This is the least expensive and most rapid way of determining the types of materials in a region and their locations. Still, it can be the least reliable because the information is not based on firsthand inspection.

Another type of reconnaissance involves the use of **remote sensing**—observation at a distance. For example, aerial photographs can be studied for evidence of archaeological sites and land-use patterns (Figure 2–7). Likewise, materials hidden beneath the ground can be detected without disturbing the subsurface by the use of various sensitive pieces of equipment, including the **proton magnetometer** (Figure 2–8).

The most common type of reconnaissance remains the direct inspection of the ground surface, however. This on-ground reconnaissance is usually conducted by actually walking over the landscape in a prescribed pattern and carefully recording what is seen, and where. While this pedestrian method is most popular because it is most sensitive, some researchers have elected to ride on horseback, and even in

reconnaissance
The determination of the type and location of the materials to be studied.

remote sensing
Reconnaissance and survey techniques that involve observation and recording from a distance.

proton magnetometer
An instrument used in remote sensing that measures the strength of magnetism passing through the ground, revealing subsurface archaeological features.

Figure 2-7
A contour map drawn using stereo photographs along with an aerial photograph of Pueblo Alto in Chaco Canyon, New Mexico.

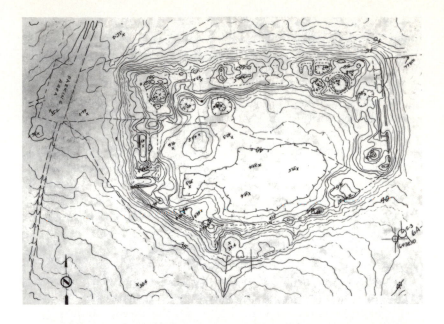

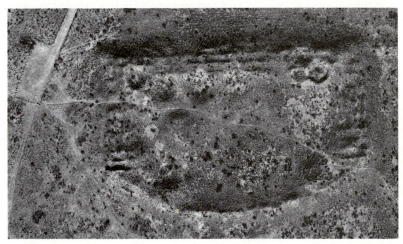

motor vehicles, to get the job done faster. Fairly obviously, a paleoanthropologist or archaeologist in a car or truck will cover more ground but will see things in much less detail!

A reconnaissance can cover an entire region or only a portion of it, and the regional sample can be chosen in a number of ways. Still, the common goal of all reconnaissance is to learn more about the subject under investigation, and thus to determine more precisely where intensive work should be concentrated.

survey
Preliminary study of archaeological resources, usually covering a large area; often immediately follows a reconnaissance.

Survey   **Survey** is usually the next step in a field project, if indeed a next step is called for in the research design. It is somewhat more intensive then reconnaissance because it involves the initial study of the materials that have been located. Most materials will be recorded in the field in some degree of detail. A sample might even be collected for more detailed analysis in the lab.

Similar to reconnaissance, surveys can cover relatively large areas in short periods of time. Both are thus useful methods because they can rapidly and inexpensively supply archaeological information about regions. Yet most of these exercises depend on the assumption that surface patterns of material reflect in a predictable fashion the unseen patterns of **artifacts** below the surface. This is not always the case, as many studies of surface-subsurface relationships have demonstrated. The relationships can be very complex and difficult to comprehend.

At the site of Fort Fillmore, in southern New Mexico, a surface survey and collection was conducted for several reasons. Fort Fillmore was a Civil War-period frontier military outpost that today is located within a thriving pecan farm (Figure 2–9). It is a large site, covering many acres, and several years ago the landowner decided to plant trees over much of it. Archaeologists were called in to determine where important archaeological remains might be located and preserved, and they decided that a survey would be most appropriate.

A surface grid was established over the most threatened portion of the site, and it consisted of 10×10-meter collection units. Alternate units were surface collected, leading to a 50 percent sample in the form of a checkerboard (Figure 2–10). All visible artifacts were counted and weighed by material type, and density maps were generated. The goal was to locate "hot spots," or areas of high-density artifact concentrations. Two hot spots were discovered, and it was assumed that important subsurface archaeological remains would be found nearby.

Indeed, important remains were found in the vicinity of the hot spots, although their exact locations were determined by additional factors—topography and climate were influential. The important lesson is, nevertheless, that a survey of a large area can lead to the discovery of subsurface resources if all factors are taken into account, and it can do so quite economically. The ultimate result of the Fort Fillmore survey was that many archaeological remains were recovered before the pecan orchard was expanded.

Excavation   Excavation, the controlled removal of materials from beneath the ground surface, remains an important method of recovering material in the field. It is time consuming, expensive, and destructive, as discussed previously, but it can result in the most detailed record of material remains. These are, in turn, often the best preserved that can be found, since the ground (or matrix) often serves to protect them from disturbance.

The goal of excavation is to recover materials without damaging them and, more important, to recover information about the relationships between materials and aspects of the matrix in which they lie. Anthropologists often speak of the **associations** of materials—their rela-

artifact

Any portable item of material culture.

Figure 2-8
Archaeologists conducting a survey with a proton magnetometer.

association

The locations of artifacts with respect to one another.

Figure 2-9
The site of Fort Fillmore, in southern New Mexico, lies within a large pecan orchard.

Figure 2-10
Surface survey and collection grid at Fort Fillmore.

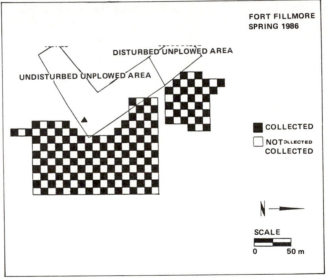

context
The characteristics of archaeological material resulting from past cultural and environmental processes.

provenience
Precise three-dimensional location of any archaeological resource.

tionships in space—and recognize that knowing the associations is most important in reconstructing past activities and processes. This knowledge is far more important than anything the individual artifacts themselves can tell us, making careful, controlled excavation imperative.

Knowing the associations of materials and matrix allows the anthropologist to reconstruct the **context**—the nature of the material record. This information is recorded by locating materials precisely in three dimensions—at a place known as the **provenience** of the material. Often, the researcher will use a grid system to determine the horizontal provenience, while vertical provenience will be measured with reference to some arbitrary elevation and to stratigraphy (see below). All materials are related spatially to a **datum,** or a single point within the three dimensions.

Stratigraphic analysis is an integral part of all excavations. It is the interpretation of geologic layers (*strata*) and the materials they contain. Strata differ because environmental circumstances change as the matrix is formed. Sometimes strata are easy to distinguish, by color or texture, and sometimes they are recognizable only by subtle variations. Regardless, it remains necessary to recognize them and interpret them correctly.

Proper stratigraphic analysis allows the anthropologist to place materials and reconstructed events in a chronological sequence. It is not possible, however, to determine the precise ages or durations of various portions of the sequence at this point. Thus, we define stratigraphic analysis as a *relative dating* technique. Using relative dating, you can know only whether a material or event is older or younger than another material or event. No measurable amount of time is determined, and the question of *how much* older (or younger) remains unanswered for the time being. Other dating techniques are discussed below.

We depend on the law of superposition when performing stratigraphic analysis, which states that the order in which strata are deposited is reflected in their sequence. For any two strata, the one deposited earlier will occur below the one deposited later. Note, however, that this law says nothing certain about the age of the strata nor about the age of the materials they contain. Note also that superposition refers only to the sequence of deposition so observed—the latest sequence of deposition—and that such complicating factors as erosion, redeposition, and other land alterations can make the stratigraphic record quite complex. In order to interpret it correctly, the researcher must consider the complete context of the material carefully.

Aware of these potential complications, we routinely record stratigraphy in the form of **profiles**—scale drawings of strata, described in detail and highlighting the locations of material (Figure 2–11). These profiles are useful documents for establishing the relative order of events, including the relative times at which various species evolved or artifact forms and styles were manufactured. This information is then combined with the results of other dating methods (see below) to reach more precise and complete chronologies.

Learning all available excavation methods takes time and experience—the kind of experience one cannot gain from a book. When conducting any excavation, however, the researcher should always keep in mind one simple rule—record the maximum amount of information with a minimum of effort. The rule is simple, though it can demand great skill in decision making to follow. Conditions of the excavation are always changing, and the need to assess and reevaluate the best approach to the situation is constant. Good excavation requires good judgment. This is true when it comes to *where* to dig as well as *how* to dig.

datum

A reference point to which proveniences are related as they are recorded; more generally, any piece of evidence; singular of *data*.

profile

Precise diagram of a geologic "slice" of the subsurface, showing associated archaeological resources.

What are the primary tools of the anthropologist conducting an excavation? Most people would name the delicate paintbrush, the tiny dental pick, and the ever-present trowel; and indeed, these are commonly used (Figure 2–12). But it is also appropriate, at times, to use shovels, and even backhoes, which are useful when deep strata containing little information lie over important material or when the nature of the subsurface must be determined rapidly.

It is also commonly thought that we always screen the matrix through wire mesh so that no materials are lost. This is a common practice, and sometimes the fieldworker will go one step further by using the method of **flotation**, whereby collectable items (primarily organic, that is, living or formerly living) are floated on water to separate them from the soil. Yet screening and flotation are not practiced all the time—the rule of maximum return for minimum effort always holds.

DATA GENERATION IN THE LAB

Once the fieldwork is completed, the recovered materials are moved to the lab, where they can be analyzed in detail. Diverse lab methods exist,

flotation

Separating small materials (often organic) from matrix by having them rise to the surface of water; the heavier matrix sinks.

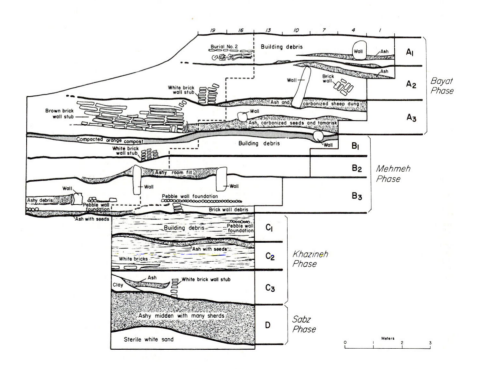

Figure 2-11

A profile showing the stratigraphy at the site of Tepe Sabz, Iran. Approximately 1,500 years of deposition are represented by this profile.

and the ones chosen depend on the research questions being asked and the available facilities. Almost all researchers, however, conduct certain standard lab exercises including cataloging, dating, and data manipulation. The goal of these endeavors is the testing of the hypotheses posed in the research design.

Cataloging   Cataloging involves identifying and measuring the materials recovered in the field. It is the most basic and common laboratory method, and it is usually the first to be conducted.

Resources from the field are sorted by provenience, by the recorded location of recovery, and often by the kind of material or the artifact class. For instance, artifacts from an archaeological field project are bagged by excavation unit and stratigraphic level, and also by whether they are ceramic (pottery), lithic (stone), bone, glass, metal, or a host of other materials. In the lab, however, other attributes play a role in the sorting procedure as the artifacts are cataloged.

The kind of object the artifact represents (called the artifact type) becomes important. Ceramics are subdivided into bowls, pots, ollas, plates, and so on. Glass artifacts are sorted into bottles, windowpane, drinking glasses, and others. Lithics are subdivided into points, other tools, and debitage (the waste products of stone tool manufacture).

The sorting does not stop there. Also considered is the *part* of an original object represented by an artifact. Parts of ceramic bowls, for example, include rim, body, and base sherds. Parts of glass bottles include necks and bases. Other attributes measured during cataloging include the *dimensions* of the original object, its *color*, and its particular *shape* (Figure 2–13).

Once artifacts are subdivided by these various measures, they are usually counted and weighed. It is then possible to compare the relative amounts of each artifact category across the archaeological region or site.

catalog

To measure, sort, and identify recovered archaeological materials.

Figure 2-12
The Marshalltown trowel—a ubiquitous excavation tool.

Figure 2-13
Much of the analysis of archaeological remains occurs in a laboratory.

But this is not the end goal of cataloging. Information regarding the distribution and frequency of *artifacts* would not require consideration of all the various attributes considered, so we must be after something else. Indeed, what is of much greater interest is the distribution and frequency of once-whole *objects* because this tells us much more about patterns of behavior. Getting this information requires a bit more work.

It is not easy to estimate the number of whole objects represented by fragments, or artifacts, and there is no general agreement on how to accomplish this. Following is one method, emphasizing ceramic and glass vessels. From each provenience (excavation unit and level), the following rules apply: 1) Each rim sherd (from ceramics) or neck fragment (from bottles) counts as one vessel if it was of obviously different form or style from the others or did not fit together (cross-mend); 2) each base (from ceramics or bottles) counts as one vessel if it was obviously of a different form or style from the others or did not cross-mend; 3) all body sherds or fragments of similar appearance (that is, that could have come from the same vessel) count as one vessel—those of obviously different form or style are counted separately. While the first two rules most likely result in an overestimate of vessels, it is thought that the third would act to underestimate the count, thus serving as a balance.

There is no simpler way of counting once-complete vessels from artifacts. It is not possible, for example, simply to divide total artifact weights by known whole-vessel weights because it cannot be assumed that complete vessels were recovered, albeit in fragments.

Archaeologists also commonly encounter not only cultural artifacts, but also biological remains. From bones of animals collected from the site, zooarchaeologists can determine the species present and whether it was wild or domesticated. From patterns in the assemblages of bones, inferences can be made as to what the inhabitants were hunting and preferentially eating. Similar inferences can be made from the study of preserved vegetable remains, such as corncobs and pollen.

Human remains often give direct data on many otherwise inaccessible questions. Working with the archaeologist, a physical anthropologist can identify the skeletal remains and, depending upon the state and extent of preservation, identify the age and sex of the individuals. From the osteological remains in a site, one can test hypotheses about changes in population density and composition, changes in nutritional status, and other biological aspects of the human population that once occupied the site.

After object distributions and frequencies across a region or site are known (or at least estimated), the researcher can begin manipulating the data in various ways to answer research questions (see below). First, however, it is necessary to date the various materials, a fundamental research endeavor that bridges basic cataloging and higher-level analyses.

Dating   Laboratories use three general kinds of dating. Relative dating, which we introduced previously, involves determining only whether materials or events are older or younger than other materials or events. Seriation (see below) is a relative dating technique. *Chronometric dating* involves assigning a bracketing range of probable dates during which materials or events are thought to have occurred. Examples of chronometric dating methods include radiometric dating (see below). *Absolute dating*, on the other hand, involves the assignment of a specific calendar date (or dates) to materials or events. Chronometric dates differ from absolute dates in that specific years are not provided by the former—only statements of probability regarding a range of time. The historical archaeologist is able to rely on many absolute dates because of the availability of written materials (Chapter 15). However, this kind of information is usually unavailable or unreliable for a researcher interested in prehistory, who must rely on other techniques.

Dating artifacts most often involves invoking another archaeological law: the law of association, which formalizes the relationship between materials from the same stratum. They are, by the law of association, from approximately the same time. Archaeologists are often obliged to subject to a dating method not the artifacts of greatest interest, but something found along with them. For example, the tree rings from a wooden beam in an ancient residence may be of little intrinsic interest; but if one can learn from them that the tree used to build the residence was felled in the year A.D. 892, that may help to date the more interesting artifacts.

Seriation   We have already discussed stratigraphic analysis, a relative dating technique that is often conducted in the field. Another example of relative dating, more commonly done in the lab, is **seriation**, developed by the Egyptologist Flinders Petrie. Actually, seriation consists of a number of relative dating methods that all rely on the following assumption: The more similar patterns of material appear, the closer the materials are in time. Artifacts and features can thus often be recognized as a time series. The archaeological chronologies that result from seriation are analogous to the phylogenies generated by physical anthropologists (Chapter 10). The two basic types of seriation concern patterns of style and patterns of frequency. Stylistic seriation allows artifacts to be put in a sequence based on the degrees to which artifact styles are the same. Frequency seriation allows artifacts to be put in a comparable sequence based on the degree to which patterns among clusters of artifacts, or type occurrences, are the same.

Stylistic seriation is the physical equivalent of the children's game "telephone," in which each child in turn repeats a whispered message to the next child. Inevitably, mistakes are made along the way, and when the last child announces the message to the group, it is often nothing

seriation
Arranging artifacts by the gradual accumulation of differences among them, based on changes in either frequency or style.

(a)

(b)

Figure 2-14. Stylistic Seriations.
(a) Sir Flinders Petrie's ordering of Egyptian pottery vessels; (b) design
changes in American cars.

like the initial communication. If you could record each child's message
in turn, you would see that the changes occur gradually and in
sequence—the changes, or in this case mistakes, are cumulative—since
each is passed on down the line. The same phenomenon occurs with
changes in artifact styles, and so the archaeologist can form sequences
(Figure 2–14).

The patterns observed in stylistic seriation can indicate either temporal or spatial variation, and care must be taken to cross-check results
with other data. In addition, there is no inherent way of telling which
end of a sequence is oldest and which end youngest. This latter limitation
is true for frequency seriation as well, and another method must be found
for establishing the polarity of the sequence.

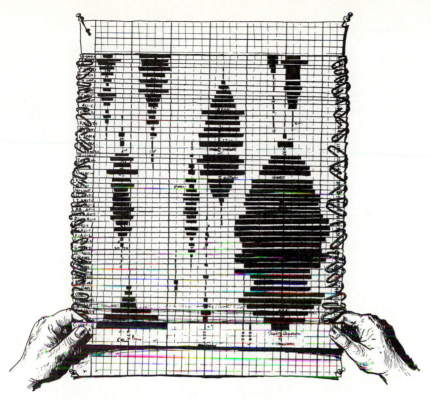

Figure 2-15
Creating a frequency seriation
by hand. Computers can do
the job much faster.

Frequency seriation is based on the observation that types appear at a certain time, after which their numbers increase through time as their popularity grows, followed by a period of decreasing occurrence as popularity wanes, and finally followed by complete disuse of the type. The length of time between initial and final use can vary a great deal, as can the lengths of time during which popularity is increasing and decreasing. Still, a diagram depicting the life of any type roughly resembles what archaeologists call a **battleship-shaped curve** (because it looks somewhat like a battleship seen from the air; see Figure 2–15). By creating these curves for available types, archaeologists can arrange sites (or deposits within sites) into relative chronological sequences.

Forming frequency seriations can be cumbersome if the number of assemblages or types is greater than a few. In recent years, however, archaeologists have designed computer programs that can generate the best sequence in a short period of time.

Dendrochronology   Tree-ring dating, or *dendrochronology*, is one of the most reliable absolute dating methods available to researchers. It is done by counting the number of tree rings in a sample of wood recovered from the field and, more importantly, comparing the pattern of the rings to established absolute tree-ring chronologies. These chronologies, often called "master chronologies," have been constructed for several regions

battleship(-shaped) curve

Diagram representing origin, popularity, and disuse of a particular type or style of material culture.

Figure 2-16
Schematic representation of how a tree-ring master chronology is built, starting from a sample of known age and overlapping successively older samples.

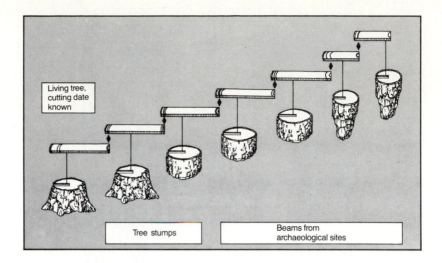

Living tree, cutting date known

Tree stumps

Beams from archaeological sites

around the world by overlapping the unique patterns of rings from trees dating from the present back as far as several thousand years. By matching a sample of wood with a specific segment of the master chronology, an absolute calendar date is reached (Figure 2–16).

Dendrochronology has a number of limitations, however. For one thing, master chronologies have not been completed for all regions. Second, only certain species of tree can be relied on to provide useful tree-ring patterns. Tree-ring dating is, after all, based on the fact that certain types of trees are sensitive to changes in the climate and grow to different extents each year. The data simply are not available for all places. Neither is the method applicable to all samples of wood.

In addition, a number of complications arise in using the method, complications that more directly reflect the complex nature of the archaeological record. First, tree-ring dates pertain to a portion of the life history of the tree, not to the time when the wood was used. Unless the bark is present on the wood, a date determined by dendrochronology might well be significantly older than the activities of interest. Second, wood is often reused in later construction, making the dendrochronological date older still. Third, and under different conditions, wooden objects are often replaced because of age and resulting weakening—in this case, a dendrochronological date might be significantly younger than the past behaviors under study.

Despite these complicating factors, tree-ring dating remains one of the more powerful dating tools, particularly in areas such as the southwest United States, where it has been used successfully for many years.

The Written Record   Another absolute dating method available to archaeologists consists of reading and analyzing the written record otherwise known as recorded history. This method actually consists of a very large number of related, complex exercises that are often overlooked.

Historical archaeology, or the archaeology of those times and places for which we have useful written materials, is a relatively new endeavor. Still, it is rapidly growing in popularity and importance. We discuss historical archaeology in more detail in Chapter 15.

Radiocarbon Dating All living things absorb both stable carbon, or ^{12}C, and a tiny amount of an unstable radioactive isotope of carbon, ^{14}C. The radioactive isotope is created in the earth's atmosphere as a result of cosmic radiation interacting with stable nitrogen, ^{14}N. As long as an organism is alive, the ratio of ^{14}C to ^{12}C within it remains the same.

At death, absorption of carbon stops. The unstable isotope in the carcass decomposes into nitrogen, and the ratio of normal carbon to radioactive carbon changes. The rate of radioactive decay is steady, however, and can be measured in terms of the **half-life** of the isotope—the length of time necessary for any given sample to be reduced by one-half. Thus, by measuring the proportion of ^{14}C in an artifact or other object, comparing that figure with the proportion of ^{14}C in the atmosphere, and applying the decay rate of the isotope, one can calculate how long it has been since the item being dated was last alive. For ^{14}C, the half-life is measured at 5730 ± 40 years.

Radiocarbon dates are derived statistically and are always expressed as probabilities—an example would be $2,000 \pm 30$ years B.P. (before present). This expression means that there is a 67 percent probability that the item being dated died between 2,030 and 1,970 years ago. In statistics, this range of dates falls within what is called the first standard deviation and means that it will be incorrect one time in three. If you want a much more reliable probability—95 percent, in fact—all you need do is double the range—2000 ± 60 years B.P. The dates 2,060 and 1,940 years ago bracket the second standard deviation. The new range would be expected to be incorrect only one time in twenty. Note that because radiocarbon dating gives you only a range of probable dates and not a date expressed as a specific number of years, it is chronometric, not absolute.

As with other dating methods, radiocarbon has its limitations and complications. For one thing, the method can be used only on once-living materials (bone, shell, wood, and charcoal, for example). In addition, it can date only objects that died less than about 70,000 years ago, even with the most advanced technological equipment—researchers cannot date earlier remains with radiocarbon because of its fairly short half-life. Third, the actual ratio of ^{14}C to ^{12}C in the atmosphere has fluctuated over time due to solar activity, compounding the uncertainty in this dating method. For the span of the last 7,000 years, therefore, radiocarbon dates have been carefully calibrated against tree-ring dates so that corrections for these fluctuations can be made.

As always, the greatest problems with radiocarbon dating stem from a lack of appreciation for the complexities of the method. It must always be remembered that the event being dated is the death of some once-living organism, and death dates are rarely the same as use dates or deposi-

half-life
The time it takes for a quantity of a radioactive isotope to decay to the extent that only half of it is left.

tion dates. If not taken into account, this could make the activity of interest appear older than it really is. So could the fact that sometimes certain organic materials, like mollusk shells, absorb inorganic carbon from surrounding rocks. On the other hand, sometimes once-living organisms can be contaminated by still-living organisms—roots growing through a buried piece of wood is an example—which introduce fresh supplies of ^{14}C. This would make the dated piece of wood seem more recent than it should.

Radiocarbon dating nevertheless remains one of the most useful methods of dating materials more recent than about 70,000 years B.P. In order to date materials from the more remote past, when hominids were first emerging (Chapters 11 and 12), we must turn to alternative chronometric measures.

Potassium-Argon Dating   Like radiocarbon, potassium-argon is a radiometric dating method, made possible because of the properties of radioactive isotopes. It is also a chronometric dating method in that a range of probable dates results from its application. Yet potassium-argon can date much older objects than can radiocarbon—objects millions of years old—because the half-life of the isotope potassium 40 (^{40}K) is 1.31 billion years.

Potassium 40 decays to form argon gas, or ^{40}Ar. When formed, rocks contain virtually no argon, which accumulates in minute amounts from the decay of the potassium isotope. Ratios of ^{40}K to ^{40}Ar in geologic samples can thus be measured to determine the date at which the rock formed. It turns out that rocks lose any argon that has accumulated when heated to very high temperatures, such as during volcanic eruptions. Thus, this method is especially useful in dating strata from volcanically active regions such as those in East Africa.

Two things must be borne in mind, however. First, a sample that was not heated sufficiently will yield a date older than it should; and a sample that has been reheated will yield a date too young. Second, this method dates rock, not artifacts or fossils. Care must be taken to ensure a good association between the geological sample and the objects of greatest interest. Often, artifacts and fossils are found to be sandwiched between two volcanic strata, and the dating of each gives a minimum and maximum time during which they could have been deposited.

A vexing problem for anthropologists is the gap of time between the minimum date that potassium-argon can reach (hundreds of thousands of years) and the maximum date of radiocarbon (tens of thousands of years). For the intervening span, other, often less reliable chronometric methods are required.

Other Dating Methods   Dating artifacts, fossils, and events obviously entails a number of assumptions. Anthropologists, therefore, try to use several dating methods to cross-check their results.

Paleoanthropologists are often aided in dating the sites of fossil hominids by studying the animals found with them. Different ages in the history of the earth are characterized by faunas of different compositions, as certain species change, become extinct, or arise. Even over a short geologic span, such as a few million years, geographical regions often have characteristic faunas. By recognizing key species and knowing approximately when they lived at other sites, one can apply the principles of **biostratigraphy**. In Europe, detailed studies of the evolutionary history of rodents called voles have shown extremely high specificity to periods of time on the order of a few hundred thousand years; therefore, any other fossil found in association with a vole can be assigned a fairly narrow range of dates with a high degree of confidence.

In Africa, however, the best biostratigraphic information has come from horses, pigs, and elephants. In one celebrated case, a potassium-argon date at a major hominid site in East Africa, called Koobi Fora, was called into question biostratigraphically. Though K-Ar dates indicated that it was about 2.5 million years old, it contained pigs and horses known to be only 2 million years old at other nearby East African sites. This suggested that perhaps the radiometric dates needed to be reexamined and redone. They were, and a concordance of dating techniques now shows that site to be about 1.8 million years old.

Researchers can use several other dating methods, a few of which we will mention below. These dating techniques are generally used in conjunction with other techniques as cross-checks, for many are new and not yet fully debugged and cannot be used confidently alone. *Thermoluminescence* is a measurement of the amount of light energy released from pottery or burnt flint during heating—and reflects the amount of time since the previous heating. *Uranium series dating* is based on the decay of uranium to thorium and protactinium and may be useful in dating seabeds or lakebeds. *Fission-track dating* is another means of dating volcanic rock, by visually examining the traces of decay of ^{238}Uranium in natural glasses. *Obsidian hydration* is a dating technique that relies on the fact that water is absorbed on exposed surfaces of obsidian at a measureable rate. It can be applied in the many regions where obsidian is found and used for tools. *Paleomagnetism* uses reversals in the earth's magnetic pole (caused by the poorly understood dynamics of the earth's core) to establish a stratigraphic pattern stretching back millions of years. *Archaeomagnetism*, on the other hand, is a technique useful over the past few thousand years, which involves the measurement of magnetic alignments within undisturbed remains that have been heated to a high enough temperature (hearths are common subjects). Because the magnetic north pole has wandered over this time, and because the iron particles in clay and other materials align themselves to the pole at high temperatures, the nature of their alignment can date the last heating.

After the recovered materials have been dated, the researcher can turn to higher-order analyses. It is at this time that the majority of the research questions can be addressed by testing the various hypotheses in the research design.

biostratigraphy

Dating events or fossils by the presence of certain species of animals known to have been associated with the events or fossils in question.

activity area

A clustered pattern of archaeological materials in space, suggesting localized specific human behaviors.

Data Manipulation   All researchers seek patterns in the data they generate in the lab. Patterns are indicative of regularities, and thus they inform anthropologists on the nature of biological and cultural evolution. Patterns are often sought in the delineation of **activity areas**—places where behaviors cluster as the result of any number of human endeavors.

Recently, historical archaeologists have concentrated their efforts on recognizing and describing various types of activity areas. For instance, Stanley South and others have recognized several functional groups, distinguishable by the relative amounts of different artifact types that occur in a given area. What is often called the Ethnic-Economic Group, for example (also called the Carolina Slave Group), contains a relatively high number of artifacts associated with kitchen activities and few artifacts associated with architecture. In contrast, the Public Access Group (or Public Interaction Group) contains little in the way of kitchen material and great amounts of architectural remains. These various groups, representing different kinds of activities, tell historical archaeologists the patterns of behavior within the regions and sites under investigation.

Other patterns that have been studied reflect social and economic status and changes of status through time. George Miller and his colleagues have documented the prices of various ceramic styles through the eighteenth and nineteenth centuries. They argue that if these prices are known, one can estimate the household investment in ceramics by charting the relative amounts of each ceramic style in the archaeological record. Thus, the researcher can observe how household members of different status practiced different consumer behaviors—important information for the interpretation of the archaeological record. These studies are complex, however, and many variables intervene to make the patterns difficult to see and interpret.

TESTING HYPOTHESES WITH STATISTICS

The patterns that researchers recognize consist of a series of measurements that relate to one another in some way. Understanding the nature of the relationships results in the testing of hypotheses and the answering of research questions.

A fundamental issue to address is whether or not the observed relationships are accidental or significant. In other words, what is the cause of the relationship—chance, or some important condition or variable? For instance, if we observe that in a group of heavy smokers, more people get emphysema than in a matched group of nonsmokers, is it accidental, or are smoking and emphysema linked in some important way? Or, if we find certain artifacts in one particular location of a site and not in another location, is this because of chance or because of some important aspect of the behaviors once occurring at the site? Obviously, this is a critical issue.

The way we determine the answer is through the use of **statistics**.

statistics

Numerical methods for briefly generalizing a description of data or for inferring probabilities of events.

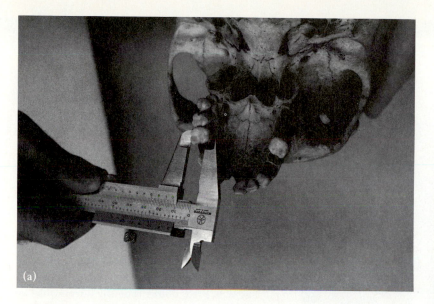

(a)

Figure 2-17
Laboratory work in physical anthropology is diverse and can include (a) analyzing teeth or other anatomical traits; and (b) studying genetic relationships from a sample of blood.

(b)

Statistical tests are designed to tell us how likely it is that a particular association between sets of measurements is accidental. Anything can happen by chance—thus, it is important to know how likely it is that the relationships we have found are due to chance occurrences.

In general, scientists accept a 95 percent confidence level from statistics. That is, if the statistics tell us that there is a 95 percent chance that the association is *not* due to chance, we accept the association as real and significant. This inference will be correct, on the average, 19 out of 20 times. Of course, this also means that 1 time in 20, on the average, we will be wrong—we will think that the association is significant when, in fact, it is due to chance. It is impossible to know when the inference is wrong, that is, when this is the 1 time in 20. Thus, hypotheses must repeatedly be tested with new data.

A Note on Experimental Anthropology

Though fieldwork is fundamental to anthropology, important data are also being collected increasingly by experimental scientists. In physical anthropology, for example, one can study the different functions of important muscle groups across species in laboratories. This can be accomplished by monitoring when the muscles fire during particular activities and can give us an idea of how the evolutionary changes in those species occurred. Judgments about fossils are generally made by comparison with reference skeletal collections, away from the field (Figure 2–17). The behavior of primates, their social and mental features specifically, can also be studied in experimental settings (Chapter 6) under controlled conditions.

Genetic relationships among primate species can be investigated by

The Shroud of Turin

Scientists are sometimes skeptical when confronted with a claim contrary to their expectations about what is likely or even possible in the universe. While they are occasionally incorrect in such dismissals ("They all laughed at Columbus" is one of the most popular sayings among cranks), they are correct far more often. Someone claiming to have invented a perpetual motion machine, or to have met aliens from the planet Venus, is likely to be snubbed by scientists without so much as a hearing. Very rarely an outlandish claim has some validity to it, but much more frequently it is a waste of time and merits a place only in the supermarket tabloids.

Yet, we hold fast to irrational beliefs about certain things. Are the accomodations really better if "George Washington Slept Here?" That illegible scrawl your grandfather showed you—does it really matter whether it is the signature of Joe DiMaggio or of somebody else? A special symbolic quality gives these objects greater value than they would otherwise have—they are not so much objects as relics. And because relics have greater value than ordinary objects, profit can often be made in the relic market.

One such relic is the famous Shroud of Turin, a cloth 14 feet 3 inches long and 3 feet 7 inches wide, which contains the faint image of a man, front and back, with the images head to head. Is it the burial shroud of Jesus Christ, whose image was formed on the cloth miraculously 2,000 years ago? Could it possibly be?

There is little doubt that the shroud has an image of Jesus upon it. Indeed, it is a man, about 5 feet 7 inches tall, with long hair (possibly tied in the back) and wearing a beard, as Jesus has been depicted in Christian art since about the sixth century. The man has holes in his wrists and his feet (indicating crucifixion), as well as several small wounds around the head (crown of thorns) and on the back (flagellation). A wound is visible between the fifth and sixth ribs on his right side, where one of the Apostles relates that Jesus was speared.

The history of this relic, however, is documented only from the fourteenth century. It became known quite suddenly in 1353 while in the possession of Geoffrey de Charny, a French nobleman. The local bishop condemned it immediately and his successor urged the Pope to prohibit its showing in 1389, citing evidence indicating it to be a forgery, including a confession by an artist. Nevertheless, it remains to this day a religious relic, not inspirational art, such as Michelangelo's *Pièta*, but to the devoted, the true burial shroud of Jesus.

History, art, and science weigh against this interpretation, however. Not only was the shroud unknown until the fourteenth century, but it was attacked as fraudulent by contemporary clergymen.

Further, that century saw a booming trade in fake religious relics carried back to Europe by the Crusaders: tears of the Virgin Mary, drops of the blood of Jesus and the martyrs, milk of the Virgin Mary, the bones, hair, and toenails of the saints, pieces of the true cross, and so on. This circumstantially tends to militate against the shroud being authentic.

Artistically, one notes no distortion of the image due to folding and wrinkling of the cloth as would be expected. Further, the limbs and fingers are very linear and longer than natural—precisely the way they were rendered by Gothic artists.

A scientific study of the apparent blood stains detected inorganic red pigments, not remnants of human blood. A pathologist noted that below the wounds to the head, the blood was trickling in discrete streams—but in real cases, the blood usually smears and becomes matted in the hair. The image shows no significant blood coagulation which is biologically unrealistic. Further, the image, the scorch-marks (from a fire in 1532), and the blood stains all fluoresce when exposed to X rays—but blood is not supposed to.

Pollen studies suggest that the shroud has been to the Middle East—but whether during the time of the Roman Empire, the time of the Crusades, or later remains open, and the quality of the studies has been strongly criticized. Why not simply date the shroud chronometrically?

The Church finally allowed samples of the shroud to be dated by ^{14}C. On 21 April 1988, samples of the shroud were given to three radiocarbon-dating labs. Each sample was approximately 50 milligrams in weight and, along with three control samples (eleventh- to twelfth-century Nubian linen, linen from a 2,000-year-old Egyptian mummy, and a French thread from about A.D. 1300), was taken to labs in Zurich, Oxford, and Tucson for analysis.

Though the analyses were not performed strictly blindly (that is, the researchers could have discovered which sample was which from the threads' appearance) none of the labs compared results, and two recoded the specimens after combustion so that the staff could not know which sample was which. The results were independently communicated to the British Museum.

The results were highly concordant. The Nubian thread was dated with 95 percent confidence to be from A.D. 1030–1160; the Egyptian mummy was dated to 10 B.C.–A.D. 80; and the French thread was dated to A.D. 1260–1280. And the Shroud of Turin? At the statistical level of 95 percent, its date is A.D. 1260–1390.

On 13 October 1989, the Archbishop of Turin made the results known publicly. To its credit, the Church chose not to challenge the results—for one's religious faith is certainly not going to stand or fall on the authenticity of the Shroud of Turin. Yet a pious physicist challenged the results with a wishful conjecture of neutrons being miraculously emanated from the body of Jesus. The response from one of the Oxford scientists was that "the likelihood they influenced the date in the way proposed is… so exceedingly remote that it beggars scientific credulity."

References:

Culliton, B. (1978). The mystery of the Shroud of Turin challenges 20th-century science. *Science*, 201:235–239.

Meacham, W. (1983). The authentication of the Turin Shroud: An issue in archaeological epistemology (with responses). *Current Anthropology*, 24:283–311.

Damon, P. E., et al. (1989). Radiocarbon dating of the Shroud of Turin. *Nature*, 337:611–615.

Phillips, T. J. (1989). Shroud irradiated with neutrons? *Nature*, 337:594. Response by R. E. M. Hedges.

analyzing protein structure or DNA sequences (Chapter 8). This can enable us to test hypotheses about phylogeny independently of the anatomy of the species in question.

Finally, experimental archaeology is also a growing field, with increasing numbers of archaeologists manufacturing their own stone tools, creating artificial archaeological sites, and carrying out controlled observations of human behavior (Chapter 16).

In each of these endeavors, however, the fundamental problems remain the same: collecting data on a pertinent problem, finding patterns among them, and testing hypotheses about our biological and cultural evolution through those patterns of data.

Summary

Science is a scholarly endeavor, though not all scholarship is scientific. The various humanities can also be scholarly. The criteria for scholarship include 1) insight, 2) a mastery of the subject matter, 3) a clear and accurate presentation of the evidence, and 4) logical reasoning.

While the sciences and humanities are both scholarly, however, they differ in important ways. While scientists try to be objective and answer the question "How?", humanists are often advocates of a particular point of view and address the question "Why?"

Science is a cultural endeavor. The work of scientists is influenced by the culture in which they live. Yet, all scientists assume that 1) the universe can be understood, and that 2) things are as they appear. Without these assumptions, science could not be undertaken. Science is also empirical, self-correcting, probabilistic, and parsimonious.

Scientific studies, including those in anthropology, can be synchronic (concerned with phenomena at one point in time) or diachronic (concerned with phenomena through time). For either, the use of proper methods is important. All scientific projects require a research design. Many projects in anthropology require fieldwork and the application of proper field and laboratory procedures. The goal is appropriately to confirm or reject various alternative hypotheses.

1. If evolution is understood through science, and science is culture bound, what implications are there for the teaching of evolution versus other theories? Are these implications different from those that exist for the teaching of gravity or electricity?

2. What are the major differences between research designs in a typical diachronic study and synchronic study?

3. What are some differences between the ways in which a paleoanthropologist would date a fossil hominid site and a historical archaeologist would date a frontier settlement?

4. What are the general differences between explanations that are considered adequate in scientific and nonscientific contexts?

Dancey, W. S. (1981). *Archaeological field methods: An introduction.* Minneapolis, MN: Burgess.

Gjertson, D. (1989). *Science and philosophy: Past and present.* London, England: Penguin.

Harrold, F. B., & Eve, R. A. (Eds.) (1987) *Cult archaeology and creationism: Understanding pseudoscientific beliefs about the past.* Iowa City, IA: University of Iowa Press.

Hester, T. R., Heizer, R. F., and Graham, J. A. (1975) *Field Methods in Archaeology.* Palo Alto: Mayfield.

Richards, S. (1987). *Philosophy and sociology of science: An introduction* (2d ed.). Oxford, England: Basil Blackwell.

The History of Evolution

The History of Evolution

Understanding Evolutionary Theory

Evolutionary theory, as all science, is a human, cultural endeavor. And like other human phenomena, in order to understand it one must understand where it comes from and how it came to be. Modern studies of evolution are dependent on strict empirical observations guided by recent theoretical frameworks. It would be a mistake, however, to think that our present ideas and research directions have not been shaped by the changing notions of the past several centuries.

Evolution in its broadest sense simply means *accumulated change over time*. This concept can be applied to many phenomena: from stars, to mammals, to societies, to ideas, and even to textbooks. In this chapter, however, we focus on evolutionary thought as it has been applied to the attributes of *Homo sapiens*. Biological evolution is the overarching theme of physical anthropology, and cultural evolution is the overarching theme of archaeology. As humans are bio-cultural animals, an understanding of their evolution can come only from considering both aspects, and an appreciation for the present state of our understanding can be gained only with a review of past states.

This can be clarified by going back to that time in European history from which evolutionary thought has had a continuous and dramatic development up to the present—**The Enlightenment**—a time of extraordinary scientific achievement spanning the eighteenth century. Unfortunately, Enlightenment scholars tended not to distinguish biological from cultural phenomena, largely because the people most culturally different from eighteenth century Europeans appeared to be the most biologically different as well.

The Enlightenment

Period of European intellectual history spanning most of the eighteenth century, during which many liberal, democratic ideals were formulated and science became an acceptable way of seeing the world.

Before the Enlightenment

Prior to the last decade of the seventeenth century, only sporadic attempts within Western society were made to come systematically and logically to terms with the human condition. Anything that appeared to be an intellectual novelty was considered anathema by the authorities of the Middle Ages, particularly those novelties that had the potential of increasing secular knowledge. In fact, as late as 1655, Isaac de la Peyrere (d. 1676), who speculated that there had existed *Pre-Adamites* (humans before Adam), was obliged to retract his views by the authorities of the Inquisition. And nearly a century after that, Count de Buffon (1707–1788) was obliged by the theology faculty at the Sorbonne to retract his radical *Theory of the Earth* (see below). Still, scientific inquiry began to emerge in Europe as early as the twelfth and thirteenth centuries with the introduction of the works of the Greeks (chiefly as Latin translations from Arabic versions). This blossoming was part of the very beginning of **the Renaissance.**

NEW METHODS OF INTERPRETATION

During the height of the Renaissance, the year 1543 can be considered something of a watershed in the history of European science. In that year, two highly influential works were published: *On the Fabric of the Human Body* by Andreas Vesalius (1514–1564)(Figure 3–1), and *On the Revolutions of the Celestial Spheres* by Nicholaus Copernicus (1473–1543).

Although these works contributed much to basic knowledge regarding the workings of the human body and of the solar system, their more significant advances lay in the improved methods of observation and interpretation they contained. Vesalius, by concentrating on the living body, by employing the experimental method, and by insisting on detailed study, was capable of developing a systemic approach to anatomy; he came to view the human organism as a dynamic system of interrelated, functioning parts rather than as essentially a bag of organs. And Copernicus, by suggesting a **heliocentric** model of our planetary system (Figure 3–2), underscored the revolutionary idea that our perspective on the universe was one that involved considerable, though regular, motion. Both works opened the door to viewing all phenomena as dynamic (not static) and regulated by laws.

The Renaissance

Period of European intellectual history spanning roughly the fourteenth through sixteenth centuries, during which there was a rebirth of many arts and sciences consciously recalling classical Greek and Roman culture.

heliocentric

Centered around the sun, as opposed to geocentric, centered around the earth.

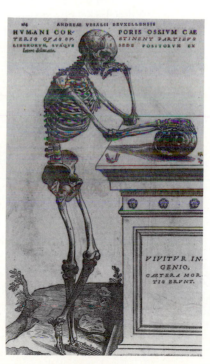

Figure 3-1

Frontispiece and second skeleton from *De Fabrica* by Vesalius, 1543.

Figure 3-2

The heliocentric solar system according to Copernicus, 1543.

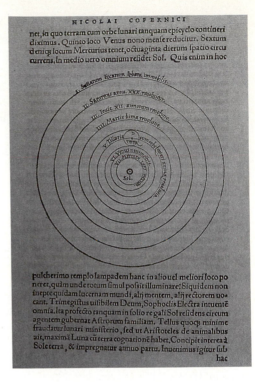

Other scholars built on these innovative perspectives during the following several decades. Some, in fact, were even more influential in shaping subsequent scientific views. William Harvey (1578–1657) published the *Anatomical Dissertation on the Motion of the Heart and Blood in Animals* in 1628, in which he described the heart as a pump that allowed the blood to circulate through a system of vessels. Galileo Galilei (1564–1642), with the help of his "optic reed" (or telescope), visually confirmed that motion and change were widespread hallmarks of the universe. Tycho Brahe (1546–1601) and Johannes Kepler (1571–1630) did the same and set out to discover mathematically what these laws of motion were. These and other initiatives culminated in Isaac Newton's (1642–1727) famous *Mathematical Principles of Natural Philosophy* (or *Principia*) in 1687.

Figure 3-3

Sir Isaac Newton

Isaac Newton   Isaac Newton (Figure 3–3) was the first scientist-hero of the modern age, a man whose work and thought defined the scope of the scientific endeavor for his generation and for many generations after. His principal achievements were in formulating mathematical regularities underlying motion and light. Newton was also privately a mystical theologian, an alchemist (trying to convert base metals into gold), and a thoroughly disagreeable fellow. The significance of Newton's work lay in demonstrating that the structure of the universe was comprehensible to mortals. There was, it appeared, fundamental order in the universe. Even if the answers to specific questions about how the universe worked were not known, at least there *were* answers. The job of the scientist was to find them.

Robert Hooke   What would today be called geology—the investigation of the history of the earth—experienced significant developments during this time also. As early as 1668, Robert Hooke (1635–1703) suggested that fossils were the remains of real plants and animals. This conclusion was contrary to the majority opinion, which was that fossils represented mere quirks of nature—stone images. Hooke noted that many marine-looking fossil organisms were located in areas far removed from any ocean. In order to explain this, he came up with the radical conclusion that the face of the earth had changed dramatically since its creation. Hooke made another important observation that would bear fruit in Germany half a century later: that a piece of cork examined microscopically seemed to be made up of tiny, similar structures he called "cells."

Some, like Nicolaus Steno (1638–1686), supported Hooke's geologic arguments and began attempting to reconstruct the dynamic history of the earth by studying the stratigraphic record and its contents. Others, like John Woodward (1665–1728), rejected the notion and clung to a static view of earth history.

SCIENTIFIC SOCIETIES

Scientific activities were occurring at greater frequency during the seventeenth century in large measure because of growing governmental support, most notable in the formation of scientific societies within western Europe. The Royal Society was chartered in England in 1662, for example, and the French Academy in 1666. These societies lessened the need for scholars to depend on the whims of wealthy private citizens for financial backing, and regular meetings of the societies allowed a greater exchange of ideas. In addition, a number of scholars (such as Galileo in Italy and Descartes in France) began publishing in modern European languages and no longer in Latin. By doing so, they made new ideas more accessible.

DEVELOPMENT OF A MODERN SCIENTIFIC WORLD VIEW

Advances in the sciences during the centuries just before the Enlightenment—especially in astronomy—heralded a fundamental shift in world view from one that saw the universe (and all things in it) as fixed and static, to one that saw everything affected by laws of motion. The planets revolved around the sun; the blood circulated through the arteries and veins. Constant movement was the newly recognized rule. Furthermore, the realization was growing that not only were there laws of motion, but that these laws could be apprehended through systematic observation and study. Finally, because of the founding of scientific societies and the growing habit of writing scientific treatises in modern languages, knowledge of these advances was no longer restricted to a tiny segment of the population. These shifts in perspective, method, and awareness, however, did not diminish the nearly universal belief among Europeans that the universe, the earth, and the life upon it were all created by God in one miraculous week.

In the eighteenth century the beginnings of modern social and political thought emerged, and with them, a modern scientific world view. As we will see, many of these advances occurred because of a continuing interest in the laws of motion and change. Such laws were refined in those subjects in which they had been previously applied and expanded to apply to a host of other phenomena as well.

The Enlightenment

We can analytically take the beginning of the Enlightenment as the publication of John Locke's (1632–1704) *An Essay Concerning Human Understanding* in 1690, three years after the appearance of Newton's *Principia*. This germinal work of Locke's was the catalyst for many fundamental concepts in the modern social sciences. It was Locke who introduced the notion that the human mind at birth was like a *tabula rasa*, a blank slate: All human thoughts and ideas, according to Locke, were acquired through the process of growing up and learning within the context of society. It was a distinctly human capability, it followed, to depend entirely on others for the development of the mind.

Figure 3-4

A Hobbesian view of primitive life.

EMPIRICISM

Locke's views were concordant with the developing scientific attitude that emphasized experience as the source of true knowledge. This is reflected in the necessity for observation and experimentation, a philosophy we call empiricism. To Locke, experience was the true source of knowledge, not only for an adult, but for a growing child as well. Thus, a child's experiences are not imparted genetically; they are all acquired, written on the child's "blank slate." Locke further criticized the earlier work of Thomas Hobbes (1588–1679), who in his *Leviathan* (1651) had asked the following question: If we were to dissolve the bonds of society, what would a human be like? Hobbes, who had suffered through the bloody Civil War in England, felt that humans without society would be hostile creatures, constantly engaged in a "war of all against all" (Figure 3–4) and that their lives would be "solitary, poore, nasty, brutish, and short." But Locke had a more optimistic view. He felt that humans were fundamentally rational beings, their capacity for reason differentiating them from other creatures. Humans existing without society, Locke concluded, would settle down to a peaceful, egalitarian existence, having nothing but their experiences and their rational powers to guide them.

Locke reached these conclusions because he saw the world as filled with societies of very different ethical and moral rules of conduct:

> **Whether there be any such moral principles, wherein all men do agree, I appeal to any who have been but moderately conversant in the history of mankind, and looked abroad beyond the smoke of their own chimneys. Where is that practical truth that is universally received without doubt or question, as it must be if innate?**

> *(quoted in Harris 1968:11)*

Granted, data regarding societies outside Europe—and available to European scholars—were not very accurate at the close of the seventeenth century. And much of these data were sensational, biased, and designed to serve the political needs of Europeans in the midst of unprecedented empire building and colonization. Nevertheless, Locke's observations were remarkably relativistic and his conclusions not unlike those of social scientists generations later: Cultural forms do exhibit a tremendous range of variation, and they impose a structure upon the way a growing human sees the world and responds to it.

BIOLOGICAL THEORIES

Repeatedly, as biological and cultural evolutionary thought emerged, theoretical advances regarding culture took the lead, while those concerning biological evolution lagged behind. At the same time as Locke was contemplating the vast array of human social conditions and the fundamen-

Figure 3-5

John Ray's influential treatise of 1691 shaped biological thought for more than a century.

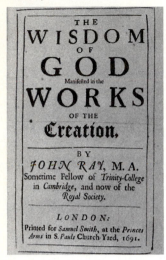

Platonic species

A group of creatures that are all slight variants on a basic ideal theme; based on the philosophy of idealism or essentialism.

tal significance of this array in terms of the human reliance on learning, the general consensus was that biological forms were immutable, unvarying, and inflexible. Indeed, in 1691, one year after Locke wrote of the *tabula rasa*, John Ray (1627–1705) introduced an extremely influential study that extended traditional Christian doctrine to all natural phenomena, including those of the biological realm. It was titled *The Wisdom of God Manifested in the Works of the Creation* (Figure 3–5), and it argued that 1) everything in the universe is created by God, 2) the structure of everything in the universe is designed according to God's intentions, 3) these intentions are never-changing, and so 4) the fundamental structures are unchangeable. This reasoning was very different from John Locke's conclusion regarding human learning and social plasticity.

Ray was aware of the emerging views of the early, pre-Enlightenment astronomers, anatomists, and geologists and was troubled by their deductions regarding matter following laws of motion. But where the physicists, following Newton, were coming to know God through underlying regularity, uniting disparate phenomena under common mechanisms, Ray as a biologist had only diversity before him. Thus, he reasoned, God must be knowable through His bounty, His generosity in creating such diverse creatures.

Yet Ray contributed to the emerging views of the universe and the things in it. He was the first to define a species as a population of organisms that produced offspring. Common reproduction defined the species, Ray argued, not appearance. His view eventually came to replace those derived from the writings of Plato.

The *Platonic concept of species* held that organisms belong to species because they look similar, being earthly, and therefore imperfect, reflections of supernatural ideals. This argument implied eternal stability for each species since, obviously, supernatural ideals cannot evolve. Ray's view of species did not include evolution but permitted later thinkers, such as Buffon, to build an evolutionary concept of the species, as it was rooted in the natural world.

GROWTH OF THE NEW PHILOSOPHY

Astronomy and the physical sciences developed rapidly in the eighteenth century. Thomas Wright (1711–1786), for example, suggested that all observable heavenly bodies were in motion and actually predicted the structure of the Milky Way galaxy in 1750. Only several decades later, William Herschel (1738–1822), the discoverer of the planet Uranus, suggested that the entire universe was made up of innumerable galaxies, an amazing deduction for the time. Throughout the Enlightenment, however, scholarly interest was increasingly focused not so much on structure as on motion—on change, and thus on origins.

The growing emphasis on motion and origins led scholars of astronomy to contemplate how the earth was formed. They did not need to begin this investigation from scratch, however; as we have seen, others had been contemplating the history of the earth before the Enlightenment.

Theories of Geological Change   During the first several decades of the Enlightenment, geological inquiry focused on the issue of how the earth's surface had changed. Due to the work of Hooke, Steno, and others during the previous century, scholars concluded that change had indeed occurred. How, after all, could one explain fossilized sea shells hundreds of miles from the sea if the earth had not undergone significant changes? The mechanisms responsible, however, were not clearly known. Even less could be said about the rate of change, a critical issue that was not systematically explored until later.

Soon, two schools of thought emerged regarding the dominant mechanisms of geological change. The Vulcanists thought that volcanic activity was the prime force shaping the earth's surface. The Neptunists, on the other hand, argued that the force of water was primary in the earth's dynamic history. Both groups focused attention on geologic *processes*, but neither sought to challenge traditional time frames that saw the earth and heavens as having been formed very recently. One traditional date for the creation was from Archbishop James Ussher, who in 1658 fixed the date of creation at October 23, 4004 B.C. by working back through the biblical patriarchs to Adam. Several years earlier, in 1642, John Lightfoot, vice-chancellor of Cambridge University, had gone so far as to calculate that the event took place at 9:00 a.m. This biblical chronology was indeed the popular European view at the time. And while the Vulcanists and Neptunists disputed the forces that governed the earth's history, they did not dare suggest that its history was longer than the clergy said it was. A radical, brilliant, and influential scholar who *did* indeed confront the popular dogma was Georges-Louis Leclerc, Count de Buffon. Buffon (Figure 3–6) was one of the principal figures in the history of scientific and evolutionary thought, primarily through a monumental thirty–six-volume series titled *Natural History, General and Particular*, one of the most widely read works of the era.

Buffon   Buffon's views regarding geology were initially expressed in detail in the first volume of his *Natural History*, published in 1749. In this work Buffon argued forcefully that earth history should be explained without reference to scripture, particularly without reference to the Great Flood of Noah as described in the book of Genesis. Clearly, this was a radical view for the time. Yet it was not the most revolutionary argument that Buffon presented. More radical, and probably having a greater impact on the development of geologic and evolutionary views, was Buffon's insistence that the nature of the earth's surface was *not* the result of a series of catastrophic miracles:

Figure 3-6
Count de Buffon

We ought not to be affected by causes which seldom act, and whose action is always sudden and violent. These have no place in the ordinary course of nature. But operations uniformly repeated, motions which succeed one another without interruption, are the causes which alone ought to be the foundation of our reasoning.

(Buffon 1749 [1791]:34)

Buffon soon learned what such radical ideas could entail. Almost immediately his views became the subject of a formal inquiry by the theology faculty at the Sorbonne, in Paris. And his only way of avoiding censure was to present a recantation of his ideas in Volume 4 of the *Natural History*, published in 1753. Yet as this work grew, he returned to his original opinions and indeed surpassed them. Before returning to issues of geology, however, Buffon developed a number of crucial concepts within biology.

As with his ideas regarding earth history, Buffon was well ahead of his time when it came to biological studies. In addition, his interest in biology ranged across virtually the entire spectrum of the eighteenth century life sciences: He considered the nature of inheritance and development, biological variation and its possible causes, and the characteristics of species. Buffon, in fact, developed a theory of **microevolution** nearly a century before Darwin, although he never accepted or developed a notion of **macroevolution**.

Buffon's ideas regarding inheritance and development were introduced in the second volume of his *Natural History*, published also in 1749. As embryology was still a nascent discipline, Buffon entered a major controversy by rejecting **preformism** in favor of **epigenesis**, the more modern view. He went on to claim that two forces allowed and directed the subsequent growth of the embryo: a store of organic molecules that acted as a "fuel" for development and an internal mold that directed its development. These conclusions were not evolutionary; the internal mold would forbid change from one species to another. Yet Buffon appreciated that biological variation could nevertheless occur— was a rule of nature, in fact—if only within prescribed limits.

Buffon felt that such variation, or intraspecific change, was possible because the nature of the "fuel" was not the same everywhere; in different environments, different food sources were available, and consequently a different set of organic molecules was present. Thus, Buffon argued for an environmental-geographical cause for the biological variation he recognized. But he went even a step farther in that he added a temporal dimension—claiming that the nature of variation within any particular species could change through time if the members of that species migrated into a new environmental setting or if the environment changed. Throughout his life Buffon championed the historical perspective in biological research, also revolutionary for the age.

microevolution

Change within a species.

macroevolution

Transspecific change; the evolution of one species into another.

preformism

The idea that an embryo is fully formed at conception and does not change, but simply grows, in the womb.

epigenesis

The idea that an embryo develops from an originally undifferentiated form (now called a fertilized egg or zygote) and changes considerably in appearance during gestation.

hierarchy

An organizing principle involving a form of ranking things one above another; there are many kinds of hierarchies, and Linnaeus and Buffon believed in different ones.

The Great Chain of Being   Buffon was not ahead of his time, however, in his adherence to the Great Chain of Being, a concept that goes back at least to Aristotle (Figure 3–7). The Great Chain of Being subsumed three ideas: 1) that every species that conceivably could exist does, in fact, exist; 2) that every species intergrades with every other; and 3) that all living species can be arranged linearly, with humans at the pinnacle. Thus, above plants came worms, above worms came fish, then whales, other mammals, monkeys, apes, and finally, humans. Variations of the Great Chain had another linear arrangement above humans that included the orders of angels leading up to God.

Western society during the Middle Ages and immediately afterward was dominated by a static social and economic **hierarchy**, and so the Great Chain was a fitting principle for organizing the world and human life both biologically and culturally. As we note throughout this book, it is still a pervasive organizing principle, though thoroughly wrong.

Linnaeus   Buffon was in many respects overshadowed by his contemporary Carolus Linnaeus (1707–1778)(Figure 3–8), with whom he disagreed about most biological issues. Buffon, greatly influenced by the work of Newton, thought that explanatory models were the ultimate goal of science; Linnaeus saw methods of arranging the data as primary. Buffon argued that the species was the only grouping of organisms having reality in nature; Linnaeus is most famous for developing a hierarchical scheme of classification that recognized more inclusive categories than the species (for example, the genus and the order). Buffon stressed the importance of a historical perspective; Linnaeus's classificatory scheme was static and

Figure 3-7

(a) The Great Chain of Being, a long-standing way of seeing the world, holds that species can be ranked along a single dimension, one above the other. The culmination of this series is the human, and some variations on this theme had a hierarchy of spiritual beings continuing up to God.
(b) Buffon's version of the Great Chain incorporated microevolution within species.

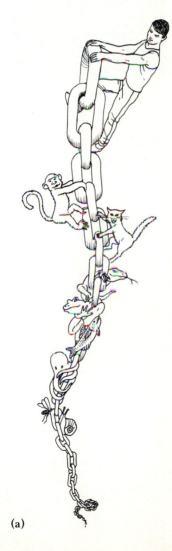

(a)

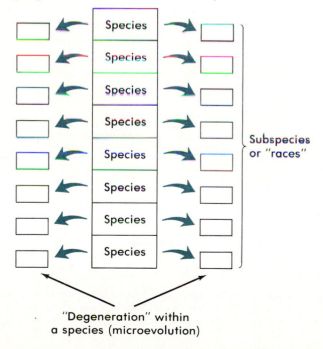

(b)

"Degeneration" within a species (microevolution)

Figure 3-8

Carl Linné (Carolus Linnaeus)

limited to the here-and-now. Buffon believed in the Great Chain of Being; Linnaeus's great contribution was to undermine it.

In the tenth edition of his great work, *System of Nature* (published in 1758, and from which modern systematics is dated), Linnaeus applied the principle of binomial nomenclature, giving every species a name consisting of two terms: Thus, *Homo sapiens* for man, and *Canis familiaris* for man's best friend (see Chapter 5). More importantly, Linnaeus grouped species into *higher categories of equal rank*. For example, humans and monkeys were for Linnaeus of equal rank, each a genus in the order Primates. And, in like manner, the order Primates and the order Carnivora were considered of equal rank, each a part of the class Mammalia (Figure 3–9). Many of the details of the classification have changed since Linnaeus's time, but the organizational principle remains the same. The Linnaean hierarchy was thus incompatible with the Great Chain: If two genera or orders were given equal rank, how could one be justifiably placed either above or below the other?

The only significant similarity between Buffon and Linnaeus—both giants in biological inquiry—was that neither was an evolutionist. This is an ironic point, for if particular views and arguments of each had been combined, a true evolutionary paradigm might have emerged much earlier than it actually did. Buffon contributed the notion of species changing through time to fit their environment, but he failed to recognize the reality of categories above that of the species. Linnaeus focused on such categories but maintained a static view of nature, always insisting that "there are no new species." In the last years of his life, observations of hybrid plants prompted him to lift that statement from the last (twelfth) edition of *System of Nature*. Darwin, a century later, finally grafted the idea of changes in species (Buffon) to that of higher taxonomic categories

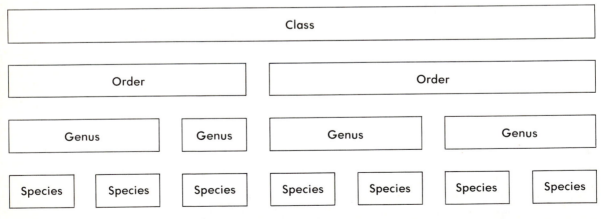

Figure 3-9

In the Linnaean hierarchy, species are grouped into clusters of genera, genera are grouped into clusters of families, and so on. Every genus has the same rank as every other genus; every family has the same rank as every other family.

(Linnaeus) and concluded that the pattern discerned in nature by Linnaeus was a relic of divergence from common ancestors.

DISCOVERY OF THE CHIMPANZEE

One of the reasons that the biological uniqueness of humans remained unchallenged in Western society for millennia is that our closest relatives, the apes, are to be found only in parts of the earth fairly remote from Europe: equatorial Africa and the East Indies. A scientific consequence of colonialism was the discovery and capture of chimpanzees and orang-utans by Europeans. There was thus little or no precedent for the study published by Edward Tyson (1650–1708), a leading English anatomist, who dissected a young chimpanzee and published his results in 1699 as *Orang-Outang, sive Homo Sylvestris, Or, the Anatomy of a Pygmie.*

What Tyson dissected was neither what we now call a pygmy nor an orang-utan. His was, however, the first anatomical analysis of an ape, an infant male chimpanzee. Tyson found thirty-four similarities between his "Pygmie" and a monkey but forty-eight similarities between his "Pygmie" and a human. Yet, it was not a human. Indeed, for the first time, a nonhuman creature was shown to be more similar to a person than to another nonhuman creature. Tyson's interpretation was that this animal was a connecting link in the Great Chain of Being, but his finding led to the important conclusion that humans are a part of the natural world, connected corporeally to the rest of the animals (Figure 3–10).

(a)

(b)

Figure 3–10

(a) Edward Tyson's "Orang-outang" or "pygmie" of 1699 was neither an orang-utan nor a pygmy, but an infant chimpanzee. Tyson drew it with a cane because it was dying when he observed it, and upon dissection he was so struck by the similarity between the chimp's anatomy and the human's that he concluded it had been designed by God to be an erect biped (and was knuckle-walking because it was ill). (b) Buffon's "Jocko" of 1766 was recognizably a chimpanzee, yet it retained the cane given by Tyson, as did virtually all pictures of apes until the 1830s.

Ultimately, therefore, the same laws that apply in nature to other animals would have to apply to our species.

ADVANCES IN CULTURAL EVOLUTIONISM

The place of humans within the organizational scheme of life was an additional area of inquiry about which Buffon and Linnaeus disagreed. Linnaeus grouped humans with apes in the order Anthropomorpha (in 1735), later called the Primates (in 1758). But Buffon argued that humans were qualitatively distinct and far removed from such morphologically similar animals as the apes because he did not group organisms on the basis of physical characteristics. Rather, Buffon emphasized the unique qualities of "mind" and rationality to be found in *Homo sapiens*, and thus was closer to the views of John Locke and subsequent Enlightenment scholars who contemplated the nonbiological characteristics of human beings:

> **Thus the ape, which philosophers, as well as the masses, have regarded as difficult to define, and whose nature was at least equivocal, and partway between that of man and the animals, is, in fact, nothing but a pure animal wearing a mask of the human figure externally, but deprived of thought, and of all that constitutes the human species.**
>
> *(Buffon 1766 [1843]:695)*

He went on to suggest that society was both a necessary and natural context for human existence; without society, there could be no humans. This conclusion was similar to Locke's insistence that humans were born without knowledge and needed social interaction in order to acquire ideas.

Much occurred, however, within the realm of cultural evolutionary studies in the century since Locke's *An Essay Concerning Human Understanding*. Indeed, during this time a fundamental shift occurred in the way scholars viewed the variety of human societies, from a traditional philosophy of **degenerationism** to an emerging view of cultural progress, or **progressionism**. Thus, not only were humans considered unique because of their particular mental capabilities and needs but also because of their potential to improve through time (Figure 3–11).

Interestingly, little in the way of archaeological field research was being conducted at this time, and archaeologists did not contribute to this philosophical shift. Although artifacts were being recovered in Europe, they were seldom recognized as very old or as the results of human behaviors. Systematic archaeological study did not emerge until the early nineteenth century.

Degenerationism had its roots in two areas. First, the ancient Greeks tended to look back upon earlier "Golden Ages" with reverence—

degenerationism

The view that various peoples have fallen from an originally better or higher state, to varying degrees.

progressionism

The view that various peoples have risen from an original baseline of primitiveness or savagery to varying degrees.

(a)

Figure 3-11

Is the "Golden Age" past or
yet ot come?
(a) Degenerationism glorifies
the life of ancient times;
(b) progressionism glorifies the
life of the future.

(b)

times when things were better and people were smarter, a theme picked
up in the Renaissance. Second, the traditional Christian interpretation of
Genesis had humankind, through Adam, falling from God's favor in the
Garden of Eden. Even Buffon, in discussing the changes that occurred to
species, called it "degeneration."

Even so, by the time of the Enlightenment, general knowledge had
grown, more European people had acquired more wealth, and the oppres-
sive bonds of feudalism and the manorial system (Chapter 15) had been
broken. A significant segment of the population consisted of upwardly
mobile traders and entrepreneurs. Surely, life for many was getting better,
not worse! And consequently, a world view developed that had philoso-

phers looking foward to the future with anticipation, not back to the past with remorse. Thus emerged the new view of cultural progress, or progressionism.

Locke himself contributed to this progressive scheme by suggesting that humans moved out of an original savage state of nature by forming social contracts, recognized agreements required for protection and for meeting mutual needs. The Enlightenment's leading scholar on this issue was Jean-Jacques Rousseau (1712–1778). Although not strictly a progressionist—because he viewed "savagery" as a generally better way of life than civilization—Rousseau held a developmental perspective that did not evoke mental or moral degeneration from an ideal past.

Rousseau   In 1755 Rousseau published his *Discourse on the Origin and Foundations of Inequality Among Men*. He argued that humans had from the beginning the unique capability of perfecting the mind. He went on, however, to suggest that society and its myriad aspects were outcomes of mental development, aspects that contained inherent and unforeseen evils. He spelled out his hypothetical sequence of human cultural development in some detail, with mental progress as the mechanism responsible for subsequent social change. Notably, however, Rousseau did not believe that biological change was a possibility. This should not be surprising; contemporary students of biology, as we have seen, were continuing to deny biological macroevolution themselves. Once more, ideas concerning cultural evolution took the lead.

Lord Monboddo (1714–1799), a Scottish jurist, held views similar to Rousseau's but focused upon the development of language as his domain for charting the progress of humankind. Language was of particular significance for evolutionary studies because clearly, European languages had been changing throughout history. Did this not suggest an explanation other than the static scriptural view of all languages being miraculously formed at the foot of the **Tower of Babel**? Indeed, Sir William Jones connected the diverse "Indo-European" languages phylogenetically in 1786 and was followed by many students of historical linguistics.

Changes in other cultural forms could also be traced backward in time. In his *Plan for Two Discourses on Universal History*, published in 1750, Anne Robert Jacques Turgot (1727–1781) presented one of the earliest general schemes for the evolution of technological and subsistence strategies. According to Turgot, humans evolved through developmental stages from hunting, to pastoralism, to farming. Similarly, Adam Ferguson (1723–1816), in his 1767 work *An Essay on the History of Civil Society*, proposed that each developmental stage is best described with reference to subsistence strategies and made the radical suggestion that peoples possessing primitive technologies were living in neither a better nor worse condition than was modern man, only a different one. John Millar, in 1771, attempted to outline the evolution of social organization, and William Robertson, in *The History of America* (1777), went so far as

Tower of Babel

The biblical story of the origin of languages given in Genesis 11: After starting to build a tower to reach heaven, people are smitten with the inability to understand one another.

to employ both ethnological and archaeological data (he was one of the few to consider archaeology at that time) to devise an evolutionary sequence that progressed from savagery, to barbarism, to civilization.

MONOGENISTS AND POLYGENISTS

Biological and cultural evolution were inextricably linked in the popular mind, if only because the most technologically simple people known appeared also to be the most biologically different from Europeans. By the eighteenth century, Europeans were therefore beginning to ask microevolutionary questions about the relationships among the different geographical groups of *Homo sapiens*. In particular, were they one species or several?

The two solutions to this question formed the positions taken by the **monogenists** and **polygenists** (Chapter 9). Most scientists found the monogenist position the more satisfactory. The polygenist position had strong backing in the United States, however, where it could be used to rationalize slavery. The debate had more than social significance, for if human groups were actually members of the same species, this would imply that a single stock could become strikingly modified over the course of time.

EMERGENCE OF BIOLOGICAL MACROEVOLUTION

As keeper of the royal gardens, Buffon secured the best possible tutor for his son, the young botanist (though soon to be zoologist) Jean Baptiste Pierre Antoine de Monet, Chevalier de Lamarck (1744–1829). Lamarck, as it turned out, went further in his biological speculations than Buffon was ever willing to go. Lamarck rejected the view that species were immutable and thus formulated the first truly macroevolutionary model for biology. Lamarck's views were also decidedly on the side of progressionism; he was the first biological scholar to adopt this perspective explicitly.

Lamarck's Model   Lamarck's reasoning went as follows:

1. The degree of development of any particular organ is determined by its degree of usefulness to the organism possessing it, which in turn is dictated by the nature of the environment.
2. Useful organs become larger and stronger, while those of little use tend to atrophy.
3. These effects of use and disuse are passed on to subsequent generations—this is Lamarck's *inheritance of acquired characteristics*.
4. Because environmental conditions change, the degrees of usefulness of different organs also change.
5. Finally, given enough time, and thus sufficient environmental change, entirely new organs and organisms can come into existence (Figure 3–12).

monogenism
The view that all humans have a single, common origin.

polygenism
The view that independent groups of people have independent origins.

inheritance of acquired characteristics (Lamarckian inheritance)
The idea that bodily alterations occurring during the lifetime of an organism can be passed on to its offspring.

Figure 3-12
Lamarckian inheritance holds that the physical effects of experiences can be stably inherited.

We know today that this model is faulty. Acquired characteristics are not inherited. But for its time, Lamarck's thinking was revolutionary, particularly in regard to the last point. Many prominent scholars rejected it out-of-hand, including the influential Georges Cuvier (1769–1832), who continued to believe that organic variation was held to specified limits.

The Problem of Extinction   In the course of their disagreements and debates, Lamarck and Cuvier were forced to deal with a new kind of biological problem, a problem that shed light on the issue of variation.

On the island of Mauritius lived a large, flightless, and unfortunately tasty bird whose name is now synonymous with extinction—the dodo (Figure 3–13). By 1700, the bird had been wiped out by hungry, visiting sailors, the first recorded instance of a species becoming extinct. However, according to the Great Chain of Being, such an occurrence was impossible. How could mortal man destroy a link created by God in His benevolence and omnipotence? Thus, John Ray had earlier rejected the possibility of extinction categorically, recognizing that under the existing ideas it would be a "dismemb'ring of the universe." Yet thoughout the eighteenth century, the Industrial Revolution led to increasing numbers of building projects of greater size and scope, leading in turn to more excavation and an increasing number of discoveries of extinct fossil animals. The dodo no longer stood alone as a freak occurrence in nature, and it became clear that many forms of life had become extinct. This is, of course, a fundamental form of change—the "flip-side" of evolution—and one that can be observed retrospectively. But how could extinction be explained?

Lamarck and Cuvier had different answers. Cuvier was the leading authority on fossil animals, the founder of vertebrate paleontology and a devoted disciple of Linnaeus. He argued that periodically the earth had been overwhelmed by catastrophes during which most or all species had been killed. This view came to be known as *catastrophism*. New and different animals, he went on, had been created to take their place. (When his work was translated into English during the Napoleonic Wars, the translator piously added to Cuvier's text the idea that the most recent catastrophe had been that of Noah's Great Flood, which wiped out the dinosaurs!)

Figure 3-13
The dodo

Lamarck, the former protegé of Buffon, saw things differently. He argued that, when faced with possible extinction, species simply change into new and different species. In essence, Lamarck saw species surviving by climbing a notch up the Great Chain of Being and thus becoming somewhat more perfect than before.

Lamarck's biological ideas resounded with progress, which the cultural evolutionists had long been using, for he thought more complex organisms continuously evolved from less complex ones. He further argued that people were not immune from such biological transformations. As early as 1809 Lamarck wrote in his *Zoological Philosophy* a possible scenario for how certain characteristics of *Homo sapiens* might have come into being:

> If some race of four-handed animals, especially one of the most perfect of them, were to lose, by force of circumstances or some other cause, the habit of climbing trees and grasping the branches with its feet in the same way as with its hands . . . in order to lay hold on to them, and if the individuals of this race were forced for a series of generations to use their feet only for walking and to give up using their feet like hands, there is no doubt . . . that these four-handed animals would at length be transformed into two-handed and that the thumbs on their feet would cease to be separated from the other digits.
>
> Furthermore, if the individuals . . . were impelled by the desire to command a large and distant view, and hence endeavored to stand upright, and continually adopted that habit from generation to generation, there is again no doubt that their feet would gradually acquire a shape suitable for supporting them in an erect attitude.
>
> Lastly, if these same animals were to give up using their jaws as weapons for biting, tearing or grasping, or as nippers for cutting grass and feeding on it, and if they were to use them only for chewing; there is again no doubt that their facial angle would become larger, that their snout would shorten more and more, and that finally it would be entirely effaced so that their incisor teeth became vertical.
>
> *(Lamarck 1809 [cf.1984:170])*

But Lamarck, anachronistically, was still wedded to the Great Chain of Being, in spite of the Linnaean school's success in demonstrating that it did not represent nature accurately. And as long as evolutionary ideas were tied to that concept, they remained unconvincing to most biologists. Furthermore, there was as yet no satisfactory suggestion regarding a mechanism for evolution—an explanation for how evolutionary change came about. That contribution was Charles Darwin's.

EARTH HISTORY

Late in life, Buffon had painted a radical view of earth history, even more radical than the one he had retracted earlier. In *Epochs of Nature* (1780), he described seven successive ages in the history of the planet, from an original molten form to the emergence of human beings. Most extraordinary, however, was Buffon's notion of the time scale involved: He published that the earth's age might be as much as 75,000 years!

Eight years after Buffon's *Epochs*, James Hutton (1726–1797) gave support to the notion that the earth was very old by introducing a strict uniformitarian view. In contrast to catastrophism, *uniformitarianism* subsumes the view that, as Buffon had earlier indicated, the only processes we can invoke to explain earth history are those of the same kind and magnitude as the ones we can observe and measure presently (Figure 3–14). John Playfair (1748–1819) soon offered great support for Hutton's conclusions and, among other things, argued that the notion of a 6,000 year old world was absurd. Soon William "Strata" Smith (1769–1839), a surveyor in England, developed a technique for tracing geological strata over large areas by reference to the fossil types contained within them, thus opening the door to a view of life history as lengthy as earth history.

Building on the work of these English geologists, Charles Lyell (1797–1875) formulated a detailed and highly influential analysis of geologic history that had strict uniformitarianism as its guiding theme. Lyell's *Principles of Geology: Being an Attempt to Explain the Former Changes of the Earth's Surface by Reference to Causes now in Operation* was published in three volumes from 1830 to 1833. Lyell summarized the state of geologic knowledge at the time and showed that a scientific uniformitarian interpretation of earth history pointed unambiguously to the conclusion that the earth must be immensely old. Lyell's contribution to evolution was that he gave it the time scale necessary for it to happen.

With advances in the study of earth history came greater understanding of cultural artifacts removed from the earth. In Denmark, Christian Jurgensen Thomsen (1788–1865) introduced his *Three Age Chronology* in the second decade of the nineteenth century, asserting that stone artifacts are oldest, bronze artifacts of intermediate age, and iron artifacts most recent. Thomsen devised this chronology to organize the vast array of materials to be housed in the Copenhagen Museum, and although many details have been added, the basic structure of the scheme remains valid. In the 1840s, several archaeologists began confirming Thomsen's views with field data, including Jens Jacob Asmussen Worsaae (1821–1885), who devoted much of his time to the archaeological study of refuse deposits in northern Europe. And by the late 1850s, certain scholars, including Jacques Boucher de Perthes (1788–1868), pushed back the span of human prehistory, showing that certain human tools were in clear association with the remains of extinct animals.

Figure 3-14. The revolution in geology of the early nineteenth century.

(a) An example of a cataclysm invoked by catastrophists.
(b) To uniformitarians, most of the observable features of the earth were explicable by recourse to normal processes acting over long periods of time.

(a)

Catastrophism   Uniformitarianism

Lightning

Earthquakes   Sun

Erupting
volcanoes   Wind

Meteorites   Rain

Floods

(b)

HERBERT SPENCER

Cultural evolution continued to be at the forefront of much of the thinking about change during the early part of the nineteenth century. Indeed, one of the most remarkable of such thinkers, Herbert Spencer (1820–1903), advocated what is now called **social Darwinism**, and before Darwin wrote his major works. This philosophy shaped much anthropological and biological thought throughout the remainder of the nineteenth century. The term *social Darwinism*, it should be recognized, is a scandalous misnomer.

During the 1840s Spencer wrote a series of papers on what he viewed as the progressive development of all phenomena in the universe, ultimately publishing them in a single volume called *Social Statics* in 1850. He combined older evolutionary ideas with new political theories. On one hand, he maintained the common Enlightenment belief that humans were perfectible in certain respects because of their ability to advance in the mental and moral realms. On the other hand—and largely because of the influence Lamarck's views had on him—he did not view human development as unique, in that he saw human achievement as merely one aspect of a universal tendency to progress. All phenomena, according to Spencer, evolve according to a single principle. This principle, which he discussed further in other works such as his *Principles of Psychology* (in 1855) and *Principles of Biology* (in 1864), he called "Survival of the Fittest." Later, Darwin borrowed the term from Spencer as a label for his own biological ideas.

Spencer's concept of "Survival of the Fittest" was simply that universal competition leads to universal progress, whether among species, cultures, or people. One consequence is that conquest of primitive cultures by complex cultures is an inevitable and natural process that will eventually result in the overall improvement of human social life.

At first glance, this appears to be a rosy view of human history and development. But Spencer saw inevitable suffering on the horizon for the vast numbers of people living in less-advanced (that is, non-Western) societies around the world.

The fact that Spencer saw such an immediate future as natural and inevitable can be explained by considering European social and political trends of the time in general and Spencer's own political convictions in particular. By 1850 much of western Europe had become highly industrialized, densely populated, and thoroughly **capitalistic** in regard to economic and political policies. Associated with capitalism is colonial development, and the degree of European colonization around the world was unprecedented during Spencer's time. Such colonization and the tendency to exploit resources and people in the search for profits led to the destruction of whole regions and societies in most of the rest of the world. By claiming it was natural, Spencer scientifically rationalized the activity; and by claiming it was progress, Spencer scientifically encouraged it.

social Darwinism

The idea that cultural evolution is progressive and driven by individual competition; widely used in the nineteenth century as a rationalization for economic oppression; associated with Malthus and Spencer.

capitalism

Economic system in which goods are privately owned and in which there is minimal governmental control, thereby promoting competition and innovation; the lack of regulation tends to promote collusion and monopolies, and the persistence of economic classes as well.

socialism

Economic system in which government strongly regulates economic practices in the attempt to foster cooperation among all members of a society and to avoid the exploitation and subjugation of the poor by the wealthy; the lack of competition tends to lead to little incentive for innovation.

Figure 3-15

Karl Marx

dialectic

Evolutionary view of philosophy or history in which an idea gives rise to its opposite, the two coexist uneasily, after which they reconcile into a new idea, which then gives rise to its opposite; associated in different ways with Hegel and Marx.

Figure 3-16
Hegel's Dialectic.

Spencer mixed science and politics more than most scholars, condemning all forms of cooperativism and **socialism**. His scholarly views were thus couched in a clearly cultural frame of reference (as are those of all scientists, though usually to a lesser degree). The combination of his individual evolutionary convictions with the general political philosophy of the time made Spencer extraordinarily influential among western European and American circles through the turn of the century.

KARL MARX

Another influential social evolutionist of the nineteenth century was Karl Marx (1818–1883)(Figure 3–15). Marx worked with a similar assumption of evolution and progress, but with a different set of political and philosophical views. His knowledge of non-European societies was scant, and he almost always supported his theoretical positions with examples from the recent history of the Western world, that is, since the time of feudalism.

Marx is responsible for formulating the philosophy of dialectical materialism. Dialectical materialism—an attempt to explain cultural evolutionary processes—is not the same as communism—a political philosophy that Marx also developed, which argues for the elimination of privately owned property and capital.

Dialectical materialism is an example of evolutionary progressionism, but of a different sort from Spencer's. Marx saw the economic configuration of society as the driving force of evolutionary change. Systems of thought, or ideology, he viewed as the outcome of economic and political systems. Thus, evolutionary developments do not occur simply because new ideas supersede old ideas, but rather because they are the inevitable outcomes of basic economic conditions.

For Marx, the nature of change from one economic system to another was more revolutionary than gradual, in that he viewed such change as rapid and rife with conflict. Here, Marx incorporated the notion of the **dialectic** from the work of Georg W. F. Hegel (1770–1831). To Hegel, the social world consisted of ideas constantly in tense relationships with their opposites. This tension, in turn, would eventually and suddenly lead to the emergence of a new synthetic mentality, as well as a new synthetic opposite, and thus the process would begin anew. The dialectic is briefly outlined in Figure 3–16. And though Marx accepted the process, he rejected the notion that it applied primarily to ideas formed in the human mind. Instead, since he saw economics as the primary determinant of history, he claimed that tensions in the economic, material world would lead to revolutionary economic syntheses; thus the term *dialectical materialism*.

Thesis + Antithesis ⟶ Synthesis

The tension of opposites, in Marx's view, was shown in the conflicting interests of economic classes, which generated class struggle and ultimately revolution, along with a new economic synthesis. History, to Marx, was therefore inadequately represented as a succession of ideas or thoughts. History needed to be placed in the context of economic and social forces because it was, after all, the economic struggle of classes that in his view shaped history.

Like Spencer, Marx saw cultural trends as difficult for many people to endure, but as eventually leading to a future paradise. Unlike Spencer, Marx thought that this future would be a dictatorship by the workers with private property abolished. Human society would thus have progressed through a series of stages from feudalism, through capitalism, to communism. Spencer, you will recall, argued that extreme capitalism would be the end-product of cultural evolution; these two great scholars stood at opposite ends of the political and scholarly spectrums. It is easy to understand, then, why Marx has played less of a role in shaping American anthropology—his notions ran strongly contrary to those inherent in the American political and social spheres.

The Darwinian Revolution

The turbulent conflict between the linear hierarchy of the Great Chain of Being, which seemed to imply that different species were closely related to one another, and the more apparently real Linnaean hierarchy, which gave rigid boundaries to the higher taxonomic categories, preoccupied biologists of the early nineteenth century. It was Charles Robert Darwin (1809–1882)(Figure 3–17) who demonstrated that the Linnaean hierarchy, that is, the pattern encountered among organisms, could be compatible with the idea of the transformation of species. He did so by reference to the biological process he called **natural selection** (Box 3–1).

THEORY OF NATURAL SELECTION

As ship's naturalist aboard the HMS *Beagle,* conducting a five-year voyage around South America during the 1830s, Darwin was struck by the observations he made on biogeography, the study of the distribution of organisms. If, as was generally reasoned, species are adapted to their environment because they were placed there by God, one would expect to find similar organisms occupying similar environments worldwide. Indeed, that was what Darwin had expected to find, having studied theology at Cambridge. Instead, he found that the species of the New World were generally more similar to one another than to any species of the Old World, regardless of environment. Furthermore, South American fossils were more similar to living South American species than to anything, living or extinct, from the Old World. Finally, species from the tropical rain forests of South America were not at all like those from the tropical rain forests of Africa. It seemed that geographical proximity, not environmen-

Figure 3-17

Charles Darwin, approximately five years before *The Origin of Species*.

natural selection

A process whereby characteristics beneficial to a species are represented in the next generation more extensively than are their alternatives, since those members of the species that possess the beneficial characteristics have a greater chance of surviving and reproducing; Darwin recognized this as the principal cause of biological adaptation.

Issues in Anthropology 3–1

Darwin's Finches Weren't Really Darwin's

Darwin's visit to the Galápagos in the 1830s convinced him that creationist biology was inadequate to explain the patterns of diversity he found among the animal species there. One of the most striking examples of such a pattern of biological diversity comes from a group of birds known as Darwin's finches.

Darwin's finches are composed primarily of the genera *Camarhynchus* and *Geospiza,* each having several species. These genera and species differ in size, diet, size and shape of beak, habitat preference, and geographic location within the islands. Yet they are all similar, products of what we now call an adaptive radiation. How could Darwin have not been impressed by this? Many current versions of the Darwin story have him being deeply impressed by the finches and appreciating the reality of evolution largely as a result of them.

In truth, it did not happen that way. Darwin was not particularly impressed by the geographical diversity of the finches, though he was the first to make a collection of them, which is why they bear his name. He did not mention them in his diary, and in the first edition of the *Voyage of the Beagle* (1839) his mention of them is cursory—only in the 1845 edition was it expanded as having newfound significance. Any impact the finches had on Darwin occurred long after he was back in London. Yet even in the *Origin of Species,* the birds of the Galápagos are discussed in a few sentences only.

Darwin, though a competent bird taxonomist, was confused by the birds of the Galápagos. Most groups of mainland birds differ only slightly in the beak but significantly in the plumage. The Galápagos finches differed greatly in beaks but little in plumage. Following what he knew, Darwin dutifully assigned them all to different genera. Upon returning to London, Darwin turned over the birds to eminent ornithologist John Gould, who came to realize that these birds were all closely related, even

tal similarity, best correlated with the distribution of biological resemblances among fossil and living species. Thus, he wrote in his *Journal of Researches into the Geology and Natural History of the Various Countries Visited by the H.M.S.* Beagle:

> This wonderful relationship in the same continent between the dead and the living, will, I do not doubt, hereafter throw more light on the appearance of organic beings on our earth, and their disappearance from it, than any other class of facts.

(Darwin 1839 [1972]:149)

Darwin also read Lyell's *Principles of Geology* while at sea and was satisfied by Lyell's arguments for the great age of the earth and for the slow and gradual nature of the changes in operation. According to Darwin's autobiography, however, the most important factor in the development of his theory was his reading the 1826 edition of *An Essay on the Principle of Population* (orig. 1798) by Thomas Malthus (1766–1834). Malthus's essay was a conservative social treatise noting

though their beaks were different. When it became clear that the geographic locality of each specimen might shed some light on their relationships, Darwin had a problem. Being a creationist biologist, geography was not important for his record keeping on the *Beagle,* so he did not know the exact origin of each specimen.

Darwin went to his shipmates, who had collected a few bird specimens of their own and who, not being scientists encumbered with prejudices about what information is significant, had actually written down the precise locality of their specimens. Darwin then tried to reconstruct from which island each of his own birds had come. He made several mistakes.

The fact that Darwin made little or no mention of the finches in his public and private writings suggests to scientific historian Frank Sulloway that they did not significantly inspire his thoughts on evolution. Rather, "it was his evolutionary views

that allowed him, retrospectively, to understand the complex case of the finches."

Later voyagers to the Galápagos brought back larger collections, and as analyzed in a book by ornithologist David Lack, they are an eloquent testimony to Darwin's ideas. His ideas, however, came from elsewhere, not from the finches.

References:

Lack, David (1947). *Darwin's finches*. Cambridge, England: Cambridge University Press.

Sulloway, Frank (1981). Darwin and his finches: The evolution of a legend. *Journal of the History of Biology,* 15:1–53.

what he perceived to be a perpetual crisis of humankind due to the inability of food production to keep up with population increases. Malthus felt that since food is always produced at a slower rate than the rate at which populations grow, poverty is a constant and natural part of human society. This, in turn, creates a "struggle for existence" in which weaker groups of people are weeded out, and society is ultimately changed for the better unless some social reformers are allowed to subvert the system. Such interference would be unnatural, argued Malthus, and therefore should be avoided.

Malthus was thus an early social Darwinist—earlier even than Spencer. His views are now considered inhumane. More importantly, they ignore the fact that human technological development allows us to increase food production dramatically. Furthermore, the poor are not poor because they have lost in a "struggle"— more often, they have not even been given a chance to compete.

What Darwin saw in Malthus was that this principle of a "struggle for existence" among people could actually be found among all species. Organisms, reasoned Darwin, always produce more offspring than are able to survive and reproduce themselves. What determines which of those offspring do, in fact, survive? The answer lay in Malthus. But in Darwin's hands, the struggle for existence took a new and different form. Darwin saw the possibility of significant biological change in the composition of a species through time because of constant population pressure. And in the face of a capricious environment, the survivors and reproducers might not be the most ordinary individuals in the species: They might be somewhat larger or smaller, or they might possess slightly different features from the average member. In the next generation, therefore, the average member of the species would appear more similar to either the larger, or smaller, or deviant individuals from the previous generation, since it was they who procreated most to produce that next generation. Thus, Darwin transformed the conservative social force of Malthus's "struggle" into a creative biological force.

The final argument Darwin felt he required was the demonstration that anatomical characters vary widely in natural populations of animals, and that populations of animals could indeed be established possessing divergent anatomical features, though clearly produced by the differential survival and reproduction of an original parent strain. For this demonstration he turned to the animal breeders of England, most particularly to the pigeon breeders. They provided strong confirmation for his theory of natural selection:

> Altogether at least a score of pigeons might be chosen, which if shown to an ornithologist, and he were told that they were wild birds, would certainly, I think, be ranked by him as well-defined species. Moreover, I do not believe that any ornithologist would place the English carrier, the short-faced tumbler, the runt, the barb, pouter and fantail in the same genus. . . .
>
> *(Darwin 1859:22–23)*

Yet all domestic pigeons are descended from a common ancestral stock. And if pigeon fanciers could create these widely divergent kinds of birds in a brief span of human history, what could nature do in the vast Lyellian expanse of earth history? The implications were profound for the study of biology:

> Although much remains obscure, and will long remain obscure, I can entertain no doubt, after the most deliberate study and dispassionate judgment of which I am capable, that the view which most naturalists entertain, and which I formerly entertained— namely, that each species has been independently created—is erroneous. I am fully convinced that species are not immutable; but that those belonging to what are called the same genera are lineal descendants of some other and generally extinct species, in

the same manner as the acknowledged varieties of any one species are the descendants of that species.

(Darwin 1859:6)

By the 1850s Darwin had earned a high reputation as a biologist by virtue of his books on the Beagle voyage and his studies of coral reefs, barnacle species, and volcanic islands. When in 1858 the naturalist Alfred Russel Wallace (1823–1913) hit upon the idea of the transformation and divergence of species due to a natural selective process, it was to Darwin that he sent his manuscript ("On the Tendency of Varieties to Depart Indefinitely from the Original Type") for advice on where to publish it. Wallace was unaware that Darwin had begun writing a book on the subject himself.

Darwin consulted his friends Charles Lyell and the botanist Joseph Dalton Hooker (1817–1911), and they presented Wallace's paper and an abstract of Darwin's book together at a meeting of the Linnaean Society, published later that year in the society's Proceedings. The society's president later summarized the events that had taken place:

> The year which has passed has not, indeed, been marked by any of those striking discoveries which at once revolutionize . . . the department of science on which they bear; it is only at remote intervals that we can reasonably expect any sudden and brilliant innovation.

(in Boorstin 1983:484)

If he failed to note then that the entire world view of modern biology had just been altered, he probably did realize it when on 24 November 1859, *On the Origin of Species by Means of Natural Selection, or the Preservation of Favoured Races in the Struggle for Life* was published. All 1,250 copies were sold that day.

EVOLUTION AND HUMANS

Darwin assiduously focused on animals other than humans in *The Origin of Species*. His only reference to *Homo sapiens* was the passing remark, "Light will be thrown on the origin of man and his history" (Darwin 1859:488). In later editions Darwin was sufficiently emboldened to change the passage to "Much ligh. . . ."

Darwin's readers, however, were aware of the implication that, if other creatures were linked genealogically, then humans were linked to them. This, in turn, implied that the present form of the human species was an alteration of some earlier, more ape-like species. As we have noted, primitive stone tools had by this time been discovered in Europe, and primitive tools implied primitive people. However, the skeptics argued that culturally primitive tools did not necessarily imply biologically primitive humans. Certainly, biologically modern people were alive at the time who were using primitive tools. And virtually no fossil human ancestors had been found or identified.

The first skull we would now call Neanderthal was found in Gibraltar in 1848. It was not recognized as belonging to an extinct human group, however, but considered to have been instead from a diseased modern person. The Neanderthal remains themselves were found in 1856, however, and described two years later, at which time they were suggested to belong to a primitive and barbaric race. It was at this time as well that those stone tools were shown unambiguously to be associated with the remains of extinct mammals, by Boucher de Perthes. Thus, not only were there primitive tools, but also evidence that their makers had used them to hunt and butcher species that were no longer extant (Figure 3–18).

Still, the role of humans in Darwinian evolution remained the most contentious part of the theory. Charles Lyell published *The Antiquity of Man* in 1863 to demonstrate that human prehistory extended far beyond what scripture would allow, but stopped short of advocating the theory that humans had emerged from ape-like predecessors. And Thomas Henry Huxley (1825–1895) wrote the first book demonstrating our kin-

Figure 3-18

Stone tools found and studied by Boucher de Perthes, published in 1857.

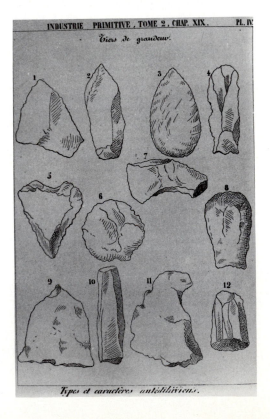

ship with the apes and discussing the meager fossil evidence for our evolution (*Man's Place in Nature*, also published in 1863), but he did not discuss in any depth the role natural selection may have played in human evolution. This was undertaken by Darwin himself, in *The Descent of Man, and Selection in Relation to Sex*, in 1871:

> **The early progenitors of man must also have tended like all other animals, to have increased beyond their means of subsistence; they must therefore occasionally have been exposed to a struggle for existence, and consequently to the rigid law of natural selection. Beneficial variations of all kinds will thus, either occasionally or habitually, have been preserved, and injurious ones eliminated. We know, for instance, that the muscles of our hands and feet, which determine our powers of movement, are liable, like those of the lower animals, to incessant variability. If then the ape-like progenitors of man which inhabited any district, especially one undergoing some change in its conditions, were divided into two equal bodies, the one half which included all the individuals best adapted by their powers of movement for gaining subsistence or for defending themselves, would on average survive in greater number and procreate more offspring than the other and less well endowed half.**
>
> *(Darwin 1871:136)*

While many social evolutionists adopted the position that people from technologically more simple cultures were biologically inferior to Europeans, Darwin and Wallace did not. Wallace, however, felt that to live in European society required more brainpower than to live in other societies. Yet those people who appeared to be living a savage lifestyle were the biological equals of civilized European people, with equally capable brains. Thus, people from "primitive" societies were not using their brains to the fullest capacity, while those in Europe were. And natural selection, Wallace reasoned, could not have produced a fully developed human brain in the head of a person who would have no need to use it.

He therefore came to the conclusion that the human brain had been formed by a supernatural agency, not by natural selection. Thus, while Wallace did not maintain the idea of European biological superiority, he foundered on the rocks of **ethnocentrism** in thinking that technologically less complex societies required less knowledge and intelligence of their members. Darwin, on the other hand, recognized that humans even "in the rudest state" had certain unique capabilities (such as language and tool use) that were the result of "observation, memory, curiosity, imagination, and reason" (Darwin 1871:137). He thus felt that even the human mind had developed by the same natural processes that were

ethnocentrism
The belief that one's own culture is superior to another; opposite of cultural relativism.

Issues in Anthropology 3–2

The Great Confrontations

Scientific issues are not settled in oral debate, but rather literature, where the combatants have the time and resources to think through and document their contentions. In the social context of science, however, this has not always been the case, and public debates have helped shape the popular consciousness in significant ways.

Shortly after the publication of *The Origin of Species* in 1870, a debate was held at Oxford between supporters and opponents of evolution and natural selection. The major spokesmen for evolution were the botanist Joseph Dalton Hooker and the zoologist Thomas Henry Huxley. The principal antagonist was Bishop of Oxford Samuel Wilberforce, renowned for his powerful oratory. Wilberforce was no ignoramus, and had been thoroughly briefed by the leading anatomist of the day, Richard Owen, who was known to loathe Huxley.

No transcripts of the debate exist, but all recollections of it agree that the climax was precipitated by Wilberforce's concluding thought. Wilberforce, with a rhetorical flourish, ended by wondering whether Huxley would claim descent from an ape on his grandfather's or grandmother's side. The audience perceived this as a personal attack, outside the proper forum of debate. Huxley later recalled whispering to the person beside him, "The Lord hath delivered him into my hands."

When called upon to respond, Huxley proclaimed that he would rather claim as grandparent the lowly ape than a person who, possessed of the gifts of intelligent and articulate speech, would compromise them in the service of ignorance and prejudice. This return volley proved to be a crowd-pleaser and helped win the day for evolution at Oxford. The more substantive issues, less often quoted, were covered by Hooker. Independently of the public debate, within a decade, virtually all scientists of note in England were evolutionists.

In 1925 in the United States, a conservative religious movement sweeping the South had enacted laws in several states banning the teaching of evolution in public schools. Although no one had been prosecuted under these laws, the American Civil Liberties Union recognized the need for a test case to decide on their constitutionality. The elders of Dayton, Tennessee, thought it might help their town if the case were tried there and so persuaded John Thomas Scopes, the local biology teacher, to be prosecuted for teaching evolution.

The prosecuting district attorney, A. T. Stewart, was unexpectedly joined by a national figure, three-time presidential candidate, Fundamentalist and stirring speaker William Jennings Bryan. Fearing that a simple trial would turn into a public rout with the great orator working for the prosecution, the defense recruited the greatest trial lawyer in America, Clarence Darrow. What was to have been a simple legal test case was now the biggest show in the nation in July, 1925.

Bryan, who was motivated by the confusion in his own mind between evolution and Social

responsible for the evolution of other characteristics of all organisms (Box 3–2).

MARX AND DARWIN

The social evolutionist Karl Marx and the biological evolutionist Charles Darwin were not unknown to each other. Marx was impressed by Darwin's demonstration of struggle leading to change in the natural world and felt that, as he wrote to his colleague Friedrich Engels in 1860, "This is the book that contains the natural-history foundation for our viewpoint" (Padover 1978:359).

Darwinism, found an eager audience in rural Tennessee. In the urban North, however, where the trial was covered in print and over the radio, he was a laughingstock.

When the defense was not allowed to call scientists as witnesses, they instead called Bryan himself as an expert witness on the authority of the Bible. As in the Oxford debate, public sentiment turned to some extent on exchanges of a personal nature. Bryan railed against the defense attorneys, whose "purpose is to cast ridicule on everybody who believes in the Bible," to which Darrow volleyed, "We have the purpose of preventing bigots and ignoramuses from controlling the education of the United States, and you know it, and that is all."

When asked how Bishop Ussher arrived at the date of 4004 b.c. for the creation of the earth, which was printed in the margins of the Bible held in evidence at the trial, Bryan hedged. Darrow pressed him, "What do you think?" Bryan responded, "I do not think about things I do not think about." Darrow asked him, sarcastically, "Do you think about things you *do* think about?"

Bryan ultimately said that he did not necessarily think that the word day in Genesis meant a literal, 24-hour day. With this concession, Darrow could now press Bryan on how there could have been mornings and evenings if the sun had not been created until the fourth day.

When Darrow finally asked how the serpent locomoted before being condemned to move on its belly after the Garden of Eden incident, Bryan exploded: "I want the world to know that this man, who does not believe in a God, is trying to use a court in Tennessee to slur at it, and, while it may require time, I am willing to take it." Darrow exploded back: "I object to your statement. I am examining you on your fool ideas that no intelligent Christian on earth believes!" At this point court was adjourned.

Scopes was found guilty, but the conviction was later overturned. Still, the law was repealed only in 1967. The paradox of the trial was that even though it was perceived as a victory for science, most American biology textbooks for the next forty years—until Sputnik motivated the teaching of science in America—avoided the subject of evolution as much as possible.

Bryan died only a few days after the conclusion of the trial. Years later, biologist and philosopher Julian Huxley (grandson of Thomas) speculated that if it had been Darrow who died directly after the trial, the religious would have interpreted his death as the judgment of God.

References:

Cole, F. C. (1959). A witness at the Scopes trial. *Scientific American*, 200(1):121–130.

Grabiner J. V., & Miller, P. D. (1974). Effects of the Scopes trial. *Science*, 185:832–837.

de Camp, L. Sprague (1969). The end of the monkey war. *Scientific American*, 220(2):15–21.

Marx, however, failed to mention Darwin at all in his major work, *Das Kapital*, first published in 1867. He sent a copy of the first volume in German to Darwin, inscribed "On the part of his sincere admirer, Karl Marx," and Darwin apparently read the first 105 pages of the total 822 (Darwin struggled with languages other than English).

What Marx did not like in *The Origin of Species* was the rejection of the idea of progress, which had formerly been linked to biological evolution in the Great Chain, and which was still linked to cultural evolution. In the Darwinian theory, biological progress was essentially an accidental outcome of the adaptive divergence of species; while in the Marxist theory, social progress was an inevitable outcome of class struggle. It does not appear that Darwin ever gave any thought to Marxism.

Evolutionary Thought after Darwin

Darwin's influence on thought regarding human biological evolution was equalled by his influence on developing notions of cultural evolution. One group of scholars—often incorrectly credited for originating cultural evolutionary studies—combined Darwin's biological theory of natural selection with Spencer's views regarding progressive cultural change. These were the unilinear evolutionists, and their ideas dominated anthropological thought through the second half of the nineteenth century.

UNILINEAR EVOLUTIONISTS

Although different individual scholars stressed different issues, the overarching rationale for *unilinear evolutionism* was as follows:

1. **All people on earth share a psychic unity; that is to say, humans have equivalent mental capabilities and drives.**
2. **Because of this psychic unity—this mental similarity—all human *societies* have evolved culturally along a single trajectory of development. It has been, in other words, a *unilinear* history.**
3. **Different societies, however, have advanced along this path at different rates and so are at different evolutionary stages at any point in time.**
4. **European societies, particularly western Europe, have advanced the farthest, and the relative evolutionary position of any society can be determined by judging its degree of similarity with the Western world (Figure 3–19).**

This scheme is notably similar to what Lamarck proposed for biological evolution, and indeed, Spencer was greatly influenced by Lamarck.

Spencer's influence on the unilinear evolutionists is seen in their equating cultural evolution with progress; societies that had advanced farther were seen as better than societies that had advanced less. Darwin's influence is seen in the unilinear evolutionists' belief that natural selection operates on cultural variability as well as on biological variability; it was generally thought that non-European groups could be "brought up to the level" of the Europeans by making their social environments more favorable for the selection of European social traits. Thus, within unilinear evolutionism existed the scientific rationale for colonization, missionary work, and enforced cultural change.

A leading figure in unilinear evolutionism was Lewis Henry Morgan (1818–1881), who conducted research among the Iroquois in the northeastern United States. Morgan, like other unilinear evolutionists, was concerned with formulating a global scheme of cultural development and

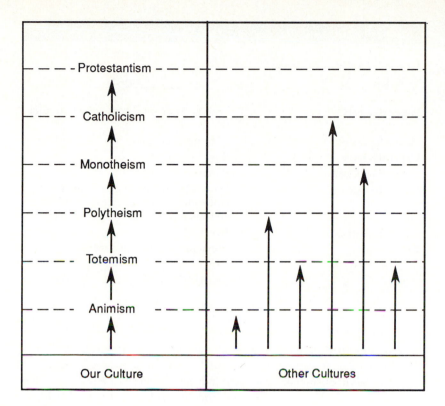

Figure 3-19
Unilinear evolution assumed that all cultures were on a common trajectory but that some had not traveled as far as others.

did so by identifying stages (and substages) of evolution and the criteria for their recognition. His scheme is given in Table 3–1. Interestingly, Morgan often emphasized differences in material culture, technology, and economy when designing his scheme, and as a result he was the favorite of nineteenth-century archaeologists and others who emphasized the material conditions of life. Karl Marx, for instance, was greatly impressed with Morgan's work.

But other unilinear evolutionists focused on different sorts of cultural criteria. Henry S. Maine (1822–1888), for instance, in his work *Ancient Law* (1861), described what he saw as a single, fundamental distinction between societies emphasizing kinship groups and societies emphasizing individuals. In the former, which were seen as primitive, a person's place and status in the larger group were determined at birth and were measured by reference to the kinship group into which he or she was born. In the latter, which were thought more complex, any individual was capable of changing status through formal agreements ("contracts") with the society at large. To Maine, evolution from the one type of society to the other was inevitable, although unlike Enlightenment scholars, he did not see the rational powers of the human mind as responsible. Similar to Morgan and the other unilinear evolutionists, Maine saw cultural evolution as the necessary outcome of social forces.

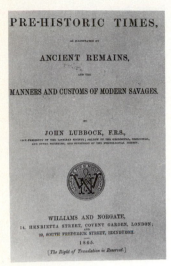

Figure 3–20
John Lubbock (later Lord Avebury) published a major work on cultural evolution in 1865.

comparative method
The study of cultural evolution by assuming that certain traits in contemporary non-Western societies are primitive, relative to Western culture. Developed by John Lubbock in the nineteenth century and similar in reasoning to modern cladistic analysis in biology (Chapter 10).

Table 3–1

Morgan's Unilinear Evolution

Stages	Criteria
Lower Savagery	Fruit and nut subsistence, the beginning of speech
Middle Savagery	Fish subsistence and fire
Upper Savagery	Bow and arrow
Lower Barbarism	Pottery
Middle Barbarism	Domestication of animals (Old World); cultivation of maize, irrigation, adobe, and stone architecture (New World)
Upper Barbarism	Iron tools
Civilization	Phonetic alphabet and writing

(Morgan 1877 [1907]:12; Harris 1968:181)

Sir John Lubbock (1834–1913) published *Prehistoric Times* in 1865, which combined emerging views of cultural and biological evolution (Figure 3–20). He wove the (unilineal) three-age archaeological theory into the fabric of human evolution and divided the Stone Age into the Paleolithic and Neolithic (i.e., Old and New). Lubbock also developed the theoretical framework that characterized much subsequent unilineal analysis, the **comparative method**. Here, one could study historical development by comparing modern society to other cultures "frozen" at earlier stages.

Edward Burnett Tylor (1832–1917) was also greatly influenced by the writings of Spencer and Darwin, and in his *Primitive Culture* (1871) he offered one of the earliest formulations of the concept of culture. Culture, to the evolutionist Tylor, was

> that complex whole which includes knowledge, belief, art, morals, law, custom, and any other capabilities and habits acquired by man as a member of society.
>
> *(Tylor 1871:1)*

By defining culture so broadly, Tylor contributed the modern view that all people live in a cultural context, no matter how primitive their society appears. His writings also stressed the differences among human social groups, and he believed, as other unilinear evolutionists did, that more complex societies those more European-like—were fundamentally more advanced and improved. Thus, despite adherence to the notion of psychic unity, this group of early anthropologists almost always disparaged non-Western peoples as backward.

Furthermore, there existed little data regarding non-European societies, and what did exist were largely inaccurate; and so, these explanations remained unchallenged for some time. Yet by the beginning of the twentieth century, a fundamental philosophical shift occurred in anthropology, brought about largely in response to the ethnocentric speculations of the cultural evolutionary paradigm.

RESPONSES TO UNILINEAR EVOLUTIONISM

One alternative to the view that different cultures had simply not progressed as far as others on the track to perfection was called **diffusionism**. It emphasized cultural continuity across space and proposed that, rather than cultures *independently* reaching the phase of pottery or architecture, major cultural innovations occur only once or a few times, and then spread (diffuse) to other societies. Possession of these innovations by cultures widely separated in space thus indicates that they were in some sort of contact (Figure 3–21). Grafton Elliot Smith (1871–1931), a leading British anatomist, for example, was of the opinion that all civilization had diffused from ancient Egypt. Other, more popular, accounts had everything diffusing from mythological Atlantis or Lemuria.

But only detailed study of several cultures was required to show that domestication, urbanization, and all other major cultural transformations

diffusionism

The cultural evolutionary view that major cultural changes have been introduced from the outside, from other cultures, not developed internally.

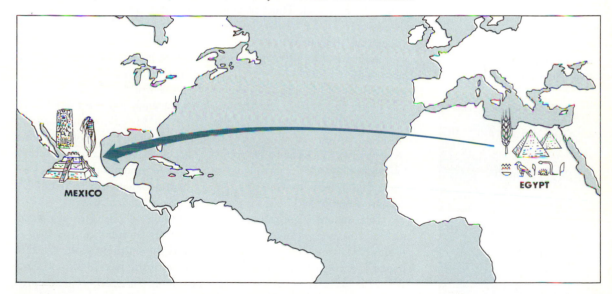

Figure 3-21

Many diffusionists rejected the notion of a single common trajectory and assumed that all things evolved only once. Therefore, any apparent similarities between cultures had to indicate contact between them.

had occurred numerous times and in numerous places. This is a less ethnocentric view—the diffusionists falsely assumed that people in other cultures were not intelligent enough to invent things on their own and had to have their achievements given to them. Certainly, cultural diffusion occurs on a small scale, but it is not the major force behind cultural evolution—humans are more clever and inventive than these thinkers believed.

The second, and far more significant, reaction against the unilinear evolutionary paradigm involved the emergence of **historical particularism**. Led by Franz Boas (1858–1942)(Figure 3–22), the major figure in anthropology in the twentieth century, this paradigm was more in line with Darwin's own contribution. Boas has often been accused of eliminating cultural evolution from the study of culture, but what he actually did was to eliminate the concept of progress, as Darwin had done in biology. And insofar as cultural evolution and progress appeared to be inextricably linked, cultural evolutionary studies subsequently suffered.

Emphasizing the importance of intensive fieldwork (as did his contemporaries in England), Boas argued that other cultures were no less advanced than our own. Their languages, customs, social relations, and myths were all recognized as immensely complex. Their knowledge of the environment was usually greater than that of the Europeans. Indeed, the only aspect of their cultures that was actually simpler was their technology, and this was merely an accident of history. Cultures differed but could not be ranked. Thus, Boas performed the same service for culture that Darwin did for biology: eliminating the idea of progress from the explanation of diversity.

Boas was also a forceful advocate of the principle of cultural relativism, which, as we have seen, is the idea that no culture is better than any other. Each provides a way of viewing the world and of coping with it. Boas further introduced the notion that each culture has its own unique history and series of responses to specific environments. It is, therefore, dangerously illogical to model human cultural evolution after the behavior of any particular primitive group, as unilinear evolutionists (following Lubbock's comparative method) had attempted. Finally, Boas argued that only by studying the specific history of a culture in detail can we learn about and account for the conditions of that culture.

Boas fought vigorously against racism and against ethnocentrism and shaped modern American anthropology. In eliminating the idea of progress, Boas and his students downplayed the cultural evolution that seemed so intimately connected to it. Not until the late 1940s and early 1950s was cultural evolution again considered an acceptable research theme in anthropology. The contributions of this later group of cultural evolutionists, including those of Leslie A. White (1900–1975) and Julian H. Steward (1902–1972), are discussed in Chapter 4.

historical particularism

The cultural evolutionary view that understanding changes in cultures can be accomplished only by detailed studies of the cultures and their internal dynamics through time; promoted by Franz Boas.

Figure 3-22

Franz Boas was the preeminent figure in American anthropology throughout the first half of this century.

EUGENICS

Another way in which the ideas of biological and cultural evolution intersected after Darwin was in the **eugenics** movement during the first few decades of this century. Eugenicists hoped to improve the genetic stock of humankind by breeding out the worst characteristics in the species. The worst traits were considered to be those such as "feeble-mindedness" and criminality and were believed to be the causes of most social problems, such as violent crime. If we bred only intelligent and noncriminal people, the eugenicists reasoned, we would be rid of social difficulties (Figure 3–23).

Of course, this program contained a number of profound mistakes. The first is *reification*, which is the assumption that the properties of an object are the same as the properties of its name. For example, the fact that we can give all forms of mental retardation the single name "feeble-mindedness" does not mean that they all have a single cause. In fact, mental retardation is the most genetically heterogeneous character known, and no amount of breeding to eliminate a specific form of retardation is likely to diminish it substantially. Thus, the journalist H. L.

eugenics

An attempt to improve human social conditions by genetic means, popular in the 1920s.

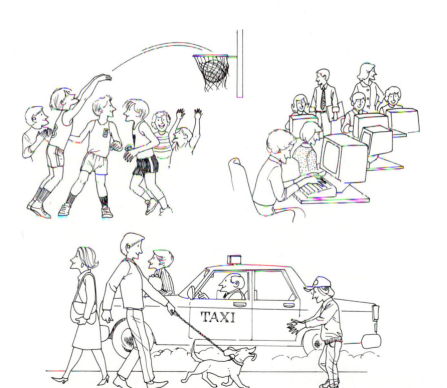

Figure 3-23

Eugenics hoped to alleviate social problems by breeding humans more selectively.

Mencken came to satirize eugenics as "the theory that charm in a woman is the same as charm in a prize-fighter."

The second mistake is *genetic determinism*, the idea that a behavioral trait like criminality is genetic in origin and can, therefore, be bred in or out. The fact that a characteristic runs in families, as criminality often does, is not evidence that it is genetic in origin. Social and environmental conditions also run in families: Poverty is most probably a leading cause of crime and is very often inherited—but not genetically.

The third mistake of eugenics is *arbitrariness*. While a general agreement might have been reached that humans would be better off if the most severely mentally disturbed people were not allowed to breed, the situation was not as clear for less disturbed people. The eugenicist Charles Benedict Davenport (1866–1944) felt that promiscuity was a sign of mental illness, and so promiscuous people deserved to get venereal disease, which, therefore, served a eugenic function. Additional personal and cultural prejudices were also the basis for many of the decisions as to which group was desirable and which was not. In the most extreme case, the Nazis not only discouraged Jews, Gypsies, and homosexuals from reproducing, but they also sought to exterminate them. With similar motivations, though less extreme actions, the United States enacted immigration laws in the 1920s to restrict the flow of "undesirable" genetic elements (such as Jews and Italians) into the United States.

Eugenics was an attempt to cure social problems by biological means, to change society without altering its fabric. We now know, however, that social problems require social solutions, not biological ones. If we wish to reduce crime, it will be more effective to end poverty than to

Figure 3-24

The synthetic theory of (biological) evolution crystallized in the 1940s with input from diverse areas of biological research.

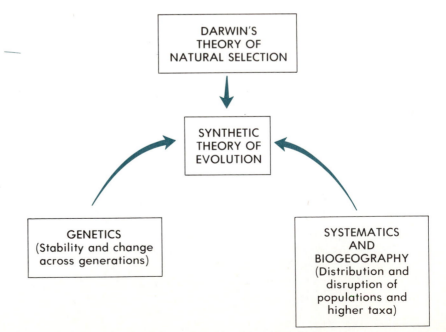

prevent criminals from breeding, for it is likely that as long as poverty exists, the criminals that concerned these social reformers will also exist. (And of course, none of these upper-class eugenicists was bothered by "white-collar" crime.)

THE MODERN SYNTHESIS

Because of his interest in eugenics, a Cambridge mathematics student named Ronald Fisher (1890–1962) turned his attention to the major evolutionary problem of his day. This problem was an apparent conflict between the intellectual heirs of Darwin and those of Gregor Mendel (1822–1884)(Chapter 7). Darwinians saw evolution as occurring by the gradual change of organisms through time. In contrast, the changes Mendel studied genetically led to discrete differences in form caused by single genes (Chapter 7). Mendel's followers saw evolutionary change in terms of the genetic processes with which they were familiar. In the case of peas, they saw round organisms replacing wrinkled ones, tall replacing dwarfed, and green replacing yellow, without any intermediates and, thus, without a suggestion of gradualism. The Darwinians, then, had a theory of evolution with no theory of genetics to generate the evolutionary variations, while the Mendelians had a theory of genetic change that appeared to contradict Darwinian evolutionism.

In 1918, Fisher showed mathematically that both points of view could be reconciled if most observable characteristics in organisms were the results of many genes, each contributing a small amount to the final physical form. By 1932, several scholars had begun to explore the consequences of genetic changes in populations, mathematically modelling the dynamics of hereditary change in populations. These studies were done and reported independently in papers and books by the Russian Sergei Chetverikov (1880–1959)("On Certain Aspects of the Evolutionary Process from the Standpoint of Modern Genetics," 1926), the English Ronald Fisher (*The Genetical Theory of Natural Selection*, 1930), the American Sewall Wright (1889–1989)("Evolution in Mendelian Populations," 1931), and the English J. B. S. Haldane (1892–1964)(*The Causes of Evolution*, 1932).

The **synthesis** of Mendelian genetics and Darwinism that emerged (Figure 3–24) holds the following tenets:

1. Morphological differences among species are the results of genetic differences between them.
2. The transformations of populations through time are the results of small changes in their genetic compositions.
3. These changes are ultimately attributable to mutations, which spread through any given population over time.
4. The spread of mutations occurs primarily by natural selection but also by other means such as migration and chance mathematical accidents.

synthetic theory of evolution

Fusion of biological ideas in the 1930s and 1940s, which resulted in a firm grounding of Darwin's ideas about evolution in the field of genetics.

Chetverikov's story is quite tragic, as he was the victim of another intersection of cultural and biological evolutionary theories. Because he lived in the Soviet Union, he was formally a follower of Marxist philosophy, which, as we have seen, is committed to the social improvement of humankind. If genetics were viewed as placing a biological limit on the extent of possible improvement, however, it could be taken as antithetical to Marxism. And indeed, Trofim Lysenko (1898–1976) suggested in the 1920s and 1930s that biological evolutionary change was due entirely to environmental factors and not to genetics at all. While this was recognized as false outside the Soviet Union, Lysenko's ideas found favor with Soviet ruling powers, in particular with Josef Stalin. Lysenko, in turn, was given absolute power in the scientific community and had virtually all the major Soviet evolutionary geneticists expelled or imprisoned. Chetverikov was banished from Moscow in 1929, although he managed to obtain a position at a junior college in 1932. From 1935 until 1948, he taught at the University of Gorky, but in August of that year, Stalin outlawed genetics. Chetverikov lived the last years of his life in poverty and died in obscurity.

Soviet genetics has never recovered from Lysenko. Soviet work on crop improvement by Lysenko's methods failed, but Lysenko himself did not fall from power until 1965. One of the most eminent victims was a leading geneticist named Nikolai Vavilov (1887–1943), who was convicted in 1940 of everything from spying to sabotaging the wheat crop, and who died in prison. One young Russian biologist, Theodosius Dobzhansky (1900–1975), was studying in the United States in the 1920s and chose not to return to the Soviet Union. He ultimately became the leading evolutionary geneticist in our country.

Dobzhansky's 1937 book, *Genetics and the Origin of Species*, marked the second phase of the evolutionary synthesis. By that time, the abstract mathematical formulations of the population geneticists were seen to be consistent with the patterns of genetic divergence of species, including the origin of reproductive incompatibilities among populations. This theme was taken up by Ernst Mayr (b. 1904), himself an emigré from Germany, in his influential *Systematics and the Origin of Species* (1942). The emergence of new taxonomic families and orders by these same principles was subsequently addressed by the paleontologist George Gaylord Simpson (1902–1984, born and brought up in the U.S.) in his *Tempo and Mode in Evolution* (1944).

These and other works converged on the conclusion that the known processes of genetics, modelled mathematically and observable in the wild, were adequate to account for all known evolutionary phenomena so far encountered. Small genetic variations, arising first as mutations in the genetic constitution of individual organisms, are passed on across the generations. If they confer an advantage upon their possessors (and occasionally, even if they do not), the new genetic variants come to characterize populations. These populations, diverging genetically from one another, come to accumulate reproductive incompatibilities and so become true species. Further, the genetic changes observable in small populations over short periods of time can be extrapolated to account for the genetic changes of large populations over long periods of time.

Although the fundamental problems have been resolved by the synthetic theory of evolution, the theory is not frozen. New questions being addressed today include the rate at which populations do change and the relations between genetic change and anatomical change. These are discussed in the next chapter.

Summary

The history of evolutionary thought enables us to appreciate current concerns and research directions. Evolutionary thought has a long history. It did not begin with Darwin in the nineteenth century but is part of a scientific way of seeing the world that has roots stretching back to at least the time of the Renaissance and its first major elaboration in the Enlightenment.

Neither biological nor cultural evolutionary thought developed in isolation—not from each other and not from other emerging sciences. Developments in astronomy, geology, and other areas of inquiry have also contributed to the growing evolutionary paradigm. And the very social fabric within which these developments occurred had an influence on their growth. Evolution, in fact, can be considered the most encompassing and most influential paradigm in all of modern Western science.

In general, theories regarding biological evolution did not influence the development of theories regarding cultural evolution. Indeed, more times than not, the influence was from the cultural to the biological realm. This is an important historical point because of a widespread and incorrect belief that biological evolutionary studies are older and more extensively elaborated than are cultural evolutionary studies.

Aspects of cultural and biological evolutionary theories have sometimes been confused with one another, resulting in ethnocentric and racist views of cultural change. Modern theories tend to recognize the two as separate processes.

Questions for Review

1. The eighteenth century was a crucial period in the emergence of contemporary ideas about our place in nature. What were the major influential ideas that arose at this time, and in what ways were they revolutionary?

2. How has the Great Chain of Being influenced the way Europeans have perceived other species and cultures? Do you think the "missing link" has been found?

3. How did Darwin arrive at the theory of evolution by natural selection? Do you think modern science would be very different if he had not?

4. How have theories of both cultural evolution and biological evolution integrated or impinged upon each other?

For Further Reading

Boorstin, D. (1983). *The discoverers*. New York: Random House.

Greene, J. C. (1959). *The death of Adam*. Ames, IA: Iowa State University Press.

Harris, M. (1968). *The rise of anthropological theory*. New York: Crowell.

Mayr, E. (1982). *The growth of biological thought*. Cambridge, MA: Harvard University Press.

Principles of Evolution

Principles of Evolution

Evolution and Science

Evolution is the major historical paradigm in science, whether physical, natural, or social science. Evolution is a statement about history—it says that the past state of any phenomenon is not identical to the present state, not recurrent or cyclical, but simply different from the present state of the phenomenon.

Thus, we can talk about the "evolution" of the solar system, which implies that the sun and planets at various past times were not in the same form as they appear today. Similarly, we can talk of the "evolution" of species or the "evolution" of cultures. We can even talk about the "evolution" of an embryo into an adult—indeed, this use (to refer to the development of an organism) was the original sense of the term in Nineteenth century biology. In each way that the term *evolution* is used, however, we mean something slightly different—for the evolution of stars, species, cultures and embryos occurs by somewhat different processes (Table 4–1).

TELEOMATIC EVOLUTION

teleomatic
Change predictable and governed by laws of physics.

To biologist Ernst Mayr, evolution in the physical world is **teleomatic.** This means that change occurs but that it is highly deterministic and predictable, governed by the laws of physics. Without knowing anything else about a star other than that it is a red giant, for example, we know the stages it passed through and can predict with a high degree of confidence what will happen to it in the future. We have this knowledge because the past, present, and future of the star are determined largely by the laws of physics.

TELEONOMIC EVOLUTION

The development of an organism from an embryo, or from a zygote, is not determined by the laws of physics but by a series of genetic instructions in the DNA of its cells. Knowing the instructions, therefore, enables a prediction of the future state. This series of changes is again highly deterministic, but in a different fashion than that of the change in form of a star, for which there are no specific "instructions." Mayr calls this kind of change—directed by a central "program"—**teleonomic.**

teleonomic
Change determined by a set of instructions.

BIOLOGICAL EVOLUTION

The evolution of species, biological evolution in its modern sense, is unpredictable in its outcome. It is partly guided by a law—natural selec-

Table 4–1

Four Different Kinds of "Evolution"

Stellar (Teleomatic)	Embryonic (Teleonomic)	Species (Darwinian)	Cultural
Highly deterministic	Less deterministic	Partly deterministic	Slightly deterministic
Linear	Linear	Linear and divergent	Linear and divergent
	Internal program	Stochastic factors	Highly arbitrary
			Can respond to desires, needs

tion—which is deterministic in that it makes a species better adapted. Yet, natural selection is only a part of the process of evolution. No program is unfolding in the evolution of a species—no inherent potential for Shakespeare to emerge from *Australopithecus afarensis* (see Chapter 11) if simply left alone. That Shakespeare happened to have A. *afarensis* in his ancestry means little. Not only many other people, but many other *species* also had that ancestor. Whatever potential A. *afarensis* may have had emerged in several directions, one of which included Shakespeare. But the Bard was no more an unfolding of a potentiality in A. *afarensis* than any of the Neanderthals was. This leads to an important insight. Unlike stellar evolution or organismal development, which involve exclusively the transformation of a single object into a new form, biological, or Darwinian, evolution adds a critically different component—the divergence of descendants from their ancestors, and from one another. Natural selection, following the splitting of a lineage, can take the two resulting lineages in different directions.

Biological evolution has other components as well as the deterministic force of natural selection. There are purely **stochastic**, or random, factors as well, namely mutation and genetic drift, which we discuss below. These factors, in addition to the divergence and intermingling of populations, make the paths of evolution virtually impossible to predict.

stochastic

Random; governed by the rules of probability; predictable in the long run but not in any specific case, such as coin tossing.

CULTURAL EVOLUTION

Cultural evolution is different from all the other preocesses we have labelled "evolution." It does contain some deterministic elements, involving the adaptation of cultures to specific environmental problems. But these adaptations can come about in a multitude of cultural ways. Most aspects of cultures involve, to some extent, arbitrary choices. For example, given that grammar is necessary in language, there are any number of ways of generating syntax, all of which appear to be equally competent. Given that clothing is necessary, there are any number of ways of being clothed, determined largely by antecedent and fashion and only partially by warmth and protection. Thus, the generation of cultural traits from any starting point involves many stochastic factors. Could anyone have predicted Nehru jackets or bell-bottom jeans (Figure 4–1)? Yet we can identify the era in which a picture was taken, given a knowledge of the variation in fashions over time; this is the same logic behind seriation (Chapter 2).

Being more inherently unpredictable, cultural evolution is different in degree from any of the other kinds of evolution we have mentioned. But *completely* unlike any of the other kinds of evolution, cultural evolution has an element of **teleology**, which (broadly defined) means action directed toward a particular goal. Teleological thinking can be religious, as when events are interpreted as the result of a divine plan. In the case of cultural evolution, however, we are talking about the plans of people and the things they do to carry out those plans. To some extent, specific cultural histories are the results of people acting toward a clear objective (Figure 4–2).

teleology

Change in a system directed toward a specific goal, such as the course of a heat-seeking missile; human behavior is often directed toward a specific goal, and thus, specific cultural evolution may have some teleological elements; but general cultural evolution does not, nor does biological evolution.

Figure 4–1

No one could have predicted that in 1968 people would actually dress like this. Unless these styles ever come back, seeing them will enable an observer to date the scene fairly precisely.

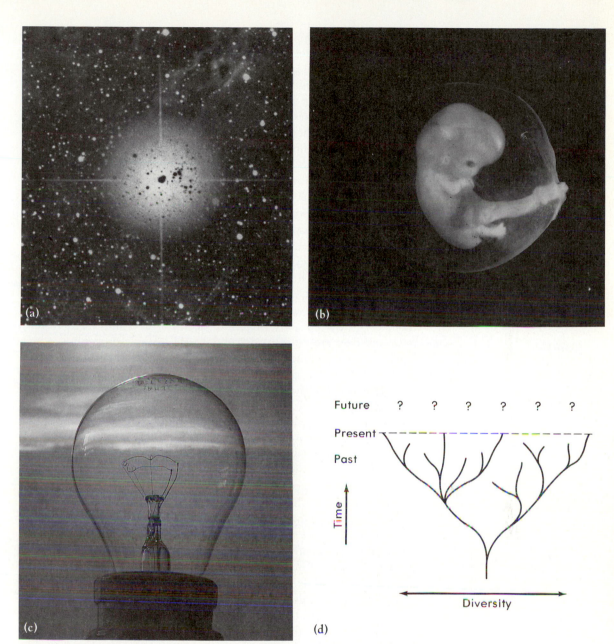

Figure 4–2. Different kinds of change may involve different kinds of "goals," or none at all.

(a) Physical laws determine a specific ultimate destiny for a star, which sometimes becomes a supernova; this is teleomatic change. (b) The genetic information, molded by eons of biological evolution, determines that an embryo will pass through fetal, infant, juvenile, and adult stages, which are therefore "goals" for the embryo; this is teleonomic change. (c) A specific invention is the result of conscious effort, a willful attempt on the part of the inventor to bring it about; this is teleological change. (d) Biological and cultural evolution do not appear to be goal-directed in any significant way: Many species are alive today, and many more extinct, none of which appears to have been a "goal" in evolution; likewise with cultures.

Progress or Relativism?

As we saw in the previous chapter, the idea of progress was one of the dominant philosophical themes of the eighteenth and nineteenth centuries. It is intrinsic to some theories of evolution, such as that of Lamarck, but it is not an intrinsic part of any modern theory of evolution except in extremely restricted senses.

In the case of both stellar evolution and embryonic development, a single trajectory is followed by the "evolving" entity. We know, therefore, that a human embryo 20 cm in length is farther along than an embryo 3 cm in length, and most 3 cm embryos, all other things being equal, will ultimately grow to 20 cm, and will do so in similar amounts of time. Thus, we can talk about a late fetus being more fully developed than an early fetus. Early fetuses will become late fetuses and are, therefore, less advanced than late fetuses.

In Darwinian evolution and cultural evolution, however, there is no single trajectory. Rather, the splitting of lineages enables them to differ from one another, that is, to diverge in different ways from their common ancestor. In no sense can we place a mouse and a deer along a single trajectory—mice do not change into deer, nor deer into mice. Instead, mice and deer are different descendants of a single progenitor, which lived perhaps 70 million years ago and whose descendants include deer, mice, and obviously, many other things.

On the other hand, could we not place a mouse and an iguana along a single trajectory? Mice are mammals, iguanas are reptiles, and mammals evolved from reptiles. Therefore, might an iguana represent an earlier stage of a mouse? Clearly not, for mice did not evolve from modern reptiles, much less from any specific modern reptile. Further, can we say that a mouse is more advanced than an iguana? Again, the answer is no. Put the two in a cage, and most likely the iguana alone will survive. The only sense in which mice can be considered more advanced than iguanas is in being more similar to humans than iguanas are, that is, if humans are the scale of measurement. While this may be philosophically tempting, it is too arbitrary to be biologically useful. If the mouse and iguana were judged in their respective degrees of advancement by comparison with a chicken, the iguana would win (Figure 4–3).

To create a scale by which to rank the relative advancement of living creatures, we need an objective standard, and no such standard exists. Humans are smarter than other creatures but are certainly less well-insulated than polar bears, are weaker than chimpanzees, are less agile than cats, have a poorly developed sense of smell, and are slower of foot than most other mammals. Creatures are different from one another, not more or less advanced than one another.

Each species is alive, adapted, and therefore not better or worse than any other species. The same is true for cultures. Human groups have many ways to exist and adapt. Each way has its strengths and weaknesses,

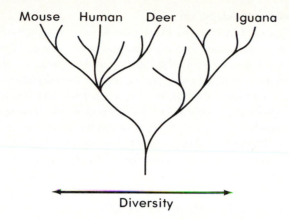

Mouse   Human   Deer   Iguana

Diversity

Figure 4–3. Living species are the products of divergence and adaptation, not steps on a ladder.

Seeing species in the Great Chain of Being is wrong. Living species differ in how recently each shares a common ancestor with the others, but none is higher or lower.

although there seems to be no single criterion for judging that one way is better or worse than another. With sophisticated modern American technology comes modern American urban violent crime, high-sugar, low-fiber diets, social alienation of the elderly and the young, our heavy emphasis on personal vanity and appearance, and the weakness of familial bonds. We do what little we can to change these, but we accept them as aspects of our society that come with our culture.

Can we then say that our culture is better than another simply on the basis of a comparison of technologies? Clearly not. At various times, people have argued that modern urban cultures are more progessive or more decadent than others. In reality, it all depends upon which aspects of culture receive focus and upon one's point of view.

Thus, cultures are neither better nor worse than others, but merely different—as we saw with reference to species earlier. This is the core of cultural relativism. Its opposite, the view that one's culture is better than others, is ethnocentrism, just as the belief that the human species is foremost among earth's creatures is *anthropocentrism*.

"Better than" or "worse than" is a value judgment, and such judgments are inapplicable in an objective way to species or to cultures. We can, however, classify cultures, as we classify species, without a value judgment. The most convenient way is by economic system or subsistence system, and we will refer to gathering-hunting, agricultural, and urban-industrial societies throughout this book. It is important to bear in mind that the use of this classification does *not* imply improvement or progress—only a different form of economic system, often with attending differences in social and cultural forms.

Divergence and Adaptation

Biological evolution in the Darwinian sense refers to change among populations of organisms, through time and across space. This change is the result of two processes: 1) the splitting and movement—the *divergence*—of populations into different places, and 2) the *adaptation* of populations to new environments. Thus, we can detect two sorts of changes operating on groups of organisms: 1) change across space, independent of time, which involves the fragmentation of groups of organisms into subgroups living in different localities, and 2) change through time, independent of space, which involves the adjustment of each subgroup to its particular environment (Figure 4–4).

POPULATION FRAGMENTATION

Population fragmentation has not been well studied empirically, although it is of great importance to evolutionary theory. The likelihood and extent of its occurrence is determined by demographic and ecological factors. How many individuals can be supported in a particular environment at one time? Is the population expanding? If so, how fast? Are there barriers to the reunion of parts of the population, or are the separations ephemeral?

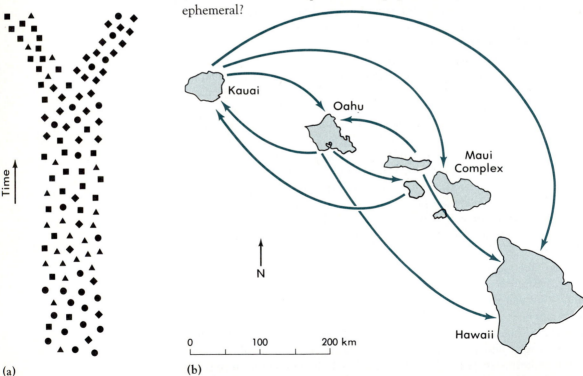

(a)   (b)

Figure 4-4. Biological evolution involves time and space.

(a) Through time, the descendants of a population can become genetically different from their ancestors.
(b) Spatial differentiation is easily evident in the fruitflies of Hawaii, in which geneticist Hampton Carson has reconstructed several founding events of species in different areas.

Figure 4–5
Yanomamo men engage in "chest pounding," an aggressive display of the social tension that often develops.

Some species tend to live in populations of great numbers that are highly mobile and fluid, while others live in small groups in clearly defined ranges. Humans, of course, live in populations of highly variable size and stability. The Yanomamo of Venezuela and Brazil tend to enter into frequent rancorous disputes when a village reaches a population of about 150–200 people. The village then splits along family lines, with sometimes half the village moving away (Figure 4–5). Were that to happen on the same scale in industrialized society, virtually no modern institutions would be possible—high schools and colleges could not exist, factories could not operate, and urbanism of any sort would be impossible.

Nevertheless, many human groups do separate from one another—people emigrate to new lands. The effect of population subdivision is to multiply the number of populations, in effect, to create two or more populations where formerly there was but one. Divergence is not the inevitable outcome of population subdivision (it could merge afterward or become extinct, for example), but it is a most important evolutionary factor in the generation of new groups.

POPULATION ADAPTATION

Once formed, a population must adjust itself to the new environment in which it is located. This it does, in time, by three general mechanisms: 1) *genetic* (or evolutionary) adaptation, 2) *physiological* adaptation (or acclimatization), and 3) *behavioral* adaptation. Because human behavior is cultural (symbolic and cumulative), the third category applied to humans can simply be called cultural adaptation. This is not true for other species, for which noncultural behavioral adaptations can help them survive. Such is the case with birds learning to pry the tops off milk containers in England, and Japanese macaques learning to wash their sweet potatoes in salt water before eating them.

For humans, the principal means of coping with the environment is culture. Culture enables us to thrive in nearly any environment on earth, to combat endemic disease, to derive sustenance from the local plants and animals, or to import non-native foods. As the earliest anthropologists discovered, members of even the most technologically primitive cultures have an extraordinarily detailed knowledge of their environment. For example, they know what is edible and inedible, how to prepare inedible food so as to make it edible, how to flavor it, how to make vessels to serve it in, how to stay warm, how to keep cool, how to make tools and utensils, and much more.

This, however, does not mean that humans never adapt in other ways. As you will see in Chapters 8 and 9, some genetic differences among human populations can most easily be interpreted as local genetic adaptations to long-term stresses, such as malaria. Other physical differences among human populations seem to be attributable to the effect of growing up under a particular stress, such as a high altitude with thin air. Usually, however, it is difficult to sort these causes out so clearly from one another. For example, skin color variation in human populations has a genetic component as well as a physiological component.

Replicators and Interactors

The processes of multiplying and adapting are fundamentally different, and both are necessary for selection to occur. **Selection** is the differential representation through time of multiplying and enduring units. In Darwinian, or *natural*, selection, those units are specific traits of an organism, or more precisely, the genes that encode the traits.

However, those units could be other things, larger or smaller. *Cultural selection* involves the differential representation through time of styles, symbols, or technologies—cultural units. Likewise, a species that tends to form new species more efficiently than others can be the focus of *species selection*—independently of its particular traits. In addition, one can think of cellular selection, in which a lineage of dividing cells is differentially represented in the body of an organism. Indeed, this is an approximation of the course of some cancers. All that is required for selec-

selection

The differential representation through time of units that can endure and replicate (or be copied); this encompasses natural selection, artificial selection, cultural selection, and so on.

tion to occur among units is that the units be *replicators* and *interactors*. A replicator is any entity of which copies can be made, however imperfect. An interactor is something that persists and participates in an environment. For selection to occur, there need only be something that can multiply through time and persist in its environment to some extent.

If the qualities of replication and interaction exist, then selection *can* occur. If there is variation in these qualities among a group of similar units, then selection *must* occur. That is, if all the units are replicating and interacting with their environments with an equal net efficiency, then no selection is occurring. If their net efficiencies differ, however—if one is even slightly relatively better at replicating or persevering than another—then selection is the result. The more efficient one will come to be disproportionately represented in the future.

Darwin's great achievement was in recognizing this principle as it applies to characteristics of organisms—what he called "natural selection"—as the cause of biological adaptations in the evolutionary process.

TYPES OF SELECTION

As shown in Table 4–2, several different kinds of selection can occur, depending upon the elements one chooses to focus on and upon the different types of replicators and interactors. As noted earlier, cells exist in a physiological environment and replicate by fission, or **mitosis**. Species interact with one another to form an ecosystem and replicate by speciation. In demic selection (*deme* is another term for population), replication is done by organisms, and the interaction is between organisms or group of organisms. In cultural selection, symbols, behaviors, and artifacts are created by people—if these are perceived as enriching the user's life, then more people adopt them.

In this book, we are principally concerned with biological (Darwinian and demic) and cultural evolution, the two processes that have combined to generate the human species as it currently exists. To understand the processes of biological evolution, we must view it at three levels: microevolution, speciation, and macroevolution. In microevolution, or evolution below the species level, the replicators are genes, and

mitosis

The process of cell division whereby one cell splits into two genetically identical copies; principally involved in growth processes.

Table 4–2

Selection by Replicators and Interactors

Type of Selection	Type of Replicator	Type of Interaction
Cellular	Cell, fission	Cell, physiological
Darwinian	Gene, in gene pool	Phenotype, in environment
Demic	Organism	Population
Species	Speciation	Biotic ecology
Cultural	Symbols, behaviors, artifacts	Language, communication

speciation

The origin of a species, either by transformation through time or by splitting from another species.

the evolutionary consequences of interest are those that allow one genetic variant to preponderate in a population. In **speciation**, or the formation of new species, the replicators are organisms, and the evolutionary consequences of interest are those that prevent the members of one population from being able to reproduce successfully with those of another. In macroevolution, or evolution above the species level, the replicators are species, and the evolutionary consequences of interest are those that allow one species to thrive while others become extinct.

Microevolution and Biological Transmission

Population genetics studies the change in genetic composition of populations over time, and this is discussed in some detail in Chapter 7. For the purposes of this chapter, we simply sketch out the ways in which microevolution is viewed.

GENE POOL

The sum of all possible genes in a population is called the *gene pool*. Therefore, when population geneticists study microevolution, they study changes in the composition of the gene pool. The gene pool is a property of a population—no single organism possesses a gene pool. Consequently, we can describe, for example, the gene pool of a population for the ABO blood group gene as being 30 percent A, 8 percent B, and 62 percent O. Yet no human could be described that way, for such a description cannot apply to a single organism. An organism, however, has a very tiny portion of the gene pool in its **genotype**, or its own genetic constitution. Thus, the

genotype

The genetic constitution of an individual.

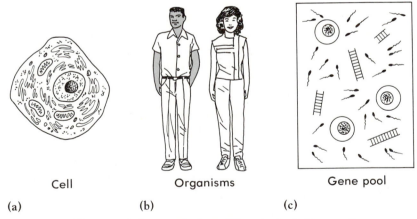

Cell   Organisms   Gene pool

(a)   (b)   (c)

Figure 4–6. Different evolutionary units have different roles in the overall process.

(a) Cells generate the fundamental genetic diversity necessary for evolution. (b) Organisms transmit the gene pool into the next generation, and by virtue of interacting with the environment, may transmit it in slightly different proportions. (c) The gene pool of the species perseveres while cells and organisms live and die; it is the evolutionary unit with long-standing cohesion and perserverance.

gene pool is continuously being apportioned into organisms. The gene pool includes all the genetic material of the species, and every new organism of the species gets a bit, but only a small bit, of the gene pool.

Organisms, however, are short-lived and have little genetic material. Consequently, in microevolutionary studies, they can be looked upon as little more than vessels for ensuring the continuity of the gene pool, for guaranteeing that it will be transmitted to the next generation (Figure 4–6). If it is transmitted perfectly, then no evolution has occurred, for there will have been no change in the gene pool.

GENETIC ADAPTATION

The major contribution of population genetics to evolutionary theory has been the recognition that only a handful of factors can actually change the composition of the gene pool. These are: 1) mutation, the generation of new variants (**alleles**) within the gene pool; 2) genetic drift, the random or accidental predominance of one allele over another in a population; 3) natural selection, the differential representation of one allele over another because of its greater efficiency of replication or longevity; and 4) gene flow, the importation or exportation of alleles to or from another population.

allele

Any genetic variant, including "normal"; produced randomly by mutation.

Genetic adaptation is produced over time by natural selection. The organisms, bearers of the genes, interact with the environment. Those possessing particular genetic constitutions may tend, on the average, to out-survive and out-reproduce others. Therefore, their genetic constitutions are preferentially represented in the gene pool of the next generation.

Individual organisms play an ambiguous part in the genetic conception of microevolution. On one hand, genes do not reproduce—organisms reproduce. Yet, on the other hand, an organism that possesses a gene enabling it to survive or reproduce more efficiently than other members of the population will ultimately produce more copies of that gene in its descendants, many of whom will have inherited the same gene and therefore survive or reproduce *themselves* more efficiently. Thus, the gene pool changes through the survival and reproduction of organisms.

Further, genes do not interact with the environment themselves. Rather, they function by producing an effect, a **phenotype**, on the organism, which in turn may affect the organism's survival and reproduction. The phenotype is what the organism "expresses" to the outside world. Thus, the organism has a phenotype, which interacts with the environment and which survives and reproduces.

phenotype

The appearance of an individual, produced by the interaction of a genotype and the environment; different genotypes can have the same phenotype, and vice-versa.

Since differential reproduction is critical to the gene pool, the speed at which the gene pool of a species can change is limited by the generation time of the organisms. Species that have short generation times can usually evolve faster than can those with long generation times, which tend more often to adapt by nongenetic means. In twenty-

Genetic Drift on Tristan da Cunha

Humans have lived in large cosmopolitan populations only since the rise of urbanism in the past few thousand years. For most of our history and prehistory, we have lived in much smaller populations in which random events would likely affect the gene pool significantly.

An elegant demonstration of this effect was performed by anthropologist Derek Roberts, studying the genes and genealogies of the inhabitants of Tristan da Cunha, an island in the Atlantic Ocean. The microevolutionary patterns in the gene pool of Tristan's population were determined largely by a series of nineteenth-century population crashes.

Tristan was colonized by a few English settlers in 1816. The population grew to a high of 103 in 1855, but two waves of emigration reduced it to 33 by March 1857. The population climbed again, but of the 106 people on Tristan in November 1885, a boating accident killed fifteen adult males. This left most of the women as widows with only four adult males on the island, of whom one was insane and

two were elderly. The population dwindled to 59 by 1891 as the widows and their children left.

The English are greatly admired by geneticists and demographers for their meticulous demographic record-keeping. On Tristan, the colonists recorded all marriages and births in their community, which enabled Roberts to trace the ancestry of each member of the population and the contribution of each founder to later generations.

Tristan's population in 1855, he determined, was descended from twenty ancestors; more than half the gene pool came from only five ancestors. By 1857, however, the entire population was traceable to only eleven ancestors. The first population crash had eliminated nine people from the ancestry of the subsequent population.

By 1884, six immigrants had contributed to the gene pool, accounting for 18 percent of the population's genetic makeup. But of the original twenty, of whom eleven were left in the ancestors, one more had been eliminated. So, 82 percent of the

five years, mice can have experienced many generations of natural selection remodeling their gene pool—but chimpanzees cannot.

Not all genetic change, however, is adaptive. If the primary force operating is natural selection, change in the gene pool will tend to be adaptive. If, however, genetic drift is the primary force working, change will tend to be nonadaptive (meaning independent of adaptive needs, not maladaptive), producing random fluctuations in the gene pool. Genetic drift usually does not have a major effect if the gene pool is large. This is because statistical fluctuations in the partitioning of the gene pool—that is, genetic drift—will tend to even out in the long run. If, however, few organisms compose a population, that is, if the gene pool is small, random fluctuations can become crucial.

Physical anthropologist Derek Roberts has shown how important genetic drift can be as a microevolutionary factor in a small population by tracking the gene pool of a population on a remote island called Tristan da Cunha (Box 4–1). In Chapter 7, we discuss how the gene pool of the Pennsylvania Amish was affected by having one of its founders carry the allele for a rare genetic disease.

gene pool had come from ten members of the founding population. Of the sixteen ancestors contributing to the 1884 gene pool, four were lost by 1891. The pattern of ancestry remained stable through the 1870s except for a few more immigrants through the years contributing a bit to the gene pool.

The population when Roberts studied it in 1961 derived 68 percent of its gene pool from the founders. The contribution of the 1884 immigrants was down from 18 to 1 percent. Twenty-three percent of the gene pool came from more recent immigrants.

Roberts then traced the contributions of individual founders as they fluctuated in the gene pools of later generations. One founder, for example, increased tenfold in genetic representation from 1855 to 1961, while ten founders vanished genetically from 1855 to 1961.

Coming from so few founders, Tristan's population became more inbred through time. The first consanguineous marriage was in 1854—the partners had few options; by 1871, there would have been no option for the couple. Roberts found that the extent of inbreeding, measured by the mean coefficient of kinship, increased from about .02 in 1850 to nearly .07 in 1870. This does not, however, appear to have caused an increase in rare genetic diseases as in other inbred populations—a fortuitous consequence of the founders' gene pool.

References:

Roberts, D. F. (1968). Genetic effects of population size reduction. *Nature*, 220:1084–1088.

Roberts, D. F. (1988). Migration in the recent past: Societies with records. From: *Biological aspects of human migration*, C. G. N. Mascie-Taylor & G. W. Lasker (Eds.). New York: Cambridge University Press.

Speciation

Species, like cells and organisms, are fundamental units in a biological hierarchy. They are held together by reproductive compatibility, the sharing of a common gene pool in which all parts of a species can participate but other species cannot. Cells generally reproduce by fission or mitosis, while organisms generally reproduce by sexual conjugation. The process by which species reproduce is called speciation.

Speciation involves the disruption of a gene pool into discontinuous parts. In other words, genetic contact between two parts of a population has been broken. Usually, this begins when a species comes to be divided among different geographical areas. Perhaps only a few individuals have entered a new territory (as often seems to be the case among fruitflies in Hawaii). Or maybe the population is structured so that small social groups are scattered fairly widely apart. As long as genetic contact (gene flow) occurs among the different segments of the gene pool, no population will diverge greatly from the others. If, in contrast, the gene flow is broken by natural environmental barriers, the populations will become genetically discrete entities. This itself is not sufficient for speciation, however. If the two populations should now come back together—if the barrier is lifted—they will be interfertile, as before.

For speciation to occur, two populations must seal off their own gene pools from one another. This is achieved while the populations are geographically apart from one another and therefore not in genetic contact, by the development of reproductive isolating mechanisms. The isolating mechanisms act to prevent genetic material of one population from being incorporated into the gene pool of another population. In other words, the function of a reproductive isolating mechanism is to curtail gene flow.

In Table 4–3 we list the ways in which two populations whose gene pools have become separated can achieve reproductive isolation. Notice that several processes are involved in compatible reproduction—identifying mates, achieving fertilization, having the offspring survive, and having the offspring reproduce. Introducing a disruption anywhere along this chain of events generates reproductive isolation, and thereby speciation.

In general, where closely related populations exhibit one of the reproductive isolating mechanisms given in Table 4–3 as numbers 4 through 7, they are considered to be separate species. In contrast, if they exhibit any of numbers 1 through 3, they are recognized as subspecies. This is because even though under ordinary circumstances there is no direct gene flow, the potential for gene flow still exists. For example, mechanical isolation clearly prevents Chihuahuas and Great Danes from producing hybrids. Nevertheless, the smaller dogs can mate with slightly larger dogs, and those dogs with even larger dogs, and so on, such that considerable potential exists for gene flow between Chihuahuas and Great Danes despite the inability of direct hybridization.

Different populations of the fruitfly *Drosophila paulistorum* will often coexist but will not mate in the wild (Figure 4–7). When mated in the laboratory, they produce living hybrids, but only the hybrid females are

---

Table 4–3

Reproductive Isolating Mechanisms

1. **Seasonal isolation:** Potential mates from different populations are not prepared to reproduce at the same time.
2. **Behavioral/sensory isolation:** Potential mates from different populations are not recognized as potential mates because they lack the appropriate identification signals—olfactory cues, dances, appearances, and so on.
3. **Mechanical isolation:** Potential mates from different populations are physically unable to mate because of size or conformation of the reproductive apparatus.
4. **Gametic mortality:** Mating is achieved, but not fertilization.
5. **Zygotic mortality:** Fertilization is achieved, but the hybrid dies *in utero.*
6. **Hybrid inviability:** The hybrid is born but fails to thrive.
7. **Hybrid infertility:** The hybrid thrives but fails to reproduce.

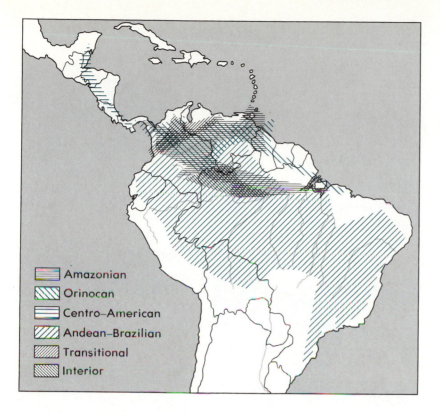

Amazonian
Orinocan
Centro-American
Andean-Brazilian
Transitional
Interior

Figure 4–7

Drosophila paulistorum, a fruitfly, is considered to be a "superspecies" consisting of several "semispecies" because its populations overlap but do not interbreed in the wild, yet can produce some fertile offspring in the laboratory (after Dobzhansky).

fertile—the males are sterile. These are considered not to be separate species, although they are presumably on their way to achieving reproductive isolation.

Similarly, different populations of gibbons (*Hylobates lar*) often have different calls or songs to attract mates. While they are not known to hybridize in the wild, they can do so quite freely in captivity. Consequently, many anthropologists feel that they should not be recognized as distinct at the species level. Nevertheless, when a lar gibbon is mated in captivity to a siamang gibbon (*Hylobates syndactylus*), a live but infertile offspring is produced. The latter situation is similar to that of the familiar horse and donkey. The horse and donkey are considered separate species, even though they can produce a viable hybrid offspring (a mule). Mules are generally sterile, although in very rare cases, a mule has reproduced successfully with a donkey.

The ability to produce hybrid offspring is not necessarily tied to how similar the parental organisms look. Usually, organisms that look similar can produce offspring and are therefore allocated to the same species. But sometimes it is difficult to tell whether different populations are, in fact, different species. Populations of savannah baboons (*Papio cynocephalus*) include the olive baboon, the guinea baboon, the yellow baboon, and the chacma baboon. All look distinctively different, yet in the wild there are hybrid zones bordering their respective ranges, where

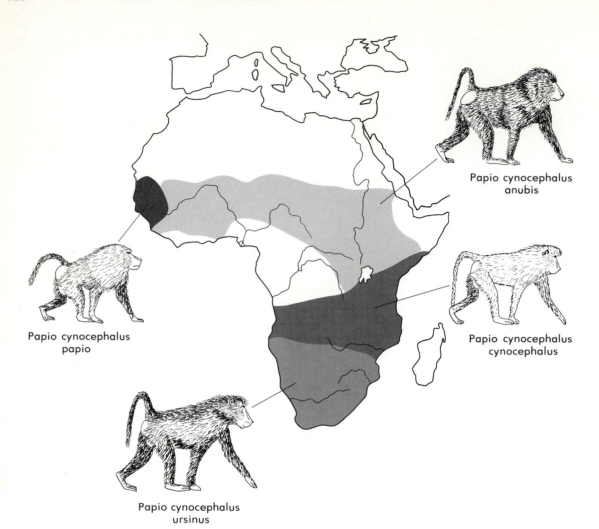

Papio cynocephalus
anubis

Papio cynocephalus
papio

Papio cynocephalus
cynocephalus

Papio cynocephalus
ursinus

Figure 4–8

The savanna baboons of Africa are grouped into the same species (*Papio cynocephalus*); they fall into four distinctive geographical subspecies, which form hybrid zones where they come into contact with one another (after Richard).

hybridization between any of the two populations regularly occurs (Figure 4–8).

The process of speciation generally has two steps, involving first **allopatry** and then the subsequent accumulation of reproductive isolating mechanisms. The final product is the divorce of the gene pools of the two populations from each other and the creation of two lineages that can now evolve independently of each other, no longer in genetic contact. They are, therefore, free to adapt to different circumstances in different ways. Their differences are then reinforced through time by the develop-

allopatry

Geographical separation between populations, which can lead to speciation; most speciation involves allopatry.

ment of a specific mate-recognition system, which in essence defines parts of a species as being what they are—potential mates. Once the organisms in two different lineages can no longer identify each other as potential mates, their gene pools are truly sealed.

The Nature of Species

Although speciation is a *process*, it can also be viewed as an *event* in the history of a lineage, not much different in principle from seeing mitosis as an event in the history of a cell line or birth as an event in the history of a family.

The species is a fundamental unit in systematics. It is also the only *objective* taxonomic category. The recognition of subspecies is made based on the degree of morphological diversity of populations and is basically a judgment call. Are these populations sufficiently distinct to be called subspecies? If so, then we will call them that. Similarly, above the level of the species, one encounters the same questions. Are these genera distinct enough to be placed in separate families or not? Again, a judgment call. The species is the only taxonomic unit for which an objective criterion exists, namely, the potential for interbreeding. Can they interbreed? Yes—then they are parts of the same species. No—then they are parts of different species. (Because speciation is a process, there are always gray areas—speciation not having been completed—but in principle, at least, the criterion exists.)

Speciation across space, or allopatric speciation, generates two coexistent species from one parental species. This is also known as *clado-genesis*, or the splitting of a species into two or more species. Evolutionary change also occurs within a single lineage over time, independent of space—this is known as *anagenesis*, the gradual transformation of one species into a different one (Figure 4–9). Anagenesis is generally regarded as the way in which a single lineage (gene pool) maintains its fit to the environment, and cladogenesis as the way in which new lineages

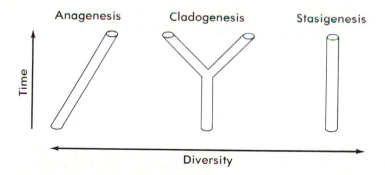

Anagenesis   **Cladogenesis**   **Stasigenesis**

Time

Diversity

Anagenesis—lineage changing through time
Cladogenesis—lineage splitting
Stasigenesis—lineage not changing or splitting

Figure 4–9

The three evolutionary modes are anagenesis, or change of a single lineage through time; cladogenesis, or the splitting of one lineage into two; and stasigenesis, the ability of a single lineage to persist without change.

are formed. Speciation can also occur by anagenesis, however, if the changes through time to a single lineage are of sufficient magnitude that reproductive isolation between the parental and descendant populations can be inferred, even though it cannot be directly tested. The evolution of *Homo erectus* into *Homo sapiens* is generally interpreted this way (Chapter 12).

If this seems somewhat arbitrary, it is. Paleontologists have a more difficult time distinguishing species than do neontologists (those who study "new" life, as opposed to "old" life). In principle, a neontologist can test hypotheses about whether two populations are species by studying their reproductive compatibility. To a paleontologist, such data are inaccessible, leaving no way to know for certain whether *Homo habilis* and *Homo erectus* could interbreed. The fact that we put them in different species indicates a value judgment that they could not have interbred.

The combination of cladogenesis (splitting) and anagenesis (change through time) accounts for the diversity of species and their adaptations. A third evolutionary mode, *stasigenesis*, refers to the persistence of a lineage without much change. This actually refers to the absence of evolution and is the reason that we still find such "living fossils" as sharks, horseshoe crabs, and coelacanths, that haven't changed much in hundreds of millions of years.

Macroevolution

Speciation also forms the bridge between microevolution, or the short-term changes that occur within a single lineage, and macroevolution, or the large-scale changes that occur to the higher taxonomic categories in the history of life. In microevolution, the units under study are characters or genes being redistributed at higher or lower frequencies in gene pools over a few generations. In macroevolution, the units are species, whose descendant species attain higher or lower frequencies in clades, or clusters of taxa descended from a common ancestor.

In microevolution, gene frequencies change because of differential survival and/or reproduction of the organisms bearing the genes. Therefore, the fate of a gene will depend upon the average longevity and fecundity of its bearer. Since the gene may be contributing to that longevity or fecundity, it carries its fate in its own hands (Box 4–2).

This, however, is only part of the picture of evolution. Organisms compose species, and species form new species. But some species have many descendant species, and others have but a few. For example, only one living species of the genus *Gorilla* exists, compared with more than twenty of the Old World monkey genus *Cercopithecus*. This is because *Cercopithecus* has a greater tendency to speciate, and/or its new species tend to persist longer. These are a set of macroevolutionary variables that are different from those affecting reproduction and longevity of *organisms*—these concern the replication and longevity of *taxa*.

What accounts for the bulk of evolutionary change discernible in the history of life? According to the traditional theory of **phyletic gradualism**, most evolutionary change occurs anagenetically, as changes to the gene pool independently of speciation. According to the theory of **punctuated equilibria**, conceived by Niles Eldredge of the American Museum of Natural History and Stephen Jay Gould of Harvard, anagenesis is only a minor part of evolution. Rather, they argue, the history of life is largely one of stasigenesis—no change, or equilibrium—which is "punctuated," they argue, by cladogenesis—where most of the change occurs.

PHYLETIC GRADUALISM

Phyletic gradualism holds that the gene pools of species are constantly adapting and changing in response to environmental stresses. While divergent speciation and lineages showing little or no change are part of the picture, the history of life is taken to be primarily the process of adapting, of constant change. In contrast, punctuated equilibria downplays adaptation, which is thought to occur only shortly after the formation of a new species, after which the species retains its integrity for a long period of time (Figure 4–10).

PUNCTUATED EQUILIBRIA

The major contribution of punctuated equilibria lies in the recognition that the formation of a species is much briefer than its duration. This implies that the gene pool is a fairly stable entity over long periods of time, not constantly changing, as phyletic gradualism has it. Rather, the gene pool, according to punctuated equilibria, undergoes radical changes due to genetic drift during speciation—the new founding population adapts, and the gene pool is fairly stable thereafter.

Splitting, stasis, and adaptation all occur, and they probably occur in all groups of organisms. The question of which is occurring to a particular group at a particular time is empirical and can be addressed only with high-quality fossil data.

phyletic gradualism

Biological evolutionary theory holding anagenesis primary and cladogenesis and stasigenesis secondary; part of the synthetic theory of evolution.

punctuated equilibria

Biological evolutionary theory holding cladogenesis and stasigenesis primary and anagenesis secondary.

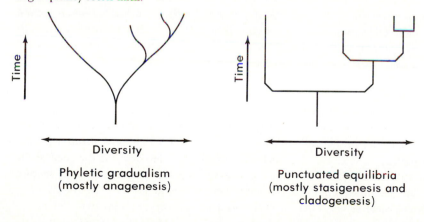

Phyletic gradualism
(mostly anagenesis)

Punctuated equilibria
(mostly stasigenesis and cladogenesis)

Figure 4–10

Phyletic gradualism and punctuated equilibria: alternative macroevolutionary models emphasizing different evolutionary modes.

Issues in Anthropology 4–2

Selfish Gene Theory

A provocative, if somewhat cynical, new way of visualizing biological and cultural evolution comes from recent work inspired by a 1976 book by biologist Richard Dawkins, *The Selfish Gene*.

Dawkins argues that primordial genes were only bits of organic molecules capable of reproduction. They did nothing but copy themselves, however inefficiently. This nevertheless set up the earliest natural selection. Linear bits of molecules that could recruit other molecules to help them copy themselves would be represented in ever greater numbers. Linear molecules (the earliest genes) that were more efficient at reproducing outcompeted other linear molecules, their alleles.

Some genes eventually became able to enhance their ability to reproduce by manufacturing proteins that aided their reproduction. These were the first phenotypes, which, Dawkins argues, originated simply as genic adaptations to enhance replication.

According to Dawkins, all cells, organisms, and species are merely vehicles that enable genes to perpetuate themselves. Cells evolved as phenotypes around genes to protect the integrity of the DNA molecule and to ensure that it copied itself precisely and rapidly. Likewise, organisms evolved around cells to ensure that the genetic material was faithfully and copiously replicated.

Next came the emergence of complex behavior, which, argues Dawkins, is an "extended phenotype"—influencing the survival of one's own genes by affecting those of another. To Dawkins, all phenotypes are best analyzed in terms of their effect on replication of the genetic material in the cells. Behavior, no matter how apparently selfless, is somehow directed at allowing one's genes to make more copies of themselves—or else, the argument runs, it would not exist, having been out-reproduced by alternative selfish genes.

This view allows only two ways in which selflessness, or altruism (sacrificing one's own interest for the good of another), could come about. The first is through kin selection, sacrificing in particular for one's relatives. Relatives share large proportions of identical genetic material, so a behavior that helps relatives at the actor's expense can be seen as actually helping the actor's genes *through* the relatives. The actor is being selfless only phenotypically—genotypically, the actor is behaving selfishly.

The second way is through reciprocal altruism, sacrificing for a nonrelative in expectation of a payback. Here one's own genes do not lose, for in the end, all the apparent altruism balances out. Again, the apparently selfless behavior is selfish in the context of the survival and proliferation of one's genes.

The selfish gene theory has major problems. First, it assumes a genetic basis for the behaviors it tries to explain. If the behavior does not depend on the differential perpetuation of genetic material, that is, by natural selection for the specific behavior, then it is not constrained to be selfish. Selfishness derives only from reproductive competition between two alternative alleles; the one that outreproduces the other must be more selfish. Why? Because the one that gives the help at its own sacrifice is going to be out-reproduced by the one that receives the help and does not sacrifice. In other words, natural selection favors selfishness.

But if one refers to alternative behaviors that do not derive from different alleles—that is, the same genes permitting different behaviors—then natural selection is not acting, for it acts upon *genetic* variation. Without genetic variation, there is no natural selection; without natural selection, there is no constraint to evolve to act in one's own genetic interests.

Another problem concerns how altruistic behavior evolves. Indeed, it can evolve in a way other than kin selection and reciprocal altruism if individuals sacrifice their interests for the good of the group—known as group selection. In other species, it is difficult to imagine group selection playing a major role even in theory, because it implies a coercive force that prevents cheaters from letting others sacrifice for the good of the group without participating themselves. Without a coercive force, a population would soon come to be composed of selfish individuals and their selfish descendants. In humans, however, culture acts as an external coercive force, suppressing those cheaters. Biologist Ernst Mayr argues that humans are probably the only species in which group selection operates. And, the selfish constraints on behavior deriving from kin selection and reciprocal altruism may not even apply to humans, where group selection may promote altruism.

A more fundamental problem lies in assuming that only genic explanations can explain behavior that occurs after the emergence of phenotypes, organisms, and brains. When only naked genes existed, competition had to be viewed in their terms. But after genes coalesced and produced phenotypes, couldn't those phenotypes compete with one another, regardless of the best interests of the genes?

Consider Virginia, which existed before the United States. Prior to the emergence of the United States, Virginia contrasted with other states and presumably always acted in its own interests. The formation of the United States helped Virginia survive, and what is good for the United States is generally good for Virginia. But is *everything* the U.S. does in the best interests of Virginia? Clearly not. Being a higher-order structure than Virginia, the U.S. has other goals than simply Virginia's interests (for example, Alaska's interests, the public concern over the long-term effect of tobacco on citizens, and so on). Virginia existed before the U.S. came into being (temporal priority), and the U.S. would not exist without the states that compose it (ontological priority). However, the U.S. has properties that Virginia lacks, and it certainly does not always act in the best interests of Virginia—though often, as noted, what is good for the U.S. is good for Virginia. Likewise with genes and organisms.

The final problem is that the selfish gene theory cannot show its necessity in explaining human behavior. While it may be *sufficient* to explain much of human behavior, it is *necessary* only if all the alternatives are rejected. While this theory may be interesting philosophy, nothing suggests that it is true. Given that actors help relatives, how can we know that they do it *because they share genes,* and not for any other reason? Given that actors help nonrelatives, how can we know that they do it only *because they expect payback?* What of actors who do not help relatives, do not help nonrelatives, help nonrelatives for no apparent payback, or help their in-laws or adoptees to whom they are not genetically related? How does one account for them? How can they even exist if these theories are true? As there is no reason for believing that this theory is better than others, it is simply another alternative in the arsenal of theories to explain human behavior.

One alternative is that there is little or no genetic variation in "human nature," and therefore all groups of people have pretty much the same basic drives, needs, and goals. Often, however, these conflict with one another, and require an individual to make complex decisions. Those decisions are based partly on internal (genetic) drives, partly on rational considerations, partly on lifetime experiences, and partly on the expectations of other social group members. Thus any behavior cannot be classified as simply selfish or altruistic; rather, it must be interpreted in the context of the individual and the culture.

References:

Alexander, R. D. (1987). *The biology of moral systems.* New York: Aldine.

Dawkins, R. (1976). *The selfish gene.* New York: Oxford University Press.

Dawkins, R. (1982). *The extended phenotype.* New York: Oxford University Press.

Kitcher, P. (1985). *Vaulting ambition.* Cambridge, MA: MIT Press.

MACROEVOLUTION AND THE NATURE OF SPECIES

The conflict over evolutionary modes and rates that is central to phyletic gradualism versus punctuated equilibria has, nevertheless, helped resolve some issues about the nature of species in the process of macroevolution. A species has a beginning (a speciation event), a duration, and an end (an extinction), giving it not only boundaries in space (its geographical range) but also boundaries in time. Further, at any given time, a species has cohesion in the form of reproductive compatibility, which excludes input from other gene pools. And it reproduces itself (speciation). It can, therefore, be considered a unit, or an **individual** (in the terminology of philosopher of science Michael Ghiselin) in much the same way that a cell or organism can be considered an individual. In some respects, cultures can be viewed as individuals as well, for similar reasons.

Extinction

The concept of a species as a spatio-temporally bounded entity, or an individual, implies that the study of the beginnings and endings of species may be as rewarding as (if not more rewarding than) the study of their "middles." In fact, what happens during the persistence of a species may be less interesting than what happens to it during its origin and terminus. Thus, speciation is currently a major area of active research in evolutionary biology. So is its opposite, **extinction**.

Extinction is a paradox. More than 99 percent of all the species that have ever lived are now extinct. As a first approximation, then, it is fair to say that all species have gone extinct! This may seem less surprising when we recognize that the origin of life represents the origin of species more than one billion years ago but that the average duration of a species detectable from the fossil record is fewer than ten million years. Clearly, a constant turnover is occurring—species becoming extinct and being succeeded by other species.

Two kinds of extinction are now recognized in the processes of macroevolution: background extinction and mass extinction. *Background extinction* occurs with the end of specific lineages, for whatever reason. The dodo, the Tasmanian wolf, and the giant gelada baboon of the African Pleistocene all experienced background extinction. *Mass extinction* is the wholesale termination of many lineages at approximately the same time (Figure 4–11).

BACKGROUND EXTINCTIONS

What causes background extinctions? Because extinction is the fate of all species, it is difficult to look for a cause. It is the nature of species to go extinct, just as it is the nature of organisms to die. We can, however, ask what makes one species more likely to go extinct rather than another. In other words, we can treat extinction as a probability, just as we can study the causes of organismal death probabilistically.

individual

Any spatio-temporally bounded entity; a system having a beginning, middle, and end, localized in space.

extinction

Termination of a species or of a culture.

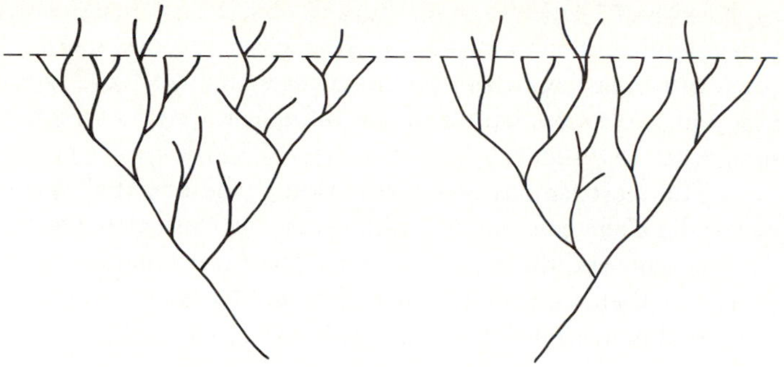

Mass
Extinction ─

Figure 4-11
A mass extinction involves the termination of many species in distantly related groups at roughly the same time.

The factors that tend to increase the chance of extinction are given in Table 4–4. A small population size means that a species is near extinction to begin with and requires little in the way of an ecological setback to become extinct. A fluctuating population size will occasionally bring the species near extinction, while the maintenance of a large population does not. Large body size, which is usually coupled to a long generation time, makes it more difficult for a species to recover its numbers in the face of a population crash. Endemic species, restricted to a localized geographical area, face the prospect of a population's local extinction being equivalent to the extinction of a taxon. For example, in the Pleistocene, *Archaeolemur* became extinct on Madagascar, the only place it existed. In contrast, *Equus* became extinct in North America but not in the Old World, where it existed as well. Thus, horses continue in existence today. Finally, ecological specialization makes it difficult for a species to survive if its local habitat or principal dietary staple crashes—a eucalyptus crisis would precipitate a koala crisis. For this reason, tropical-dwelling species tend to be more likely to become extinct than temperate-dwelling species, which are adapted to seasonal changes and environmental diversity.

MASS EXTINCTIONS

Mass extinctions, on the other hand, appear to be the result of major ecological traumas, wiping out many taxa at roughly the same time. Jack

Table 4–4

Factors Likely to Increase the Probability of Extinction

1. Small population size
2. Fluctuating population size
3. Large body size, long generation time
4. Endemism
5. Specialization

Sepkoski and David Raup of the University of Chicago calculate that background extinction rates encompass about 180–300 species per million years, while mass extinctions occur at rates of about 1,200 species per million years. At such high rates, it is difficult to predict which species will survive such a disaster.

The most famous mass extinction is the one that occurred at the end of the *Cretaceous* era, 65 million years ago, associated with the end of the dinosaurs and the explosive radiation of the mammals, who had been around by then for over 100 million years. Nevertheless, this occurrence is dwarfed in scope by the mass extinction at the end of the Permian era, nearly 250 million years ago. David Raup has calculated that over half the existing taxonomic *families* of marine vertebrates and invertebrates became extinct at approximately that time.

What causes mass extinctions? Does each mass extinction have a unique explanation for its occurrence, or is there a common thread that unites them? Raup and Sepkoski have found that in the history of life over the last 250 million years, mass extinctions have occurred roughly every 26 million years. This apparent periodicity is too lengthy to have a terrestrial explanation, they reasoned; therefore, an astronomical explanation may be required. Various scenarios have been proposed to account for the apparent periodicity of mass extinctions. These include asteroid impacts, comet showers, oscillations of the solar system through the galactic plane, an unknown companion star to the sun (called "Nemesis"), and an unknown planet called "Planet X" (Figure 4–12).

Effects of Mass Extinction   Regardless of the causes, which are obviously largely speculative, the effects of mass extinctions may be critical to our understanding long-term patterns in the history of life. If a large random component determines which species go extinct, and a large number of species go extinct, then there follows a great deal of "ecological space"—free niches—which the surviving species can fill without much competition. This may be the reason that mammals have achieved terrestrial dominance for the past 65 million years although they had not done so for 100 million years previously, while the dinosaurs lived.

The overall patterns in the history of life may be inherently unpredictable—roughly every 26 million years, a significant fraction of living species dies, and an ecological free-for-all among the survivors ensues.

Cultural Causes   Another cause of mass extinctions is better known and neither terrestrial nor astronomical—but cultural. Humans were the cause of the first recorded extinction, that of the large, flightless dodo in the 1600s, and have been the cause of many other extinctions before and since. Between about 12,000 and 8,000 years B.P., many large-bodied mammals became extinct in the New World. This coincided roughly with both the end of the Pleistocene and the first large-scale settlement of the New World by Upper Paleolithic people (see Chapter 12). Fifty-seven species, including the sabre-tooth cat and mastodon, are known to have died out.

The Shasta ground sloth became extinct in two different environments at this time, which suggests that climatic change was not the cause of the sloth's demise. Further, the advances and retreats of the glaciers through the Pleistocene, indicating major environmental changes, do not seem to correlate well with major extinctions. On the other hand, moose and bison, two perennial favorites among hunters, survived. And certain species of bird became extinct despite being seemingly ignored by people. Was it the hunters, the climate, or some combination of the two that was responsible?

The situation is less ambiguous for the megafauna of Madagascar. There, about 1,000 years ago, giant lemurs, large birds, and hippopotamuses all became extinct at about the same time as the island was first settled by humans. There seems little doubt that humans were fundamentally involved in their extinction, whether by hunting them or by destroying their habitats.

Although extinction is obviously a fact of life, humans are the only species aware of it. We are also the species most directly involved in most extinctions and the only species capable of preventing it. If extinction is a fact of life, however, why should we be bothered with it? Should it matter to us that there are no more Tasmanian wolves?

The ultimate fate of the Tasmanian wolf, or the humpback whale, or the gorilla is likely to be exactly the same as the fate of *Homo sapiens*—all have become or will become extinct—but the absence of Tasmanian wolves, from the point of view of understanding the natural world, means an absence of data about a possible means of adapting and living in a particular environment. Each species occupies a unique **niche** in nature, and the extinction of a species means we can no longer study the way that

niche

A nebulous ecological term referring to the range of environmental variability within which a species can survive and proliferate.

Figure 4-12

A popular group of scenarios for the extinction of the dinosaurs at the end of the Cretaceous involves extraterrestrial phenomena triggering ecological chain reactions that affected the mammals less drastically.

one species coped with its environment. Extinction means that the ecosystem the species lived in is now different, so other ecological changes will occur as a result of the extinction. Further, if the species in question is a close relative of ours, such as the gorilla, it may mean the loss of a small window into our own past. Once a species is extinct, it can never be recovered—it is the analog of death to an organism.

Cultural Evolution

Humans are subject to another form of change in addition to their genetic adaptations to environments and rates of speciation and extinction. The predominant means of adapting among humans is culture—the accumulated knowledge and lifeways of a society. Different groups, or societies, adapt culturally in different ways and change through time in a patterned fashion. Thus, we can speak of cultural evolution.

Cultural evolution affects our lives much more directly and dramatically than does either biological microevolution or macroevolution. Our material surroundings are nearly entirely the products of culture, and they are constantly changing. Our behaviors change in turn, and our values and ways of viewing the world respond in kind. The study of human history demonstrates the pervasiveness of cultural evolution and the operation of its processes, which leads us to appreciate its trends.

MODES OF CULTURAL TRANSMISSION

Cultural evolution can be viewed on a grand, global scale, consisting of gradual, though fundamental, changes in the ways people cope with their environments. Yet, cultural evolution is also an intragenerational phenomenon. While changes in the gene pool are tied to biological reproduction, changes in culture can occur within a single generation, making cultural evolution very effective in enabling the human species to cope.

The potentially great speed of cultural change is a result of the unique means by which cultural information is transmitted among individuals. People depend a great deal on language and other symbols to learn how to deal with the environment, and language is the most effective, responsive, and creative form of communication. Further, the use of symbols allows one person to transmit cultural information to many other people at one time. Genetic information cannot be transmitted in this way (Figure 4–13).

Cultural and biological evolution differ additionally in that new cultural information can sometimes be accepted or rejected by societies almost capriciously. New items may be accepted, such as the VCR and CD player, or soundly rejected, such as the quadraphonic stereo and the Edsel. What determines whether new cultural elements will be accepted or rejected? No one knows for certain, although a number of societal conditions and resulting judgments appear to play a role.

These conditions form a cultural and environmental matrix into which any new bit of cultural information must be embedded—it must fit in, to some degree, in order to be adopted. The judgments are the decisions made by society regarding the appropriateness of the new information. Measures of economy, symbolic suitability, and aesthetics are taken into account, as is the cultural analog of inertia—if something already exists or is being done in one way, why change?

It is important to understand that these are group decisions, not easily affected by individual members of society. It is also necessary to appreciate that the group's judgments are themselves cultural entities, the products of cultural evolutionary processes, for one thinks the way one is trained to think. Cultural evolution can thus be viewed as occurring for primarily cultural, and not individual psychological, reasons. It must be studied from this perspective to be understood.

It is sometimes difficult to accept that cultural evolution operates nearly independently of the needs and desires of specific individuals. This is particularly true for members of complex, Western nations, where a strong cultural tradition holds that individuals have free will to determine their fates. It can also be difficult to appreciate the societal judgments that are made at times, particularly if one is not a member of the society.

The Wheel　　One classic case is the adoption of the wheel for transportation. This change occurred on a large scale only in the Old

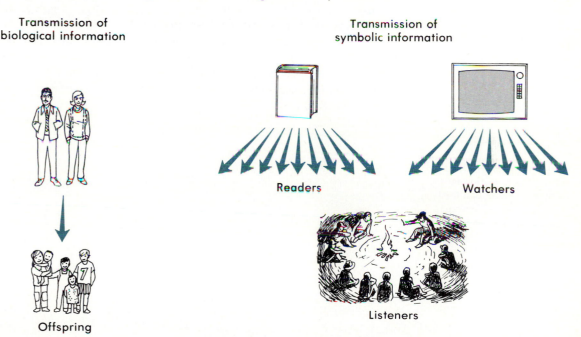

Figure 4-13

While the transmission of biological information is limited by the reproductive capabilities and desires of humans, the transmission of cultural information can be much more efficient and prolific. A storyteller in any human society can influence many people; a published book or television program can influence many more.

World, where wheeled vehicles were used first for ritual and ceremonial purposes, next as instruments of war, and finally for purposes of transport. In pre-Columbian Mesoamerica, however, where societies had reached comparable levels of complexity, large-wheeled vehicles for transportation never existed. It was not that Mesoamerican people were ignorant of the wheel, which could be found on small toys (Figure 4–14). Rather, it was the case that wheeled transport would not have fit well into the Mesoamerican cultural and environmental matrix.

In preindustrial societies, large-wheeled vehicles are efficient only if a society uses draft animals and resides on a fairly clear and flat terrain. This was the situation in many areas of the Old World where complex societies initially evolved (Chapter 14). The proper matrix did not exist in Mesoamerica, however, where powerful domesticated animals were not present, and where much of the landscape was mountainous or covered by a rapidly growing tropical flora.

ACCEPTANCE OF CULTURAL DEVELOPMENTS

A new cultural element can also be rejected because it does not fit into the symbolic system of a group of people. For example, the Tsimshian of the northwest coast of North America strongly resisted the substitution of rowboats for their dugout canoes. While the function would be identical, the methods of manufacture were different (splitting, chopping, and steaming planks versus hollowing out tree trunks), and as a result, the symbolic meanings were absent for rowboats. Anthropologist Homer Barnett found that the rowboat "was judged to be something entirely distinct from the canoe because it was put together differently. My informants found the suggestion of a transfer of the ritual associations to the rowboat rather ludicrous."

Figure 4–14

Wheeled vehicles were not used for transportation in Mesoamerica, although toys like this one from Veracruz indicate that Mesoamericans certainly understood the principle (after Miller).

Similarly, although the Bronze Age preceded the Iron Age in the Old World, bronze continued to be used for many centuries after iron was obtainable. Bronze was softer, less abundant, and no easier to extract than iron, but for many items it was considered more attractive. In this case, aesthetics had an impact on the decision to reject a new cultural element.

In some cases, societies operate according to the rule of inertia—not accepting new cultural information merely because it is different from the information that already exists. The decimal metric system is a very efficient way of measuring weight, volume, and length. However, although it is used throughout the world, the United States has refused to adopt it. We use it only in our monetary system, and always have—the English did not adopt a metric monetary system until the 1960s. There seems to be no reason for the U.S. to reject the metric system in other ways, but neither any reason compelling enough to change our behavior. Thus, grams and centimeters tend to be used in the United States only by scientists and by those deeply involved in international commerce.

USE OF CULTURAL DEVELOPMENTS

The economic, symbolic, and aesthetic judgments of a society may conflict with one another, as well as with the force of stability. In addition, when a cultural element diffuses to and transforms a culture in some way, it is itself transformed by the new cultural and environmental matrix. Tobacco, used by Native Americans primarily in ritual contexts, spread rapidly through the Old World after 1492 (Figure 4–15) and is now used in a completely secular, profane context. In our society, we tend to associate it principally with high-stress secular situations and with sex. In a similar fashion, gunpowder, used primarily for amusement in fireworks by the Chinese, quickly was modified in creative ways for in killing people when it diffused to Medieval Europe.

Indeed, it is often difficult to predict how a new cultural element will be used. Thomas Edison, for example, was very slow to concede that the principal use of his 1877 invention, the phonograph, was for home entertainment. He had envisioned it for a host of other purposes—taking dictation without a stenographer, recording talking books for the blind, teaching public speaking, preserving family reminiscences, using talking clocks, and learning foreign pronunciations.

Social Context of Cultural Developments   A discovery or invention can be made only when the appropriate social factors and technological components are present; and when they are present, the discovery or invention is essentially inevitable. This is not to demean the contribution of great thinkers and creators but to emphasize that in any individual case, had the person who ultimately received credit for it *not* made the crucial discovery, someone else would have. Indeed, the history of science and technology shows us that someone else virtually always does.

For example, Darwin and Wallace formulated theories of natural selection at the same time; Leibnitz and Newton invented calculus at the same time; Sutton and Boveri formulated the chromosome theory of inheritance at the same time. This pattern of invention holds for major transformations in cultural history as well—plant and animal domestication occurred independently in several places, at about the same time (Chapter 13). There are always people of insight and genius, but their influence on cultural evolution derives from the time and situation, not from their intrinsic greatness. They are great *because of* their situation; they contribute to that particular milieu and are remembered for their contribution to that setting. Albert Einstein in eighth century Ireland would not have come up with a theory of relativity, but someone else in the early twentieth century would have. Watson and Crick in pre-Dynastic Egypt would not have derived the structure of DNA, but someone else in the twentieth century would have. In fact, it probably would have been the chemist Linus Pauling, against whom Watson and Crick were competing.

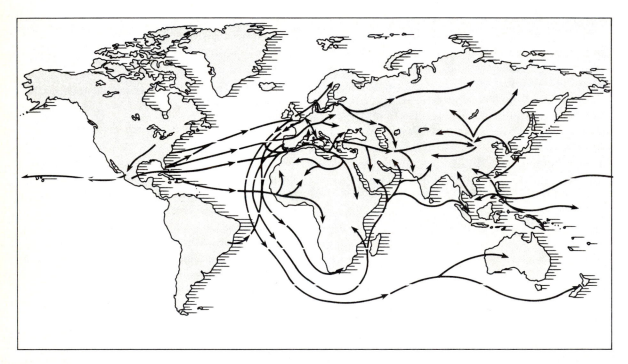

Figure 4-15

The earliest record of tobacco is from Mesoamerica in the fifth century A.D., with strong theological associations. Though it has no nutritional value, it was domesticated and brought to the Old World in the early 1500s. The eponymous Jean Nicot, French ambassador to Portugal, purchased some tobacco seeds in Lisbon and grew it in Europe; Sir Walter Raleigh helped make tobacco fashionable in England, although it was initially controversial. It was rolled in cigars, smoked in pipes, or crystallized and inhaled as snuff.

Thus, the force that drives general cultural evolution is societal, not individual. The accomplishments of individuals are significant as history, but history is in large measure the documentation and explanation of unique events. Joe Namath's role in the 1969 Super Bowl was significant and great, as was Omar Bradley's role in World War II. Without them, history would be different; they filled in its details and are important for the documentation of the cultural history in question. But this is *specific* cultural evolution—what happened to a particular culture at a particular time, and why.

General cultural evolution is different. As we discuss next, cultural evolution can be described as a process with regularities, and as such, it is amenable to scientific analysis for which unique events and individuals rarely have explanatory power. One cannot study the inventor of domestication any more than one can study the first biped or the first mammal. We *can* study how it happened, where it happened, when it happened, perhaps why it happened, and the regularities of its occurrence in various places and times.

GENERAL CULTURAL EVOLUTION

In 1960 Marshall Sahlins and Elman Service distinguished between two forms of cultural evolution—general and specific. By **general evolution** they meant the cultural trends evident in the history of our species—the kinds of phenomena emphasized by anthropologist Leslie White through the 1940s and 1950s. By **specific evolution** they meant the cultural history of a particular society—how it copes with its environment in particular ways and how its relationship with the environment changes over time.

General evolution has no clear parallel in biology. We can see cultural trends, such as gathering-hunting preceding agriculture, and both emerging before complex society and industrialization (Chapters 13–15), and this may superficially resemble the paleontological recognition that fish evolved into amphibians, then into reptiles, and finally into mammals. Yet, where we seem to see a historical trend in biological evolution (fish to mammal) that may parallel a historical trend in cultural evolution (gatherer-hunter to industrialist), there is an important contrast between them. This contrast resides in the fact that fish are still plentiful *although* other kinds of organisms have subsequently evolved, while gatherer-hunters are not *because* other kinds of cultures have evolved. Thus, where biological evolution can generate new forms without an adverse impact on the old, cultural evolution apparently cannot. Why is this so?

One reason is that all human societies, regardless of their degree of complexity, are composed of people belonging to a single species—in fact, a single subspecies (Chapter 12). This has been the case for approximately 35,000 years. The basic biological similarities among all people have been fundamental in importance, despite the more visible (and

general cultural evolution
Major cultural changes that have occurred on a worldwide scale, due primarily to changes in technology.

specific cultural evolution
Local history of a particular society.

more recent) cultural differences that have emerged in technology and social organization. Further, these fundamental similarities have been most clearly reflected in the equal capacity, among all people, to use language and symbols in order to communicate. In other words, cultural information can be transmitted quite effectively from any to all societies because the members of all societies have the same cultural capacity. As people migrate and interbreed, they bring their culture with them.

ROLE OF COMPLEX SOCIETIES IN CULTURAL EVOLUTION

Why, then, have the more recent, complex, and industrial societies contributed the vast majority of the new cultural information? Why have they come to dominate the world at the expense of gatherer-hunters and nonindustrial agriculturalists? Apparently, the general evolution of cultural complexity brings with it the increased ability to diffuse cultural elements to other societies. Several reasons explain why this is so.

First, more complex societies are relatively large, in terms of both population and territory. Further, they tend to expand in size as their complexity grows. Relatively simple (and small) gatherer-hunters and agriculturalist populations have been literally enveloped by more complex societies.

Second, complex societies are more heterogeneous internally. There is greater specialization of activities and tasks, with numerous groups of people concentrating on specific endeavors. Standing armies and full-time missionaries, for example, are possible in complex societies, and these groups can focus their attention on bringing new cultural information to others. Gatherer-hunters and noncomplex agriculturalists generally exhibit little, if any, specialization of this kind.

More complex societies are also internally more highly integrated. Effective integration and coordination of activities is essential where there is great heterogeneity, and complex societies have evolved centralized bureaucracies and communication technologies to meet the need. Greater integration makes possible a more unified and effective effort at diffusing cultural information (Figure 4–16).

Finally, and perhaps most importantly, more complex societies can harness a greater amount of energy than can simpler societies, if not more efficiently. This might be the most obvious of the general evolutionary trends. Currently, it is necessary only to observe that a society possessing nuclear weapons can have a greater impact on other cultures than can one with nothing more powerful than spears. Thus, the nuclear-age culture has been the one to diffuse throughout the world most readily in the past half-century.

CULTURAL COMPLEXITY: SOME POSSIBLE CAUSES

Understanding that complex societies *can* diffuse cultural information easily does not explain *why* they have done so. The latter, more interesting question is difficult to answer and leads to an additional concern.

Figure 4-16

Social complexity permits the development of full-time institutions devoted to enculturation and education, such as schools, universities, and libraries.

Does complexity emerge and diffuse easily because of some ultimate plan, some intent or purpose? In other words, is the growth of cultural complexity and technological intensification teleological by its very nature, reflecting some underlying aspect of God's will or of the human spirit?

Some philosophers have argued that indeed it is, that the course of cultural evolution is the expression of a drive toward something—greater freedom, or greater decay from original purity, or redemption for the human race, or simply a cosmic drama whose conclusion is known only to deities. However, the general course of cultural evolution, like that of biological evolution, has no discernible goal.

This is not to say, however, that people fail to act toward their own goals. They certainly do, and the history of specific cultures contains many obvious examples of goal-directed behavior—of people faced with a problem taking steps to overcome it. The spring-wound clock was invented because of the need for accurate timekeeping and navigation at sea, where the pendulum clock had failed. Many years later the atomic clock was developed to measure small increments of time very accurately, thus allowing scientists to study a number of fundamental physical processes. Indeed, the history of technology abounds with examples of new tools and machines that made possible desired, though previously impossible, achievements.

There is, however, no grand scheme to cultural evolution. Why not? Because every problem has multiple solutions, and every solution that people devise has consequences they did not count on, which in turn create new cultural forms and new problems to solve. While people may succeed in solving immediate problems, they can rarely predict accurately the ultimate results of their actions.

Soviets decide to pursue a space program; U.S. responds by revamping science education, ultimately commits to moon landing.

Krushchev places missiles in Cuba, escalates Cold War.

John Kennedy assassinated in Dallas.

Beatles dump Pete Best, pick up Ringo Starr; tour U.S.; become slightly more popular than Dave Clark Five, inherit their fans.

Foreign policy embraces domino theory—if one nation goes Communist, all will; overvalues South Vietnam.

Figure 4-17

Specific cultural evolution is the result of a historical sequence of contingencies. For any given case there exist a number of possible outcomes or choices, of which only one actually happens. These outcomes determine the actual trajectory of the evolution of the culture and affect later decisions, behaviors, and attitudes.

The course of human history contains many examples of people attempting one thing and, because of that attempt, unwittingly allowing something very different to occur. Perhaps the best-studied and most significant example of this is the rise of domestication, a major cultural watershed that we discuss at length in Chapter 13. Under changing environmental conditions and growing environmental stress, certain gatherer-hunter groups responded in various ways in a deliberate attempt to maintain their standard of living—especially to keep the necessary workload to a minimum. Yet these very responses, including spending greater periods of time in areas rich in wild resources, altered the groups' lifestyle so that the domestication they adopted ultimately became a necessity. Ironically, domestication required almost everyone to work harder, and for longer hours, than did gathering and hunting. It forced them to rely on a narrower range of foods than their ancestors had gathered and hunted, which left them generally more poorly nourished. Further, it had social consequences, including the emergence of social inequality and (particularly with agricultural intensification) the gradual shift of women's roles from subsistence to domesticity. The plan, the deliberate goal, then, was very different from the cultural evolutionary outcome.

Consider, as another example closer to home, the visions of the future illustrated in old science-fiction movies. Scenes of personal cars that could fly through the air, huge glass apartment buildings floating in the stratosphere, and a governing body of contemplative scholars in long, flowing robes—are quaint, aren't they? But they never reflect the future (which, in many cases, is today) very accurately, even though people are always planning for it and trying to envision it. The reason, again, is that each action in the present has a number of unforeseen consequences for the future that must be dealt with in turn and that create the problems with which the next generation must cope.

Oil embargo drives inflation higher; smaller foreign cars favored.	Buckner boots grounder; loses World Series for Red Sox.	NASA officials launch Challenger despite cold weather and warnings of possible O–ring failure; space program is crippled.	Department of Housing and Urban Development left unregulated by Reagan administration; millions earmarked for social programs lost.	Gorbachev's policy of *Perestroika* begins to diminish intensity of Cold War.

We conclude that in the long term, general cultural evolution is not teleological. Yet, elements of goal-directed behavior in specific cultures can be seen when viewed over relatively short periods of time.

Cultural Ecology

When we look at the cultural history of any particular society, we often see a series of problem-solving endeavors in the face of perceived environmental stress. All human groups make decisions in order to make their lives easier—to maximize economic returns at a minimum investment of energy. That these decisions are often ineffective need not concern us here. Much of what they do is not adaptive in any apparent way but does result in a unique history for the group. We must note that environments, conditions, and social stresses differ somewhat for each society. Thus, each one displays a unique set of responses that together form its cultural history (Figure 4–17).

The study of how societies respond to different environments is called *cultural ecology*, developed by the anthropologist Julian Steward. Steward was also responsible for formulating the notion of **multilinear evolution**, which recognizes that each society follows a unique cultural history and thus follows a particular path. Steward did not emphasize the differences among societies as much as he did the convergent and parallel evolutionary paths that different societies can follow. Convergent and parallel evolution occur, he argued, when environments and situations are similar enough to dictate similar evolutionary responses.

Steward, like Leslie White and the unilinear evolutionists (Chapter 3), thought cultural evolutionary processes followed predictable paths that could be understood by application of scientific methods. Unlike White, Steward advocated the study of individual cultures, at least initially, and concentrated on the environment as a stimulus to cul-

multilinear evolution

A theory of cultural evolution that focuses on specific cultural evolution and the local histories of cultures within particular environments.

tural forms. The environment was seen as playing a critical role in cultural evolution by posing problems for cultures to solve creatively. Steward, then, emphasized specific cultural evolution, while White emphasized general cultural evolution.

One of the classic studies in cultural ecology, showing that similar evolutionary changes can occur in different societies facing similar conditions, is Robert Murphy's and Julian Steward's work on tropical forest "tappers" and subarctic "trappers." The Mundurucu of the Amazon Basin were horticulturalists for many generations. Many of them entered the commercial rubber production industry as the region entered the global market economy—they became rubber-tree tappers. In a similar fashion, many of the Montagnais of northeastern Canada abandoned hunting as the commercial fur industry grew—they became fur trappers. Murphy and Steward note that despite the very different physical environment and outside appearances, the social conditions of cultural contact and change were so similar as to lead both groups to similar responses. Both groups sought Western trade goods. Both groups devoted increased time to raising specialized cash crops and producing trade items. And both societies experienced a shift in the way work was conducted—from a situation of group cooperation and autonomy to a situation of individual effort and dependence on an outside authority. The end result was that both groups shared a breakdown of traditional social order—a kind of extinction of tradition.

Societies cannot always respond successfully to the environmental problems they confront. People, and the societies they compose, make mistakes or face obstacles that simply overwhelm them. And, as discussed earlier, cultural innovations do not always result in the desired, or even the expected, outcome. Indeed, environmental stresses (including the stresses of neighboring societies) can be so severe that entire societies—entire cultural systems—can vanish completely. Thus, cultural evolution exhibits a property analogous to biological extinction.

Cultural Extinction

Franz Boas, the father of American anthropology, was instrumental in developing the methods of ethnographic research. Notable was his insistence on participant observation—living within a society for an extended period of time, both participating as a member of that society and still observing it as an outsider. Boas argued that this method would lead to intimate and detailed knowledge and viewed it as particularly important in cases in which societies were rapidly changing or disappearing in the face of European contact.

CAUSES OF CULTURAL EXTINCTION

Boas recognized that cultural extinction was an inevitable product of cultural evolution; as cultures change, the old ways vanish. Thus, it is important to document cultures as much as possible before they disappear.

Indeed, it appears that all cultures are destined to face extinction, and the majority of societies once present, like the majority of species, are no longer in existence.

Different types of societies become extinct for different reasons. Gatherer-hunters especially, and many agriculturalists and pastoralists, are inherently stable groups. Yet they have faced extinction because of contact with more complex social orders—on a massive scale during the past several centuries. Colonialism and conflict, often accompanied by economic suppression and even genocide, are violent means by which complex and industrial societies have destroyed many other groups. More peaceful, though no less destructive, has been the continuous diffusion of cultural information from the more to the less complex, with the consequent eradication of the receiving culture's traditions.

But relatively simple societies are not the only ones to have faced the threat of extinction. Complex societies appear to be inherently unstable. Indeed, a general cultural evolutionary rule seems to be that greater complexity leads to greater internal instability and precariousness. Currently, nuclear war could destroy our living planet in less than one hour. This unforeseen consequence of early nuclear physics did not exist when technology was less complex. What is the source of this instability and precariousness? Apparently, it lies in the short-term nature of the responses cultures make to the problems facing them, which pose new and greater problems, and end in the collapse of the cultural system.

Norman Yoffee, an archaeologist at the University of Arizona, has suggested that the Babylonian empire collapsed precisely because of poor, short-term responses to perceived stresses. Around 1700 B.C., the Babylonian bureaucracy decided to expand its role in overseeing agricultural production, its goal being to make the operation more efficient. The rise in the number of administrative officials was accompanied by a drop in available farm labor, and fields were divided into smaller and smaller administrative units. Farming became less efficient through time, and the bureaucracy became more concerned with preserving itself than in managing the society. In a relatively short period of time, the Babylonian empire collapsed.

Similar mismanagement can be seen in more recent times, and even today. The historian Paul Kennedy has suggested that much of Western history consists of a series of economic and military struggles among nations. National power rises and falls relative to other countries and in large measure is determined by the economic efficiency by which a country can conduct warfare. War is expensive, especially in recent times, and national bureaucracies can easily overspend on military concerns. According to Kennedy, such mismanagement of economic resources has led to the collapse of some very powerful and complex societies.

The somewhat discouraging view presented here is tempered by the fact that humans remain the only species capable of preventing extinction, either biological or cultural, or at least of delaying it. Further, it is important that we do so—just as it matters that there are no more Tasmanian wolves, it matters that there are no more Tasmanian native people.

EFFECTS OF CULTURAL EXTINCTION

As each culture vanishes, so does some potential knowledge about the cultural world. Because culture plays such an important role in shaping our existence, extinction means that we actually lose critical knowledge regarding what it means to be human. The breadth and scope of human existence is irretrievably diminished by cultural extinction, and it is this breadth of the human experience that defines for us the boundaries of humanity. Boas understood this, and we must continue to appreciate it today.

Yet, perhaps more importantly, there is an ethical issue related to the extinction of human societies and cultural diversity. As members of the subspecies *Homo sapiens sapiens* (Chapter 12), equally sharing the unique ability to culturally adapt to our environments, we owe it to ourselves and one another to preserve the vast array of cultural forms that we encounter. A homogeneous, global culture would be a tragedy, not to mention an exceeding bore. Indeed, some social scientists believe that the rise of ethnic and group consciousness in Western society in the 1970s is a form of response to the impending homogeneity of Western culture. Faced with the prospect of being exactly like everyone else in a great "melting pot," people have responded with heightened group identifications: Native American, African American, Jew, gay, woman, Hispanic, and so on. The same process is occurring in Europe and Asia today. It remains to be seen what the social consequences of this response may be.

Summary

The word *evolution* can be applied to many phenomena; however, we are principally concerned with characterizing and documenting the biological and cultural evolution of humans. Neither of these can be shown to exhibit progress in any general sense—things merely change. These things—biological characters or cultural artifacts—change according to certain rules and principles. Yet, neither all the biological attributes of an organism nor all the attributes of a culture change together for better or worse. Each simply derives relative to an ancestral form or state.

Evolution entails the properties of multiplying and adapting. Thus, we can consider evolving entities to be both replicators and interactors. Biological replication occurs in three fundamental ways: through cell division (mitosis), organismal reproduction (meiosis and fertilization), and the splitting of lineages (speciation).

The ongoing processes within a species, which continually alter it genetically in small but significant ways, are subsumed under the label of microevolution. The splitting of a lineage into two involves the acquisition of reproductive isolation. And the processes occurring to species or to groups of species is known as macroevolution. The contrasting macroevolutionary models of gradualism and punctuated equilibria hold different assumptions concerning the pace at which evolution occurs and the processes playing the major roles.

Cultural evolution is not as well understood as biological evolution. Modes of change are different, and the transmission of information can be much quicker, allowing cultural evolution to occur much more rapidly. Still, we recognize different scales of cultural evolutionary change—general cultural evolution, which concerns global trends, and specific cultural evolution, which concerns trends within individual societies.

Extinction is an irreversible fate, and if it occurs, information is irretrievable. Biological extinction results in the loss of a way in which life on earth can exist and has existed. Cultural extinction results in the loss of knowledge about the many ways we can be human.

Questions for Review

1. Is a dog more advanced than a frog? Why or why not? Is a dog more advanced than an earthworm?

2. Why do you think general cultural evolution is in large measure the development and expansion of increasingly complex societies? How is this different from the general pattern of biological macroevolution?

3. In which ways is evolution deterministic? In which ways is it stochastic? Which implications do you think this may have for the future evolution of our species?

4. Some people have argued that natural selection is a tautology because natural selection is survival of the fittest, and the fittest are simply those which have survived; therefore, natural selection is simply survival of the survivors. What do you think?

For Further Reading

Gould, S. G. (1980). Is a new and general theory of evolution emerging? *Paleobiology*, 6:119–130.

Hull, D. (1980). Individuality and selection. *Annual Review of Ecology and Systematics*, 11:311–332.

Sahlins, M. D., & Service, E. R. (Eds.). (1960). *Evolution and culture*. Ann Arbor: University of Michigan Press.

Simpson, G. G. (1953). *The major features of evolution*. New York: Columbia University Press.

The Products of Evolution: Synchronic Studies

CHAPTER 5
Primate Systematics

CHAPTER 6
Primate Behavior

Primate Systematics

Primate Systematics

Classification

Classifying things, arranging them into some sort of meaningful order, is the way we begin to make sense of them. There are many ways of organizing things, including animals, and each society uses its own criteria for deciding on which categories to recognize. Our method of classifying animals derives ultimately from the work of the eighteenth-century naturalist Carolus Linnaeus (Carl Linné—see Chapter 3) and is now recognized to represent general evolutionary relationships.

As with all sciences, the specialized language of biology and physical anthropology is encoded in a **classification**, in this case, a method of referring to species or groups of species. The adoption of a classification helps ensure that one person can discuss the family Cercopithecidae, for example, and that another person will know that the speaker is talking about a specific group of primates—one that includes baboons among others, but not gorillas. In other words, a classification is a linguistic device that facilitates communication.

All classifications impose some order or structure on what would otherwise be an imponderable jumble in the natural world. As anthropologist Mary Douglas has shown in a classic example, the ancient Hebrews devised an elaborate system for classifying the animals with which they were familiar, based on these animals' habitats, their ways of moving, and aspects of their digestive systems and foot anatomies (Table 5–1). Animals that did not fit neatly into the categories became **taboo**, and as a consequence, it was forbidden to consume them or even come into contact with them. Understanding the classification and its basis is important in our understanding of how these people perceived the animal world.

Like other linguistic systems, classifications subtly affect the way we think about the things we have classified. Some good examples of this phenomenon come from the world of physical anthropology. For example, in 1949, Sherwood Washburn and Bryan Patterson suggested that the best way to classify fossil **hominids** was in two genera, *Homo* and *Australopithecus*. By the mid-1960s virtually all physical anthropologists regarded them similarly. This classification, however, carries the subtle idea that any one species of *Australopithecus* is more closely related to the other species of *Australopithecus* than it is to *Homo*, and anthropologists tended to regard the "gracile" and "robust" *Australopithecus* species as variants of each other. Currently, however, it appears that the "gracile"

classification

A system for organizing the diverse phenomena one encounters in order to make generalizations about classes of things.

taboo

A cultural prohibition whose violation may incur supernatural (or actual) wrath.

hominid

Belonging to the Family Hominidae: humans and their close fossil relatives.

Australopithecus species is more closely related to *Homo* than it is to the "robust" form. It is probable that calling the two by the same name hindered the appreciation that they most likely fall on different evolutionary lines.

Table 5–1

Classification of Animals from Leviticus xi and Deuteronomy xiv

Living on the Ground

Animals with hooves

Split hoof and chews cud

ox	sheep	goat
hart	gazelle	roebuck
wild goat	pygarg (ibex)	
antelope	mountain sheep	

Split hoof but does not chew cud

camel	hare	rock-badger

Whole hoof and chews cud

pig

Animals with paws

Animals that creep or swarm

weasel	mouse	lizard
gecko	crocodile	chameleon

Animals that travel on belly

Animals with many feet

Living in the Water

Animals with fins and scales

Animals without fins and scales

Living in the Air

Animals that fly

eagle	vulture	osprey
kite	falcon	raven
ostrich	hawk	sea-mew
owl	cormorant	pelican
heron	hoopoe	bat

Animals that swarm, with wings and jointed legs

locust	grasshopper	cricket

Animals that swarm, with four feet

The modern system of classification is based on different criteria than that of the ancient Hebrews. It is based ultimately on the work of Linnaeus, a Swedish botanist of the eighteenth century who saw the order of nature as a *nested hierarchy* (Chapter 3). That is, he saw a system of levels or categories, each category subsuming the ones below it, and including fewer and fewer groups of species as one reached progressively lower categories. Thus, the class Mammalia included (among others) the order Primates and the order Carnivora; the order Primates included (among others) the genera *Homo* (humans) and *Lemur* (lemurs). The genus *Homo*, for its part, included two species—*Homo sapiens* and *Homo troglodytes*—actually, this latter species existed only in the imagination of Linnaeus.

It was Charles Darwin, in the middle of the nineteenth century, who recognized that the nested order perceived by Linnaeus was a result of the fact that these groups shared a series of successively more recent common ancestors. We can classify humans and lemurs as primates because they are descended from a common ancestor, from whom they have subsequently diverged, but who left its imprint upon them. Similarly, we can classify primates and carnivores as mammals, diverged from a common mammalian ancestor, from whom they both inherited the suite of characters we recognize as "mammalian."

As shown in Table 5–2, mammals can be identified and distinguished from other creatures (such as reptiles) by the presence of specializations in virtually every bodily system (Figure 5–1). Following Darwin, we interpret the existence of these features in a restricted number of all living animals as signs of common ancestry. We possess these features for no better reason than that our ancestors possessed them.

Figure 5–1

Mammals and reptiles differ in many profound ways. For example, the limbs of a reptile tend to be splayed outward, while those of a mammal are directly under the body.

Reptile   Mammal

Although Linnaeus was not an evolutionist, part of the success of Darwin's theory was in explaining this pattern of similarity in the natural world.

What are some alternative explanations? Could species like baboons, chimpanzees, and humans have naturally arisen one by one and independently acquired these sets of resemblances? They could have, but this is extremely unlikely. And as science deals with the most probable explanations for things, this idea is not given much credence. Could similar species have been supernaturally formed one by one, but fall into a narrow range of body plans as a result of the creator's ideas? Again possibly, but supernatural explanations fall outside the realm of modern scientific inquiry. Furthermore, this view devalues the imagination and power of the creator. Could a creator have such a limited imagination as to build the thousands of mammal species along a single plan, rather than create thousands of plans? Even the theologically minded scientists of the nineteenth century found the hypothesis of a common plan unsustainable.

Table 5–2

Features of Mammals

Skin Specializations

Hair	Sweat glands

Reproductive Specializations

Viviparity	Lactation

Postcranial Skeletal Specializations

Limbs oriented less laterally, more ventrally	Fusion of epiphyses to bone shafts at end of growth period
Fused pelvic girdle	Ribs only on thoracic vertebrae

Cranial Specializations

Two sets of teeth	Single jawbone
Different kinds of teeth	Secondary palate
Complex posterior teeth	Pair of occipital condyles
Bony ear, external ear	Corpus callosum of brain
Ethmoturbinal bones in nasal cavity	

Physiological Specializations

High body temperature, regulated, internally generated	Red blood cells lose nucleus
Diaphragm	Bladder for excretion
	Four-chambered heart

Given that the theory of common descent explains the nested pattern of similarity evident among the species of the earth, what is the best way to express that similarity? This is what a scientific classification does (in contrast to classifications by people from other cultures that are not based upon patterns of common descent). In all systems, a group of organisms at any level, however established, is called a *taxon*, and the study of the procedures for establishing taxa comprise the science of *taxonomy*. The basis of our classification is *phylogeny*, the evolutionary history of species.

TRAITS AND DISTANCES

Two principal ways exist of gauging the relationship of two species to each other. The first is the occurrence of key characters, evolutionary novelties, or *apomorphies*. If a character is unique to a species, it is an **autapomorphy**, and the number of autapomorphies on a particular lineage tells us how divergent one species is from its closest relatives. If an evolutionary novelty is shared by a few species, it is a **synapomorphy** and indicates that the species shared a common ancestor from which they each inherited the trait. These concepts are discussed in greater detail in Chapter 10. Table 5–2 is a list of the synapomorphies of mammals. These traits are shared derived characters, inherited from a unique mammalian ancestor, linking living mammals as each other's closest relatives and excluding amphibians, fish, and all other living things.

Alternatively, one can measure the degree of similarity among organisms by using mathematical *distances*, which describe their differences from one another in anatomy, behavior, and so on, rather than in the presence or absence of traits reflecting their common ancestry. These distances can be calculated by measuring a large number of attributes of the animals and then using a computer program to collapse these measurements of many taxa into combinations or associations of traits and taxa. Such a method has the advantage of being less subjective than a trait-by-trait study because the same statistics and analyses can be repeated, even by researchers lacking a detailed knowledge of the morphology under study; but it has the disadvantage of being highly abstract and often not clearly related to the biology of the organisms under study.

In addition to morphological distances, one can calculate genetic distances, by measuring some attributes of the genes of the taxa under consideration. Some genetic distances are derived from measuring the extent of immunological reactions, or protein similarity, or the stability of DNA molecules artificially constructed from pairs of species.

The primary disadvantage of using distances, however, is that they do not distinguish among those things unique to a taxon and those things shared with other taxa. One simply generates a table of distances between pairs of taxa and then allows a computer to make certain assumptions in linking up the taxa into a branching diagram. The procedure is, there-

autapomorphy

A derived character possessed by a single species.

synapomorphy

A derived character possessed by several species, indicating that they inherited it from a recent common ancestor.

fore, based upon overall similarity of the taxa being compared, not upon their evolutionary novelties, and consequently, it tends to be sensitive to fluctuations in evolutionary rates. Major changes in a single lineage (autapomorphies) may result in that taxon being incorrectly placed far from close relatives with whom it may have only a few shared features (synapomorphies)—but these features may be crucial.

Some taxonomists prefer to use distances, while others prefer to use traits. Likewise, some prefer genetic data, while others prefer anatomical data. The advantages of anatomical data are that: 1) They are readily observable and measureable, and 2) they are present in fossils. The advantages of genetic data are that they reflect to a much lesser extent the influence of the environment. Thus, genetic data are freer of the effects of convergent adaptive evolution—animals changing in similar ways to similar conditions.

On the other hand, anatomies are extraordinarily variable and yield many differences and similarities to analyze. Genes are composed of sequences of only four nucleotides (Chapter 8). Such a limited range of alterations makes it possible that there will be a broad base of random *convergent evolution*—similarity between taxa due not to similar responses to similar environments, but due to the fact that there are only four possible things a particular nucleotide can be. Thus, any DNA sequence from any organism will be 25 percent similar to another randomly chosen DNA sequence from any other species purely by chance.

Fortunately, these different approaches most often yield similar results, which is eloquent testimony to the fact that a common ancestry, or phylogeny, constrains related animals to be fairly similar.

HOW SHOULD WE CLASSIFY THINGS?

Like all aspects of the scientific endeavor, there are schools of thought on the best way to generate a classification. These schools are known as **classical systematics** or **evolutionary systematics**, and **phylogenetic systematics** or **cladistics**. These differ largely in how they perceive the relationship between phylogeny and classification, which may not always be simple.

Evolutionary Systematics   This school of thought is based principally on the modern writings of paleontologist George Gaylord Simpson and ornithologist Ernst Mayr. To Simpson, a classification involves "the ordering of animals into groups . . . on the basis of . . . associations by contiguity, similarity, or both." What this means is that we can group by common ancestry, though there have been occasions when species have diverged from close relatives fairly rapidly and fairly radically. In such cases, we would have one divergent unique species and a cluster of similar species that may not be each other's closest relatives but that nevertheless are similar by virtue of lacking the uniqueness of the other species. When these situations occur, we can group things by similarity.

evolutionary systematics

Theory of classification by descent and divergence, or synapomorphy and autapomorphy, or contiguity and similarity.

cladistics

Theory of classification by only synapomorphy, or descent, or contiguity.

Consider, for example, trying to classify turtles, crocodiles, and birds (Figure 5–2). Detailed anatomical and biochemical analyses have shown that birds are closely related to crocodiles, though they have diverged radically from them. That is, from a common ancestor, birds have changed a lot, but crocodiles have changed only a little. Thus, crocodiles and turtles, lacking the specializations that distinguish the birds, appear to us to be more similar to each other—we call them both reptiles. We have, therefore, classified them as reptiles (class Reptilia) not on the basis of contiguity, but on the basis of similarity. If we classified them solely on the basis of contiguity, we would put the crocodiles and birds together, not the crocodiles and turtles, for crocodiles and birds are the closer relatives.

Phylogenetic Systematics   In phylogenetic systematics (or cladistics, founded by the German entomologist Willi Hennig), classification cannot be based on similarity, only on contiguity. That is, a classification must reflect only phylogenetic relationships and not the extent of divergence of any taxon. Thus, in the previous example, a cladist would indeed classify the crocodiles and birds together.

Both these systems have strengths and weaknesses. Classical systematics applies criteria inconsistently. How do we decide whether to classify by contiguity or by similarity in any case? There is no set answer. Further, confusion can easily result if a particular taxon has been created on the basis of similarity but if subsequent practitioners (or students) naïvely assume that it represents phylogeny. On the other hand, phylogenetic systematics creates taxa that are inherently unstable. Because we are constantly rearranging the details of family trees, we should constantly be revising our classifications as well. Yet classifications are linguistic systems devised to minimize confusion, and a system of classification that constantly changed would be extremely confusing.

Furthermore, knowing the rate of evolutionary change—whether one group has changed much more than another over the same period of

Figure 5-2

Although we consider turtles and crocodiles to be reptiles, crocodiles are actually more closely related to birds than to turtles.

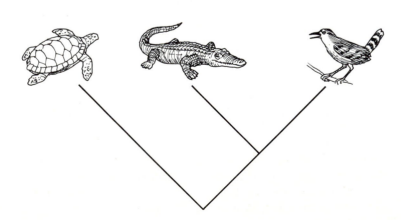

time—is very important. To ignore it at the expense of phylogenetic relationships is to cut down the amount of biological information in the classification. Of course, on the other hand, to include that information means mixing two sets of information in a single classification.

Finally, relations by similarity have an advantage in being commonsensical. Because lungfish have lungs, they are more closely related to frogs than they are to trout. To a cladist, lungfish must be classified with frogs rather than with trout. That same lungfish is, nevertheless, a fish on the basis of overall similarity. It has changed very little since its ancestors acquired lungs, while the ancestor of the frog has changed a lot. To a cladist, the concept of *fish* must be abandoned since some fish are more closely related to amphibians than they are to other fish. In the same way, the concept of *reptile* must be abandoned since some reptiles are more closely related to birds than they are to other reptiles. Nevertheless, we tend strongly to perceive the categories *fish* and *reptiles*, in spite of the fact that they are not strict, phylogenetic assemblages. In classical systematics, this is not a problem, for one can keep those categories.

In this text we classify the primates by both contiguity and similarity, according to classical systematics. Usually it is by contiguity—the two major exceptions involve the placement of the tarsier and the human. Nevertheless, the principles of inferring phylogeny have been very well developed by the cladists. We have already discussed them to a limited extent in this chapter, and although we do not use them as a rigid basis for classification here, the principles of phylogenetic inference derived from cladistics are discussed in greater detail in Chapter 10.

Primates among the Mammals

Primates are principally tree-dwelling (arboreal) mammals. The few primates that live on the ground give ample testimony to a tree-living ancestry. Primates are not the only mammals that live in trees, however, so it seems likely that the specializations of primates are adaptations not only to arboreality, but to a specific means of subsistence in trees. Anthropologist Matt Cartmill has shown that a likely explanation for the unique features of primates is *visual predation,* associated with insect hunting, while in the trees.

To a tree-dwelling predatory species, certain specializations would be extremely useful. In terms of locomotion, the ability to grab and hold branches (as well as prey) would be a considerable advantage. On an irregular substrate, such as a tree limb, paws do not perform very well— one needs to be able to cling. Though squirrels cling with sharp claws, primates do it with their hands and feet, particularly with the thumb and big toe, which close in opposition to the other digits. Further, primates have flexible shoulders, which permit other locomotory postures such as hanging (or holding on for dear life, as the case may be).

The sensory apparatus might also become specialized. While cattle in a herd on the plains rely heavily on their sense of smell, primates in the trees depend primarily on their sense of sight—to see each other among the leaves, to see the next branch, and to see food.

What we note among the primates, therefore, are a number of modifications of principally the cranium and locomotor apparatus:

1. Primates tend to have forward-directed eyes, or *orbital convergence*. While most mammals have eyes directed laterally, primates have eyes that face directly forward. This gives each eyeball a field of vision that overlaps with that of the other eye, permitting acute three-dimensional perception (Figure 5–3). This rotation of the eye also puts part of the ethmoid bone of the skull into the structure of the eye orbit, a diagnostic primate feature lacked only by a small group of lemurs.

2. Primates tend to have well-protected eyes. Unlike most other mammals, the eyes of primates are surrounded by a bony ring, the postorbital bar. This appears to serve as a buttress to absorb, in relatively large-eyed creatures, heavy chewing forces. In a restricted group of primates, the anthropoids, the eyeball is completely enclosed around the back by a bony socket (and nearly so in the tarsier; Figure 5–4).

3. The elaboration of the visual apparatus comes at the expense of olfaction, the sense of smell. Primates tend to have small snouts (except in species in which the snout is enlarged to accommodate huge canine teeth, such as baboons). Further, the parts of the brain that govern olfaction tend to be reduced at the expense of those parts that govern vision.

4. Primates tend to have flat nails, not curved claws (Figure 5–5). All primates have a nail on the big toe, reflecting a grasping, rather than clinging, mode of support in the trees. Most primates

Figure 5-3

Primates tend to be able to see in three-dimensional space better than other mammals because the forward rotation of their eyes gives them considerable overlap of the two visual fields.

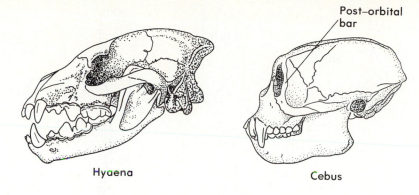

Post-orbital bar

Hyaena

Cebus

Figure 5-4
Primates tend to have well-protected eyes (after Gregory).

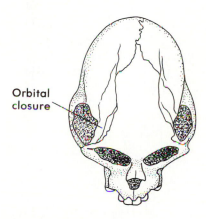

Orbital closure

have nails on all digits of the hands and feet, although prosimians have at least one toe with a claw used for grooming, and others (marmosets and aye-ayes) have re-evolved a form of claws.

5.   Primates tend to have a grasping thumb and big toe. The major exception to the latter, of course, is humans, whose feet have adapted to bearing the body's weight on the ground. Many primate species, however, have had their thumbs secondarily reduced or lost.

6.   The flexibility of primate limbs enables them to be moved in a diagonal pattern, that is, the *right* forelimb extended forward along with the *left* hindlimb. This pattern appears to derive from a strong tendency to have the center of gravity closer to the hindlimbs. In other mammals, by contrast, either the two forelimbs stride together, or the two limbs on the same side stride together (Figure 5-6).

7.   Primate hands and feet tend to be sensitive. Pads with tactile ridges (dermatoglyphics or fingerprints), sweat glands, and specialized structures called Meissner's corpuscles help to reduce slippage and increase sensitivity in arboreal support.

Figure 5-5

Primate hands and feet are distinctive in their grasping abilities, sensitive ridges, and nails (after Schultz).

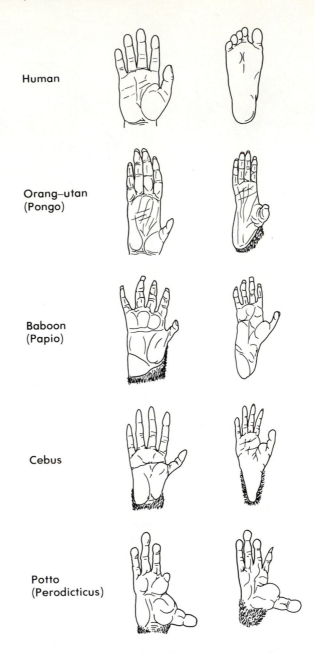

Human

Orang–utan
(Pongo)

Baboon
(Papio)

Cebus

Potto
(Perodicticus)

Other primate specializations include aspects of their life histories and unique aspects of other body parts.

8. Primates tend to have relatively large brains, given overall body size, that are particularly evident before birth. Primates tend to grow more slowly than do other mammals, reach sexual maturity late, and have long life-spans. This means that they tend to devote a considerable portion of their lives to learning.

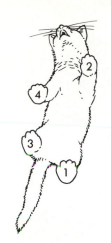
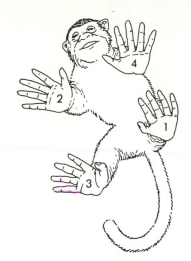

**Lateral Sequence
of limb movements,
characteristic of
non–primates**

**Diagonal Sequence
of limb movements,
characteristic
of primates**

(a)

Figure 5–6. Primates are also distinctive in the sequence of motion of their four limbs.

(a) Unlike most mammals, who use a lateral sequence of footfalls on the ground, primates use a diagonal sequence. (b) This results in having a forelimb and the opposite hindlimb extended together for long intervals during the gait. When humans walk bipedally, they carry on this primate tendency by extending the left arm and right leg together in a stride, unlike the bipedalism of other vertebrates such as kangaroos and birds.

(b)

9.   Male primates are unique in that their testes permanently descend fairly early in life into a scrotum, below the penis. Female primates tend to lack a urogenital sinus, into which the vagina and urethra enter in many other mammals. Most female primates also have only a single pair of nipples, located high on the chest, rather than on the abdomen.

10. The bony ear of primates is formed in a unique way. The ear of a living primate has a bony chamber, or bulla, whose base, or floor, is formed principally by the petrosal part of the temporal bone of the skull. Variations on this theme are diagnostic of the skulls of primate subgroups (Figure 5–7).

11. The molar teeth of primates tend generally to be unspecialized, lacking the ever-growing capabilities, or zigzig system of crests, or the scissorslike shearing developed in other mammalian groups.

PROSIMIANS

The major division we recognize within the Order Primates divides them into the suborder Prosimii (lemurs, lorises, tarsiers) and the suborder Anthropoidea (monkeys, apes, and humans). This is, however, a classification by similarity rather than by contiguity, since the tarsier is now recognized to be more closely related to the anthropoids than to the other prosimians (Table 5–3).

The three groups of **prosimians** are the lemurs (found only on the island of Madagascar), the lorises (including galagos, and found in central Africa and southern Asia), and the tarsiers (found on Borneo and several neighboring islands—Figure 5–8).

prosimian

Lemur, loris, galago, tarsier; member of the suborder Prosimii.

Figure 5-7

(a) Primate outer ear bones are distinctive, involving the relationships between the tympanic bone and the petrous part of the temporal bone. (b) In a lemur, the tympanic bone is suspended within a chamber at the skull base; in a New World monkey, the tympanic bone forms a ring at the margin of the chamber; and in monkeys, apes, and humans, the tympanic bone extends outward as a solid tube (after Fleagle).

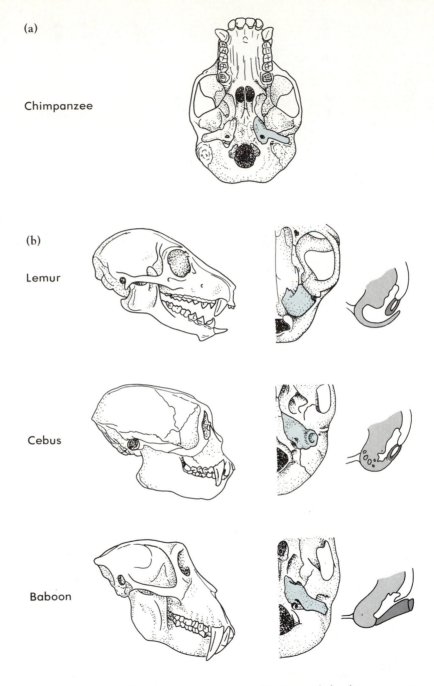

(a)

Chimpanzee

(b)

Lemur

Cebus

Baboon

Lemurs and lorises possess a specialization of the lower anterior teeth, which jut outward to form a *tooth-comb*, a diagnostic feature of this group (Figure 5–9). It is used in grooming (see Chapter 6) and also for feeding—the animals can gouge the bark of trees to eat the resins. The

Table 5–3

Classification of Living Primates Used in This Book

Order Primates
   Suborder Prosimii
         Superfamily Lemuroidea
         Superfamily Lorisoidea
         Superfamily Tarsioidea
   Suborder Anthropoidea
     Infraorder Platyrrhini
         Family Cebidae
         Family Callitrichidae
     Infraorder Catarrhini
       Superfamily Cercopithecoidea
         Family Cercopithecidae
            Subfamily Cercopithecinae
            Subfamily Colobinae
       Superfamily Hominoidea
         Family Hylobatidae
            Genus *Hylobates*
         Family Pongidae
            Genus *Pongo*
            Genus *Gorilla*
            Genus *Pan*
         Family Hominidae
            Genus *Homo*

tooth-comb is composed of three pairs of teeth, two incisors and a canine on either side, although in a few species only two pairs of teeth are involved.

Prosimians practice various kinds of locomotion. Many propel themselves from tree to tree using their hindlimbs, starting from a crouching position, and holding their trunk erect. This locomotion is called vertical clinging and leaping. Other species, such as the lorises, climb slowly from branch to branch, while still other, smaller species scramble around in the branches. Some species of lemurs hop or lope bipedally when on the ground (but do not often find themselves out of the trees).

Prosimians have a greater reliance on smell than do other primates, but compared with other mammals, they have made an unambiguous biological commitment to vision—a primate character.

Lemurs   The lemurs of Madagascar are extraordinarily interesting. Creatures very similar to them are not found anywhere else in the world. Furthermore, they are quite diverse in locomotion and behavior,

Figure 5-8

Distribution of extant prosimians.

Figure 5-9

Living prosimians, like this *Lemur fulvus* (a), have a specialization of their lower jaws known as a tooth-comb (b).

Figure 5-10
A ring-tailed lemur (*Lemur catta*).

representing an adaptive radiaton of a distant primate group. While lemurs may look superficially more like dogs or raccoons, a detailed analysis shows them to be primates (Figure 5–10). Unlike carnivores, they have opposable thumbs (and big toes), nails on all digits (except the second toe, which is used for grooming), and eyes that face forward. Dentally, few similarities occur between lemurs and carnivores. And their biology, behavior, and postcranial anatomy reveal them to be adapted for moving in the trees, like primates, not for running on the ground.

Anthropologist Earnest Hooton eulogized the lemur in verse many years ago:

The lemur is a lowly brute;
His primate status some dispute
He has a damp and longish snout
With lower front teeth leaning out.
He parts his fur with this comb-jaw,
And scratches with a single claw
That still adorns a hinder digit
Whenever itching makes him fidget.
He is arboreal and omnivorous;
From more about him, Lord deliver us!

On Madagascar, the lemurs are a unique group of **endemic** animals. They are diverse enough to be classified as five separate families and dozens of species. Nevertheless, their present diversity is misleading, for only a few thousand years ago, there were many more species. Since Madagascar was settled by humans, many species have become extinct and are known only as subfossils, whose bones are incompletely mineral-

endemic

Narrowly localized and isolated geographically.

Figure 5-11

(a) A member of the loris family, the potto (*Perodicticus*); (b) A galago (*Galago*).

ized. If the living lemurs are not protected, many more species will face extinction in the near future, particularly as their native forests are cut down.

The subfossil lemurs are closely related to the extant lemurs; they can all be classified within the five families. Generally, the extinct ones were larger. For example, the weight of *Megaladapis* can be estimated from its remains to have been approximately 150 kg—considerably greater than its closest living relative, the sportive lemur, which might weigh 1 kg after a full meal.

Lorises and Galagos   The lorises and galagos (Figure 5–11), distributed more broadly across Asia and Africa, are considerably less diverse than their prosimian relatives, the lemurs. This pattern is best explained by the fact that the lemurs never faced competition from other primate taxa on Madagascar, which split off from the African mainland before anthropoids had evolved. Faced with competition from primate taxa that had new adaptive strategies, the living lorises and galagos survived by virtue of being nocturnal. The monkeys and apes are diurnal: The only nocturnal anthropoid primate is the night monkey (*Aotus*) of South America, and there are no nocturnal anthropoids in Asia or Africa, where the lorises and galagos exist.

These prosimians, consequently, are classified into only two families. The galagos are specialized for a leaping form of locomotion and have big ears and long, bushy tails. The lorises, by contrast, stay still for long periods, and move by climbing slowly. They have reduced tails and only a stub for an index finger, which helps allow a great spread of the hand.

The Ambiguous Position of the Tarsier   The tarsier (genus *Tarsius*) is probably the closest living relative of the anthropoids, not of the other prosimians. The tarsier is not a monkey or ape, however, and is a nocturnal arboreal leaper, like the galagos. It also has grooming claws on its feet. Unlike the galagos, the tarsier's tail is not bushy, and it derives its name from the extreme length of its tarsal (ankle) bones, which give the tarsier, in effect, a built-in springboard for a foot (Figure 5–12). This unique propulsive mechanism is augmented by the fusion of its lower leg bones, the tibia and fibula, for most of their length—which apparently resist the bending forces that accompany the tarsier's leaps.

Another unique feature of the tarsier is its relatively enormous eyes, which are so large that they cannot be moved efficiently by their surrounding muscles. Consequently, the tarsier rotates its head to see and can do so nearly as extensively as an owl. Its eyes, in fact, are so large that each alone is more massive than the tarsier's brain. Those eyes, in the nocturnal creature, are also very sensitive to light but not to color.

Thus, the tarsier lives and moves like other prosimians but has certain unique characteristics, as well. Like the monkeys and apes, however, the tarsier does not have a tooth-comb. It also has a nearly complete bony eye socket, like the anthropoids. Its retina has a structure called a fovea that it shares with anthropoids; and behind the retina, the tarsier lacks a reflective layer present in other nocturnal prosimians (and other mammals), but lacking in anthropoids. Its placenta differs from that of the other prosimians and is similar to the anthropoid variety in being hemochorial, allowing considerable contact between the blood of the mother and fetus. Likewise, the tarsier's uterus has only one horn, like monkeys and apes, rather than two, like other prosimians.

Figure 5-12

A tarsier (*Tarsius*)

Figure 5-13

The number and types of teeth can be a diagnostic feature; in each jaw quadrant, a platyrrhine has one more premolar than a catarrhine.

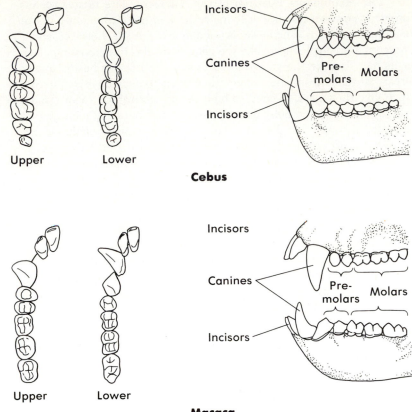

Upper   Lower

Cebus

Upper   Lower

Macaca

The tarsier's nose is dry and lacks sensitive whiskers or vibrissae like anthropoids but unlike prosimians and most other mammals. Neither is its upper lip split down the middle, again a feature shared with anthropoids. The pattern of blood flow to the brain (emphasizing the promontory artery) also links the tarsier to the anthropoids. And the tarsier, like the monkey, ape, and human, has lost the ability to synthesize its own vitamin C.

Thus, the tarsier seems to have broad, primitive features linking it to prosimians and detailed features linking it to anthropoids. Yet it is neither a monkey nor an ape—it is a primate that diverged from the lemurs, lorises, and galagos before the living monkeys and apes evolved. It does not readily fall into either of our two major primate categories, principally because there is only one genus of tarsiers and so many genera of prosimians (on one hand) and monkeys (on the other). As indicated earlier, we recognize this unique and bizarre creature as the closest living primate relative of the monkey, ape, and human, though not one of them itself. An alternative cladistic classification based only on the phylogenetic relationships would call the tarsiers, monkeys, apes, and humans the suborder Haplorhini and the remaining lemurs, lorises, and galagos the suborder Strepsirhini.

TEETH: IMPORTANT TAXONOMIC CHARACTERS

We often refer to dental characteristics in talking about the evolutionary relationships of primates. We do this for several reasons. Principally, teeth are very often diagnostic of a taxon, usually diagnostic of a genus, but almost always diagnostic of a family. And second, they are the most abundant parts of the body in the vertebrate fossil record and have consequently received a lot of attention. We give them greater attention in Chapter 11.

Cheek teeth (molars) preserve many anatomical details, mostly on the chewing, or *occlusal*, surface, where always-present bumps, grooves, and ridges can serve as taxonomic landmarks. Not only the surface of the tooth may be important, though—often, simply the spatial pattern or the number of teeth identifies a group.

Mammals have four kinds of teeth—incisors, canines, premolars, and molars, moving from the front to the back of the mouth (Figure 5–13). The mouth is bilaterally symmetrical, but the upper and lower jaws may differ in the number of teeth they hold. We can establish a *dental formula* for a species by taking the number of upper and lower teeth it has on one side. For example, the tarsier has the dental formula $\frac{2.1.3.3}{1.1.3.3}$. This means that it has two incisors, one canine, three premolars, and three molars on each side of its upper jaw and one incisor, one canine, three premolars, and three molars on each side of its lower jaw.

Prosimians are much more diverse in dental formula than are anthropoids. The aye-aye has the fewest teeth, with a formula of $\frac{1.0.1.3}{1.0.0.3}$ (Box 5–1); at the other extreme are many lemurs with $\frac{3.1.3.3}{3.1.3.3}$.

Anthropoids are more uniform in dental formula. Humans have a dental formula of $\frac{2.1.2.3}{2.1.2.3}$, as do all the apes and all the Old World monkeys. Indeed, as we shall see, this dental formula is a defining feature of the **catarrhine** primates (Old World anthropoids). The **platyrrhine** primates (New World anthropoids) are divided into two groups, the family Cebidae ($\frac{2.1.3.3}{2.1.3.3}$) and the Family Callitrichidae ($\frac{2.1.3.3}{2.1.3.2}$). Thus, all species of Catarrhini have one premolar less in each quadrant of the jaw than have species of Platyrrhini. In addition, the Callitrichidae have lost a molar in each quadrant of the jaw.

More importantly, however, the number and pattern of cusps on the occlusal surface of the molar teeth give highly specific information about the taxonomic group from which the animal came. For example, the upper molar of a mammal is derived from a triangular pattern built around three cusps: protocone, paracone, and metacone. Two smaller cusps, the paraconule and metaconule, lay on the occlusal table of the crown, near the base of the paracone and metacone. From a surrounding rim of enamel, called the cingulum, another cusp (the hypocone) devel-

catarrhine

Belonging to the infraorder Catarrhini: Old World monkeys, apes, and humans.

platyrrhine

Belonging to the infraorder Platyrrhini: New World monkeys.

Issues in Anthropology 5–1

The Aye-Aye, Daubentonia madagascariensis

Other than *Homo sapiens,* the most bizarre living primate is certainly the rare and unique aye-aye of Madagascar. First encountered by Europeans in the 1780s, its nature and affinities were widely debated until a detailed study by the anti-Darwinian anatomist Richard Owen in 1863 showed that it was, in fact, allied to the primates.

The aye-aye is an example of the divergence that can evolve from within the primate group, as aye-ayes have radiated from a common stock to become specialized in many ways. Since many more species have become extinct than are currently alive, we can easily underestimate the variety of species in any particular group if we judge by only the organisms alive today. Thus, we are very fortu-

nate that the aye-aye, another unique branch of the primate tree, is still with us.

The aye-aye is related to the lemur (the only other nonhuman primate on Madagascar) and has black hair, oversized ears, a large, bushy tail, and a weight of about 3 kg. Its most unusual skeletal features are its teeth and hands. Its central incisors are strikingly enlarged at the expense of its other teeth, so that its dental formula is 1.0.1.3/1.0.0.3. Indeed, its incisors recall a rodent or lagomorph more readily than they do a primate, although its deciduous (baby) teeth are more primatelike. Other aspects of its skull are readily identifiable as primatelike, as well—the aye-aye is simply very autapomorphic.

Its digits are equipped with clawlike nails (except for the big toe, which has a regular, primate nail). Its third finger is extremely slender and bony, and is used for tapping, scratching, and spearing. The aye-aye taps the trunk of a tree with its finger and uses its enlarged ears to listen to the sound, which will tell whether an insect larva or grub is in the tree. Then, with its incisors and claws, it scratches and gnaws the bark until it exposes the grub, spears it, and eats it.

Anthropologist Matt Cartmill argues that the

ops outside these cusps (Figure 5–14). On the lower molars, the five main cusps are called protoconid, paraconid, metaconid, hypoconid, and entoconid (see Chapter 11). The orientation of these cusps, the ridges of enamel that join them, the relative sizes of these cusps, and other additional cusps and grooves serve to differentiate the teeth of primate taxa from one another. Thus, for example, the tarsier is unique among living primates in the possession of a paraconid on its lower molars, for the lemurs and lorises as well as the anthropoids have lost it; and the callitrichids are unique in lacking a hypocone on their upper molars. As in any scholarly endeavor, one can often be dazzled by the details; and doubly so with things as seemingly simple and mundane as teeth. Nevertheless, it is important to appreciate that they can be a tremendous store of taxonomic information for anthropologists.

aye-aye has evolved among the mammals to fill the ecological niche usually occupied by woodpeckers among the birds on Madagascar—as the striped opossum appears to have done in Australia. Both have evolved superficially similar adaptations that aid in prying and gnawing chunks of wood and extracting the prey. Indeed members of another extinct mammalian lineage, the apatemyids, have now been suggested to fill a similar niche through the evolution of large incisors and a long, thin, spearlike finger.

The aye-aye has a much larger brain than is expected in a prosimian of its size, especially the cerebellum, although we do not know why. Other skull specializations are related to the dissipation of chewing forces generated by the gnawing activity uncharacteristic of primates. It also has a curious arrangement of skull bones forming the eye socket, very rare among primates.

The aye-aye supplements its diet of insects with fruits and nuts, again using its large front teeth. It builds nests in trees during the day and, like most prosimians, is active only at night. For this reason, not much is known about its social life.

Anthropologist Earnest Hooton eulogized *Daubentonia madagascariensis* as follows:

In Madagascar dwells the Aye-Aye,
Who would be better named the Why-Why.
His chisel teeth recall a rabbit
And are connected with the habit
Of digging grubs out from their holes
In boughs of trees or even boles.
He pokes his wirelike middle finger
Into the ends where larvae linger,
Impales them on this one-tined spear,
And forks them in with right good cheer.
By now you doubtless have surmised
The Aye-Aye is too specialized
For living on one kind of grub.
If this should fail—"Aye, there's the rub."

References:

Cartmill, M. (1974). Daubentonia, Dactylopsila, woodpeckers and klinorhynchy. In R. D. Martin, G. A. Doyle, & A. C. Walker (Eds.), *Prosimian Biology*, (pp. 655–670). London: Duckworth.

Fleagle, J. (1988). *Primate adaptation and evolution*. San Diego: Academic Press.

Koenigswald, W. V., & Schierning, H. P. (1987). The ecological niche of an extinct group of mammals, the early Tertiary apatemyids. *Nature*, 326:595–597.

THE ANTHROPOIDEA

Tarsiers, monkeys, apes and humans share a number of features, as noted above, which distinguish them from the lemurs, lorises, and galagos. The monkeys, apes, and humans (collectively suborder Anthropoidea, or **anthropoids**) have several features that they share with one another, distinguishing them from living prosimians, including tarsiers. In addition to the features of the placenta, snout, bony ear, and cranial blood vessels shared by anthropoids and tarsiers, anthropoids are distinguished from tarsiers by having an eye orbit fully closed at the rear. Nails are found on all digits (except in the Callitrichidae, which have re-evolved claws on all digits but the big toe).

The left and right halves of the anthropoid lower jaw fuse together at the midline. So do the left and right halves of the frontal bone of the

anthropoid

Monkeys, apes, and humans; member of the suborder Anthropoidea.

Figure 5-14
Many landmarks—bumps, furrows, and ridges—can be seen on the occlusal surface of a molar tooth. Indicated are the main cusps of a left upper first molar from an extinct ape known as *Pliopithecus* (after Simons).

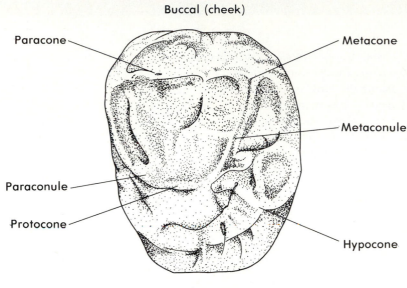

Buccal (cheek)

Paracone

Metacone

Metaconule

Paraconule

Protocone

Hypocone

Lingual (tongue)

skull. The eye orbits are completely closed at the rear, and a bone known as the lacrimal takes part in composing the eye orbit (in prosimians, this bone lies in front of the eye orbit). These appear to be synapomorphies of living anthropoids, although fusion of the jaw is known in some extinct nonanthropoid primates (Figure 5–15).

New World Monkeys: The Platyrrhini No modern primates other than humans are indigenous to North America; however, many other anthropoid species exist in Central and South America. These fall into two broad groups, the family Cebidae and the family Callitrichidae.

The Cebidae are the more familiar New World monkeys, such as the spider monkey, and have a **prehensile** tail. The Callitrichidae are smaller and generally less well known, the marmosets and tamarins. Both groups have widely spaced nostrils, which distinguish them from the Catarrhini, or Old World anthropoids.

The Callitrichidae are unique among anthropoids in having principally claws on their digits, although these are believed to be secondary modifications of nails. Further, they ordinarily give birth to twins, unlike the customary single primate birth. They have also lost a molar tooth in each jaw quadrant, as mentioned, so that their dental formula is $\frac{2.1.3.2}{2.1.3.2}$. They are by far the smallest anthropoids and are also striking for their lack of sexual dimorphism—males and females look fairly alike, and males take a very active role in caring for the offspring (Figure 5–16).

The Cebidae, on the other hand, have a dental formula of $\frac{2.1.3.3}{2.1.3.3}$ and nails on all digits. They include several genera with prehensile tails (Figure 5–17), used as fifth limbs for locomotion in the trees. The Cebidae are also quite diverse, including the roaring howler monkey, the

prehensile
Able to grasp, like a hand.

Anthropoids

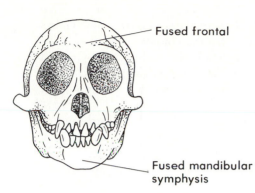

Fused frontal

Fused mandibular symphysis

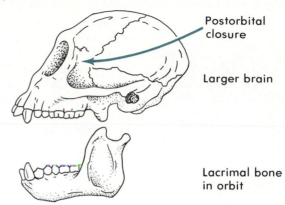

Postorbital closure

Larger brain

Lacrimal bone in orbit

Prosimians

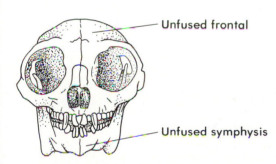

Unfused frontal

Unfused symphysis

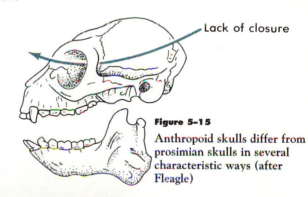

Lack of closure

Figure 5-15

Anthropoid skulls differ from prosimian skulls in several characteristic ways (after Fleagle)

Figure 5-16

A callitrichid, the moustached tamarin (*Saguinus mystax*), having a typical primate meal.

Figure 5-17

Many cebids have prehensile tails that they can use as fifth limbs.

bizarre uakari, the dextrous capuchin (or organ-grinder monkey), and the night monkey, the only nocturnal anthropoid. Indeed, it is now widely thought that some cebids are more closely related to callitrichids than to other cebids; thus, again we classify these primates into two broad groups by similarity as well as by contiguity, rather than by contiguity alone.

Falling somewhat between the cebids and callitrichids, Goeldi's marmoset (*Callimico goeldii*) has claws like other callitrichids, except on the big toe; single births, unlike other callitrichids; and extremely reduced third molars.

Old World Anthropoids: The Catarrhini The catarrhine primates are the anthropoids of the Old World, and they share a number of distinctive features. Their name comes from the characteristics of their nose, which has nostrils that are narrowly separated and that open downward rather than out to the sides, as in the platyrrhines. Further, their

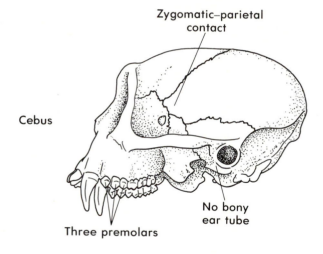

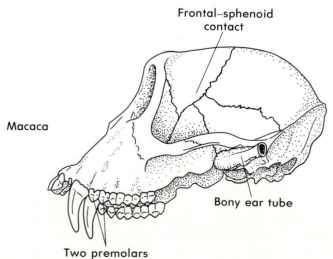

Figure 5-18

The skulls of platyrrhines and catarrhines have several characteristic differences (after Fleagle).

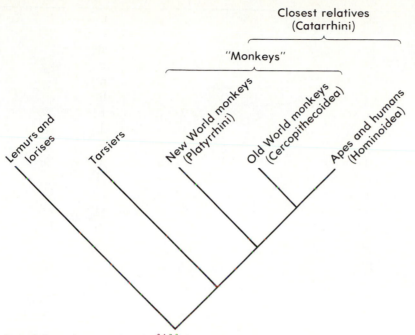

Figure 5-19

Cladogram showing the relationships of the extant primates. Although the New World and Old World both are home to monkeys, the monkeys of the Old World are more closely related to the apes than to the monkeys of the New World.

dental formula is uniformly $\frac{2.1.2.3}{2.1.2.3}$, having one less premolar in each quadrant than the Platyrrhini. The tympanic bone in the auditory region of the skull is expanded to form a true tube in the Catarrhini rather than the fairly narrow ring shape it possesses in the Platyrrhini. Further, the arrangement of the bones at the side of the skull is characteristic for the two groups: in platyrrhines, the zygomatic bone and parietal bone border each other, but in catarrhines, the frontal and sphenoid bones jut out between them (Figure 5–18).

The two main groups of Catarrhini are the superfamily Cercopithecoidea, which includes all the Old World monkeys, and the superfamily Hominoidea, which includes the apes and humans (Figure 5–19). Despite the fact that we call both the Platyrrhini and the Cercopithecoidea monkeys, the Cercopithecoidea are more closely related to humans and apes than they are to the New World monkeys. Thus, the category *monkey* is evolutionarily artificial.

One important catarrhine feature concerns its rear end. On a bone called the ischium (of the pelvis) is a bulge known as the ischial tuberosity. In most catarrhines, this is quite large and is associated with prominent skin hardenings on either side of the anus, called the *ischial callosities*. These structures are part of the catarrhine heritage, possessed prominently by cercopithecoids and by gibbons but secondarily quite reduced in the great apes and completely absent in humans.

Cercopithecoids are arguably the most successful primate group, subsuming the baboons of Africa, the langurs of Asia, the macaques, the rhesus monkeys, and the extraordinarily diverse guenons of Africa. Yet all these diverse cercopithecoids have a similar specialization of the molar

Figure 5-20

A molar tooth of the Old World monkeys has two pairs of cusps, each pair of which is connected by a sharp ridge.

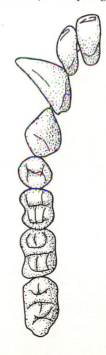

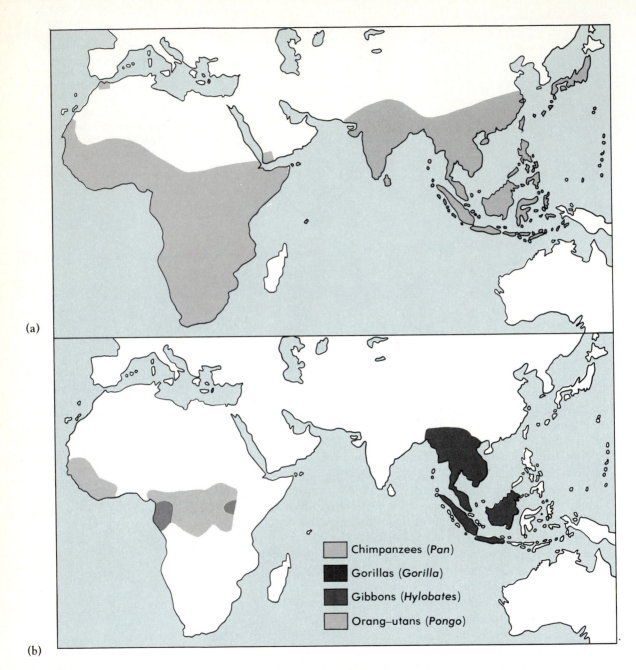

(a)

(b)

Chimpanzees (*Pan*)

Gorillas (*Gorilla*)

Gibbons (*Hylobates*)

Orang–utans (*Pongo*)

Figure 5-21

(a) Distribution of living cercopithecoids;
(b) distribution of living hominoids.

teeth, which involves the connection of the two anterior and two posterior cusps by ridges of enamel. The resulting condition is known as a *bilophodont* molar (Figure 5–20).

While the New World monkeys live only in the tropical forests, Old World monkeys live in a great range of habitats, from the forest to the savanna, and even in the urban environments of India and Pakistan (Figure 5–21). Although none of the cercopithecoids has a prehensile tail, tail length varies considerably. For the most arboreal species, the tail often acts as a counterweight for balance. In other, more terrestrial species, the tail is sometimes so reduced as to be a mere rudiment, as in the so-called "stump-tailed" macaque.

Cercopithecoids are exclusively diurnal (active during the day) and crepuscular (at dawn and dusk)—none are nocturnal. They are generally much larger than New World monkeys. Though most cercopithecoids spend most of their time in the trees, some spend a considerable portion of their time on the ground. In the trees, the Old World monkeys tend to walk or run on branches and to jump from branch to branch. On the ground, they walk quadrupedally, the palms and soles making contact with the earth.

Many cercopithecoids are highly sexually dimorphic, males being considerably larger than females (Figure 5–22). This appears to be related to their social organization, which is usually **polygynous**. This appears to be the result of competition among males for reproductive partners and choices on the part of females (Chapter 6).

The superfamily Cercopithecoidea comprises only one family, the family Cercopithecidae, but a broad division between these Old World monkeys is recognized at the subfamily level. The colobines (subfamily Colobinae) are mostly Asian and are notable for a diet that emphasizes leaves. This entails adaptations of the teeth (which have higher cusps and sharper crests), of the stomach (which permits extended digestion and fermentation of the leaves), and even of biochemicals, as the enzyme lysozyme (involved in the breakdown of foods in the stomach) has some convergent similarity with the cow's version of that enzyme. Colobines

polygyny
Social system in which several females are associated with each male.

Figure 5-22

In most primate species, males are larger than females; in some, this difference is pronounced.

Figure 5-23. The apes.
(a) A gibbon; (b) orang-utans; (c) chimpanzees; (d) a gorilla.

(a)

(b)

(c)

(d)

also have very small thumbs and longer legs and tails than their close relatives. This group includes the langurs of Asia and the colobus monkeys of Africa.

The cercopithecines (subfamily Cercopithecinae) have a narrower interorbital distance (distance between the eye orbits) than that of the colobines and also have cheek pouches for storage and initial processing of food. They tend to feed more on fruits, nuts, and seeds than on leaves. These monkeys represent one of the most successful radiations of primates, having many species that occupy diverse niches from the treetops to the ground. Many of these species are distinguished from one another by patterns of bright coloration on either the face or rump. This group includes the baboons of Africa, macaques of Africa and Asia, and vervets and guenons of Africa.

Apes and Humans: The Hominoidea   The closest relatives of the superfamily Cercopithecoidea are the other catarrhine primates, members of the superfamily Hominoidea. The **hominoids** subsume five living genera of primates—*Hylobates*, the gibbons of southeast Asia; *Pongo*, the orang-utan of Borneo and Sumatra; *Pan*, the chimpanzee of central and western Africa; *Gorilla*, the gorilla of central and western Africa; and *Homo*, humans (Figure 5–23).

We classify these genera into families by similarity rather than by contiguity. The gibbons are placed in their own family, the Hylobatidae, and they are recognized to be quite distantly related to the other apes and humans. Genetical analyses and detailed anatomical studies have shown that among the remaining genera, humans, chimpanzees, and gorillas are more closely related to one another than any of them is to the orang-utan. Nevertheless, the unique anatomical and behavioral divergences of the human has created a more natural division between the great apes on one hand and humans on the other. Although there is some scholarly disagreement regarding the best way to classify these genera, we will continue to recognize these relationships here and classify the chimps, gorillas, and orangs into the family Pongidae and the humans into their own family, Hominidae.

The apes are differentiated from the Old World monkeys in several fundamental ways (Figure 5–24). First, the apes have completely lost their tails, except as embryos. Second, their molar teeth have low, rounded cusps, lacking the crests or ridges on those of the cercopithecoids. Third, most hominoids are arboreal and have adopted a climbing form of locomotion, which often involves hanging or swinging from branches rather than walking upon them. Numerous anatomical changes have accompanied this postural and locomotory change.

Because apes climb and hang from branches rather than walk on them, they require stronger and more flexible shoulders than do Old World monkeys. The scapula, or shoulderblade, has been rotated to the back in apes rather than to the side (Figure 5–25). To support the reori-

hominoid

Belonging to the superfamily Hominoidea: apes and humans.

Figure 5–24

Apes and monkeys differ skeletally in several characteristic ways, notably in the spine, thorax, and shoulder (after Schultz).

Figure 5-25

Looking down the spinal
column of a monkey and a
hominoid, one is struck by the
different position of the
scapula as well as by the shape
of the thorax (after Schultz).

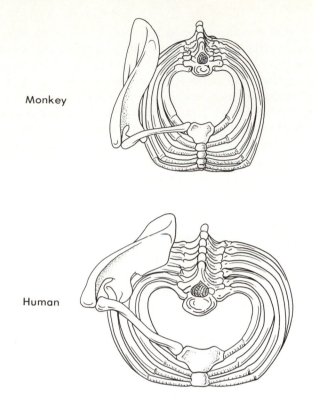

Monkey

Human

entation of the shoulders and the attendant musculature, the thorax has
expanded, yielding a generally broader chest in apes than in monkeys.
Similarly, the function of the arm joints (elbow and wrist) has changed
from one of supporting the body's weight above the arm to having the
body suspended below it. As different functions usually entail different
structures, we find consistent differences in the elbows and wrists of monkeys and apes. These features in apes allow full extension of these joints
(remember that the apes are hanging by their hands) and rotation of the
wrists with greater ease.

Along with this change in locomotion has come a change in habitual posture. Monkeys are habitually *pronograde*, with their trunks parallel
to the ground. Apes, on the other hand, tend to be more *orthograde*, as
the suspensory posture maintains the body more perpendicular to the
ground (Figure 5–26). An important correlate of this is a more compact,
less flexible vertebral column. Further, the chest no longer hangs down
from the vertebral column, as in a pronograde primate, but supports it as
a vertical strut. This involves a change in the shape of the thorax and a
subtle migration inward of the vertebral column to give the chest rigidity.

The life histories of apes and monkeys are also significantly different. Apes are larger and longer-lived and take longer to reach maturity.
They have larger brains and spend even more of their lifetimes learning.

Humans as Hominoid Primates

Thomas Huxley, in the late nineteenth century, delighted in pointing out that there were no *qualitative* differences between humans and apes—that is, there was no structure possessed by humans that apes could be shown to lack completely. Therefore, it could *not* be maintained that humans were *different* from all other animals. Rather, the issue involved *where* humans fit in the animal scheme.

As early as the mid-eighteenth century, Linnaeus had classified humans on the basis of their anatomical similarities to other organisms. He concluded that the genus *Homo* was among the mammals and, within the mammals, among the primates. The accumulated knowledge of more than 200 intervening years has enabled us to locate our position with even greater precision.

The bodies of the apes are extraordinarily similar in form to those of humans, except for three human specializations that we discuss shortly. The molar teeth are very similar in humans and apes, bearing five small cusps. In spite of the divergence of humans, the bones of humans and apes are very similar. The scapula of a human is in a similar position to that of an ape, the bones of the skull fit together in a similar fashion (this is diagnostic of many primate groups), both humans and apes lack tails, and the life history of apes, with a long period of learning and immaturity, is like that of humans. In brief, humans bear the marks of an ape ancestry and fit into the nested hierarchy of living beings noted by Linnaeus (Table 5–4).

Humans also bear the catarrhine dental formula ($\frac{2.1.2.3}{2.1.2.3}$), have placentas, noses, and enclosed eye sockets like other anthropoids, and have nails, fingerprints, and forward-facing eyes, like other primates. An independent check of the evolutionary significance of these anatomical relationships is afforded by molecular genetics (Chapter 8).

Figure 5-26

The typical position of a cercopithecoid is pronograde, while that of an ape is orthograde.

Table 5–4

Classification of Humans

Kingdom Animalia
(excluding other multicellular organisms)
  Phylum Chordata
  (excluding starfish, insects, and other animals lacking a hollow cord
  down their backs)
    Subphylum Vertebrata
    (excluding chordates without backbones)
      Superclass Amniota
      (excluding fish and amphibians, lacking amniotic egg)
        Class Mammalia
        (excluding reptiles and birds)
          Infraclass Eutheria
          (excluding monotremes and marsupials)
            Order Primates
              Suborder Anthropoidea
                Infraorder Catarrhini
                  Superfamily Hominoidea
                    Family Hominidae
                      Subfamily Homininae
                        Genus *Homo*
                          Species *Homo sapiens*

Humans as Unique Primates

Although humans fall among the apes anatomically and genetically, they nevertheless are secondarily divergent from them in several important ways. Humans are uniquely divergent apes by virtue of their mode of locomotion (bipedalism), reduction in canine teeth, and expansion of the brain. These three things are of paramount significance because they can be traced historically in the fossil record, at least in principle.

Bipedalism, or the habit of walking on two legs, comes with anatomical specializations that are uniquely human and that are discussed in detail in Chapter 11. These include changes in the head, vertebral column, hip, knee, ankle, foot, and toes. Other primates are sometimes bipedal when on the ground (such as the sifaka, which has a fairly comical running and jumping gait). Our closest relatives, the apes, have a clumsy, shambling stride when obliged to walk on two legs rather than use their hands for support, as is their inclination.

Human teeth are distinguished by the lack of large canines, the absence of a diastema between the lower canine and lower first premolar (for the upper canine to fit into when the jaws are closed), and the lack of a **sectorial premolar** next to the lower canine, on which the upper canine

sectorial premolar

First lower premolar in most catarrhines with a single cusp, against which the upper canine is sharpened.

sharpens itself (Figure 5–27). Not only are human canines ineffective as weapons, but they cannot even serve the same communicative functions—as display organs—as they do in other primate societies. The former function has been taken over by technology, the latter by language.

Brain expansion is the last of the three skeletally detectable differences between humans and the apes to appear in the fossil record. It is obviously related in some way to the greater intelligence of humans relative to other primates. Unfortunately, the relationship between brain size and intelligence is not very clear. Although tools are detectable in the archaeological record over 2 million years ago, the hominids that used them had brains slightly larger than those of the average modern chimpanzee (400 cc). Neanderthals had brains larger than ours on the average (1500 cc), and people with brains anywhere from 1000 to 2000 cc have been found with normal intelligence. It is *not* now the case that larger brains are required for the manufacture and use of finer tools, and it is, therefore, not clear that it *was* the case in the Stone Age. Nevertheless, until the emergence of *Homo sapiens* a few hundred thousand years ago, an empirical correlation exists between brain size and tool quality. Regardless of why the skull expanded (and the brain within it), this is one of the key differences between humans and apes, insofar as this information fossilizes, and may be a clue to intelligence.

Yet humans are distinguished in other ways as well, which we cannot track in the material record. For example, humans have lost their covering of fur. In other primates, fur not only provides thermoregulation but something for an infant primate to cling to when being carried by its mother. In humans, the thermoregulatory function of fur has been taken over culturally by clothing, and the infant-carrying function has been taken over by either the practice of supporting the child on wide hips or culturally, by cradleboards or other similar devices.

Heat dissipation is also something of a problem in primates. Other primates, and most other mammals, cool off by panting. In humans, however, the mouth is preoccupied with another specialization—speech. Humans manage to cool down by a different method—evaporation, that is, sweating.

Figure 5-27

Chimpanzee jaws and human jaws differ greatly in canine size and in the shape of the lower anterior premolar.

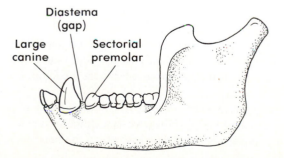

Diastema
(gap)

Large
canine

Sectorial
premolar

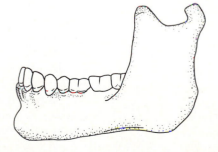

Our Closest Living Relative

Perhaps the fundamental question we can ask when confronted with the fact of evolution and the similarities between humans and primates is, "Which is closest to us?" Darwin and Huxley targeted the African apes (gorilla and chimpanzee) as most closely related to each other and then to us. Most data now bear out that judgment. Yet other primates have, on occasion, been put forth in that role.

In the 1920s, anatomist Frederic Wood Jones proposed the tarsier, but his arguments were not persuasive to many. English anatomist Grafton Elliot Smith argued for only the gorilla, and slightly later, Nazi anthropologist Hans Weinert argued for only the chimpanzee. The American Dudley Morton and the British Charles Sonntag favored the chimp-gorilla group, but most anthropologists followed Adolph Schultz of Johns Hopkins in the inference that all the great apes (chimp, gorilla, and orang-utan) formed a cluster that was the closest relative of the human. This view was dominant through the 1950s.

Genetic studies of phylogeny in the 1960s showed that the orang-utan really belonged outside the human-chimp-gorilla group as Darwin, Huxley, Morton, and Sonntag had believed. But ignoring these newer studies, paleontologist Bjorn Kurten argued that the Old World monkeys are our closest relatives. Likewise, in the 1980s anthropologist Jeffrey Schwartz published a series of anatomical arguments supporting the orang-utan as our closest relative. Neither garnered much support because they defied many genetic studies showing a close relationship among human, chimpanzee, and gorilla.

Within that threesome, however, genetic studies have had difficulty showing which *pair* are closest, for they are all exceedingly close. DNA sequencing of one gene region (pseudo-eta globin) suggests human-chimp, while another (involucrin) suggests chimp-gorilla. The technique of DNA hybridization suggested to some geneticists a human-chimp link, but considerable controversy has surrounded the application of this technique and its ability to resolve phylogenetic branchings at such a fine scale. Even the honesty with which the results have been reported was controversial.

If we accept that genetic studies do define a cluster of humans, chimpanzees, and gorillas, we

Indeed, sweating is one of our most interesting features. There are two major kinds of sweat glands in the primate skin. Apocrine glands secrete a viscous substance that is broken down by bacteria, causing body odor. In animals such as prosimians, which mark territories via smelly secretions from these glands, they are common. They are also present all over the human fetus. They are subsequently lost in humans, however, and are found in adults only at the armpits, nipples, navel, anogenital region, and in the ear. Eccrine glands are nearly as plentiful as apocrine glands in the skin of apes, but in humans, they are far more predominant, as they secrete sweat.

Sweating has several functions. In addition to thermoregulation, it plays a role during states of emotional arousal (sweaty palms) in humans. But its major function in primates is to provide friction to the hands and

can return to anatomy to complement the studies and resolve which pair may be closest. Most anthropologists accept two principal lines of anatomical evidence linking chimpanzee and gorilla.

First, the chimp and gorilla share a unique mode of locomotion on the ground that is not present in orangs or the ancestors of humans. Chimps and gorillas bear their weight on the knuckles of their hands, reflected in several anatomical specializations of the hand and wrist not present in humans or orang-utans. Second, chimpanzees and gorillas have thinner enamel on the surface of their molar teeth than do humans and orangs, suggesting that a recent common ancestor of the African apes evolved thinner enamel than did its relatives, which eventually became modern humans and orangs on different lines. Other ancillary data are concordant with this interpretation, such as the presence of bands at the tips of the chromosomes of the chimp and gorilla but not the human and orang.

Thus, different analyses can give us information on the relationships of primates to one another. Most often, different lines of analysis give concordant results. Where they conflict, we must think carefully about each one and decide which is more likely to be right or wrong.

There will always be people with other ideas, and the scientific community is enriched by the presence of iconoclasts. These people cause us to rethink our basis for holding particular ideas and views, and to formalize more clearly the basis for believing certain things. A scientific community in which there is total agreement is one where nothing interesting is occurring and where no intellectual activity exists. And, once in a while, one of these iconoclasts turns out to be right.

References:

Fleagle, J. G., & Jungers, W. L. (1982). Fifty years of higher primate phylogeny. In F. Spencer (Ed.), *A history of American physical anthropology, 1930–1980* (pp. 187–230) New York: Academic Press.

Andrews, P., & Martin, L. (1987). Cladistic relationships of extant and fossil hominoids. *Journal of Human Evolution*, 16:101–118.

Marks, J., Schmid, C. W., & Sarich, V. M. (1988). DNA hybridization as a guide to phylogeny: Relations of the Hominoidea. *Journal of Human Evolution*, 17:769–786.

soles for a better grasp in the trees. In humans, the major function has been totally subsumed by evaporative cooling. Nevertheless, we still encounter its ancestral primate function in our own bodies—and when shooting a game of pool, it can be very annoying.

Another important specialization of the human anatomy is the modification of the vocal tract and oral musculature, which permits the wide possibilities for sound production necessary to speech. In addition to speech (the utterances made), parts of the human brain have taken on the function of processing the mental rules governing those utterances, what we call language.

Another mental function involves precise neuromuscular control over the hands. Most primates are capable of manually manipulating objects to a considerable extent. Humans, however, whose hands are not

Figure 5-28

Sexual dimorphism in humans is not so much a matter of body size and canine teeth, but rather of shape, body composition, and distribution of hair.

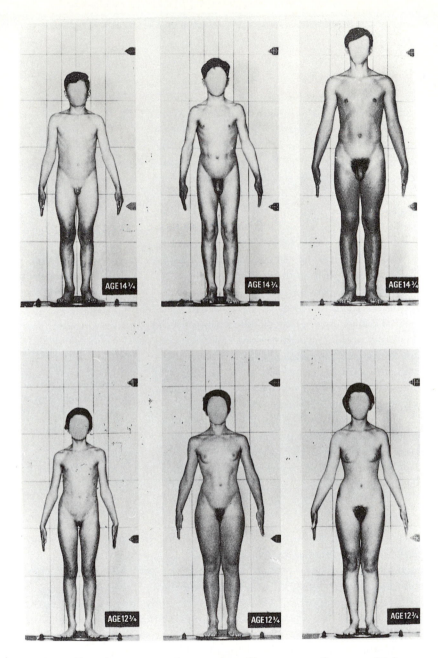

precision grip

The ability to grasp objects delicately, as in holding a pencil; apparently an autapomorphy of humans.

used at all in locomotion, have especially sensitive fingers, which are capable of a wider spectrum of grips and movements than are those of other primates. In particular, the way one holds a pen (and other, similar objects) is known as the **precision grip**—and even our closest primate relatives cannot manipulate objects with such delicacy and skill.

Perhaps the most striking human difference is in reproductive physiology and behavior. Human females have the largest breasts, and males the largest penises, of any primate. Human males are the only catarrhine primates lacking a bone in the penis, the *os baculum*. Further, human females do not go through a breeding season, or cycles of sexual activity, as other primates do. Instead, they can be sexually active at any time.

In addition to these differences in sexual activity, there are differences between humans and other primates in sexual dimorphism, or in how different males and females of the same species appear. In most anthropoid primates, males are substantially larger than females and have much larger canine teeth. A few exceptions to this generalization are the gibbons and some callitrichids. In humans, however, these differences are slighter, and sexual dimorphism involves largely the accumulation of subcutaneous fat deposits in females, resulting in a "figure," and growth of body hair, especially facial hair, in males (Figure 5–28).

Physiologically, these changes take place in humans during a period of rapid growth usually occurring between the ages of 12 and 14, known as the *adolescent growth spurt*. Human males tend to be somewhat larger

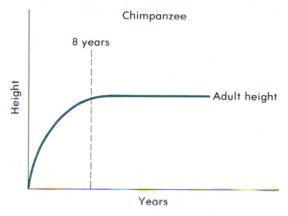

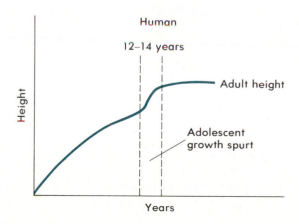

Figure 5-29

While a human experiences a distinct period of accelerated growth during adolescence, nonhuman primates do not seeem to.

than females due to a longer growth spurt, but the adolescent growth spurt does not appear to be a component of the growth of other primates, who grow at roughly the same rate until reaching maturity (Figure 5–29).

Humans also reach maturity later than other primates. The great apes are sexually mature by their eighth year, but humans not until their thirteenth or fourteenth, and growth is often not completed until the eighteenth year or later. In a sense, humans are simply carrying late maturity, one of the primate characteristics discussed earlier, to an extreme.

Humans, then, like all creatures, are a composite of features shared with other related animals and unique to themselves. To understand the biology of humans, we have to understand first that evolution consists of both ancestry and divergence—the adaptations of your species' ancestors and those of your species. These result in two suites of biological characters, called by paleontologist William King Gregory "heritage" and "habitus." Distinguishing these features from each other is often difficult and always requires an extremely detailed examination of the characters in question. Of singular interest and difficulty is the issue of behavior—whether what we do is the result of our great ape heritage or the result of our uniquely human habitus.

Summary

There are many ways of classifying, or imposing order upon the various species on earth. The classification we currently use is based upon that of Linnaeus, who perceived that nature could best be represented as a nested hierarchy. Thus, each genus is composed of species, each family composed of genera, each order composed of families, and so on. It was the subsequent insight of Darwin, a century later, to perceive that this pattern of similarity resulted from proximity of common descent.

At this time, relationships can be inferred in many ways. Anatomical and genetical data are both useful, and these relationships can be inferred by calculating similarities among taxa as distances or by keying on certain traits shared by a group of closest relatives. A characteristic shared by a group of closest relatives is a synapomorphy, and a characteristic shared uniquely by a single species is an autapomorphy. While some biologists prefer to classify solely on the basis of synapomorphy, others prefer to include autapomorphy, to indicate divergence where they deem it appropriate. We do the latter, which has relevance directly for the placement of both the tarsier and the human.

Mammals possess a suite of characters, or synapomorphies, that distinguish them from other vertebrates, and primates possess a more restricted set of features that distinguish them from other mammals. The major division within the primates is between the prosimians and anthropoids, with the tarsier occupying an ambiguous position. Within the anthropoids, we recognize those of the New World (platyrrhines) and the Old World (catarrhines). Within the Catarrhini, we distinguish the Cercopithecoidea (Old World monkeys) from the Hominoidea (apes and humans).

Humans share many synapomorphies with other hominoids, and yet, they also have many autapomorphies that distinguish them from the apes. The autapomorphies given the most weight (since their material remains can readily be studied) are in the locomotory apparatus, the dentition, and the skull. Humans are, however, unique in several other ways. But in order to appreciate the position of humans in the natural world, one must become familiar with the evolutionary context in which we came to be.

Questions for Review

1. What is the purpose of a classification? What is implied by putting humans in a different family from the great apes or placing them in the same family as the chimpanzee and gorilla?

2. What are the features of your own body that convince you that you are a primate? What are the features that convince you that you are a hominoid? What are the features that convince you that you are not a gorilla?

3. Why do you think humans are not very sexually dimorphic in the same way as other primates? What implications do you think this has for understanding human biology or for human social interactions?

For Further Reading

Douglas, M. (1966). *Purity and danger.* London: Routledge and Kegan Paul.

Fleagle, J. (1988). *Primate adaptation and evolution.* San Diego, CA: Academic Press.

Groves, C. (1989). *A theory of human and primate evolution.* New York: Oxford University Press.

Martin, R. (1990). *Primate origins and evolution.* London: Chapman and Hall.

Szalay, F., & Delson, E. (1979). *Evolutionary history of the primates.* New York: Academic Press.

Primate Behavior

Primate Behavior

totemic clan

Kin group symbolically associated with a natural object, often an animal.

Humans and Other Animals

One of the most pervasive human attributes is that of group identification. Whether the group is a **totemic clan**, a baseball team, an alma mater, a nation, a special-interest group, or a family, humans have a strong tendency to "belong." This trait not only promotes the solidarity of the group that we belong to but also defines another group in opposition to it—the one that we are *not* a member of.

GROUP IDENTIFICATION

Since group identification is a cultural process, it is generally strongly symbolic in nature. Sometimes these symbols are as obvious as a shared secret ritual, wearing the same color, or speaking the same language. Or the symbols can be more subtle; very often, the boundaries of our group are reinforced by assigning their group certain behavioral characteristics in opposition to our own. We—that is, our group, "normal" people—do not eat human flesh, have rules governing sexual activity, and are intelligent. Our social counterparts, or their group, the argument often runs, have subhuman characteristics—they eat human flesh, are sexually licentious, and, of course, are dumb as bricks to boot.

These three characteristics are common cross-cultural symbols of *human* as opposed to *nonhuman* or *animal*. The divisive concept of race, which (as we will see in Chapter 9) is a social device that sets one human group apart from another, is often associated with the subjugation of one group to another. And one of the most efficient ways to rationalize the subjugation of another human group is to suggest that its members are really subhuman—in other words, to dehumanize the group—and thereby suggest that it deserves such subjugation. How? By attributing to it symbolically nonhuman attributes.

We can recognize the eating of human flesh, lasciviousness, and low intelligence as cultural stereotypes of various oppressed groups throughout history. For example, during Medieval times, Jews were often accused of extreme sexuality and of eating Christian babies (Figure 6–1). At the turn of the century, Jews were accused of having low intelligence. Likewise, the pagans accused the Christians of eating pagan babies in Roman times, and later Europeans accused many primitive societies of cannibalism. The accusations of lasciviousness and low intelligence are still widespread with reference to African Americans and Hispanic Americans.

Figure 6-1
Imaginary scene of fifteenth-century Jews (each of whom wears a badge) preparing to kill and drain the blood of a Christian baby. Stories like these dehumanize the accused group and are widespread, although the accusing group and the accused group vary widely.

These accusations symbolically juxtapose one human group against another and dehumanize the accused. But not only are the accusations false with respect to other human groups, as we shall see, they are false even with respect to the animals with which they attempt to associate the other group. Not only do our close nonhuman primate relatives rarely eat meat, much less the meat of their own species, they are generally rarely sexually active. And certainly, as the concept of the Great Chain of Being is false, there is no such thing as subhuman—only nonhuman.

HUMAN AND NONHUMAN PRIMATE BEHAVIOR

It is in this important social context that we introduce the study of the behavior of our closest relatives, the nonhuman primates. We study nonhuman primate behavior in hope of illuminating certain aspects of the evolution of human behavior. Yet the similarities among the behaviors of *all* human groups overwhelm the differences. The behavior of all human groups is cultural (symbolic and cumulative), and nonhuman primate behavior is not. It follows that any human behavior is more profoundly similar to other human behavior than it is to any nonhuman primate behavior. Consequently, no human group can be more animal-like in its behavior than any other human group. Any suggestion that we can compare the behavior of a chimpanzee to, say, the South African !Kung San gatherer-hunters more logically than to the population of Terre Haute,

Indiana, is false as well as dehumanizing. One might as readily compare apartment-dwelling New Yorkers to gibbons living high in the canopy of the forest. We can study nonhuman primate behavior to come to a better understanding of the behavior of our species, not of any particular segment of it.

The other misleading approach to primate behavioral studies involves a question that was current among philosophers of the Enlightenment—What is the natural state of humans, or what would a human be like without culture? Perhaps the study of primate behavior can enable us to infer what a cultureless human would be like—what the "native" state of humans is.

We know, however, that culture *preceded* the emergence of our species. *Homo sapiens* was born into a culture already possessed by its ancestor, *Homo erectus* (Chapter 12). Our species has always been a cultural one—a human without culture is a contradiction in terms, an oxymoron. The question of what humans would be like without culture is like asking what a duck would be like with lips instead of a bill. It would not be a duck; the question is nonsense.

Humans are a composite of primitive and derived characteristics, as are all species. As humans are the only cultural primates, there is no primate model we can use to study the evolution of culture directly. As humans are the only habitually bipedal primates, there is no primate model we can use to directly study bipedalism. As humans are the only language-using primates, there is no primate model we can use to directly study the evolution of language. These are all uniquely derived aspects of the human species. Nevertheless, humans do many things that other primates do: socialize, eat, use tools, and copulate, for example. These are ancestral characteristics of our species.

The variety of social, dietary, and sexual variations that the human species can devise, and the importance of cultural context for all these, indicates that there is no natural, no noncultural, state for these things. We can use data from the nonhuman primates, however, to learn something about the possible precursors of modern human behavior—the possible ancestral forms that these characteristics took. We can try to infer what the noncultural ancestors of *Homo* might have been like to learn about the *antecedents* of human behavior and the sorts of changes that occurred in the evolution of *modern* humans. Like other uses of the comparative method, though, we must remember that in studying nonhuman primates, we are studying not the antecedents of humans, but different and divergent species. The importance of these particular species is that, as primates, they have a background similar to humans, a lengthy common evolutionary heritage, and are subject to similar sorts of biological demands.

One would be wiser to reason from baboons to humans than from ants to humans because fewer than 30 million years of evolution separate baboons from humans, while hundreds of millions separate ants from humans. Because of our relatively recent common ancestry, baboon physiology is more similar to a human than is ant physiology, and a baboon's relationship to the environment will likewise be more similar.

The Study and Interpretation of Primate Behavior

Because there are no primates more exotic than *Homo sapiens* native to either North America or Europe, most primatologists are faced with a situation similar to that of most ethnographers—to make an accurate record and interpretation of behavior in distant locales. For this reason, most reports of primate behavior prior to the turn of the century were based on legend and hearsay rather than on direct observation. For the same reason, the reports were often confused and inaccurate.

Did the chimpanzee walk erect, with white, curly hair, communicating in whistles, as Linnaeus thought in the eighteenth century (Figure 6–2)? Were gorillas ferocious killers, as late nineteenth-century explorers often said? And what implications might either of these observations have for our own nature? The only way to know, as the maturing sciences appreciated, was to study the primates as they lived and to find out firsthand.

STUDIES OF PRIMATES IN CAPTIVITY

The first, and easiest, solution chosen by primatologists was to use the growing facilities of zoos to study the behavior of captive animals. Probably the most notorious of these studies was that of the hamadryas baboons of Monkey Hill in the London Zoological Gardens in the 1920s, performed by Solly Zuckerman (later Lord Zuckerman). Sixty hamadryas baboons were released in 1925 into a 100-foot by 60-foot enclosure. This

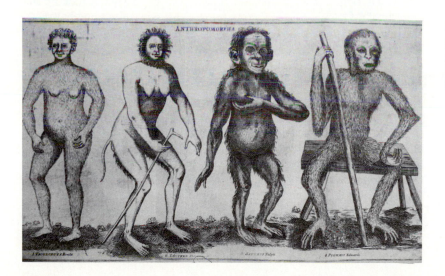

Figure 6–2

Eighteenth-century views of the chimpanzee, as it was known to Linnaeus, through the work of his student Hoppius.

group was almost entirely male. Two years later, thirty females were introduced. Within a month, half had been killed by the males, literally torn to pieces. This set primatologists to thinking.

Why had such carnage occurred? Hamadryas baboons in the wild, we now know, live in single-male "harem" groups, with each male maintaining fairly strict control over his females. When the females were introduced at the zoo, each adult male sought immediately to establish his own harem at the same time—a situation that would never occur in nature. In fact, wild hamadryas baboons do not regularly steal mates from one another, nor do they kill females in what Zuckerman called "sexual fights." Rather, a maturing male begins to hug, carry, and protect a juvenile female until she is old enough to mate, and conditions her to limit her movements by issuing light bites to her neck and back. The adopted female follows her mate closely, competes with other females for his attention, and seeks his protection.

This is a small part of only one of the many social systems encountered among the primates. But imagine the social chaos to a large troop of male baboons programmed to establish a harem and nip at any female who strays outside the limits established by her male, when a few females are suddenly dumped on them! The moral is that the behavior of captive primates in artificial situations may not reflect their behavior in their native environment.

STUDIES OF PRIMATES IN THE WILD

Certainly the most significant student of primates in the first half of this century was Robert Yerkes of Yale University. Yerkes was a psychobiologist, principally interested in the cognitive skills of apes, as he was in those of humans. Yerkes established the first ape colonies in the United States. He trained several students, of whom C. R. Carpenter took up the mantle of primate behavior. Carpenter was the pioneer of primate behavior in the wild and even before World War II had published monographs on the behavior of gibbons in Southeast Asia and howler monkeys on Barro Colorado island, off Panama. Carpenter's research, unfortunately, did not have a strong impact, although it was widely cited. He was unable to attract students to follow up his work, and it stood alone for nearly two decades.

In the late 1950s, however, renewed interest in primate behavior led Sherwood Washburn of the University of Chicago (and later, Berkeley) and his student Irven DeVore to the African savanna, where they studied baboon troops for several months. The main significance of the work was in the context of human evolution—humans had diverged from ancestral apes by leaving the trees and becoming terrestrial, so perhaps the study of this other terrestrial anthropoid could tell us something about ourselves.

Figure 6-3
Jane Goodall and two primate friends prepare to film the Gombe chimps.

By the early 1960s, it was widely appreciated that a study of wild chimpanzee behavior might be more directly relevant to human behavior, as chimpanzees are more closely related to us than are baboons. Accordingly, under the auspices of paleontologist Louis Leakey, Jane Goodall began a long-term study of chimpanzees at Gombe Stream National Reserve in Tanzania. Her 1971 book, *In the Shadow of Man*, became a best-seller, and her work is probably the best-known in primatology (Figure 6–3).

Since Goodall's work, other long-term field studies of the great apes have been conducted. Dian Fossey's turbulent life and work among the gorillas of central Africa has been documented in *Gorillas in the Mist*, a best-selling book and movie. Many other anthropologists now work in the field studying these apes and the other diverse species of primates.

ADVANTAGES AND DISADVANTAGES OF CAPTIVE AND WILD STUDIES

There are many ways to study the behavior of primates. The primary division is between captive and wild studies. The advantage of a captive study is that the animals are accessible and always present. If one wished to test a hypothesis about primate behavior, like any experimental protocol, one would have to establish controls. Is the behavior of a group of primates affected by phenomenon X? To establish this, one must record not only their behavior in the presence of X, but their behavior in the absence of X, and, of course, record a large sample of observations for each. In the absence of sufficient experimental controls, the connection between X and behavior is merely anecdotal. However, often such controls are simply impossible to obtain in the wild, and lab studies are often necessary to establish conclusions rigorously. Further, psychological and physiological studies are usually next to impossible in the wild.

On the other hand, captivity alters the behavior of nonhuman primates, as we have seen. One could not, after all, generalize about the behavior of the human species from studying the behavior of inmates in a prison. Captivity has many biological effects on primates, making them, for example, generally larger and sexually mature at an earlier age than their wild counterparts.

We also need to distinguish what a primate is capable of from what a primate actually does. Often, laboratory studies get at the former, and field studies get at the latter, although this is not always the case, for a field study may be conducted under aberrant conditions. Sometimes, for example, a field researcher must feed the animals in the wild in order to get close enough to study them. In so doing, however, the researcher changes their behavior. The behavior of captive primates, on the other hand, may tell us what various species are *capable* of doing, but not what they *ordinarily* do.

Another important distinction is long-term versus short-term studies. Because the weather, and therefore, the environment, varies seasonally, to document the behavior of a group of primates accurately and comprehensively entails observing them for an extended period. Further, if there is climatic variation, for example, if it is rainier during one rainy season than during the next, the primate behavior may vary accordingly. And finally, for many aspects of primate society such as demography—rates of birth, causes of death, group composition and stability, and so on—a study of many years is necessary.

Unfortunately, a study of many years in the wild is usually not practical. Long-term organization, continuous funding, and permanent facilities are required. While the chimpanzees of Gombe have been under study for nearly thirty years, this is rare among primatological work. Other long-studied primates are the savanna baboons at Amboseli, in Kenya, the macaques of Japan, the vervet monkeys at Kibale, and the howler monkeys of Barro Colorado Island, which have been continuously observed for decades.

On the other hand, one can never hope to document all the diverse behaviors of a primate group over either the short term or the long term. A more narrowly focused research project, therefore, may permit us to learn more about the behavior of a particular species than will a long-term, ethnographic study. Thus, a short-term project can allow a primatologist to test a specific hypothesis by focusing on a particular suite of behaviors, rather than trying to document everything the animals do and hoping that something useful falls out of the data collection.

Factors that Influence Primate Behavior

What influences the behavior of a primate? Behavior is a response to two sets of factors: the nature of the environment and the biology of the species. In the environment, what a primate does will be molded by what sorts of foods are available, the abundance of these foods, the climate, and whether predators are present. The social environment—other animals that are present—also affects its behavior.

The other major influence on behavior is biology. First, many taxa have feeding specializations—for gnawing, digesting foliage, manipulating small objects, or grabbing insects. These specializations have evolved in synergism with the behaviors, by natural selection. Yet it is fairly obvious that any species with a particular anatomy will attempt to use that anatomy to its advantage. Aye-ayes, with their chisel-like incisors, are known to use them to gnaw through coconut husks.

Another biological influence on behavior is body size. A small animal will have different constraints placed upon it, and different opportunities, than will a large animal. This can be demonstrated by considering two extremes—the elephant and the ant. The small animal can walk on the ceiling but can become trapped in a drop of water because, at its size and weight, the surface tension of water is a greater hazard than gravity. The elephant would fall off the ceiling but not mind the drop of water, for the opposite reason. Within the range of body sizes among the primates, different factors must be considered, but clearly, body size can affect the behavioral capabilities of an animal. A small primate has a higher metabolic rate (which influences its diet), faces greater danger from predators (which influences where it stays and when it is active), and has less chance of breaking the branch it jumps on (which influences how it moves). Thus, an animal's biology places strong constraints on, as well as affords useful opportunities for, its behavior (Box 6–1).

We will discuss five principal categories of behavior: locomotor, feeding, cognitive, social, and sexual behavior. Each varies widely within the primate order, although we focus on the behavior of our closest relatives, the other hominoids.

LOCOMOTOR BEHAVIOR

Primates move in a number of ways. The way humans move is one of the most distinctive things about our species relative to the other primates. Consequently, locomotor behavior is of interest in the study of primates because it relates to how they interact with their environment, and also because it can enable us to frame hypotheses about the evolution of the human bipedal condition by comparing human locomotion to that of other species.

Because the vast majority of human locomotion is **bipedal**—humans fit clearly into a single category—it is tempting to try to assign

bipedalism
Locomotion on two legs; characteristic of humans.

The Effect of Size on Primates

Size affects many aspects of an organism, including metabolic rate and, therefore, diet, as well as considerations of where and how it can live and of what it should be afraid. Equally as significant, however, is the effect that a change in body size has on body form. This is because living organisms are subject to the laws of physics and geometry.

A muscle, for example, is strong in proportion to its cross-sectional area, a two-dimensional quantity. If an organism evolves to ten times its former size, the muscle will be roughly 10 times 10, or 100 times as strong as it was. But the function of a muscle is to move a mass, and mass (and volume) is a three-dimensional quantity. Thus, in the same time that the muscle has increased in strength a hundredfold, the job it must do has increased a thousandfold (10 times 10 times 10). To maintain its strength at a larger size, the muscle must increase in size much more than simple linear scaling suggests. If the muscle simply increases a hundredfold with the rest of the body, it will be proportionately a tenth as strong as it was at the smaller size.

Thus, at a larger size, the animal must either alter its behavior and overall biology to reflect the weaker musculature or become relatively more muscular in order to maintain the same strength. The leg bone of a gorilla, reduced to the same size as that of a pygmy marmoset, would still be stouter. This is why there could never be (as science-fiction movies occasionally show) giant people or giant gorillas that are simply expanded versions of their more diminutive selves. They are physically obliged to change shape to maintain equivalence of function at a different size.

Many other biological features function in pro-

each primate to a category. This, however, would be very misleading. Humans are not only unique in being bipedal, they are rare, if not unique as well, in being *exclusive* in their manner of locomotion. All humans in all cultures virtually always go from place to place bipedally. (An argument could be made for a cultural modification of this habit since many humans go from place to place while sitting—on an animal, in a car, or in a plane. This is an example of how culture has altered a biologically-based behavior pattern.) In contrast, most primates have a predominant form of locomotion, yet move in other ways as well. Thus, *Macaca fascicularis*, which we would group as a quadruped, actually was found to move that way only 68 percent of the time. The rest of its time in locomotion was spent climbing (26 percent) and leaping (6 percent).

The reason for this diversity is fairly simple. Primates are mostly arboreal, but environments are heterogeneous. A primate may specialize in one part of the environment but carry on some activities in another. A baboon troop, for example, will usually travel and feed on the ground but sleep in the trees. An orang-utan will spend about 90 percent of its time in the trees, climbing and hanging, descending to the ground only about 10 percent of the time, where it moves in a unique quadrupedal manner—supporting its weight on its clenched fists. When the chimpanzee and gorilla move on the ground, which they do about 50 percent and 90 percent of the time, respectively, they support their weight on their second knuckles.

portion to their areas and fail to operate as efficiently at larger volumes of body size. One of these is respiration in insects; an insect takes in oxygen through its skin, which is limited by the surface area of the insect's body. A larger insect has a greater volume and mass, requiring much more oxygen; but as the surface area has increased proportionately less than the volume it now must serve, it is getting only a little more oxygen (which is why there are no foot-long insects, much less gigantic ones such as Mothra, the giant moth of old Japanese sci-fi movies).

The study of form can show empirically how particular features scale at different body sizes across species, across ages, or simply across individuals. If a character varies in direct proportion to variation in body size, that character is changing *isometrically*. If the trait varies so that it is proportionally larger or smaller than a simple calculation from body size would predict, then the trait is changing *allometrically*. Positive allometry means that the rate of increase of a character is greater than the expansion in body size; negative allometry means that a character changes at a rate smaller than the increase in body size. The human brain, for example, is about three times as large as one would predict for a primate of our size.

Reference:

Jungers, W. L. (Ed.). (1985). *Size and scaling in primate biology*. New York: Plenum Press.

Even the forest is heterogeneous. The forest floor and canopy are very different in composition and, consequently, require different sorts of adaptations to navigate them efficiently. The kinds of branches, the kinds of foods, the kinds of predators, all vary—consequently, so must the behavior of the primates that interact with them.

Table 6–1 summarizes the main ways in which primates move about. Most prosimians, and especially the lemurs, are principally leapers. Their manner of leaping, however, is somewhat different from that of leaping anthropoids. A leaping prosimian uses its long legs for both propulsion and a feet-first landing (Figure 6–4). Anthropoids, whose arms are usually as long as or longer than their legs, land hands-first when leaping from branch to branch. Yet descending occasionally to the ground, the lemurs are also quadrupedal, and some of the Lemuroidea adopt a unique, bipedal running gait (Figure 6–5).

Other prosimians, such as the potto, move by climbing very slowly through the trees, grasping each branch tightly with a hand-span enlarged by the loss of its index finger. This anatomical feature enables the animal to clamp its hands tightly to the branch. Its motion is deliberate, with three of its four limbs virtually always in contact with its substrate. Other primates, lacking this feature, are also sometimes quadrupedal in the trees but in different ways.

Among the anthropoids, we encounter diverse forms of locomotion. The cercopithecoid monkeys tend to be principally arboreally

Table 6-1

Categories of Locomotion in Primates

Leaping

Quadrupedalism

  Arboreal

  Terrestrial

    Open-handed

    Knuckle-walking

Suspensory

  Semibrachiation

  True Brachiation

Bipedalism

Figure 6-4

(a) Prosimians, such as this ring-tailed lemur, push off with their feet, and then (b) land feet first, such as this sifaka.

quadrupedal, although baboons and macaques are principally terrestrial quadrupeds. The hominoids, characterized by a strong and flexible shoulder, tend to adopt a suspensory posture when moving in the trees. Thus, where a monkey would be walking on the branch, an ape would be swinging beneath it.

Although the apes are usually forest dwellers, when they descend to the ground, each moves in a unique way. The gibbon moves bipedally, balancing with its absurdly long arms that otherwise enable it to **brachiate** through the forest canopy. The orang, as noted, quadrupedally bears its weight on the fists of its forelimbs. And the chimpanzee and gorilla balance their weight on the second knuckles of their hands, in a posture reminiscent of a football lineman (Figure 6–6).

The locomotor behavior of humans is unique among primates, and the way in which it evolved is one of the most fundamental research problems in physical anthropology (Chapter 11). As in other primates, our locomotor behavior is closely related to our anatomy, our environment, and our mode of subsistence.

FEEDING BEHAVIOR

Two of the most important components of a diet are protein (for growth and cell regeneration) and carbohydrates (for energy). Primates have

brachiation

Posture or locomotion involving suspension by the arms.

Figure 6–5

When on the ground, sifakas (*Propithecus*) adopt a bipedal running gait.

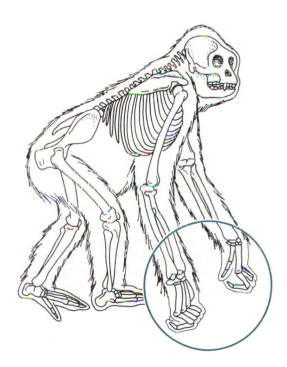

Figure 6–6

Gorillas (and chimpanzees) bear their weight on the knuckles of their hands when walking on the ground, unlike other primates, whose hands are open, and whose weight falls on the palms or fingers.

quite diverse diets and feeding behaviors, but some generalities can be noted.

Meat   Humans are unique among the primates in the quantity of meat consumed in their diet. Among the Hominoidea, the percentage of meat consumed by all species other than *Homo sapiens* is effectively zero. Only chimpanzees among the Hominoidea occasionally, but rarely, eat meat in the wild. Yet of the varied diets of modern human groups, even among cultures whose nutrition derives mainly from plants, such as the !Kung San, meat is often 20–30 percent of their diet. At the other extreme of a wide range of human dietary behaviors, most Arctic peoples eat virtually nothing but meat.

Meat is a rich source of both protein and carbohydrates (and fat), and humans consume more of it than do any other primates. The dietary shift in humans, its causes and consequences, can be analyzed only by reference to nonhuman primates. After all, the only way to know what the shift entailed is to know what the ancestral diet was (or diets were), and obviously, it had to have been more similar to the diets of other hominoid primates.

Many primates get most of their protein from eating animals, and the animals of choice are usually insects. Chimpanzees are known to select a twig, trim it of leaves, moisten it, and fish for termites by poking the twig into a termite hole and eating the insects that cling to it when withdrawn (Figure 6–7). **Insectivory** as a main feature of the diet, however, is limited to smaller primates. The exoskeleton of an insect is difficult to digest, and it would require a tremendous number of insects to fuel a large primate such as a chimpanzee in the absence of other staples, so catching an insect means more to a small primate than it does to a large one. For a small primate such as the tarsier, insects can constitute virtually the entire diet. Most prosimians, therefore, tend to be insectivores, while some larger catarrhines (cercopithecoids) also eat vertebrates, such as lizards, young antelope, or other species of monkeys.

Fruit and Foliage   The most common theme of primate diets, however, is fruit. This is the most popular source of carbohydrates (sugars) across the primates, and every anthropoid family has at least one species of **frugivore**. Some primates eat flowers, which are a poorer source of carbohydrates. A **folivorous** diet of leaves and stems, such as those of gorillas and colobine monkeys, requires adaptations of the digestive tract, because the cellulose in the cell walls of leaves is largely indigestible. These adaptations may include symbiotic bacteria and enlarged stomachs or large intestines for a longer digestive process. A few primates supplement their diets with seeds. Very few eat a large number of seeds, as seeds are also difficult to digest.

Some primates go for sap and gum in the trees, which are difficult to digest, though usually available. Baboons are known to eat roots and bulbs, in contrast to most primates. In general, we find that prosimians

---

insectivory

A diet consisting principally of insects.

frugivory

A diet consisting principally of fruit.

folivory

A diet consisting principally of leaves and stems.

Figure 6-7
Termiting by a chimpanzee.

tend to eat insects as a source of protein and fruit or gum as a source of carbohydrates, while anthropoids tend to eat insects or leaves for protein and fruit for carbohydrates.

Environmental Influence on Diet   Primates do not, however, eat haphazardly. Each species has a series of strategies for exploiting its environment. Some resources are evenly distributed, and others are available only in certain localities or at certain times of the year. Some are riskier to get than others, some are tastier than others, and some are simply easier to acquire than others. Primate groups determine the quality and quantity of foodstuffs and organize their behavior accordingly. Primates are very selective about their fruit, for example, sniffing and tasting many samples while testing for ripeness.

Many ecological consequences occur as a result of primate dietary habits. For example, a folivore will tend not to travel as far each day as a frugivore of the same body weight because foliage is more evenly distributed than is fruit across the environment. In other words, if you walk through the forest, you will constantly encounter leaves (though not all are edible) and only intermittently encounter fruit. Consequently, there will also tend to be a higher density of folivores than of frugivores per given area—for there will be more for a folivore to eat in the same area. But it will also be of less nutritional value and require anatomical specializations to utilize efficiently.

We should avoid stereotyping the diet of any species. What most primates eat depends mainly upon what is available, which in turn depends upon the environment and the season. While many primates have dietary specializations, others can be surprisingly eclectic in their diets, not unlike humans. Gorillas, for example, while strictly vegetarian in the wild, will eat meat in captivity. We can, therefore, make statements about the food *preferences* of species—we can find some consistency in the diet of many species in spite of seasonal and environmental variability.

Food Sharing   We also have to remember, as we try to apply this knowledge to the evolution of the human diet, that behaviors other than simply food *choice* are unique among humans. Two other important behaviors relating to food are also present in humans. The first is food sharing, the distribution of food outside the nuclear family (many species provision their offspring, which does not count). Food is an economic and social commodity in human societies as in no other primate species. In other words, even something as mundane as food occurs in a cultural context and has meanings other than simple nutrition. The other important behavior is cooking, which is often social and tied to food sharing, but also breaks down otherwise inedible foods, or indigestible parts of foods, and so expands the range of possible food sources available to human groups.

Did food sharing arise in humans as the social correlate of a shift to more meat? Interestingly, the only other *ape* known to eat meat occasionally, the chimpanzee, is also known to share it. Among chimpanzees, meat is predominantly a male meal (although sometimes, some is given to females), so a shift toward more dietary meat might well imply a division of labor. Among Old World monkeys that hunt, likewise, the males are the ones who get the meat. But there is little sharing here—it is every baboon for itself.

Several reports note cooperation among chimpanzees as they have been seen to hunt down a prey, such as an infant baboon or a bush pig. But in these infrequently carnivorous primates, the meat is acquired on an opportunistic basis rather than as a foresighted activity—an injured antelope here, a young colobus monkey there. The chimp who makes the kill appears to have propriety over the carcass, as larger, more dominant males will beg for meat rather than grab at it. What is not shared, however, is the brain, which the chimps appear to savor. Their delight in eating the prey's brain is not well understood.

Many anthropologists take the contrast in meat eating with nonhuman primates as the core of a model for human evolution. Not only do humans routinely share food in a cultural setting, they do it at a **home base** (Chapter 12). All other primates eat as they forage, and any sharing they may do occurs on the spot. Humans not only regularly divide their food according to culturally specified rules, but do so only after returning to this central place. The sharing of food in a specific location rather than on the fly also has social implications. A home base can serve as a location where sick and elderly members can stay while healthier, younger individuals take over the economic functions of the group.

home base

A camp where individuals gather and cluster socially for at least a few days, usually longer; characteristic of humans.

Nonhuman primates, such as chimpanzees and gorillas, invariably have all the group members on the move every day. Sleeping nests are used for one night only. By contrast, in human societies, while people in many cultures do not live in the same place year-round, even the most nomadic people have home bases that they occupy for days or weeks at a time.

COGNITIVE BEHAVIOR

Primates make decisions routinely: what to eat, where to get it, how to get there, and so on. Are they capable of thought or language, or even the rudiments? Some of the earliest interest in nonhuman primates involved studying them as models for the development of human thought. In the 1920s and 1930s, several researchers raised primates at home to study their intellectual growth. Indeed, psychobiologist Robert Yerkes reared his children with chimpanzees as virtual siblings.

Studies of Primate Intelligence   There are now many well-documented studies of ape intelligence, but much remains anecdotal, based on observations made by a caretaker of a captive animal. Yerkes and his associates raised many chimpanzees (usually not as pseudohumans) and studied their behavior carefully. Unfortunately, studies of primate thought and language like these are hindered by the fact that upon reaching sexual maturity, nonhuman primates' behavior becomes more erratic and their strength prodigious. Thus, a great ape can be raised in a human environment only until about age 7 or 8, after which it becomes physically too risky, even though the animal has not reached its full intellectual potential.

One of the more famous (or infamous) stories about raising an ape as a human child involves a wealthy couple in the 1930s. Kenneth and Maria Hoyt, after having killed eight other gorillas in a hunting expedition, kept the ninth, an infant they named Toto, and raised her as a human baby. They succeeded in spoiling her completely and ended up with a moody brat that had the strength of twenty men. Upon reaching sexual maturity, Toto was given to the circus (Figure 6–8).

Nonhuman primates are extremely intelligent, at least by the criteria human primates use to judge them. In addition to Yerkes, pioneering studies by the Russian Nadya Kohts and the German Wolfgang Kohler established the impressive learning and problem-solving abilities of chimpanzees. Many later studies have expanded on their work. For example, confronted by a mirror, most nonprimates will react as if another member of their species were present but will ultimately become accustomed to the mirror image. Most apes, by contrast, react initially in a similar fashion but soon use the mirror image to examine themselves in places they can't ordinarily see. When a red spot is painted on their foreheads, they will use the mirror as a guide to touch the spot and often sniff their fingers after touching the spot. These apes *know* that the image is theirs. Other animals, including Old World monkeys, do not behave in this way.

Figure 6-8

As an adult, Toto still showed affection for her surrogate human mother.

speech

The production of linguistic sounds by the vocal apparatus.

language

Symbolic communication; characteristic of humans.

Studies of Primate Linguistics   Given that they are intelligent, why don't the apes talk to us? Early studies in the 1940s included one by Keith and Cathy Hayes, who raised a chimpanzee named Viki and tried to teach her to talk. After many months of repetition and of physically molding Viki's mouth to the appropriate shape for the sound desired, the Hayeses conceded to nature with Viki barely able to say "mama," "papa," "cup," and "up" (and even that is stretching it quite a bit, judging from the existing films of Viki).

In the 1960s, however, a revival of interest in primate linguistic capabilities began. Partly as a result of an emerging consciousness for the rights of the handicapped and an emerging technology for communication with deaf and mute people, primate language was approached from a new perspective. **Speech** and **language** are, after all, different. A parrot can speak but does not know what it is saying, and a mute has something to say but is physically unable to say it. Perhaps, it was now reasoned, the apes are unable to speak not for intellectual reasons, but simply because they have different vocal musculature and sound-production areas than humans. Given a nonvocal medium, perhaps they did have some sort of language capabilities.

This approach was taken in two directions by now-classic studies: American Sign Language, taught to Washoe and others by Allen and Beatrice Gardner; and computer symbols, taught to Lana and others by Duane Rumbaugh and Sue Savage-Rumbaugh. The chimps took to both media with astonishing ease, and it soon became clear that they were quite competent at describing their surroundings, expressing their feelings and desires, and grasping the rudiments of grammar, such as the distinction between subject and object (Figure 6–9).

The most carefully analyzed results have been those of Nim Chimpsky (punning on the name of linguist Noam Chomsky). Nim's signing never revealed the consistent ability to form sentences of more than two "words." This may suggest the limits of ape cognitive skills. On the other hand, Nim was reared under highly abnormal conditions (60 trainers over four years, preventing close bonds from forming), and the possibility has been raised that Nim was "retarded" on account of this deprivation.

Because the sign-language studies involved extensive interaction between chimps and humans, some doubts were subsequently raised about the interpretation of some of the anecdotal feats of Washoe. For example, when Washoe saw a swan for the first time and signed "water-bird," was she extending and combining concepts (water and bird) she already possessed in a new and creative way, or was she statically describing what she saw—water and a bird? Somewhat less ambiguous may be the sign language made by Koko the gorilla for Francine Patterson, which included calling a Pinocchio doll "elephant baby."

Figure 6-9
When taught by humans or by another chimp who has already been taught, apes can demonstrate some linguistic abilities using nonvocal media.

Nevertheless, these experiments have shown that chimpanzees and gorillas have some sort of cognitive capacities that include the ability to manipulate symbols in a linguistic fashion. They can use signs in ways similar to that in which humans use words. Indeed, a human child, on learning a new word, will often overapply it until learning its precise application. An ape child appears to learn in a similar fashion—when Koko was taught the sign for "drinking straw," she applied it to any long, thin objects she encountered, including a cigarette, a pen, a hose, and a car antenna.

Apes, however, have only been able to use symbolic systems devised by humans and do not, apparently, have the ability (or desire?) to generate their own symbolic systems of **communication**. It is also far from clear exactly what the relationship of these laboratory results might be to the life of apes in the forest. Washoe is now teaching her own offspring sign language.

Primate language studies, however, did not fulfill the expectations of early researchers. Underlying them was a naïve hope that once a chimp and a human could open a communications bridge, the conversations would be fascinating, opening the mind of an entirely different species. Perhaps they would sit down and explain themselves to us: "You know, old boy, it is exciting to be an ape. Would you like to hear about our social system? Or perhaps our foraging strategies?" Instead, the researchers heard such things as, "Come, gimme fruit. Tickle now."

communication

The transmission and reception of information.

Issues in Anthropology 6–2

Can You Trust a Chimpanzee?

We humans sometimes take a perverse pride in believing we are the only species capable of rational thought, and a behavioral consequence of rational thought is the possibility of rationally deceiving others. It is clear, however, that deception and manipulation of others is within the capabilities of chimpanzees—much as this may diminish them in our eyes from being the pure and innocent creatures we imagined.

In an experiment, some chimpanzees watched as food was hidden under a container. Each chimp learned quickly to point to the container with the food for a cooperative and sympathetic human who then shared the food with the chimps. But for a human who did not share, the chimps learned *not* to tell where the food was; and the oldest chimp learned to misinform the selfish human.

Jane Goodall cites several cases of deceptive behavior among the wild chimpanzees of Gombe. Sometimes a chimp will distract a dominant individual by grooming in order to acquire something that the dominant individual would keep it from getting. Most common, however, among the Gombe chimpanzee deceptions is "concealment of interest." Goodall cites the example of Figan, a young male, who was eating a dead colobus monkey. Surprisingly, his mother, Flo, who was an avid eater of flesh (for a chimpanzee), paid little attention. Flo did, however, move closer to Figan every few minutes, all the while grooming herself and appearing disinterested. Suddenly, Flo grabbed at the monkey carcass's tail to steal it from Figan; but Figan was ready and jumped away. Flo tried a few more times during the next hour, unsuccessfully.

A quarter of a century later, these are the kinds of things that the only species to ever have spoken to us have had to say. The apes appear to have complex emotional states, anxieties, and fears, but usually, they talk about lunch. On one hand, these studies have yielded fascinating results about the mental capabilities of the apes; but on the other hand, they have been frustrating. Further, virtually all these studies have tried to fit the nonhuman's communication into a human mold, and nearly nothing is known about whether, or how, humans can communicate like nonhuman primates.

Despite the information that has been forthcoming on linguistic potentials in captive apes, exceedingly little is known about their communication in the wild. Unlike humans, who communicate principally by auditory/vocal means, other primates make fuller use of tactile, olfactory, and visual systems of communication. Most prosimians demarcate their territories by secreting pheromones or by marking the spot with urine. Many cercopithecine monkeys communicate important social information through facial expressions. Because we lack a "dictionary," it is extraordinarily difficult to understand or interpret these signals. They highlight, however, the differences between the ways humans and other primates principally communicate.

This is not to say, however, that other primates do not communicate vocally. It has been known for several years that vervet monkeys

Goodall relates that when Figan matured, he became proficient at the technique of seizing meat after feigning disinterest.

Goodall also contrasts the behavior of a chimp named Evered with that of the crafty Figan in another context. Boxes were designed to open and reveal bananas after a chimp unscrewed a nut and bolt and released a handle. Evered, a quick learner, would unscrew the apparatus, excitedly release the handle, and then watch as the dominant adult males ate the bananas. Figan, changed the technique a bit: He performed all but the last operation and then sat and waited. When the dominant males left, he quietly released the handle and took the bananas himself.

Figan also learned to get more food for himself in a more directly deceitful manner. Goodall observed him, after other chimps had gotten bananas and he had not, to get up and lead his group away, presumably toward some food. A few minutes later, he simply snuck back and took some bananas himself. Having seen this more than once, Goodall concluded that this misdirection was intentional.

Finally, even sign language can be subverted by chimps to untruthful ends. After defecating in the living room, a signing chimpanzee named Lucy tried to convince a human (Roger Fouts) that she hadn't done it, accusing instead the humans, only admitting culpability afterward.

Reference:

Goodall, J. (1986). *The chimpanzees of Gombe.* Cambridge, MA: Harvard University Press.

---

give different alarm calls for ground predators (such as leopards), air predators (such as eagles), and snakes. When tape recordings of these calls were played to a group of vervets in the wild, they responded in patterned ways. To the leopard alarm, they ran into the trees. To the eagle alarm, they looked up or hid in the bushes. And to the snake alarm, they began to look down at the grass. It appears that the nonsymbolic mode of communication among these cercopithecines is complex, and we have barely begun to scratch its surface.

Studies of Primates and Tools   Another area of cognitive behavior that received a jolt from close studies of primates—this time in the wild—was the idea of humans as the only tool users. What Jane Goodall saw on 4 November 1960 was that a Gombe chimpanzee named David Greybeard would eat termites, which he obtained by fishing for them with a twig (that is, a **tool**) after first carefully selecting it and trimming its leaves for the purpose (modification). She later observed others doing the same thing. So not only did chimps *use* tools, they also *made* them—crude tools, to be sure, but tools by anyone's definition. Interestingly, some other chimpanzee groups have not been observed to do this, and it therefore appears to be a group-specific behavior.

Captive studies had shown that chimps could modify items in their environment to achieve an end, for example, stacking boxes to reach a reward located far above them. This required foresight, and the stacked

tool

Any part of the environment that is used to solve a particular problem.

Figure 6-10

Grooming is an important social interaction for primates such as these patas monkeys (*Erythrocebus patas*).

groom

Social interaction among primates involving close contact and manual or oral activity.

boxes could be considered as a makeshift stepladder, a tool. Yet termite fishing was the first evidence of nonhuman primates *in their native habitat* altering elements of their environment to achieve a goal. Goodall later observed the Gombe chimpanzees using leaves as we would use napkins or towels—sometimes to wipe a wound, to wipe off excrement, or to wipe off the tip of the penis after mating.

Nearly twenty species of anthropoids have been observed sporadically to use tools in many different ways, including throwing projectiles, hitting an intruder with a stick, smashing open nuts between two rocks, and using leaves as a sponge. Apes do this more frequently than monkeys. For example, when chimps and baboons competed for food left out by Goodall at Gombe, chimps would occasionally throw objects at the baboons to drive them away, but the baboons never did it to the chimps.

Three principal contexts in which primates have been observed to use tools, as the previous discussion indicates, are: 1) in the acquisition of food; 2) when threatened or threatening another; and 3) in bodily care.

Thus, the behavior of nonhuman primates allows us to test a hypothesis about the evolution of human behavior—was the ability to make and use tools the key factor in becoming human? The answer must be *no*: The ability to make and to use tools is present in our relatives and, therefore, by inference in our common ancestors. It seems, rather, to have been a combination of the ability to use tools with a unique body that did not have to occupy its hands in locomotion that enabled humans to develop and rely on material culture to the extent that they have.

SOCIAL BEHAVIOR

The life of a nonhuman primate is structured by complex social relationships still understood only in their rudiments.

Grooming   **Grooming** is perhaps the most important activity in primate society (Figure 6–10). It involves close attention and touching, parting the fur, and removing particles if any are found (often, none are). It seems that in addition to playing a practical utilitarian role, grooming is the way in which primates establish and maintain their relationships with one another.

Some species tend to groom relatives preferentially, and others tend to groom nonrelatives of the opposite sex preferentially. Other patterns are more subtle. For example, in macaques, a daughter will groom its mother more frequently than a son will, but chimpanzees do it equally. Lemurs and lorises use their tooth-combs for grooming, while other primates groom manually. Grooming behavior can relieve an otherwise aggressive encounter, can reassure a frightened infant, or can establish bonds of association among nonrelatives and potential mates.

Many other interactions among nonhuman primates are also quite complex, and most involve a number of different kinds of behaviors in addition to grooming, some of which involve vocalizations, some of which are visual or olfactory, and others of which are simply tactile. Primate societies, especially the well-studied baboons, are now known to be very complex and involve intricate decisions on the part of the baboons—decisions about when to display a threat, how to establish alliances, when to transfer into a new group, how to make friends in a new group, and most importantly, how to survive and procreate, which is only possible in a social context.

Primate Social Systems   The composition of a primate group can be described by four variables: age, sex, kinship, and **dominance**. In general, there are infants, subadults, and adults; males and females; relatives and nonrelatives; and high-ranking and low-ranking. A primate who is consistently able to displace another primate in an aggressive (or merely direct) encounter is said to be dominant, and dominant animals are defined as the higher ranking in the hierarchy. Alternatively, a primate to whom another individual exhibits submissive signals (such as avoiding eye contact, or crouching) can be regarded as dominant. Dominance can be achieved by frightening or defeating another individual. For example, among the Gombe chimpanzees, one named Mike achieved dominance by banging empty kerosene cans together and frightening off other males.

Such encounters are sometimes aggressive and may result in a stare-down or even a death. In some primate societies, a dominant animal appears to have preferential access to resources, food and sexual partners principal among them.   But often they do not—a primate who can displace another with a look may not be able to take food away because of the other primate's friends and relatives. And the first primate usually knows it. Thus, primate societies are not without their checks and balances, and they are not at all the savage societies like those envisioned by Thomas Hobbes (Chapter 3). Rather, they involve intelligence, foresight, and decision-making strategies on the part of the animals.

For example, there appear to be three clear-cut ways in which a male savanna baboon can have a good shot at reproduction. (In many primate societies, savanna baboons among them, it is difficult to know who the father of an offspring is since several males copulate with a fertile female. We discuss the evolutionary consequences of this below.) First, he can fight his way to the top in the expectation of gaining preferential access to the females. This is extremely risky, however. Second, he can form alliances with other male baboons to ward off attacks by dominant individuals and so have access to fertile females. Or third, as documented at length by Barbara Smuts of the University of Michigan, he may "make friends" with a particular female and establish a long-term bond with her. When she becomes fertile, he will often have preferential sexual access to her.

Not all primates are baboons, however. Primate social behavior is quite variable across species. Still, we can find a number of generaliza-

dominance

Social relationship among primates, often measured by the ability of one individual to displace another, though not necessarily through an aggressive confrontation.

tions. For example, primate social interactions are regulated in several ways. The dominance hierarchy, in which each individual knows its place, is one—although many primate species lack a dominance hierarchy. Grooming behavior (which all primates have) is a second. A third involves the transfer of a primate away from its natal group (the one into which it was born). Thus, a primate must learn how to adjust to new neighbors, both as an immigrant and as a resident. And the regularity of group transfer makes it a common safety valve in times of conflict. The fourth general mediator of social interactions is the prevalence of threat displays, which communicate to other members of the group the possibility of aggression by the actor. Such displays, while broadly common among the primates, vary considerably in detail (Figure 6–11). A prosimian, *Lemur catta*, waves its conspicuous tail (it is known as the ring-tailed lemur) after daubing it with pheromones—the signal is both visual and olfactory. A male squirrel monkey (*Saimiri sciureus*) accomplishes the same end by displaying its erect penis. A baboon does it by yawning to show its large canine teeth or by flashing its eyebrows. And a gorilla does it by adopting a bipedal stance and pounding on its chest.

PRIMATES IN GROUPS

Primate groups are highly variable in size, from the usually solitary orang-utan to the scores of baboons that may compose a troop. Most primates live in groups of small or large size. Members of few species exist alone, like the orang-utan. Why do they bother to be social? Why should primates live in groups at all? There appear to be four factors that lead to the formation of groups.

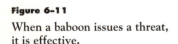

Figure 6-11

When a baboon issues a threat, it is effective.

First is *access to resources*. If food is evenly distributed throughout the environment, then small groups and loners can cope easily. If, however, food is to be found only in certain places, then being a member of a group is a great advantage, for it enables one primate to benefit from the foraging of others and facilitates protection of the resource, if need be. Second is *protection*, a particular necessity if one considers the predators that roam the savannas. The average primate is not much of a contest for the average leopard, but a group of baboons is generally too much for a leopard to handle. Third is *assistance in parenting*—a primate mother with slow-growing offspring may often need others to assist in protecting and raising the infant. And last, living in groups is probably the easiest way to ensure that an organism has *access to sexual partners*—a solitary species must have other social mechanisms of bringing males and females together at appropriate times if they don't ordinarily live together. And this would lead to competition for mates, a feature of primates who live in large groups.

Only a few species lack the social gregariousness so common among primates. The orang-utan is the only such anthropoid—the other species are nocturnal prosimians. The causes of such solitary behavior among these few primates are not completely understood, and it is possible that each has a unique explanation. For example, some of the solitary nocturnal prosimians are primarily insectivores, and it is possible that the favored prey are most easily caught by individuals acting alone and that capturing prey may be disturbed by the presence of larger groups. Whatever the explanations, these nongregarious primates serve to highlight the breadth of adaptations and the diversity of social systems that exist among the primates.

A few primates, such as the gibbons and some of the smaller New World monkeys, are **monogamous**. Again, the causes are not well understood but appear to be different in each case. Gibbon monogamy involves the establishment of defensible territories by females and high rates of aggression against other females. Among some of the smaller New World monkeys, it appears as though the infant is such a large fraction of the mother's weight at birth that she requires a resident male to care for it.

Most primates, however, live in single-male or multi-male groups—one or several males with two to more than twenty females and their offspring (Figure 6–12). What determines the size of the social group? In general, the same three factors that determine solitary versus group living also determine whether one lives in a small or a large group—distribution of food, defensibility of resources, and predator pressure. Additionally, a number of correlations suggest other factors in determining group size.

For example, terrestrial primates tend to live in larger groups than do arboreal primates, probably because of ground predators. Frugivores tend to live in larger groups than do folivores, probably because of the

Figure 6–12

Primates generally live in social groups.

monogamy

Social system in which one male and one female associate exclusively; technically, the term means "one marriage," and should contrast with "polygamy," but is generally used in primatology to contrast with polygyny (several females) and polyandry (several males).

diurnal
Active during the day.

nocturnal
Active during the night.

less even distribution of fruit than of foliage. **Diurnal** primates tend to live in larger groups than do **nocturnal** primates, perhaps again because of predators. But also, large-bodied primates tend to live in larger groups than do small-bodied primates, and primates that have a large home range tend to live in larger groups than do primates with a small home range. Many of these correlations, it must be appreciated, are loose and may often conflict across species, making predictions about group size almost impossible. We could probably not know without directly studying them that the folivorous but larger-bodied gorilla lives in smaller groups than does the frugivorous but smaller-bodied chimpanzee.

These correlations may also be the result of other, common factors. Thus, arboreal primates, which tend to live in smaller groups than do their close terrestrial relatives, have a number of other adaptations that relate to their tree-dwelling mode of life. They tend to be smaller (trees being less sturdy than the ground), they tend to communicate by calling (it being easier to hear than to see another primate up in the trees), and they tend to be nocturnal.

THE DIVERSITY OF PRIMATE SOCIAL BEHAVIOR

Sifakas: A Prosimian Matriarchy   Sifakas (genus *Propithecus*) are large prosimians who live on Madagascar (Figure 6–13) and who have been studied in detail by Alison Richard of Yale University. They are diurnal and generally do not move around or socialize much. They move by leaping and subsist on an eclectic diet of fruit, flowers, leaves, and bark. Sifakas live in groups averaging about five individuals, and when food is at stake, a dominance hierarchy emerges. As expected, immature individuals will give way to mature individuals, but in stark contrast to the situation in baboons, a male sifaka will give way to a female sifaka.

Males transfer out of their natal groups, but a female will generally spend her entire life in one group. In the dry forests of southern Madagascar, *Propithecus* territories do not overlap much, and sifakas defend their territories by leaping back and forth across common boundaries instead of by fighting. In northern Madagascar, where the population density is higher because of a wetter forest, home ranges overlap, and defending them consistently would be futile. Interactions in these circumstances are variable, ranging from ignoring the other group to actually fighting it.

Sifakas do not fight much, though, or exhibit much in the way of overt aggression except during the mating season (a few days in January or February). At that time, male sifakas leave their own groups to try to mate with receptive females in other groups. These attempts lead to fights with resident males. If the visitor loses, he will return to his own group, but a winner has options—he may stay in the new group (if his status and rank was low in the old group, this is a good choice for him), or he may return to his old group. Sometimes, however, there is no fight

Figure 6–13
A sifaka.

Figure 6-14
Howler monkeys.

at all. The visiting male mates with the female with no interference from the rest of her group. Perhaps this variation reflects social networks larger than simply the troop.

Howler Monkeys of the New World   Howlers (genus *Alouatta*) are among the largest of the New World primates, and several species occupy the forests of Central and South America. Howler monkeys derive their name from their vocalizations. They have an enlarged hyoid bone of their throat, which enables their voices to resonate impressively and be heard over long distances (Figure 6–14).

A social group consists of usually ten to fifteen individuals, with one to three adult males and two to seven adult females. These groups, however, are rather fluid because both males and females transfer from group to group. Some females stay and breed in their natal groups, but most do not. They either enter another troop (and are resisted by the females there), or, more commonly, they start a new troop with other males and females. Males have a relatively short tenure as adults in a given troop and may often alternate between group membership and a solitary peripheral existence.

Males dominate females among howlers. Not only are males somewhat larger than females, but in some species, they are also different colors. The significance of this **sexual dichromatism** is not known, but a few other primate species are characterized by it, notably some species of lemurs and gibbons, which are also highly vocal arboreal animals. Howlers howl early in the morning, often males howling alone, but sometimes entire troops howling. They also howl upon encountering strangers or neighboring troops.

Uncharacteristically for primates, howlers do not do a lot of grooming, spending an average of less than 2 percent of their time at it and

sexual dichromatism

Males and females of the same species being differently colored.

having each grooming bout last only about a minute. Usually, adult females groom their offspring or adult males.

Howlers eat principally fruit and leaves, preferring figs to other foods. Although they have been studied since the 1930s on Barro Colorado Island, off Panama, significant differences appear to exist between howler populations in different areas of South America. For example, while the supplanting of a resident male by an outsider is a generally peaceful process among howlers in Costa Rica, it can be accompanied by fierce fights among Venezuelan howlers.

The flexibility of howler monkey society has been tracked over time on Barro Colorado. In the 1960s, a population increase, which led to higher population densities, ultimately resulted in smaller group size, smaller territories for those groups, and more exclusive use of those territories. Previously, group ranges had overlapped. This serves to emphasize that primate social behavior is sensitive not only to the environment, but to the demography of the population as well—the same population in the same place may well behave differently under different densities of population. If we then begin to consider variation in behavior due to environmental and seasonal differences, describing the behavior of any species comprehensively seems a daunting prospect. The best we can ever hope for is an adequate *sample* of the group's behavior.

Gorillas: The Largest Living Primates   Gorillas are among our closest relatives, but among the least studied of all primates when it comes to group behavior. They are highly endangered (a total of fewer than 40,000 exist, most belonging to only one of the three subspecies) and are restricted to the highlands and lowlands of central and western Africa, although they have only two natural predators. These predators are leopards and humans, and it is the latter who are driving gorillas to the brink of extinction (Figure 6–15).

Gorillas are almost exclusively folivorous, rarely supplementing their diverse roots, stems, and leaves with insects or fruit. They live in the forest in groups that typically consist of an adult dominant male, some younger males, adult females and young. The older, dominant male is easily distinguished by a saddle-shaped grey area on his back—he is known as the "silverback." Silverbacks have priority of access to fertile females in the group, but overt sexual activity among gorillas is surprisingly rare. A silverback may remain in his position of authority for as long as ten years.

Gorillas travel less than 1 kilometer per day and do not defend territories, which they freely share with other groups. At night, they carefully make nests of branches and leaves to sleep on. Males become sexually mature at about 15 years of age, and females at about 10 years of age. Adult males are nearly twice the size of females and have larger facial muscles and canine teeth. Grooming occupies much of their behavior, but there are few clear trends in who grooms whom—it varies from group to group.

Figure 6-15
Gorillas

Females usually transfer from their natal group, often more than once. Males leave their groups less frequently but do not transfer into another group. Rather, they become solitary after they leave. Juveniles in a gorilla group are strongly bonded to the silverback, who treats them with little more than disaffected tolerance, except during threatening situations, when he shields them. He also breaks up fights between group members by intervening on behalf of the younger combatant.

Aggressive interactions are rare among gorillas within the group and usually take the form of vocalization rather than action. This makes it difficult to detect dominance relationships among the females. The males, on the other hand, have to defend the group, and especially the females, from solitary silverbacks. These solitary males will occasionally try to take over a group by attacking, sometimes killing an infant and leaving with the infant's mother (or any female who will join him)—thus forming his own group.

THE SEX LIFE OF PRIMATES

Most primates know when the females of their species are ovulating. This is because of **estrus**, a period of sexual activity on the part of females in which they solicit (proceptivity) and accept (receptivity) sexual attention. For most prosimians and New World monkeys, females are sexually receptive only during a restricted breeding season, and in many primate species, the testicles of the males are functional only during these periods.

In apes, humans, and most Old World monkeys, the period of fertility is cyclical and includes a periodic discard of the lining of the uterus, the menstrual cycle. Menstruation is characteristic of the Catarrhini, and

estrus

Period of behavioral, olfactory, and sometimes visual changes in females, during which they may solicit sexual activity or be more responsive to males.

occasional observations of small amounts of vaginal blood in New World monkeys have been reported. The estrus cycle is more flexible in hominoids, with the time of peak receptivity generally lengthened. Captivity changes hormonal levels in primates and tends to introduce changes into the estrus cycle, which makes the observations of sexual behavior in captive primates difficult to evaluate.

Humans appear to be unique among primates in lacking a cycle of peak times for sexual activity, though obviously maintaining a cycle of fertility. While most hominoid primates lack an obvious sexual swelling (see below), significant changes in the behavior of females promote sexual activity at certain times. The reasons for the lack of such temporal variation in the sexual receptivity of human females are not well understood.

Sexual Cues   Sexual cues in primates are both visual and olfactory. Most primate males initiate sexual activity by touching and smelling the vaginal secretions of their prospective partners. In many species, there are subtle morphological changes in the female genitalia, for example, a slight swelling or a darkening in color, at the time of sexual receptivity. In some species, however, female receptivity is signaled visually by a great swelling of the tissues around the genitalia, which develop into a striking reddish or purple sexual skin or *sexual swelling* (Figure 6–16). Interestingly, the species in which this morphological feature is present (some colobines, some cercopithecines, and chimpanzees) all have a common social feature as well—a multi-male breeding system.

In the savanna baboons, the sexual swelling will rise gradually over the course of two to three weeks, during which time the female will mate with juvenile and subadult males. It reaches its maximum size just before ovulation, at which time there is strong competition among the adult males to form an exclusive bond with the female for the next few days. Females, however, are not altogether passive, and they have apparent preferences for the particular adult with which they pair off.

A contrasting pattern has frequently been observed in chimpanzees, although the behavior of chimpanzee females varies considerably. Jane Goodall described the estrus she observed in a female named Flo at the Gombe Stream Reserve:

Figure 6-16

(a) An estrus swelling on a female baboon; (b) a male begins to take sexual interest in a female.

Flo crouched to the ground, presenting Goliath with her pink posterior, and he mated with her in the typical nonchalant manner of the chimpanzee, squatting in an upright position, one fruit-laden hand laid tightly on Flo's back and the other resting on the ground beside him.

Chimpanzees have the briefest possible intercourse—normally the male remains mounted for only ten to fifteen seconds. . . .

The next day Flo arrived very early in the morning. Her suitors of the previous day [Goliath and David Graybeard] were with her; once again they courted and mated before eating their bananas. . . . And then, from the corner of his eye, Hugo [van Lawick] saw another black shape in the bushes. As we peered we saw another, and another, and another. . . . Almost immediately I recognized. . . . just about all the adult males I knew. And there were some adolescents, females, and youngsters in the group as well.

We remained inside the tent. Soon Flo moved up into the bushes and there was mated by every male in turn. . . .

For the next week Flo was followed everywhere by her large male retinue. It was impossible for her to sit up or lie down without several pairs of eyes instantly swiveling in her direction, and if she got up to move on, the males were on their feet in no time. Every time there was any sort of excitement in the group—when they arrived at a food source, when they left their nests in the morning, when other chimps joined them—then, one after the other, all the adult males mated Flo. We saw no fighting over this very popular female; each male simply took his turn. Only once, when David Graybeard was mating Flo, did one of the other males show signs of impatience: irascible J. B. started to leap up and down as he swayed a large low branch so that the end beat down on David's head. But David merely pressed himself close to Flo and closed his eyes—and J. B. did not attack him. . . .

On the eighth day of her swelling Flo arrived in camp with a torn and bleeding bottom. The injury must have just occurred. Within another couple of hours her swelling had gone. She looked somewhat tattered and exhausted by then and we were relieved for her sake that everything was over. At least we thought it was over, for normally a swelling only lasts about ten days. But five days later, to our utter astonishment Flo was fully pink again. She arrived, as before, with a large following of attendant males. This time her swelling lasted for three consecutive weeks, during which time the ardor of her suitors did not appear to abate in any way.

agonistic buffer

Using another individual to de-escalate an aggressive encounter.

Why would something as odd as sexual swellings evolve, and why would it do so repeatedly in species sharing social similarities? Anthropologist Sarah Blaffer Hrdy has argued that this announcement of fertility and concomitant mass mating has the principal effect of confusing paternity in these species. If the offspring in a troop might belong to any given male, then males might generally be expected to tolerate and protect all of them, indeed to treat them better than if the offspring were known to belong to someone else. And given the volatility of dominance relationships and the slow development and maturation of a chimpanzee, it would certainly be advantageous to the child to be tolerated by all the adult males in a group.

This hypothesis can be supported by two lines of evidence. First, in baboons, aggression between males is often abated by **agonistic buffering**, in which one of the males shields himself physically with an infant. Adult males are strongly disinclined to attack infants from their own troop. Second, in langur monkeys, where troops are occasionally taken over by males from the outside, a successful invader will sometimes kill infants in the troop. In the first case, there is the possibility that the aggressor is the father of the infant, and so he will not attack—in the second case, there is no such possibility.

Most primates, however, do not mate with such abandon. Indeed, the females in some multi-male groups do not have obvious sexual swellings. Among the hominoids, the chimpanzees appear to be unique in this advertisement for sexual activity and subsequent promiscuity. Gibbons, orangs, and gorillas are much more reserved, and females show no obvious signs of estrus. Gibbons, in fact, are monogamously pair-bonded for life and live in nuclear family social groups. Actual matings of gibbons or of gorillas in the wild have rarely been observed.

Orang-utan sexual behavior has some interesting and poorly understood aspects. These large, arboreal apes travel through the forests of Borneo and Sumatra, most frequently alone. Copulation is rare, and when a female and male encounter each other, she usually avoids or ignores him. For his part, the male either ignores her or follows her around. Sometimes, a female will permit an adult male to travel with her for several days as a consort, during which they may mate a few times. This relationship may recur over a period of months. However, a subadult male encountering an adult female may try to mate with her against her will. Such forced copulations by subadult males will often be terminated by the arrival of an adult male. Though the female actively resists, she is rarely successful. These matings, though, do not appear to have a reproductive impact, as the female is probably not fertile when they occur.

Sexual Selection   Multi-male breeding systems, such as those of the chimpanzee and savanna baboon, have another interesting side effect on the biology of the species. Given a situation in which several males can mate with the same fertile female, what determines which male's genes will be represented in the next generation?   The answer seems to be that dominant males will tend to have greater access to fertile females. And the achievement of dominance is to some extent the result of large body size and fighting ability.

Therefore, in such a breeding system, there will tend to be competition among males for mates, with large body size and fighting ability favored. This is what Charles Darwin called **sexual selection**—evolutionary pressure placed on one sex but not on the other. The result of this selection is *sexual dimorphism*, a morphological divergence between the sexes, such as we find in body size and canine teeth among baboons and chimpanzees. In monogamous primates, such as the gibbons, such competition for mates is largely absent, and we find both sexes to be similar in both their overall size and in their canine teeth.

Many other factors are involved in sexual selection, however, and sexual dimorphism can apparently develop under somewhat different circumstances than those just described. One important complicating factor, for example, is the fact that the female is not passive and may take an active role in choosing a sexual partner. While this is apparently not often the case in the more promiscuous primate females, such as Flo the chimpanzee, it appears to be a factor in the gorillas and orangs, which are also highly sexually dimorphic, though with different breeding systems.

sexual selection
Differential, nonrandom reproduction among individuals of the same sex.

Models for Human Evolution

The study of primate behavior has afforded opportunities to model human evolution on the behavior of select species, each for a particular reason. Two principal ways of modeling human behavior on that of nonhuman primate behavior are by evolutionary analogy and by evolutionary homology. The first approach uses the concept of parallel evolution, or homoplasy (discussed in Chapter 10). Because similar evolutionary pressures may stimulate different taxa to evolve in similar ways, it is reasoned that nonhuman primates that have ecological similarities to early hominids may give us insight into the evolution of human behavior; after all, humans had to adapt in a similar fashion. The second approach uses evolutionary homology, a shared common ancestry, to model the ancestral hominid social behavior. Both these approaches also have what can be termed narrow and broad applications, depending on whether they are based on a comparison to only one or several species.

EVOLUTIONARY ANALOGY

The argument by ecological parallel, or evolutionary analogy, was formulated in its narrow application with reference to *Papio cynocephalus*, the savanna baboon. The baboon model, popular in the 1950s and 1960s, was based on an ecological parallel in baboon and human evolution. Baboons have become adapted to terrestrial life on the savanna in the past few million years, although their ancestors (and closest relatives) were strictly forest dwellers. This sounded familiar to researchers—it is a capsule view of hominid evolution, too (Chapter 11). Perhaps, therefore, baboon social behavior is an ecological adaptation to similar pressures faced by early hominids, and if so, perhaps hominids evolved socially in similar ways.

And perhaps, it was reasoned in the 1950s, there may be significant parallels. Baboons have a rigid dominance hierarchy. Males are larger, more aggressive, and dominant over females. According to this model, this aggression was adaptive for the troop, and it was used and controlled in the context of a central male hierarchy. The most aggressive, dominant males got to reproduce preferentially. And further, as baboons were not observed to hunt, hunting was taken as a uniquely human attribute, indeed perhaps *the* attribute that distinguished hominid savanna social behavior from baboon savanna social behavior.

More fieldwork, however, has destroyed the edifice of the baboon analogy to human evolution. The model seems to have been as much a product of its times and values as it was of what baboons really do. We now know, for example, that the male hierarchy is real but ephemeral. Since a male baboon transfers out of his natal group and often transfers repeatedly, the hierarchical position he occupies at any time is very flexible and unstable. Since females do not transfer but remain in the same troop their entire lives, it is they who give the baboon society its stable core, and it is the *female* dominance relationships that are pervasive, long-lasting, and most significant in baboon society. We also know that baboons do hunt: A troop of yellow baboons (*Papio cynocephalus anubis*) at Gilgil, studied by Shirley Strum, found itself in an ecological situation with much game and few predators, and, being smart, adaptable primates, they took the chance they had and began to augment their diet with meat.

Further, they often cooperated through coordinated relay chases— one baboon would chase the prey, and then another would pick up the chase until the prey was tired out.

Finally, it appears that aggression is not the key to reproductive success in baboons, either. Females tend to mate preferentially with long-term residents, not with the most aggressive male. As discussed earlier, many social strategies are open to a baboon, of which individual aggression is but one, and the riskiest. Although new males in a troop are often aggressively dominant, older residents tend to receive preferential access to resources and estrous females. Thus, the baboon model probably tells us more about the way our culture saw the world in the 1950s than it tells us about either baboons or humans.

The broad perspective of ecological analogy asks a different sort of question. Rather than asking, "What single species can we compare to humans?" it asks, "Under what ecological circumstances has a certain behavior evolved in different species, and when those circumstances are found in humans, does the behavior appear?" That is, it focuses on a specific behavior, not on a particular species—and importantly, it recognizes the variability in human behavior and attempts to account for the variations.

For example, the combination of monogamous mating systems (one male and one female) and **neolocal** residence occurs among some humans and in some primate species (about 12 percent of the latter). This system is consequently one in which the **nuclear family** is the social unit rather than the **extended family**, or larger group. Primatologist Warren Kinzey has argued that the nuclear family social unit in nonhuman primates is an adaptation to dispersed, uneven resources, which require defense. In human societies, where the nuclear family is often more significant than the extended family (especially among gatherer-hunters and Western industrial societies), Kinzey argues that sociocultural adaptations parallel those in nonhuman primates. These are, perhaps, similar adaptive social responses to similar ecological circumstances.

EVOLUTIONARY HOMOLOGY

The argument from homology takes a different approach. A narrow version of this argument, popular in the 1970s and 1980s, is the chimpanzee model of human evolution. Here, instead of arguing from ecological analogy, the argument is from phylogeny: Chimpanzees are our close relatives; therefore, their behavior stands in a special evolutionary relationship to our own. The model is based not on the assumption of analogy, but on homology.

The underlying assumption of this model, however, is that chimpanzee social behavior is primitive and, therefore, represents the primitive state of human behavior as well. Comparative research, however, shows that chimp social behavior is probably highly derived and, as such, not a good ancestral model. For example, the prominent female estrus display and concomitant sexual behaviors are present in chimpanzees, but not in any other hominoid primate. This suggests that it may be a recent development unique to the chimpanzee lineage and of little or no significance in modeling the evolution of human behavior. Indeed, it is an interesting coincidence that two of the best-studied nonhuman primates, chimpanzees and savanna baboons, both have prominent sexual swellings—it is likely a biological adaptation to the social patterns they share, multi-male breeding systems.

The argument from evolutionary homology hinges strongly on the distinction between ancestral and derived characteristics. If we wish to reason backwards from the behavior of a living nonhuman primate to that of prehistoric humans, we must find characters in the nonhuman primate that are ancestral for the **clade**. Ancestral characters are more likely to be found in several species than in only one. Therefore, behavioral characters unique to chimpanzees are likely to be derived characters and not useful for phylogenetic reconstruction.

The argument from homology will require examining behavioral characters shared by more than one of our close relatives. For example, behaviors shared by both chimps and gorillas are more likely to be good ancestors for the human condition than are behaviors possessed by only

neolocal

Residence pattern whereby a husband, wife, and any dependent offspring live together but not with either spouse's family; contrasted with matrilocal (living with the wife's family) and patrilocal (living with the husband's family).

nuclear family

Small group of related individuals, generally encompassing two generations: parents and dependent children.

extended family

Larger group of related individuals, generally encompassing more than two generations and more distant relatives.

clade

A group of closely related species, defined by the presence of synapomorphies and including all the species that have the synapomorphies; the Hominoidea form a clade, but the "great apes" do not (because they omit humans).

one of the species. But the social behaviors of these species are very different. A broad version of the argument from homology would have to be based on few traits shared by more species.

Primatologist Richard Wrangham has analyzed the social behavior of chimps and gorillas in this way to suggest ancestral characters that might be appropriate for consideration as primitive for humans as well. He finds that, in contrast to the baboons, where females stay in the troop and males transfer, in both gorillas and chimps, females *do* transfer, which suggests that this might be a characteristic of early hominids. Further, in both chimps and gorillas, hostilities often occur between groups that encounter one another, and it is males that take the lead in hostile intergroup encounters. Interestingly, in many Old World monkeys, when aggression occurs between social groups, females often play a strong participatory role, unlike chimpanzees and gorillas. And finally, in both chimps and gorillas, a male will tend to have a sexual relationship with more than one female at the same time. In chimps, the reverse is also true—a female will mate with several males at the same time. This is not the case with gorillas, where generally, a female mates with only the dominant silverback.

The result is a series of hypotheses about the social behavior of early hominids, based on phylogenetic reasoning rather than simple modeling after a single species. These hypotheses, of course, have yet to be satisfactorily tested, but they demonstrate the ways in which we can use modern primates to construct strong hypotheses about the ancestry of human behavior.

Summary

The dichotomy of "human versus animal" has greater symbolic importance than biological importance. Biologically, humans have a large and interesting set of autapomorphies; but focusing on them alone would present a very narrow view of the historical connections among living primate species.

We study the behavior of nonhuman primates to learn about the evolutionary roots of human behavior, although the behavioral diversity of nonhuman primates and within the human species makes it difficult to arrive at inferences about precursors. Nevertheless, detailed observations coupled with theoretical advances are currently enabling us to test new and interesting hypotheses about the evolution of human behavior.

1. To what extent is the study of nonhuman primate behavior relevant to understanding our own behavior? What kinds of human behaviors can be illuminated by primate studies?

2. What are the advantages and disadvantages of using ecological analogies versus phylogenetic homologies in reasoning from nonhuman primate societies to human behavior?

3. How are human diets different from the diets of nonhuman primates? How do these differences relate to aspects of human social behavior?

4. Why do anthropologists no longer maintain that human males are naturally aggressive and dominant to females?

Jolly, A. (1985). *The evolution of primate behavior*, (2d ed). New York: Macmillan.

Kinzey, W. (Ed.). (1987). *The evolution of human behavior: Primate models*. Albany, NY: SUNY Press.

Richard, A. (1985). *Primates in nature*. San Francisco, CA: W. H. Freeman.

Smuts, B., Cheney, D., Seyfarth, R., Wrangham, R., & Struhsaker, T. (Eds.). (1986). *Primate societies*. Chicago, IL: University of Chicago Press.

The Processes of Evolution: Synchronic Studies

CHAPTER 7

The Generation of Biological Diversity

The Generation of Biological Diversity

We have seen in previous chapters some of the results of evolution, the diversity of primate species. Now we examine evolution mechanistically to learn not what *has* happened, but *how* it happens and has happened. The two approaches are complementary in physical anthropology: We can study variety and its history (evolutionary products) or the mechanisms that produce it (evolutionary processes). The products of evolution are new and different species with unique adaptations, many of which we have already surveyed. The processes of evolution are studied within the field of genetics.

The study of genetic evolution centers around the resolution of a theoretical conflict between the fundamentally conservative nature of heredity and the processes of change that constitute evolution. Two questions to be kept in mind while reading this chapter are "How are similarities perpetuated across generations?" and "How are stable changes generated?"

The Gene Pool

Biological evolution subsumes any change in the hereditary composition of populations. The hereditary composition of any population is called its gene pool. We cannot hold or see the gene pool: It is the hypothetical summation of all the hereditary information—all the genes—in a population. It is, therefore, not a tangible entity. We can, however, infer certain properties of the gene pool: We can sample it statistically, and we can describe its composition.

If we are interested in the diversity and adaptations of organisms, why do we study genes and gene pools? Because the presence and range of expression of any character in an organism is set by its genes. While we may be interested in the phenomena of bipedalism and cranial expansion that characterize hominids, these are actually manifestations of changes in the genes of hominid populations. We do not know precisely which genes or precisely what the genetic changes were, but it is certain that genetic changes are at the root of these unique hominid specializations. Genes control, or set the range of expression of, every biological function in our bodies, from cell division, to the digestive chemical reactions in our stomachs, to the likelihood of our contracting cancer.

It is important to keep in mind that often what the genes do is establish a normal range of expression, the specific value of which is determined by other factors. Thus, the genes determine that a normal

Figure 7–1

Range of heights for a sample of college students (women). Some are taller than average, and some are shorter than average, but all are "normal."

American will ordinarily achieve a height of, say, between 5 feet and 6 ½ feet (Figure 7–1). Whether a particular person grows to 5 feet 3 inches or 6 feet 3 inches will depend on other things, such as whether male or female hormones are secreted during adolescence and the person's nutritional status. Furthermore, tall parents tend to have tall children, and there exists a set of cryptic genetic factors (perhaps an entirely different set of genes) that affects the specific height any person will achieve. Some changes can lead to dwarfism or gigantism, taking a person outside the normal range of variation for human height (Figure 7–2), but these are rare and pathological.

CHANGES IN THE GENE POOL

Changes in the gene pool, which are changes in the genetic constitution of a population, can be of two kinds. The first kind of genetic change accumulates over time and often makes the organisms composing the population better adapted to their environment. Or, these changes may have no effect at all on the organisms. In either case, their net effect is to make the gene pool of a species at one time different from the gene pool of the same species at a different time. The process of gradual change in the gene pool through time is called anagenesis and is especially important in the study of microevolution. The second kind of genetic change can make a population reproductively incompatible with other populations of the same species. This incompatibility leads to the splitting of one species into two, or cladogenesis, as we noted in Chapter 4.

Neither anagenesis nor cladogenesis is exclusively associated with anatomical changes in organisms because it is the gene pool, and not necessarily the anatomy, that is changing in both situations. Cladogenesis may occur in the absence of any anatomical modification, as in sibling species that may be identical to the eye but genetically disjunct from one another. Or, profound anatomical changes may occur in the absence of species formation, as in the cases of extreme polymorphism or polytypy (Chapters 8 and 9), widely known in many species.

Figure 7–2

Robert Wadlow, the Alton giant, stood 8½ feet tall in 1937, at age 19.

Genes

Evolution is any change in the gene pool. The gene pool is a summation of all the genes in a population. What, however, are we referring to by the word "gene?" A *gene* is the fundamental unit of heredity. It is a unit of information passed down intact across generations.

THE NATURE OF GENES

The intact nature of genetic units is the key to the rules of inheritance formalized by Gregor Mendel, based on his experiments with peas in the 1850s and 1860s. What Mendel's followers developed in the 1900s, especially William Bateson in England and Thomas Hunt Morgan in the United States, was a *particulate* theory of inheritance, in contrast to *blending* theories. A blending theory of inheritance is one that hypothesizes that the process of heredity is similar to the mixing of fluids of different colors: if you mix a red liquid with a yellow liquid, you obtain something intermediate—an orange liquid. The red and yellow components can no longer be recovered because they have been modified by each other's presence to generate the orange result. Thus, it was supposed that a child was the mixture of its parents and intermediate between them in its outward aspects (Figure 7–3).

Of course, it was known that many features run in families and are not blended away, but recur generation after generation. An early example is polydactyly (extra digits), tracked through four generations by Maupertuis in the 1740s. Nevertheless, it was observed as well that quite often, features such as skin color will indeed be inherited in a blended fashion. But the commonsense inference of a blending *mechanism* from a blending *pattern* is incorrect. While some characters appear to blend in the offspring of parents who differ noticeably, the reason they do so is not that they physically intermingle. Instead, the genes for such characters occur in different *combinations* in different individual organisms (see

Figure 7-3

According to the theory of blending inheritance, a child is midway between its parents in its characteristics. But this mechanism cannot account for traits that "run in families" and are consequently transmitted only by one parent. Thus, the observation of a blending *pattern* does not imply a blending *mechanism* of inheritance.

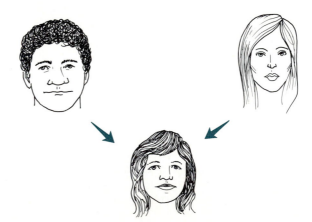

below). The genes retain their individuality completely intact across generational lines. Genes are like particles, not like fluids: this is the essence of Mendelism.

THE FUNCTION OF GENES

Hereditary instructions are encoded and retrieved in identical ways by the genetic systems of all unicellular and multicellular creatures: Bacteria, sponges, house plants, turtles, daffodils, sea urchins, orangutans, and human beings all have their genetic information stored in the structure of DNA molecules. *DNA* (deoxyribonucleic acid) is a *polymer*, that is, a long chain of elementary subunits (Figure 7–4). Its subunits are called *nucleotides*, of which there are four. Each of the four contains a phosphate (derived from phosphoric acid), a sugar (deoxyribose, or ribose missing an oxygen molecule), and one of four bases: Adenine (A),

Figure 7-4

(a) DNA is a polymer, built up from nucleotide subunits. A sugar, phosphate, and base compose a nucleotide. The backbone of the molecule consists of alternating sugars and phosphates, while the bases bind to complementary bases from the other DNA strand.
(b) In its most physiologically stable form, DNA is a double helix.

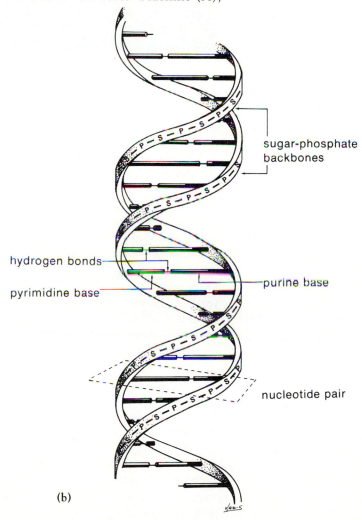

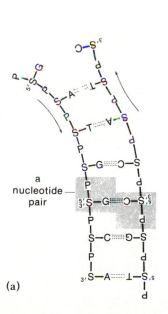

(a)   (b)

Figure 7-5

The fact that DNA strands are complementary enables the DNA molecule to make two identical copies of itself by using both original strands as templates and synthesizing a new complementary strand on each.

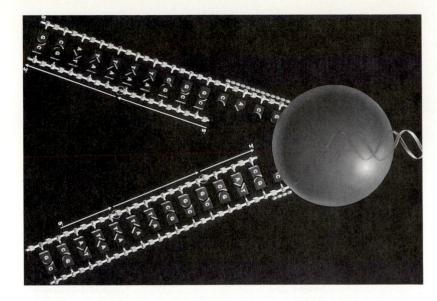

replication

The copying of a DNA molecule, creating two identical, double-stranded DNA molecules.

transcription

The formation of an RNA molecule from one strand of a DNA molecule, creating a sequence of RNA nucleotides complementary to one DNA strand and similar to the other.

Guanine (G), Cytosine (C), or Thymine (T). The DNA polymer is constructed so that the sugars and phosphates alternate down either side of the molecule, forming two backbones. The bases lie in the center of the molecule and pair with each other by means of weak interactions. This pairing is highly ordered, however: Adenine always pairs with thymine, and guanine with cytosine. The order in which the nucleotides fall encodes the genetic information, and the pairing specificity means that knowing one side of the DNA molecule enables cells (and students) to construct the other side of the molecule. The two halves of a DNA molecule are said to be *complementary* to each other; note that a functional gene, being a stretch of DNA, will have its instructions encoded on *one strand*—the other strand will simply be complementary to it.

A gene is, in a very tangible and mechanistic sense, a stretch of DNA with a particular function. Genes do two things actively: **replicate** (make DNA copies of themselves) and **transcribe** (make RNA copies of themselves to implement the instructions they encode). DNA replication always precedes cell division and is an integral part of organismal growth and development (Figure 7–5). RNA transcription is what allows a gene to perform a function. In addition, some genes perform a passive function, serving as stretches of DNA to which other molecules may bind, which may affect the active function of nearby genes.

RNA   RNA (ribonucleic acid) is a derivative molecule, similar in structure to DNA but: (1) built upon the sugar ribose, (2) normally single stranded, and (3) substituting the base uracil for thymine. RNA contains a sequence of bases derived directly from a DNA gene and is therefore complementary to it (and almost identical to the *other* DNA strand). Some classes of RNA have their own function, but other RNAs simply transfer the information stored in the DNA gene to a location in the cell where that information is used to construct a specific protein. The latter class of RNAs are called messenger RNA, or mRNA.

   Proteins   *Proteins* perform the majority of biochemical tasks in the cell and in the body. They include structural proteins, such as keratin in the hair and collagen in the bones; transportation proteins, such as hemoglobin, which carries oxygen in the blood; hormones, such as insulin, which travel through various tissues and act as biochemical signals and regulators; antibodies, which attack foreign substances in the blood of vertebrates; contractile proteins, such as actin in muscle; storage proteins, such as ferritin, which stores iron in the spleen; and enzymes, which catalyze biological reactions. All these proteins exist as the direct result of gene function: transcription of a DNA message into an RNA message and then **translation** of the RNA message into a protein structure.

   Like DNA, proteins are polymers, though of a very different kind. Although the information on how to construct specific proteins is encoded in the genes, the protein is built up from entirely different subunits than those comprising DNA. The subunits of proteins are *amino acids*, of which there are twenty—each of which bears a positively charged amine (NH_2^+) group at one end and a negatively charged carboxylic acid ($COOH^-$) group at the other end. These can be biochemically linked up, head to tail, liberating a water (H_2O) molecule from between each pair of amino acids. The genetic code—the relationship between a specific DNA sequence and a specific protein sequence derived from it—involves a specificity of three consecutive nucleotides (a triplet in DNA and a codon in RNA) for one of the twenty amino acids. Thus, a sequence of twelve nucleotides in a gene, for example, specifies a sequence of four amino acids to be added to the protein polymer (Figure 7–6). Proteins are of highly variable lengths. Some brain hormones are but five amino acids in length, while the beta chain of hemoglobin is 146 amino acids in length. Other proteins can be thousands of amino acids long.

   Thus, in controlling the production of proteins, the genes contain the information that ultimately encodes all bodily biological functions, that is, the information required to construct and maintain a living organism. Changes in these genes must result in changed organisms, and the transmission of these entities across generations is of vital interest in the study of evolution. In humans, as in fruitflies and peas, the rules for the transmission of genes follow those first formulated by Gregor Mendel.

Mendel's Laws

For several reasons, Mendelian heredity is most easily observable in non-human organisms. First, many such organisms, like flies, can be mated to each other for experimental purposes without moral or ethical dilemmas. Second, these same organisms have relatively short generation times and large litter sizes, compared with humans. For genetic purposes and statis-

translation

The production of a protein from a messenger RNA molecule by the genetic code's specificity of an amino acid for each sequence of three nucleotides.

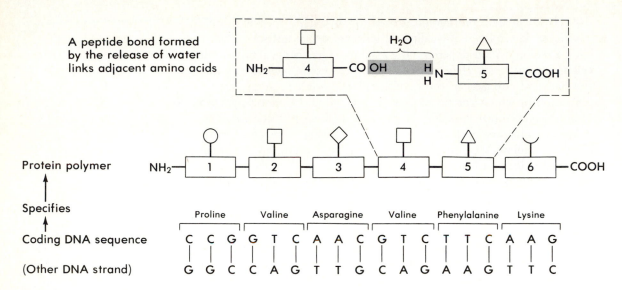

A peptide bond formed
by the release of water
links adjacent amino acids

Figure 7-6

The sequence of nucleotides in a gene determines the sequence of amino acids in an active protein. A protein is a polymer of amino acids connected by peptide bonds, which are created when the amino group of one reacts with the acid group of another, liberating a molecule of water.

tical reasons, one would ideally wish to study many offspring to understand hereditary patterns and would not want to wait fifteen to twenty years to obtain them.

Third, most human characters of simple inheritance, while copious enough (over 4,300 are listed in the 1988 catalog compiled by Victor A. McKusick, called *Mendelian Inheritance in Man*), are by the very nature of their detection pathologies. Normal characters are generally of complex inheritance, the products of many genes working together. But consider the difficulty in proceeding *from* the information, for example, that hemophilia is caused by an alteration in a specific gene involved in the formation of blood clots *to* a reasonably complete description of the genetics of blood clotting. In other words, genetic diseases, by their nature, interrupt a complex chain of biochemical and developmental events. But how do you reconstruct a chain with only the knowledge derived from the breakage of a single link?

While we recognize that inheritance in humans follows the same principles as Mendelian inheritance in other organisms, most of our knowledge of these principles is derived from those other organisms.

Mendel's experiments with seven characters in peas (*Pisum sativum*) demonstrated two regularities in the inheritance of these characters. They now bear his name as Mendel's First Law ("Segregation") and Mendel's Second Law ("Independent Assortment"). Mendel inferred these laws as a result of his mathematical treatment of inheritance.

MENDEL'S FIRST LAW: SEGREGATION

Mendel's First Law (segregation) states that a character, say seed color, is determined in the plant by *two* factors that we now call genes. At some stage of the reproductive cycle, these genes separate from each other so that each **gamete** (pollen or ovule in plants, sperm or egg in animals) has only *one* gene for each character. When fertilization occurs, the two-gene state is restored in the fertilized egg (or **zygote**) and therefore in the next generation (Figure 7–7).

Mendel's First Law is applicable to multicellular organisms in general as well to peas and fruitflies as to humans. For pod color in peas, he distinguished two varieties, green and yellow. These outward properties are phenotypes. The yellow pod color is the result of the presence of two identical copies of a gene, g and g; we can represent the genotype (genetic determinants) of this single character as gg. The green pod color phenotype, however, can be produced by either of two genotypes, Gg or GG. Variant forms of the same gene, such as G and g, are called alleles. The two genotypes that produce green pod color, therefore, differ in that one is composed of two copies of the same allele, while the other is com-

gamete

A reproductive cell containing half the amount of genetic information as other cells.

zygote

The result of fertilization, the fusion of two gametes from different sexes, containing the full amount of genetic information.

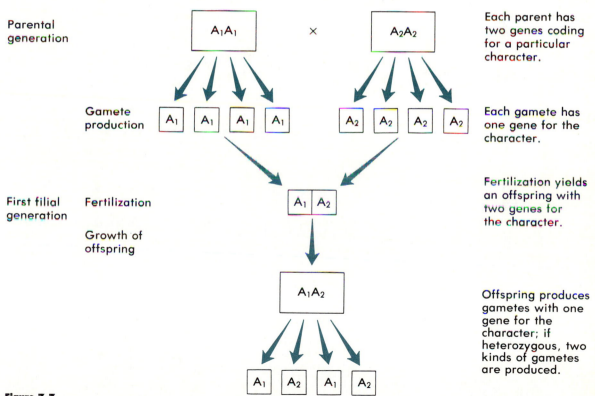

Parental generation — Each parent has two genes coding for a particular character.

Gamete production — Each gamete has one gene for the character.

First filial generation — Fertilization — Fertilization yields an offspring with two genes for the character.

Growth of offspring

Offspring produces gametes with one gene for the character; if heterozygous, two kinds of gametes are produced.

Figure 7-7

Mendel's First Law governs the inheritance of a single gene.

homozygous

Having both the maternal and paternal alleles for a particular gene be the same; the organism is a homozygote.

heterozygous

Having the maternal and paternal alleles for a particular gene be different; the organism is a heterozygote.

posed of one copy each of two different alleles. A genotype that consists of two identical alleles is **homozygous**, while a genotype consisting of two different alleles is **heterozygous**.

The gametes contain only one gene from each gene pair in the genotype. A homozygous organism can, therefore, produce only one kind of gamete, while the heterozygote can produce two kinds of gametes.

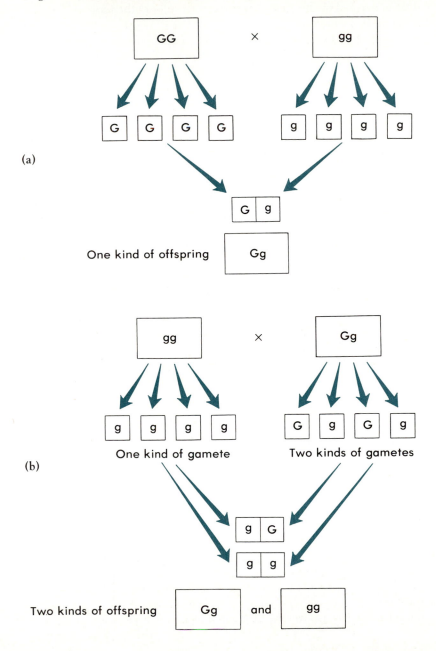

Figure 7-8

(a) GG × gg yields all Gg progeny; (b) gg × Gg yields Gg and gg progeny in equal numbers.

That is, a GG (green pod) plant produces only G gametes; a gg (yellow pod) plant produces only g gametes; but a Gg (green pod) plant produces both G and g gametes in equal proportions.

When a GG (green pod) plant is mated to a gg (yellow pod) plant, the offspring are all Gg (green pod—Figure 7–8). The green-pod parent can donate only a G allele to an offspring through its gamete, and the yellow-pod parent can donate only a g. As a result, all offspring from this mating will be heterozygous. In terms of phenotype, the mating produces a green-pod plant due to factors of dominance, discussed in greater detail below. The observation that the heterozygous condition leads to green pods is critical, as it is impossible to reconcile with the principles of blending inheritance. Under blending inheritance theory, you will recall, a green-pod plant crossed to a yellow-pod plant would be expected to yield a plant with greenish-yellowish pods. The fact that the offspring phenotype was the same as one of the parental phenotypes, and not intermediate between them, convinced Mendel that the essence of heredity was particulate, not blending.

The mating between a yellow-pod plant (gg) and a heterozygous green-pod plant (Gg) can be analyzed as follows (Figure 7–8). One parent can produce only g gametes, while the other produces G and g in equal proportions. Fertilization, therefore, can unite g with g or g with G. The progeny of a gg by Gg cross results in a genotypic ratio in the offspring of 1 gg:1 Gg and in a phenotypic ratio of 1 yellow:1 green.

The mating between two heterozygous green-pod plants can be analyzed in a similar fashion. Each Gg parent can produce G and g gametes. They combine in zygotes in a ratio of 1 GG:2 Gg:1 gg. This 1:2:1 genotypic ratio, however, results in simply a 3:1 phenotypic ratio since the GG and Gg genotypes yield the same phenotype.

The same principles hold for other multicellular species. A fruitfly with two vg ("vestigial") alleles, for example, develops with wings that are deformed and stunted (Figure 7–9). Crossing two heterozygotes will produce the same 1:2:1 genotypic ratio (homozygous vestigial to heterozygous to homozygous normal) and 3:1 phenotypic ratio (normal to vestigial) as in the pea example.

In humans, the gene responsible for producing an enzyme called phenylalanine hydroxylase has an allele that does not produce a working enzyme. Homozygotes for this allele have the genetic disease known as PKU, or phenylketonuria. Lacking the enzyme, which biochemically converts the amino acid phenylalanine to the amino acid tyrosine (which can then be further metabolized), leads homozygotes to accumulate abnormally high amounts of phenylalanine. Forced to be metabolized by other biochemical pathways, the phenylalanine is converted to toxic phenylketones, which are ordinarily present only in minuscule quantities. These phenylketones affect the developing nervous system of children, and one of the major phenotypic results is severe mental retardation.

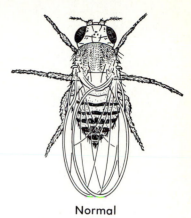

Normal

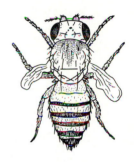

Vestigial

Figure 7-9

The recessive allele vg causes a fruitfly to have vestigial wings (after Sturtevant and Beadle).

Heterozygotes for PKU are phenotypically normal, but their mating produces homozygotes with this condition one-quarter of the time, on average. This occurs because, following the same rules that hold for peas and fruitflies, two heterozygotes (say, Pp and Pp) produce one-fourth PP, one-half Pp, and one-fourth pp genotypes in their offspring, or three phenotypically normal offspring to every one phenylketonuric. Fortunately, medical science has learned how to compensate for the condition, primarily through diet early in childhood. This is, in addition to being a human example of Mendel's First Law, a demonstration of how knowledge and cultural practices can transcend biology.

THE CHROMOSOME THEORY OF INHERITANCE

About the same time as the principles of Mendelian heredity were being rediscovered, cell biologists were beginning to work out the cellular basis of reproduction and inheritance. **Cells** in humans are composed of two basic domains (Figure 7–10): a *nucleus*, containing genetic instructions; and *cytoplasm*, in which these instructions are carried out and the cell's functions are actually performed. For example, the function of a nerve cell is to transmit a small electrical impulse: The information on how to do this is stored in the nucleus, while the actual transmission of the impulse is carried out by the cytoplasm.

In the 1860s, the biologist and anthropologist Rudolf Virchow argued that cells were the fundamental units of all life and that all cells come from previously existing cells. Thus, while nerve cells, muscle cells, liver cells, and blood cells in the same body are all the lineal descendants of a single, fertilized egg, or zygote, this zygote is itself the result of a fusion of egg and sperm, which are lineal descendants of the cells of the parents. It follows that all life is a continuum, and while we may choose culturally to mark the beginning of a new organism from the point of fertilization, this is an arbitrary point in the life cycle from the perspective of the cells.

In the 1880s, August Weismann emphasized the fundamental differences between reproductive cells and cells of the rest of the body. A fertilized egg begins to divide and reproduce by the fission process we now call mitosis (Figure 7–11). Mitosis creates two identical daughter cells that have the same genetic material as the original cell. Thus, all the descendant cells of a single zygote contain exactly the same genetic information, or in plain terms, virtually every cell in your body is genetically identical. Weismann recognized that there was an important exception to this generalization. At some point in the growth of the organism, a particular group of cells begins to divide somewhat differently, generating daughter cells with *only half* the amount of genetic material as the originals. These cells are specialized reproductive cells—the gametes we considered earlier—and are the organism's only biological link to the next generation. Anything that happens to the growing and developing body

cell

Fundamental unit of life.

Figure 7-10

Cells are the basic materials of which organisms are constructed. Within each cell, a structure called the nucleus contains the heridITary material, while most of the cell's activity occurs in the cytoplasm.

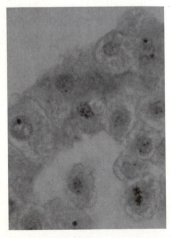

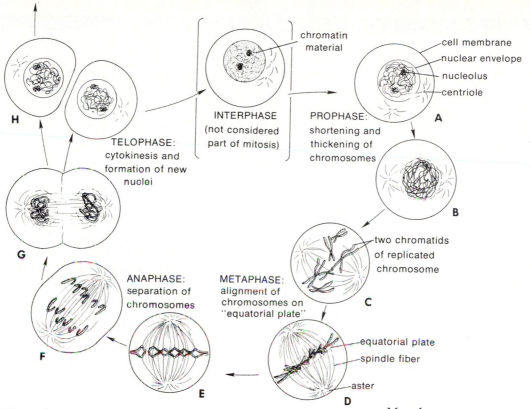

Figure 7-11

Mitosis. The chromosomes replicate and condense and then gather in the center of the cell. Each doubled chromosome splits, and the chromatids migrate to opposite ends of the cell. The result is two cells identical in genetic constitution to the original.

Metaphase

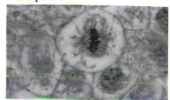

Anaphase

Telophase

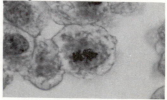

subsequent to gamete formation will not be passed on to its offspring since the cells from which the next generation will arise have already been set aside. Weismann thus formally distinguished between the *germ* cells, or reproductive organs, and the *somatic* cells, those composing the rest of the body.

This doctrine is thoroughly incompatible with Lamarckian inheritance: the inheritance of acquired characters. If a bodily character is acquired during one's lifetime, it is acquired by the soma, the body, but can have no effect upon the germ cells, as these are already present and complete. The character, therefore, cannot be passed on to the offspring. Consider the tail of a mouse. If we were to cut the tails off mice for twenty generations, would a mouse born in the twenty-first generation have a shorter tail than the original mouse? Weismann performed such an experiment and found the tails to be equally long, no matter how many generations of tail amputations he performed. A change in the tail

---

Issues in Anthropology 7–1

The X Chromosome

Mendel properly deduced that two functioning copies of each gene exist in the cells of a normal individual. While the copies may be slight variants of each other, the genetic system is attuned to the presence of two, and only two, copies of each segment of genetic information.

Having only one copy of a chromosome, or part of a chromosome, is called *monosomy*. In humans, this is nearly always incompatible with life; at best, it results in severe birth defects. Likewise, having three copies of a chromosome, *trisomy*, is usually incompatible with life. Trisomy for a small chromosome, number 21, is compatible with life, but results in the well-known congenital condition of Down's syndrome.

An exception to the rule of two copies of each genetic instruction occurs in the sex chromosomes. Female mammals, who are XX, have two copies of each gene on the X chromosome; males, who are XY, have only one copy of each gene on the X chromosome, while the Y chromosome has very few genes on it. How can both males and females be genetically normal? If one copy of the X chromosome is normal, females should be like trisomics; and if two copies of the X chromosome is normal, males should be like monosomics. How can the dosage of X chromosome material result in normal phenotypes in both cases?

The answer to this paradox was deduced by geneticist Mary Lyon in the 1960s. At a specific point in the development of a female embryo, at around the sixty-four-cell stage, a signal is given that randomly shuts off one or the other X chromosome in each cell. The chromosome shuts off by becoming tightly coiled and condensed, rendering it incapable of transcription.

This inactive X chromosome is passed to the daughter cells after each cell division, so a cell's

---

meiosis

Process of cell division producing gametes; division of one diploid cell into four genetically different haploid cells; in mitosis in somatic cells, one diploid cell divides into two genetically identical diploid cells.

chromosome

A structure in the nucleus, visible during cell division, which contains the hereditary material; a long stretch of DNA and attendant proteins.

is a somatic change and cannot be communicated to the germ cells (Figure 7–12).

The setting aside of germ cells occurs by a different form of cell division, called **meiosis**. Because an offspring is formed by the fusion of two parental cells, the process of fertilization involves a doubling of the genetic material. Offspring, therefore, would have twice as much genetic material per cell as their parents if meiosis did not occur, and there would be consequent doublings every generation. What meiosis involves, therefore, is a *halving* of the genetic material every generation—before the doubling of fertilization—and this halving allows the amount of genetic material to remain constant every generation.

It had also been observed that the products of a meiotic cell division actually contained half as many of a particular cellular component as the original cell. These components were called **chromosomes**, or "colored bodies," and were consequently suggested (in 1902, by Theodor Boveri in Germany and Walter Sutton in America) to be themselves the genetic material.

Any somatic cell has twice as many chromosomes as any germ cell. A somatic human cell contains forty-six chromosomes, which can be

descendants all have the same X chromosome inactivated. It is visible under the microscope as a small blob in the nucleus of female mammalian cells but not in male cells. The shutdown is random at the sixty-four-cell stage, so adult females have some cells in which one X chromosome is functioning and some in which the other is functioning.

The demonstration that women are genetic mosaics involved studying women who were known (by their parents' genotypes) to be heterozygous for a gene on the X chromosome. The gene was for an enzyme called glucose-6-phosphate dehydrogenase, or G6PD. It has two alleles, G6PD-A and G6PD-B. When biopsies from different tissues of these women were taken and cloned populations of cells were grown from the biopsies, each cell population had *either* G6PD-A *or* G6PD-B, but not both. It was as if the women were composed of two types of haploid cells, not of one type of heterozygous diploid cell. Female mammals are consequently recognized as genetic mosaics for the X chromosome.

The inactivation of the X chromosome is not complete, as several loci are now known to escape inactivation. Further, the inactivation does not occur in the germ line, so an active X is passed on in the eggs, no matter which X it is.

References:

Lyon, M. F. (1988). X-chromosome inactivation and the location and expression of X-linked genes. *American Journal of Human Genetics*, 42:8–16.

Davidson, R. G., Nitowsky, H. M., & Childs, B. (1963). Demonstration of cells in the human female heterozygous for glucose-6-phosphate dehydrogenase variants. *Proceedings of the National Academy of Sciences, USA*, 50:481–485.

considered as either twenty-three pairs of chromosomes or as two sets of twenty-three chromosomes each. If we say twenty-three pairs, we emphasize the fact that each chromosome has a distinct recognizable morphology and that there are twenty-three of them. If we say two sets, we emphasize the fact that twenty-three chromosomes (one of each set) were donated by the father (that is, the sperm that fertilized the egg) and that twenty-three chromosomes were donated by the mother (in the egg). Thus, each parent makes an equal genetic contribution to the zygote and to the next generation.

Mendel's law of segregation actually describes the effects of meiotic reduction of the chromosome number, from twenty-three pairs to twenty-three individual chromosomes in humans. Thus, in meiosis, each chromosome separates from its partner, and the two chromosomes of each pair end up in different gametes. Furthermore, we have in meiosis visual evidence for the operation of Mendel's law of segregation. By 1920, considerable evidence had accumulated, particularly from studies of the fruitfly *Drosophila*, to indicate that every gene is located somewhere on a chromosome, and when the chromosomes segregate at meiosis, the genes segregate with them, as Mendel described.

Figure 7-12

According to Weismann's theory, each body is a dead end, for the continuity between generations is provided by only the reproductive cells, which have been formed early in development and receive no input from the rest of the cells of the body. Therefore, Lamarckian inheritance is impossible, for the activities of the body (soma) cannot be passed on to the next generation.

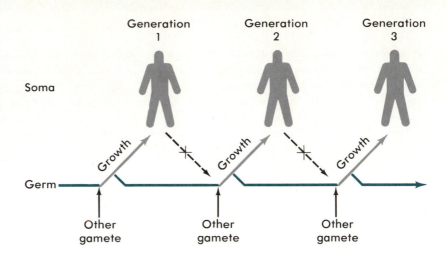

diploid

The state of having two sets of chromosomes or two sets of genes, one from each parent, as in somatic cells.

MENDEL'S SECOND LAW: INDEPENDENT ASSORTMENT

The somatic human cells contain two sets of twenty-three chromosomes each; we say, therefore, that the **diploid** chromosome number for humans is forty-six. One set is of paternal origin, and the other is of maternal origin. Let us call these chromosomes 1P and 1M, 2P and 2M, 3P and 3M, and so on, up to 23P and 23M. We know that 1P will separate from 1M—that is the essence of Mendel's First Law—but what of the segregation of 1P with respect to chromosomes 2P and 2M? 2P and 2M segregate from each other as well, and it is legitimate to ask whether chromosome 1P will end up in a gamete with chromosome 2P. The answer is in Mendel's Second Law, known as the law of independent assortment.

Assume that an individual is heterozygous for type Rh-positive blood and is also heterozygous for a disease known as alpha-thalassemia. Rh-positive blood type is dominant over Rh-negative, and this gene is located on chromosome 1. Alpha-thalassemia is recessive and is located on chromosome 16. It follows that this individual has Rh+ and Rh– on chromosome 1 and T (normal) and t (thalassemia) on chromosome 16.

Assume further that the Rh+ allele is on the paternal chromosome 1 and that the Rh– allele is on the maternal chromosome 1; and that the thalassemia allele is on paternal chromosome 16 and the normal allele on the maternal chromosome 16. This person consequently can be described as having Rh+(1P), Rh–(1M); and t(16P), T(16M). Any gamete, after meiosis, will have either the Rh+ allele or the Rh– allele since it will have only one chromosome 1. It will also have either the t or the T allele, as it will have only one chromosome 16. Of course, any functional gamete will have one each of the other chromosomes as well.

Mendel's Second Law tells us that genes of different chromosomes assort into gametes independently of one another. This means that chromosome 1P might end up in a gamete with *either* chromosome 16P or chromosome 16M (Figure 7–13). Likewise, chromosome 1M might end up in a gamete with either chromosome 16P or chromosome 16M. There are, consequently, four possible gametes that can occur in this individual, even when considering only two of the twenty-three chromosome pairs, and only two genes: 1P/16P, 1P/16M, 1M/16P, and 1M/16M. Because any particular cell can have any of these four outcomes, all four of these

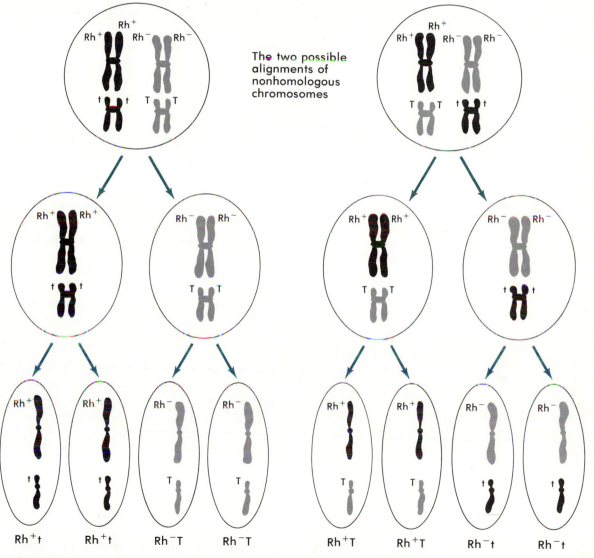

The two possible alignments of nonhomologous chromosomes

Figure 7-13

The doubly-heterozygous individual has chromosomes in black from one parent and in color from the other parent. Four different kinds of gametes can be produced by a person with this genotype because of Mendel's Second Law, which governs the inheritance of genes on different chromosomes.

gametes will actually be present in virtually equal numbers. Thus, if we follow the genes on the chromosomes, four genotypic classes of gametes correspond to the four chromosome classes:

1P/16P	1P/16M	1M/16P	1M/16M	Chromosomal
Rh+/t	Rh+/T	Rh-/t	Rh-/T	Genotypic

All four of these genotypes are produced in theoretically equal numbers by the meiotically dividing cells of our subject.

Our doubly heterozygous individual marries, and by a coincidence, the spouse is also a double-heterozygote for these same two genes. What genotypes and phenotypes can be expected? We know that there will be four genotypic classes of sperm and the same four genotypic classes of egg. Any sperm presumably has an equal chance of fertilizing any egg. If we make a chart, listing the four sperm categories across the top and the four egg categories down the side, we can then bring them all together by filling in the sixteen genotypic classes of the offspring. Such a chart is known as a Punnett Square (Figure 7–14).

Each of the sixteen genotypic possibilities for the new zygote represents a diploid fertilized egg and, therefore, has two of each gene. If we organize the genotypic results into phenotypic classes based on which characters are dominant and which recessive, we find four such possible phenotypes: Rh-positive and normal, Rh-positive and thalassemic, Rh-negative and normal, and Rh-negative and thalassemic. These occur in the ratio 9:3:3:1. Thus, if our couple has a child, we predict that it has a 9 in 16 chance of being Rh-positive and normal, a 3 in 16 chance of being Rh-positive and thalassemic, a 3 in 16 chance of being Rh-negative and normal, and a 1 in 16 chance of being Rh-negative and thalassemic.

It would be nice, genetically, if our couple produced hundreds of offspring, for then we could observe these probabilities in action first-hand. That, however, is an impossibility for any human couple. Consequently, we have relied on other organisms, such as peas and flies, to discover these statistical regularities. They hold true when large numbers of offspring are produced, but for any particular offspring, we can make only a statistical educated guess. That is to say, there is a better-than-even chance of any particular child being Rh-positive and normal ("even" being 8 in 16) but only a very small chance of any particular child turning out to be Rh-negative and thalassemic.

Mendel actually deduced the mode of inheritance for double-heterozygotes by observing the phenotypic ratios of appropriate crosses, exactly the reverse of what we have done. Mendel showed that two genes on different chromosomes will assort into gametes independently of each other. Studying his peas, in which yellow seed color (Y) is dominant to green (y) (note that this is the opposite of pod color discussed earlier) and in which round seed shape (R) is dominant to wrinkled (r), Mendel mated double-heterozygotes (YyRr) and counted the progeny. He found 315 round, yellow seeds; 108 round, green seeds; 101 wrinkled, yellow seeds, and 32 wrinkled, green seeds: nearly a perfect 9:3:3:1 ratio.

On the basis of these and other crosses, Mendel concluded that the genes for seed color and seed shape were assorted independently of each other. There are other possibilities. Suppose that for each heterozygote,

Genotypic classes of zygotes

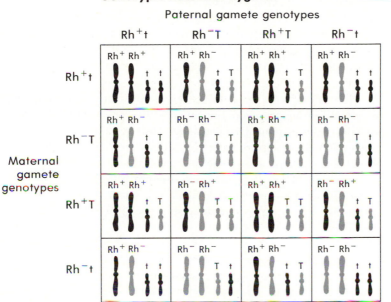

Figure 7-14

Using a Punnett Square, we can see that the expected phenotypic ratio from a mating of two people both heterozygous for two genes on different chromosomes will be 9:3:3:1.

Phenotypic classes of zygotes

Rh+ thalassemic	Rh+ normal	Rh+ normal	Rh+ thalassemic
Rh+ normal	Rh− normal	Rh+ normal	Rh− normal
Rh+ normal	Rh+ normal	Rh+ normal	Rh+ normal
Rh+ thalassemic	Rh− normal	Rh+ normal	Rh− thalassemic

the two dominant alleles (yellow and round) are maternal in origin and the two recessive alleles (green and wrinkled) are paternal. They might well be. Now let us hypothesize that instead of assorting randomly, the paternal chromosomes always go into one gamete, the maternal chromosomes into another. If that were the case, we would find only two genotypic classes in the gametes of the doubly heterozygous subject, namely Y/R and y/r. Following fertilization, we would expect to find among the offspring (by constructing a Punnett Square) ¾ yellow and round, and ¼ green and wrinkled, or a 3:1 ratio.

The double-heterozygote cross, however, *does* yield a 9:3:3:1 ratio when the genes in question are on different chromosomes because chromosomes assort independently of one another during meiosis. The paternal or maternal origin of each allele has no effect upon its subsequent segregation.

The principle of independent assortment can occasionally help us understand certain aspects of human genetics. For example, the fact that two hemoglobin variants (sickle-cell and Hopkins-2) were found to assort independently in heterozygotes led directly to the recognition that hemoglobin is composed of two subunits, produced by genes on different chromosomes. More often, however, complicating factors can mask or impact upon the effect of independent assortment, making the study of human genetics a complex task, indeed.

Linkage

haploid

The state of having one set of chromosomes or genes, as in germ cells.

In a human **haploid** genome—the genetic material in a gamete—there are twenty-three chromosomes. These chromosomes, however, carry tens of thousands of genes. Clearly, numerous genes must be located on each individual chromosome. Two genes that happen to be located on the same chromosome do not assort independently; they are obliged to travel together. Such genes are said to be *linked*.

If we take as our subject an individual heterozygous for two genes, A and B, where allele A is dominant to a and allele B is dominant to b, we can express our subject's genotype as AaBb. If the genes are *not* linked, they will assort randomly as Mendel's Second Law dictates, and we will expect to find four classes of gametes produced: AB, Ab, aB, and ab. Suppose, instead, that the two genes are on the *same* chromosome. Since our subject is diploid and is heterozygous for the two genes, the genotype is still AaBb—regardless of whether or not the genes are linked. Even if we do know that the genes are, in fact, linked, we still do not know which *alleles* are linked. The subject could have AB on one chromosome and ab on the other; or Ab on one chromosome and aB on the other. In either case, the genotype is still the same, so how can we tell which chromosomal configuration is present?

It would not be easy with humans, but with fruitflies, we could make a *testcross:* We could mate our subject to a double-recessive homozygote (aabb) and analyze the offspring (Figure 7–15). We know the double-recessive homozygote can make only one kind of gamete: ab. If our subject has AB on one chromosome and ab on the other, then its two

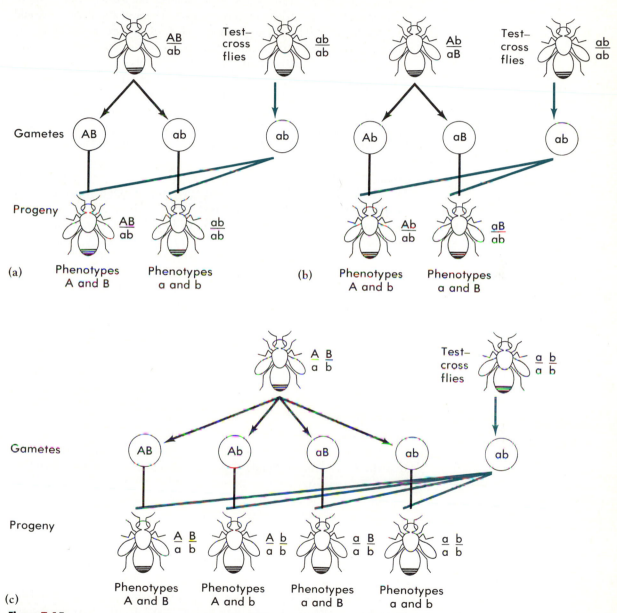

Figure 7-15

A testcross can distinguish among various hypotheses of linkage. (a) If A is linked to allele B (not b), two classes of progeny are expected; (b) if A is linked to allele b (not B), two different classes of progeny are expected; (c) if genes A and B are not linked, four classes of progeny are expected.

classes of gametes will be AB and ab. And the offspring of this subject and the double-recessive homozygote would display two phenotypic classes: double-dominant (AaBb) and double-recessive (aabb), in equal proportions. On the other hand, if our subject has Ab on one chromosome and aB on the other, the phenotypic classes of the progeny would be quite different. The progeny would consist of two groups, each having as a phenotype one of the dominant characters and one of the recessive characters. The genotypes would be Aabb and aaBb.

Thus, a testcross enables us to distinguish among the possible linkage relationships of a heterozygote. Note that, in our example, if the genes are actually on *different* chromosomes and therefore *not* linked, we would get four different phenotypic classes in the progeny of a testcross. These correspond to the genotypes AaBb, Aabb, aaBb, and aabb.

Genetic Recombination

The recessive alleles for purple eyes (pr) and vestigial wings (vg) are located on the same chromosome in the fruitfly *Drosophila*. It is customary in fruitfly genetics to designate the wild-type allele, the normal allele found in the wild, by a + sign. We use this sign, therefore, to designate normal eyes (which are red) and normal-sized wings.

Calvin Bridges, one of the major figures in genetics during the early decades of this century, established a line of fruitflies in which he knew that the pr and vg alleles were linked to each other. He testcrossed the double-heterozygote to the double-recessive homozygote as follows:

$$\frac{pr\ vg}{+\ +} \times \frac{pr\ vg}{pr\ vg}$$

The alleles above the lines are on one chromosome, and the alleles below the lines are on the other chromosome. Bridges knew that the homozygote could produce only pr vg gametes and, since the alleles were linked, that the heterozygotes could produce pr vg *and* + + gametes. Therefore, Bridges anticipated obtaining only two phenotypic classes in the offspring, normal and double-recessive, from the expected genotypes:

$$\frac{pr\ vg}{pr\ vg} \quad and \quad \frac{pr\ vg}{+\ +}$$

Bridges counted 1,195 flies of the first type and 1,339 flies of the second type, very much according to his expectations. However, he also found 151 flies with normal eyes and vestigial wings and 154 flies with purple eyes and normal wings. He (and his supervisor, Thomas Hunt Morgan) reasoned that somehow the alleles, in a small proportion of the gametes, had become recombined. Instead of pr being linked invariably to vg, it had become unlinked about 11 percent of the time. Instead of obtaining only the $\frac{pr\ vg}{pr\ vg}$ and $\frac{pr\ vg}{+\ +}$ progeny, there were now some individuals with the genotypes $\frac{pr\ +}{pr\ vg}$ and $\frac{+\ vg}{pr\ vg}$. The explanation for this phenomenon lies in the process of meiosis itself and is called **crossing over**. It represents the actual, physical exchange of genetic material between chromosomes.

Crossing Over: The Physical Basis of Recombination

Because each chromosome contains a large number of genes, it must be recognized that linkage and crossing over are rules, not exceptions. Crossing over occurs in every chromosome at every meiosis and continually reorganizes alleles into new combinations. We can track genes A and B on different parts of chromosome 1 during meiosis (Figure 7–16). The chromosomes (1P and 1M) begin in the meiotic cell as long, diffuse strings of DNA complexed with proteins. The DNA then replicates, so that there is now twice as much in the cell, and each chromosome has an identical twin attached to it. The point of attachment is called the *centromere*. Note that although the DNA has replicated, the centromere is still a single unit. Therefore, we still count two sets of chromosomes and not four, even though each set is now twice as large as it formerly was. On either side of the centromere are *sister chromatids*, genetically identical to each other.

The doubled chromosomes condense dramatically, to the point that they are visible as regular structures in the cell. Then the paternal and maternal copies of each chromosome (called **homologous chromosomes**, or homologs) pair up with each other. The pairing is so intimate that each chromosome pair (four chromatids in all) actually appears as a single mass. During this pairing, called synapsis, the homologs overlap, break, and rejoin to each other. Thus, during this process, the portion of a chromatid that carries allele A may become attached to the portion of a chromatid carrying allele b. Where we began with A linked to B, and a linked to b, we now have four different chromatids, of which two retain the original linkage relationships, one has a linked to B, and one has A linked to b. Crossing over is observable in cells, and several crossovers may occur along any single pair of homologous chromosomes (Figure 7–17). The result of this process is the formation of new allelic combinations, and thus the production of genotypic variation in the population.

This is precisely how the vestigial wing and purple eye alleles of the fruitfly came to be found in the odd combinations discovered by Bridges and Morgan. Their colleague, A. H. Sturtevant, recognized that a crossover was more likely to occur between genes far apart on the same chromosome than between genes close together. Thus, by crossing the appropriate flies and analyzing the phenotypes of thousands of offspring, it became possible to construct a genetic map of several genes on the

crossing-over

Meiotic process by which chromosomes originally from different parents exchange segments, resulting in a chromosome containing linked maternal and paternal alleles.

homologous chromosomes

Chromosomes from different individuals, containing the same genes but probably different alleles; different from the concept of homology in evolution.

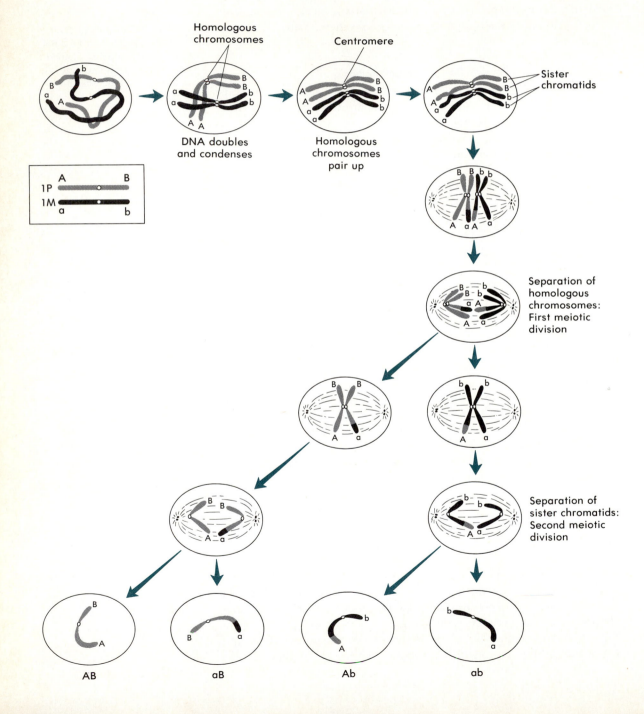

fruitfly's chromosomes, giving the relative and approximate positions of several genes on the same chromosome.

Recent biochemical techniques have permitted the mapping of many genes on human chromosomes (Figure 7–18). Most of the genes and other pieces of DNA that have been mapped to human chromosomes so far are of obscure function.

Interactions among Genes

So far in this chapter, we have focused on gene transmission: how genes are passed on from parent to offspring in successive generations. Intertwined with this issue is the physiological problem of gene action: how genes function and interact with one another in controlling the body's biological machinery. The molecular basis of gene action is presented in Chapter 8.

SICKLE-CELL ANEMIA

Sickle-cell anemia is physical anthropology's best example of nearly everything. Hemoglobin is one of the most abundant proteins in the human body, transporting oxygen in the bloodstream. Indeed, red blood cells, or erythrocytes, can be very properly regarded as simply traveling bags of hemoglobin. These bags, however, take on a characteristic shape much like that of a space station in old science-fiction movies, technically called a biconcave disc. The hemoglobin molecules, which fill the erythrocytes, consist of four protein chains that contain one iron-binding, or heme, molecule each. The four protein chains consist of two identical alpha chains, each 141 amino acids in length, and two beta chains, each 146 amino acids in length. The alpha-globin protein is produced by a gene on chromosome 16. The gene that produces beta-globin is located

Figure 7-17

(a) Crossing over in a generic animal cell; (b) meiosis in a human, showing twenty-three pairs of synapsed chromosomes (the linear chromosome is the X, with the Y paired to only a short stretch of it).

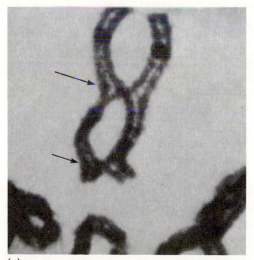

(a)

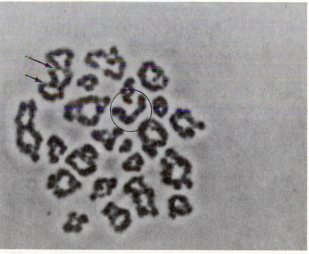

(b)

Issues in Anthropology 7–2

Homeoboxes: How Do You Build a Fruitfly?

Developmental genetics, the study of the hereditary control of embryological growth, is a hot area of research because it ties into two central issues in biology: how genes get turned on and off, and how phenotypes emerge from genotypes.

Two organisms are in the forefront of this research: a nematode worm called *Caenorhabditis elegans*, and our friend, the fruitfly *Drosophila melanogaster*. In C. *elegans*, the fate of every cell from the fertilized egg to the adult organism is mapped out: which cells will become sex organs, which will become skin, gut, and so on. How this occurs is unknown, but mapping the cell fates for C. *elegans* was a major accomplishment.

In *Drosophila*, a different story is unfolding. Fruitflies, like other insects, are segmented, developing from a series of repetitive elements. Of the three segments of thorax, the third contains the fly's wings, and the second contains club-shaped balancing organs known as halteres. In 1918, Calvin Bridges isolated a fruitfly mutant whose halteres extraordinarily had been replaced by partial wings. This came to be known as a *homeotic mutation*, one that directs the construction of a body part in the wrong place, and the gene came to be known as bithorax.

Bithorax is now understood as one of a cluster of genes (the bithorax complex), and in 1933, Bridges and Dobzhanzky discovered another cluster of homeotic genes, the antennapedia complex. These genes replaced the fly's antennas with legs, eyes with wings, and other comparably bizarre anatomical substitutions. Genetic analyses in the 1980s have revealed two interesting facts about these genes. First, they are involved fundamentally in determining the anterior-posterior polarity of the developing fly. The mutations are not so much instructions for putting the wrong part in a particular place as they are confusions in the ability of a particular cluster of cells to distinguish where it is relative to the head or tail of the developing fly. The cells are fated to develop into some structure, and which structure they develop into depends upon their ability to receive and process spatial signals in the fruitfly embryo. If they misinterpret their location, they develop into the wrong structures.

The other fact concerns a part of each homeotic

---

on chromosome 11. The sickle-cell gene is an allele of this beta-globin gene.

Individuals with the sickle-cell allele produce a different kind of beta-globin product than do other people, which also complexes with alpha-globin to form a tetrameric molecule called hemoglobin S (Hb S). Hb S has different properties for binding and releasing oxygen than does normal hemoglobin (Hb A). Furthermore, the hemoglobin has slightly different physical properties, so the molecules tend to stack up rigidly. If there is no Hb A, that is, if the individual is homozygous for sickle-cell, this physical property of Hb S deforms the erythrocyte into the shape of a crescent, or sickle (Figure 7–19). Not only does the hemoglobin function poorly, but the shape of the cells makes them clog the capillaries and rupture easily. Oxygen transport is impeded, the heart is over taxed, the spleen (which recycles red blood cells) is over taxed, and the brain, which requires great quantities of oxygen, is deprived. Thus, numerous

gene itself. Most appear to contain a sequence of 180 nucleotides, coding for sixty amino acids of a protein product. This sequence of nucleotides is known as the *homeobox,* and there are eight to twenty copies of it throughout the DNA of the fruitfly. An unexpected discovery, however, is that homeoboxes were also found in the genes of mammals—most specifically, in mice and humans.

There is very little about mammals and insects that is similar, either anatomically or genetically, except for the most fundamental biological operations, and so it was quickly appreciated that the homeobox must be performing a fundamental biological operation. But what operation? Humans and flies develop in very different ways; what function could a common genetic structure have in the development of both organisms?

We now believe that the homeobox codes for a segment of sixty amino acids that bind to DNA molecules. This is inferred on the basis that the amino acids of the protein transcript of the homeobox (known as the homeo domain) are highly alkaline (positively charged) and that the DNA double helix is highly acidic (negatively charged).

Further, the predicted shape of the homeo domain suggests that it could wrap snugly around a piece of DNA.

The inference is that the homeotic genes are coding for proteins, which in turn bind to other genes and turn them on or off. The homeotic genes are part of a regulatory cascade in which banks of genes are controlled by other genes that function earlier in development. These genes help encode the signals that give cells their spatial orientation in the developing embryo—fly, mouse, or human—and permit the proper structures to form in the proper places. In vertebrates, genes containing homeoboxes function in the anterior-posterior subdivision of parts of the central nervous system, very early in embryonic life.

References:

Gehring, W. J. (1987). Homeoboxes in the study of development. *Science,* 236:1245–1252.

Ingham, P. W. (1988). The molecular genetics of embryonic pattern information in *Drosophila. Nature,* 335:25–34.

Lewis, J. (1989). Genes and segmentation. *Nature,* 341:382–383.

physiological problems, including anemia and mental retardation, are the results of homozygosity for this single allele. Such multiple phenotypic effects from a single gene are called pleiotropic effects, or *pleiotropy* (Figure 7–20).

THE MECHANISM OF GENE ACTION

Now, what sort of hemoglobin would we expect to find in the blood of a heterozygote? If inheritance of sickle-cell worked exactly as it does with Mendel's peas, we would probably expect to find either Hb A or Hb S, depending on which is dominant. Instead, however, we find *both* Hb A and Hb S: The alleles are co-dominant with respect to this particular phenotype. The explanation for this finding lies in the mechanism of gene action.

As we have seen, genes do things. In the current example, a gene makes beta-globin. An allele of the beta-globin gene could conceivably

Figure 7-18.

Map of human chromosome 18, showing forty pieces of DNA whose locations are known to be on this chromosome. The function of most of these is unknown, and many have not been localized to a particular segment of the chromosome.

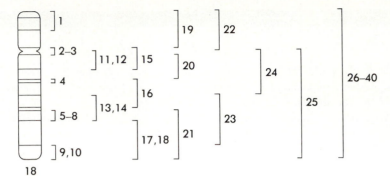

18

1 single copy DNA, chromosome 18,#3
2 highly repetitive DNA, chromosome 18,#1
3 highly repetitive DNA, chromosome 18,#2
4 fragile site, aphidicolin type, common, fra(18)(q12.2)
5 B cell CLL/lymphoma 2
6 fragile site, aphidicolin type, common, fra(18)(q21.3)
7 Yamaguchi sarcoma viral (v–yes–1) oncogene homolog 1
8 single copy DNA, chromosome 18,#8
9 peptidase A
10 single copy DNA, chromosome 18,#11
11 hepatitis B virus integration site 7
12 single copy DNA, chromosome 18,#7
13 gastrin releasing peptide
14 simian sarcoma–associated virus 1/gibbon ape leukemia virus–related endogenous retroviral element
15 alpha–2–plasmin inhibitor
16 phosphogluconate dehydrogenase–like 1
17 endogenous retroviral sequence 1
18 myelin basic protein
19 laminin, A polypeptide

20 prealbumin
21 single copy DNA, chromosome 18,#5
22 single copy DNA, chromosome 18,#6
23 plasminogen activator inhibitor, type II (arginine–serpin)
24 Kidd blood group
25 repetitive DNA family 19, chromosome 18, member #7
26 actin, beta pseudogene 3
27 dihydrofolate reductase pseudogene 1
28 glyceraldehyde–3–phosphate dehydrogenase–like 11
29 metallothionein–like 3
30 asparaginyl–tRNA synthetase
31 repetitive DNA family 3, chromosome 18, member #3
32 single copy DNA, chromosome 18,#1
33 single copy DNA, chromosome 18,#4
34 single copy DNA, chromosome 18,#10
35 single copy DNA, chromosome 18,#12–4
36 single copy DNA, chromosome 18,#16–9
37 single copy DNA, chromosome 18,#21–5
38 single copy DNA, chromosome 18,#27
39 single copy DNA, chromosome 18,#29
40 thymidylate synthetase

Figure 7-19

Sickled and normal red blood cells.

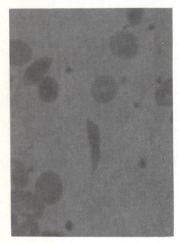

silent

A mutation that has no observable phenotypic effect; most commonly in noncoding DNA or in coding DNA for which the same amino acid is encoded.

do any of five things: (1) also make beta-globin; (2) make something other than beta-globin; (3) make nothing at all; (4) make too little beta-globin; or (5) make too much beta-globin. In technical terms, an allele could be (1) **silent**; (2) *co-dominant*; (3) *null*; (4) *partially or incompletely dominant*; or (5) *over-dominant* with respect to the particular phenotype in question.

Mendel's pea alleles were most likely null alleles, such that the product of the normal allele was simply absent in the recessive strain. Most biochemical phenotypes, however, are co-dominant—the allele produces something that works, but the structure of the protein product is slightly different and is detectable as such. This is the case with the sickle-cell allele. The other categories are also common: silent alleles are genetically different yet yield the same phenotype. These are the most common form of mutation, although being unexpressed, they are not particularly interesting except to molecular geneticists and will be discussed in the next chapter. Partial or incomplete dominance occurs when the phenotype of a heterozygote is intermediate (although not necessarily exactly intermediate) between the two homozygotes. Such an expression, you will recall, was the expectation under theories of blending inheritance. We now know that this is the case when an allele produces a protein that is less active or produces less of the protein than its normal allele. Finally, some alleles actually produce a more extreme phenotype in heterozygotes than in homozygotes. These are called overdominant. Overdominance is probably the cause of hybrid vigor, in which two inbred (homozygous) strains of plants or animals are crossed to produce an outbred (heterozygous) offspring that is often more fertile and more vigorous than its parental types.

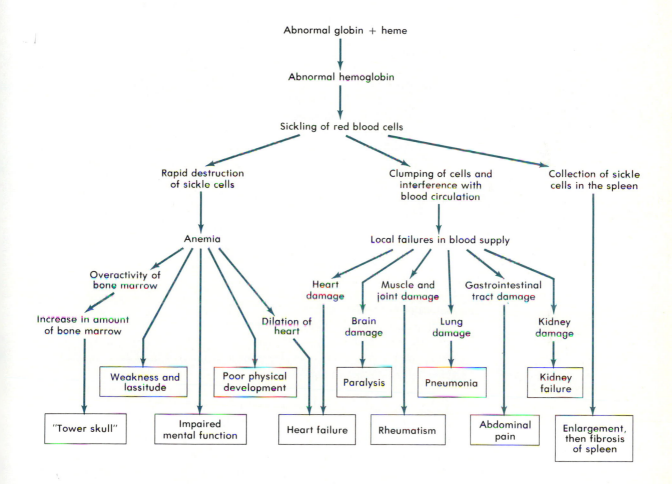

Figure 7-20

The sickle-cell phenotypes are complex and varied, stemming from a simple genetic mutation (after Neel and Schull).

antigen

Biochemical marker on the surface of a cell, which can stimulate an immunological reaction.

To illustrate the phenotypic expressions that may exist when these various allele types are present, we can consider the ABO blood group system, discovered by Karl Landsteiner in 1901 and now known to be the product of a gene located on chromosome 9. The product of this gene is an enzyme that modifies the molecules on the cell surface of erythrocytes. These surface molecules act as biochemical flags, or **antigens**. There are three major alleles for the ABO system in the human gene pool: A and B, which are co-dominant to each other, and O, which is a null allele. A and B are both dominant to O, insofar as they are making slightly different proteins, and O is apparently not doing much of anything. We therefore have six possible genotypes for a diploid human: AA, AO, BB, BO, AB, and OO. Their corresponding phenotypes are as follows:

Genotypes	AA	AO	BB	BO	AB	OO
Phenotypes		A		B	AB	O

Notice that the phenotype of type A blood is the result of either of two genotypes, AA or AO. Similarly, the phenotype B is the result of either BB or BO. However, the phenotypes O blood and AB blood result from only one genotype each. Furthermore, the heterozygotes AO and BO express the phenotype of only one allele, while the heterozygote AB expresses the phenotypes of both alleles.

Thus, while Mendel led us in the right direction with his experiments on peas, he did not uncover the whole story. Dominance relationships exist in many forms across gene systems, or as the ABO gene shows, even within the same gene system.

PLEIOTROPY

Pleiotropy is the determination of several phenotypes by the action of a single gene. Since the human genome encompasses a complex genetic network, with perhaps 100,000 genes coordinately operating to govern the maintenance of bodily development and function, it is likely that all genes are pleiotropic to some degree.

The geneticist Sewall Wright considered the common occurrence of pleiotropy a "universal principle." In mice, for example, the single allele Tabby, which generates the familiar tabby coat markings, also changes the number of whiskers a mouse may have. Pleiotropy can come about in either of two ways. First, the functional gene product, say an enzyme, may function in several different biochemical manners. Consequently, an allele for such a gene could well function differently along several biochemical pathways. This is possibly why the Tabby allele affects both coat markings and whisker number in mice.

In PKU (phenylketonuria), where the only genetic difference is the activity of the enzyme phenylalanine hydroxylase, the serious difficulties (previously noted) result from a buildup of phenylketones. However, other major problems occur in phenylketonurics as a result of the fact that the PKU allele lies at a crossroads of several biochemical pathways. Because of the blockage in the synthesis of melanin (which gives skin, eyes, and hair their dark color), PKU homozygotes tend to be blond-haired and blue-eyed, even if these traits do not ordinarily run in their families. A high proportion also exhibit behavioral abnormalities, brain-wave anomalies as measured on electroencephalograms, and other neuro-muscular or mental disorders as a result of the blockage in the synthesis of dopamine (which is a chemical active in the neurons of the brain) and the thyroid hormone thyroxine (Figure 7–21).

More often, however, pleiotropy is the result of a gene with a single function that has cascading developmental effects. One example of this kind of pleiotropy occurs in the common rat (*Rattus norvegicus*). Here, a single allele that causes cartilage to develop abnormally ultimately results in death by virtue of multiple defects in the respiratory apparatus. Similarly, sickle-cell homozygosity, as we have already noted, ultimately affects many body organs. Again, recall that only a tiny genetic difference causes all the sickle-cell problems: a single amino acid difference in the sixth position of the 146 amino acids in beta-hemoglobin.

Another, more bizarre example of this sort of pleiotropy occurs in victims of Lesch-Nyhan syndrome, caused by an allele for the gene that produces the enzyme hypoxanthine-guanine phosphoribosyl transferase, or (mercifully) HPRT. HPRT catalyzes the breakdown of hypoxanthine, a chemical similar to the adenine and guanine in DNA. Indeed, hypoxanthine is occasionally present in the structure of RNA molecules. Nevertheless, when the metabolism of hypoxanthine is prevented by the Lesch-Nyhan allele, the result is a terrible and uncontrollable compulsion to bite off one's own lips and fingertips. Affected children must be forcibly restrained and flail about destructively, even when strapped to a chair or bed. Exactly how this phenotype comes to exist is not known,

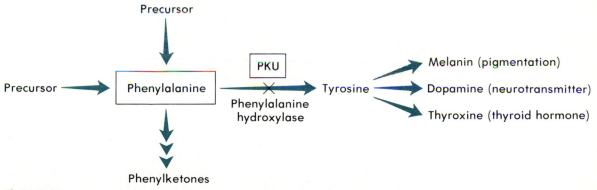

Figure 7-21

Phenylalanine lies at a metabolic crossroads: Mutations to the gene that codes for the enzyme phenylalanine hydroxylase cause PKU, which has diverse pleiotropic effects upon the phenotype.

Figure 7-22

(a) Hemoglobin is produced by the cooperative action of the alpha-globin gene on chromosome 16 and beta-globin gene on chromosome 11; (b) the functional hemoglobin protein consists of two alphas and two betas, each with a heme group, which contains an iron molecule.

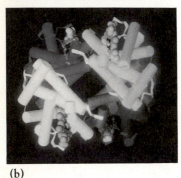

(b)

(a)

β–globin gene

α–globin gene

Functional hemoglobin protein

16

11

but it is the distinct result of a simple inability to break down enzymatically the hypoxanthine molecule.

Lesch-Nyhan syndrome affords an instructive example of how misleading it may be to infer the function of a gene from an observation of the phenotypic effects of its alleles. Although the allele leads to self-mutilation, it would be quite incorrect to assert that the normal allele has the function of preventing self-mutilation. Its function is to make HPRT; the bizarre phenotype is a developmental consequence of the absence of this enzyme. The fact that we can describe what goes wrong in the human body in the absence of proper gene functioning does not mean that we can describe the normal function of the gene or the way in which a normal phenotype is produced.

EPISTASIS

If pleiotropy is considered to be the production of several phenotypes from one gene, the other side of the coin is *epistasis*, the contribution of several genes to a single phenotype.

The most obvious form of epistasis occurs in the production of a protein composed of different subunits, each encoded by a separate gene. Hemoglobin, as we have seen, is formed by the products of two genes: an alpha-globin gene on chromosome 16 and the beta-globin gene on chromosome 11. If the beta-globin gene is present as an allelic variant, *it will not matter what allele is present in the alpha-globin gene:* An abnormal hemoglobin will be produced. Thus, normal hemoglobin is produced by the action of two genes, both of which are necessary for the emergence of the normal phenotype (Figure 7–22).

Epistasis is also the result of the complexity of biochemical affairs in the body. In *Drosophila,* for example, more than fifty different genes are known whose alleles produce a phenotype different from the normal red eye color. Again, this does not mean that there are fifty genes whose function is the trivial one of ensuring that the eyes come out red. Rather, it means that interrupting a large number of biochemical steps will lead to abnormal phenotypes. The nature of these biochemical steps is not known. Indeed, the very first *Drosophila* allele isolated, shortly after the turn of the century, causes the fly's eye to be white. It is still not known, however, exactly what the gene's protein actually does.

Just as in the case of Lesch-Nyhan syndrome, we would be incorrect to say that the PKU allele is "for" blondness, even though that is usually one of its phenotypes. Similarly, the fruitfly genes are not genes "for" eye color, although their presence may be necessary for the normal phenotype to emerge. They are, rather, links along a network of developmental and biochemical chains required for normal development, chains that can be broken at any point.

A final example of epistasis occurs in the case of the ABO blood group gene where, as we have seen, any one of four phenotypes can be present in humans: A, B, AB, or O. Some people, however, test as type O despite the fact that they do not have the O alleles. These people, it turns out, are homozygous for a rare allele (h) of a different gene (H). H actually works earlier in the biochemical chain of events than the ABO gene. As discussed previously, the ABO gene appears to plant a biochemical flag on the surface of an erythrocyte. This marker molecule, or antigen, ordinarily consists of a protein base with sugars attached (Figure 7–23). The tip of the antigen at one point consists of three sugars: galactose, N-acetylglucosamine, and another galactose. The H (normal) allele encodes an enzyme that adds a molecule of the sugar fucose to the end of the chain. To the new antigen, ending with four sugars, the enzyme product of the ABO gene adds either nothing (allele O), N-acetylgalactosamine (allele A), or galactose (allele B). Note that the tip of the antigen has just four sugars if the O allele is the only one active, but five sugars if A or B is active.

The h allele has the effect of preventing the *fourth* sugar, the one normally added by the product of the H allele, from attaching to the chain. As a result, people homozygous for h do not add a fifth sugar (the action of the ABO gene) because they do not have a fourth to add it to.

What is the phenotypic effect? None in the sense of health, longevity, or fertility, as far as anyone knows. However, if a blood test is given to an hh homozygote to check blood type, it invariably shows up as type O, regardless of the alleles that are actually present at the ABO gene. This is because the ABO gene product cannot work on a sugar chain only three sugars long; it requires a substrate four sugars long. And in the absence of a four-sugar chain, the ABO gene product does nothing. That is, it functions as a null allele, which is what the O allele is. Therefore, the H allele is required in order for the ABO gene to be expressed.

A person homozygous for hh—who appears to have blood type O but does not really—is said to have the Bombay phenotype, named for where it was first discovered. This phenotype may cause difficulties when such people receive blood—when the blood bearing the normal H-substance is transfused into a person with the Bombay phenotype, the regular A and B alleles that the recipient may have can now act upon it, creating A or B type blood, which is foreign to the recipient's system.

Genes in Populations

The study of genes, genotypes, and phenotypes is important to the study of evolution only insofar as it can be applied to the study of populations. As noted at the outset of this chapter, evolution is a change in the genetic composition of populations. Individual organisms are unique constellations of phenotypes, formed in part by unique combinations of genes. However, the lifetime of the individual organism is very short in comparison with that of the population or species of which it is a part.

In terms of the great amount of time needed to study evolution, therefore, the individual organism is a transient being. The organism represents, genetically, a very short-lived combination of genes in a single time, at a single place. It can thus have little significance in the evolution

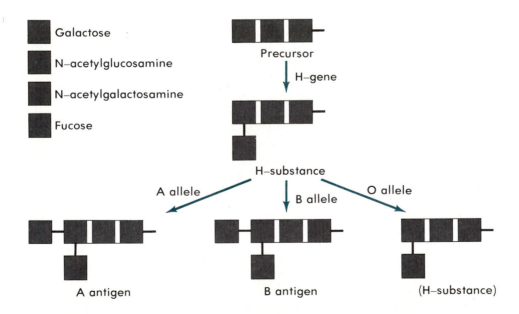

Figure 7-23

The ABO locus encodes an enzyme that modifies the H-substance. Allele A adds one sugar, allele B adds a different one, and allele O adds none.

of species, which occurs over long durations of time (thousands to millions of years) and across large geographic areas.

The structure that perseveres relatively intact for long enough periods of time, that can be studied over a wide geographic range, and that is, therefore, the structure of greatest interest to students of evolution, is not the organism, but the gene pool. Recall that the gene pool is the sum total of all the genes in a population. Changes in this gene pool constitute evolution.

Thus, evolution is *not* the change of one organism into another, but the change of one gene pool of a population into another. We consequently must turn from the genetics of individual organisms to the genetics of populations in order to understand the processes of evolution.

Furthermore, most phenotypic characters of interest to us are not the results of the action of single genes. Traits such as skin color, height, weight, body build, cranial volume, or tooth size vary continuously; that is, the phenotypes are not discrete, but grade into one another. Observation informs us that there are not simply dark and light people, or tall and short people. Rather, in any population, there are people with average height and pigmentation and other people with greater than average and less than average. (There are also certain rare alleles that lead to albinism or dwarfism as phenotypes, but we are considering only the normal population here.)

The inheritance of these continuously varying traits is complex. We know that taller-than-average people tend to have taller-than-average offspring, all other things being equal, so somehow genes are involved. However, it also is true that people growing up in the United States tend to be taller than their close relatives growing up elsewhere, which suggests a strong environmental component as well.

These complex characters are difficult to deal with at the level of the individual organism. We are all too familiar with the controversial issues of whether traits such as intelligence, cancer, or musical ability have a genetic component, and if so, how much of a genetic component. There are no good answers to such questions currently, as we simply do not know enough about the physiological processes that occur in the developing human to understand the emergence of these phenotypes in specific organisms. However, we can take a different approach by studying the distribution of phenotypes in populations. All we need to assume is that (1) these phenotypes have some sort of underlying genetic basis (remember, biological evolution is a change in the *genetic* composition of populations); (2) the genetic basis, however large or small, is the same in all members of the population; and (3) this genetic basis is the result of several genes, each contributing a little to the phenotype. We can then study changes in the distribution of phenotypes in a population through time and regard them as a reflection of underlying changes in the genetic structure of the population.

Figure 7-24

Distribution of a quantitative
trait in a population. In this
case the trait is height, and the
population is Hawaiian
women.

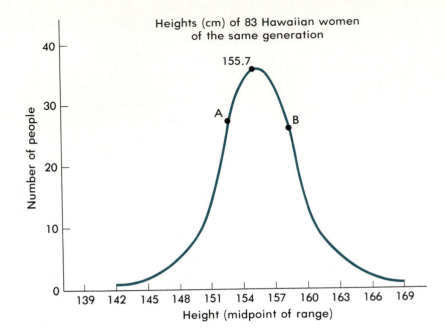

Polygenic Inheritance

The study of phenotypic characters caused by the interaction of many
genes—which are the characters of real interest—is called *polygenic inheritance, or quantitative characters,* since the phenotypic differences being
examined are differences of quantity. This field was founded by Francis
Galton in the late nineteenth century. His own work, however, was quite
naïve. For example, he thought he had shown that prominence was
genetic because the offspring of prominent people are often themselves
prominent. Of course, with his sample of the aristocracy of Victorian
England, Galton showed nothing more than that money is usually inherited—and prominence comes along with money. Fortunately, the modern
science of quantitative genetics is much more sophisticated. It deals with
the distribution of traits without regard to the actual physiological basis
of those traits. Indeed, the science of statistics was developed in large part
within the field of quantitative genetics by Galton's successors Karl
Pearson and Ronald Fisher.

INHERITED TRAITS

Consider a population of people who have had their heights measured.
The group can be represented graphically (Figure 7–24). This graph is
bell shaped, or normal, which is very common for such quantitative characters. Here, we happen to have measurements of height for 104
Hawaiian women, collected earlier this century. Notice that we can
describe this population with respect to an average value, or mean; and
we can classify any individual by her deviation from the population's

mean. Thus, in this population, the mean height is 155.7 cm, and person A falls 3 cm below the mean, while person B falls 3 cm above it.

Most organismal phenotypes of most populations can be described in this way. If we were to examine the descendants of a population 100 years in the future, we could expect to find that any of four things happened. First, the new curve might be identical to that of the original population (Figure 7–25a). There would consequently be no change in either the mean of the population or the shape of the curve. In this case, the distribution of phenotypes and presumably, then, of the underlying genotypes is unchanged through time. Apparently, the population has been simply reproducing itself and not changing. (Bear in mind that complex traits such as height are strongly influenced by environmental factors as well; changes in the distribution of phenotypes are *evolutionary* only if they represent changes to the gene pool.)

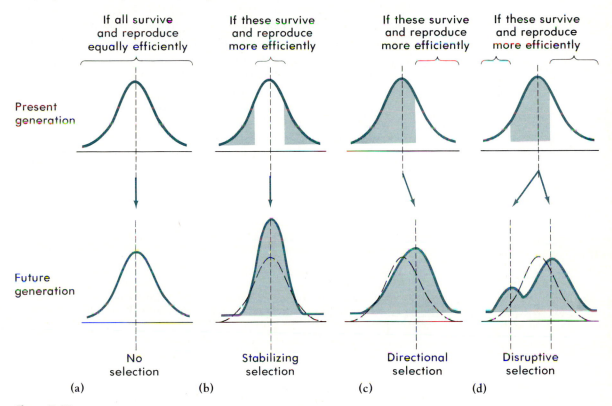

Figure 7-25

Over time, the distribution of a quantitative trait is affected by the reproduction of the members of a population. (a) If people anywhere on the distribution survive and reproduce with equal efficiency, there is no change in the future generation. (b) If people near the center of the distribution are favored, stabilizing selection is acting, and the distribution will become taller and narrower. (c) If people at one end of the distribution are favored, directional selection is occurring: The mean will shift, and the curve may become skewed in that direction. (d) If both ends are favored, disruptive selection is acting, and the result is morphological bifurcation of the population.

Second, we could find that the mean value has not changed but that the *shape* of the curve has. The curve has become narrower, and there are more people close to the mean value than there were before (Figure 7–25b). Obviously, the people with values close to the mean have done a better job of surviving and reproducing themselves and their phenotypes.

While an explanation for this trend in the case of height in a human population may not be easy to come up with, consider a study by Hermon Bumpus (in 1899) of the length of birds' wings. Bumpus examined sparrows that had died during a storm and compared several quantitative characters, notably wing size, against those birds that had survived. He found that much more variability occurred among the dead birds than among the survivors—that the live birds were distributed more closely around the mean value than were the dead birds. Apparently, it was advantageous for birds to have "normal-sized" wings, and not to have large or small wings (Figure 7–26). This process, the greater rate of survival and reproduction of organisms with phenotypes near the mean value, is called *stabilizing* natural selection.

Stabilizing Natural Selection   Stabilizing natural selection is conservative. It changes the genetic composition of a population by eliminating the phenotypic extremes in the group, birds with very large and very small wings, for example. Nevertheless, the selective agent (the storm) did not change the average length of the wings, as it was nearly the same before and after the storm. Therefore, evolution has occurred, but only in a very conservative sense: The gene pool has changed, but the average phenotype has not.

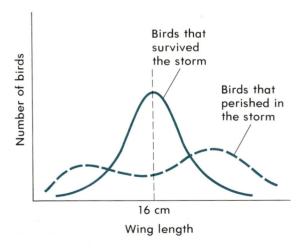

Figure 7-26

Bumpus found that survivors of the storm clustered around a mean value, while the wing lengths of those that perished in the storm were more widely distributed.

In humans, the classic illustration of stabilizing selection was made by M. Karn and L. S. Penrose in 1949 for birth weight. They showed that the phenotype of birth weight was distributed in a similar bell-shaped fashion, that the average birth weight in their sample of British babies was approximately 7.5 pounds, and that babies weighing below approximately 4.0 pounds and above approximately 10.0 pounds had difficulty surviving.

The third possible outcome of our analysis of the normally distributed phenotype at a later time is that the mean value has changed, but not the shape of the curve. In this case, individuals at one end of the normal curve have been more successful in surviving and reproducing than individuals around the mean or at the other end of the distribution (Figure 7–25c). This is *directional* natural selection, and the recognition of it is the major contribution to biology of Darwin and Wallace.

Directional Natural Selection   The direct result of directional natural selection is a descendant population in which the average member is different from the average member of the ancestral population. Directional selection, therefore, results in the transformation of a population through time, phenotypically and (insofar as the phenotype is produced by genes) genotypically as well. Directional selection is the major cause of adaptation in nature, because the environment constrains certain parts of the population to survive and reproduce more efficiently than others. In this sense, then, the population is changing its average phenotype to fit the demands of the environment and so becomes better adapted to the environment.

Consider a hypothetical population of *Homo erectus* (Chapter 12), with cranial capacities distributed normally around 900 cc. Some of these individuals possess 1,000 cc, while others possess 800 cc. If those with the larger skulls, and presumably the brains to fill them, are better able to survive and reproduce, and if this advantageous phenotype has a hereditary component, then succeeding generations will have a mean value slightly higher than that of the original population. Such a trend has proven very difficult to measure directly because the actual reproductive difference between the contrasting phenotypes may be very small yet produce dramatic effects over the eons of geologic time. Directional natural selection remains the most plausible and most powerful explanation for evolutionary trends in the historical succession of life. The effects of allowing organisms with certain phenotypes to survive and reproduce preferentially are, of course, readily available in our domesticated plants and animals (Figure 7–27).

Disruptive Natural Selection   The final possibility for a normally distributed trait is that the extremes may reproduce more efficiently than the mean, which would be selection against the mean (Figure 7–25d). This is called *disruptive* natural selection and results in the fragmentation of an ancestral population into two phenotypically different daughter populations (an important first step in some modes of speciation). In a patchy environmental setting, disruptive selection might be expected to make parts of a population well suited to one microhabitat and other parts well suited to a different one. The average member, however, might not be particularly well suited to either. Unfortunately, there are few well-studied cases of disruptive selection.

These processes operating on phenotypic distributions are evolutionary only insofar as the different phenotypes are caused in part by different interacting alleles. Therefore, as the one phenotype becomes more and more prevalent in a population, so, too, do the alleles in the gene pool that cause it to develop. This trend constitutes a change in the gene pool and is evolution as the term is applied to biological phenomena in modern times. Complex traits, such as height, can change dramatically in a single generation as a simple result of environmental effects; therefore, a change in the frequency distribution may not be indicative of evolution. This is the difficulty we face in knowing that evolution is at root a genetic process but in having access only to phenotypes.

The Hardy-Weinberg Law

The distribution of genes in a population can, in theory, be followed algebraically, as was recognized by the mathematicians G. H. Hardy and W.

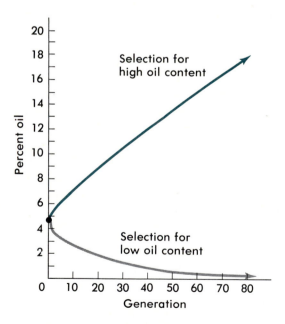

Figure 7-27

Since 1896, selection has been practiced for high-oil content and low-oil content in corn seeds. Despite minor short-term fluctuations, the results have shown fairly continuous change in both directions.

Weinberg and by the geneticist W. E. Castle, around the turn of the century. The Hardy-Weinberg Law (named by the geneticist Curt Stern in 1943) forms the basis for tracing the spread of genes through time—regardless of phenotypes.

Consider a gene pool in which there are two alleles, A1 and A2. A1 occurs in the population with a **frequency** "p," and A2 occurs with a frequency "q." These are the only two alleles present, so probability theory leads us to state that p + q = 1. The frequency of the A1A1 homozygous genotype should be equal to the probability of drawing two A1 alleles from the gene pool one after the other, or $p \times p = p^2$. The frequency of the A1A2 heterozygote should be equal to the probability of drawing an A1 allele and an A2 allele, but this can be done in two ways—either A1 and then A2, or A2 and then A1. Therefore, the frequency of the A1A2 heterozygote is $2 \times p \times q = 2pq$. The frequency of the A2 homozygote is the probability of drawing an A2 allele followed by another, or $q \times q = q^2$.

Because there are only three possible genotypes (A1A1, A1A2, and A2A2), their frequencies must sum to 1. Therefore, we can write:

$$p^2 + 2pq + q^2 = 1$$

where p^2 is the proportion of A1 homozygotes, 2pq is the proportion of heterozygotes, and q^2 is the proportion of A2 homozygotes. The Hardy-Weinberg Law thus generalizes the relationship between the proportion of alleles in the gene pool and the proportion of genotypes in the population. Furthermore, this generalization will hold and remain unchanged in all future generations.

The Hardy-Weinberg Law is an equilibrium law. The genotype proportions equilibrate with respect to one another and stay at the equilibrium values. It is, therefore, a nonevolutionary statement, that is, a generalization about heredity in the absence of evolution. More specifically, the Hardy-Weinberg Law tells us that if Mendelian segregation is the only force operating on a gene pool, evolution will not occur. Heredity is conservative: Populations tend to reproduce themselves faithfully.

Population Genetics

What, then, are the ways in which we can upset this equilibrium? The Hardy-Weinberg Law gives us a ground state by which we can compare real populations and decide whether they are changing or not. Five forces cause populations to deviate from the Hardy-Weinberg equilibrium and allow evolution to occur.

1. *Mutation.* In the Hardy-Weinberg case, we consider only two alleles. The introduction of a new allele by a change in the genetic constitution in the gamete of an individual organism produces added genetic variation. All alleles are ultimately the results of mutations.

frequency
Proportion of one item relative to the total.

2. *Natural Selection.* When organisms with one genotype have greater reproductive success than those with other genotypes, the conditions of the Hardy-Weinberg Law are violated, and the composition of the gene pool will be altered. We assumed implicitly in deriving the law that, for example, A1A1 and A2A2 individuals enjoy equal success in contributing genetic information to the next generation. Suppose, however, that A2A2 individuals enjoy a reproductive advantage over A1A1 and A1A2. Because they produce only A2 gametes, it follows that, to some degree, they will flood the next generation with A2 alleles. Therefore, the gene pool of the next generation would have the A2 allele over-represented, and evolution would have occurred.

Notice that we were discussing natural selection on phenotypes earlier and are now modeling natural selection on genotypes. These two ways of looking at natural selection relate to each other insofar as genotypes may cause or be correlated with the appearance of certain phenotypes.

3. *Gene Flow.* The influx of genetic material from an outside source by interbreeding alters the genetic composition of a population. Since the outside population may have a very different gene pool, it follows that contact between the two populations will change their gene pools and make them more alike than they had been previously. The gene pool of African Americans, for example, is generally intermediate between that of African blacks and American whites, reflecting centuries of genetic contact between the ancestral gene pools. Similarly, the gene pools of populations of European Jews are consistently found to be less similar to one another than they are to the gene pools of the local non-Jewish populations.

4. *Genetic Drift.* Genetic drift is quite different from gene flow and should not be confused with it, although it often is, by students. Genetic drift is a statistical concept, deriving from the small size of normal populations of real organisms. Recall the mating of two heterozygotes:

$$A1A2 \times A1A2 \rightarrow 1\ A1A1 + 2\ A1A2 + 1\ A2A2$$

Suppose, however, that this couple has only two children. We can make a statistical guess at the genotype of each one, but the only thing we can say for certain is that the genotypes would sort into Mendelian ratios *if they had an infinite number of offspring.* Obviously, they will not. The larger the number of offspring they have, the more likely they are to fall into, or extremely close to, the expected Mendelian ratios. The fewer offspring they have, the less likely are the Mendelian ratios to appear. And clearly, if they have fewer than four children, it is *impossible* to expect the Mendelian ratios to be present.

This problem of small population size violates the assumptions of the Hardy-Weinberg Law, in which we assume that Mendelian ratios will always appear, and by implication, that populations are infinitely large.

However, animals, especially mammals, and more especially primates and humans, tend to have offspring in much smaller numbers than they conceivably could. The smaller the number of offspring, the greater the likelihood and magnitude of deviation from the theoretical expectation. Similarly, the smaller the size of a population, the less likely is the gene pool to segregate exactly according to the Mendelian expectations. Elaboration of the role of genetic drift as an evolutionary force is due to the geneticist Sewall Wright.

A related concept is **founder effect**, wherein a small population is generated from a larger ancestral population. The larger the founding population, the more likely it is to be a fair genetic representation of the ancestral population. The *smaller* the founding population, the *less* so. Consequently, the genetic effect of a very rare allele may be considerably magnified if the allele happens to be in the small founding gene pool of a new population. This has indeed been shown to have occurred repeatedly in human groups.

One well-studied genetic isolate are the Amish of Lancaster County, Pennsylvania. A genetic study in 1964 by Victor McKusick and his colleagues found a frequency of the allele causing Ellis-van Creveld syndrome (which involves dwarfism, extra fingers, and heart deformities) to be approximately 7.3 percent (Figure 7–28). Outside this community and in other Amish communities, the frequency of the allele is less than 0.1 percent. The explanation for this anomalous gene pool of the Pennsylvania Amish is that among the relatively few early settlers of the area were a Mr. and Mrs. Samuel King, who arrived in 1744, and the present-day bearers of the Ellis-van Creveld syndrome allele are all lineal descendants of that couple.

5. *Nonrandom Mating.* In the Hardy-Weinberg case, we bring alleles (actually gametes containing alleles) together at random to create genotypes. Most commonly, however, similar organisms tend to mate with one another. This is called *assortative mating*. In human populations, for example, there is a strong tendency to mate assortatively for features such as height, skin color, educational level, and religion. These characters are obviously quite diverse in the degree to which they may be correlated with genetic variations. Nevertheless, assortative mating will tend to create an excess of homozygotes, by virtue the fact that (1), people phenotypically alike are often genotypically alike as well; and (2), homozygotes "breed true," while heterozygotes do not. An A1A1 × A1A1 mating can yield only A1A1 offspring, whereas an A1A1 × A2A2 mating will yield heterozygotes. As long as assortative mating is occurring, there will be a small but consistent drain on the frequency of heterozygotes. Assortative mating, therefore, tends to reduce heterozygosity and increase homozygosity. This outcome changes the genotype frequencies but does not in itself affect the allele frequencies. So, it shuffles alleles around within the gene pool but does not actually change the composition of the

founder effect

Microevolutionary process whereby a new population originates from a small, nonrepresentative sample of an older population, making the two populations somewhat genetically different from each other on the average. The smaller the founding population, the larger the magnitude of the difference; this is generally subsumed under genetic drift.

Figure 7-28

Ellis-van Creveld syndrome in a Pennsylvania Amish baby. In addition to several other phenotypes, polydactyly is part of this syndrome. Count the child's fingers.

gene pool. In creating an excess of homozygotes, however, assortative mating may give extreme phenotypes to a larger proportion of the population and thus allow directional natural selection more raw material on which to work. Assortative mating is a more general concept than **inbreeding**, where individuals mate with relatives (not only phenotypically similar individuals) at a higher-than-chance frequency.

Microevolution

The principles of population genetics describe mathematically the short-term changes in genetic structure that can occur in a species. Mutation is the source of variation, generating new alleles, but has little effect alone on a population, given that any specific mutation occurs very infrequently. It is the other forces that allow a new genetic variant to affect a population significantly.

Natural selection has several effects. Directional selection makes populations genetically different from one another, as they adapt to their local environments. Even adapting to a similar environment can occur through different genetic mechanisms: For example, populations in different parts of the world have adapted in genetically heterogeneous ways in response to malaria. Disruptive selection also makes populations different. On the other hand, stabilizing selection tends to homogenize populations because variants are being selected against.

Gene flow is the major force keeping populations homogeneous. Interbreeding of two genetically different populations makes each one more like the other. It also, however, can introduce new genetic variation into a particular population. Thus, gene flow reduces variation among populations but increases variation within a group. For speciation to occur, gene flow must be curtailed.

inbreeding

Preferential mating with genetic relatives (cultural relatives, such as in-laws, do not count). This increases the probability of a rare allele being homozygous in an offspring; in the population at large, one would have to calculate the probability of two copies of the rare allele coming together randomly (which would be remote), but here, they can both come from a recent common ancestor of the parents.

Figure 7-29

The action of genetic drift. In each of six small populations, both A1 and A2 alleles are present. If the allele frequencies fluctuate randomly, sooner or later, one allele will go extinct in each small population. We cannot predict what will happen in any particular population, but over time, half will come to have only A1, and half will have only A2. Thus, there is greater heterogeneity across populations but greater homogeneity within each population.

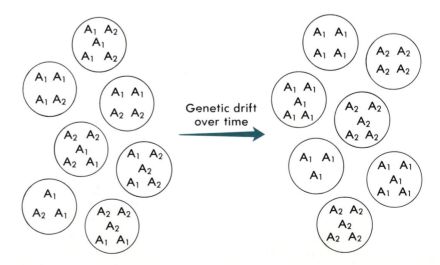

Genetic drift works in precisely the opposite way. The allele frequencies of two separate, small populations will generally diverge from each other; thus, genetic drift increases genetic variation among groups. Genetic drift, however, additionally leads to the loss of alleles in a population. This is because the frequency of a particular allele can fluctuate randomly at any value—except at zero. Once the frequency of the allele hits zero, it is lost and cannot be recovered until a new mutation occurs. Yet, by genetic drift, sooner or later the value of a drifting allele will hit zero.

Imagine a small population with two alleles, A1 and A2, at equal frequencies (both 50 percent) and of equal selective value, so that their spread will be governed only by genetic drift. Sooner or later, one of them will reach zero. Which one? It is impossible to tell in a particular circumstance, since this is a random process. However, if there are a lot of these populations, we can predict that half of them will ultimately have A1 go extinct (that is, reach zero frequency), and half will have A2 go extinct. Obviously, the gene pool of each small population has changed, from 50–50 to 100 percent of one of the alleles. Also, a specific small population (having only A1) is now likely to be different from its neighbor (having only A2).

Genetic drift, then, increases the variation among populations but reduces the variation within each population (Figure 7–29). Unlike natural selection, which can have the same effect on variation, genetic drift

Table 7–1

Effects of Microevolutiuonary Forces

Mutation

      Creates variation

Natural Selection

    Directional, Disruptive

      Increases between-group variation

      Reduces within-group variation

      Leads to adaptation

    Stabilizing

      Reduces within-group variation

Gene Flow

      Reduces between-group variation

      Increases within-group variation

Genetic Drift

      Increases between-group variation

      Reduces within-group variation

Inbreeding

      Increases homozygosity

does not make a population better adapted to its environment. This is nonadaptive change.

Inbreeding pushes genotypes toward homozygosity through time. Homozygotes can produce only more homozygotes, while heterozygotes produce some heterozygotes and some homozygotes. Therefore, in a situation in which individuals tend to mate with individuals genetically like themselves (namely, their relatives), fewer and fewer heterozygotes will be born. Nevertheless, while the alleles may find themselves arranged in a different set of vessels (genotypes), the composition of the gene pool remains the same. The gene pool of a population consisting of all heterozygotes is identical to the gene pool of a population consisting of half of one homozygote and half of the other homozygote—both will be 50–50 for each allele. If, however, there is selection for one or the other homozygote, inbreeding (by producing more homozygotes) can make that selective force work more efficiently (Table 7–1).

Summary

The processes of evolution are consequences of the processes of hereditary continuity. The fundamental units of biological heredity are known as genes. Two copies of each gene exist in almost every cell of the body, although an individual passes only one copy to a child. Which particular allele is passed on in a specific case is random and can therefore be envisioned only in terms of probabilities.

Biological diversity is maintained in a population in three ways. Mutations create new pools of alleles every generation, but their contribution to evolution is indirect because each mutation arises only rarely. Different combinations of alleles are put together on the same chromosome through the process of crossing over; and different combinations of chromosomes are put into the same cell by the processes of independent assortment and sexual reproduction.

A particular allele (which arises by mutation or which is introduced by gene flow from outside) can spread in a population through time in two ways. It can spread deterministically if it improves the survival and/or reproduction of the organism it helps to construct. Alternatively, it can spread stochastically if the population size is fairly small. In the former circumstance, the spread of the allele is under the control of natural selection. In the latter case, it is under the control of genetic drift.

1. How is biological variation created and perpetuated in a species?

2. Can paleontologists, who conceive of evolution as anatomical change, and geneticists, who conceive of evolution as genetical change, have the same evolutionary models?

3. What kinds of differences can you perceive between evolution in sexually reproducing organisms and in asexually reproducing organisms?

4. Which microevolutionary forces act in opposition to one another? How do you think their relative importance for humans has changed over the past few thousand years?

For Further Reading

Dobzhansky, T. (1970). *Genetics of the evolutionary process*. New York: Columbia University Press.

Mange A., & Mange, E. (1990). *Genetics: Human aspects* (2d ed.). Sunderland, MA: Sinauer.

Wallace, B. (1980). *Basic population genetics*. New York: Columbia University Press.

Molecular Genetics and Evolution

Molecular Genetics and Evolution

Immunology

We saw in the last chapter that the ABO blood-group system exemplifies many aspects of simple inheritance. The specific gene in question is located on chromosome 9 and contains the instructions for the production of an enzyme that attaches the final sugar to the antigenic coating of the red blood cell. Three major alleles are at the locus, two of which (A and B) cause different sugars to be attached, and the third of which (O) causes no sugar to be attached.

Mammals have evolved a complex system of defense against infection by foreign cells that centers on the recognition and distinction of the antigens that are supposed to be present in the body (self) from those that are not supposed to be present (nonself). From a practical standpoint, it means that if someone with type A blood receives a transfusion from someone with type B blood, the recipient's own system will recognize the antigens as foreign and attack the cells, obviously doing the patient little good. This, of course, is the basis for matching blood types before transfusing (Box 8–1).

IMMUNE SYSTEMS

An immune system will react against blood with foreign antigens, but not against blood with similar antigens or no antigens at all. Thus, as shown below, a person with type A blood can receive only type A blood or type O blood—blood with type B antigens (B or AB) will be rejected. By this reasoning, someone with type AB blood can be seen as a universal recipient, and someone with type O can be seen as a universal donor.

Phenotype	A	B	AB	O
Can receive blood from	A, O	B, O	A, B, AB, O	O
Can donate blood to	A, AB	B, AB	AB	A,B,AB,O

When presented with the same foreign antigen repeatedly, the immune system acquires the capacity to produce large amounts of highly specific **antibodies** to destroy the antigen or the cell which possesses the antigen. The organism is now immunized against the antigen, and this is the basis for vaccinations (Figure 8–1).

Antigens are universal on the cells of our bodies, and a complex antigen system called HLA governs skin transplantation. This system consists of a large cluster of genes and has so many different alleles that

antibody

Specific protein produced by the immune system to destroy or inactivate a foreign substance whose antigens stimulate the production of the antibody.

Figure 8-1
Some aspects of the immune
system.

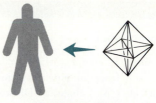

Foreign antigen
enters body

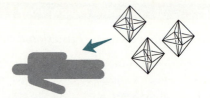

Antigen (in this case, a
pathogenic virus) reproduces.
Part of the immune system is
stimulated to produce antibodies.
Host body gets sick.

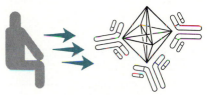

Some B–lymphocytes in blood
ultimately begin to produce the
"right" antibodies of many
possible ones coded by genes—
it is highly specific to this
antigen, and subsequently
inactivate or destroy it.

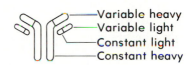

Variable heavy
Variable light
Constant light
Constant heavy

Antibody protein
or immunoglobulin

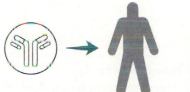

Immune system "remembers"
antigen; has specific antibodies
ready. Subsequent reinvasion by
same antigen is terminated quickly.

until the development of immunosuppressive drugs, only skin from
another part of the same body or from a very close relative could be
transplanted with confidence.

In addition to the ABO antigens, other red blood cell antigens are
known. The Rh antigen was discovered in 1939, when a rabbit immunized against the blood antigens of a rhesus macaque produced a strong
antibody reaction against human blood as well. It was later found that
about 85 percent of humans have the Rh antigen (Rh-positive), while 15

The Immune System, Functional and Dysfunctional

The immune system is our primary means of staying healthy and alive. It consists of a complex network of genetic and physiological systems: several gene clusters, which have many alleles and which function in a highly regular fashion to combat infection by foreign cells or molecules.

The class of cells which have a primary responsibility in the immune reaction are called *lymphocytes*. There are two kinds of lymphocytes: those produced by the thymus, and those produced by the bone marrow. From there, they migrate to characteristic regions of the throat, underarm, spleen, lower back, and genital area—the areas that become tender when one has "swollen glands."

Lymphocytes from the bone marrow produce large quantities of proteins called *immunoglobulins*, which actually carry out the business of neutralizing the foreign entity. There are five classes of immunoglobulins, each with different properties: IgA, IgD, IgE, IgG, and IgM. IgG, for example, helps fight infection in fetuses, as it is small enough to cross the placenta and travel from mother to fetus, while IgA and IgM fight infection in babies, being transported in breast milk.

Each immunoglobulin molecule consists of distinct protein chains, coded for by several regions of DNA. For example, an IgG protein consists of a light protein chain of about 220 amino acids and a heavy protein chain of about 440 amino acids. Each chain, heavy or light, consists of a variable region and a constant region, and sometimes a junction region as well, between them. And there are about 1000 genes coding for each variable region (hence, "variable"), while less than 10 code for each constant region.

The immunological specificity of each cell comes through a process of somatic splicing of DNA. In other words, by a series of processes not well understood, after being stimulated by an antigen, a cell "selects" a gene for a variable region and brings it into close spatial contact with genes for other parts of the immunoglobulin protein molecule. Thus, the instructions for a heavy chain of an IgG molecule result from the physical union of the genes for a variable ("V") chain, a "D" segment, a joining ("J") region, then three constant chains, and the subsequent transcription of a single mRNA after the bits of DNA have been spliced together. (Note that this is DNA splicing, not RNA splicing! RNA splicing does happen, but only after the DNA rearranges and a transcript is made.) The cell continues to produce this specific protein throughout its lifespan, although it had many possibilities at the outset.

Though there is a potentially huge number of antibodies each lymphocyte could make, each cell nevertheless makes only one highly specific one. The immunological reactions involve a process of clonal selection—whereby the lymphocytes manufacturing the appropriate immunoglobulin become prolific and create a genetically identical colony of cells, a clone, which makes the same specific immunoglobulin protein.

Since there are many genes, several kinds of immunoglobulins, several kinds of immunological reactions possible, and many other facets to the immune system, it is extremely flexible. This genetic system is also highly polymorphic, which is why some people are more resistant to certain diseases than other people.

Sometimes, however, the immune system works too efficiently, and the results can range from benign if bothersome (allergies) to life threatening (diseases such as lupus and myasthenia gravis). On the other hand, sometimes the immune system can fail to respond adequately. Indeed, undoubtedly the greatest concern in the area of public health at present centers around a failure of the immune system—Acquired Immune Deficiency Syndrome, or AIDS.

There are three ways of contracting AIDS: 1) being born to a mother who has AIDS; 2) from the blood of someone who has AIDS; and 3) having sexual contact with someone who has AIDS. Thus, most adult cases in the United States are either among intravenous drug abusers who share needles or among those who contract it venereally.

By an accident of history, the earliest U.S. cases of the disease were diagnosed in homosexual males, so that a decade later, that community is disproportionately represented among AIDS victims, and there are more U.S. men afflicted with AIDS than women. Nevertheless, it is equally transmissible heterosexually; and in Africa, where the disease has been spread by prostitutes, males and females are stricken in equal proportions, principally through heterosexual contact. The likelihood of sexual transmission, however, is very unpredictable in any specific case.

AIDS appears to be caused by a virus known as HIV, or human immunodeficiency virus. Presence of the virus appears to be necessary to develop the syndrome, but it may be many years between the time the virus is acquired and the symptoms begin to appear. Nevertheless, the test for AIDS is actually a test for the HIV virus, and those who are HIV-positive are considered at great risk of developing AIDS in the future and of transmitting it to others.

As the biological similarity of nonhuman primates to humans was critical in understanding and eradicating polio and kuru (see Chapter 17), so, too, are primates being used in the fight against AIDS. This obviously creates a moral dilemma—sacrificing the lives of nonhuman primates in the hopes of saving the lives of humans (Chapter 18). One discovery already has been the difficulty in getting a chimpanzee to become HIV-positive and the inability (thus far) of getting a chimpanzee to express the symptoms. Since chimpanzees are generally susceptible to all human diseases, this suggests that AIDS is a very recently evolved virus with a very specific host organism. A virus resembling HIV has been detected in *Cercopithecus*, and it was once thought that the disease originated in these monkeys and was subsequently transmitted to humans—but this is now considered very unlikely.

Until there is a cure or vaccine, the strongest weapon we have is education and behavior modification. Blood banks now routinely screen for HIV, and practicing safe sex is the watchword for the 1990s. Unfortunately, AIDS intersects a number of strong taboos in our culture—venereal disease, homosexuality, and drug abuse—which sometimes renders it difficult to discuss openly. Indeed, one all-too-common, if grossly inhumane, attitude is that the disease is a judgment on the wicked and that therefore, the victims of AIDS somehow deserve it.

This is highly reminiscent of the attitudes surrounding syphilis in the early part of the twentieth century. Such attitudes retarded efforts to treat and cure syphilis and, indeed, often helped it to spread—by curtailing educational efforts through censorship; by stigmatizing the affected and forcing them underground; by denying the realities of its transmission and replacing them with misinformation such as contraction of the disease through toilet seats and casual contact; by seeing the disease as a moral rather than an epidemiological problem, as if sex were the issue, not the disease; and most importantly, by taking the focus away from how to control and combat the disease.

AIDS presents us with a series of powerful social conflicts about the meaning and the risks of sexuality, as did syphilis before it. It also raises the same questions about the role of the state in providing and protecting public health, and the potential conflict of individual civil liberties with the common welfare.

References:

Alt, F. W., Blackwell, T. K., & Vancopoulos, G. D. (1987). Development of the primary antibody repertoire. *Science*, 238:1079–1087.

Brandt, A. M. (1988). The syphilis epidemic and its relation to AIDS. *Science*, 239:375–380.

percent do not (Rh-negative). The genetics of the Rh antigen are not as well understood as ABO, and the subtly different phenotypes are thought to be produced either by three genes with several alleles or by a single gene with many alleles. Nevertheless, the Rh system can be painted in broad strokes as a one-gene system with two alleles (Rh+ and Rh−), with the positive allele dominant and the negative allele recessive.

The proper functioning of the immune system can sometimes work against the organism's best interests. ABO incompatibility was the cause of many deaths before the discovery of blood groups. In the case of Rh, a female recessive homozygote (Rh-negative/Rh-negative) who marries either a heterozygote (Rh-negative/Rh-positive) or a dominant homozygote (Rh-positive/Rh-positive), has a good chance via Mendel's First Law of carrying in her body a fetus possessing Rh antigens, even though she herself does not. The placenta successfully keeps the fetal blood separate from the maternal blood, but at birth, some fetal cells enter the mother's bloodstream and can immunize her against the Rh antigen. Once a mother is immunized against the Rh antigen, her system will recognize the next Rh-positive fetus as foreign and attack it. The result is called hemolytic disease of the newborn, or erythroblastosis fetalis. If the Rh phenotypes of the parents are known, the disease can now be prevented medically.

STUDYING EVOLUTIONARY RELATIONS THROUGH IMMUNOLOGY

The immune system has a useful property which enables us to study evolution, the property of *cross-reactivity*. When an organism has been immunized against an antigen, it can be stimulated to produce antibodies not only by another exposure to the original antigen, but by a slightly different antigen as well. In this case, however, the intensity of the immune reaction will be somewhat weaker, depending upon just how similar the antigen is to the original one.

Let us suppose, therefore, that we immunize a test animal, say a rabbit, against a specific antigen, say the human protein albumin. We know that every time we expose the rabbit's system to human blood, a strong immunological reaction will occur. If, however, we decide to fool the rabbit's immune system and give it not human albumin, but *gorilla* albumin, what will happen? The rabbit blood will react, but not quite as strongly. And if we give it baboon albumin, it will react less strongly still. If we could measure the intensity of these immunological reactions, then we could get an idea of exactly how similar human albumin, gorilla albumin, and baboon albumin are to one another.

Crude experiments of this sort were performed as early as the turn of the century by G. H. Nuttall; however, with technical refinements, it was the work of Morris Goodman in the early 1960s that made molecular anthropology a viable research area. Goodman used an *Ouchterlony plate*, as shown in Figure 8–2. In the bottom well was placed the serum drawn from a rabbit which had been immunized against a specific antigenic protein and, therefore, contained antibodies against it. In the upper wells were placed similar antigens from two other primate species. The antigens and antibodies were allowed to diffuse through the agar matrix of the Ouchterlony plate (this technique is called agar gel diffusion). If the rabbit serum encountered an antigen similar to the one it was immunized against, it reacted strongly; and if it encountered an antigen not very similar, it reacted weakly. Goodman was thus able to test pairs of primate species against one another to see which antigen of a pair of primates was more similar to that of a third primate. The more similar of the two showed a *spur* where the antigens and antibodies met.

Since the proteins that were being used as antigens were a reflection of a small bit of the genetic instructions of these primates, Goodman argued that he was getting at the true genetic relationships of these pri-

Figure 8–2

Using rabbit antibodies to study the relationships of primate proteins.

Rabbit is immunized against an antigen—say, a human protein

Blood containing antibodies against human protein is drawn

Is human protein more similar to gorilla or to baboon? Will the antibodies made against human protein react more strongly to gorilla or baboon protein?

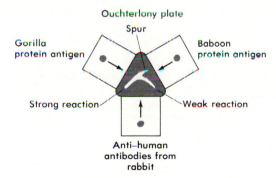

Ouchterlony plate

Spur

Gorilla protein antigen

Baboon protein antigen

Strong reaction

Weak reaction

Anti–human antibodies from rabbit

Rabbit serum containing antibodies against human protein are placed in bottom well. Gorilla and baboon antigenic proteins are placed in upper wells and allowed to react with antibodies against human. Reaction against gorilla's antigen is much stronger than reaction against baboon antigen. This implies that gorilla's protein is more similar to human than baboon is. Note the spur hanging over the side of the stronger reaction.

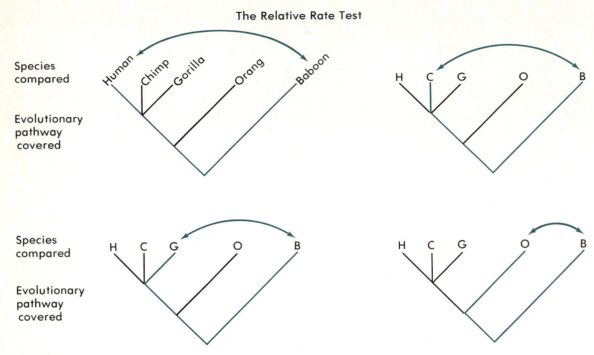

Figure 8-3

Though each of these four evolutionary pathways spans the same amount of evolutionary time (the time since the cercopithecoids and hominoids diverged from one another), a difference in evolutionary rate would make some of the immunological distances appear larger or smaller than others. Sarich and Wilson found that the immunological distances across the four evolutionary pathways were very similar; thus, they inferred that the rates of change along each lineage were about the same.

mates. He was comparing the similarity of proteins of different species with one another, which was a reflection of their genes, using the immune system of a rabbit as his instrument. The results he obtained were highly concordant with the phenotypic relations of the primates, with one interesting exception. The orang-utan, which looks somewhat like the chimpanzee and gorilla—they are all great apes—turned out to be relatively genetically distant from a tight group consisting of chimpanzee, gorilla, and human.

    In the late 1960s, a different immunological technique called microcomplement fixation was adopted by Vincent Sarich and Allan Wilson. While the fundamental principle remained the same, Sarich and Wilson's technique enabled them not only to compare the relative intensity of two immunological reactions, but actually to measure the intensity of a given reaction numerically. They were thus able to calculate an **immunological distance** between any two species, which they interpreted as an estimate of how genetically different the two species were.

immunological distance

Measurement of the amount of difference between the antigens of two species, judged by the extent to which the antigens of one species cross-react with the antigens of the other. To the extent that the antigens are genetically coded, this is also a genetic distance.

The Molecular Clock

Sarich and Wilson found that the rate of accumulation of immunologi-cal/genetic differences did not fluctuate widely across hominoid taxa by means of a *relative rate test* (Figure 8–3). This involved comparing each hominoid to a specific nonhominoid relative, such as a baboon. Since the same 30 million or so years separates the cercopithecoid from *all* homi-noids, would the amount of immunological evolution between the cercop-ithecoid and each hominoid be roughly the same, or would some lineages have accumulated more change than others? It turned out that the immunological distance between a baboon and a gorilla was about the same as the immunological distance between a baboon and a chimpanzee, a baboon and an orang-utan, or a baboon and a human. Note from Figure 8–3 that if the immunological distance between, say, baboon and chim-panzee turned out to be much greater than the baboon–human, baboon–gorilla, or baboon–orang distances, one could conclude that the antigens of the chimpanzee were changing faster than those of the human, gorilla, or orang.

If these rates of change did *not* vary widely across lineages—which is what was found—then they could be used as a **molecular clock** to date the divergence of any two species from each other. One need only know the rate of change, and then, from the immunological distance between any two species, one could calculate how long it has been since they began accumulating antigenic differences from each other. Such a calcu-lation is not highly technical: If you are in a car going 30 miles per hour and you have traveled 60 miles, then you have been driving for two hours.

Sarich and Wilson found a very small difference between human, chimpanzee, and gorilla antigens. They then performed a molecular clock calculation and concluded that if the Cercopithecoidea and Hominoidea diverged 30 million years ago, then human, chimpanzee, and gorilla diverged from one another only about 4–5 million years ago.

This challenged two orthodox ideas that were deeply ingrained in 1967. First, chimpanzees and gorillas are very similar creatures anatomi-cally, and both are fairly distinct from humans. Yet genetically, all three seemed to be virtually indistinguishable from one another. This seemed to imply that although organic evolution is caused by genetic change, one could note very little genetic change causing very much organismal change in the human lineage (Figure 8–4). Second, the date of 5 million years seemed far too recent for the emergence of the human lineage. Dental fragments from 14 million years ago (*Ramapithecus*, Chapter 11) were suggestive human in form, indicating to most paleontologists the existence of a human lineage at least that old.

Three objections could be raised to Sarich and Wilson's work. First, the observation of very little genetic difference between human, chim-panzee, and gorilla could be explained equally well by either (1) an equal rate of change and a 5-million-year divergence date for all three species,

molecular clock

The observation that the rate of accumulation of genetic differ-ence between two species is roughly proportional to the time since they have diverged from each other.

Figure 8-4

Though one could easily distinguish actress Dorothy Lamour from Jiggs the chimpanzee phenotypically, the differences are far smaller genotypically.

as Sarich and Wilson argued; or (2) a slower rate of change in the human lineage, leading to an *equal amount* of change over a *longer* period of time—hence, a more ancient divergence simply being underestimated by Sarich and Wilson (Figure 8–5).

Second, the molecular clock was being calibrated with a divergence date of 30 million years for Hominoidea-Cercopithecoidea obtained from the fossil record and was challenging a fossil-based divergence of humans, chimpanzees, and gorillas. There is, argued opponents of the molecular clock, considerable circularity in using one fossil-based date to challenge another.

Third, the immunological distance provided a very crude estimate of the genetic relationships of organisms. The genetic material encompassed far more than the tiny portion being estimated by these techniques. Perhaps other, more direct genetic studies would reveal different evolutionary patterns than those found immunologically.

The conclusions of Sarich and Wilson have stood up remarkably well, given the potential difficulties. The divergence of humans and African apes is no longer considered to be over 14 million years, but closer to 5 million years ago—perhaps 7 or 8 million years ago. And the patterns they found using proteins as substitutes for actual examinations of DNA tend to be supported by the DNA itself.

The genetic relationships of primates can be studied in many ways that differ according to the methods used, the remoteness of the phenotype being studied from the genotype itself (after all, immunological reactions are still phenotypes), and the ease of interpretation of the results. Molecular studies can provide an independent test of phylogenetic hypotheses derived from anatomical studies and can tell us about how the genetic material itself changes through time. It is, therefore, useful to take a close look at the structure of genes and gene products in order to appreciate the kinds of genetic evolutionary comparisons we can make.

Chromosome Structure and Evolution

The twenty-three pairs of human chromosomes can be seen during cell division and can be stained to reveal at least two major patterns of bands across each individual chromosome. The first pattern, called *G-bands*, allows the clear identification of each pair of chromosomes from every other pair (Figure 8–6). It also allows clinicians to detect rearrangements of the chromosomes. In general, people with chromosomal rearrangements have no clinical abnormalities themselves, but the addition or deletion of chromosomes or segments of chromosomes almost invariably has drastic harmful phenotypic effects.

For example, deletion of part of one of the chromosome 5 pair causes *Cri-du-Chat syndrome*, which includes heart defects and retardation (and also causes a "cat's cry" from the afflicted baby). On the other hand, the addition of a third chromosome 21 causes the well-known *Down's syndrome*, the phenotype of which includes retardation, short stature, stubby hands and feet, a "simian crease" on the palm of the hand, epicanthal folds of the eye, and heart defects.

Figure 8–5

(a) If the proteins of humans and chimpanzees were evolving at the same rate, then they appeared to diverge from one another 4–5 million years ago. But (b) if humans have slowed down and most of the difference in the human-chimp comparison is on the chimp line, the divergence could be earlier.

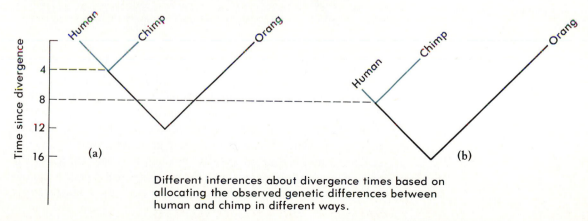

Different inferences about divergence times based on allocating the observed genetic differences between human and chimp in different ways.

Figure 8-6

G-banded chromosomes of a normal male.

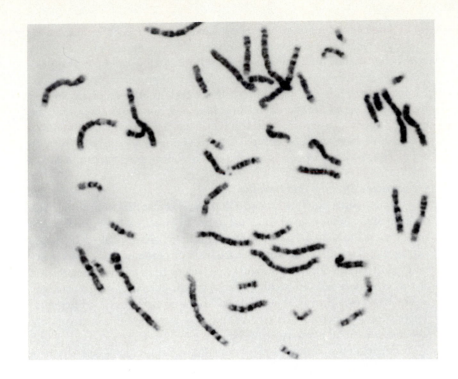

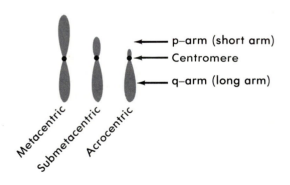

Figure 8-7

A chromosome is characterized by the position of the centromere, which divides it into two arms.

A chromosome (Figure 8–7) is analytically divisible into two parts, a long arm (q-arm) and a short arm (p-arm). The arms are separated by a centromere, which is involved in moving chromosomes to opposite ends of the cell during cell division. If the chromosome has arms of equal length, it is *metacentric*. If the arms are of slightly different lengths, it is *submetacentric*, and if they are greatly unequal, it is *acrocentric*. In the evolution of humans, two acrocentric chromosomes still found in the living apes and some monkeys have fused to form the large submetacentric chromosome we call human chromosome 2 (Figure 8–8). This changed the number of chromosome pairs from twenty-four to twenty-three, though it did not change the quantity or the quality of the genetic information.

The **genome** is very strongly constrained to the presence of two, and only two, copies of every piece of genetic information. Curiously, some parts of the genome tolerate fluctuations in quantity well. These regions are noninformational (devoid of genes) and a major class of these gene-less regions is stained by the other major banding pattern, *C-banding*.

C-bands appear at the centromere of every chromosome. In humans, four regions have additional C-bands. These are just below the centromere on chromosomes 1, 9, and 16, and at the end of the long arm of the Y chromosome (Figure 8–9a). Although these probably have no phenotypic effect, it is interesting to note that these four C-bands are not present in the apes. Instead, chimps and gorillas have C-bands at the tips of most of their chromosomes in addition to the C-bands at the centromeres (Figure 8–9b). Orangs have C-bands only at the centromeres. It is not known why, but C-bands generally appear to vary widely in size *within* a species and in location *between* species.

CHROMOSOME ORGANIZATION

Each chromosome consists of one long strand of DNA, with attendant proteins, packaged in a very regular way, though it is not known exactly how. If we were to strip a chromosome, we would be left with a protein scaffold and a veritable ocean of DNA (Figure 8–10). If we focus on a small segment of the DNA and stretch it taut, we find fundamental units

genome

The entire DNA sequence of one (haploid) cell.

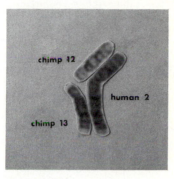

Figure 8-8

In the human lineage, a fusion of two chromosomes has resulted in the formation of human chromosome 2, reducing the haploid number from 24 to 23, though the G-banding pattern is preserved.

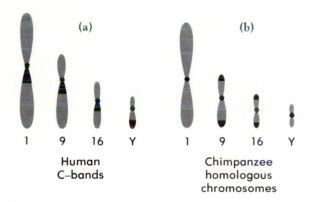

Figure 8-9

(a) C-banded chromosome of a human male; note that each chromosome looks much the same as the others, except for 1, 9, 16, and Y, which bear distinctive C-bands. (b) In the chimpanzee these regions are not present, but C-bands are present at the tips of many chromosomes, unlike humans.

histone

Alkaline protein which binds to DNA to form the nucleosome structure.

denature

To heat a solution of DNA, breaking apart the molecule at the midline, into single strands.

of chromosomal organization called *nucleosomes*. These are composed of 200 base-pairs (bp) of DNA tightly wrapped around a cluster of eight proteins called **histones**. A ninth histone protein attaches to the DNA between nucleosome bodies. Removing the histones leaves us nothing but the DNA double helix (Figure 8–11).

Comparing Genomes Across Species: DNA Hybridization　　A useful technique for comparing the DNA of one species with another is called DNA hybridization. Here we make use of the fact that DNA is a double-stranded molecule whose strands are held together by weak hydrogen bonds connecting the nucleotide pairs A–T and G–C. The strands can be separated or **denatured** when the bonds are broken by the addition of energy in the form of heat.

By taking the DNA of one species, denaturing it, and mixing it with a vast excess of denatured DNA from a different species, we can fool the first species' DNA into pairing with DNA from the second (Figure 8–12).

Figure 8-10

Most of the proteins have been removed from the DNA of this chromosome, leaving only a scaffold and a mass of DNA loops.

Figure 8-11

Though chromosomes are large packages of DNA, little is known about the manner in which DNA folds so precisely into compact shapes. The lowest level of DNA packaging, the nucleosomes, are fairly well understood, but above that, there is mostly conjecture.

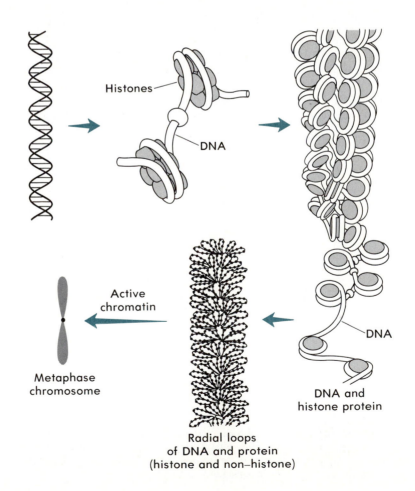

Histones

DNA

Active chromatin

Metaphase chromosome

Radial loops of DNA and protein (histone and non–histone)

DNA

DNA and histone protein

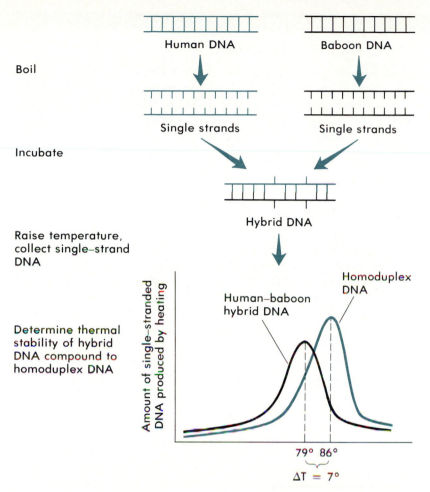

Boil

Human DNA

Baboon DNA

Single strands

Single strands

Incubate

Hybrid DNA

Raise temperature, collect single–strand DNA

Determine thermal stability of hybrid DNA compound to homoduplex DNA

Amount of single–stranded DNA produced by heating

Homoduplex DNA

Human–baboon hybrid DNA

79° 86°

ΔT = 7°

Figure 8-12

DNA hybridization is a two-part procedure. First, hybrids are made by radioactively labelling the DNA of one species, denaturing it, and mixing it with a large amount of DNA from another species. The second part makes use of the fact that hydroxylapatite, a chemical found naturally in bone, traps double-stranded DNA but not single-stranded DNA. Thus, as the heat is raised on a mixture of hybrid DNA on hydroxylapatite, it denatures into single strands and is released.

The resulting double-stranded DNA is hybrid, or **heteroduplex** DNA, consisting of one strand from one species and one strand from another species. Since the DNA comes from two different species, it is not as perfectly bonded as **homoduplex** DNA, whose strands are both from the same species. The reason for the less perfect bonding is that mutations have arisen in each lineage since the divergence of the two species, and their DNA consequently differs by virtue of those mutations. Because there are fewer bonds holding the hybrid DNA together, it requires less energy (less heat) to denature it. The difference, therefore, between the temperature at which heteroduplex DNA denatures and that at which homoduplex DNA denatures gives a crude estimate of how similar the DNA is from the two species forming the heteroduplex.

In general, heteroduplexes formed between any combination of human, chimpanzee, and gorilla DNA will denature at about 1 or 2 degrees less than homoduplex DNA. DNA composed of hybrids between

heteroduplex

DNA molecule in which the two complementary strands are from different species.

homoduplex

DNA molecule in which the two complementary strands are from the same species.

The Cystic Fibrosis Gene

Molecular genetic techniques are increasing our understanding of the genetic basis of many diseases. In a few cases, "reverse genetics" has been used to identify the primary defect involved.

In traditional genetic analyses, one attempts to isolate a variant protein or RNA from a patient, characterize it, and map it to a chromosomal location. Chromosomal mapping in this case can be performed by using the isolated DNA as a probe, tagging it with a radioactive or fluorescent marker, making it single-stranded, and then allowing it to find a partner on a microscope slide of metaphase chromosomes. When the DNA probe hybridizes to a complementary sequence on the chromosome, a photograph or X-ray exposure will reveal where the probe has bound, and therefore, where the gene is located.

In reverse genetics, the sequence of isolation and mapping is switched. Cystic fibrosis, the most prevalent genetic disorder among Caucasians, affects one in 2,000 newborns in the United States. The isolation of this gene in 1989 was an important step in clinical genetic applications of molecular techniques.

First, pedigrees were analyzed for genetic mark-ers, regions of DNA that accompanied the cystic fibrosis gene across generations, without being separated from it by crossing-over. Cystic fibrosis could be seen to be inherited with DNA markers on chromosome 7—but there are hundreds of millions of nucleotides on that chromosome. These markers were labelled and used as DNA probes for further analysis. Cloned bits of human DNA were then isolated by virtue of hybridizing to these DNA probes (Figure 8–13). The end of one clone was then used as a probe to locate another DNA clone that would hybridize to it, which would extend the known region farther. Then the end of the new clone was used as a probe. By using a variant of this method of "chromosome walking," researchers accumulated 280,000 continuous base-pairs of DNA clones near or around the cystic fibrosis gene. They then applied evolutionary logic.

Since intergenic DNA evolves rapidly, and coding, genic DNA slowly, they reasoned that the cystic fibrosis gene would be distinguishable from the morass of noncoding DNA by being conserved across species. Consequently, when these DNA clones were isolated, they were used as probes to detect sequence similarity between the cloned

probe

A short piece of DNA which can be used in molecular genetics to locate DNA with a similar sequence, since it will hybridize, by virtue of being complementary to the other strand of DNA.

any of these three species and the orang-utan will denature at about 3 degrees lower than homoduplex DNA. Hybrids between these four species and the gibbon will show a reduction of about 4 degrees, and those from these hominoids and a cercopithecoid monkey will show a reduction of about 7 degrees.

The principle of DNA hybridization has broader applications. Any single-stranded DNA sequence will spontaneously hybridize to a sequence nearly complementary to it. This allows geneticists to isolate any precisely defined stretch of DNA from the billions of nucleotides in the genome by simply using a known sequence as a labelled **probe** and hybridizing it to the unknown DNA. The probe finds a complementary mate in the unknown DNA, which tells the investigator the location of a DNA sequence similar to the probe used (Box 8–2).

human DNA and the homologous DNA of a cow, mouse, and hamster. The detection of hybridization across these mammalian orders suggested similarity in DNA sequence, which suggested the presence of a conserved region in the DNA clone, which in turn suggested the presence of a gene.

The next step involved characterizing the gene product using the new, conserved DNA probe, which contained at least part of the cystic fibrosis gene. Only certain types of cells express the gene, and one type of cell was found in sweat glands. From these cells, mRNA was isolated. An enzyme called reverse transcriptase makes DNA copies from RNA templates, and adding the enzyme to the RNA from these cells enabled the researchers to make DNA copies of all the mRNAs in the cell. Using their conserved DNA probe against the DNA derived from the cellular mRNA permitted them to isolate the whole message, more than 6 kilobases (kb) in length.

This message, however, was derived from a mature messenger RNA, one whose introns had already been spliced out and whose complexity was still not fully known. Now using the newly isolated message (known as a complementary DNA, or cDNA, since it is derived from RNA) as a probe, the researchers were able to isolate and clone the gene itself.

The cystic fibrosis gene is more than 250 kb long (alpha hemoglobin is about 1 kb) and consists of twenty-four exons (alpha hemoglobin has 3). Of the 1,480 amino acids in the normal protein product, number 508 is phenylalanine and is absent (deleted) in most cystic fibrosis patients. The protein itself appears to sit in the cell membrane of the lungs and facilitates the secretion of ions and water through the cells of the lungs. The defective protein is unable to secrete efficiently, causing the lungs to accumulate a thick mucus, which leads to serious infection to which the patient ultimately succumbs.

Cloning and characterizing the gene and the defect will aid immediately in diagnosis and in genetic counseling for risks of passing it on. It still remains to be cured.

Reference:

Marx, Jean L. (1989). The cystic fibrosis gene is found. *Science*, 245:923–925.

GENOME STRUCTURE

Genes, the genetic information encoded in the DNA molecule, are located on chromosomes at specific locations. The chromosomes of multicellular organisms, however, contain much more than just genes—they contain extra DNA. The function and origin of this extra DNA is one of the larger mysteries of biology at present.

If we consider the protein-coding part of the genome to be the hereditary information, there appears to be about fifty times more DNA in a cell than is necessary to encode it all. We do not know what this extra DNA does, if anything. *Satellite DNA*, for example, accounts for about 4 percent of the human genome, and consists of simple nucleotide sequences (from a few up to about 300 nucleotides) repeated millions of times, one next to another. Short interspersed elements (*SINEs*) are distributed apparently at random throughout the genome. One class of these, called *Alu repeats*, consists of nearly a million copies of a DNA sequence 300 nucleotides long, scattered throughout the genome with no apparent rhyme or reason. These are found only in the genomes of anthropoids, although prosimians appear to have related sequences, and other mammals have other kinds of interspersed elements. While we do

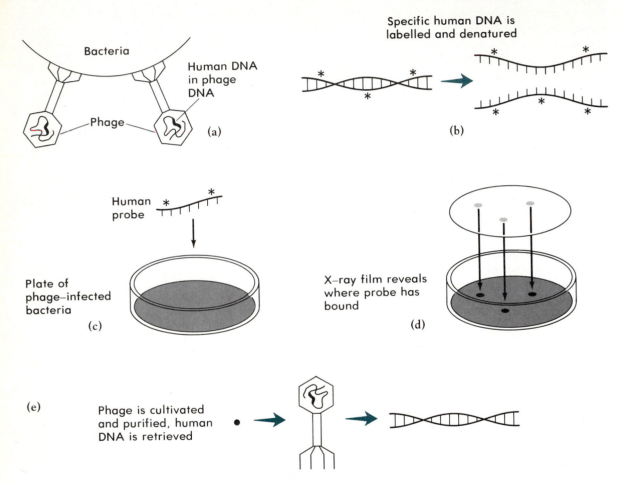

Figure 8-13

Locating bits of human DNA using hybridizing probes. (a) Human DNA is divided and inserted into millions of microorganisms called phage. Phage parasitize bacteria; they make many copies of themselves, and incidentally also copy the bit of human DNA they contain. (b) Human DNA probe is labelled and denatured. (c) Phage "library" of human DNA is screened with probe by adding probe to dish of phage-infected bacteria. Probe is allowed to hybridize, and excess is washed away. (d) Where probe binds to complementary DNA indicates presence of phage with the appropriate piece of human DNA. This is detected by applying X-ray film to surface of dish and observing where radioactive probe exposes a small area of film. (e) The specific phage is cultivated in bacteria, and the human DNA it contains is isolated from the phage DNA. This can be used as a probe itself (as in chromosome walking) or it can be analyzed.

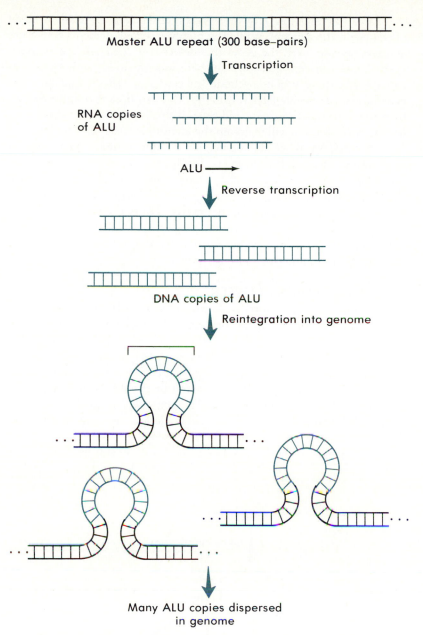

Master ALU repeat (300 base–pairs)

Transcription

RNA copies of ALU

ALU ⟶

Reverse transcription

DNA copies of ALU

Reintegration into genome

Many ALU copies dispersed in genome

Figure 8-14

Alu repeats are numerous and interspersed throughout the genomes of anthropoids. They apparently spread by transcribing copies of themselves, making DNA copies of the transcripts, and reinserting elsewhere. If they reinsert in the coding sequence of a gene, the effect is like having any other kind of mutation.

not know the extent of variation within a species in the number of Alu sequences per genome, it seems likely that there have been regular amplifications of Alu DNA sequences independently in different primate lineages at different times. They appear to spread by having a master copy transcribe many RNA copies of the Alu sequence and then having these RNA copies reverse-transcribed to DNA copies and integrated into the genome (Figure 8–14).

The amplification of DNA segments seems a be a prevalent mode of change in the genome. While the highly repeated elements constitute an extreme case, even the genes themselves will duplicate occasionally, creating two adjacent genes where there was previously only one. This can easily be thought of as a genetic "rubber-stamp" effect. The duplicate gene has three possible fates (Figure 8–15). First, it can continue to perform the same function as the old gene. If this is beneficial to the organism, natural selection will maintain the identity between the two genes.

Second, it can accumulate mutations through time which render it inoperative. After all, if one gene is already present, a second one may be superfluous—and if it deteriorated through time, it would not be missed. We then call it a **pseudogene** since, upon examination, it turns out to be structurally similar to a gene but not active. Third, the newly made copy can begin to diverge in structure and, therefore, in function from the old gene and take on a different but related role through time. In this way, clusters of gene families are built up in the genome.

THE BETA-GLOBIN CLUSTER

One well-known gene cluster is shown in Figure 8–16. This cluster controls the production of part of the protein hemoglobin. Hemoglobin, as we have seen, transports oxygen in the bloodstream and is composed at all stages of the life cycle of two subunits of 141 amino acids in length and two subunits of 146 amino acids in length. The genes which code for the 141-amino-acid subunit are located in the alpha-globin cluster, located on human chromosome 16. The genes which code for the 146-amino-acid subunit are located in the beta-globin cluster on chromosome 11. Scattered among them are nine Alu repeats.

The genes in the beta-globin cluster perform similar functions at different stages of life. Epsilon (ϵ) is functional only in the earliest embry-

pseudogene

Stretch of DNA that resembles a gene but that is not itself functional; presumably, it was once functional but superfluous and has shut down due to the accumulation of mutations debilitating to the gene but not to the organism.

Figure 8-15

Gene duplication is a widespread process and results in the formation of gene families in the genome. Three possible fates are shown for a duplicate gene.

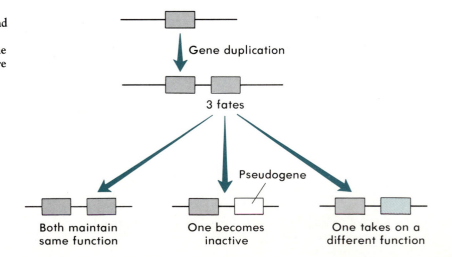

Gene duplication

3 fates

Pseudogene

Both maintain same function

One becomes inactive

One takes on a different function

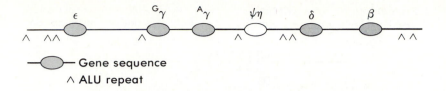

—⬭— Gene sequence

∧ ALU repeat

Figure 8-16
The beta-globin gene cluster on chromosome 11. There are five functional genes, one pseudogene, and nine Alu repeats. Sickle-cell anemia is the result of a single nucleotide substitution in the beta-globin gene, at the far right. The length of DNA shown is about 60,000 nucleotides.

onic stages, producing a 146-amino-acid-long globin molecule that is specialized for oxygen transport in embryonic tissues. From about two months' gestation until about a month after birth, the two gamma (γ) genes contribute the relevant subunit to fetal hemoglobin, which comprises nearly all the circulating hemoglobin until shortly after birth. These two genes differ from each other by only one amino acid, number 136, which does not seem to affect the function of the protein. A single amino acid change, as we know, can have drastic phenotypic effects—but this one does not. Pseudo-eta (ψη) is not functional in primates and is therefore a pseudogene; it does, however, function in the genome of some other mammals. Delta (δ) is functional at a very low level throughout fetal and adult life in humans and contributes to less than 3 percent of the total hemoglobin proteins at any time. Beta (β) produces most of the 146-amino-acid hemoglobin subunits from approximately a month after birth onward. Elucidating the specific signals that turn these genes on and off at the appropriate times is currently a major research focus.

Gene Structure and Function

By convention, we call the left end of a DNA sequence the 5′ ("five-prime") end, or "upstream," and the right end 3′ ("three-prime"), or "downstream". (The names 5′ and 3′ derive from the orientation of the deoxyribose sugars in the DNA molecule and need not concern us.)

Transcription, the manufacture of an RNA copy of the gene's DNA instructions, begins at a specific site upstream from the coding sequence of the gene (Figure 8–17). Transcription proceeds past the end of the coding sequence to an unspecified point downstream from the end of the gene. Three things then happen to the RNA molecule. First, the transcription initiation site is biochemically modified, or "capped." The transcription initiation site is consequently also known as the "cap" site. Second, the other end of the RNA is cleaved at a precise point, and a string of adenines ("A"s; thus, a "poly-A tail") is added to the transcript. Third, several internal segments are spliced out. All these processes occur in the nucleus of the cell.

The RNA molecule is then transported into the cytoplasm, where its encoded instructions are translated into a protein (Figure 8–18). The instructions are read in groups of three nucleotides, called *codons*, beginning at a specific initiation codon (and not at the beginning of the RNA molecule) and ending with any of three termination codons (and not at

Figure 8-17

A simple gene with three exons has several identifiable landmarks in its DNA sequence. After transcription, the precursor RNA goes through processing as shown to become a functional messenger RNA. DNA sequence given is from one of the two strands.

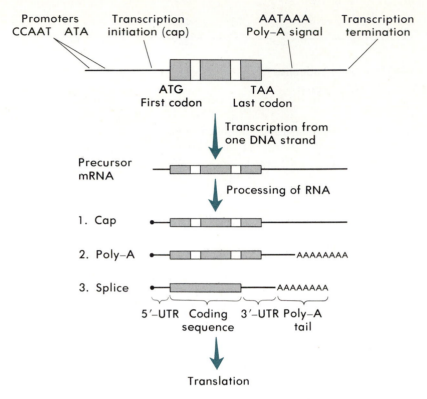

the end of the RNA molecule). Each codon specifies an amino acid, which is added to a growing protein chain as the RNA message is translated. The coding sequence of beta-globin has three nucleotides per codon times 146 codons (excluding the initiation and termination codons), which multiplies to 438 nucleotides.

We can, therefore, distinguish certain structural elements in the beta-globin gene, based on the processes that will occur to its derivative RNA (Figure 8–17). Farthest upstream are *promoter elements,* DNA sequences that must be present in order to ensure the efficient transcription of the RNA copy from the gene. A defect in the promoter region can dramatically lower a gene's output: This is actually what has happened to the delta-globin gene. The *cap site* defines the beginning of the RNA transcript, and the *initiation codon* (ATG in DNA; AUG in the mRNA copy) defines the beginning of the protein-coding instructions. Between these two sites, the DNA is transcribed into RNA but not translated into protein; consequently, it is the 5′-*untranslated region,* or 5′-UTR. The coding regions that are spliced together in the mRNA are **exons,** and those which are deleted are **introns**. The globin genes all contain three exons, or coding sequences, and these are separated by two introns, or intervening sequences. The end of the last coding sequence is marked by a *termination codon* (TAA, TGA, or TAG in DNA; UAA, UGA, or UAG in the mRNA copy). Downstream from the termination

exon

Region of a gene that actually contains a protein-coding instruction; in messenger RNA, these are spliced together to form a long, contiguous message.

intron

Region of a gene that interrupts the coding sequence; in messenger RNA, these are spliced out.

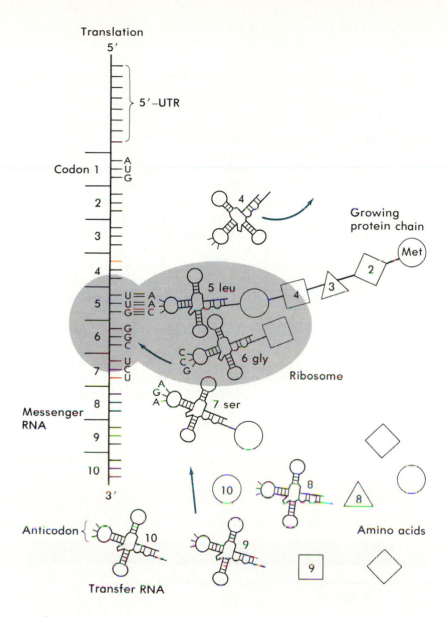

Translation

5′

5′–UTR

Codon 1

2

3

4

5 leu

6

7

8

Messenger RNA

9

10

3′

Anticodon

Transfer RNA

Growing protein chain

Met

2

3

4

5 leu

6 gly

Ribosome

7 ser

10

8

9

Amino acids

Figure 8-18

Translation involves the formation of a specific protein from the message carried by an mRNA. This occurs in the cytoplasm on an organelle called the ribosome, with the aid of transfer RNA molecules. Each tRNA bears an amino acid at one end and adds it to the growing protein, as the particular codon in the mRNA specifies.

codon is DNA that is transcribed into RNA but not translated into protein; hence, the *3′-untranslated region* or *3′-UTR*. Near the end of the 3′-untranslated region is a sequence of nucleotides (often AATAAA), which apparently signals that polyadenylation of the RNA is to occur shortly downstream: This is the *poly-A signal*. And the site at which the "A"s will be added to the RNA is called the **poly-A site**.

Notice that only a fraction of the DNA sequence of the gene actually results in a phenotype, the protein. The DNAs which are spliced out and which comprise both untranslated regions are not expressed in any

poly-A site

Nucleotide at which a tail of adenines is added to the messenger RNA; this is not the same as the end of transcription, which is currently unknown.

readily apparent way. Since natural selection operates on phenotypes through their interaction with the environment, it follows that the effect of selection can be only very weak at best on the noncoding sequences. Therefore, when mutations arise in the DNA, we may expect them to be preferentially eliminated from the coding sequence (by natural selection) and rather more slowly, if at all, from the noncoding sequence.

THE EVOLUTION OF GENE PRODUCTS

As Goodman, Sarich, and Wilson had shown in the 1960s, the more distantly related two primate species are, the more different their gene products are. At that time, however, they had been able to sample gene products only very indirectly by measuring the intensity of immunological reactions against similar antigens. Concurrently, it was becoming clear that if one compared the amino acid sequence of proteins against one another—that is, the *direct* gene products—across species, one would obtain nearly the same results as the indirect immunological studies.

Table 8–1 gives the number of differences one finds in comparing the amino acid sequence of human beta-globin to that of various other primates. Notice that the number of differences becomes larger as the comparison involves species more distantly related from humans—but that this relationship is not perfect. Although the Old World monkeys are more closely related to humans than are New World monkeys, we do not find significantly more differences between the New World monkey and human globin than we do between the Old World monkey and human globin. Thus, our globin clock is only fairly accurate; on the other hand, it was astounding to many in the 1960s that we could take but a single molecule and trace anthropoid relations with *any* degree of accuracy!

A comparison of the number of differences or similarities between species like the one we have just performed is a **phenetic** comparison. Consider, however, the effect of evolutionary rate on such a study. If the Old World monkey globin proteins were changing slightly faster than the globin proteins of other lineages, then they would be more different in a

phenetic

Comparison based on extent of similarity and difference.

Table 8–1

Number of Amino Acid Differences from the Human Sequence in the Beta Chain of Hemoglobin

Human	—
Chimpanzee	0
Gorilla	1
Orang-utan	2
Gibbon	2
Cercopithecines	4–9
Platyrrhini	5–8
Tarsier	15

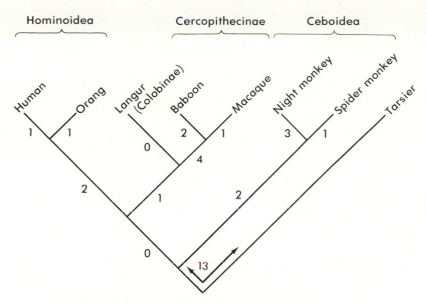

Figure 8-19

Tree constructed from the data in Table 8–2, requiring the occurrence of thirty-one mutational steps to account for all the differences seen among these taxa. It is not the only tree possible from these data, nor is it the only one that takes the minimum thirty-one steps. But it is consistent with the relationships of these taxa that the anatomical evidence affords. To construct the tree, we have invoked a single evolutionary event at sites 6, 13, 19, 21, 22, 33, 58, 69, 73, 75, 76, 104, 125, 126, and 139. Two events must be invoked at the following sites, and we have interpreted them as follows (though there are other possibilities): 5: P to A (Tarsier), P to G (Spider, Night); 9: A to N (Baboon, Macaque), A to S (Human, Orang-utan); 50: T to S (Night), T to S (Langur, Baboon, Macaque); 52: D to A (Baboon), D to A (Tarsier); 56: M to S (Spider, Night), S to N (Night). Three events must be invoked at the following sites, and we have interpreted them as follows: 43: E to D (Tarsier), E to D (Night), E to D (Baboon); 87: Q to K (Tarsier), Q to T (Human, Orang-utan), T to K (Orang-utan).

phenetic comparison from other lineages and, therefore, appear to be more distantly related than perhaps they really are. This might explain why the Old World monkey beta-globin was as different from the human as the New World monkey beta-globin appeared to be.

A different approach to these molecular data, therefore, is called the *parsimony* method. Here we examine not only the *number* of amino acid substitutions that differentiate taxa, but the specific *nature* of those differences as well, and we assume that a change from one amino acid to another occurs rarely. We then ask what phylogeny can be drawn from these amino acid substitutions, assuming the *fewest* number of evolutionary events? And how many events have occurred along each lineage?

From the data given in Table 8–2, there are a few equally likely phylogenetic trees and several ways to distribute the (at least) thirty-one amino acid substitutions over them. We show one tree in Figure 8–19, which happens to be fully concordant with the anatomical characters discussed in other chapters.

How do we know that this tree is correct? Since it is extremely unlikely that the exact branching order of all primates would emerge from the study of a single protein, there are a number of alternative phylogenies that we cannot reject from these beta-globin data. For example, it is possible that the Old World monkeys and New World monkeys are more closely related than the Old World monkeys and hominoids. It is possible because by moving the Old World monkey branch to the New World stem, we will not have to add any more mutational steps to the thirty-one we already have—the two trees are equally parsimonious. If, however, we wish to move the baboon from its present position to the langur branch, we would have to invoke additional mutations (Figure 8–20). For

Table 8–2

Amino Acid Sequences of the Beta-Globin Molecule in Various Primates

	10	20	30	40	50
Human	VHLTPEEKSA	VTALWGKVNV	DEVGGEALGR	LLVVYPWTQR	FFESFGDLST
Orang-utan					
Langur	A				S
Baboon	N	T		D	S
Macaque	N	T		L	S
Spider	G A				
Night	G A			D	S
Tarsier	AD A	D	ED	D	

	60	70	80	90	100
Human	PDAVMGNPKV	KAHGKKVLGA	FSDGLAHLDN	LKGTFATLSE	LHCDKLHVDP
Orang-utan				K	
Langur				Q	
Baboon	A		N	Q	
Macaque			N	Q	
Spider	S			Q	
Night	N			Q	
Tarsier	A A		N E M	K	

	110	120	130	140	
Human	ENFRLLGNVL	VCVLAHHFGK	EFTPPVQAAY	QKVVAGVANA	LAHKYH
Orang-utan			Q		
Langur			Q		
Baboon	K		Q		
Macaque	K		Q		
Spider			QL		
Night			Q		
Tarsier			Q	T	

A—alanine
R—arginine
N—asparagine
D—aspartic acid
C—cysteine
E—glutamic acid
Q—glutamine
G—glycine
H—histidine
I—isoleucine

L—leucine
K—lysine
M—methionine
F—phenylalanine
P—proline
S—serine
T—threonine
W—tryptophan
Y—tyrosine
V—valine

example, at position 76, the baboon and macaque have N, while the other primates have A. We have scored this as a single change in the common ancestor of the cercopithecines from the ancestral A to the derived N. If, however, we move the baboon to the langur (colobine) branch, we have to hypothesize an A to N change in the macaque and also independently in the baboon, or an A to N change in the Cercopithecoidea and a change back to A in the langur—either way, two mutations, not one. This is not impossible, simply less likely than the alternative of one mutation.

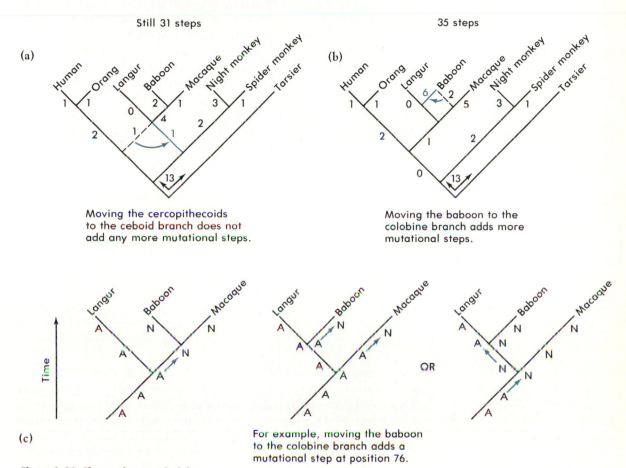

Figure 8-20. The parsimony principle.

(a) These data cannot falsify a phylogenetic hypothesis that links cercopithecoids to Platyrrhines rather than to hominoids, as there are no more mutational steps that must be invoked. (b) These data can be taken as a falsification of the phylogenetic hypothesis that places the baboon with the colobine rather than with the other cercopithecine, for this would require that four more evolutionary events, or steps, be added. (c) For example, at position 76, we invoke a single mutational step or evolutionary event to have occurred in the common ancestor of baboon and macaque, substituting asparagine for alanine. If we place the baboon on the colobine branch, we need at least one more evolutionary event to account for the pattern of data we find. In general, the tree with the fewest mutational steps is the better one.

PATTERNS OF PROTEIN EVOLUTION

From Table 8–2, we can make several observations about the pattern of amino acid substitutions throughout the beta-globin molecule in primate history. First, there are certain regions that are absolutely invariant across all taxa, for example positions 24–32. These positions are invariant because they are of great functional significance to the beta-globin protein and any alteration in this region would prove harmful to the oxygen-transportation capabilities of the primate bearing it. Natural selection has weeded out any variants which have arisen in that part of the protein. In general, the fewer the variations at a particular amino acid site across taxa, the more important we can infer that amino acid site to be.

Second, there are twenty amino acids, but the substitutions that occur across taxa are not random. For example, at position 43, all the primates have glutamic acid, except the baboon, tarsier, and night monkey (*Aotus trivirgatus,* a platyrrhine), which have aspartic acid. Since the baboon and night monkey are not closely related, this must reflect substitutional events in different lineages (rearranging the tree to put the baboon and night monkey together would add more steps; try it and see). This change can occur in different lineages because glutamic acid and aspartic acid have similar properties; amino acids that have similar properties tend to be preferentially substituted for one another. The reason, of course, is that such a conservative substitution is less likely to disrupt the protein's function than is the substitution of an amino acid that has different properties.

Genic Evolution

The genetic code has an interesting property that arises from the fact that it encodes a total of twenty different amino acids. There are four possible nucleotides in the instructions, read in groups of three, and by a simple arithmetical calculation, sixty-four codons are possible. Three of these are terminations (TAA, TGA, and TAG), and one (ATG) serves as translation initiator as well as coding for the amino acid methionine. This leaves sixty codons to code for the other nineteen amino acids. Obviously, some different codons must be coding for the same amino acid. This property of the genetic code is called *degeneracy,* and it usually occurs in the third codon position. Thus, CTC, CTA, CTG, and CTT all code for the amino acid leucine (Table 8–3). This has important evolutionary implications.

THE ROLE OF DNA IN GENIC EVOLUTION

If the DNA coding sequence GAG mutates to GAA, what will happen? The original DNA codes for glutamic acid, and the mutant DNA also codes for glutamic acid. If the same amino acid is placed into the protein, then the phenotype produced by this genetic change will be unaltered. This is a silent mutation because the mutant is "silent" phenotypically. Since natural selection operates on phenotypes, that is, selecting different

Table 8–3

The Genetic Code (mRNA Codons)

Alanine Ala	Arginine Arg	Aspartic Acid Asp	Asparagine Asn	Cysteine Cys
GCA	AGA	GAC	AAC	UGC
GCC	AGG	GAU	AAU	UGU
GCG	CGA			
GCU	CGC			
	CGG			
	CGU			

Glutamic Acid Glu	Glutamine Gln	Glycine Gly	Histidine His	Isoleucine Ile	Leucine Leu
GAA	CAA	GGA	CAC	AUA	UUA
GAG	CAG	GGC	CAU	AUC	UUG
		GGG		AUU	CUA
		GGU			CUC
					CUG
					CUU

Lysine Lys	Methionine Met, INI	Phenylalanine Phe	Proline Pro	Serine Ser
AAA	AUG	UUC	CCA	AGC
AAG		UUU	CCC	AGU
			CCG	UCA
			CCU	UCC
				UCG
				UCU

Threonine Thr	Tryptophan Trp	Tyrosine Tyr	Valine Val	"Stop" TER
ACA	UGG	UAC	GUA	UAA
ACC		UCU	GUC	UAG
ACG			GUG	UGA
ACU			GUU	

traits by virtue of their interaction with the environment, natural selection cannot easily operate here. Why? Because the different genetic sequences produce essentially the same trait. Changes in the third nucleotide of a codon usually result in silent mutations.

If, however, the same DNA coding sequence GAG mutates to GTG, it provides a different instruction for the translational machinery.

Now, instead of inserting glutamic acid into the growing protein chain, the machinery will insert valine. While this change may not seem like much, it may be sufficient to give the protein different structural properties, which will aid or impair the reproductive success of its bearer. Indeed, this is precisely the change that causes sickle-cell anemia.

There is no particular physiological reason for animals that look alike to necessarily have hemoglobin molecules that look alike, much less have unexpressed DNA sequences that look alike. Thus, when we examine the nucleotide sequence of, say, the alpha-globin gene on chromosome 16 and find it to be nearly identical in humans and orang-utans, we interpret this as evidence that humans and orangs have been accumulating mutational differences in their alpha-globin genes for a relatively short time. That is, humans and orangs share a recent (geologically speaking) common ancestor from whose DNA sequence both human and orang DNA have been diverging. The nucleotide sequence of the human and orang-utan alpha-globin genes are given in Table 8–4 on pages 314–315.

THE ROLE OF NATURAL SELECTION IN GENIC EVOLUTION

Locate the exons and introns of the alpha-globin genes. Notice that there seem to be proportionally more differences between human and orang-utan in the noncoding regions than in the coding regions. Overall, there is about a 2.6 percent difference in the coding regions and about a 3.6 percent difference in the non-coding regions. Why?

Next, notice the distribution of differences in the coding sequence. Of eleven differences, one is in the first codon position, one is in the second codon position, and nine are in the third codon position. Of those nine changes in the third codon position, eight are silent. If natural selection were not operating, we would expect the differences in the coding sequence between human and orang-utan to be randomly distributed among the first, second, and third codon positions. The fact that we find many more silent than **substitution mutations** indicates that natural selection has been screening out most mutations affecting the alpha-globin protein that have arisen since the divergence of humans and orang-utans.

substitution mutation

Nucleotide substitution in a gene resulting in a different amino acid being encoded in the protein.

Generally, we find that replacement mutations in DNA accumulate most slowly, silent mutations next most slowly, untranslated DNA in genes (introns, promoters, and the flanking untranslated regions) somewhat more rapidly, and intergenic or nongenic DNA fastest. This represents the progressive decline of the influence of stabilizing natural selection constraining the evolution of these DNA sequences. The bulk of the most rapidly evolving sequences, nongenic and nonfunctional DNA, are **neutral** to natural selection.

neutral mutation

Nucleotide substitution with no phenotypic effect or with an effect perfectly equivalent to its alternatives.

Geneticist Motoo Kimura showed in the 1960s that neutral mutations should spread through a population at a rate simply proportional to how often they arise. Most will not spread at all and will become extinct within one or a few generations. Very few, however, will manage to spread in a population. The reason neutral mutations can spread is because of the action of genetic drift, the statistical fluctuations in Mendelian ratios due to small population size. Since natural selection is not affecting these neutral mutations (that is what *neutral* means), only genetic drift is. And since they arise at very low frequencies, any specific neutral mutations have a very small chance of spreading over an entire population. But since they are continually arising and since evolutionary time is very long, a few neutral mutations do spread, and they do so at a rate that is roughly constant over the long run and roughly equal to the rate at which they arise.

Thus, because much of the DNA is unexpressed, the evolutionary process operating on DNA sequences is primarily genetic drift, allowing DNA mutations that do not affect the phenotype to spread through a population over time with a small but appreciable probability. Those few changes that do affect the phenotype will come under the influence of natural selection; either stabilizing selection to weed out harmful mutations from the population, or directional selection, which will allow a beneficial mutation to spread.

MOLECULAR MICROEVOLUTION: SICKLE-CELL ANEMIA

The same techniques we use to study evolutionary divergence at the level of the species can be used at the microevolutionary level to study genetic variation within a species. The most famous example of this is a single nucleotide change in the sixth codon of the beta-globin molecule in which the GAG codon for glutamic acid is changed to GTG (valine).

Ordinarily, we might expect one of two things to occur: Either the mutation would not affect the functional integrity of the hemoglobin molecule, in which case the mutation could spread through time by genetic drift; or it might affect (beneficially or adversely) the molecule, in which case natural selection would either spread it or get rid of it. A different situation altogether is the case for sickle-cell anemia. The valine in position 6 changes the properties of the hemgolobin protein in a dramatic way, as we have already noted. This single nucleotide substitution and consequent amino acid substitution affects the conformation of the hemoglobin molecule. The shape of the hemoglobin molecules affects the shape of the red blood cell that contains them, changing it from a fairly flexible doughnut into a pointed sickle. These sickle-shaped cells clog the capillaries and impair circulation of the blood. We discussed the cascading pleiotropic effects of the sickle-cell genotype in Chapter 7.

The paradox of sickle-cell lies in the frequency of such an obviously harmful allele: up to 20 percent in parts of Africa. Why wouldn't such an obviously harmful allele simply be eliminated by purifying natural selection? The answer lies in the culture history and ecology of West Africa and in the nature of the sickle-cell heterozygote.

Plasmodium falciparum is a parasitic microorganism which divides its life cycle between two macroorganisms: a mosquito (*Anopheles gambiae*) and a human. While in a mosquito, it undergoes the sexual phase of its

Table 8–4

DNA Sequence of an Alpha-Globin Gene in Human and Orang-utan

```
Human        ----------------------------------c---------------------
Orang-utan   ccaatgagcgccgcccggccgggcgtgcccctgcgccccaagcataaaccctgg
```

```
H   -------------g-----------------------------g------------ --- --- ---
O   cgcgctcgcggccccgcactcttctggtccccacagactcagaaagaacccaccATG GTG CTG TCT
                                                          INI Val Leu Ser
```

```
                                        Ala
H   --- --- --- --- --- --- --- --- G-- --- --- —T --- --- --- --- ---
O   CCT GCC GAC AAG ACC AAC GTC AAG ACC GCC TGG GGG AAG GTC GGC GCG CAC
    Pro Ala Asp Lys Thr Asn Val Lys Thr Ala Trp Gly Lys Val Gly Ala His
```

```
        Glu
H   --T --- --G --- --- --- --- --- --- --- -- ------------------------
O   GCC GGC GAC TAT GGT GCG GAG GCC CTG GAG AG gtgaggctccctcccctgctccgacc
    Ala Gly Asp Tyr Gly Ala Glu Ala Leu Glu Ar
```

```
H   ------------------g-------a----------------------------------------
O   cgggctcctcgcccgccctgacccaccggccaccctcaaccgtcctggccccggacccaaacccaccc
```

```
H   --------------------- - --- --- --- --- --- --- --- --- --- --- ---
O   ctcactctgcttctccccgcag G ATG TTC CTG TCC TTC CCC ACC ACC AAG ACC TAC
                          g Met Phe Leu Ser Phe Pro Thr Thr Lys Thr Tyr
```

```
                                                        Gly
H   --- --G --- --- --- --- --- --C --- --- --- --- --- --- -G- --- ---
O   TTC CCC CAC TTC GAC CTG AGC CAT GGC TCT GCC CAG GTT AAG GAC CAC GGC
    Phe Pro His Phe Asp Leu Ser His Gly Ser Ala Gln Val Lys Asp His Gly
```

```
H   --- --- --- --- --- --C --- --- --- --- --- --- --- --- --- --- ---
O   AAG AAG GTG GCC GAC GCG CTG ACC AAC GCC GTG GCG CAC GTG GAC GAC ATG
    Lys Lys Val Ala Asp Ala Leu Thr Asn Ala Val Ala His Val Asp Asp Met
```

```
H   --- --- --- --- --- --- --- --- --- --G --- --- --- --- ---  --- ---
O   CCC AAC GCG CTG TCC GCC CTG AGC GAC CTG CAC GCT CAC AAG CTT CGG GTG
    Pro Asn Ala Leu Ser Ala Leu Ser Asp Leu His Ala His Lys Leu Arg Val


H   --- --- --- --- --- --- -------------------------------------------
O   GAC CCG GTC AAC TTC AAG gtgagcggcgggccgggagcgatctgggtcgaggggcgagatg
    Asp Pro Val Asn Phe Lys


H   --------------------g---a----------------------------c----------
O   gcgccttcctcgcagggcagagcatcccgcgggttgcgggaggtgtagcgcaggcggtggctgcgggcc


H   *t-ggccctc------------------------- --- --A --- --- --- --- ---
O   ccg*******ggccccactgaccctcttctctgcacag CTC CTG AGC CAC TGC CTG CTG
                                           Leu Leu Ser His Cys Leu Leu


H   --- --- --- --- --- --- --- --C --- --- --- --- --- --- --- --- ---
O   GTG ACC CTG GCC GCC CAC CTC CCT GCC GAG TTC ACC CCT GCG GTG CAC GCC
    Val Thr Leu Ala Ala His Leu Pro Ala Glu Phe Thr Pro Ala Val His Ala


H   --- --- --- --- --- --- --- --- --- --- --- --- --- --- --- --- --- ---
O   TCC CTG GAC AAG TTC CTG GCT TCT GTG AGC ACC GTG CTG ACC TCC AAA TAC
    Ser Leu Asp Lys Phe Leu Ala Ser Val Ser Thr Val Leu Thr Ser Lys Tyr


H   --- ----------c------------------------------c-----c----c--*----------
O   CGT TAAgctggagactcggtggccatgcttcttgccccttggg*ctcccgccaggccctcctcccctt
    Arg Ter


H   -----------------g---------------------------------------------------
O   cctgcacccgtaccccctggtctttgaataaagtctgagtgggcggcagcctgtgtgtgcctgagttt


H   t------------c------a-------
O   cttccctcagcaaatgtgccaggcatggg
```

life cycle and (without apparent ill effect to the insect) sends some progeny to the mosquito's salivary gland. The next time the mosquito bites a human, it infects the human with some of the *Plasmodium* parasites, which then go through a phase of asexual reproduction in the red blood cells of the human host. The result is malaria, a debilitating disease with alternating bouts of chills and high fever, and a great threat to life in many areas of the world, particularly in West Africa.

Malaria is most prevalent where the *Anopheles gambiae* mosquito, its vector, is common. This mosquito species thrives in open, sunny areas with standing water, unlike related species, which prefer shaded river and tropical forest environments. With the advent of irrigation agriculture in equatorial Africa some 2,000 years ago, the area became a happy hunting ground for *Anopheles gambiae* and for the malaria parasites they harbor.

When the *Plasmodium falciparum* enters the bloodstream of a sickle-cell anemia heterozygote, something remarkable happens. These individuals carry both Hb A (normal: two alpha and two beta protein chains) and Hb S (sickle: two alpha and two beta/sickle chains) in each of their red blood cells. Ordinarily, these cells function adequately in the transport of oxygen. When the heterozygote is stressed for oxygen, however (which rarely occurs under ordinary conditions), some sickling of these cells results. The entry of a malarial parasite into a red blood cell places that cell under stress, and it sickles. It is consequently flushed out of the circulating bloodstream and into the spleen, *before the parasite has a chance to complete its life cycle.*

Ultimately, therefore, the sickle-cell heterozygote neither suffers from sickle-cell anemia nor from malaria. The relatively high frequency of an allele that is so deadly in double dose is explained by its great benefits in single dose. The survival and reproductive advantage to the heterozygote is called *balancing natural selection*, which reflects the balance between the harmful effects of being either homozygote. Remember that in the mating of two heterozygotes, only half their offspring will themselves be heterozygotes. Thus, the homozygotes, even though at a disadvantage, are nevertheless continually produced by the mating of the favored heterozygotes.

The advantage that accrues to sickle-cell heterozygotes is useful only in malarial environments. In nonmalarial environments, the normal genotype (Hb A/Hb A) will have an advantage over the heterozygote (Hb A/Hb S), since as parents, the latter will be producing sickle-cell anemics with a predictable frequency, while the normal genotypes will not.

Among African-Americans, approximately 1 in 12 people is a sickle-cell heterozygote. Since one-quarter of the offspring of two heterozygotes will have sickle-cell anemia, about 20 in 10,000 births to African-Americans have sickle-cell anemia. This high frequency is due to their high proportion of West African ancestry. And the sickle cell story is the result of a single nucleotide substitution in the beta-globin gene.

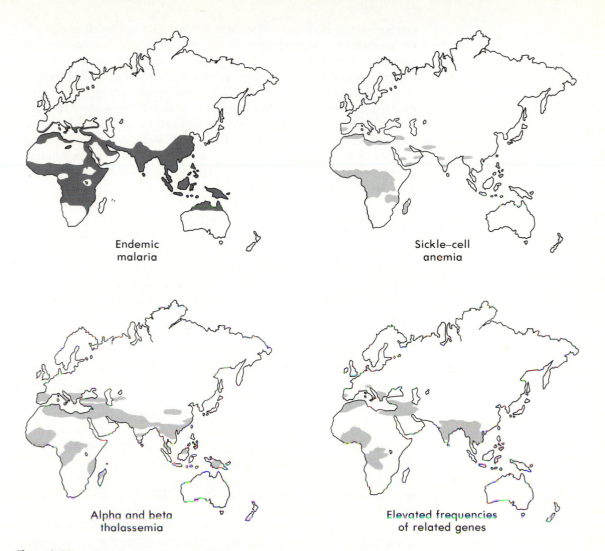

Endemic
malaria

Sickle–cell
anemia

Alpha and beta
thalassemia

Elevated frequencies
of related genes

Figure 8-21

Geographical distribution among aboriginal populations of the Old World of endemic malaria, greater than 1 percent frequency of the sickle-cell allele, greater than 1 percent frequency of alpha and beta thalassemia, and elevated frequencies of related genes, such as glucose-6-phosphate dehydrogenase (G-6-PD) deficiency, and hemoglobins C and E.

Many populations have genetically adapted in parallel to the stress of malaria. Molecular genetic analysis indicates that the sickle-cell allele originated and spread at least three different times in different parts of Africa. There appear to be three distinct genetic configurations around the sickle-cell allele, which are geographically localized in Africa, suggesting independent origins for each. Further, the sickle-cell mutation is not confined to Africa nor to people of African ancestry—it has achieved a significant frequency virtually anywhere malaria is a threat to health. Other populations, however, have adapted genetically in other ways.

Thalassemia, a genetic disease in which the hemoglobin is structurally sound but in which too little is produced, appears to have the same beneficial effects to heterozygotes as sickle-cell. In the Mediterranean and in southeast Asia, where sickle-cell is less common but where agriculture and malaria are present, a similar microevolutionary role appears to be played by thalassemia as well as by other hemoglobin variants (Figure 8–21).

TAY-SACHS' DISEASE: SELECTION OR DRIFT?

Other genetic diseases are found in higher frequencies in specific populations. We have already discussed Ellis-van Creveld syndrome, found among the Pennsylvania Amish more frequently than in other populations, and due to founder effect. A similar situation exists for a disease known as *porphyria*, which is caused by a dominant allele and leads ordinarily to sensitive skin, especially on the back of the hand. In the presence of certain chemicals, such as barbiturates, porphyria causes acute abdominal pain, red urine, and hysteria. It is rare throughout the world except in the white population of South Africa, where it reaches a frequency of about 1 in 300. Affected individuals are the descendants of Jacomijntje van Rooyen, an eighteenth-century settler.

Sometimes it is not so easy to determine whether an elevated genetic frequency is due to selection, as in sickle-cell, or to founder effect, as in Ellis-van Creveld and porphyria. In the case of *Tay-Sachs' disease*, molecular genetics affords a test of these alternative hypotheses.

Tay-Sachs' is a recessive lethal allele, affecting the gene that codes for an enzyme called hexosaminidase A. This enzyme is involved in breaking down a large lipid molecule that accumulates in the neurons of the brain. The gene, on chromosome 15, encodes 529 amino acids, stretched across 14 exons, spanning 50,000 nucleotides. Heterozygotes are completely normal, but homozygotes (one-quarter of the offspring of two heterozygotes) die by their second year of life of neural degeneration—obviously, a family tragedy of considerable gravity.

The allele is carried by about 1 in 30 Jews of eastern European ancestry, about ten times more frequent than in other populations. Is the elevated frequency due to founder effect or to some element of balancing selection?

In the Jewish ghettos of eastern Europe, one of the major causes of death was tuberculosis. The geneticists Myrianthopoulos and Aronson suggested that perhaps heterozygosity for Tay-Sachs' might confer a measure of resistance to the disease. They found that the distribution of Tay-Sachs' parallels that of tuberculosis, and that the grandparents of

Tay-Sachs' victims were less likely to have died of tuberculosis than a comparative control group. Eastern European Jews are also known to have elevated frequencies of other related genetic diseases involving the central nervous system, such as Gaucher's and Niemann-Pick's. Why would a cluster of diseases on the same metabolic pathway all be elevated by genetic drift? It seemed difficult to explain and so suggested that perhaps balancing selection for tuberculosis was instead involved. This was not a very persuasive argument, however, since Tay-Sachs' was known to be elevated in some small non-Jewish, isolated populations: Clearly, it *could* be elevated by genetic drift, so why not among the Jews as well?

Molecular genetics recently provided a test of these hypotheses. If genetic drift were the cause of the elevated frequency, one would expect that all the alleles for Tay-Sachs' would be the same, since this would simply represent the increase in frequency of one particular allele. If, on the other hand, selection was at work, then one might expect some genetic heterogeneity among the alleles for Tay-Sachs' (as found for sickle-cell). In other words, different mutations all causing the same phenotype would be independently elevated by natural selection—but not by genetic drift.

Recent molecular studies have shown that while about one-quarter of all Tay-Sachs' alleles analyzed were caused by a defect in splicing out the twelfth intron, there is also considerable heterogeneity within the population. Thus, Tay-Sachs' among eastern European Jews has several different alleles, elevated in frequency together, as a cause. This does not prove the tuberculosis connection, but it is incompatible with the idea that genetic drift alone has caused the elevated allele frequency in this population.

Summary

Biological evolution is a change in the genetic composition of populations. Studying the actual genetic relationships among species allows us to infer phylogenetic relationships, evolutionary rates, and the specific evolutionary changes that have occurred in each lineage. This study is still in its infancy.

We can examine genetic relationships by comparing proteins, DNA, or chromosome morphology. In comparing genes across species, we also learn about the structure and function of genes and about the relative evolutionary importance of certain parts of the genome. Those parts that differ the most across species are thought to be the least important, and those that are the most well-conserved parts are thought to be the most important and fundamental to the survival and reproduction of the organism. In some cases, most notably sickle-cell anemia, we can find specific molecular causes for the existence and prevalence of the disease in human populations.

Questions for Review

1. What might be some explanations for cases in which molecular evidence for phylogenetic relationships conflicts with anatomical evidence?

2. How can one infer the operation of natural selection from a comparison of DNA sequences from different species? If you wanted to infer phylogenetic relationships among species, would you be better off using coding or noncoding sequences?

3. Anthropologists often have difficulty arriving at a precise and rigorous definition of "culture" that they can all agree upon, since there are many ambiguous areas and different ways of studying it; likewise with biologists and "species." What problems can you perceive in establishing a precise and rigorous definition of "gene" that all geneticists can agree on?

For Further Reading

Goodman, M., & Cronin, J. (1982). Molecular anthropology: Its development and current directions. In A *history of American physical anthropology, 1930–1980,* F. Spencer (Ed.). New York: Academic Press.

Lewin, B. (1990). *Genes IV.* New York: John Wiley and Sons.

MacIntyre, R. (1985). *Molecular evolutionary genetics.* New York: Plenum.

Marks, J. (1989). Molecular micro and macro-evolution in the primate alpha-globin gene family. *American Journal of Human Biology,* 1:555–566.

Watson, J., Hopkins, N., Roberts, J., Steitz, J., & Weiner, A. (1987). *Molecular biology of the gene* (4th ed.). Menlo Park, CA: Benjamin/Cummings.

Human Variation

Human Variation

Human Origin

Human groups differ biologically from one another by virtue of microevolution. The study of human differences has traditionally focused on the variation among human groups, although we now recognize that to be an exceedingly small biological problem. That approach focuses on a very few genes with obvious phenotypes affecting the form and shape of parts of the face, the hair, and the skin. While these features do differ among human populations, any two humans drawn from the same population differ genetically and anatomically at least as much as any people drawn from different populations. This is because most of the detectable variation in humans is within-group variation, differentiating people from one another in height, body build, metabolism, facial morphology, blood antigens, and so on.

Unfortunately, the widespread tendency toward **typological thinking** has often led us to ignore *within-group* biological variation and instead focus on *between-group* biological variation, which is more obvious and certainly augmented by differences in language and culture among groups. The fact that such differences are obvious does not mean that they are biologically important, however.

typological thinking
Emphasizing differences among groups of biological individuals and ignoring or downplaying the differences within each group.

THEORIES OF HUMAN ORIGIN

By the middle of the eighteenth century, two clear schools of thought had arisen on the subject of human origins (Chapter 3). The monogenists held that all kinds of people belonged to a single species and that all observable variation had arisen since the single divine origin of our species. They maintained the fundamental unity of mankind. The polygenists, in contrast, held that the different major human groups had no ancestry in common and were the results of distinct and separate acts of creation (Figure 9–1).

This controversy polarized people in a way that may seem odd today. The monogenists were social liberals, citing the Bible as their justification for a single creative origin for all and for subsequent biological divergence. They were, therefore, early modern evolutionists—microevolutionists, of course. The polygenists, on the other hand, held that the Bible should not be taken so literally, for Adam was not the father of everyone. Thus, the more theologically liberal, the polygenists, were those who denied evolution, while the more theologically conservative element, the monogenists, were social liberals advocating evolution.

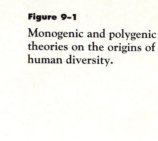

Figure 9-1
Monogenic and polygenic
theories on the origins of
human diversity.

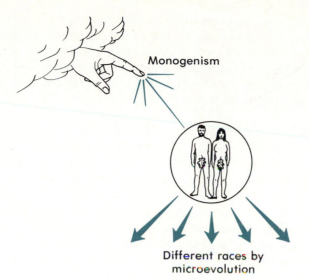

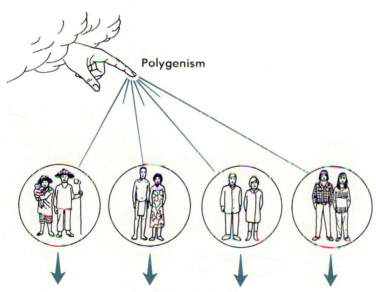

This issue had both social and biological relevance. If it could be shown that other human groups were actually different species, this could be used to rationalize the subjugation and maltreatment they often received. On the other hand, if these diverse human groups were members of the same species, this would imply that a single stock could become strikingly modified over the course of time.

Most contemporary scientists recognized that humans constituted a single species. Even those biological rivals of the eighteenth century, Linnaeus and Buffon, both adopted the monogenist position. As late as 1948, however, a Harvard geneticist published a book attempting to maintain that human groups had actually evolved as different species. (He didn't manage to convince anyone.)

TWO APPROACHES: LINNAEUS AND BUFFON

Although both Linnaeus and Buffon agreed that all humans had a single common origin and had radiated somehow from it, they treated the issue of human groups in different ways. Linnaeus, the great classifier, simply incorporated them into his classification as subspecies, and listed six: *Homo sapiens ferus*, wild children found abandoned in the forest; *Homo sapiens americanus*; *Homo sapiens europaeus*; *Homo sapiens asiaticus*; *Homo sapiens afer*, Africans; and *Homo sapiens monstrosus*, incorporating mythological populations, Hottentots (Khoi), and people with birth defects. Linnaeus then gave a second human species, *Homo troglodytes*, in which he incorporated some of the more anthropomorphic descriptions of chimpanzees and orang-utans.

Buffon was less interested in categorizing groups of people than he was in describing and explaining the differences among them. He was the first to use the word *race* to refer to a local population, and he believed that local environmental conditions (especially food) were the cause of local variations in appearance.

Clearly, both Buffon and Linnaeus were scientifically naïve by modern standards, but note their two approaches to the problem. The Linnaean approach is to categorize and pigeonhole; the Buffonian approach is to illustrate and interpret the differences among groups. The history of physical anthropology is the history of the largely Linnaean approach—only since the 1950s has the other approach begun to hold sway.

Racial Studies

The scientific study of race begins a generation later than Buffon and Linnaeus, with Johann Friedrich Blumenbach, often called the father of physical anthropology. Blumenbach concluded that the people of the world could be divided into five essentially arbitrary divisions by continent. He called these the Caucasian, Ethiopian, Mongolian, American, and Malay races.

Since these divisions were arbitrary, a major question soon surfaced: How far can we subdivide these races and still obtain significant divisions? Could we not, after all, take the race localized to Europe and recognize Nordic, Mediterranean, and Alpine geographical races within it? Presumably we could, given the arbitrary nature of the original division. Yet, as all human issues ultimately are, this biological question became overlaid with a social issue. In nineteenth-century Europe, where Jews constituted a significant minority population, interest centered on the nature of their differences from the Christian majority. In nineteenth-century America, where black people constituted a significant minority population, interest centered on the nature of their differences from the white majority. In both cases, centuries of oppression stood to be rationalized if innate biological (and especially behavioral and mental) features could be seen as differentiating the oppressed from the oppressors. And, as we noted in Chapter 6, along with oppression often comes dehumanization (Figure 9–2).

It is worthwhile to distinguish at this point between *racial* studies and *racist* studies. The study of the biological relationships among major groups of humans is a legitimate scientific endeavor, and it can be done in theory just as one might study the biological relationships between groups of clams, groups of sparrows, or groups of mice. There are, however, only two major ways in which one can study groups of, say, mice: competently and incompetently. That is, there are standards to which biological work on mice can be held and against which it can be judged whether the work was done well or not. A study of humans, however, can be done not only *competently* or not, but also *morally* or not. This is because we live in a society in which humans have culturally defined rights and equal worth as individuals.

A **racist** study is one in which individuals are characterized according to properties of a group and their worth evaluated on the basis of their group membership. Such a study is immoral for two reasons: First, it conflicts with our culture's principles of equal rights for all people as individuals; and second, it is not at all clear that human groups are empirically different in such a manner as to make one better or worse than

racist
Judging individuals on the basis of a group to which they belong.

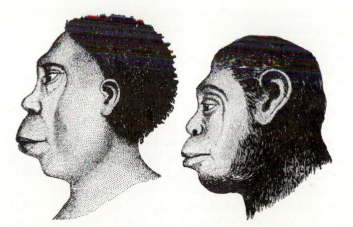

Figure 9-2
From a nineteenth-century book on human variation, this picture attempts to dehumanize Hottentots (and by extension, all Africans) by showing imaginary resemblances to gorillas. In fact, the Khoi peoples tend to have relatively flat faces and high foreheads—so the depiction of *neither* the gorilla *nor* the person is accurate.

racial

A study of the differences among human groups.

another. Average biological differences may exist among human groups—elucidating this point is the empirical goal of **racial** studies, but in the words of the American physical anthropologist Earnest Hooton,

> the range and mean of individual capacity within the several human races has never been proved to differ significantly. Each has, in all probability, its own array of points of strength, offset by weaknesses; and these points do not always coincide in all of the different races. Add them all together in any single race, and I am afraid that it amounts to zero—or, in other words, it comes out even. Thus, all races are equal.
>
> *(E. A. Hooton,* Twilight of Man, *p. 64)*

Unfortunately, throughout much of the history of physical anthropology, it has been difficult to distinguish studies of race from racist studies. This is because many of the studies undertaken on the subject of race were done with the goal of justifying widely held prejudices and values. This goal was accomplished by attempting to show that some groups are more intelligent than others and that this property of intelligence was part of the unalterable hereditary composition of the group.

The Heredity and Innateness of Intelligence

There is some primitive logic to the syllogism that goes: cultural achievements are the product of the human mind; mental activities are located in the brain; therefore, differences in the brains of people of various cultures are the cause of the different achievements of those cultures (Figure 9–3). We now recognize that cultural achievements are the results of: (1) a collectivity of minds, called culture; (2) circumstances; and (3) local history; and further, that (4) the relationship between brain and mind is extremely complex. Nevertheless, early biologists sought materialistically to document and explain cultural history in the size and shape of the skull.

SKULL SIZE

One such study was performed by Samuel George Morton (1799–1851), who amassed a collection of literally hundreds of skulls from all over the world and measured the quantities of mustard seed or lead shot needed to fill each one. He concluded that the skulls of Caucasians averaged about 92 cubic inches; Malays, 85; Chinese, 82; American Indians, 79; and Africans, 83. Yet his analysis contains a number of errors detectable with modern analysis, as shown by Stephen Jay Gould. Gould recalculated these values with the knowledge that the size of the skull varies in proportion to the size of the body and found that all the groups represented

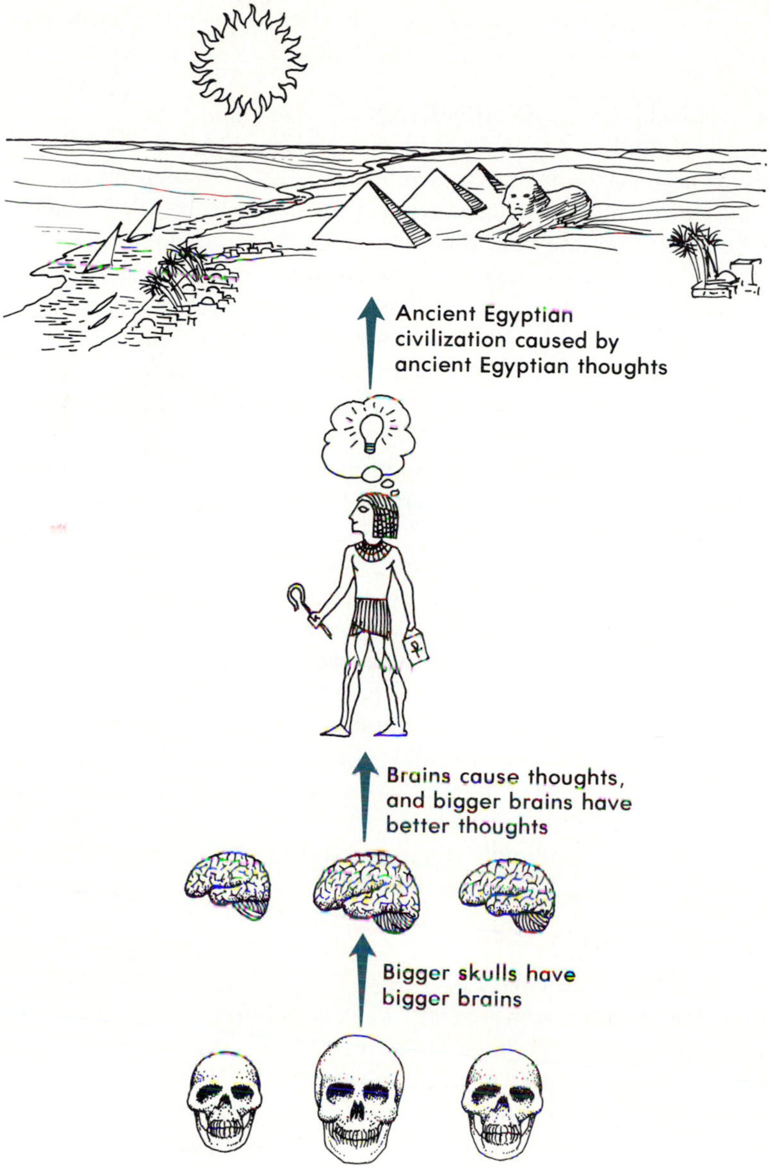

Figure 9-3
The logic of relating skulls to
cultural achievements.

Ancient Egyptian
civilization caused by
ancient Egyptian thoughts

Brains cause thoughts,
and bigger brains have
better thoughts

Bigger skulls have
bigger brains

in Morton's sample averaged about 85 (1,392 cubic centimeters), with no
statistically significant differences among them. Gould also found some
minor errors in calculations and significant omissions on Morton's part,
all of which unconsciously prejudiced the results in the direction Morton
expected to find. We now recognize that individual human skulls vary

widely in size (from about 1,000 cc. to about 2,000 cc.) with no apparent effect on mental function at the individual level, much less at the group level.

INTELLIGENCE QUOTIENT (IQ)

The size of skulls was soon dropped as an indicator of native intelligence only to be replaced by a new number, the IQ. A French psychologist named Alfred Binet developed a set of mental tasks by 1911 which he used to determine the tasks that an average French child at a given age could accomplish. The tasks were progressively more difficult for older children, and each child was assigned a "mental age" based on performance, which could be contrasted with chronological age. In 1914, a German psychologist named William Stern suggested dividing the mental age by the chronological age (hence, "quotient") and multiplying by 100. The resulting number came to be known as IQ.

Lewis Terman of Stanford University translated Binet's work and developed a set of norms for American children. Terman, however, had another set of beliefs about the IQ. He thought it was constant throughout life and that it measured innate ability rather than simply academic achievement at a particular time. Terman devised general tests for adults as well, which tested in essence their knowledge of American culture and aesthetics. An IQ movement, led by Terman and Robert Yerkes of Yale, gave IQ tests to a large battery of people, especially immigrants and World War I army recruits. The immigrant studies showed that eastern and southern European peasants did poorly, and this was used as an argument to restrict immigration from those areas. This, in fact, was a cornerstone of the eugenics movement discussed in Chapter 3: These immigrants were hereditarily stupid and should not be allowed to immigrate, it was argued, lest they interbreed and make future generations of Americans stupid!

THE ROLE OF HEREDITY

The connection between heredity and intelligence was also an integral part of a larger social program. If social problems, which always exist, are seen as intrinsic to the constitution of certain individuals—that is, if social problems are caused by an excess of bad people—then the problems could conceivably be solved by dispatching the bad people or by assuring they did not reproduce. This was the core of the eugenics movement. If, on the other hand, the problems were caused not by defective organisms but by a defect in the structure of society—in the oppression of the poor and the erection of subtle but effective barriers to their advancement—then the only way the situation could be improved would be via a major overhaul of the social system. Obviously, people who are successfully operating within the system would not be favorably disposed toward overhauling it. Therefore, the idea of social problems being caused by too many defective people was more attractive, for it meant that the problems of society were not "our" fault, but "their" fault. Further, the targeted people had to be incurable, for if the defect were temporary or could be improved, then the humane response would be to cure the defect (Figure 9–4).

Consequently, a great deal of time and energy was expended to prove that intelligence, or more precisely its opposite, "feeblemindedness," was ingrained in the constitution of certain humans and groups of humans, and was passed on to their offspring. For then, social problems could be seen as "their" fault and could be dealt with as such. The major promoter of these studies was Charles B. Davenport, who founded the prestigious Cold Spring Harbor laboratory (now a respectable molecular genetics center) with that goal in mind.

The Kallikak Study   One classic (now infamous) study was published by Henry H. Goddard in 1912, as a hereditary study of feeblemindedness in a pseudonymous family, the Kallikaks. Martin Kallikak was a young man from a good family during the Revolutionary War and had a brief fling with a "nameless feeble-minded tavern girl," who had his son, Martin Kallikak, Jr. (Figure 9–5). He later married within his station, however, and by his Quaker wife had another son, Frederick. Martin Jr., the illegitimate son, had left 480 descendants when the study was done in 1912, of whom 143 were feebleminded. Frederick, the other son, had 496 descendants, none of whom was feebleminded and, except for two alcoholic doctors, were all prominent and respected citizens. Goddard, the author, interpreted these data as showing that the good Kallikak blood

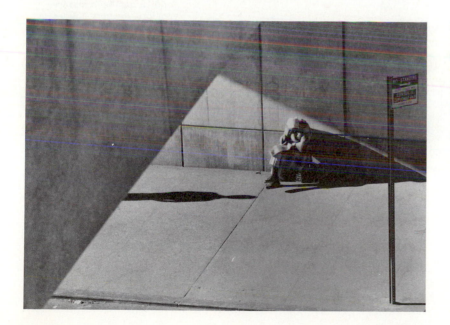

Figure 9-4

Are the problems of homeless people their own fault, or ours? If we can convince ourselves that they are their own fault—that their problems have an intrinsic cause—then we do not have to burden our own consciences.

Martin Kallikak

He had an affair with a nameless feeble-minded tavern girl.

She bore a son known as "Old Horror," who had left 480 descendants by the year 1912.

He married a Quakeress named Rachel.

She bore a son named Frederick, who had left 496 descendants by the year 1912.

From this side, there were 143 feeble-minded, 33 sexually immoral, 24 alcoholics, 3 epileptics, 82 deaths in infancy, and 8 who ran houses of prostitution; only 46 of his descendants could be judged to be "normal."

From this side, there were 0 feeble-minded, 0 illegitimate, and 15 deaths in infancy; doctors, lawyers, judges, educators, traders—respected citizens.

Figure 9-5

The Kallikak story, in which myths of class and myths of genetics combine in a social morality tale.

had been tainted by the defective tavern girl, such that her offspring were defective; while the good-blooded wife had produced only worthy citizens—thus proving the heredity of feeblemindedness.

Critics charged that it proved the heredity of poverty and misery, not of feeblemindedness. But there were more serious difficulties. How, for example, could they have known the tavern girl was feebleminded

Figure 9–6

The Depression, when it became glaringly obvious that poverty was not necessarily a genetic defect.

when they didn't even know her name? (They obviously couldn't, and Goddard is now known to have lied publicly about it.) The basis of the diagnosis of living subjects was usually not even an IQ test, but an interview by one of Goddard's amateur assistants, and often the assessment was made on a glance. And the diagnosis of dead relatives was based simply on hearsay and innuendo. Nevertheless, it was necessary that mental abilities be largely hereditary in order for the social program of eugenics to have any validity. And so it was: The moral of the tale said simply that the bad Kallikaks (and others like them) are the root of social ills such as street crime and poverty. Their misery is in their makeup, their problems are incurable, no amount of welfare will improve them, and if there were simply no bad Kallikaks, we would all be better off for it.

This line of research ended with the Depression, when formerly wealthy and powerful people learned first-hand that being poor does not mean being genetically feebleminded (Figure 9–6).

Army IQ Tests   The army IQ tests purported to show that black recruits were less intelligent than white recruits. Nevertheless, more careful analysis of the data showed that northern blacks scored higher than southern whites and that the major factor explaining the distribution of

IQ scores was not ancestry but the average state expenditure on education per year. Persons, white or black, from states which spent large amounts of money on educational programs scored higher than persons from states which did not. Thus, the IQ was not an innate character of the group, but responded strongly to external social variables.

Twin Studies   The final line of evidence for the inborn basis of intellectual qualities came from twin studies. Identical twins are genetical clones of each other, and if reared in different environments, they could comprise an experimental laboratory for the contributions of genes and circumstances to the general properties of intelligence.

Sir Cyril Burt amassed a large sample of identical twins reared apart and was regarded for decades as the world's leading authority on the basis of intelligence. His data indicated very strongly that, raised together or apart, identical twins had identical IQs. Princeton psychologist Leon Kamin, however, has raised a number of questions about Burt's study, for example: Very little reference was made to the actual data or its manner of collection; absolutely no change occurred in the statistical results between 1955 and 1966, despite an increase in the sample from 21 pairs of identical twins reared apart to 53 pairs; and all the data were destroyed upon Burt's death.

As if that were not strange enough, Oliver Gillie, a medical reporter for the London Times, decided in 1976 to investigate the allegations beginning to surface about Sir Cyril Burt. Since much of Burt's data had been collected by his assistants, Miss Conway and Miss Howard, who had co-authored papers with Burt, Gillie sought them out. What he found, however, was that there was no documentary evidence that Miss Conway and Miss Howard had ever actually existed. They had apparently been fabricated by Sir Cyril Burt, along with the widely cited data.

More recent studies of identical twins are more honest than Burt's but also more difficult to interpret. Often they try to establish not only the heredity of intelligence, but the heredity of personality generally and the psychic contact between twins (see Chapter 17). Nevertheless, twin studies tell us nothing about the differences that may exist in the ranges of variation among human groups. At present, there seems to be no good evidence for any substantial input of genetic differences to the range of variation in intelligence (however that may be measured) among human groups.

NORMAL INTELLIGENCE

In the area of intelligence, therefore, it appears that there is a broad range of normal intelligence in which humans from all cultures can participate equally. IQ tests, however, have tended to be strongly bound by culture—and not only in the kinds of answers solicited. The first researcher to try to give IQ tests to Australian aborigines was inducted as an honorary member of the group and then beset with questions for help on the exam.

He considered it cheating; they considered it absurd to try to answer a difficult question without soliciting advice from one's seniors. Who was more intelligent?

Intelligence is a complex entity and cannot be collapsed into a single number. IQ *is* but a single number that can be compared across individuals, but it is not clear exactly what IQ measures. IQ is changeable over the course of an individual's life. IQ runs in families, but because it is responsive to economic, social, and health factors, the fact that it is inheritable probably does not mean that it is largely *genetically* inheritable (remember, there are other modes of inheritance). Though there may well be some genetic differences that contribute to differences in IQ among people, many other things contribute to IQ differences as well—things such as nutritional status, family size, economic status, and rate of physical growth. The burden of proof is on anyone suggesting that a particular detectable difference among the IQs of human groups is due to genetic differences and not to other causes. Thus far, that burden has never been met, and it seems unlikely that it ever will. In sum, no solid basis exists for the argument that because intelligence is an inborn character, which is measured by IQ, certain human groups are superior to others as a result of being more intelligent.

Three Flaws in Racist Studies

Three important problems are evident in the attempts to demonstrate hereditary differences in intelligence among human groups. The first is a confusion between culture and biology, the assumption that technologically simpler cultures are composed of less intelligent people. This is, as we have seen, not true, since the processes of cultural evolution occur without recourse to the intelligence of the individuals in the culture. The achievements of a culture do not reflect upon the qualities of its members; they comprise a cumulative historical sequence of events in a social context. Our culture can build home computers from raw materials, but none of us can as individuals. The rapid technological leaps we are currently making do not seem to be accompanied by, much less caused by, an increase in the proportion of geniuses arising. Thus, achievements of individuals or of the group to which they belong is not an indication of individual ability.

The second fallacy is the Great Chain of Being. In the nineteenth century, it was implicitly assumed that groups of humans could be ranked, generally according to the cumulative achievements of their cultures. This, to the European mind, put the Europeans on top, Asians next, and Native Americans, Australians, Africans, and others last. This is related to the first fallacy in that the people (i.e., the organisms) were being ranked along a linear hierarchy derived from the achievements of their cultures. Yet the diversity of cultures—like the diversity of organisms—is the result of a historical *branching* process, not a single track along which

Issues in Anthropology 9–1

Racial Purity

One of the most pernicious applications of typological thought in anthropology has been in the search for "pure" races. In the late nineteenth and early twentieth centuries there was widespread belief that history could be understood in terms of primordial migrations of pure races, whose purity was subsequently lost as they commingled with one another, which resulted in the decay not only of their genetic makeup, but of their civilizations as well.

This is wrong for several reasons. First, and most transparently, it equates civilization and genetics, which has no discernible justification.

Second, it assumes that there are, or have been, pure races, that is, people who all looked much the same and had much the same alleles. How can we identify these races? Theorists pointed to the most extreme human phenotypes they could find and considered them "purest." But what is the justification for equating *"most extreme"* with pure? The most extreme phenotypes are simply those whose ancestors were adapted to the most extreme environments. Why should the fact that one can find extreme phenotypes imply that they were drawn from populations that had little or no variability?

The confusion of individuals for populations is typology, and it was rampant in this line of theorizing.

Indeed, there seems little reason to think that, with the exception of small breeding isolates, human populations of the past were any less genetically variable than human populations of the present. There was polytypy and a great deal of polymorphism. In fact, it appears that genetic purity is bad for a population—after all, the more homozygous a population becomes, the less vigorous it becomes, a phenomenon long known to breeders as "inbreeding depression." Its remedy is the infusion of new genetic variability and resulting "hybrid vigor"—the advantages of heterozygosity over homozygosity.

One instructive example of the importance of genetic variation comes from a distant mammalian relative, the cheetah. The cheetah is the fastest living mammal, an impressive predator that once roamed over most of the world. Now, only a few thousand survive in the wild, and cheetah cubs have a high mortality rate due to disease susceptibility. Further, the cheetah does not breed well in captivity, and studies of cheetah sperm revealed a

some groups proceed farther or faster than others. Instead, every group must be understood in a *historical* context (where they have come from), not a *teleological* context (where you think they are going, on the assumption that everyone is going the same way).

The third fallacy is that of typology, the failure to appreciate the great amount of variation for any trait that exists within any group. This failure leads to treating individuals as merely representatives of an abstract racial "type," which may rarely or never exist in reality. Because our interest, as scientists, is in the description of empirical reality, it follows that typology is of little use to us (Box 9–1). This recognition as applied to other species was one of Darwin's major contributions.

Grouping Humans: Racial Studies

Since humans obviously occur in groups, a series of questions were easily posed by students of human diversity. How many of these groups, or

tenfold reduction in sperm count relative to the domestic cat, with nearly three times as many abnormal sperm.

The problem seems to be that cheetahs have almost no genetic variation—they are virtual clones of one another. Several techniques were used to study the genetic differences among individual cheetahs, and all concluded that there is astonishingly little genetic variation among them.

One battery of such tests involved the genes of the major histocompatibility complex, or MHC (called HLA in humans). This is a cluster of genes that code for cellular antigens and determine whether or not tissue or skin grafts are possible. Because there are several genes in the MHC and many alleles for each gene, it is almost impossible to receive a skin graft from another person. Unless it comes from another part of the same body or from a very close relative, the skin will have different MHC antigens, be recognized as foreign, and be rejected.

In the cheetahs, three kinds of grafts were performed. These were *autografts,* from the same individual but from a different part of the body; *allografts,* from a different cheetah; and *xenografts,* from a different species. If the experiments were performed in humans, we would expect the autograft to work and the allograft and xenograft to be rejected. In the cheetahs, in contrast, the autografts and allografts worked, and only the xenografts were rejected.

This means that the cheetah's immune system is functioning, for it was able to reject the xenograft readily. But where most vertebrates have extremely high amounts of polymorphism for the MHC genes, the cheetah has virtually none. All cheetahs appear to have the same MHC alleles, for they are able to graft skin freely to one another. Other genetic tests have borne out the conclusion that the cheetah is lacking in much genetic variation.

Thus, the cheetah appears to be what those nineteenth and twentieth century theorists yearned for—a genetically pure race. And headed for extinction because of it.

Reference:

O'Brien, Stephen J., Wildt David E., & Bush, Mitchell (1986). The cheetah in genetic peril. *Scientific American* 254(5):84–92.

races, are there? What are they? What traits or features should be used to distinguish them? What is the significance of this biological diversity among human races? Unfortunately, there are no objective criteria we can use for grouping organisms below the level of the species. One **species** is defined as different from another if it is reproductively incompetent with the other species. But how do we define whether a **subspecies** is different from another? We might be tempted to say, "If it looks different." But how different? What kinds of differences do we score as significant? These questions can be answered, but the answers will be *arbitrary.* Different people will use different criteria and come up with different groups and different numbers of groups.

What sorts of characters would be useful for distinguishing human races? Early anthropologists used features such as language (for example, inferring the Aryan people from an Aryan linguistic family) and other cultural attributes, but by the early years of this century, serious students

race

A population that differs from others in a manner perceived as significant.

species

A series of reproductively compatible populations in space or time.

subspecies

An arbitrary division, often geographic, of a species.

Figure 9-7

Noses vary in many ways, within and among populations.

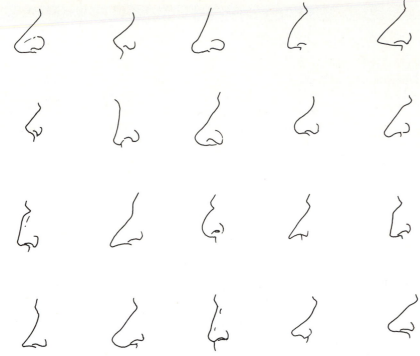

of human biological variation recognized that these were too labile and could change radically within a single generation. A racial trait would have to be stable and hereditary and be variable between groups. Skin color, hair texture, and nasal form satisfied these requirements but varied continuously—that is, any grade of intermediacy between any two skin colors, hair textures, and nose shapes was easy to see (Figure 9–7).

One could, of course, find general differences among populations in these traits. There were two problems, however: these were hard to measure in a precise scientific way, and as anthropologists went out into the field, they found that many of the traits they assumed to be uniform within a population were really variable and often did not occur together in the "right" combinations. This made it difficult not only to place individuals into racial groups, but also to relate racial groups to one another.

These problems appeared to be solved by the use of the *cephalic index,* a measure of head shape (Figure 9–8). This was a statistic developed by a Swedish anatomist named Anders Retzius in 1842 and simply involved the maximum breadth of the head divided by the maximum length, multiplied by 100. Since these were measurements, they could be made with a fair amount of precision; further, they were found to be very strongly characteristic of specific populations and could be recorded from prehistoric skeletal material to obtain time depth. Further, the cephalic index measured the skull, which enclosed the brain, which was the material basis of mental processes, which were responsible for culture. It therefore *had* to be important.

Soon the science of **craniometry** had pigeonholed the populations of the world into the *brachycephalic,* or broad-headed, people (cephalic index greater than 80), *dolichocephalic,* or long-headed, people (cephalic index less than 75), and *mesocephalic* (between 75 and 80). The French, for example, were largely brachycephalic, the Germans dolichocephalic.

But even this system broke down. Most West African tribes turned out to be dolichocephalic, which would align them with the Germans as opposed to the French. Two of the most brachycephalic peoples in the world turn out to be the Hawaiians and the Lapps of Norway. This struck many observers as consequently a somewhat artificial classification.

The most telling blow to craniometry, however, was the study of U.S. immigrants published by Franz Boas in 1910. Boas (Chapter 3) contrasted the heads of two immigrant groups: the brachycephalic Sicilians and the dolichocephalic eastern European Jews. When he compared the skull shapes of newly arrived immigrants to those of their relatives who had been living in the United States, he found that the skulls of both groups became more mesocephalic! Although both groups were endogamous (marrying within their group), the broad-headed Sicilians acquired longer heads, and the long-headed Jews acquired broader heads. The major factors influencing skull shape appeared to be whether you were born in the United States or in the "old country" and how long your mother had lived in the U.S. before you were born.

The Boas study showed that skull shape is a very unstable character, influenced radically by the environment. The basis for this influence is still not known, but it severely undercut the use of the cephalic index as a racial marker.

At the same time that the cephalic index was being shown not to be a strictly inborn character, a new technology was emerging for the

craniometry

The science of head measuring.

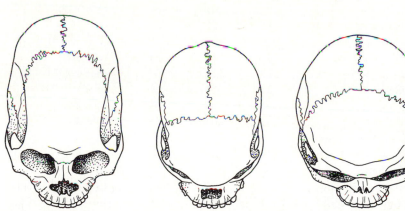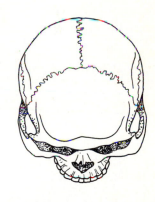

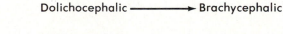
Dolichocephalic ⟶ Brachycephalic

Figure 9-8

Head shapes vary from very round to very long, but they turn out to be influenced strongly by the environment.

polymorphic

Variance within a population such that two closely related individuals may be different from one another.

study of races: genetics. The discovery of **polymorphic** blood groups at the beginning of the century made possible the characterization of different populations in terms of the frequencies of the various alleles they contained. Thus, by determining the ABO blood types of many members of a population, one could mathematically calculate the frequency of the A, B, and O alleles in that population. Table 9–1 shows such a series of calculations.

Certain generalizations can be made about these data. Notice, for example, that high proportions of allele B are found in Asian populations. Allele O is the most common everywhere, but in many Native Americans it is virtually the exclusive allele.

But what about relationships among populations? The Belgians and the Germans differ by fairly little, as we might expect—they are much more similar in their ABO frequencies than, say, the Germans and the Pima/Papago of southern Arizona. And yet the German frequencies are virtually identical to those found among the inhabitants of New Guinea (Figure 9–9).

Table 9–1

ABO Frequencies in Various Populations

Population	Allele A	Frequencies B	O	Number Tested
Japan	.28	.17	.55	(n = 29,799)
Belgium	.26	.06	.68	(n = 3,500)
China (Fukien)	.19	.16	.65	(n = 3,885)
China (Canton)	.16	.17	.67	(n = 992)
Swinomish (NW)	.10	.01	.89	(n = 149)
Navajo	.13	.00	.87	(n = 359)
Estonia	.26	.17	.59	(n = 1,844)
New Guinea	.29	.10	.61	(n = 500)
Pygmies (Africa)	.23	.22	.55	(n = 1,032)
Germany	.29	.11	.60	(n = 39,174)
West Australia	.31	.00	.69	(n = 243)
Eskimo	.33	.03	.64	(n = 484)
New York (white)	.25	.10	.65	(n = 1,077)
New York (black)	.28	.09	.63	(n = 582)
Bushman	.17	.06	.77	(n = 268)
West Africa (Ewe)	.15	.17	.68	(n = 161)
Yap (Micronesia)	.13	.11	.75	(n = 213)
Pima/Papago	.03	.00	.97	(n = 600)

Frequencies of A, B, and O alleles in various populations from Boyd, 1950; Mourant et al., 1976.

Figure 9-9
Germans and New Guineans have similar ABO frequencies, although they are as physically different as any two human populations.

The ABO system as a racial marker has two obvious problems: first, it characterizes populations but says nothing about how to classify an individual. An individual of any blood type could be from any population (with the exception of the extreme unlikelihood of a Type AB person coming from a Native American population). Second, how different do two gene frequencies have to be before they tell us we are looking at two different populations? Are the frequencies of the Fukien and Canton Chinese populations close enough to be the same, or should we regard them as different? What about the Estonians and the Japanese? The answer to this question will depend on the number of people actually studied and will require a statistical test to decide. And both sets of Chinese frequencies are similar to those of the African pygmies, to whom they are probably not very closely related.

Perhaps if we had another set of allele frequencies from a different gene system, the picture would become clearer. For example, a different blood antigen system with two alleles (M and N) gives the data shown in Table 9–2. With the information from this gene, the Pacific peoples (Australians, Melanesians, Polynesians) separate from other groups on the basis of having very low frequencies of allele M—even though their ABO frequencies did not show them clearly as a cluster. This, then, would distinguish the Germans from the New Guineans, who have similar ABO frequencies but different MN frequencies.

However, we still can't distinguish the Estonians of eastern Europe from the Japanese of eastern Asia based on these two genes (Figure 9–10), nor from the Pygmies of central Africa, for that matter.

Perhaps what we need is another gene to tell these populations apart. But notice what happens: The more genes we use, the more differences we

Figure 9-10

The populations of Estonia and Japan have similar ABO and MN frequencies.

Table 9–2

MN frequencies in various populations

Population	Allele M	Frequencies N	Number tested
Japan	.54	.46	(n = 3232)
Belgium	.54	.46	(n = 3100)
China (Fukien)	.55	.45	(n = 422)
China (Canton)	.60	.40	(n = 4648)
Swinomish (NW)	.75	.25	(n = 147)
Navajo	.61	.39	(n = 104)
Estonia	.60	.40	(n = 310)
New Guinea	.06	.94	(n = 1148)
Pygmies (Africa)	.50	.50	(n = 126)
Germany	.54	.46	(n = 10000)
West Australia	.16	.84	(n = 243)
Eskimo	.74	.26	(n = 2081)
New York (white)	.57	.43	(n = 3268)
New York (black)	.48	.52	(n = 500)
Bushman	.61	.39	(n = 112)
West Africa (Ewe)	.57	.43	(n = 853)
Yap (Micronesia)	.23	.77	(n = 450)
Pima/Papago	.70	.30	(n = 485)

Frequencies of M and N alleles in various populations from Boyd, 1950; Mourant et al., 1976.

find among populations. How does this help us decide how many races there are or what these races are? All we are doing is showing that *populations are different from one another*, and if we used many genes, we would ultimately be able to show that all populations are distinct. But this tells us very little, if anything, about race. Two races could be considered populations genetically different from each other, but we can ultimately distinguish any population genetically. And how different is different? Thirty percent? Twenty-five percent? Any decision is arbitrary and subject to the same problems that arise when using other kinds of data.

Polymorphic and Polytypic Variation

We have also made a subtle shift in the way we are looking at these data on human variation. Human groups are both polymorphic and **polytypic;** this means that each population contains diversity and is different from other populations. The study of racial difference classically focuses on polytypy, differences among groups. But the advent of genetics didn't reveal an "Asian" allele or a "Nordic" allele for any genes. Rather, it uses different extents of polymorphic variation (within a population) to make statements about relationships among populations. Thus, we didn't say that the Oceanic peoples are distinct because they have allele N—only that they have relatively more N than other populations do. The circumpolar peoples, such as the Eskimos, fall at the other end, having relatively more M than other populations.

Yet, where we started looking at genes to study *polytypic* variation in humans, we have instead charted the differences that exist in *polymorphic* variation among groups. The distinction is subtle but critical. Years of searching has not enabled us to find a gene that can distinguish a random African Yoruba from a European Swede or a South American Yanomamo. The genetic differences we are using to distinguish populations are not alleles that most or all of one group have and most or all of the other group lack; rather, they are alleles that coexist in both groups in different proportions (Figure 9–11).

polytypic

Variance between populations such that the members of one group can be distinguished from the members of another.

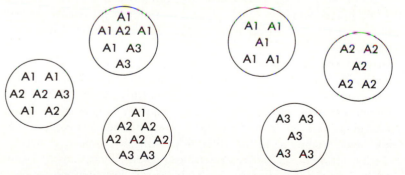

Polymorphism
(differences within a population)

Polytypism
(differences among population)

Figure 9–11

Polymorphic differences and polytypic differences: Patterns of human variation indicate that there is far less between-group variation than there is within-group variation. This tends to emphasize the genetic unity of the species and undermine the significance of studying polytypy.

cline

Variance both within and among populations such that the frequency of a trait changes gradually across a geographic gradient.

Many blood group antigen systems are now known, and while they can often be used to distinguish *populations* from one another, they rarely tell us anything about *individuals*. Why? Because these are polymorphic variations and therefore vary among individuals in a given population. The Diego blood group antigen (Di+), for example, is unknown in European and African populations. It has a frequency of less than 15 percent in eastern Asian populations and in North American Indians. It may reach over 40 percent, however, in South American Indians. Yet any South American Indian can obviously be Diego negative, just as any eastern Asian can be Diego positive.

A gradual geographic change in the frequency of a character (in this case, an allele) is called a **cline**. What we find when we look at a map plotting the frequencies of the various ABO alleles in Figure 9–12 is that there is a gradient in the distribution of these alleles across the world's populations. Thus, the A allele is quite common in northern Europe, southern Australia, and western Canada, and declines in frequency in all directions from those three areas. Similarly, the B allele is common in central Asia and declines in frequency elsewhere.

But why did we do genetic studies on human populations in the first place? To find differences among populations and track patterns of racial variation. But now, instead of finding objective criteria to define differences among races, we have simply found that all populations are genetically different from one another and that particular alleles are distributed clinally across most populations.

Genetics thus contained the seeds of its own destruction as a method of racial analysis. It was found that the vast majority of detectable genetic variation in the human species is variation within groups, not between groups. The geneticist Richard Lewontin calculates that 85 percent of the genetic variation located in *Homo sapiens* is polymorphic variation, with only 15 percent being polytypic variation. If we are interested in genetic variation in the human species, then the genetic differences among races define an exceedingly trivial biological problem. If most of the genetic variation occurs within groups, then it follows that our interests should be focused on *that* variation rather than on the little bit that happens to correlate with obvious cultural differences (Box 9–2).

Polytypic Variation in Humans

Obviously, human groups do vary from one another. People of West African ancestry look different from people of Irish ancestry. But we have still not solved the problem of how to recognize this polytypic variation in a formal scientific way. We could follow Linnaeus and designate the aboriginal inhabitants of the different continents as racial subspecies, thereby setting down Native Americans, Asians, Europeans, Africans, and (following Blumenbach now) Melanesians. But then we are faced with the classic problem: Are an Iroquois from New York, an Eskimo

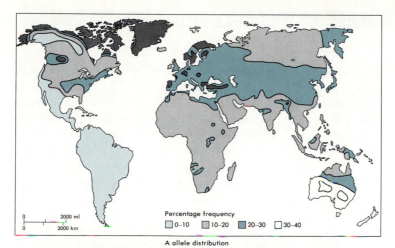

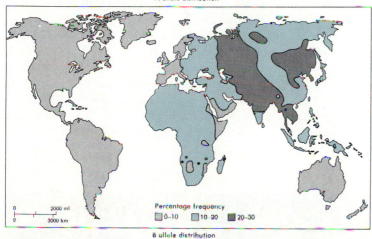

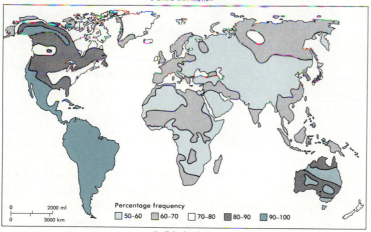

Figure 9-12
The clinal distribution of the
ABO alleles.

Issues in Anthropology 9–2

Sex—The Most Prevalent Polymorphism

Probably the most significant way in which humans in a population differ from one another is in the fact that half are men and half are women. While ape males and females differ principally from one another in overall size and in canine tooth size, humans express their sexual dimorphism in fundamentally different ways.

A human adult male is, on the average, about 8 percent taller and 19 percent heavier than an average adult female. This is comparable to the size difference between male and female pygmy chimpanzees (*Pan paniscus*) but a far smaller difference than among the larger apes. Among human populations, there is variation in sexual dimorphism for size and stature, and generally smaller peoples are less dimorphic in this way. However, differences in diet, exercise levels, and nutritional status affect these measurements greatly, and consequently, it is difficult to explain differences in these measurements across different populations.

Nevertheless, all human populations are very sexually dimorphic in other ways.

Puberty signals a change in the rate of growth of both males and females, resulting in a recognizable adolescent growth spurt (Chapter 5). Males begin theirs slightly later than females but tend to have a slightly larger change in growth rate and have it last for a longer period of time. This change in rate of growth at puberty is not easily apparent in the growth of nonhuman primates. More significantly, however, while males and females both develop pubic and axillary hair, males grow much more body hair, and more facial hair.

Most noticeably, at puberty, the body composition of males and females begins to change significantly. Men tend to build muscle mass to a larger extent than women; women tend to accumulate fat reserves, particularly noticeable in the hips and breasts, to a larger extent than men. Thus, where an average American adult male may be composed

Figure 9–13

Iroquois, Eskimo, and Yanomamo, from the New World.

from Alaska, and a Yanomamo from Venezuela so similar as to be a single race, or should the "Native American race" be subdivided further (Figure 9–13)? If so, by what criteria? How about a Ukrainian, an Ainu from Japan, and a Cambodian (Figure 9–14)? One race or more? Or are they the same as the Native American race? A !Kung San, a Nuer, and a

of 16 percent fat and 40 percent muscle, an average adult female will be about 25 percent fat and 36 percent muscle. Evidence supports the idea that a critical percentage of body fat is necessary for normal female menstrual cycling to take place; female athletes and bodybuilders are often amenorrheic.

The differences in size and muscle mass often enable anthropologists to determine the sex of a skull with a high degree of certainty, for males will tend to have larger crania with more muscular attachment area. Differences in the size of neck musculature, which correlate with differences in the size of certain ridges on the surface of the skull, can allow the identification of the sex of a skull. This is not always possible, however, since there is considerable variation in size among human beings—is any particular skull from a fairly small man or from a fairly large woman?

The pelvis is considerably less ambiguous in permitting the sex of a skeleton to be established. The autapomorphies of human childbirth have placed structural constraints on the pelvis that are sexually dimorphic. Males generally have a narrower sciatic notch, a different shape to the pubic bone, and other differences.

Among living people, biological differences between males and females are typically augmented culturally, in decoration, dress, and roles. This makes it even more difficult to separate the effects of biological endowment from those of social acquisition. Men and women are physically different, and this is the most pervasive anatomical polymorphism in the human species. Certainly, women differ from men in behavior as well, as any two groups of humans can be found to differ. But whether the behavioral differences are primarily the results of differences in morpho-physiology, or are acquired socially, is an open question. It is probably the latter.

Tuareg from Africa (Figure 9–15)? A Polynesian, Micronesian, and an Australian (Figure 9–16)?

Couple this difficulty with the fact that wherever two populations meet, what Cole Porter called "the urge to merge" invariably expresses itself, and we are left with tremendous subjectivity in the delineation of

Figure 9–14

Ukrainian, Ainu, and Cambodian, from Asia.

Figure 9-15
!Kung San, Nuer, and Tuareg, from Africa.

Table 9-3

How Many Races Are There?

Researcher	Year	Number of Races
Haeckel	1873	12
	1879	34
Topinard	1878	16
	1885	19
Deniker	1889	13 races, 30 subdivisions
	1900	17 groups, 29 races
Hooton	1931	4 groups, 29 races and subraces
	1946	3 primary races, 7 composite races, 15 subraces
Boyd	1950	6
	1963	7 groups, 13 races
Coon	1962	5
Garn	1971	9 geographical races, 32 local races
Birdsell	1972	4

the number of races there are, what they are, and who belongs to them. This is true regardless of whether anatomical or genetic criteria are used.

In Table 9–3, we see the result of lifetimes spent trying to delineate the races of *Homo sapiens:* that all the experts disagree. The problem is not with the experts, who controlled all the relevant data and were the most highly respected workers in the field at the time their work was published. The problem is with humans, whose social patterns produce large, variable groups that generally resist classification.

Thus, the physical anthropologist Frederick Hulse has argued that we should recognize a race as simply an "evolutionary episode," a transient package of allele frequencies molded by natural selection as a response to local environmental conditions.

Race as a Social Marker

The primary reason that races are so difficult to delineate in humans is that human variation is generally continuous, rather than discrete. The second reason is that human groups are polymorphic, subsuming a range of variation for each character, just as they are polymorphic for genetic alleles. The third reason is that races are not exclusively, or even primarily, biological categories: They are *social* categories.

Consider the following problem. A man of African ancestry and a woman of European ancestry have a child. To what race does the child belong? Biologically, it should be obvious that the child shares equally in an African and European ancestry, for it receives the same amount of genetic contribution from its mother as from its father. Yet almost invariably, the child will be *socially* defined as black and will identify consequently with the black community. Thus, the biological and social realities about this child contradict each other. Socially, one can either be black or white, yet biologically, one can be anything in between.

This means that the definition of race, and who belongs to each one, is principally defined in accordance with social rules, not biological rules. Unfortunately, these rules are only slightly less extreme than those pronounced by the racist author Madison Grant in 1916: "The cross between a white man and an Indian is an Indian; the cross between a white man and a negro is a negro; the cross between a white man and a Hindu is a Hindu; and the cross between any of the three European races and a Jew is a Jew." The problem is that Grant thought he was making a statement of *biological* significance, when actually he was merely *observing the social facts*. The social facts are that wherever a privileged population coexists with another, less privileged population, a great deal of status difference is attached to a relatively small amount of genetic variation.

Many states had laws passed years ago prohibiting the marriage of people belonging to different races, or miscegenation. In order to enforce such a law, definitions of each race had to be obtained. Typical was Indiana's statute 44–104, which made it illegal for a white person to marry someone "possessed of one-eighth or more of negro blood." Thus,

Figure 9-16

Hawaiian, Australian, and Yap, from Oceania.

having one great-grandparent of African ancestry defined one as black, while having seven great-grandparents of European ancestry was not sufficient to define one as white. The 1935 Nuremberg laws which prohibited "marriages between Jews and citizens of German or related blood" similarly defined a small fraction of Jewish ancestry as sufficient to define a person as Jewish, in obvious contradiction of the biological facts.

Thus, the issue of race is more a social issue than a biological issue. The German Nuremberg laws and American miscegenation laws emphasized not the biological contribution of Jewish or African ancestry to a given person, but its symbolic contribution. The fact that it takes very little racial ancestry to define a person as belonging to that race emphasizes the symbolic nature of the entire endeavor: In earlier days, it was said that one's blood was "polluted" or "tainted" by only a small dose of ethnic ancestry.

The problem is not whether groups of humans differ biologically from one another, but whether the categories we set up to recognize those differences are biological categories or social categories. The answer is that human groups do differ biologically from one another, but we acknowledge those differences as socially defined and symbolically marked categories. The social groups we tend to recognize correlate somewhat with biological differences among populations, but the social differences are much more significant, and indeed, membership in the group is defined largely socially.

Therefore, the trouble with race is twofold: (1) the confusion of biological and social categories, and (2) differential treatment of different groups. Neither kind of category is intrinsically good or bad, for all human groups differentiate themselves socially from other groups—but confusing biological categories for social ones is a mistake. Unfortunately, much of the literature on race involves exactly this confusion. The different treatment that groups receive is what places great significance on the allocation of individuals to one group or another. This different treatment is, of course, a social problem and can be dealt with only socially.

Population Differences as Local Adaptations

Populations differ from one another as a result of microevolution, the principles of which have already been covered. Generally, differences among populations can be either adaptive, as a result of natural selection, or nonadaptive, as a result of genetic drift.

MALARIA

An example of adaptive microevolution is the sickle-cell anemia polymorphism, discussed earlier. In a malarial environment, equatorial African populations have evolved higher frequencies of the allele, which, in single dosage confers resistance to the disease. Other populations also carry this allele. For example, Mediterranean and Asian groups, also in malarial environments, are known to have the sickle-cell gene (thus, it is not a reliable marker of African ancestry).

But populations have adapted to malaria in other ways as well. Wherever malaria is present, there is strong pressure on human groups to adapt in any way they can. But to adapt genetically, a population is constrained by the alleles that are present: If there is no sickle-cell allele, a population cannot create one to combat malaria. However, other alleles that are present may do the trick, for example, Hemoglobin C, which changes the same sixth amino acid in the beta chain, but to lysine instead of valine as in the sickle-cell or Hemglobin S allele. Hemoglobin E changes position 26 from glutamic acid to lysine. These two alleles (Hb C and Hb E) are found at elevated frequencies throughout the Mediterranean, equatorial African, and southeast Asian populations— performing the same adaptive function as the more common Hb S, conferring resistance to malaria upon heterozygotes.

Thalassemia is a constellation of blood diseases in which the hemoglobin is structurally normal but is simply not produced in sufficient quantities. There can either be not enough alpha-globin (alpha-thalassemia) or not enough beta-globin (beta-thalassemia), and there are several different alleles that produce the alpha- or beta-thalassemia phenotype. The distribution of these alleles also parallels malaria. One alpha-thalassemia allele has been estimated to reach a frequency of about 20 percent in West Africans, a different one is common in southeast Asia, and all alpha-thalassemia alleles together reach a frequency of 60 percent in parts of Papua New Guinea. Beta-thalassemia alleles are common throughout all of the Mediterranean and southern Asia (see Chapter 8).

Again, heterozygotes are protected from malaria; they reproduce more efficiently; they pass on the allele to their offspring but also generate homozygotes. This is natural selection (balancing) producing a series of microevolutionary adaptations in different populations, producing multiple genetic solutions to a similar problem. This is, consequently, a major source of genetic difference among populations.

LACTOSE TOLERANCE

Milk is the perfect food for a mammalian infant. It contains a precise blend of sugar, carbohydrates, and proteins adjusted by natural selection for the needs of the young of each species. The sugar contained in milk is called *lactose*; an enzyme in the small intestine breaks down this sugar to the simpler glucose and galactose, which can then be further metabolized. This enzyme is called *lactase*, and if it is not present, several things happen: The lactose molecules persist in the intestine, increasing the particle content of the intestinal fluid, which then draws water from the surrounding tissue into the intestine (result: diarrhea); also, the lactose is not metabolized by the proper enzymes and so is fermented by intestinal bacteria (result: gas).

Table 9–4

Lactose Intolerance

Population	Percent Lactose Tolerant	Percent Intolerant	Number Studied
U.S. white	78	22	913
U.S. black	35	65	390
Native Americans	5	95	221
Mexico	17	83	401
U.S. Chicano	48	52	305
Spain	85	15	265
Sweden	99	1	400
Australian white	95	5	133
Australian aborigines	33	67	145
Somali	24	76	244
Jordan	21	79	204
Jordanian bedouins (dairying nomads)	76	24	162
Beja Sudanese (dairying nomads)	83	17	303
Hungary	63	37	535
Estonia	72	28	650
Central Thailand	3	97	279

Data from Flatz, 1987.

Virtually all human infants have the enzyme lactase. Thus, milk is the perfect food for infants. But what about for adults? While among certain populations, lactase is plentiful throughout adulthood, in most populations, the gene that produces lactase switches off by age five. Having lactase as an adult is the minority state, and in fact, only certain groups have lactase as adults; we call these adults "lactose tolerant." The genetic basis for this phenotype is not well understood, but it is strongly associated with a cultural historical dependence on pastoralism and dairy farming. Thus, the two groups that can tolerate lactose (that is, can drink milk) are Europeans and African or Asian pastoralists. In Table 9–4, we see some percentages of the lactose tolerant and intolerant phenotype among various populations. Interestingly, this polymorphism tracks both cultural history and biological ancestry. Notice that the hybrid population of Mexico has percentages between those of Native Americans and those of Spaniards, that all the European groups and their descendants are over 60 percent lactose tolerant, but also that the two groups of Jordanians differ from each other.

The origin of this polytypic difference may have been a response to the availability of milk as a dietary supplement, which is very nutritious if it doesn't make you sick. Again, however, we find that this is first and foremost a polymorphic variation: The two variants exist in virtually all populations; only their relative magnitude differs between populations.

BODY BUILD

One interesting way in which human groups have adapted biologically to extreme environmental conditions involves differences in body build. For populations living in cold climates, one would ideally wish to retain heat as efficiently as possible. The efficiency of heat retention at a given volume or weight depends upon minimizing the surface area through which heat will be radiated. A form that has a large surface area will radiate more heat and retain less at a given weight or volume than will a form that has less surface area.

The geometric form with smallest surface area per volume is the sphere. A cylinder, for example, has more surface area for a given volume than a sphere. One might, therefore, expect that where heat retention is at a premium, organisms would evolve to a more massive, rounder form. This is found in most mammalian species and is known as *Bergmann's Rule:* In a variable species, body mass increases with decreasing external temperature. Why? Because a large object has less surface area per volume than a small object (Chapter 6). And among humans, the smallest people in the world, the pygmies of Africa and Micronesia, are found in tropical climates (Figure 9–17).

Allen's Rule makes another generalization about body build and temperature for the same reason. In a variable species, bodily appendages tend to increase in size with an increase in temperature. Thus, rabbits in cold climates have smaller ears than rabbits in warm climates, which aids in heat retention. Again, in human populations, we tend to find people with shorter limbs and relatively larger trunks in colder environments and those with longer limbs and relatively shorter trunks in warmer environments (Figure 9–18).

SKIN COLOR

Skin color is the most conspicuous of human polytypic variations. Variation in skin color results from the relative proportions of three molecules present in the skin: *melanin* (black/brown), carotene (yellow/orange) in the fat cells of the skin, and hemoglobin (red when oxygenated/blue when deoxygenated) in the blood vessels. Skin performs several diverse functions: thermoregulation, immunity, sensory input, social signaling (blushing), and most importantly, protection. Protection from what? Therein lies the explanation for the variation in melanin content.

Melanin occurs in specialized cells called melanocytes, which originate in the nervous tissue and migrate upward to the outer layer of the skin. At a given place on the skin, all humans (even albinos) have roughly the same number of melanocytes. Each melanocyte, however, contains melanin granules called melanosomes, whose size, number, and arrangement is variable. Dark-skinned people have more and larger melanosomes than light-skinned people. The function of melanin is to absorb ultraviolet light; thus, at the same thickness of skin, about 3.5 times more ultraviolet light passes through the skin of a light person than of a dark person.

Ultraviolet light, as sunbathers are now regularly warned, can

Figure 9-17
Pygmies of New Guinea with neighbors.

induce basal skin carcinomas—it causes skin cancer. Dark-skinned people very rarely get this cancer. The amount of ultraviolet radiation varies geographically: The rate of skin cancer for a white male is 28/100,000 in England but 265/100,000 in Queensland, Australia. It is, then, an adaptive advantage to be darkly pigmented when located in an area at risk for skin cancer—as the inhabitants of tropical Africa and most of India, Melanesia, and Australia are.

But ultraviolet light serves another function: It converts a molecule of 7-dehydrocholesterol into vitamin D in the skin, which regulates the absorption of calcium into bones. The lack of sufficient vitamin D leads to rickets, the symptoms of which are brittle, soft bones, knock-knees, curvature of the spine, and other skeletal deformities. These are most pronounced in children. It requires about twelve times as much ultraviolet light to maximize vitamin D production in a dark-skinned person as it does in a light-skinned person. Why? Because melanin is screening out the ultraviolet light so efficiently. Rickets is not a problem where ultraviolet light is plentiful.

But when some prehistoric human groups migrated to regions where little ultraviolet light got through, such as Pleistocene Europe, it became critical for them to maximize their vitamin D production. Their long-term adaptation was to become depigmented.

In the modern urban ghettos of temperate North America, rickets became a serious health problem, particularly for dark-skinned people—but as well for other groups. Thus, biological problems were posed for light-skinned people living in tropical areas (cancer) and for dark-skinned people living in urban temperate areas (rickets). In both cases, the biological problems have been overcome by cultural means: the development of sunscreens and the supplementing of milk with vitamin D.

Thus, the most obvious variation in human skin color is attributable to the adaptive presence or absence of large amounts of melanin. The geneticist Curt Stern showed that the range of variation in human skin color from darkest to lightest could be explained by as few as four interacting genes.

To those who would classify Europeans differently from Africans on the basis of skin color, the presence of very dark-skinned people in Pakistan (usually classified nevertheless as "Caucasoid") and somewhat lighter-skinned people in South Africa (usually classified nevertheless as "Negroid") tends to belie the existence of those categories. Again, like the blood groups, human skin color is distributed as a cline (Figure 9–19) and represents simply local adaptations to environmental circumstances—evolutionary episodes.

Adaptive Human Variation

Variation in skin color, however, is influenced by another property of human organisms: the ability to make physiological adaptations. Such

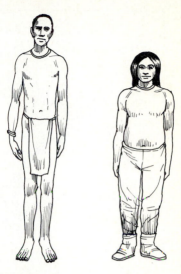

Figure 9-18

Allen's Rule explains geographic variation in body build adaptively.

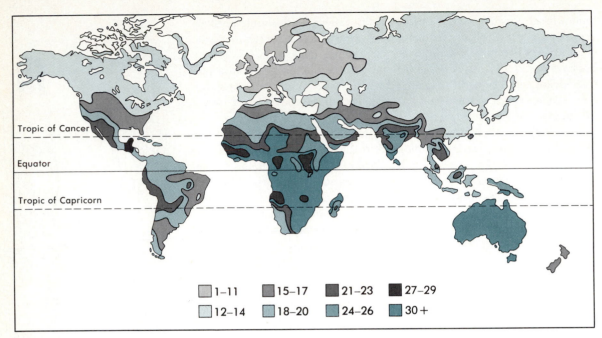

▢ 1–11	▨ 15–17	▨ 21–23	■ 27–29
▢ 12–14	▨ 18–20	▨ 24–26	▨ 30+

Figure 9-19

Skin color in humans is distributed as a cline.

hypoxia

Less than normal quantities of oxygen.

adaptive responses are neither genetic (evolutionary) nor behavioral (cultural)—but they are another cause for humans differing phenotypically from one another. In the case of skin color, the physiological change is tanning: Two members of the same population, one of whom works indoors and one outdoors, will have different degrees of pigmentation.

A similar explanation is at the root of the unique physiology of the Quechua Indians (Figure 9–20), living high in the mountains of Peru, and the Sherpas, living in the mountains of Nepal. The problem faced by these populations is the decreased oxygen level in the atmosphere at high altitude. This is called oxygen stress or **hypoxia**. A person from sea level who visits an altitude of 10,000 feet or higher will often develop high altitude sickness—shortness of breath, physical and mental fatigue, a rapid pulse, headaches, and digestive disorders. After several days, the body is able to make physiological adjustments, but one will still be unable to function as efficiently as a person from a native highland population.

If we compare a Quechua with a lowland native, we find the Quechua to have a larger lung capacity (to take in more oxygen), a broader chest, more viscous blood (containing more red blood cells to transport oxygen), larger capillaries (to facilitate the movement of the more viscous blood), and hypertrophy of the right ventricle of the heart (for pumping the more viscous blood).

Most of these adaptations seem to be physiological in nature.   A lowland native who grows up as a child under hypoxic stress will develop the suite of characteristics common to the high-altitude native populations. This suggests that these adaptations are not unique genetic microevolutionary adaptations of these populations, but rather unique expressions of a developmental program common to all humans and stimulated in these cases.

Nonadaptive Human Variation

Not all differences can be ascribed to functional responses to stress. Differences in allele frequencies, for example, are often attributable to the random effects of genetic drift—although some equivocal evidence has been suggested to link certain blood groups to resistance to certain diseases, such as bubonic plague and duodenal ulcers.

Nevertheless, we no longer recognize the need to explain everything—every part of the body, every allele—in terms of adaptation. In fact, it is frightening, and rather morbid, to think of an organism being pulled simultaneously in so many different directions by natural selection. There are many shapes that a nose or a skull can take: and while there is often polytypic variation, there is always much more polymorphic variation. One can make an informed guess that a skull with a sloping forehead is more likely to be Melanesian, or one with high, wide cheekbones

Figure 9-20

Quechua, from the highlands of the Andes.

Figure 9-21

Possible relationships of groups of human populations. The south African (!Kung, etc.) peoples are very genetically heterogeneous and may be the most ancient human populations. Since all these groups can and do interbreed with one another, this diagram reflects at best the gross biological history of these groups, not necessarily the ancestry of modern populations or individuals.

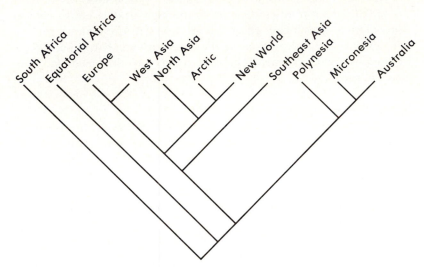

is more likely to be Eskimo, but one may not always be right. In fact, one may not even be right most of the time.

It seems that, in addition to the adaptive differences we can find among populations, a normal human feature can have a broad range of variation without being pathological. Some of this variation is geographically patterned; we recognize a curved nose form as characteristic of some Mediterranean populations, an epicanthal eyefold as characteristic of certain Asian, Native American, and South African populations, and blond hair color as characteristic of certain European populations. Flat faces are characteristic of south Asians and some south Africans. What is the significance of such variation? Probably very little.

Tabulating these sorts of variations helps us to distinguish populations from one another and to characterize populations uniquely, just as the gene frequency data did. But they tell us little more than that. Now that we recognize that (1) human populations are biologically different from one another, (2) different does not imply better or worse, (3) there is much more diversity within a group than between groups, and (4) biological differences often interplay in a complicated way with cultural differences, the "scientific" question of race becomes a quaint historical note with little biological significance. The *social* question of race, however, remains very significant (Box 9–3).

Many of the aboriginal populations of the world may be related as shown in Figure 9–21. Based on genetic and anatomical data, we can construct the cladogram shown. Studies of mitochondrial DNA have suggested that the deepest root of the human family tree is in Africa (see Chapter 12). Thus, we find that African populations are more genetically diverse than other continental populations; and Europeans may be more genetically related to some African populations than those African populations may be to other African populations. The Oceanic, European, Asian, and American peoples form clusters of their own, with Asians and Native Americans being closest relatives. The Australian branch has been seen as closely related to the European, but genetic data place it closer to the Asian.

Of course, the figure becomes less and less relevant as populations become more and more intermixed and as technological advancement removes many of the selective pressures that have helped mold the differences between populations. The tree is a representation of prehistory, but recent history, the present, and the future have the branches of the biological relationships in the tree tending to come together.

Summary

Humans are a highly variable species, biologically and behaviorally. While variation can be seen among human groups, much more can be found within any group. This was overlooked by early physical anthropologists, who sought to describe abstract types rather than real biological entities. Genetic data are supported by morphological data in affirming that the human species is *not* composed of types, within which people are similar and between which people are different. Rather, the human species is composed of populations, each of which is adapted to its environment, and each of which contains a great deal of variability. The problem of race stems primarily from a confusion between biological and social categories, the biological categories being geographically localized populations and the social categories being symbolically marked abstractions. In a society where groups are treated unequally, this confusion can be particularly pernicious.

Questions for Review

1. Why is eugenics, the "improvement movement," no longer a viable program?

2. Do you think that if more people understood the insecure biological foundations of the concept of human races, there would be less racism?

3. IQ is known to be a good predictor of future performance in our school system. Can you explain why that is so?

Issues in Anthropology 9-3

The Saga of Miss Saigon

Race is, as we have noted, biologically trivial but socially significant. Nowhere was this more "dramatically" demonstrated than in a controversy over a Broadway musical. The musical is a distinctly American art form, but with roots in English operettas, continental grand opera, and vaudeville sketches. And like all art, Broadway musicals often reflect life and the sentiments and insecurities of the people and the era.

Some of the most memorable musicals have dealt sympathetically with issues of race, particularly during times when popular consciousness was not highly raised. For example, at the same time as the eugenics movement was working to restrict immigration, Oscar Hammerstein and Jerome Kern opened *Showboat* on Broadway. This 1927 musical not only had blacks as central characters and a black singer stop the show with "Ol' Man River," but brought audiences face to face with miscegenation laws and the harsh fact of economic oppression. The 1935 *Porgy and Bess* by George Gershwin, Ira Gershwin, and Dubose Hayward attempted to bring the pathos and solidarity within a rural black ghetto to the musical stage—giving white characters only the small and nonsinging parts.

Throughout the years, other social conflicts have been played out on the musical stage, in shows as popular as *South Pacific* (Polynesian/American), *West Side Story* (Puerto Rican/Anglo), and *Fiddler on the Roof* (Jew/Gentile).

When producer Cameron Mackintosh announced in 1990 that the biggest hit in London, *Miss Saigon*—centering on the relationship between a Vietnamese woman and an American man—was going to come to Broadway, it was greeted with the largest advance ticket sale in theater history, about 25 million dollars' worth. It would come with the London star, Jonathan Pryce, recreating his role as the engineer, for which he had already garnered major awards.

The plans hit a snag, however, when the actors' union in New York refused to allow Pryce to play the part of a Vietnamese because he was English. The action was taken in support of Asian union members who were offended at the major role being portrayed by someone of the "wrong" race.

And yet, noted former New York mayor, Ed Koch, the role in question was that of a half-Asian, half-European man in the first place. Why should only the Asian half of the character's ancestry be relevant to the casting?

But that was hardly the point. Would it thereby have been legitimate to bar an English actor from playing a *completely* Vietnamese character? Certainly not. The part of Porgy or Richard III need not be played by handicapped people, nor Peter Pan by men, nor Eliza Doolittle by Cockneys, nor Mister Spock by extraterrestrials; that is, after all, why they call it "acting." Critics may debate whether Laurence Olivier's portrayal of Othello compared favorably to Paul Robeson's, but the verdict has far less to do with the fact that Olivier was white and Robeson was black than with the fact that both were brilliant tragedians.

The debate over *Miss Saigon*, once again, involves the confusion of discrete social categories for fairly nebulous biological and geographical categories. The fact that one can be labelled (or label oneself) as Asian does not mean that the label defines a discrete group of people who partake of some hereditary biological essence. Thus, one may well ask the offended actors whether only a Vietnamese could be allowed to play the engineer, or would a Cambodian be acceptable for the part, too? If the quality of *Asian* extends beyond Vietnam, then how far does it extend? Could a south Chinese be allowed to play the role? A north Chinese? A Siberian? A Pakistani? An Eskimo? An Apache?

Could a Jew be allowed to play the role? After all, to nineteenth-century European anti-Semites, Jews were considered to be Asians—stemming, as they did, from *west* Asia.

That, however, is not what the offended actors had in mind. Rather, they appropriated (or had appropriated to them) the entire continent of Asia as a *social* label to subsume American immigrants (and their descendants) from various nations of principally *southeast* Asia. Once we appreciate that this immediately reflects a fairly arbitrary division of the continent, we can then ask: An ancestry from *which* nations permits one to be a member of this social group, and *how much* ancestry does it take?

Ultimately, the answers to these questions are fully arbitrary and without a basis in human biological variation. Human biological variation is continuous, not discrete, and highly polymorphic, not typological. Asian, like black and Jew, is *not* a distinct and objective biological category whose essence is imparted to individuals with a precise amount of ancestry from a certain group of nations. Rather, it is a category whose membership is defined by a combination of self-identification, vague overall looks, upbringing, and external imposition. It correlates to a limited extent with some human biogeography, but its primary significance is as a social category, for its members are defined according to highly arbitrary standards.

It is only when we fully appreciate that the categories by which we classify people are constructed, not natural, that we will be able to liberate ourselves from thinking "racially" and see ourselves as we really are. What are we? We are a single species, with a great deal of biological variation within populations, with some biological variation between populations, but with most outward characteristics diffusing gradually over geographic gradients; and with a strong tendency to classify things and one another and to reinforce with an inequality of money or status the symbolic boundaries that inhere in a classification.

For Further Reading

Dobzhansky, T. (1962). *Mankind evolving*. New Haven, CT: Yale University Press.

Frisancho, A. R. (1979). *Human adaptation*. St. Louis, MO: C. V. Mosby.

Gould, S. J. (1981). *The mismeasure of man*. New York: W. W. Norton.

Lewontin, R. (1982). *Human diversity*. New York: Scientific American Library.

Montagu, A. (Ed.). (1964). *The concept of race*. New York: Free Press.

Roots of the Human Species: Diachronic Studies

Principles of Historical Inference

Principles of Historical Inference

major concern of physical anthropology is to reconstruct the biological history of our species and its relatives. A major concern of archaeology is to reconstruct cultural history. In paleoanthropology, relationships are constructed based upon the bony remains of an animal. In archaeology, relationships are based on patterns of material culture. Species are closed systems, with genetic information unable to travel into other species (the rare exception to this is the possible transfer of DNA by viruses). Societies and their cultures, on the other hand, often receive information and materials from other societies readily. As a result, the reconstruction of archaeological cultures is considerably more difficult. To trace biological macroevolutionary relationships, we can assume that taxa and the characters we use to identify them are in the process of constant divergence. Cultural evolution, however, can be **reticulate**, with diverse strands coming back together. This can happen on a trait-by-trait basis or due to the large-scale merging of populations and cultures.

Both physical anthropologists and archaeologists nevertheless attempt to infer historical relations from patterns of remains. The problems they must grapple with are often similar, and their solutions to them often converge.

reticulate

Having many fine branches that sometimes diverge and somtimes merge. In biology, most evolution above the species level is divergent; some is convergent (different species evolving in similar ways to similar environmental pressures, resulting in superficial similarities), but there can be no merging.

Abandoning the Great Chain of Being

The primates have been characterized by several major *adaptive radiations*—evolutionary divergences into many closely related taxa over a short period of time. Although it may be tempting to think of primate evolution along the lines of a "Great Chain" (prosimians, tarsiers, monkeys, apes, humans), what we find in the paleontological record is that different groups have flourished in different places at different times. Apes flourished in the early-to-mid-Miocene, but the prosimian lemurs of Madagascar reached their greatest diversity in the Pleistocene. The African monkeys are flourishing at the present time. There is only one species of *Homo* now, but twenty species of *Cercopithecus*.

Furthermore, lemurs, tarsiers, monkeys and apes are all contemporaries. It is difficult to envision one extant group evolving into another, insofar as evolution is a statement about time, and contemporary taxa have little or no time depth. However, we can refer to the *earliest appearance* of a group—and we see that at one time, in the Eocene, all the known primates were recognizably prosimians. Apes and monkeys appear later, in the Oligocene, while the prosimians continue to exist. And humans emerge from an ape line in the Pliocene, while all the other groups persist—evolution is principally a branching process, not a linear one.

To study the phylogenetic history of humans, we therefore have to abandon the Great Chain of Being, for its imagery does not reflect the evolutionary process as we currently know it. We must then develop a set of rules for interpreting the great structural variability we encounter in nature and learn how to group species by their evolutionary relations.

Unilinear, chainlike models of cultural evolution have to be abandoned as well (Chapters 3 and 4). Much of the evidence for the complex, multidimensional and multilinear nature of culture history has come from archaeology. We now know that societies and their cultures can change for a variety of reasons, including various forms of contact with other groups and the need to adapt in the face of diverse environmental stresses. It is also known that different aspects or parts of societies—all things, from artifact styles and forms to modes of technology and social organization—change at different times during a culture's history as well as at different rates. No single standard of cultural evolution can be described on anything but the most general level.

In this chapter, we first consider the complex picture of biological history that physical anthropology provides. We then introduce the more complicated culture history offered by archaeology. Details of both kinds of historical, or diachronic, analysis are presented in subsequent chapters.

Cladistic Analysis: How We Infer Phylogeny

At any given time, many primate species are or were thriving. How can we link close relatives and say with some degree of assurance that species A is more closely related to species B than either is to species C (Figure 10–1)? The answer is given by a methodology that has been practiced for

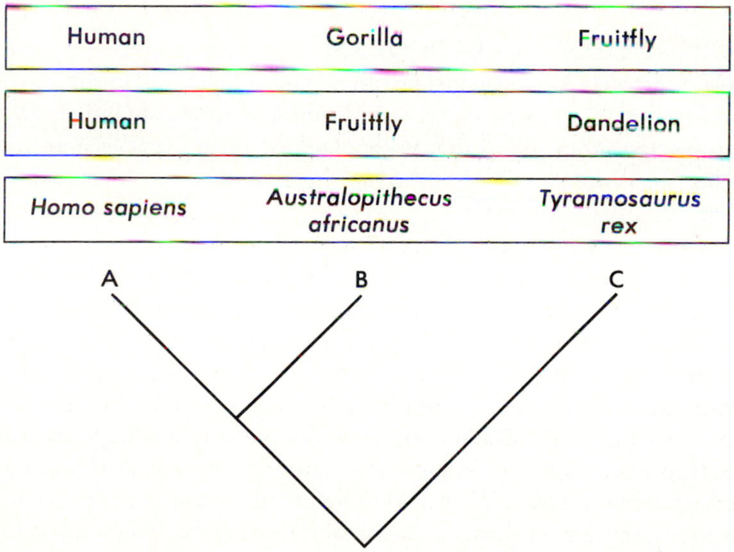

Figure 10-1

A cladogram is a generalized statement about relationships between closest relatives (sister taxa) and a more distant relative (out-group).

many decades but which has only been codified and made explicit since the late 1960s. This is called phylogenetic systematics, or cladistics, developed by the German entomologist Willi Hennig (Chapter 5).

In cladistics, the fundamental unit of analysis involves three taxa. These consist of two closest relatives, or **sister groups**, and a reference species, or **out-group**. Since all species are ultimately related to one another, any statement about the relationship of two species is meaningful only when reference is made to a third species. Thus, humans are related to gorillas. Humans are related to fruitflies. Humans are related to dandelions. Each of these statements is true, but none is very informative. However, the statement "Humans and gorillas are more closely related to each other than either is to a fruitfly" gives us a significant piece of historical information. Similarly, "Humans and fruitflies are more closely related to each other than either is to a dandelion" tells us that two of the three taxa under discussion intimately share a part of history not shared by the third.

The way we express this information is through a **cladogram**, a simple branching diagram. Each branch on the cladogram represents a taxon, and tracing any two taxa downward leads to their joining at a *node*. Any taxa within a node are more closely related to each other than either is to any taxa outside that node. Thus, for the cladogram in Figure 10–1, we can substitute human, gorilla, and fruitfly for A, B, and C; or human, fruitfly, and dandelion for A, B, and C. A cladogram is, thus, a generalized statement about relationship.

A cladogram lacks a time dimension. It gives only the relative branching order of taxa, regardless of when they lived. Thus, for the same cladogram, we can substitute *Homo sapiens, Australopithecus africanus,* and *Tyrannosaurus rex,* even though none of these species overlapped in time.

CONSTRUCTING A CLADOGRAM

How do we construct a cladogram? In examining any organism, we find characters or traits of which it is composed. Some traits are unique to the given species—they tell us that we are looking at this species and not at another one. Most traits, however, are shared by the species in question and by other species as well.

Evolution represents change through time. This means that certain traits have become altered over the course of time in certain taxa. Thus, each character has two states—the original, or *primitive,* condition, and the altered, or *derived,* condition. For example, if we were studying a human, a rhesus macaque, and a horse, we might recognize that the human and macaque have eyes pointed forward, while the horse has eyes pointed to the side (Chapter 5). Most other mammals have outward-directing eyes, like the horse—the orientation of the human and macaque eyes is a rarity. We would therefore infer that this represents an alteration (or series of them) in the skull reflecting the common ancestry

sister group

The closest relative of a taxon, from the taxa being considered, determined on the basis of possessing synapomorphies.

out-group

A more distant relative, determined on the basis of having plesiomorphies (primitive character states) where the two sister groups have synapomorphies.

cladogram

A branching diagram without a time dimension, showing the closest relatives among a group of taxa from the distribution of synapomorphies.

of the human and macaque. That is, there existed a creature in the ancestry of the macaque and human, but not of the horse, who developed this trait (eye socket rotation) and from whom the macaque and human have inherited the trait. Forward-facing eye sockets therefore constitute a shared derived character or synapomorphy linking human and macaque, with the horse as an out-group.

Every species is a mosaic of primitive and derived features. Thus, no contemporary species is more advanced than another. Remember, there is no Great Chain of Being. Nevertheless, each particular species has some unique, derived traits (which distinguish it from other species), some shared, derived traits (which tell you what species it is related to), and some primitive traits (which it has retained from its ancestors). Different species may have more or fewer primitive traits, but it is the trait that is primitive, not the organism.

Take, for example, modern gorillas (Figure 10-2). They are larger than other living primates—their size is a uniquely derived feature. The position of their shoulder blade (scapula) is to the rear of the body, giving the shoulder great mobility. This is a derived trait shared as well by gibbons, orangs, chimps, and humans. Other primates have the shoulder blades oriented more laterally. Further, the gorilla has a dense coat of body hair, like other primates, but unlike humans—this is a primitive character for the gorilla.

Two things require comment. First, note that the sharing of primitive characters does not define a group of closely related species. Dense body hair has been retained in many primate lineages and lost in one. Loss of hair is the derived condition; the retention of it is the primitive. But "all primates with dense body hair" is not a group of close relatives because the evolutionary event in question occurred in the other group,

Figure 10-2

A gorilla, like all species, is a mixture of primitive and derived traits.

Dog

Bird

Gorilla

Octopus

Starfish

Fly

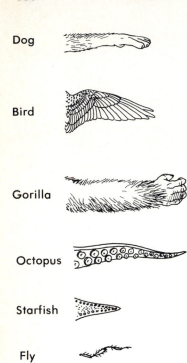

Figure 10-3

Extremities have evolved several times in the animal kingdom; in making a comparison across taxa, one needs to make certain assumptions about homology.

homology

Fundamental structural similarity due to common ancestry.

homoplasy

Superficial similarity due to different species changing in similar ways.

the one that lost its coat. We define a *clade*, or a group of closest relatives, by the occurrence of specific evolutionary events, not by their lack of occurrence. Somewhat paradoxically, in this case, the absence of a trait (dense body hair) represents the occurrence of an evolutionary event (loss of it). The presence of the character tells us only that the other species were evolving in different ways and that little of interest was going on with respect to their hair.

Second, note that even an "advanced" primate like the gorilla is full of primitive characters. This is because there is no such thing as an advanced organism, only derived characters. Humans, as we will see, have many derived features. But if we contrast the hands of that quintessentially "advanced" primate, *Homo sapiens*, with those of the gorilla, we find that the knuckles of the gorilla are enlarged and have thick pads of skin, complete with fingerprint-like ridges and specialized sweat glands—on their knuckles! This is clearly related to their mode of terrestrial locomotion. Nevertheless, it is a derived character in the gorilla (shared only with the chimpanzee). Humans retain the primitive character state of their knuckles, along with other primates.

How can we determine which character is the derived one and which is the primitive one? This is the central question in phylogenetic reconstruction. There are no sure-fire guidelines, but there are some regularities to assist us. First, the trait more widely distributed across different species is likely to be primitive. This is because the derived character evolved later and, therefore, presumably fewer descendant species possess it. Second, the character that first appears in the fossil record is obviously more likely to be primitive. Third, the primitive character may often manifest itself during the development of an organism that ordinarily expresses a derived character. Thus, embryonic humans have gill slits, tails, and a two-chambered heart at various times: This may suggest that lungs, taillessness, and a four-chambered heart are derived states.

Homology   A key concept in phylogenetic analysis is **homology**, a particular relationship that may exist between two traits in different species. The divergence and modification of species through time implies that two descendant species may have features that are different from each other but that are fundamentally similar in structure and development, even if not in outward appearance and function. For example, a dog's forelimb, bird's wing, and gorilla's arm are all related through descent from the forelimb of an early tetrapod that lived pehaps 300 million years ago. They are not related to the arms of an octopus, starfish, or fly, which independently acquired limbs of very different kinds at various times in the history of life (Figure 10–3).

Homoplasy   The greatest difficulty in phylogenetic analysis is in the recognition of characters which have been independently derived in different lineages. This is called *parallel evolution*, or **homoplasy**, and distinguishing it from homology is critical. In the example above, the tetra-

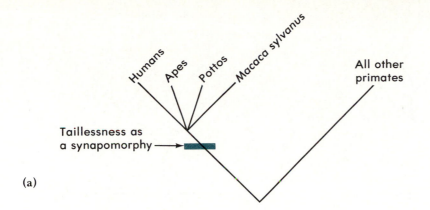

Humans   Apes   Pottos   *Macaca sylvanus*   All other primates

Taillessness as a synapomorphy ⟶

(a)

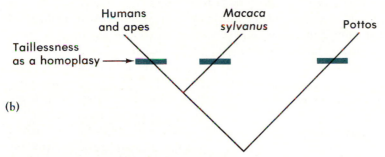

Humans and apes   *Macaca sylvanus*   Pottos

Taillessness as a homoplasy ⟶

(b)

pod (amphibian, reptile, bird, mammal) limbs are homologous to one another; and the tetrapod, cephalopod (octopus), arthropod (fly), and echinoderm (starfish) are homoplasies.

To give another example, the hominoid apes have lost their tails. Nevertheless, so have the prosimian pottos, and in some species of macaques, the tail has become markedly reduced. We could naïvely hypothesize that pottos, apes, humans, and *Macaca sylvanus* are all, therefore, very closely related—assuming the loss of the tail occurred once, a unique evolutionary event. However, this hypothesis can be tested and rejected—we can find no other characters that yield such a phylogenetic grouping. Virtually all the anatomical and genetic data yield the phylogeny given in Chapter 5, therefore indicating that taillessness has evolved independently at least three times in the primates (Figure 10–4).

This method accounts for why we often have to rely on very obscure anatomical parts for our assessment of relationships among taxa. We require characters that are different among the taxa we wish to study—but of course, in most ways, closely related species are very similar to one another. We need characters that also tend not to vary greatly so that we can assume we are avoiding homoplastic traits, which evolved in parallel in different lineages. And further, we need characters in which an out-group has the primitive condition for the character that varies in

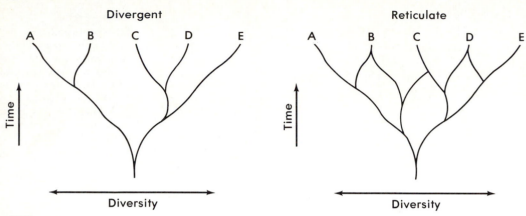

Figure 10-5

In strictly divergent modes of evolution, such as macroevolution, the determination of what is more closely related to what is less complicated than in evolutionary modes that permit fusion of lineages and result in reticulate evolutionary patterns.

polarity

The determination of which homologous feature is derived (say, bipedalism in primates) and which is ancestral (say, quadrupedalism); the proposition of an evolutionary event in the common ancestry of a group of species.

the species under examination. This way, we can assume we are avoiding traits that have been retained independently in distantly related species. These three conditions impose strong constraints on the number of anatomical traits that are cladistically informative or useful. As a result, quite often the placement of a species will turn on the shape of its elbow, a bump on its tooth, or the relative distance between landmarks on its skull. Nevertheless, it is because these characters pass the stringent requirements we have laid down that we give them weight.

When dealing with fairly closely related animals or fossilized and incompletely preserved animals, it becomes more difficult to distinguish homology from homoplasy, and that is why phylogenetic hypotheses often differ among researchers in their details. Independent analyses of different parts of the same species, for example, chromosomes, DNA structure, or other anatomical features, can indicate whether one has assigned homology or **polarity** to a specific feature mistakenly. Thus, different traits and analyses are tests that can be used to falsify hypotheses of relationship. Further, this method assumes that lineages are diverging from one another, which holds only for macroevolutionary analyses. When lineages can come back together, as in reticulate biological microevolution or cultural evolution, the judgment of "closest relatives" becomes far more complex and somewhat less meaningful (Figure 10–5).

Phylogenies

When we have our homologous characters chosen, our polarities (primitive/derived) assigned, and our cladogram constructed, we have completed the first and simplest step in phylogenetic analysis. We have ordered the taxa with respect to their relative branchings from one another, but we have not made any hypotheses concerning which taxa are *ancestral* to others. This judgment will depend upon when the taxa in question lived and thus requires additional data about time as well as the distribution of characters upon which the cladogram was constructed.

PHYLOGENETIC TREE

The addition of time to a cladogram yields a **phylogenetic tree**. Thus, the probable descent of *Homo sapiens* from *Australopithecus afarensis* will not be represented in a cladogram, but will be represented in a phylogenetic tree. Contrast the cladogram and tree depicting the relationships of *Aegyptopithecus zeuxis*, *Australopithecus afarensis*, *Homo sapiens*, *Pan troglodytes*, *Pongo pygmaeus*, and *Sivapithecus sivalensis* in Figure 10–6.

phylogenetic tree

A branching diagram which indicates when certain species lived and diverged from others; it contains all the information in a cladogram, and temporal data and more inferences as well.

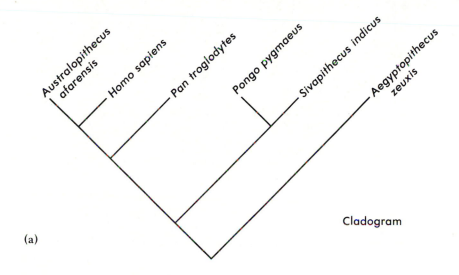

(a)

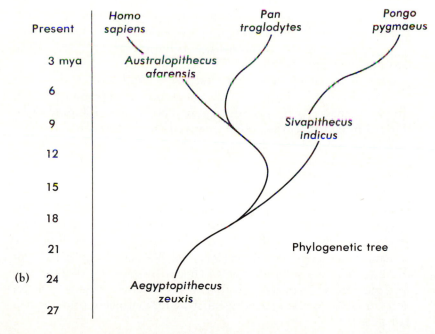

(b)

Figure 10–6

(a) Cladogram representing the relationships among six catarrhine species. (b) Phylogenetic tree representing the relationships, temporal positions, and possible ancestor-descendant statuses of those six species.

Figure 10-7

Hypothetical phylogenetic tree. At the present, there are three extant species (A, B, C), but at time "t" there were thirteen species in this clade. The chances of finding and identifying the three species directly ancestral to the three living ones are fairly small.

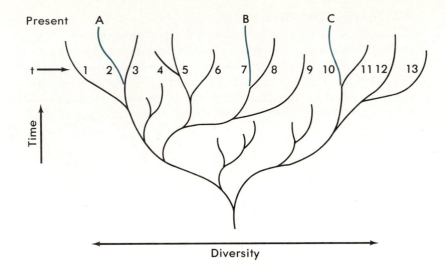

The phylogenetic tree gives more information than the clado-gram—not only branchings, but possible ancestor-descendant relation-ships and absolute divergence times as well. This is because it builds in more information, and more assumptions, than the cladogram. Thus, many phylogenetic trees may be consistent with a single cladogram, depending on the temporal placement of the taxa in the cladogram.

Unfortunately, we rarely can say with any certainty that one taxon is ancestral to another. There are two reasons for this. First, as we go back in time, we sample a smaller percentage of the taxa which lived at that time. Therefore, it is increasingly likely that the actual ancestor of the taxon which lived at a later time is not represented in the fossil sample. What we are likely to have, however, is a close contemporary relative of that direct ancestor (Figure 10–7). Second, even if we had the direct ancestor in our sample, it would be difficult to tell that it was the direct ancestor. We do not find an individual of one extinct species fossilized in the act of giving birth to another species. Such relationships must be inferred from an identification of derived characters in the putative descendant and primitive characters in the putative ancestor.

EVOLUTIONARY SCENARIOS

evolutionary scenario

Explanation for a phylogenetic tree, based on the tree and incorporating other information and inferences.

We fill out the phylogenetic tree by making inferences about selective pressures and inferring causes of the evolutionary divergences we have traced. This information can come from studies of paleoclimatology, paleoecology, or other sorts of data. As an example, one **evolutionary scenario** resulting from such inferences may include an explanation for the acquisition of the bipedal habit in hominids—not only do we recog-nize the derived character and that it was inherited from a common ancestor (*Australopithecus afarensis*), but we try to explain it now as well (Chapter 11).

Just as many different trees are compatible with a single cladogram, many different scenarios are compatible with a single tree. An evolutionary scenario will give us the most information, but it will also contain the most assumptions. In contrast, as we have seen, a cladogram will have the least information and the fewest assumptions. That is why it is the first and most fundamental step to take in historical biological reconstructions.

Interpreting Anatomical Variation

Let us say we encounter two skulls in the fossil record. Obviously, they are going to be different from each other in certain ways—they can't be clones, after all. Granting that the two skulls we have will not be identical, how do we interpret the differences we encounter? This is the most critical problem in historical biology—interpreting the morphological variation we detect among fossils. There are nine different causes of anatomical diversity among organisms, each of which must be considered in analyzing fossil material.

TAXONOMIC VARIATION

Much of the variation in the fossil record is interpreted as representing taxonomic diversity. Different species almost always look different from one another, and there is a vast number of extant species (Figure 10–8). Therefore, two fossils which look different could well be from different species. A tendency to interpret too much of the observable diversity as taxonomic results in *splitting*—splitters are scientists who divide fossils into too many taxa. Louis Leakey was known as a splitter, placing his robust australopithecine fossil in the brand-new genus *Zinjanthropus*, for example.

A tendency to interpret too little of the observable diversity as taxonomic results in *lumping*, or placing what were probably different species in the same taxonomic entity. In the 1960s, for example, David Pilbeam and Elwyn Simons of Yale University spearheaded a movement to collapse the diverse hominoids of the Miocene, which they considered to be greatly oversplit, into relatively few taxa. They concluded that the genus

Figure 10–8

(a) Yellow baboons (*Papio cynocephalus*) and (b) barbary macaques (*Macaca sylvanus*) are closely related species and are clearly distinguishable from each other.

Proconsul and the genus *Dryopithecus* were actually both *Dryopithecus*. More fossils and subsequent analyses led Peter Andrews of the British Museum (Natural History) to conclude in 1978 that Simons and Pilbeam had in turn overlumped the Miocene apes. This has begun a pendulum swing back toward recognizing great taxonomic diversity in the sample— and we now recognize *Proconsul* as a valid genus once more.

SEXUAL DIMORPHISM

Males and females of most primate species look different, especially skeletally. Males tend to be larger, have larger canine teeth, and have larger crests for larger muscles to attach. The failure to appreciate sexual dimorphism is probably the cause of most splitting. But how can you tell a fossilized male skull from that of a female of the same species? Fleagle, Kay, and Simons found that in their sample of *Aegyptopithecus zeuxis*, molar teeth were all about the same size, while canine teeth were either large or small. This suggested that, based on the general pattern in catarrhine primates, the ones with large canines were the males, and the ones with small canines were the females.

Some workers in the 1960s held that the large, "robust" australopithecines and the small, "gracile" australopithecines, who lived in Africa 1–3 million years ago (Chapter 11) might simply be males and females. But several arguments about their patterns of sexual dimorphism and geographical distribution militated against this view. Later finds of female "robust" fossils and other contemporaneous morphologies suggest that lumping these fossils would underestimate their taxonomic diversity. The *single species hypothesis* is no longer maintained.

Whether the hominids from Hadar, Ethiopia, represent a single very sexually dimorphic species (*Australopithecus afarensis*—Chapter 11) or a mixture of two related species, one large and one small, is a hotly contested issue. Most workers are willing to regard it as a single species.

ONTOGENETIC VARIATION

The end of the preformism-epigenesis debate in the eighteenth century (Chapter 3) resolved once and for all that at all stages of life, organisms do more than simply grow—they also change (Figure 10–9). Animals are dynamic entities through time and possess an **ontogeny**. This, of course, leads to a problem if most of the species which have ever lived are extinct, which they are. The problem is, how do you link a juvenile form of an extinct species with an adult? If we are lucky, we might find only one species of a particular group extant in a particular time and place— therefore, if immature specimens are found (for example, the *Homo erectus* child's skull from Modjokerto, Java), they most likely belong to that species.

But suppose we find a child's skull in a context for which there are more than one hominid species, such as the case with the Plio-

ontogeny

The growth and development of an organism, from embryo to old age.

Figure 10-9
Animals change appearance as they grow older. When dealing with an unknown species, having a juvenile specimen may not tell you what the adults looked like.

Pleistocene hominids in southern Africa about 2–3 million years ago. How do we know to which hominid species it belongs? We have to rely on more subjective criteria. In fact, the Taung skull (Chapter 11) has occasionally been suggested to be a junior "robust" australopithecine, rather than the junior "gracile" australopithecine it is usually considered. In the absence of direct knowledge of just what immature individuals of each species looked like, it is difficult to allocate isolated immature specimens to one or another species.

RACIAL VARIATION

Variation at the subspecies level is certainly common in animals. There are several subspecies of chimpanzees, each subtly but consistently different from the other. The subspecies of gorillas (*Gorilla gorilla gorilla*—the lowland gorilla, *Gorilla gorilla graueri*—the eastern lowland gorilla, and *Gorilla gorilla beringei*—the mountain gorilla) differ in their general length of hair, width of nostrils, breadth of chest, aspects of skull form, and aspects of hands and feet. The two subspecies of orang-utans (*Pongo pygmaeus pygmaeus*—the Borneo orang-utan, and *Pongo pygmaeus abelii*—the Sumatra orang-utan) have consistent differences in the structure of their faces and in their facial hair (Figure 10–10).

But how would we know to make these different subspecies, as opposed to different species or the same subspecies, if we found them as fossils? Again, we would be forced to make partly subjective decisions, based upon the amount of morphological difference we take to be appropriate at the subspecies level. We recognize, for a significant example, the two different subspecies *Homo sapiens sapiens* (modern humans) and *Homo sapiens neanderthalensis* (Neanderthals). Most European anthropol-

Figure 10-10

The two subspecies of orangutan show subtle but regular differences.

ogists, however, have regarded the two groups as different species. Bear this in mind when we cover Neanderthals in Chapter 12, and then decide whether you think the data support one taxonomic placement or the other.

ECOTYPIC VARIATION

Biological systems have built-in plasticity in development. This means that from the same genetic background, a growing organism can develop in different ways due to environmental pressures. For example, genetically identical plants grown at different altitudes will grow to different sizes, as a classic experiment showed. As you saw in Chapter 9, people living at high altitude tend to develop certain anatomical and physiological responses to the long-term stress of breathing the thin air. Such developmental adjustments will not be, strictly speaking, inherited, but they will appear as stable traits of the population as long as the environmental stimulus is present.

Ecotypes are stable developmental responses by populations to different environmental pressures in the absence of significant genetic differences between them. Therefore, if we find two fossils, similar but slightly different, we need to consider the possibility that the differences between them are due only to environmental stress and developmental plasticity. Would anthropologists of the future be able to tell that the young adults of the 1990s, being considerably taller, and their great-grandparents, the young adults of the 1890s, are not different subspecies?

POLYMORPHIC VARIATION

In any population, people look different. Some are tall, some are short, some are thin, some are fat, some are muscular. These are hereditary differences attributable to the shuffling of genes which occurs as a result of reproduction. In interpreting differences between any two fossils, therefore, we need to consider the possibility that their differences are simply a sample of the normal genetic diversity which exists in any population.

PATHOLOGICAL VARIATION

It would be nice if all fossils represented healthy individuals in the prime of life. But disease existed, even for prehistoric populations. They faced the same sorts of real problems as living populations. Some diseases, such as syphylis, tuberculosis, and various vitamin deficiencies, leave their marks on the victims' bones and can be studied in the subdiscipline called *paleopathology*. Traumatic injuries or birth defects can also create major skeletal differences among individuals. Additionally among humans, we find that often cultural practices result in dramatic changes to certain parts of the body, notably artifical cranial deformation (Figure 10–11). While not strictly examples of pathological variation, the outcome is the same—a different morphology that must be interpreted.

These sorts of variants can be detected by having a large sample of skeletal material. If there are normal individuals, the pathologies will stand out. Suppose, however, you find the first fossil remains of a creature with which there is nothing to compare—can you assume it was normal? Some anatomists, as we saw in Chapter 3, felt that the fossil remains from the Neander Valley in Germany belonged to a prehistoric creature different from ourselves. Others, however, argued that they belonged to a somewhat brutish Mongolian Cossack deserter of the Czar's army during Napoleon's invasion of Russia. Subsequent discoveries, of course, vindicated the former interpretation.

In 1913, the French paleontologist Marcellin Boule competently reconstructed a skeleton (which we now recognize as Neanderthal) as permitting only a bent-over, stooped kind of walking. While this passed into popular imagination as the way Neanderthals got around, other finds suggested otherwise. A reanalysis by W. L. Straus of Johns Hopkins in the 1950s showed that Boule's reconstruction was essentially correct—only

Figure 10–11

Cultural practices (deliberate or not) often deform the skulls of people; this has no known effect on mental functions but has sometimes been done for vanity.

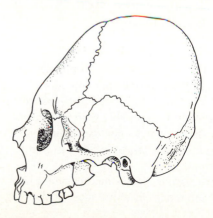
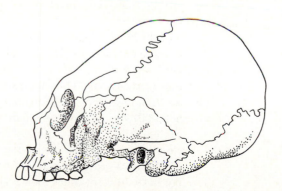

Figure 10-12
Boule reconstructed the arthritic, old Neanderthal man (left) as walking with a stooped gait, unlike normal modern humans (right), but other Neanderthals did not walk that way.

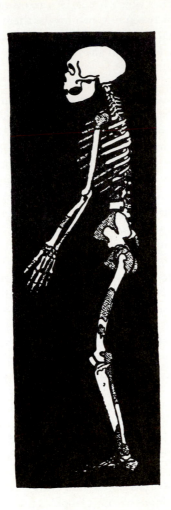
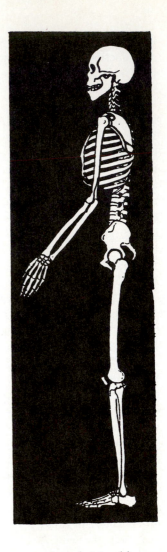

that the specimen in question belonged to a seriously arthritic old man. The generalization about Neanderthals was, therefore, unfounded based on this one specimen (Figure 10–12).

TEMPORAL VARIATION

Because evolution is change through time, we often find that populations of organisms living at one time are slightly different from populations living at other times. Thus, for example, the fossils attributed to *Homo erectus* from Ngandong and Sangiran, both in Java, probably span upwards of 500,000 years. Despite the fact that they are from the same place and similar enough to be attributed to the same species, they differ in significant aspects of skull shape and size (Figure 10–13).

If two groups of remains from the same species at the same place but from different times show regular differences, then we must be doubly cautious in interpreting biological variation among fossils from different times and different places.

TAPHONOMY

Finding a fossil does not automatically guarantee a blueprint of the part of the organism it came from. After all, fossils lie in the ground for much longer than bones ever lie in an animal's body. As a result, fossils are subjected to the ravages of chemical, biological, and mechanical forces—the stresses of destruction, deterioration, and deformation. The subdiscipline of *taphonomy* studies what happens to a bone between the time an organism dies and a paleontologist uncovers it.

Often, for example, fossils will be found as part of the remains of a prehistoric carnivore's den. Not only, therefore, must the fossil be interpreted in light of the chemical alteration of bone into fossil and the geological stresses of being buried and embedded in rock for millions of years, but as well in light of the fact that it was ravaged by a massive pair of (possibly) hyena jaws! Bones are often trampled by herds of animals as they lay exposed on the African savanna. Often, since flowing water concentrates bone collections, the action of a stream influences the nature of the fossil assemblage (Box 10–1).

While taphonomic processes must be considered in explaining aspects of the appearance of some fossils, the study of taphonomy forms a bridge between paleoanthropological and archaeological investigations. If we attempt to infer aspects of behavior from hominid fossils, taphonomy becomes critical for testing hypotheses. For example, the proportions, parts, and patterns of breakage of animal bones found in South Africa alongside hominid fossils suggested to Raymond Dart that they had been modified by the hominids as part of an early tool kit. He termed this the *osteodontokeratic* culture, meaning that the tools were probably made of such perishable materials as bones, teeth, and horns. Subsequent tapho-

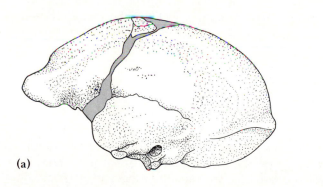
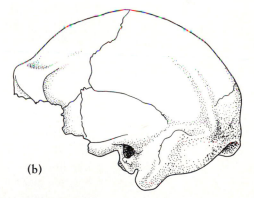

(a)   (b)

Figure 10-13

Homo erectus skulls from (a) Sangiran (Pithecanthropus II) and (b) Ngandong (Solo XI) are both from Java but separated by several hundred thousand years.

How Was This Creature Ever Found?

Long ago, a monkey fell out of a tree. It fell 150 feet to the forest floor, where it died instantly and painlessly. Thereupon, its body was rapidly decomposed by the acidic soil of the forest floor, and there was nothing left.

Or perhaps instead, the tree was by a lake, and the ground soil was neutral or slightly alkaline, so the body didn't decompose. It lay there until the scent drifted to the nearby vultures and carnivores, some of which ate the meat off the carcass, and others of which crunched its bones, until there was nothing left of its body.

Or perhaps instead, rather than lying there to be crunched by carnivores, the carcass was quickly buried under the earth. Some of its meat was eaten by scavengers (mammals and birds) and insects, but the bones were not chewed up by hyenas. Thereafter, it lay just under the surface, being trampled into little bits by all the other animals that walked past the tree by the lake, until there was nothing left.

Or perhaps instead, rather than being trampled,

it was buried sufficiently deeply and sufficiently quickly that it remained relatively intact in the ground. Thereafter, bacterial action decomposed the remains, so that nothing was left.

Or perhaps instead, rather than suffer bacterial decomposition, the bones lay buried in a fairly sterile environment. After a while, the chemistry of the ground simply decomposed them.

Or perhaps instead, rather than being decomposed by the soil chemistry, there was a high concentration of inorganic salts present, such that ions in the bones could be passively exchanged for those in the ground. After a long while, the bones became fossilized. Geological activity proceeded to distort the earlier shape of the fossils, deform them, and move the bones and the parts of bones away from one another spatially.

Then, after several million years, geological processes permitted the fossils to weather out to the surface of the ground, whereupon the forces of climatic erosion soon disintegrated the fossils.

Or perhaps instead, they weathered out just

---

nomic work, however, suggests that the features cited by Dart may well be due to natural processes.

Butchering with stone tools leaves distinctive markings on bone, and when combined with ethnographic knowledge of which animal parts are taken, how the butchering is performed, and how the animal skeleton is disarticulated, taphonomy can help in making inferences about prehistoric human behavior.

Arranging Archaeological Data: Form and Space

The diachronic aspects of physical anthropology are principally concerned with establishing biological ties among species and with discovering patterns in their evolution. The diachronic aspects of archaeology deal with the reconstruction and explanation of behavior among various hominid and human groups. As the physical anthropologist begins by creating cladograms, the archaeologist initially arranges artifacts according to their physical properties. Similar to cladograms, these arrangements are made initially independent of both the spatial and temporal

enough to be seen by someone before they eroded away, whereupon the person took the fossil, making it impossible for a scientist to study.

Or perhaps instead, the fossils weathered out, and the first person to locate them happened to be a paleontologist or simply a lover of science. That person donated the fossils to a museum, which enabled the bones to be studied.

Given the highly improbable circumstances of the fossilized bones even coming into existence, much less being found and put in the hands of the scientific community, can we tell anything about the creature's life? For example, did it die of natural causes, or was it hunted? Was its meat eaten? If so, was it chewed off the bone, or was it sliced off with a tool (which would indicate the presence of hominids)? Did it live where its fossils were found, or were the bones transported by other agencies, such as a carnivore or the action of a flowing stream?

To answer these questions, paleoanthropologists make use of studies of taphonomy: analyzing what happens to bones between the time the organism dies and its fossilized remains are found. Most often, several processes interact to create complex patterns of post-mortem features to a collection of fossils; and only isolated parts of any animal actually make it to the point of discovery. Thus, the paleontologist is faced with a series of interpretative questions beyond simply identifying the species to which the fossil belongs. This is analogous to the problems faced by archaeologists in trying to reconstruct the use of artifacts from their context.

References:

Behrensmeyer, A. K., & Hill, A. P. (1980). *Fossils in the making*. Chicago: University of Chicago Press.

Brain, C. K. (1981). *The hunters or the hunted?* Chicago: University of Chicago Press.

dimensions. Archaeologists accomplish this task by considering various formal characteristics of artifacts—called **attributes**—including size, shape, material composition, and so forth. Groups of artifacts that exhibit a cluster of similar attribute measures are arranged into types, and artifact types are then compared with one another so that the overall range of artifact formal variability can be measured and a **typology** can be produced.

IDENTIFYING ATTRIBUTES

Though the concept of the artifact type might seem straightforward, it is often quite difficult to recognize types and understand the reason or reasons for their existence. Consider the large collection of objects we commonly group together under the term *chair*. We all know what is and what is not a chair. Yet it is difficult to identify the specific formal attributes that precisely define this type (Figure 10–14).

Many chairs have four legs, but this is not a defining attribute. Chairs can have any number of legs or no legs at all, as long as they main-

attribute

A measureable characteristic of an artifact or other archaeological resource.

typology

A collection of similar artifact types, or groups of artifacts that share similar attributes.

tain balance and support. Similarly, most chairs have backs and seats, though the range of sizes and shapes these attributes can take make them nearly useless in defining the type. When does a chair become a stool or an ottoman? When does a chair become a bench? Indeed, chairs can take such a wide variety of forms that they are sometimes unrecognizable—but most times, we can agree what is and what is not a chair. Why? Because of their function.

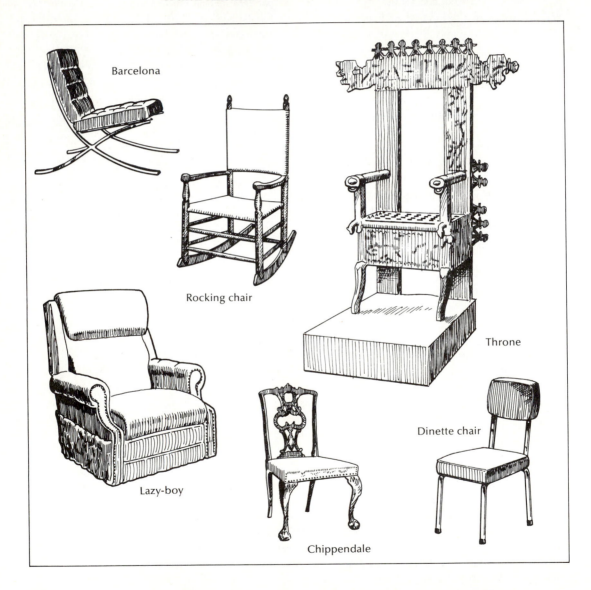

Figure 10-14

Various types of chairs. Note that they serve different social and ideological functions in addition to having different forms.

FUNCTION

Chairs, let us say, are those artifacts that primarily function to support a person who is sitting. Note that this is not a perfect definition. Chairs do have secondary functions—they can symbolize status (an expensive chair or a designer chair) or power (a throne or an executive chair). Certain chairs also serve special functions (wheelchairs and the electric chair). People use chairs for a variety of purposes unforeseen by chair designers—as footrests, as step ladders, and simply as convenient surfaces on which to stack books and papers. And people use other pieces of furniture (tables, for example) as if they were intended to be chairs. Finally, certain other objects serve the same primary function of chairs—the stool, ottoman, and bench mentioned earlier are examples. But undeniably, every chair has a single primary function—to hold up a seated person—and this is how we can best discriminate chairs from the host of other objects in our environment. This is how many meaningful artifact types must be defined.

In many instances, however, the archaeologist cannot observe the functions of artifacts or artifact types. Often, the only way for archaeologists to recognize meaningful, functional types is by analogy and inference. This is not easy, as crucial information regarding form–function relationships is often missing or difficult to interpret. Many functions, and thus many types, will remain forever best guesses, not certainties.

SPATIAL ARRANGEMENTS

Archaeologists also study the spatial arrangements of artifacts and other archaeological resources. They do so to observe which artifact types are associated with one another and so suggest how these associations might reflect past behavioral patterns.

Spatial arrangements in the archaeological record can be studied at various scales, both within and among sites. The distribution of artifacts within a single room or intramural area might be the subject of investigation. Alternatively, the arrangement of rooms within a single household might be the focus of study. How households and various structures are arranged in a single settlement might be of interest, or instead, attention could be given to the arrangement of settlements across a region. These various spatial arrangements at different scales are indicative of various social groups and behaviors, and so the scale chosen depends on the research issues of greatest interest.

A classic study of spatial arrangements within a single, small area was conducted at an Apache wickiup in Arizona by William A. Longacre and James Ayres (Figure 10–15). The archaeologists carefully recorded the locations of artifacts and features at the dwelling, abandoned only two years before the study. They concluded, among other things, that an Apache nuclear family (mother, father, and young, dependent children) once occupied the site. Artifacts related to female activities predominated, however. In addition, it appeared that the structure was used

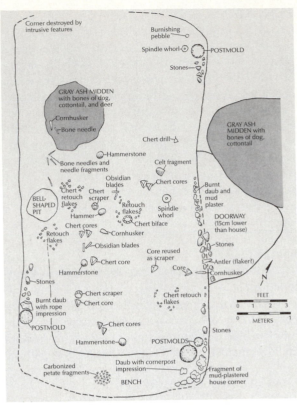

Figure 10-15

The modern Apache wickiup, studied by Longacre and Ayres.

primarily for storage and cooking, with occupants sleeping within it only during bad weather.

Subsequent interviews with the Apache confirmed many of the archaeological inferences. An Apache family did live there, though the father was away much of the time. Storage and cooking did occur in and around the structure. Longacre and Ayres demonstrated both the importance of careful spatial analysis and the usefulness of ethnographic analogy (Chapter 16).

William Longacre also conducted one of the best-known studies of spatial arrangements at the level of studying sites. This work focused on the prehistoric pueblo known as Carter Ranch (Figure 10–16), in eastern-central Arizona. Longacre was interested in inferring social organization from patterns of material culture and thought he could do so by studying distributions of decorated pottery sherds. He observed that styles of decoration tended to correlate with different areas of the site, forming spatial clusters. He further noted that pottery making among modern pueblo dwellers, including the Hopi, is a family affair, with mothers apparently teaching daughters the nuances of manufacture and design. This observation was critical, given the nature of Hopi living arrangements.

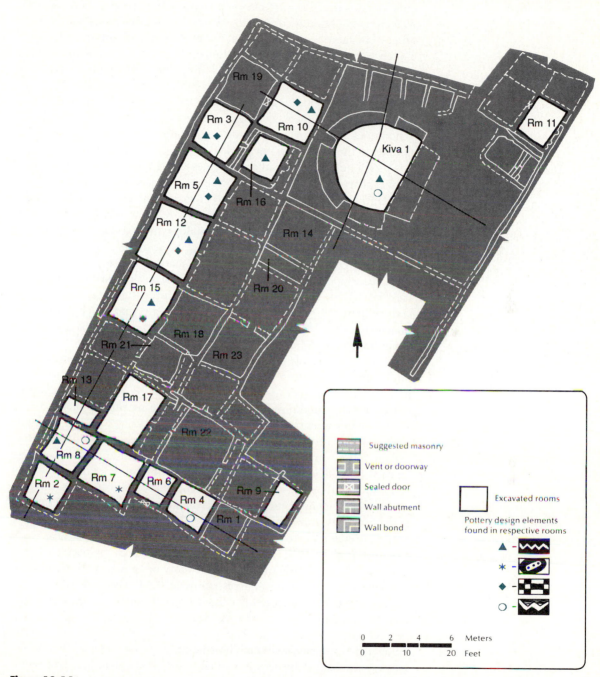

Figure 10-16

A plan of Carter Ranch pueblo, showing the distribution of decorated pottery.

The Hopi are *matrilocal*—after marriage, a couple lives near the parents of the wife. They are also *matrilineal*—they trace descent through women, with children considering themselves members of their mother's group. Longacre reasoned that if the prehistoric inhabitants of Carter Ranch were matrilocal and matrilineal also, and if they manufactured pottery in the same manner as the living Hopi, with mothers teaching daughters, then there might be a sociocultural explanation for the clustering of design elements among the decorated ceramic debris he found at the site. Indeed, if mothers taught daughters, and daughters through the generations lived in the same site area, slight variations of style might develop in the different room blocks.

This and similar studies by James Deetz and James N. Hill have been criticized on several grounds. Some anthropologists have questioned whether Hopi mothers are actually the major influence on their daughters when it comes to pottery manufacture. Others have questioned the great dependence on ethnographic analogy this type of work requires (Chapter 16). Perhaps most critical have been those observing that the places in a pueblo (or any site, for that matter) where people live and work are seldom the places where they throw away their broken pottery (see below). Still, Longacre's research at Carter Ranch was innovative and influential—he demonstrated convincingly that much about past human life could be reconstructed by a careful analysis of the spatial dimension.

It is perhaps on the regional level that this sort of work is most important. Many patterns of behavior and sociocultural interaction can be understood only on a grand scale, particularly those that relate to environmental conditions. Archaeologists have recently concluded that spatial studies across large regions are essential, though one of the earliest investigations of this kind occurred nearly forty years ago. It was conducted in the Viru Valley of Peru, under the supervision of archaeologists Gordon R. Willey and James Ford. What Willey and Ford discovered, by carefully recording the locations of settlements in the valley, was that the type and placement of sites were related and that both reflected environmental variability and the nature of social interactions. The structures of entire societies could be suggested by a region's **settlement pattern**. Since this work in the 1940s, regional studies have grown in sophistication and importance, particularly over the past twenty or so years with the special requirements of cultural resources management (Chapter 18). Yet even Willey and Ford recognized the need to consider one additional variable—time.

Arranging Archaeological Data: Chronologies

Having arranged their data in formal and spatial categories, archaeologists find it necessary to arrange these data in a *temporal* fashion, that is, by time. These arrangements are often called **chronologies**—they are the

settlement pattern

The distribution of archaeological resources across a region, reflecting the settlement patterns of human groups.

chronology

An ordering of cultural and environmental events through time.

archaeological analogies to the phylogenetic trees of physical anthropology. The archaeologist has available a number of diverse ways of creating chronologies—these ways are called dating methods.

As we discussed in Chapter 2, there are three general kinds of dating methods. Relative dating involves determining only whether an archaeological resource or event is older or younger than another resource or event. No specific amount of time is determined. Chronometric dating involves assigning a range of probable dates during which an archaeological resource or event is thought to have occurred. Finally, absolute dating involves the assignment of a specific calendar date (or dates) to an archaeological resource or event.

As phylogenetic trees in physical anthropology supply more information than cladograms, chronologies in archaeology supply more information than typologies. They permit various formal and spatial arrangements to be viewed in a new way, along the dimension of time, and thus make it possible for archaeologists to explain observed patterns more completely. Since both species and cultures evolve, the temporal element is crucial to this explanation. Still, more assumptions are needed to accept a chronology over a typology, and several chronologies can be consistent with a single typological scheme. In this way, also, there is an analogy with phylogenetic trees and cladograms.

Archaeological Scenarios

Once artifacts and other archaeological resources are arranged in the three dimensions of form, space, and time, the archaeologist can begin considering explanations for the observed arrangements. These **archaeological scenarios** are analogous to the evolutionary scenarios discussed previously. As such, we can see that archaeological scenarios, while supplying the most information, will be based on the greatest number of assumptions.

Scenarios in physical anthropology attempt to answer questions about the specific nature of selective pressures, or the reasons that a particular pattern of biological diversity is found. Scenarios in archaeology similarly are proposed to explain diversity, as observed in the material world or archaeological record. Effective archaeological explanation, based on solid theory, is a difficult goal to reach, but one that is necessary if we are ever truly to understand the nature of cultural history and cultural evolution. For good explanations to be possible, it is important that we properly interpret the variation seen in the archaeological record along each of the three dimensions discussed above.

Interpreting Variation in the Archaeological Record

The archaeological record of the past is not a "fossil" of past social systems. Numerous forces help to shape and reshape what is eventually available for the archaeologist to study. We can say that the archaeologi-

archaeological scenario
Explanation for the arrangements of archaeological resources that result from analysis, based on the arrangements and incorporating other information and inferences.

Figure 10-17

Michael B. Schiffer, in the Laboratory of Traditional Technology at the University of Arizona.

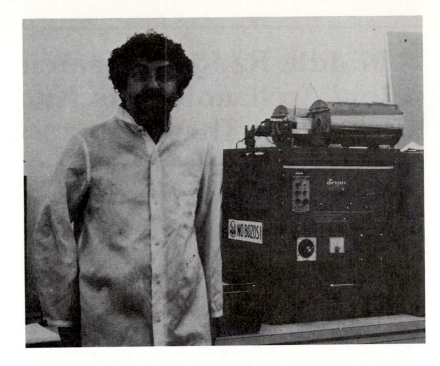

formation process

Any force that shapes the archaeological record, cultural (resulting from human activity) or environmental (resulting from interactions between archaeological resources and the natural setting).

cal record is indeed formed by the complex interaction of many processes—these are, logically, called **formation processes.**

Archaeologist Michael B. Schiffer (Figure 10–17) has systematically explored the nature and impacts of formation processes on archaeological resources. He divides these processes into two large groups—*cultural formation processes,* those that result from human activities, and *environmental formation processes,* those that result from interactions between archaeological resources and the natural setting. A sample of each is briefly considered here.

REUSE

The cultural formation processes known as *reuse* occur whenever the user or the use of an object changes. Schiffer recognizes several types of reuse, including 1) *recycling,* the modification of an object into a different kind of object; 2) *secondary use,* a change in use that does not require any change in the object itself; 3) *lateral cycling,* in which the user of an object changes, but not the use of the object; and 4) *conservation,* a process by which objects are intentionally saved.

Many examples of the different kinds of reuse are recognizable. Newspapers and aluminum cans are recycled into new products. Cinder blocks and bricks are secondarily used to build bookcases. Thousands of items are laterally cycled each weekend at garage sales and swap meets. And museums are striking examples of the importance our society places on the conservation of certain objects. Schiffer's important contributions, however, have been twofold. First, he recognizes that a significant portion of the material world is (and has been) subject to reuse—these processes have a profound effect on the shaping of the archaeological record. Second, he observes that reuse processes are patterned—they can be measured and understood. Studying them can shed light on the nature of human behavior.

All reuse tends to keep objects out of the archaeological record, at least for a certain duration. In Schiffer's terms, reuse extends the time during which objects remain in **systemic context** (in an ongoing society) and postpones the time they enter **archaeological context** (in the archaeological record). Reuse does this primarily by making objects seem useful for longer periods of time than would otherwise be the case. As a result of reuse, we can say that objects move within systemic context. Both the nature of the object and the nature of society help determine whether reuse will occur, and in what form.

DEPOSITION

Deposition consists of a number of cultural formation processes that take objects out of systemic context and place them in archaeological context. Types of deposition include 1) *discard*, the intentional throwing away of objects no longer considered useful; 2) *loss*, which happens when objects are misplaced and not recovered by anyone else; 3) *caching*, the purposeful burying of items so that they can be recovered at a later time, and 4) *burial*, or placing the dead into the archaeological record.

Schiffer has noted that, like reuse, the practice of deposition is patterned, and the patterns are shaped largely by sociocultural factors. Similarly, the nature of depositional processes can have enormous impacts on the nature of the archaeological record. For example, discard sometimes results in *primary refuse*—trash deposited at the location of use. More often it results in *secondary refuse*—trash deposited away from the location of use. Most uncommon, however, is *de facto refuse*—archaeological materials, sometimes still useful, that are discarded because an area is abandoned. All are examples of discard, yet all lead to very different material culture patterns that suggest very different behaviors and conditions. Archaeologists must always observe the archaeological record carefully in order to infer accurately which type of deposition was once occurring.

RECLAMATION

The group of cultural formation processes Schiffer calls *reclamation* can be viewed as the opposite of deposition—they result in the movement of objects from archaeological context to systemic context. Perhaps the best example of reclamation is *archaeological recovery*, though it is clearly not the most important in terms of impacts on the archaeological record.

systemic context

A condition of material culture when it is participating within an ongoing society.

archaeological context

A condition of material culture when it is not participating within an ongoing society.

Much more significant are *scavenging*, the retrieval of a settlement's archaeological materials by residents of the same settlement, and *collecting*, which happens when residents of one community take archaeological materials from another. Treasure hunting is a particular type of collecting that is dramatically different from archaeological recovery (Chapter 18).

DISTURBANCE

The final type of cultural formation process we consider is *disturbance*— the movement of objects within archaeological context. There are many types of disturbance, brought about by numerous causes, ranging from a casual, unconscious kick of an artifact across the land surface to the devastating impacts of an earthquake. One of the best studied disturbance processes is plowing—the churning of the subsurface made necessary by the demands of agriculture. Plowing has disturbed many archaeological resources, and archaeologists have found it necessary to study the effects of this activity in order to interpret many of their findings adequately.

FAUNALTURBATION

A natural formation process, *faunalturbation* consists of the various effects nonhuman animals can have on the archaeological record. The vast majority of these impacts, which can be substantial, are caused by animals that spend all or a portion of their lives underground. Results of their activities include the movement of archaeological resources, the ingestion of archaeological resources (particularly organic materials), and the accumulation of animal waste (and thus substantial alterations in the matrix). Archaeologists must always be wary of these impacts, as they are complex, significant, and not always obvious at first glance.

FLORALTURBATION

Another natural formation process is known as *floralturbation*, the effects of living plant life on archaeological resources. Possibly the most significant of these effects results from root growth, which can greatly disturb archaeological deposits. In addition, large trees often fall after they die, causing the roots violently to rip from the subsurface and scatter archaeological materials. The impacts can be enormous on a site and its distribution of artifacts.

Plants also act to obscure archaeological resources on the surface— sites in a dense forest are often much more difficult to locate during survey than sites in the desert. Archaeologists must carefully consider the effects of plant cover when making interpretations.

CRYOTURBATION

A third natural formation process is known as *cryoturbation*, an impact on the archaeological record that results from the freezing and thawing of the ground. Included are frost heave, which causes artifacts to rise and

Issues in Anthropology 10–2

The History of an Artifact

You can go to any flea market and see hundreds of plates, cups, bowls, and other assorted pieces of china. Assume you have just moved into the college dorms and need a single soup bowl (you have a hot plate and pot for late-night snacks). You find one that has a nice, blue pastoral scene at the swap meet—where did it come from? How did it get to your dorm room?

It was manufactured in East Liverpool, Ohio, by the Homer Laughlin China Company, in 1922. It was shipped as part of a set—eight place settings—to St. Louis, Missouri, where it was purchased by a rather wealthy family. Over the next twelve years, it was used many times at the dinner table. That big chip along the rim happened in 1930, although the bowl was not relegated to the back of the cabinet, and finally to the servants table, until four years later. The family, economically hurt by the Depression, could not afford new china until then.

The maid used the bowl for several more years and then gave it to her daughter, who stored it away for the future when she would have a family of her own. She took it with her when she was married, used it at the dinner table several times, but later gave it to her first child as a toy. It was lost somewhere in the move to Denver.

It turned up many years later as a treasure hunter searched for historical bottles at an abandoned railroad depot. Frequently passing from hand to hand, for little money, it eventually ended up at the flea market, to be purchased by you, so that you could eat soup while studying anthropology and consider the formation processes it went through!

assume a vertical orientation, and thrust, which results in the horizontal movement of materials. Obviously, cryoturbation occurs only in environments that become cold enough for some portion of the subsurface to freeze. This is quite common in many places, however, and the effects of this formation process can be considerable.

There are many other cultural and natural formation processes in addition to those discussed here. Indeed, hundreds of various forces are constantly impacting all archaeological sites and artifacts (Box 10–2). These forces operate to varying degrees at each site, depending on the nature of the site and its environment. And the relative impact of each force changes over time. It is a very complex task to reconstruct formation processes and their effects. Still, the task is necessary if we are to reconstruct and explain the past.

Species, Cultures, and the Problem of Diffusion

In attempting to understand change through time, archaeology and physical anthropology face analogous problems. Analogous steps have been developed to accomplish the task. Yet in one regard, the archaeologist has a much more difficult undertaking than the physical anthropologist—an increased difficulty emerging from a fundamental difference between how cultures interact and species interact. Genetic information cannot move from one species to another. Each species is, by definition, a closed system. But cultural information travels freely from one society to another, often back and forth, allowing different cultures to diverge and converge over and over in a complex fashion. Reconstructing and explaining culture history accurately is a formidable business.

The movement of ideas or materials, cultural information, from one society to another is known as diffusion (Chapter 3). Here we are using the term in a very broad sense, and it occurs as the result of such diverse mechanisms of information exchange as trade, migration, and warfare. Anthropologists have been studying diffusion since the nineteenth century, with varying degrees of success. Curiously, ideas regarding the importance of diffusion in determining culture history have usually tended to be extreme. For example, at some times, diffusion has been generally viewed as the most significant, if not the only, shaper of history. This was the case for certain anthropologists in the early twentieth century, when Grafton Elliot Smith and others were claiming that all civilization had diffused from ancient Egypt.

In contrast, at other times, certain anthropologists have completely rejected diffusion as a cultural occurrence of any importance. Many archaeologists in the 1960s felt this way, arguing that the important phenomenon was the *acceptance* of an idea or object by the members of a society, not the means by which the information reached them. If people are prepared to accept something new, it was reasoned, it does not matter whether the novelty was derived from within or brought from without. The same situation would result in either case.

Diffusion should not be viewed as either extremely important or totally insignificant. As with most occurrences, the relative importance of diffusion in culture history has varied, depending on historical circumstances. The challenge is not to judge the importance of diffusion in general, but to determine empirically the role it has played under various circumstances. In other words, we must find a way, on a case-by-case basis, of distinguishing independent cultural evolutionary development within societies from the results of external influence.

Homoplasy and independent invention are analogous between biological and cultural evolution, but there is an important difference. In general, we tend to find that the key evolutionary events in biological history have happened only once, in a single group, and that their descendants benefited genetically and radiated adaptively as a result. In cultural evolution, it seems that of the three identifiable historical watersheds (domestication, social complexity, and industrialization), certainly the first two have happened in parallel in several different societies, presumably the result of humans responding creatively to a specific set of problems in similar ways, producing characteristic and irreversible changes in their societies.

Summary

The reconstruction of biological and cultural histories is a major goal of physical anthropology and archaeology. In order to accomplish this, it is necessary to abandon archaic notions such as the Great Chain of Being—we have to think in terms of evolution.

Physical anthropologists begin by constructing cladograms, which are evolutionary relationships without consideration for the time dimension. Then, phylogenetic trees are designed. These do involve time. Finally, evolutionary scenarios are suggested. These fill out the phylogenetic trees by including inferences about and explanations for evolutionary events.

Archaeologists follow a similar procedure. First, artifacts are arranged by form into types, and consideration is given to the spatial component. This is equivalent to forming a cladogram. Then, chronologies are created by adding the time dimension. Chronologies are like phylogenetic trees. Finally, archaeological scenarios are constructed.

As one moves from cladograms or types, to phylogenetic trees or chronologies, to evolutionary or archaeological scenarios, the amount of explanatory information increases. Likewise, the number of assumptions one must hold increases, making conclusions less certain and more qualified.

Both organisms and artifacts can exhibit diversity, brought about by many forces. Historical analysis is similar in physical anthropology and archaeology. Yet the reconstruction of cultural histories involves one major complicating factor not associated with biological histories. Cultures are open systems (species are not) and thus are candidates for the impacts of diffusion; but humans are ingenuous and resourceful, and it is critical to distinguish between what any society developed itself and what it borrowed.

Questions for Review

1. Do you think all characters in the construction of a cladogram should be given equal weight, or should one "good" character outweigh several "bad" characters that give a different phylogeny? What criteria would you establish to decide between "good" and "bad" phylogenetic characters in a cladistic analysis?

2. Often, there is as much information subtly loaded into the narrative structure of a scenario (the way it is told) as there is in its formal content (what it says). Are scenarios scientific? How could we perform science without them?

3. Why do you think independent invention in cultural evolution is more prevalent than homoplasy in biological evolution?

4. Why is it important to understand formation processes when interpreting the archaeological record? Are accurate interpretations possible if the formation processes are so numerous and complex?

For Further Reading

Cracraft, J., & Eldredge, N. (1979). *Phylogenetic analysis and paleontology.* New York: Columbia University Press.

Schiffer, M. B. (1976). *Behavioral archaeology.* New York: Academic Press.

Schiffer, M. B. (1987). *Formation processes of the archaeological record.* Albuquerque: University of New Mexico Press.

Simpson, G. G. (1983). *Fossils and the history of life.* New York: Scientific American Books.

Primate Phylogeny and Human Origins

Primate Phylogeny and Human Origins

In this chapter we trace the biological evolution of the primates in gross outline to show the stock from which our species emerged. That stock is primate, anthropoid, catarrhine, and hominoid, and the ancestors of these increasingly narrow groups of primates lived in successively later periods. The three main skeletal differences between humans and their closest relatives are in the locomotor anatomy, the reduction of the front teeth, especially the canines, and the size of the cranium. We find in the fossil record that these occurred in the following order: bipedalism, dentition, cranium. Our earliest detectable unique ancestors were, therefore, apes with a peculiarly specialized form of locomotion.

The Earliest Primates

Primate history is principally localized within the **Tertiary** period, beginning about 65 million years ago with the extinction of the dinosaurs and the explosive adaptive radiation of the mammals. The Tertiary period is given in Figure 11–1, beginning with the Paleocene epoch at 65 million years ago, and ending with the Pleistocene-Recent boundary only 10,000

Tertiary

Geological period beginning about 65 million years ago. The Quaternary began with the Pleistocene, about 1.7 million years ago.

Figure 11-1

Geologic time scale for primate evolution and the origins of major primate groups.

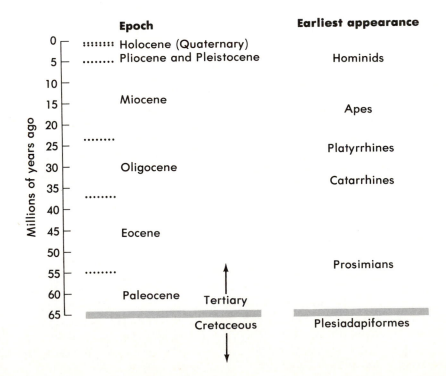

Figure 11-2
Plesiadapiform primates coexisted with dinosaurs in the late Cretaceous, although they were probably not the bipedal tool users that this facetious drawing indicates.

years ago. A single tooth from a common Paleocene "primate" genus (*Purgatorius*) represents the Cretaceous "primates," found in present-day Montana, and contemporary with some of the last *Triceratops* (Figure 11–2).

The Paleocene "primates" are known as Plesiadapiformes, and their interpretation is currently in a state of flux. Usually grouped into six families, it is now thought that at least one of them, the Paromomyidae, is not closely related to the living primates at all, but to a group of gliding mammals known as colugos, sole living members of the Order Dermoptera. On the other hand, at least one other Paleocene family, the Plesiadapidae, seems to have molar teeth and a bony ear region similar to modern primates. Therefore, the Plesiadapiformes probably do not form a clade, a group of animals more closely related to one another than to anything else. Apparently, only some of them—if any—are at the base of the primate lineage.

Unfortunately, the strong tendency is to try to link extinct primates directly to specific known living primates, although many fossil groups under study are likely to have become extinct without leaving direct descendants. If we appreciate that we are only sampling a small part of a larger adaptive radiation of animals, we may come to understand that any fossil group we see may not itself have been directly ancestral to anything now living, but may instead have been a close relative of a species that was ancestral. There are always many more species that were *not* ancestors than those that *were* ancestors. And the differences between the ancestors and nonancestors will be very subtle because they are parts of the same radiation of closely related creatures.

In particular, the Paleocene was a time in which many of the modern orders of mammals were originating, as the dinosaurs had only recently become extinct. It should not be surprising that consequently, many of the small, arboreal creatures we encounter are only slightly different from one another and yet evolved into different groups.

The "primates" of the Paleocene would hardly be recognized as such if they were alive today. They had few of the diagnostic features we use to identify primates, and many looked superficially more like rodents than like lemurs (Figure 11–3). These archaic "primates" contrast with later **euprimates**, those that look modern—for their nonprimate characters are much more apparent. Their eye sockets were not completely encircled by bone, their fingers and toes were clawed, their snouts were long, and their incisors were enlarged in a way that immediately calls rodents to mind. These, however, are not synapomorphies (shared, derived characters: Chapter 10). They are primitive mammalian characteristics, except for the incisors, which probably evolved in parallel with the rodents.

In possessing some, but not all, of the defining primate characteristics, and in antedating all the true primates or euprimates, these archaic creatures are widely regarded as fairly good candidates for the ancestry of the modern primates. These appear to be the roots of the primate tree,

euprimates

Primates that, unlike the plesiadapiformes, have most of the characteristics that distinguish primates from other mammals.

Figure 11-3

Though they may have had some derived features characteristic of modern primates, the Plesiadapiformes were overall quite different from modern primates.

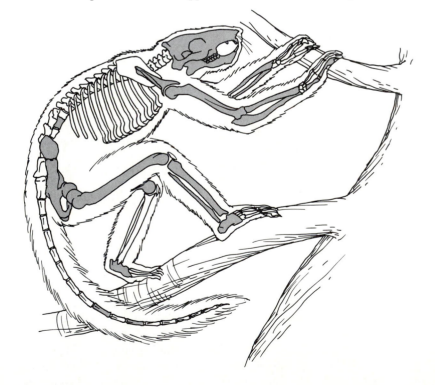

our remote forebears, and they have no living models because they were less primatelike than even the oddest prosimians.

True Primates of the Eocene

From the Eocene, 55–38 million years ago, we find the first euprimates: animals that were *obvious* primates. They had an eye orbit surrounded by a bony ring, the postorbital bar; nails rather than claws on at least some digits; shorter faces; forward-pointing eyes; and a grasping big toe. The Eocene primates are known from all over the Northern hemisphere, and with a few exceptions, they fall into two large groups, the *adapids* (Family Adapidae) and the *omomyids* (Family Omomyidae).

What kind of primates were they? What are the relations among the living primates and the adapids and omomyids? Fortunately, we have many well-preserved fossil specimens of these Eocene primates—and not only of teeth and jaws, but of nearly entire animals. Unfortunately, they have not made the relationships among these animals completely clear. Modern lemurs and lorises share the tooth-comb as an obvious synapomorphy, and neither group of Eocene primates possesses it. Therefore, the modern lemurs and lorises are all more closely related to one another than any is to an adapid or omomyid. Yet since the tooth-comb is derived, these creatures could be ancestors in whom the trait had not yet developed.

ADAPIDS

Adapids and living lemurs and lorises appear to be directly linked by aspects of the ankle and wrist joints. These aspects particularly link the modern forms with the European adapids, as opposed to the North American ones. Therefore, we may infer that adapids diverged in Europe from the ancestor of modern prosimians before the development of a tooth-comb.

One of the best-known adapids is *Notharctus* from North America, shown in Figure 11–4, whose limbs indicate a grasping ability, a specialization of modern primates. The crests on its molar teeth are suggestive of a folivorous (leafy) diet, its eye orbits suggest a diurnal lifestyle, and much of its postcranial skeleton is very similar to that of living lemurs. It had long hindlimbs and is believed to have been a leaper and quadrupedal runner. It further appears to have had a rather small opening for the maxillary nerve, which in turn suggests a reduction in emphasis upon the tactile whiskers of prosimians.

Some adapids appear to have had a fusion of the midline of the jaw (the mandibular symphysis), like anthropoids. Some have the stapedial artery as the main source of blood flow to the brain, as in lemurs; others emphasize the promontory artery, like anthropoids. Thus, it is possible that the adapids are similar members of a radiation that ultimately diverged into quite different kinds of primates.

Figure 11-4

The Eocene *Notharctus* is a well-known adapid genus.

OMOMYIDS

The omomyids are even more ambiguous. While the adapids had a ring-shaped tympanic bone like the lemurs and lorises, the omomyids had a tube-shaped tympanic bone, like most anthropoids. The *Necrolemur*, shown in Figure 11–5, has been widely thought to be an Eocene relative of the tarsier. This is based on the interpretation of three principal features as synapomorphies: elongated ankle bone, fused lower leg bones (tibia and fibula) in some species, and enlarged eye sockets. Others, from detailed analyses of the skull base, feel that the omomyids are unique primates without close living relatives. It is always critical to bear in mind that over the great expanse of geologic history, there have been many adaptive radiations of creatures that are fairly closely related and that then adapt to specific environments in often characteristically similar ways.

If the omomyids are not the closest relatives of tarsiers, then those similarities to tarsiers would not be considered synapomorphies, but parallel acquisitions, or homoplasies (Chapter 10). The issue is still unresolved; however, new skulls of a genus called *Shoshonius* have recently reinforced the link between tarsiers and at least *some* omomyids.

The Eocene of southeast Asia may well have been home to the stem lineage of the anthropoids, as teeth and jaw fragments of two genera known as *Amphipithecus* and *Pondaungia* have suggested relationships to the living anthropoids. Little, however, is known about them.

Teeth: Most of the Primate Fossil Record

We have already noted that some of the major distinguishing features of primate groups are dental in nature. The loss of a premolar from each jaw quadrant, for example, is an important synapomorphy defining the catarrhine primates relative to other groups. Teeth are important in paleoanthropology for four primary reasons. First, their shapes are often highly characteristic of specific groups and therefore diagnostic of most taxa. Second, aspects of tooth morphology often permit inferences about the diet of the organism that possessed the tooth. Third, teeth erupt at different times throughout the lifespan of the organisms, and inferences can therefore be made about the age of the individual from an examination of its teeth. Finally, teeth are the hardest and best-preserved part of the body and therefore constitute the bulk of the primate fossil record.

KINDS OF MAMMALIAN TEETH

With the exception of sloths, whales, and dolphins, all mammals are *heterodont,* that is, they have different kinds of teeth. These teeth are of four basic kinds: *incisors* for biting, scraping, or gnawing; *canines* for puncturing, gripping, or slashing; *premolars* for chewing and for sharpening the canine; and *molars* for crushing and grinding, or for cutting. Different primate groups may adapt specific kinds of teeth for a specialized function. Lemurs and lorises, as we have seen, have specialized lower incisors and canines forming a tooth-comb. Baboons, as we have also seen, have large canines functioning socially during threat displays. Robust australopithecines, as we shall see, had their premolars expanded to look like and function as additional molars.

Figure 11-5

The Eocene *Necrolemur* is a well-known omomyid.

Figure 11-6

Lower left first molars of a hominoid and cercopithecoid showing the Y-5 pattern on the hominoid tooth and the bilophodont pattern on the cercopithecoid tooth.

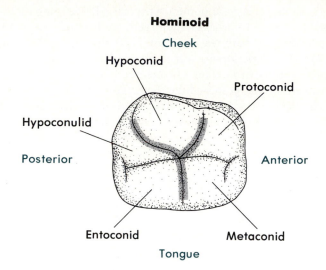

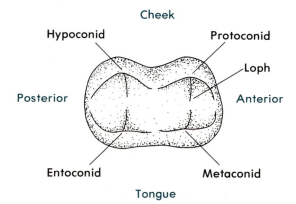

The rear (posterior) teeth, however, have many distinctive features—each molar is, in essence, a landscape whose terrain enables pale-ontologists to identify the animal from whom the tooth is derived. The occlusal, or chewing, surface of a molar has a characteristic pattern of cusps, or bumps. (The human premolar has two such bumps, which is why your dentist calls it a bicuspid.) Two cusps may be connected by a crest or loph, hence the bilophodont molars of the cercopithecine monkeys.

If we compare the lower first molar of a cercopithecoid and a hominoid in a very generalized sense, we find in the monkey that of the four identifiable cusps, the protoconid and metaconid are connected by one ridge, and the hypoconid and entoconid by another. A fifth cusp, the hypoconulid, is present in the hominoid tooth. Further, the hypoconid (on the buccal, or cheek, side) is surrounded by two deep fissures, recalling the arms of the letter "Y"—the fissure then continues to separate the metaconid and entoconid. This creates the characteristic Y-5 pattern highly diagnostic of the hominoid lower molar (Figure 11–6). It may not, however, be a synapomorphy, as many workers now interpet this pattern as ancestral for catarrhines and then lost in cercopithecoids.

The inside of a molar also has important information concerning the rates at which enamel is laid down on the tooth and the overall thickness of the enamel layer. As anthropologist Lawrence Martin has shown, chimpanzees and gorillas have relatively thin enamel, humans have thick enamel, and orang-utans have intermediate thickness. Humans form their enamel rapidly, while all the great apes form theirs slowly, which indicates that the thin enamel of chimps and gorillas is probably a synapomorphy (Figure 11–7).

The details of the occlusal surface of a molar can thus yield many characters diagnostic of a particular group of species. In addition, features of the teeth often allow us to reconstruct aspects of a fossil organism's life-style—filling in part of an evolutionary scenario. For example, living species that eat primarily insects have relatively high pointed cusps, presumably useful in puncturing the **chitinous** exoskeleton of the food. Living species that rely on leafy foods usually have crests connecting their cusps, which may help in shearing the leaves. We can use these and other correlations between morphology and behavior to infer (by analogy) the behavior of fossil primates.

chitin

A protein that composes the hard exoskeleton of an insect.

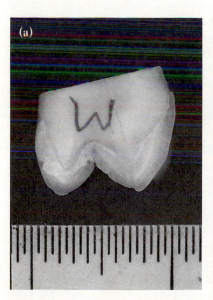
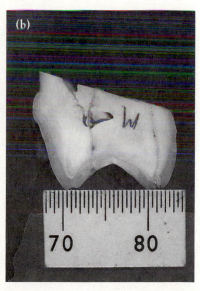

Figure 11–7

Cross-sections of hominoid teeth can also contain key pieces of information about relationships. (a) Humans have thick tooth enamel, while gorillas (b) have appreciably thinner tooth enamel.

Figure 11-8

An Oligocene scene.

The Parapithecidae: Stem Anthropoids?

During the Oligocene, 38–23 million years ago, the principal radiations of anthropoids and of catarrhines occurred. Unfortunately, most of our information on this critical time comes from a single site, the Jebel Qatrani Formation of the Fayum region in Egypt.

Paleoecological studies have shown that 30–40 million years ago, this presently arid region was a lush swamp bordered by forest. Plants similar to those in present day tropical southeast Asian could be found with fossil water-birds, principally jacanas and shoebilled storks, suggesting an environment conducive to most modern primates (Figure 11–8).

Although it is possible that anthropoids first appeared in the late Eocene, they are first unambiguously identifiable in the earliest Oligocene. The Parapithecidae subsume several genera, of which *Qatrania* is the earliest and smallest—indeed, smaller than any extant Old World anthropoid. Its relative, *Parapithecus*, was about ten times larger, however, which indicates that then (as now) primates tended to diversify widely in appearance. *Parapithecus* had lost its lower incisors completely, which is unique in primates and presumably excludes *Parapithecus* from the direct ancestry of any living anthropoid.

The best-known of these parapithecids is called *Apidium*, which displays several derived features for anthropoids: fused left and right sides of the lower jaw, fused left and right frontal bones of the skull, and an eye orbit entirely sealed off from behind. Interestingly, its lower leg bones were pressed tightly together for nearly half their length (though not fused into a single bone), recalling the tarsier and omomyids but also suggesting very limited mobility at the ankle joint. This in turn indicates the likelihood that it made its way by leaping from branch to branch. Its small eye orbits suggest daytime activity, and thick tooth enamel suggests hard foods in its diet.

All the parapithecids had three premolars per jaw quadrant, which makes them plausible ancestors of both catarrhine and platyrrhine primates (remember, loss of a premolar is a derived feature in catarrhines). They do not seem to show derived features that would put them specifically in the catarrhine lineage—even though they are found, obviously, in the Old World. In virtually all the ways in which catarrhine primates have a derived anatomical feature and platyrrhines have a primitive one, *Apidium* has the primitive, platyrrhine feature. This is particularly true for details of the inner ear, which are often diagnostic of primate taxa. Similarly, the ischial tuberosities of the pelvis of catarrhines are absent from the pelvis of *Apidium*.

Some details of the teeth (a new cusp, the hypoconulid, and a particular pattern of wear on the teeth unique to catarrhines) have been taken to indicate that parapithecids may have been on the catarrhine lineage after the divergence of the Platyrrhini. The bulk of the anatomy, however, indicates that these were primitive anthropoids—that platyrrhines and catarrhines were each other's closest relatives and that parapithecids were an early and primitive out-group (Figure 11–9).

AEGYPTOPITHECUS: A STEM CATARRHINE

Another kind of primate was living in the Fayum at the same time as the known parapithecids. This kind of primate (known collectively as the Family Propliopithecidae, or propliopithecids) is best represented by the species *Aegyptopithecus zeuxis*.

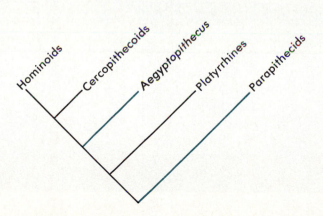

Figure 11-9

Cladogram showing the probable relationships of Oligocene and modern anthropoids.

Aegyptopithecus had lost its anterior premolar, so its dental formula was $\frac{2.1.2.3}{2.1.2.3}$, synapomorphic with other catarrhines—putting this creature firmly on the catarrhine branch. Another possibly synapomorphic feature indicating a relationship specifically to the catarrhines involves the arrangement of skull bones at the side of the skull. In most other respects, however, its skull and limbs are primitive—more reminiscent of New World monkeys and the parapithecids (Figure 11–10). In the ear region, for example, this species had a ring of bone similar to modern platyrrhines rather than the tube that characterizes modern catarrhines. And above the elbow, *Aegyptopithecus* had a small hole called the entepicondylar foramen, which is primitive and not present in living catarrhines.

Sexual dimorphism, as far as can be discerned, existed in the canines of *Aegyptopithecus*, which in turn implies a polygynous social system by analogy to most modern sexually dimorphic Old World primates. In addition to several skulls, postcranial remains include bones of arm, foot, and tail. Overall, its morphology is most consistent with a tree-living, quadrupedal animal active in the day and eating primarily fruit.

Oddly, the Oligocene primate fauna was lacking in some of the characteristic features we have come to take for granted in catarrhine primates. There is no evidence that any of the species—despite considerable variation in size—was particularly large. There is also very little evidence of adaptations for leaf eating, for seed eating, or for living on the ground—features that are common in their descendants.

We place *Aegyptopithecus* as a sister group or closest relative of the living catarrhines. Its placement in time makes it an excellent candidate for the ancestor of these primates.

Figure 11–10

There are several skulls and some postcranial material known for *Aegyptopithecus zeuxis*, an early catarrhine.

ORIGIN OF THE PLATYRRHINES

A genus of Oligocene primates is known in the New World (Bolivia), related to the extant New World monkeys and perhaps directly ancestral to them. *Branisella* dates from about 26 million years ago and is known only from dental and jaw fragments. From the Miocene, about 17 million years ago, several other genera are known from Argentina and Colombia, and some nearly complete skulls have been recovered.

The most interesting question at the present is also the most fundamental: Where did the platyrrhines come from? South America in the Oligocene was an island continent considerably closer to Africa than it is today, but still geographically far removed. Since the early African anthropoids have many platyrrhine-like features, it is generally believed that the platyrrhines are derived from an African anthropoid stock (rather than from an indigenous North American prosimian stock). But how?

We have no particularly convincing answers at the present. The best explanation may reside in a view of the widening Atlantic as a geologically dynamic system, producing short-lived chains of islands that, through time, permitted an east-west crossing, perhaps by the islands themselves moving and by the primates moving from island to island across a shallows. These island "rafts" would have had to contain their own collection of flora and fauna and perhaps, over the course of a million years, could conceivably have permitted a group of primarily arboreal primates to colonize the forest of an isolated island continent.

Miocene Radiation of the Apes

During the Miocene, which lasted from about 23 to 5.5 million years ago, there was an extensive diversification of apelike creatures. We may call them apes for lack of a better word, since if one were seen today it would be called an ape, even though a detailed examination would reveal it to be quite different from any living ape.

Miocene apes exhibited not only great diversity in shape and size, but in distribution as well: They have been found throughout Europe, Africa, and Asia. The earliest ones, however, are only from Africa. During the Oligocene, Africa was a lowland tropical rain forest, but during the early Miocene, the environment became much more diverse, challenging the stem catarrhines to adapt to new habitats. Partly, greater fluctuations in climate during the seasons led to greater variation in conditions at a single place, but more importantly, areas of grassland and savanna expanded at the expense of the tropical rain forest.

Why was the climate changing? Partly because the continent of Africa was moving northward. At the beginning of the Miocene, Africa and Arabia formed a southern island continent, isolated from Eurasia by the Tethys Sea. Thus, the Atlantic and Indian Oceans were connected. The Mediterranean is all that is left of the Tethys. The geological action of plate tectonics caused a collision between the southern and northern continents about 17 million years ago, which resulted in new geological features and, therefore, in new climatic patterns. For the apes, in particular, it had important effects in releasing them to colonize an area that previously had no such creatures. The result of this environmental diversity was the great biological diversity among Miocene hominoids.

Early Miocene hominoids are found only in Africa; later Miocene hominoids are found throughout the Old World. Of the latest Miocene hominoid species, which appear to have been somewhat fewer in number than their immediate predecessors, one became bipedal. This one was our ancestor. Unfortunately, we have not yet found it. Consequently, we focus on the diverse forms we have already found, and whose numbers are constantly increasing as more fossil specimens are discovered.

Anthropologists once attempted to group all these creatures into two categories—those ancestral to humans, and those ancestral to the other extant apes (see Box 11–1 on page 410). We now know, however, that few of the Miocene hominoids fall into those two categories since there are so many kinds of Miocene hominoids, and so few modern ones. Most of the extinct Miocene forms left no living descendants, and it is difficult to tell which are the few that did. We will focus on four of these creatures to show what some representative members of the Miocene fossil record look like, and to highlight some of the difficulties in understanding the roots of the Hominidae.

PROCONSUL: A STEM HOMINOID

Proconsul is an early Miocene ape genus from Africa well enough known to be divided into three species differing principally in size and spanning nearly the entire range of body sizes for extant apes. The best representative of *Proconsul* is a skull found by Mary Leakey in 1948 on Rusinga Island in Lake Victoria. Postcranial remains were found at the same site three years later (Figure 11–11). This genus is at least 22 million years old, and perhaps as young as about 13 million.

Proconsul looked in many ways like a monkey, particularly in its distal extremities (hands and feet). Its skeleton has an overall look like that of a cercopithecine. However, of the synapomorphies shared by cercopithecines, we find none in *Proconsul*. It looked essentially like a generalized monkey with some key hominoid or apelike parts. Indeed, its sinuses have been noted as very similar to those of humans, chimps, and gorillas.

Proconsul appears from its postcrania to have been principally an arboreal quadruped, though some of the larger species of *Proconsul* were probably somewhat terrestrial. In general, therefore, it was like many modern monkeys and like the Oligocene primates that preceded it—lacking the specializations for suspension or brachiation that are synapomorphic among the apes. This is obviously a primitive or ancestral morphology and does not give us information on its relationships. Its teeth, however, are distinctively hominoid, notably in details of the canines and premolars. Its molar teeth, interestingly, retain many primitive features not seen in later hominoids. For example, it had fairly thin dental enamel, which is different from most of the later Miocene hominoids, presumably the direct ancestors of the living hominoids.

Proconsul was consequently a mosaic of derived hominoid and primitive features, just as we would expect an ancestor of the Hominoidea to be. Paleontologist Peter Andrews has shown that despite its primitive aspects, *Proconsul* shares eight specific derived characters with living hominoids in the shoulder, elbow, jaws, teeth, and head.

SIVAPITHECUS: A RELATIVE OF THE ORANG-UTAN

By the later Miocene, the apes had diverged sufficiently in their diets that we can find major differences in the thickness of enamel on the crown of their molar teeth, those with thick enamel being more specifically related to the ancestry of living apes and humans. Like modern hominoids, and unlike *Proconsul*, some of these apes had their molar cusps closer to the edge of the tooth.

One of these apes with both dental features just mentioned, *Sivapithecus*, is known from Asia (principally India, Pakistan, China, and

Figure 11-11

Proconsul, a Miocene hominoid from Africa.

I Remember Rama

In the 1960s, Elwyn Simons and David Pilbeam, then at Yale University, launched a campaign to rehabilitate an extinct Miocene primate. Named in 1932 by G. E. Lewis, *Ramapithecus brevirostris* was an apelike primate with a short face and fairly small canines. True, it was known only from tooth and jaw fragments, yet it appeared to be like humans and unlike chimpanzees in a number of significant ways.

In addition to the small size of the canines and shortness of the face, *Ramapithecus* had thick enamel on its molar teeth, like humans and unlike chimps. Further, it appeared to have a tooth-row diverging at the rear (shaped like a parabola, like humans), not parallel (U-shaped, as in chimps). A few other features as well seemed to ally it more with humans than with chimps.

Further, Simons and Pilbeam felt that Miocene primates were taxonomically oversplit, that there were more names than the fossils justified, and collapsed some fossils from Africa known as *Kenyapithecus* into the new human ancestor, *Ramapithecus*.

Not only did *Ramapithecus* appear to be specifically allied with humans, but if it included *Kenyapithecus*, then it would have to be at least 14 million years old, the known age of *Kenyapithecus*. Thus, Simons and Pilbeam argued for the split of humans and apes prior to 14 million years ago, when the first creature unlike chimps but like humans, at least dentally, could be detected.

With the aid of hindsight, we can now detect some hidden faulty assumptions in the thinking of Simons and Pilbeam. First, they assumed that similarity indicates proximity of descent. This, however, easily leads to a confusion of symplesiomorphies and synapomorphies. Only the latter really indicate close common ancestry. Second, Simons and Pilbeam assumed that the diversity of apes in the Miocene was comparable to the diversity of apes living now. There are only a handful of ape genera presently; if the diversity back then was comparably low, then linking the modern and the fossil forms together should not be all that difficult.

Third, and most significantly, they implicitly divided the fossils into two categories: us/not us, or more specifically, human and ape. This subtle but significant anthropocentrism tended to imply that the apes were all more closely related to one another than any was to humans and that all the evolutionary change occurred in the human lineage. Therefore, humans must be full of derived features, and any similarities between a human and a Miocene ape must be a synapomorphy. And those synapomorphies could begin to be detected as early as 14 million years ago.

This interpretation was challenged by studies of molecular evolutionary rates in the late 1960s. If the molecular data were being interpreted properly, then the 14-million-year date for the divergence of human and apes might be as much as a three-fold overestimate. Humans, chimps, and gorillas were so genetically similar that they could not have been separate lineages for that long. Thus, Vincent

Turkey) and probably Europe as well. This genus is well dated as early as 12 million years ago and as late as 8 million years ago, so it clearly was successful. After all, the genus *Homo* is not even 3 million years old.

The affinities of *Sivapithecus* have been debated since the turn of the century, when it was known from only jaws and teeth. As early as 1915, Guy E. Pilgrim suggested derived similarities between *Sivapithecus* and humans, while later that year, the great paleontologist William King Gregory suggested it was instead closely related to the orang-utan. With

Sarich argued that *Ramapithecus* could not possibly be a hominid at 14 million years ago, "no matter what it looked like," for there was no uniquely hominid line at the time. It didn't come into being until much later.

Subsequent discoveries in Turkey and Pakistan showed that *Ramapithecus* was most similar neither to the human nor to the chimpanzee, but rather to the orang-utan! Certain of the traits shared by humans and *Ramapithecus*—for example, thick molar tooth enamel—are indeed shared by them and not by chimps, but by orangs. They are consequently now interpreted as symplesiomorphies. The evolutionary event in question was a *thinning* of the tooth enamel, and it occurred in the common ancestry of the chimps and gorillas. Other characteristics, such as the parabolic dental arcade, were only reconstructed wishfully. The new fossils clearly indicated that Simons and Pilbeam had misinterpreted the old fossils.

Further, the Miocene apes are now recognized to have been exceedingly diverse, considerably more so than contemporary apes. Only one species of these varied creatures at any time was in our ancestry, and only a handful are in the ancestry of all the living apes; most are extinct without living issue. This means that to try and isolate *the* specific one that gave rise to us is going to be very difficult, perhaps even futile.

And finally, grouping all apes that were not like us into a single category created a very phylogenetically heterogeneous group. By assuming that anything like us is closely related to us and that anything not like us is closely related to any other thing not like us—in other words, by failing to differentiate between similarity and synapomorphy—Simons and Pilbeam were making much weaker phylogenetic inferences than they imagined. *Ramapithecus* is now widely accepted to be the female of *Sivapithecus*, and both are closely related to the orangs. *Kenyapithecus* is a genus of its own again, and it may yet emerge to be ancestral to some or all of the living apes and humans.

The *Ramapithecus* episode dramatically demonstrates three important issues. First, it highlights the difficulty in inferring ancestral-descendant relationships from the fossil record, especially in the presence of deeply seated, unarticulated biases. Second, it illustrates the self-correcting nature of science. And third, it shows how genetic data can be used to test hypotheses about the evolutionary relationships of organisms independently of anatomy.

References:

Andrews, P., & Cronin, J. (1982). The relationships of *Sivapithecus* and *Ramapithecus* and the evolution of the orang-utan. *Nature*, 297: 541–546.

Lewin, R. (1988). *Bones of contention*. New York: Simon and Schuster.

only a few scrappy fragments of tooth and bones, of course, different interpretations are possible. More substantial remains allow the rejection of some hypotheses of relationship.

By the 1960s and early 1970s, more dental fragments suggested to Elwyn Simons and David Pilbeam a connection between *Sivapithecus* (then called *Ramapithecus*—Box 11–1) and humans. To others, such as Alan Walker and Peter Andrews, certain key features, such as the shape of the dental arcade, were not clearly similar between *Sivapithecus* and

Figure 11-12

In several key facial features, the orang-utan differs from the chimpanzee, and *Sivapithecus* shares the derived condition with the orang-utan (after Ward and Kimbel; Conroy).

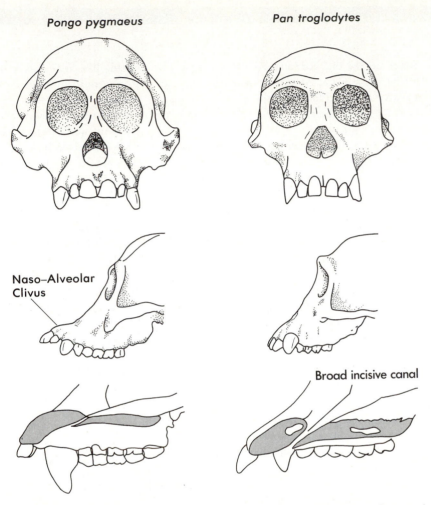

humans. Not until the late 1970s and early 1980s were faces of *Sivapithecus* discovered in Turkey and Pakistan, which suggested independently to Andrews and to Pilbeam the *Sivapithecus-Pongo* connection.

Three principal facial details link *Sivapithecus* to the orang-utan. The first is the interorbital septum, or the distance between the eye sockets. Only in *Sivapithecus* and *Pongo* is it so narrow. The second feature is the naso-alveolar clivus, or the upper jaw below the nose. In profile it has a very distinctive curvature, again seen only in these two genera. The third derived feature is the incisive canal, in the palate between the nose and the mouth, through which a nerve passes. In orang-utans and in *Sivapithecus* it is very narrow, while in earlier and other, later apes it is broad (Figure 11–12). Other features of the nasal area, cheekbones, and upper palate have also been suggested to link these two genera.

These features make *Sivapithecus* a probable unique ancestor of the orang-utan. The discovery and analysis of postcranial remains will help to elucidate the details of the orang's evolution (and the postcranial bones of *Sivapithecus* are curiously different from those of orang-utans), but from the neck up, it looks like the orang-utan is almost a living fossil, very similar in striking detail to animals which lived about 10 million years ago.

LOOK OUT FOR *GIGANTOPITHECUS*

Along with *Sivapithecus*, other thick-enamel-toothed apes flourished in the Miocene. Among them was the aptly named *Gigantopithecus*, which survived well into the Pleistocene in Asia. *Gigantopithecus* is known only from teeth and jaw fragments (and a possible elbow fragment), but what teeth and jaw fragments they are (Figure 11–13)!

The genus was named by the Dutch paleontologist G. H. R. von Koenigswald in 1935, on the basis of an enormous hominoid molar he had purchased in a traditional Hong Kong pharmacy. Its teeth are now known from India, Pakistan, and China, and they recall the thick-enamelled Miocene hominoids of the middle Miocene, but at a much larger size. Further, its reduced canines and vertical (rather than sticking out) lower incisors have suggested to some researchers a special connection to humans. Most consider it a parallel dental development.

If its body size were proportional to its tooth size, which presumably it ought to have been, *Gigantopithecus* may have weighed 600 pounds and stood 9 feet tall, making this enigmatic animal far larger than a gorilla and the largest known primate.

OREOPITHECUS—AFFINITIES AMBIGUOUS

Sometimes, as it happens, having more body parts available for comparison actually makes it harder to place the taxon phylogenetically. This may be for several reasons: 1) because we are dealing with a creature lacking close living relatives and therefore lacking a model, 2) because it was adaptively convergent on one group while more closely related to another, or 3) because it was so adaptively divergent that its affinities are hard to discern. An example of such a genus, well known but poorly understood, is the late Miocene *Oreopithecus* (Figure 11–14).

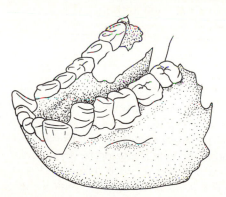
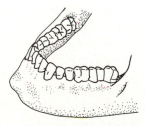

Figure 11-13

If the rest of *Gigantopithecus* was as big as its jaws and teeth (left) suggest, it would have been impressively large when compared to a human jaw (right) (after Eckhardt).

Figure 11-14

Compared to other fossil genera, there is a great deal of *Oreopithecus* material, including the cranial remains shown here; nevertheless, its relationships still remain unclear.

Oreopithecus is known from northern Italy, where it occupied a swampy forest about 8 million years ago. It is the only primate known from these sites, whose occupants included many mammals and reptiles. Yet even this assemblage is a unique and motley group, some related to African, and some to European forms that arrived in Italy at various times before the Mediterranean Sea existed as it does today.

In its molars, *Oreopithecus* has suggested to some a derivation of the cercopithecoid cusp pattern, though it has more cusps and wrinkles than the teeth of any known Old World monkey. Yet it also had no diastema, and did have a bicuspid front premolar and small canines, all like humans. Further, its long arms and generalized postcranial skeleton recalled an arboreal hominoid ape, while its feet suggested a terrestrial monkey.

Most workers believe that *Oreopithecus* was a hominoid, perhaps as closely related to the gibbons as to the modern great ape and human clade. Nevertheless, this is far from a unanimous opinion. *Oreopithecus* was clearly a unique creature, not easily placed into the groups of primates now alive.

Bipedalism: Hallmark of the Hominids

Many Miocene ape localities have yielded diverse fossil remains, including material from Fort Ternan in Kenya, where a genus named *Kenyapithecus* lived about 14 million years ago. There are fossil monkeys (such as *Victoriapithecus*) and fossil prosimians (such as the tiny *Komba*) known from the Miocene. We tend to focus on the Miocene apes because they are more directly relevant to our own ancestry (Figure 11–15). There are, however, precious few hominoid fossils from the late

Miocene–early Pliocene time, when the human lineage appears to have emerged. Indeed, in a recent review, Andrew Hill and Steven Ward concluded that only eleven African fossil specimens could be clearly identified as hominoid between 14 and 4 million years ago (the time between the sites of Fort Ternan and Laetoli; see below). However, some, such as the teeth and mandible fragment from a site called Tabarin in Kenya, are dated to between 5 and 6 million years and fall on the hominid clade. Yet the teeth are not the key feature differentiating the human clade from the other hominoids.

Sometime in the late Miocene, a group of hominoids began walking on the ground on their two hind limbs, rather than suspending themselves from trees, or climbing, or using all four limbs on the ground. These were our ancestors, the first hominids—whose adaptations for terrestrial bipedalism we have inherited. Who were they? Unfortunately, as already noted, the fossil record from this range is extremely sparse, so when we can peek in again at about 3.7 million years ago, we find some hominoids already possessing many of the principal features of bipedalism.

ANATOMICAL BASIS FOR BIPEDALISM

Walking is a unique form of locomotion, and, of the criteria by which we distinguish humans from apes, it is the one which is detectable earliest in our ancestry. Thus, the hominids (that is, in the human family, a subcategory of the human-and-ape superfamily) of 3.7 million years ago had apelike brains and teeth, but had the peculiarly human trait of getting from place to place primarily on two legs. On what basis can we infer this? Let us examine the anatomical basis for this significantly human behavior.

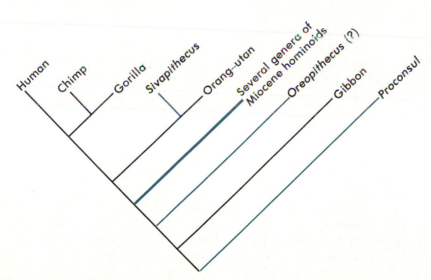

Figure 11-15

Cladogram showing the relationships of several Miocene apes and modern genera.

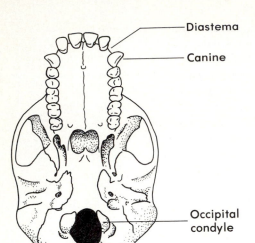

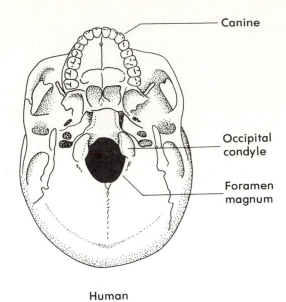

Chimpanzee

Human

Figure 11-16

Basicranium of ape and human.

occipital condyles

Paired bumps on the base of the skull, on either side of the foramen magnum, on which the skull rests atop the vertebral column.

foramen magnum

Large hole in the base of the skull through which the spinal cord enters the brain.

lumbar curve

Additional curve to the human spine not present in apes; associated with bipedalism.

ilium

Broad, flat bone of the pelvis.

If we compare the locomotor anatomy of apes to that of humans, we find a number of significant differences, all of which reflect structural modifications of the human skeleton for bipedalism. First, we find on the skull that the **occipital condyles** lie directly beneath, and not toward the rear, since the head is held vertically. Similarly, the **foramen magnum**, the hole through which the spinal column emerges, is directly beneath the skull (Figure 11–16).

Second, the human vertebral column has more marked curves than that of the apes. A new curve, the **lumbar curve** in the lower back, appears in the human spine. This makes the lower back stronger in its new role of helping to support the body's weight (Figure 11–17).

Third, the pelvis takes on a new function as well, that of bearing the brunt of the upper body's weight—in a walking human, the pelvis is located directly beneath the trunk, whereas in the natural ground locomotion of an ape, the pelvis is behind the trunk. The **iliac blades** have become shortened and rotated, forming what is essentially a bowl structure (Figure 11–18).

Fourth, the lower limbs have become longer and more muscular relative to the upper limbs (Figure 11–19). The lower limbs constitute more than 30 percent of the weight of a human but less than 20 percent of the total weight of a chimpanzee.

Fifth, the hip joint (formed by the head of the femur inserting into the **acetabulum** of the pelvis) has been strengthened and reoriented—part of the joint's new roles have been taken over by a greatly expanded gluteus maximus in the human buttock. Other muscles rotate the hips in humans, keeping the center of gravity stable during walking, in contrast to the side-to-side swaying one sees in apes walking in such a fashion.

Sixth, the knees, which are always bent to some extent in the apes, can fully straighten in humans, necessary in our mode of locomotion. This involves an inward, or medial, orientation of the knee-joint as well, compared with that of an ape (Figure 11–20). This can be thought of as torsion or twisting of the femur and tibia, reorienting the knees but keeping the feet and body facing forward. The result is a very characteristic hominid knee, called a valgus knee, in which the knees are brought inward, under the body's center of gravity. As the human gait requires briefly balancing on one leg while the other swings forward, the valgus knee keeps the body stable during a phase of potential instability. For the same reason, the inner condyle of the femur is larger in humans (the medial, or inner, condyle and lateral, or outer, condyle are about the same size in apes).

Seventh, the human foot bears weight in three places during a stride: the heel, ball, and big toe. All three of these areas are expanded in humans for this reason. As a result, the human foot is a less flexible structure than its ape counterpart due to the development of strong ligaments. The big toe, in addition to being enlarged, is now aligned with the other toes. Thus, it is no longer capable of acting like a thumb, as it does in the apes. The human foot has lost much of its movement capabilites in a trade-off for stability (Figure 11–21).

acetabulum

Socket at the side of the pelvis into which the head of the femur fits.

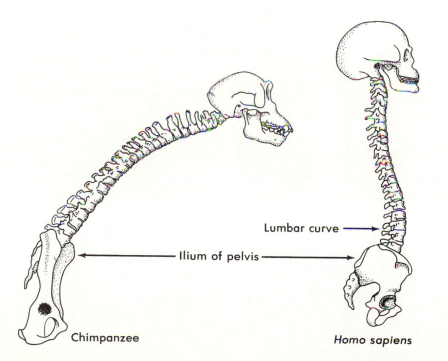

Lumbar curve

Ilium of pelvis

Chimpanzee

Homo sapiens

Figure 11-17

Vertebral column of ape and human (after Le Gros Clark).

Of great importance here is that these features of the muscular and skeletal systems can be detected in fossils and, therefore, can be used to infer the bipedal gait in extinct species. Habitual bipedalism has evolved several times among animals (dinosaurs and kangaroos may come to mind), but these are examples of convergence since the locomotor mechanics in these groups are actually very different from one another. We assume that since there are no other living bipedal primates than our own species, bipedalism must be a synapomorphy between any extinct species and us. In other words, we assume bipedalism has arisen only once among the hominoids, and any species possessing that trait will be closely related. We use this trait now to define the extinct species (and the one extant species) within the family Hominidae, the hominids.

Figure 11-18

Pelvis of ape and human.

Chimpanzee   Human

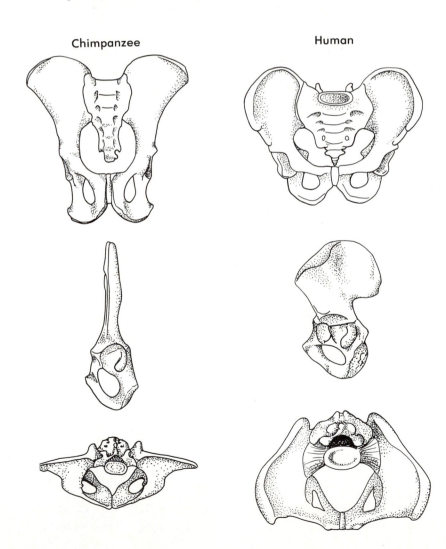

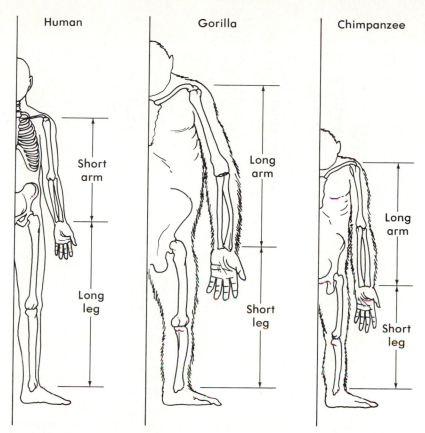

Figure 11-19

Relative limb length of human and apes (after Schultz).

Pliocene Emergence of the Hominids—First Evidence of Bipedalism

The earliest evidence for bipedalism in the hominid fossil record is actually quite indirect. It was discovered when paleoanthropologist Andrew Hill, working with Mary Leakey at a site called Laetoli in Tanzania, evaded a bit of dried elephant dung which had been playfully flung at him by a fellow field worker one evening. He found himself in a dry riverbed which contained a layer of volcanic ash with several depressions within it. The depressions, it turned out, were footprints of various animals, including identifiable gazelles, giraffes, elephants, pigs, monkeys—and bipedal primates, hominids. Further, the fact that the prints occurred in volcanic ash made it possible to date them by the potassium-argon method. They turned out to be 3.7 million years old.

The feet that made those prints were fairly short and wide, a little more than 6 inches long and 4 inches wide. Nevertheless, they had a large big toe aligned with the other toes, and they transferred weight during stride in the same manner as modern humans. Further, if the general proportions of modern foot size to body height are similar to those that existed in these earliest hominids, then two individuals, one about 4 feet tall, and the other about 4 ½ feet tall, are identifiable.

Figure 11-20

Orientation of the knee in human and ape (after Johanson and Edey).

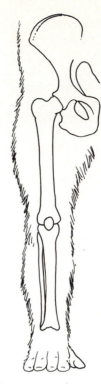
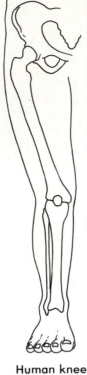

Human knee   Ape knee

australopithecine

A hominid of the Plio-Pleistocene, not specifically recognized as a very close relative or ancestor of *Homo sapiens*; contrasted with hominine.

Hominid fossils (jaws and teeth) from the Laetoli site have been given the name *Australopithecus afarensis* and are slightly older than similar fossils from the site of Hadar in Ethiopia. These populations formed the roots of the hominid phylogenetic tree as it is presently known.

Since the earliest fossil hominids are from Africa, we believe that Africa is the continent within which a group of hominoids evolved into the first hominids during the late Miocene. Pliocene fossil sites yielding the remains of **australopithecines**, these early hominids, are found in southern and eastern Africa (Figure 11–22) and range in age from 5–6 million years (the mandibular fragment and teeth from Tabarin identified as *Australopithecus afarensis*) to slightly more than 1 million years, in the Pleistocene.

When dealing with the hominid fossils of this age, it is useful to refer to certain key specimens since the taxonomic relationships of these specimens are not always clear. Certain fossils, as a result of the often gradual nature of evolutionary change, span the morphological gaps that we would like to believe exist between species. These fossils take on special significance by helping us tell which of the extinct populations were most closely related to one another.

PLIOCENE HOMINIDS

We divide the Pliocene hominids into three closely related groups: 1) the earliest, or basal, australopithecines, *Australopithecus afarensis;* 2) the later, "gracile" australopithecines, *Australopithecus africanus* (with generally smaller faces and jaws than the next group); and 3) the later, "robust" australopithecines (larger in face and jaws), which many workers now place in a separate genus, *Paranthropus* (Figure 11–23). Though all were bipedal hominids, the biological diversity that existed among them reflects an adaptive radiation—a successful new adaptation leading to the emergence of several new taxa. It contrasts strikingly with the modern situation, in which only one species of hominid exists.

THE BASAL AUSTRALOPITHECINES

The *Australopithecus afarensis* remains from Hadar, Ethiopia, constitute one of the most important finds in the history of paleoanthropology. These fossils were discovered in the 1970s by an American-French expedition led by Donald Johanson and Maurice Taieb and are very similar to the few Laetoli fossils. The Hadar fossils are dated to about 3 million years ago. A large range of anatomical variation is represented by the Hadar fossil hominids, which was initially interpreted as different species

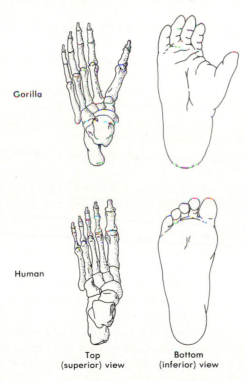

Gorilla

Human

Top (superior) view   Bottom (inferior) view

Figure 11-21

Foot of ape and human (after Gregory).

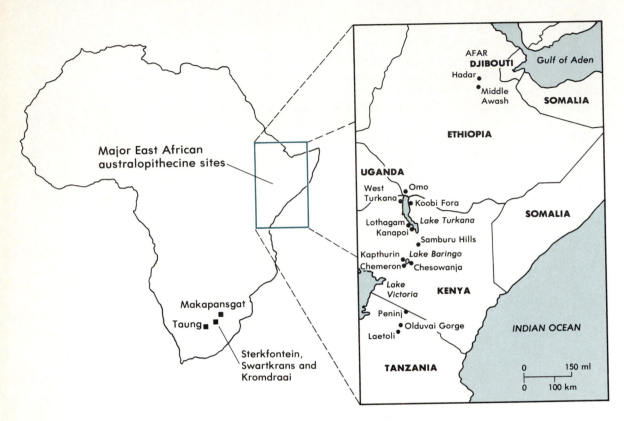

Figure 11-22

Locations of the main sites of early hominids.

coexisting at the site, a view still maintained by some workers. Most pale-oanthropologists, however, follow the interpretations of Donald Johanson and Tim White in seeing the diversity as a result of a great deal of sexual dimorphism in this primitive hominid species.

"Lucy" is a 40-percent-complete skeleton of a female who stood less than 4 feet tall, weighing about 60 pounds, and so named because she was discovered while the Beatles' "Lucy in the Sky with Diamonds" was play-ing on a tape recorder in camp (Figure 11–24). Her teeth are primitive, with a diastema separating a larger-than-modern canine from the first premolar. Little of her skull remains, but from other specimens it is clear that the brain was small, like an ape's (about 400 cubic centimeters, less than one-third of an average human)—but some details of the brain of this species can be detected from imprints left on the inside of skull frag-ments. These may suggest a brain differently organized from that of an ape, perhaps ancestral to the human form.

Lucy's pelvis, knee, and foot indicate unambiguous bipedal adapta-tions. Nevertheless, there remain many nonhuman features in Lucy. Her arms were much longer in proportion to her legs, compared with a mod-ern human, her toes were long and curved, her cervical vertebrae had areas for large and powerful shoulder muscles to attach, and the orienta-

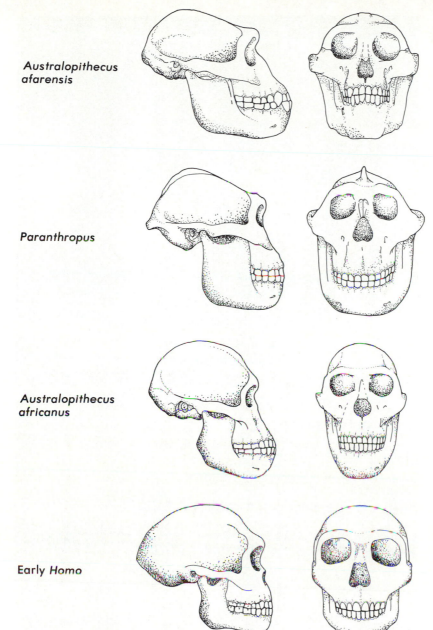

Australopithecus afarensis

Paranthropus

Australopithecus africanus

Early *Homo*

Figure 11-23

At least four general categories of hominids are recognized in the Plio-Pleistocene: *Australopithecus afarensis, Paranthropus, Australopithecus africanus,* and *Homo.*

tion of her shoulder joint suggests a greater range of motion than that in modern humans. These anatomical forms suggest that the basal australopithecines were more efficient climbers than modern people—in addition to having fully terrestrial capabilities.

An important correlate of pelvic shape not only relates to the mode of locomotion but to the process of giving birth as well. Since the shape

Figure 11-24

(a) Lucy, a specimen of *Australopithecus afarensis*, more than 3 million years old, from Ethiopia. (b) Footprints from Laetoli, Tanzania, were probably made by hominids like Lucy, with feet that were short and broad relative to those of a modern human.

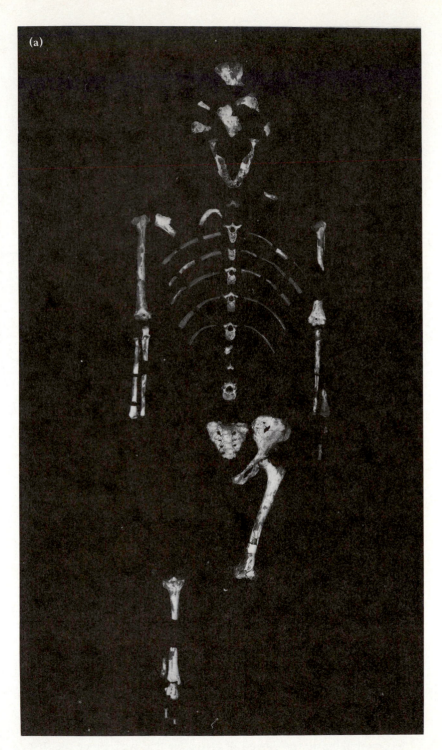

(a)

(b)

Chimpanzee   Lucy   Human

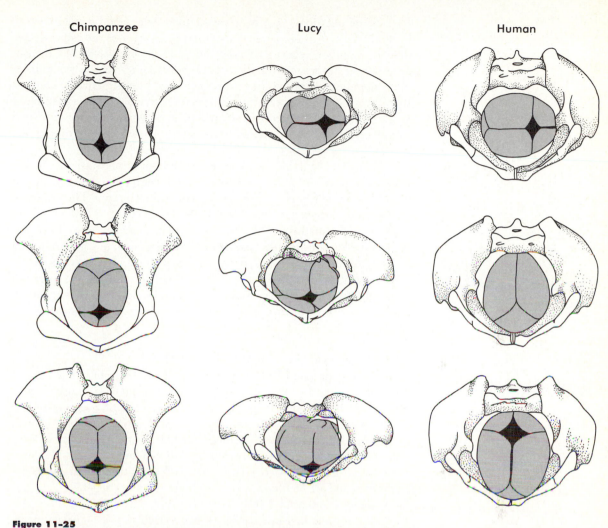

Figure 11-25

Passage of a baby through the birth canal in an ape, australopithecine, and modern human. The fontanelle (shaded) is toward the front of the baby's head (after Tague and Lovejoy).

of Lucy's birth canal is somewhat different from that of a modern woman, Robert Tague and Owen Lovejoy have been able to infer aspects of australopithecine obstetrics. In particular, Lucy had a very wide, shallow pelvis (*platypelloid*), while modern women have a broad, oval shape to the birth canal. Human babies enter the birth canal with their heads sideways and then rotate their heads in the birth canal, generally coming out facing away from the mother. Lucy's pelvis apparently would have obliged a baby not to rotate its head and to be born facing sideways (Figure 11–25).

Some questions have been raised about whether the creature that made the footprints at Laetoli 3.7 million years ago was the same species as Lucy, 3 million years ago. Russell Tuttle of the University of Chicago, for example, has argued that the curved toes of Lucy's species would have made different footprints from those found at Laetoli. This means that there would have been two bipedal species (presumably diverged from a common ancestor even earlier). However, most workers are now satisfied to interpret the early australopithecines as a single, sexually dimorphic, bipedal species.

Australopithecus afarensis appears as a uniquely intermediate species, retaining a mosaic of many primitive features, yet having developed some derived hominid features. Strikingly mosaic is the cranium. The primitive canine teeth (larger than ours but smaller than a chimp's) cause the jaws to jut out—**prognathism**—like those of an ape. The back teeth, however, are very large. They possess **post-canine megadontia**, like a hominid. The descendants of this species appear to have diverged along two lines: the robust group, with a striking development of the molars and chewing apparatus; and the gracile group, whose brains became their primary adaptations. To chew or to think—a fateful crossroads in human evolution!

prognathism

Having jaws jutting forward.

post-canine megadontia

Having large back teeth.

THE "ROBUST" AUSTRALOPITHECINES

In 1938, paleontologist Robert Broom announced the remains of the first robust australopithecines from the site of Kromdraai in South Africa. Similar fossils have since been discovered at the site of Swartkrans, also in South Africa, and in several places in East Africa, notably Olduvai Gorge, Tanzania, and along the shores of Lake Turkana, Kenya. In general, the East African fossils are better preserved and more readily dated since they are found in geological strata. The South African fossils are from caves and are embedded in a hard limestone matrix.

Olduvai Hominid 5 (OH-5) is also known as "Zinj" because after its 1959 discovery by Mary Leakey, it was placed by Louis Leakey in the taxon *Zinjanthropus boisei*, which is no longer recognized. This individual lived approximately 1.75 million years ago, and these hominids are known from about 2.5 to about 1.2 million years ago. Slightly younger than "Zinj" is ER-406 (from East of Lake Rudolph, now Lake Turkana).

sagittal crest

A ridge of bone across the top of the skull, from front to back, which permits additional surface area for the attachment of enlarged jaw musculature.

While its **sagittal crest** may superficially recall an ape, its teeth do not (Figure 11–26). The function of a sagittal crest is to provide a surface for the attachment of large chewing muscles, and the development of large chewing muscles in some apes and some hominids is an example of homoplasy. How do we know this? Postcranial remains from South Africa, as well as the base of the skull, indicate bipedalism in these creatures. Further, their small canines and flat faces are fundamentally non-apelike characters.

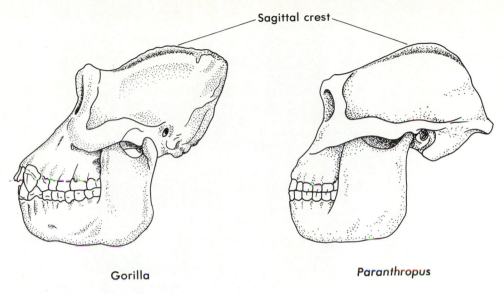

Gorilla

Paranthropus

Figure 11-26

The sagittal crest of *Paranthropus* is only superficially similar to that of a gorilla—*Paranthropus* was bipedal and had hominid teeth.

Interestingly, if we consider the fundamental dental differences between humans and apes to be in small canine size and reliance on back teeth rather than on front teeth, the robust australopithecines appear to have been hyper-human. That is, they possessed the hominid dental pattern to an even greater extent than do modern humans. Not only were their molars extremely large, but their premolars took on a **molariform** appearance. Thus, they had in effect not simply three molars per jaw quadrant, but five. This emphasis on the rear teeth and their grinding function explains the sagittal crest and wide cheekbones in this group. To use those teeth efficiently, large temporalis muscles for chewing originated on the top of the skull and passed through the cheek.

Where the major change characteristic of the earliest australopithecines was the emergence of bipedalism, the later australopithecines seem to have been characterized by a new adaptation to feeding. It was once believed that "gracile" australopithecines ate principally meat and that "robust" australopithecines ate principally vegetables, but this is no longer believed because of newer analyses of teeth. It now appears that both genera were likely to have been principally vegetarian. However, studies of the microstructure and wear patterns of the molar teeth indicate that *Paranthropus* species were crushing and grinding gritty objects, perhaps seeds and tubers, to a much greater extent than was *Australopithecus*.

molariform
In the form of a molar.

Figure 11-27

KNM-WT-17000, a link between *Australopithecus afarensis* and *Paranthropus*.

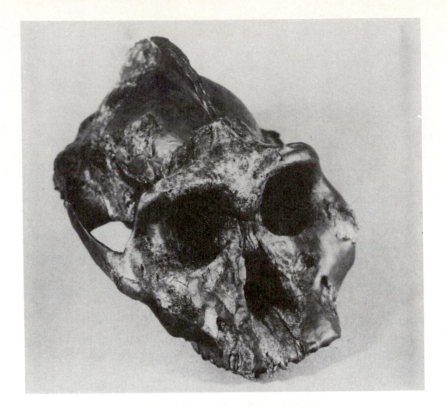

Although its cranial form is much different from our own, with unique specializations for crushing and grinding foods, there is little reason to think that the robust group was actually less intelligent than its contemporaries. Early stone tools (see Chapter 12) have been found in association with them, although these are usually attributed to other hominids since those other hominids look more like us. A study of the hand bones of *Paranthropus* from South Africa by Randall Susman, however, has concluded that these robust hominids were capable of the fine manipulation required for tool manufacture.

A specimen in a unique phylogenetic position is WT-17000 (West Turkana), discovered in 1985 by Alan Walker of The Johns Hopkins University (Figure 11–27). Being the oldest representative of the robust australopithecine lineage, having their characteristic chewing adaptations, it nevertheless has far more primitive characters, similar to *Australopithecus afarensis*, than any other member of its lineage. For example, its face juts out like the earlier australopithecines, and the base of its cranium is strikingly similar to theirs. By virtue of its age and its preservation of ancestral features, this specimen is an excellent intermediate between *Australopithecus afarensis* and *Paranthropus*. (Taxonomic splitters place this fossil in the species *Paranthropus aethiopicus*.)

THE "GRACILE" AUSTRALOPITHECINES

The first australopithecine discovered is known as the Taung child (Figure 11–28), found by miners in a cave in Taungs, South Africa, in 1924. It was brought to the attention of anatomist Raymond Dart, who recognized a unique constellation of features in this creature, which was only an infant at the time of its death more than 2 million years ago (Box 11–2).

The preserved parts were its face, its jaw, and (curiously enough) a fossil cast of its brain, though not the outer skull itself. When Dart compared the skull with those of apes and humans, he came to the conclusion that it showed a mosaic of features common to both apes and humans. Even though its **deciduous** canines were large for a human, they were small for an ape, and the rest of its baby teeth were clearly human in appearance. Further, despite the general apish appearance of the face, the brain and base of the skull suggested human affinities. Consequently, Dart interpreted this fossil as a "missing link" between apes and humans. Now we see it as a species preserving many primitive characters but also sharing derived characters with humans, and we retain the name Dart gave it, *Australopithecus africanus*. Although Dart's find was initially greeted with skepticism when published in 1925, later corroborative discoveries in the 1930s by Robert Broom helped sway the scientific community to the opinion that these australopithecines were, in fact, primitive hominids.

Other "gracile" australopithecines, which lived (coarsely) between 2 and 3 million years ago, have been found at the sites of Sterkfontein and Makapansgat in South Africa. One well-preserved cranium is called STS-5 (from Sterkfontein) and is informally known as "Mrs. Ples," since Robert Broom initially called this specimen *"Plesianthropus,"* a name no

deciduous

Something that is shed or falls off after a period of time, such as the leaves of certain trees and baby teeth.

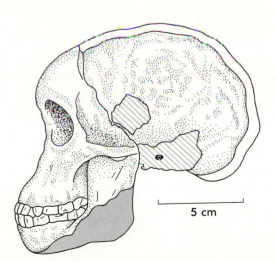

Figure 11-28

The Taung child, described by Raymond Dart in 1925 (after Montagu; Eldredge and Tattersall).

5 cm

The Age of Little Hominids

When Raymond Dart encountered the first fossil of an australopithecine in 1924, the Taung child, he naturally attempted to ascertain how old it was when it died. Knowing the sequence of eruption of human teeth enabled Dart to make an inference about its age at death. It had a full set of deciduous (baby) teeth, and its adult first molars had erupted. Dart took caution and mentioned only that this state corresponded to a modern human child of about six years of age. Later, in the 1970s, Alan Mann of the University of Pennsylvania, studying a large sample of hominid remains, generalized the idea that early hominids had dental development and maturation patterns like those of modern humans.

The first challenge to Dart's inference came in 1985, from Timothy Bromage and Christopher Dean in England. They studied the fine structure of dental enamel and noted that fine bands called perikymata circle around the front incisor teeth as they grow and are laid down according to a fairly regular weekly rhythm. They can be seen even by the naked eye in a mirror but are readily analyzed by the scanning electron microscope. Counting the perikymata on the enamel of incompletely formed incisors, which happen to begin to form at birth in apes and humans, is like counting the weeks of the specimen's life and can permit an independent cross-check of the age at death of the hominid.

Bromage and Dean found that in a sample of human teeth, the perikymata count on the incisors matched the age of the individual inferred from standard measures of tooth development. Yet humans develop slowly, compared with apes, and mature biologically much later. Apes, therefore, have a different schedule of tooth development, which is accelerated relative to humans. Thus, a

human of age six would have teeth comparable to a chimpanzee of just over age three.

What did the perikymata say about the age of fossil hominids? Bromage and Dean found that for *Australopithecus*, *Paranthropus*, and early *Homo*, for example, a specimen aged about three years by perikymata already had its first permanent molars erupting. This is like the apes, several years shy of a modern human child's age of eruption for this tooth. Their conclusion: Hominids of the Plio-Pleistocene were on a maturation schedule not like modern humans, but like modern apes!

Holly Smith of the University of Michigan showed in 1986 that the general pattern of dental maturation for the fossil hominids was more similar to living apes than to living humans, but somewhat out of synchrony with both. Thus, inferring the age of various fossils tooth by tooth, she found that the upper dentition of STS-24 (a child's jaws from Sterkfontein) suggested a range from 2 to 6.1 years on a human schedule, depending upon which tooth one examined; judged from an ape's schedule, the range was only 2.8 to 4.3. Thus, although there was variation from tooth to tooth, the schedule of an ape gave greater consistency in the estimation of age than did the schedule of a human. Similarly, the upper canine of STW-151 (also an infant's jaw from Sterkfontein) suggested that it was 3.8 years old, while its first upper molar suggested that it was 7.3 years old, based on a human schedule. Based on an ape schedule, the canine suggested 5.5 and the molar 5.7, considerably greater consistency.

When Smith examined the same specimens as Bromage and Dean and estimated the age from an ape's dental development schedule, she found high concordance with their age estimates based on perikymata counts. She concluded that fossil hominids of the Plio-Pleistocene had not yet begun to develop in the long, slow manner of modern humans, but were maturing early, like modern apes, and, like Bromage and Dean, she concluded that the ages at death of immature fossil hominids had been considerably overestimated.

Complementing the analysis of the perikymata on the incisors and the schedule of dental maturation, Beynon and Wood in England performed a careful analysis of the development of the molars. Using specimens whose molars had been chipped or broken when discovered, which exposed underlying portions of enamel to analysis, they found, once again, that the fossil hominids developed along a schedule that was accelerated relative to humans and similar to apes.

These new findings suggested that the first and most famous australopithecine, the Taung skull, should be reanalyzed. But since that fossil came from a limestone cave and was highly mineralized, it was difficult to study. At the sixtieth-anniversary celebration of the initial publication of the Taung find, in 1985, Bromage predicted that the Taung child would have an apelike pattern of development as well. In particular, he suggested that the Taung child's permanent central incisors would be well within the jaws, would have an enamel crown, but would show little or no root formation—like a three-year-old ape, not a six-year-old human. In 1987, Glenn Conroy and Michael Vannier of Washington University were able to subject the Taung skull to computerized tomography, or CT ("cat") scanning. This permitted them to see internal structures—in particular, partly formed and unerupted teeth—which would enable a more thorough analysis and a better estimate of the fossil's age.

In humans, the first molars and incisors erupt at about the same time. In apes, the first incisor does not erupt until about two years after the first molar. The CT scan showed that while the crowns of the incisors were developed, no discernible development of the roots had yet taken place. This was similar to the apes. Likewise, roots of the canines and front premolar are also present when the first molar erupts in humans—but not in apes, and not in the Taung child. The conclusion of the CT-scan study is that "overall, the pattern of the Taung specimen is most like that of a 3.0–4.0-year-old pongid."

Thus, we have an example of the mosaic nature of evolution at work. The australopithecines, though clearly hominids from the derived form of their teeth and skeletons, nevertheless matured early, like their plesiomorphic ancestors and like living apes. The maturational patterns characteristic of modern humans appear to have evolved in their descendants. And continuing studies are tending to find differences in the dental maturation patterns between *Paranthropus* and *Australopithecus* as well.

References:

Bromage, T. G., & Dean, M. C., (1985). Re-evaluation of the age at death of immature fossil hominids. *Nature*, 317:525–527.

Smith, B. H. (1986). Dental development in *Australopithecus* and early *Homo*. *Nature*, 323:327–330.

Conroy, G. C. & Vannier, M. W. (1987). Dental development of the Taung skull from computerized tomography. *Nature*, 329:625–627.

Beynon, A. D. & Dean, M. C. (1988). Distinct dental development patterns in early fossil hominids. *Nature*, 335:509–514.

Figure 11–29

Paranthropus looks overall somewhat less like us than *Australopithecus* does, but the two were probably not very different in most ways.

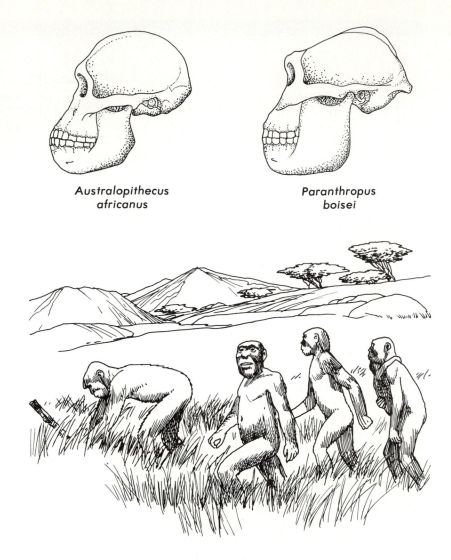

Australopithecus
africanus

Paranthropus
boisei

longer recognized. Though smaller than the robust group, the cheek teeth of this species are still considerably larger than those of modern humans. Postcranial remains, including a pelvis, indicate that these were bipedal hominids.

Overall, their faces jut out more than the faces of their robust cousins, and their lack of the massive chewing specializations give the "gracile" australopithecines an overall look more similar to us (Figure 11–29). In specimens such as ER-1813 (again from East Rudolph/Turkana), anatomical similarities between "gracile" australopithecines and early *Homo* are evident. It is to these early *Homo* creatures that the earliest stone tools are usually attributed, as the tools are found alongside both early *Homo* and *Paranthropus*.

In general, the "gracile" australopithecines had teeth and jaws larger than our own and brains much smaller. The molars and premolars are smaller than those of *Paranthropus*, and the average cranial capacity of 440 cc. is more comparable to a chimpanzee than to a human, which averages about 1400 cc. They were, nevertheless, hominids, and thereby our close relatives, as they were fully bipedal. Whether their bipedalism was precisely the same as ours remains open to question through studies of biomechanics, but there is no reason to suppose that it must have been *exactly* like our own form of bipedalism.

Relationships among the Plio-Pleistocene Hominids

Arguments were put forth in the 1960s that perhaps the robust forms were males and the gracile forms were females of the same species. While it is certainly important to take into account sexual dimorphism in interpreting the fossil record, it is now clear that such a simple interpretation is impossible to maintain. The robust and gracile forms are found in different sites; the robust forms outlived the gracile forms by nearly a million years; and the gracile forms (presumptive females) have larger canines than the robust forms (presumptive males). They are now recognized as being fundamentally different species and are, as noted, allocated to different genera.

We noted in Chapter 5 that the names one gives to groups can affect how they come to be seen. The fact that we contrast australopithecines with our own direct ancestors, the **hominines**, may imply something linguistically about the unity of the autralopithecines which is not present biologically. In other words, simply because we call *Paranthropus*, *Australopithecus africanus*, and *Australopithecus afarensis* "australopithecines," it does not necessarily follow that they are one another's closest relatives. The name merely serves as a contrast to "hominines," the group reserved for the genus *Homo*. This is simply another manifestation of the widespread tendency to focus on our own closest relatives, put them in one category (ours), and lump everything else into another category.

Another problem of nomenclature involves the use of the terms "gracile" and "robust," which are very firmly entrenched in the literature. While these have often been taken to mean "small" and "large," it is not very clear that these groups differed in body size significantly. Henry McHenry of the University of California at Davis has shown that apparently considerable sexual dimorphism in body size existed for each group, as judged from the sample of femurs known from these species. But the mean value for each group is remarkably similar (about 46 kg, or 100 lbs); what seems to vary across the groups is the size of their chewing apparatus. Thus, *Australopithecus africanus* and *Paranthropus* appear to have been similar-sized hominids with different feeding adaptations.

The cladistic relationships among *Paranthropus*, *Homo*, and *Australopithecus africanus* are far from absolutely clear, but a growing con-

hominine

Belonging to the subfamily Homininae, humans and their very close relatives; in contrast to australopithecines, which are hominids and merely close relatives.

sensus at present sees the latter two as each other's closest relatives. This is due to the apparent antiquity of the *Paranthropus* morphology, as shown by WT-17000, and to certain features of the skull, such as the pattern of blood circulation at the rear of skull, noted by Dean Falk and Glenn Conroy. This feature is variable but appears to unite *Homo* with the graciles having a synapomorphic pattern, and *Paranthropus* with A. *afarensis* having a plesiomorphic pattern. Similarly, the shape of the nasal bones and aspects of the mastoid processes of the skull base have been shown by Todd Olson to link the graciles and *Homo*, in spite of some morphological variability.

Australopithecus afarensis is probably the ancestral taxon of all three groups, evolving into (on one hand) *Paranthropus* and (on the other hand) *Australopithecus africanus*. Some populations of the latter species probably evolved into the genus *Homo*. Nevertheless, any proposed pattern of cladistic relationships among the three groups carries with it the implication of considerable homoplasy in several parts of the body.

Figure 11–30 summarizes the probable relationships of the early hominids. *Australopithecus afarensis* is probably equally closely related to both the "gracile" and "robust" australopithecines, while the genus *Homo* shares a special relationship with the "gracile" australopithecines. In the phylogenetic tree, we see that A. *afarensis* is likely to have been a common ancestor of both australopithecine lineages.

Scenarios: Fetal Chimps and Hairy Dolphins

Why did the earliest australopithecines become bipedal? Why did our ancestors and relatives come to develop the way they did? These questions are difficult to answer, for they involve events that occurred only once. And while we can study phylogenetic relationships from morphology, we can never reconstruct precisely the reasons for the emergence of a particular morphology. The best we can do is to infer use from structure, although use and cause may be very different.

EVOLUTION OF THE HAND AND BRAIN

Consider, for example, the human hand. It can be used for many things: writing, punching, making tools, making love. We are reasonably certain that the modern human hand evolved by natural selection, but selection for what? Not for writing, since writing was invented long after the human hand assumed its modern aspect. But the human right uppercut has no counterpart in the primates, the tool-making behavior of apes is rudimentary at best, and humans have far more tactile exploration during sexual activity than apes. So which of these alternatives was the unique selective advantage that molded the human hand, and which remaining alternatives were simply uses to which the new structure could be put? It is impossible to know since these are untestable hypotheses. We generally think that tool use is the force that molded the human hand, but there is no way of knowing for certain because we cannot retrace our steps.

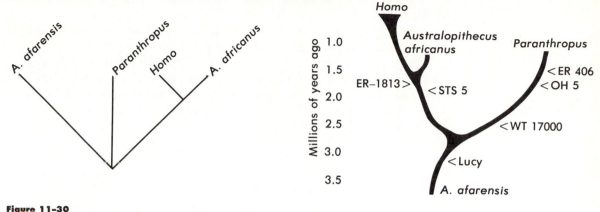

Figure 11-30

Probable relationships of the hominids. *Australopithecus afarensis,* being ancestral to two lineages, would therefore be the closest relative or sister group of both.

A similar argument applies to the expansion of the human brain, later in the evolution of our lineage—the brain has many functions, and its expansion may have been driven by any of them. Was it the ability to symbolize, or to imagine, or to enter trance. Perhaps it was problem solving and the ability to create ever more specialized forms of material culture that selected large brains in our ancestors. But we cannot know for certain, as we cannot recreate the past. And that is why we leave evolutionary scenarios for last.

BIPEDALISM SCENARIOS

What about bipedalism, the first unique specialization of our line? Why was that first step taken? Several answers have been proposed.

One popular scenario from the 1950s and 1960s had male bands of hunters at the center of hominid evolution. Quadrupeds are faster over the short run—any monkey or ape can outrun a human—but bipedalism appears to give an advantage to humans in endurance. Therefore, bipedalism might have been a significant advantage to hunting bands in stalking game over long distances. Further, since bipedalism left the hands free of locomotor functions, a bipedal primate could develop the use of weapons concurrently to assist in bringing down the prey.

It turns out, however, that bipedalism precedes the earliest evidence of the most rudimentary tools by a cool million years. Of course, bipedal primates could have been using wood or bone tools before stone tools, and these would not have been preserved in the archaeological record. But it is also not clear that the earliest hominids were eating significant amounts of meat—indeed, the analysis of microwear patterns on their enamel suggests that their diet included no more meat than the diet of a baboon or other savanna primate. Thus, although cooperative hunting could well have been within the capabilities of these early hominids, it probably was not a frequent enough activity (meat was not a significant enough part of their diet) to make a major difference in their survival. On the other hand, perhaps during the lean times, hunting managed to see the hominids through when other primates succumbed.

Two other scenarios emerged in the 1970s and are not mutually exclusive. As contrasted with the "man the hunter" scenario above, the "woman the gatherer" scenario emphasizes female roles in food procurement as being the more significant aspect. Among most living people who subsist by gathering and hunting, the females come up with most of the calories and nutrition in the form of plant food, and the males come up fairly infrequently with high-quality animal food. This is a sexual division of labor; of special note in this context is the sharing of gathered food with other members of the band.

Perhaps bipedalism developed as an efficient way to transport food and materials to a home base. A species whose arms are preoccupied with locomotion cannot use them to carry things—a chimpanzee carries things clumsily and only for short distances. If this scenario is true, what were these early hominids carrying? Possibly plant food, this scenario argues. The females spent their day gathering food and carrying it back to a home base, where it was then shared with other members of the band.

This scenario emphasizes cooperation rather than aggression, female roles rather than male roles, and the day-to-day survival of the hominids rather than the once-in-a-while hunting jackpot.

Yet humans have more meat in their diet than any other primates. Meat is prized food in all cultures, perhaps because it has been risky for technologically simple societies to obtain. Another scenario incorporates elements of both previous ones. Bipedalism emerged, it argues, not for hunting meat, but for *scavenging* meat. Hominids, it is argued, followed the migrating herds over the African savanna, living off weakened or dead animals. When such a feast was encountered, the hominids may have opportunistically stripped the meat off the carcass. Here, the advantage that bipeds have in endurance, to follow the migrating herds, is emphasized. Further, the entire band came along, females carrying infants on their hips, which is common behavior among humans but not among other primates.

There are many other possible scenarios, although the scenarios we have just discussed contain two good features. First, they rely upon the known behaviors of humans and nonhuman primates in accounting for the shift to bipedalism. Certainly, if we can account for a phenomenon by recourse to ordinary events or behaviors, we have a better explanation than one that makes recourse to extraordinary ones. Second, they relate the locomotor innovation to other important behaviorally unique qualities of humans, treating bipedalism as part of a major system rather than standing alone or being part of an unrelated group of traits. Third, with only minor adjustments, they are all compatible with the evidence as it stands.

GRAND SCHEME SCENARIOS

Less useful scenarios are those in which the fossil record and primate behavior are ignored or glossed over in favor of a grand scheme, which cannot be easily tested, as it purports to explain remote and unique events. Two examples are the "fetalization hypothesis" and the "aquatic ape hypothesis."

Fetalization Hypothesis   The fetalization hypothesis notes that in certain ways, a baby ape resembles an adult human more than an adult ape does. Thus, the baby ape has a flatter face, has a larger brain in proportion to its body size, and carries its trunk more vertically. Perhaps, therefore, early hominids simply became more like babies, retaining infantile characters even through adulthood. Hence, the flat face, large brain, and vertical posture of humans, and the long period of pre-adult dependency. According to this scenario, we may be, in essence, fetal chimps.

The scenario, however, treats these three traits as unrelated except insofar as they are all infantile. And what about all the other characters of infant chimps—their high metabolism and general physiology, for example? Certainly, adult humans lack the metabolism and activity level of infants. And there is no evidence that our teeth are more like baby teeth or our feet more like baby feet. Indeed, all the human characters that are not apparently fetal remain unexplained. Why would only some traits become fetalized and not others? And what about the social and behavioral uniquenesses of humans—where do they come from if they are not part of the general explanation for bipedalism? Brian Shea of Northwestern University has shown that the general features of human anatomy result from several kinds of changes in growth rate and timing, not from an overarching "immaturity" program. Thus, in arriving at a simple explanation for a few disparate features of the human form, the fetal chimp hypothesis raises more questions than it answers.

Aquatic Ape Hypothesis   The aquatic ape hypothesis suffers from the same problems, only in a more extreme form. This scenario argues that the fundamental hominid adaptation is to water. Humans are the only ape that can tolerate a good swim. Perhaps, therefore, our ancestors lived on the lakeshore and waded into the lake. The buoyant properties of the water then could have made them more vertically erect, the argument goes. Further, like the other aquatic mammals, hominids could have lost their fur coat. The subcutaneous fat layer in humans is also explained in this way, a parallel acquisition to whale blubber. Thus, humans are here regarded as "hairy dolphins."

The same problems emerge as did with the fetalization hypothesis. Why would we respond by losing our body fur but not our axillary hair, which contains distinctive odors fairly useless in the water? Why would we lose our hair, like aquatic animals, but not our mobile limbs, as they have? Why have our teeth remained specialized, unlike those of the cetaceans? Why have our eyes and noses remained in front of our faces and our nostrils remained pointing down, unlike other wading animals such as capybaras and hippopotamuses, whose nostrils have moved upward?

Again, disparate characters are specially selected for explanation, without considering the many characters that might be expected to have changed as well but did not. Further, the unique social aspects of humans are systematically ignored, as only the changes in the human body *form* are thought even to require explanation—and only a few of those are addressed. The theory, therefore, raises far more questions than it answers, and we do not find it useful, even though there is no direct evidence to refute it.

Summary

Primates of the past are considerably more diverse than those of the present. The earliest primates of the Paleocene have no living analogs, while the Eocene primates look much more like modern primates. The sparse fossil record of the Oligocene appears to hold the origins of the Anthropoidea and Catarrhini. The early and middle Miocene saw the diversification of the apes to a much greater extent than their present descendants would suggest. The late Miocene is tantalizingly poor in terms of its fossil material but seems to hold the key to the divergence of the bipedal hominids from the other apes in Africa.

Humans emerged from a group of Pliocene australopithecines, who shared an innovation among primates—bipedalism. This change in locomotion involved alterations in most parts of the skeleton, so the behavior is readily recognizable in the fossil record. The earliest bipeds had fairly large canine teeth, so the reduction in size of these teeth occurred after the evolution of bipedalism. Finally, they all had small brains, so the evolution of the human skull was the last of the three major skeletal differences between humans and apes to have occurred. In the next chapter, we discuss the evolution of humans and of culture.

Questions For Review

1. Why do you think there were so many more ape species at any point in the Miocene than there are now?

2. Most primates are small and live in forests: How do you think this affects their chances of being located in the fossil record? If you found one, what parts of the body would you hope to find, and how much information would it take to establish the category into which the animal could be placed?

3. Why do you think early hominids became bipedal? How would you test your ideas about it?

For Further Reading

Conroy, G. (1990). *Primate evolution*. New York: W. W. Norton.

Fleagle, J. (1988). *Primate adaptation and evolution*. San Diego: Academic Press.

Grine, F., (Ed.). (1988). *Evolutionary history of the "robust" australo-pithecines*. Hawthorne, NY: Aldine de Gruyter.

Wood, B., Martin, L., & Andrews, P. (Eds.). (1986). *Major topics in primate and human evolution*. Cambridge, England: Cambridge University Press.

CHAPTER 12

Biological and Cultural Evolution in the Genus *Homo*

Biological and Cultural Evolution in the Genus *Homo*

With the emergence of the genus *Homo*, biological diversity in the hominid family begins to decline. Where in the Pliocene several species, indeed, several genera, of hominids are discernible, we are left with but one species, *Homo erectus*, shortly after the beginning of the Pleistocene. The reason seems to be that having made a commitment to material culture as their principal means of adapting, *Homo erectus* drove other hominid taxa to extinction. This successful competition was not necessarily head to head, but simply involved greater average survival and reproduction of members of this species than of others. Throughout the biological history of the human family, an increase in cultural complexity was accompanied by a reduction in biological variation. First, several species were cut back to one, and then several subspecies of *Homo sapiens* were cut back to one.

Homo erectus migrated from Africa to the rest of the Old World, living in diverse climates. Their descendants are our species, *Homo sapiens*; and *Homo erectus* fossils are difficult to distinguish from early *Homo sapiens* fossils. One variant of this species is the subspecies *Homo sapiens neanderthalensis*, Neanderthals, which flourished in western Europe and the Near East tens of thousands of years ago. The other major variant, *Homo sapiens sapiens*, appears to have originated in Africa more than 100,000 years ago. Thus, the two subspecies coexisted for a considerable amount of time. By 30,000 years ago, however, no Neanderthals remained. Not only is no taxonomic diversity now recognized among hominids at the species level, but none is recognized at the subspecies level, either. All modern humans are part of *Homo sapiens sapiens*.

Early *Homo*

The earliest representatives of our genus, *Homo*, are from East Africa, usually fragmentary, and often difficult to distinguish from gracile australopithecines. Nevertheless, a temporal bone (the rounded bottom of the side of the cranium, which contains several diagnostic features of the bony part of the ear and skull base) from the Chemeron formation near Lake Baringo in Kenya and older than 2.4 million years, is unambiguously diagnosed as *Homo*, not *Australopithecus*.

Generally, *Homo* has smaller teeth (especially molars and premolars), a larger brain, more limited pneumatization (air-filled regions) of the temporal bone and less prognathism when compared with *Australopithecus africanus*. The earliest species recognized as *Homo* is *Homo habilis*, named on the basis of cranial and dental fragments found in

Figure 12-1

KNM-ER-1470, a fossil from Koobi Fora, East Turkana, Kenya, identified as *Homo habilis* and dating from the beginning of the Pleistocene, about 1.7 million years ago.

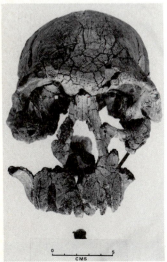

Olduvai Gorge by Louis Leakey in the early 1960s. Other specimens from East Africa, such as ER-1470 (Figure 12–1), found in 1972 by Richard Leakey's team in East Turkana, Kenya, have been attributed to *Homo habilis*. This skull is dated to about 1.8 million years ago.

But is *Homo habilis* the only species of early *Homo*? Many paleoanthropologists now believe that a second species can be recognized, which would bear the name *Homo ergaster*. Some specimens fall clearly into neither *Australopithecus africanus* nor *Homo habilis*, such as ER-1813 (Figure 12–2). Perhaps these anthropologists are over-splitting these hominids, however. Given the fragmentary nature of the remains and the various explanations for morphological variability given in Chapter 10, this is a possibility. But it is equally as likely that over-lumping these specimens into a single species of *Homo* across Africa and over hundreds of thousands of years might obscure patterns of macroevolution that would otherwise be detectable. The resolution must come from formulating better testable hypotheses for the existing fossil specimens and from finding more fossils.

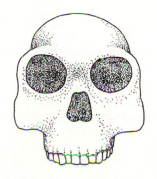

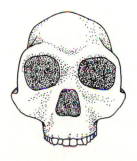

Figure 12-2

Reconstructions of KNM-ER-1470 and 1813. Many anthropologists believe that they are from the same species, but some would place 1813 in a different species, *Homo ergaster.*

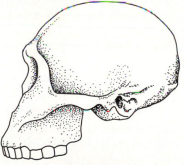

KNM–ER 1470
(reconstruction)

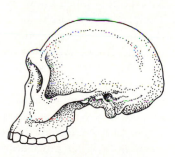

KNM–ER 1813
(reconstruction)

Later cranial remains from South Africa (both Sterkfontein and Swartkrans) are also attributed to early *Homo,* as are the earliest dental remains from Indonesia. These are most likely slightly older than 1 million years but have proven difficult to date accurately.

These hominids were smaller than we are and had smaller brains, though larger teeth, especially rear teeth. Their canines were not particularly large, though larger than those of late *Australopithecus,* as were their incisors. They were, of course, bipedal, like the hominids before and after them. But in one interesting aspect they may have been strikingly primitive—the aspect of body proportions. The recently discovered OH-62 in Olduvai Gorge consists of fragments of an associated skeleton, which identify the organism in question as *Homo habilis* and date to about 1.8 million years ago. But it had relatively long arms (compared with modern humans) like "Lucy," who lived more than a million years earlier. Perhaps, therefore, these early representatives of our genus had primitive body proportions like apes—relatively long arms and short legs—even though they were bipedal tool makers. The body proportions would have evolved into the modern human form (short arms, long legs) with the emergence of *Homo erectus,* for which associated skeletal material is also known.

Early Material Culture

How did these early members of our genus live? Were they furry philosophers or simply clever, upright apes? The information at our disposal in the Lower Paleolithic (the earliest period of the "Old Stone Age") record makes it difficult to address these questions directly but affords us some clues as to the behavioral capabilities of these creatures.

EARLY TOOLS

Over many hominid sites in eastern and southern Africa sharp stones are scattered on the ground and embedded in the ground itself. These stones are the earliest detectable tools. They are simply rocks whose surfaces have been smashed a few times with other rocks, leaving a sharp edge. They are of two kinds: flakes, and cores from which flakes were struck (Figure 12–3). These forms do not occur naturally.

Such tools were first recognized in Olduvai Gorge, along with the remains of *Paranthropus,* in deposits dating to 1.75 million years ago. Louis Leakey, therefore, concluded that these hominids were toolmakers. He changed his mind, however, when early *Homo* was found at the same site, on the assumption that there could have been only one tool-making species at a single time and that it had to be the species most like us. Nothing, however, precludes the possibility that these tools were made by other hominids as well. The earliest tools, from the Middle Awash, Ethiopia, are older than 2.4 million years, which is as old as the earliest known representatives of *Homo.*

Figure 12-3.

Stone tools of the Oldowan industry.

These earliest tools are called **Oldowan** and were probably used for processing vegetable matter, sharpening softer materials (such as wood), and most radically, for skinning and butchering animals. This suggestion is supported by the recognition of cut-marks along the joints and shafts of fossil animal bones found at the same sites as the tools and hominids. Examination of these marks under the electron microscope by Rick Potts and Pat Shipman demonstrated that no other explanation (canine teeth of carnivores, incisor teeth of rodents, erosion, excavation, and so on) was adequate to explain the marks. They were made by sharpened stone edges being deliberately run along the animal's bone. Why? To remove the skin for protection, the meat and bone marrow for food, and perhaps the tendons for tying. At some sites, cut-marked bones are found miles from the nearest tools; at others, the source of the raw material is miles from the site. This suggests that the hominids may have held on to their tools rather than discarding them after a single use.

Archaeologist Nicholas Toth has found that stone tools prepared with blows from the right hand can be distinguished from those prepared with blows from the left. The earliest tool-making hominids at 2 million years ago were overwhelmingly right-handed. Nonhuman primates, by contrast, generally are 50% right-handed and 50% left-handed, while more than 90 percent of modern humans are right-handed.

The fact that hominids apparently butchered animals to supplement their diets does not necessarily indicate that they hunted animals. Many anthropologists feel that the early hominids were not so much hunters as they were scavengers, competing with hyenas, leopards, and other predators on the African savanna. The large game which appear to

Oldowan

Pebble tool industry associated with hominids of the late Pliocene and early Pleistocene.

have been butchered would be daunting to any hominid equipped with only sharp stones. Therefore, hominids probably waited until the large carnivores made a kill and moved in to scavenge the remains of the carcass once the carnivore had had its fill. But it is also unclear whether hominids could have efficiently displaced the other species of scavengers themselves, for there are carnivore marks on some hominid fossils as well as on other faunal remains. The issue remains unresolved.

The stone tools were large pebbles of lava, which, when repeatedly bashed in a particular way, yielded small, sharp flakes and larger cores. Many flakes could be made from a single core, and both kinds of tools were probably used for different purposes. These were probably not the first tools, but simply the first recognizable ones in the archaeological record. Wooden tools and worked animal skins, for example, would not be preserved and therefore cannot be identified, although the earliest tool makers presumably were ingenious enough to make use of them.

Oldowan sites were considered in the 1970s to represent the earliest evidence for "home bases," a particularly human feature, a position advanced by paleoanthropologist Glynn Isaac. More recent considerations of taphonomy and formation processes indicate that such a conclusion is premature. Nevertheless, at sites like FLK Zinj in Olduvai Gorge, hominids were clearly doing something new and interesting, for about 2,500 tools and 60,000 animal bones, many with cut-marks, and mostly remains of the meatiest parts of the animals, have been excavated. The interpretation of these materials has proven controversial in light of modern archaeological theory, but these hominids were clearly processing animal remains in ways and degrees unknown in other primates—except humans.

And Then There Was One: *Homo erectus*

At the same time as *Homo habilis* and *Paranthropus* coexisted at what is now the site of **Koobi Fora**, on the eastern shores of Lake Turkana in Kenya, a third hominid species lived as well. This was the earliest representative of *Homo erectus*, dating to more than 1.6 million years ago.

Homo erectus has a distinct morphology, which varies slightly through time and across space and can be recognized as existing in prehistoric Africa and Asia for more than a million years. The evidence of *Homo erectus* in Europe is more equivocal, consisting of only tools, not skulls. By 1 million years ago, it was the only hominid species remaining.

FIRST DISCOVERY OF *HOMO ERECTUS*

The first discovery of *Homo erectus* was made in 1891 by a Dutch physician, Eugene Dubois, who was searching for fossils in the Dutch colony of Batavia in Java. The skullcap, two teeth, and femur that he found in the Solo riverbeds, near the town of Trinil, came to be known as "**Java Man**" and provoked intense controversy in the 1890s. Dubois interpreted the remains as belonging to a missing link, a new erect ape-man—

Koobi Fora

Major hominid site on the eastern side of Lake Turkana, Kenya.

Java Man

Colloquial name for hominid remains now allocated to *Homo erectus*, from various sites (such as Sangiran and Trinil) in Java.

Pithecanthropus erectus. Other anatomists, however, felt that the fossils were perhaps modern but of a "low" type, while still others attributed the remains to a fossil gibbon. The controversy these fossils engendered drove Dubois into a depression, and he stowed the fossils away, not allowing anyone to see them for the rest of his life. We now know that while Dubois's phylogenetic intuition about the skull was correct, the femur is actually from a different stratum from the skullcap and probably belongs to *Homo sapiens,* not *Homo erectus* after all.

In 1927, a Canadian anatomist named Davidson Black, working in Peking (modern Beijing), encountered a fossil hominid tooth which, he quickly decided, belonged to a new species of hominid—"*Sinanthropus pekinensis*". The following year, from the same cave site at Chou Kou Tien (modern Zhoukoudian), some lower jaw and skull fragments were recovered. And in 1929, a nearly complete skullcap was found. The fossil sample grew, and after Black's death in 1934, supervisory work was carried on by Franz Weidenreich, a German-Jewish refugee.

By 1938, fossil material had been recovered from about forty individuals, including five skullcaps. At the same time, further investigations caried out in Java by G. H. R. von Koenigswald, a Dutch paleontologist, found more fossils like Dubois's original. Weidenreich and von Koenigswald noted the striking resemblances between "Java Man" and "**Peking Man**" in jointly authored papers.

Unfortunately, the situation was becoming tense politically. The Japanese empire had invaded China, and hostilities were open between the Chinese and Japanese in the late 1930s. In mid-1941, fearing for the safety of the valuable fossils and for his life, Weidenreich evacuated China for America. He had already made accurate casts of the fossils and arranged to have the originals transported to the United States for safekeeping. In November, the fossils were packed in crates, delivered to the U.S. Embassy, and placed in the care of the U.S. Marines to be transported from China to the safety of a U.S. naval base on the SS *President Harrison*. That ship left port on December 8, 1941—which was December 7, 1941, on the other side of the International Date Line— Pearl Harbor Day. Those "Peking Man" fossils have never been seen since.

Fortunately, Weidenreich's casts and reconstructions were of excellent quality (Figure 12–4), and more recent Chinese excavations have found many other fossils from the same cave. In fact, skull parts recovered in May 1966 from the identical locality as the prewar excavations fit perfectly with the casts of one of the incomplete skulls found in 1934. Six skulls, 12 other cranial fragments, 15 mandibular fragments, 157 teeth, and 13 postcranial bones have now been recorded from various places in the cave.

Louis Leakey found other specimens in East Africa very similar to the Asian fossils, coming from the higher strata of Olduvai Gorge. *Homo erectus* has also been found at other sites in East Africa, and the most

Peking Man

Colloquial name for hominid remains now allocated to *Homo erectus*, from the lower part of the cave site at Zhoukoudian.

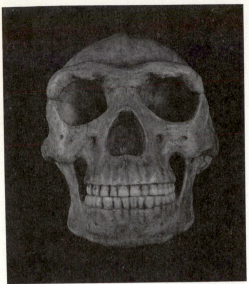

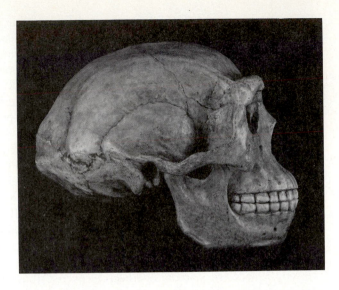

Figure 12-4

The cast of a skull of Peking Man, from the cave at Zhoukoudian.

complete skeletal remains have come from around Lake Turkana. These African fossils, though found later than the Asian fossils, are geologically older, with *Homo erectus* from East Turkana dated to more than 1.6 million years ago, from Olduvai Gorge about 1.2 million years ago, and from Ternifine in northern Africa about 0.6 million years ago. Of the Asian specimens, none is reliably dated to over 0.8 million years ago, and most are 0.4 to 0.5 million years old.

WHO WAS *HOMO ERECTUS*?

Homo erectus displays a great deal of variability, which is partially attributable to microevolutionary divergence over time and across continents. Nevertheless, this species shows a broad continuity of features which distinguish it from those who came before and those who came after.

Skull Features   A *Homo erectus* skull can be fairly easily identified (Figure 12–5). Its teeth are intermediate in size between early *Homo* and modern *Homo*. But its skull bones are very thick, up to one-half-inch thick in adult males, and the shape of its skull is quite distinct. While a modern human skull is round in appearance, the *Homo erectus* skull is long and low, with prominent brows at the front and a sharply angled occipital region in the back. And while a modern human face is relatively small and flat, the *Homo erectus* face is large and protruding. Much of the appearance of the *Homo erectus* skull is attributable to smaller brain size and much heavier cranial and neck musculature than our own. The angled occiput contains a wide attachment region for strong nuchal mus-

Post-orbital constriction

"Pinching" between the brows and braincase in a skull, when viewed from above.

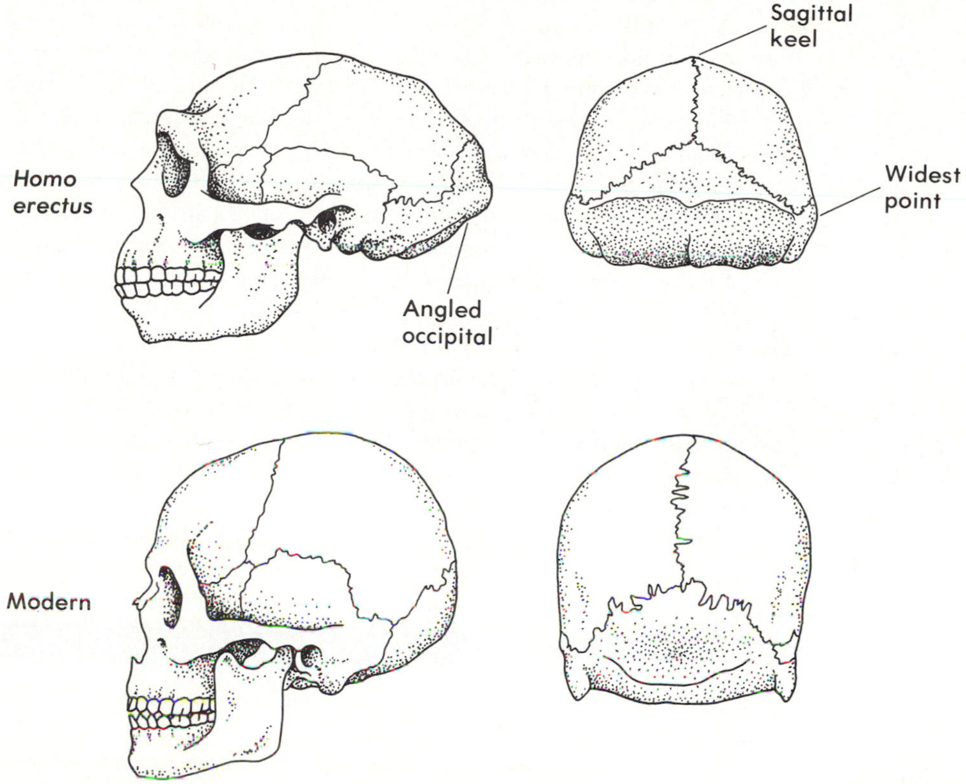

Figure 12-5

Homo erectus and modern human skulls.

Sagittal keel

Homo erectus

Widest point

Angled occipital

Modern

cles, and the attachment of heavy chewing muscles left horizontal stria-
tions on the parietal bones. The large brows and small frontal region of
the skull resulted in a **post-orbital constriction** when seen from above.
The extreme thickness of the skull bones appears to cause a bulge down
the midline of the skull, the sagittal keel. The jaws and teeth were larger
and stronger than our own, although post-cranially, the remains of *Homo
erectus* and modern *Homo sapiens* are not very different. One curiosity,
however, is that the femur of *Homo erectus* had a considerably different
cross-sectional shape from those of modern humans.

Skeleton   A nearly complete skeleton from West Turkana (WT-
15000), about 1.6 million years old, tells us other things (Figure 12–6).
The skull possesses an impression of Broca's area, a part of the brain lacking in apes that appears to be related to language capacity in humans.
Further, the skeleton is that of a 12-year-old boy and is nearly as tall as a
modern American boy of the same age. The limb proportions are virtually the same as those in modern humans and strikingly different from
those of *Homo habilis* (OH-62), which it probably overlapped in time.
Christopher Ruff of Johns Hopkins argues that WT-15000 shows the

Figure 12-6

WT-15000, skull of a very early *Homo erectus* youth.

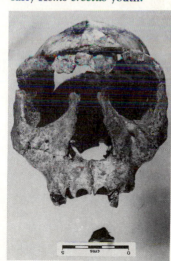

effects of Allen's Rule (Chapter 9), where life near the equator favors a linear body build in *Homo erectus* as in modern populations of *Homo sapiens*: a case of parallel microevolution.

Most anthropologists maintain that the majority of cranial expansion in hominid evolution occurred in *Homo erectus*, whose earliest representatives have cranial capacities between 800–900 cc and whose latest representatives have skull sizes well within the range of modern humans, more than 1200 cc. Further, the earliest *Homo erectus* specimens show many similarities to early *Homo* in East Africa, while the latest show many similarities to Neanderthals. Thus, there appears to be considerable anagenesis in this species. Generalizations about this species may be difficult to make because the species spans so much time, space, and anatomy.

HOW DID *HOMO ERECTUS* LIVE?

Since *Homo erectus* persisted a long time and occupied many different lands (Table 12–1), there was certainly no uniformity in life-style for the species. Considering the diversity of life-style of modern humans, who have not been around nearly as long as *Homo erectus* survived, this conclusion should not be surprising.

Tools   The most uniform aspect of the culture of this species was a sharpened, flat, usually teardrop-shaped, pointed stone tool worked on

Table 12–1

Some Major Sites of Homo erectus *and Their Approximate Dates*

Millions of Years Ago	Africa	Indonesia	China	Europe
0.3				Archaic *Homo sapiens*
0.4		Ngandong		
0.5			Zhoukoudian	
0.6	Ternifine	Djetis	Lantian	
0.7	Olduvai Bed IV	Trinil	Yuanmou	
			Gongwangling	
0.8				
0.9				
1.0				
	Swartkrans			
1.1				
1.2	Olduvai Bed II			
1.3				
1.4				
1.5				
1.6	Lake Turkana			

Figure 12-7

Acheulean hand-axes. The one on the right is more recent and shows marked improvement in tool-making efficiency.

both surfaces (Figure 12–7). Many other kinds of stone tools were used by *Homo erectus,* but this **Acheulean hand-axe** is the most characteristic. This type of tool is found in prehistoric sites over most of the Old World, although it is curiously absent from southeastern Asia. Other aspects of the Acheulean tool-kit include scrapers, cleavers, and many other kinds of bifaces—tools worked on both surfaces. Paleolithic archaeologists find that through time, the Acheulean bifaces became thinner, flatter, and more symmetrical, in short, more aesthetically refined and probably more efficient.

It is not clear how the tool was actually used because the side that was presumably held was also sharpened, which would be counterproductive. Perhaps it was hafted to a wooden or bone handle, or perhaps it was a projectile. Perhaps it was even flung. It is also possible that these hand-axes were not themselves tools, but rather cores off of which sharp tools were cut. In any case, their manufacture reflects a degree of planning and forethought not apparent in earlier hominids, while their stability (more than a million years of using the same tools) suggests a degree of behavioral consistency not found in later hominids. Still, these tools reflect a growing efficiency in the use of raw materials, providing a much greater length of usable sharp edge than did their Oldowan counterparts.

Hunting   The new technology probably enabled this species to hunt more successfully and spend less time foraging and scavenging. Microscopic studies of wearing of the edges of hand-axes at European sites indicate their use in butchery, which supports this idea. At the site of Olorgesailie, in East Africa, giant gelada baboons were possibly butchered by these hominids, who left us many tools at the site but, unfortunately, no fossils of themselves; but one needs to consider taphonomic processes here.

Acheulean hand-axe

A relatively large biface stone tool of roughly triangular shape, manufactured during the late Lower Paleolithic and early Middle Paleolithic. Associated with *Homo erectus.*

Distinguishing active hunting from scavenging remains difficult, however. The problem is to recognize immediate access to a dead animal from delayed access—but there is a possible solution. Observation of contemporary hunting and scavenging indicates that certain parts of the dead animals' bodies—including certain bones—are chewed and eaten first. Other parts and bones are eaten only later, and still others are commonly left behind at the place of the animal's death. For instance, forelegs are often taken before hindlegs, and vertebrae are often left behind by primary predators. Tabulating the number of each type of bone at a *Homo erectus* site can thus suggest whether the meat was obtained by actually hunting and killing a prey or merely by picking up what was left behind by a predator.

Similar evidence is available from tabulating the number of young victims relative to adults. Hunters, both hominid and otherwise, usually select the young whenever possible because they are less dangerous and easier to kill. Scavengers, by contrast, take whatever is available. A *Homo erectus* site containing the bones of many adolescent animals would suggest hunting, therefore, while one containing a mix of adolescents and adults might reflect scavenging activity. These inferences obviously remain tentative, and there is no sure way of determining how meat was, in fact, obtained. As archaeologist Lewis Binford has cautioned, there is often no simple way even to recognize hominid from non-hominid activities.

Skeletons   Another suggestive piece of fossil evidence for this behavioral shift is a female *Homo erectus* partial skeleton from East Turkana, ER-1808. In the longbone shafts of this specimen is evidence of trauma to the skeleton, particularly to the cross-sectional structure of the bones. Apparently, she had an affliction to the membrane of the bone, which led to bleeding and clotting and to formation of bone in the blood clots. This diagnosis is consistent with a large dietary excess of vitamin A, which is easy to get by eating the livers of carnivores. (It is also consistent with severe infection.) Nevertheless, since bony invasion of the blood clots is detectable in the fossil, the woman must have survived for a short period with the disease in order for ossification to have occurred. The only way she could have survived for even a few weeks is by having water and provisions brought to her—which might tell us something about society among *Homo erectus*.

HOMO ERECTUS AND THE GLACIERS: OTHER ASPECTS OF CULTURE

The Pleistocene environment posed a series of challenges for tool-using hominids emigrating from Africa, who may have reached Israel ('Ubeidiya) and Europe (Soleihac and Le Vallonnet) by 1 million years ago. The inference about *Homo erectus* in Europe is problematic, as no clear European fossils from this taxon are known; there are archaeological sites that contain *Homo erectus* tools, but none that contain hominid fossils (Figure 12–8). Nevertheless, in these more northerly latitudes there was more than the necessities of life, nutrition, and protection to worry about. It also was considerably cooler than the African tropics, where *Homo erectus* originated. Indeed, glaciers have advanced to cover much of the Northern Hemisphere and then retreated about every 115,000 years.

Glaciation   The advance of the glaciers is due to the cyclic nature of the earth's climatic patterns. Glaciation affects many aspects of the planet's ecology, so its history can be traced in many different ways. For example, the more ice that is taken up by glaciers, the less water is in the oceans, and the sea level drops accordingly. Particularly sensitive to such changes are microscopic invertebrates called foraminifera, some of which live at the bottom of the sea and the shells of which yield information on the composition of the ocean (and by implication, the extent of glaciation) at the time they lived.

There was not a single Ice Age, but a great many Ice Ages, or glacials, separated by climatically milder interglacials. Although *Homo erectus* probably did not interact directly with the glaciers themselves, the rest of the world was cooler during glacial periods. The geographical expansion of the species during this period thus seems even more remarkable and is probably a testimony to the quality of its cultural abilities to adapt to new environments.

Climate Changes and Emigration   In a few instances, the changes in climate occurring during the time of *Homo erectus* might have helped them emigrate from Africa. The cooler and wetter conditions in northern Africa, for instance, might have transformed the Sahara region from a desert (as it is today, also) to a savanna with enough water to allow habitation and passage. Likewise, the periodic lowering of sea level formed land bridges, where before there was shallow water, making the movement of *Homo erectus* into new territories easier. Still, it was the growing reliance on nonbiological means of adaptation—on culture and societal cooperation—that played the primary role in making *Homo erectus* the first transcontinental hominid.

Generally, contemporary tropical peoples place a greater dietary emphasis on plant foods than on animal foods. We have already considered in *Homo erectus* the possible growing reliance on hunting over foraging and scavenging, and this activity would have demanded an increasing ability to cooperate and to make decisions in the face of danger. These abilities, furthermore, would have been most important when large game were pursued. The large fauna would have been more extensively pursued in the colder environments, where many plants and smaller animals could not live. While the evidence remains questionable in many instances, there is little doubt that cultural capabilities were being exercised and expanded in *Homo erectus*.

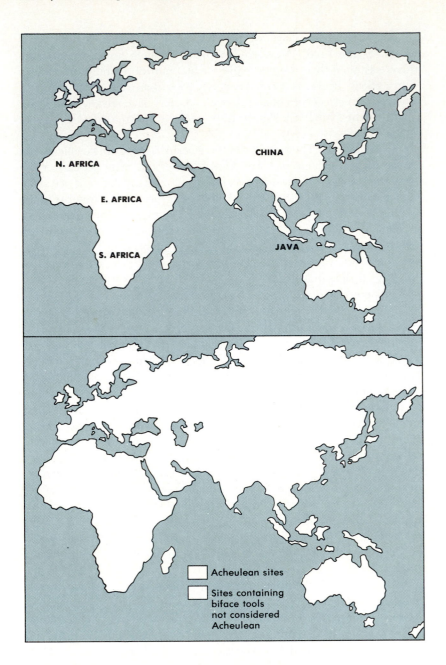

Figure 12-8

The distribution of *Homo erectus* fossils, Acheulean stone tools, and non-Acheulean stone tools. Note that no classic *Homo erectus* fossils are found in present-day Europe.

Fire   Good evidence does exist for the use and control of fire by *Homo erectus*. Probably no species had the ability to make fire on demand until the emergence of our own species. Yet for a very long time, hominids had obtained fire—and used, and controlled it—from natural occurrences such as lightning.

In sites such as Chesowanja in East Africa, some burnt clay is found with Oldowan tools from about 1.4 million years ago. Andrew Sillen and C. K. Brain have reported that fire was probably used as early as 1.2 million years ago at Swartkrans Cave in South Africa. The evidence consists of a number of antelope bones, apparently burned at a temperature too high to have been a natural occurrence. Although it is not certain, the most likely user of the fire there was *Homo erectus*. Direct and persuasive evidence for the use and control of fire comes from numerous sites hundreds of thousands of years later. Burnt materials, and even apparent hearths, have been found at the sites of Zhoukoudian, Yuanmou, and Lantian in China; Terra Amata and Vallonet in France; Torralba and Ambrona in Spain; and elsewhere. By about 300,000 years ago, fire had been controlled throughout the Old World.

Fire had a number of uses for *Homo erectus*, as it had (and has) for *Homo sapiens*. First, fire provided warmth in a fairly cold climate. While it may not have been a necessity in equatorial Africa, it was a definite necessity in the northern, Ice Age lands of Europe and Asia. (The same climate probably made clothing a necessity also, for the first time.) Besides warmth for comfort, fire was likely used to scare other animals out of desirable caves, which offered additional protection from the elements. Fire might have also helped *Homo erectus* hunt these animals, many of which were large and dangerous. Fires could have been used to drive animals into canyons or swamps, in which they would have been easier prey. There is, in addition, evidence to suggest that wooden spears were hardened in fire and thus made more effective as weapons.

Fire was also used for protection during those times when the hunter *Homo erectus* became the hunted. Predators would probably avoid the circle of light and probably flee when a burning branch or cinder was hurled in their direction. The hominids using fire were safer at night than their ancestors had ever been.

In addition, fire was used for cooking, and while we may never know when this cultural universal emerged, there is little question that it allowed *Homo erectus* to eat many new foods that would otherwise have been too tough or indigestible. Cooking made it possible for hominids to thrive in environments that were once marginal and to survive marginally in environments that were once prohibitive, by allowing a broader range of foods to be exploited.

Finally, it is likely that the use and control of fire gave *Homo erectus* a greater degree of behavioral freedom—a freedom that only a cultural adaptation can provide. No longer did the day's activities have to end with the setting of the sun. Fire offered a light around which the hominid group could gather and work, or simply socialize. Gathering around a fire and telling stories, or participating in rituals, is a widespread feature of modern peoples—and it does not seem unreasonable to suppose that fires were put to similar use by *Homo erectus*.

Shelter   The cold climate of Europe and China made shelter a necessity as well, and when protective caves could not be found or could not be used, these hominids appear to have constructed some fairly large and durable habitations. Some form of shelter might have been used by earlier hominids, for example, by *Homo habilis* in Olduvai Gorge, although the evidence is far from clear.

Some of the most widely cited evidence for shelters comes from the site of Terra Amata, in Nice, France. There, archaeologist Henry de Lumley has excavated numerous Acheulean stone tools, concentrations of animal bones (but no hominid fossils), and structural remains that consist of rows of post holes, several hearths, and a wall of stone. His reconstruction of the site shows a number of large, oval huts made from wooden posts anchored by stone in the ground (Figure 12–9). Each of

Figure 12-9

An artist's reconstruction of a dwelling at Terra Amata, along with a floor plan (after Haviland, 1989).

these was up to 50 feet long and 18 feet wide and probably housed as many as twenty hominids. In addition, stratigraphic and pollen evidence suggest that the huts were occupied repeatedly for as many as a dozen years, primarily in the spring and early summer, about 300,000 years ago.

Since de Lumley's excavations, a number of archaeologists have questioned his conclusions because of the complexity of the stratigraphic record at Terra Amata. There is growing concern that numerous site disturbances have obliterated all original living surfaces, making it very difficult to interpret the patterns of past behaviors. Still, an important fact to consider is that, even though there is the problem of formation processes to consider, there is little question that *Homo erectus* at this latitude *needed* shelters to a greater extent than did their forebears in more equatorial climates. Indeed, sites such as Terra Amata can more reliably be considered home bases—places to which individuals would return after each day, and at which the injured or the ill could remain. This would also imply that these hominids were living a more stable and organized lifestyle than their ancestors.

Social Stability   Hominids had been living in social groups well before the emergence of *Homo erectus*—indeed, modern nonhuman primates live in complex social groups, so this is not surprising. Still, certain unique patterns of modern human society emerged in *Homo erectus*.

Perhaps the temperate climate into which *Homo erectus* migrated played a role in requiring a greater dietary reliance on meat and therefore larger group sizes, greater dependence upon food sharing and cooperation, and perhaps even promotion of kinship systems and reciprocal economic obligations. Or perhaps these aspects of culture were present in *Homo erectus* before emigrating from the tropics.

Changes in the biology of the hominids themselves may have played as important a role. The only *Homo erectus* infant skull, from Modjokerto in Java, has the ossification characteristic of a modern human six-year-old in the ear region but of a two-year-old in the closure of the fontanelle at the top of the skull (there are no teeth). This suggests that infants were not as immature as modern infants of comparable age, or at least not in all their parts. The period of immaturity and learning in humans is uniquely long among primates, and this *Homo erectus* individual was ambiguously immature. Yet *Homo erectus* was depending more on symbolic learning than on genetics, the result being a better ability to communicate and socialize. And as we already know, this growing dependence on learning correlated with the evolution of an even larger brain at maturity.

Homo sapiens

Following the migration of *Homo erectus* from Africa and subsequent colonization of the rest of the Old World, the human lineage is effectively one species. However, about 300,000 years ago, another colonization

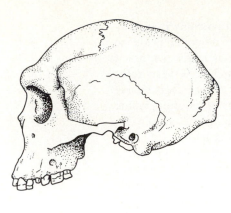

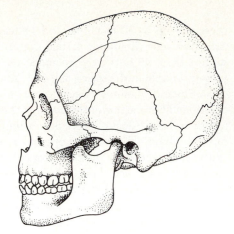

Kabwe
(Broken Hill, Rhodesian Man)

Modern human

Figure 12-10

The Kabwe ("Rhodesian Man" or Broken Hill) skull, a non-Neanderthal archaic *Homo sapiens,* contrasted to modern human.

seems to have begun, involving the replacement of these *Homo erectus* hominids by slightly larger-brained, thinner-skulled, smaller-jawed populations—archaic *Homo sapiens*.

Anthropologists currently divide the species *Homo sapiens* into three broad categories: 1) archaic *Homo sapiens* who are not Neanderthals; 2) Neanderthals, who are archaic but different from the other archaic populations; and 3) anatomically modern *Homo sapiens*. These categories reflect differentiation interpreted to have arisen below the level of the species. Thus, archaic *Homo sapiens* is properly regarded as a subspecies, although it is not formally named; Neanderthals are the subspecies *Homo sapiens neanderthalensis*, and moderns are the subspecies *Homo sapiens sapiens*. Of these, all but the last are extinct, and therefore, all modern and historic human populations are classified within the same subspecies, *Homo sapiens sapiens*.

ARCHAIC HOMO SAPIENS

Archaic (non-Neanderthal) *Homo sapiens* is distinguished from *Homo erectus* by a more rounded occipital region in the rear of the skull, a larger brain, greater bending, or flexion, of the base of the skull, and a higher skull vault. Behaviorally, the species *Homo sapiens* is usually associated with a flake tool culture, although many of the early *Homo sapiens* sites contain Acheulean tools (and some Asian *Homo erectus* sites contain flake tools). This is testimony to the gradual nature of evolutionary change and to the difficulty in attempting to match tools to taxa in a one-to-one fashion.

Several archaeological sites are attributed to archaic *Homo sapiens*, but these are generally difficult to date precisely. The majority of fossil finds are isolated specimens, so we cannot say much about behavioral changes during this time.

A face and parietal bone found in the Bodo beds in central Ethiopia in 1978 display features essentially anatomically intermediate between *Homo erectus* and *Homo sapiens* and are usually classified as archaic *Homo sapiens*. Near Lake Ndutu in Tanzania, a similar skull with features similar to both earlier *Homo erectus* and later *Homo sapiens* was found in 1973. Both of these are similar to a south African specimen found in 1921 at the site of Kabwe or Broken Hill in Zambia, with massive brow ridges, thick skull bones, and an occipital torus, yet a large cranial capacity of 1,280 cc. This skull also, interestingly, shows some of the earliest evidence of dental cavities but has been very difficult to date precisely (Figure 12–10).

In Asia, specimens from the Narmada Valley in India, Ngandong in Indonesia, and several sites in China suggest that the representatives of the genus *Homo* who lived between 400,000 and 100,000 years were considerably more modern looking than earlier *Homo erectus*. Similarly, the earliest fossils of archaic *Homo sapiens* in Europe come from this time and are widespread and fairly intermediate in morphology. Specimens are known from all over Europe, including the sites of Petralona in Greece; Verteszollos in Hungary; Steinheim, Bilzingsleben, and Mauer (the famous "Heidelberg Man", known from a mandible) in Germany; Biache, La Chaise, and Arago in France; Swanscombe in England; and Ibeas in Spain (Figure 12–11).

Figure 12-11

Non-Neanderthal archaic skulls: Steinheim from Europe, Dali from East Asia, Bodo from Africa, and Swanscombe from England.

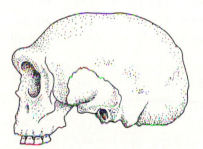

Steinheim skull

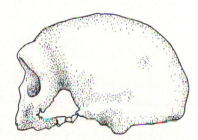

Dali skull

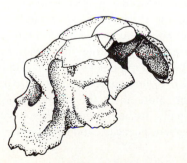

Bodo skull

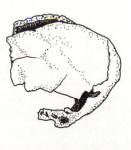

Swanscombe skull

Incontestable evidence for the widespread use of fire is abundant in many cave and open-air sites of early *Homo sapiens*. A few concentrations of artifacts are present at the site of Bilzingsleben in Germany, each about 2–3 meters in diameter, next to the remains of hearths and possibly walls. Similarly, the cave site of Le Lazaret in France has a concentration of artifacts and hearths between the cave wall and a line of boulders, probably used as a windbreak. Around the hearths are concentrations of carnivore teeth and small shells, which might be all that remain of animal skins and seaweed mats.

It is thought that different populations of archaic *Homo sapiens* diverged through time, such that the ones living in Western Europe had descendants who were noticeably different from their contemporaries elsewhere. These divergent Europeans are known as Neanderthals and are different enough from all modern people that we taxonomically place them in a separate subspecies. Modern humans appear to be descended not from these Pleistocene Europeans, but from their "cousins" in Africa.

THE NEANDERTHALS

Western Europe, during the Ice Ages, was populated by a unique and famous group of hominids. Named for a skullcap found in 1856 in the Neander valley of Germany, the Neanderthals have become very much a part of our folklore, often as savage or brutish contrasts to modern humans. There are, as we shall see, some interesting anatomical and cultural contrasts one can locate between Neanderthals and ourselves—but little to suggest that they were more brutish or more savage. Still, the relative lack of substantial differences between Neanderthals and ourselves has occasionally been overstated, as, for example, in a famous quotation by Straus and Cave in 1957:

> If he could be reincarnated and placed in a New York subway—provided he were bathed, shaved and dressed in modern clothing—it is doubtful whether he would attract any more attention than some of its other denizens.

Neanderthals, or *Homo sapiens neanderthalensis*, are found only in Europe and the circum-Mediterranean area and fall within a timespan of 130,000 to about 35,000 years ago. They developed a number of anatomical specializations that appear to preclude them from direct modern human ancestry. Consequently, they are considered to be a side branch that evolved from a European archaic population rather than from an African archaic population, as we did. All modern humans are more similar anatomically to archaic African *Homo sapiens* than to the Neanderthals. Yet we know considerably more about the Neanderthals than about our direct ancestors, principally because so many sites have been excavated in Europe since the nineteenth century, and because they buried their dead.

ANATOMICAL FEATURES OF NEANDERTHALS

What are some of the anatomical features that would tell us we are looking at a Neanderthal and not at an ordinary subway rider? First, the skull
has a long, low shape, unlike the high, rounded skull of anatomically
modern humans (Figure 12–12). Skull shape is a variable character
within and among modern humans, but no living person has a skull
shaped much like a Neanderthal. In the front, the Neanderthal skull is
characterized by very prominent brow ridges and little or no forehead,

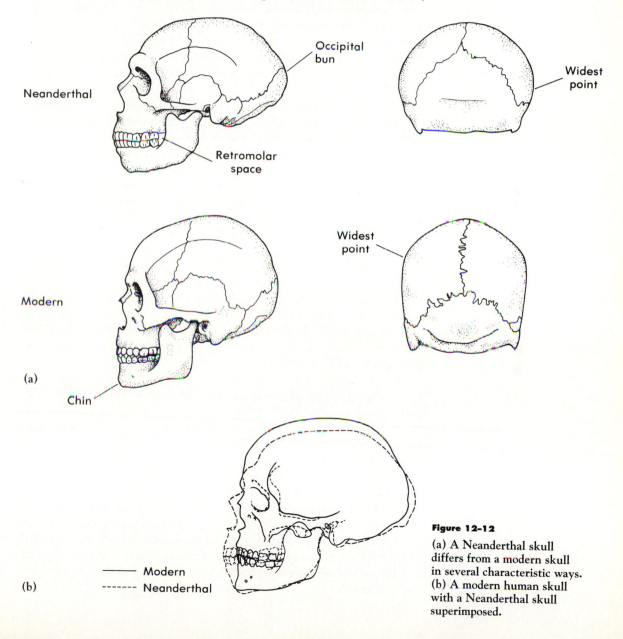

Figure 12-12

(a) A Neanderthal skull
differs from a modern skull
in several characteristic ways.
(b) A modern human skull
with a Neanderthal skull
superimposed.

while in the rear is a rounded "bun" in the occipital region. Above the bun is a small groove, the suprainiac depression, diagnostic of Neanderthals. The cranium is more rounded, or globular, than earlier populations, in which there was pronounced angularity of the skull's shape. Neanderthals are also notable for having small mastoid processes, behind the ear.

The Neanderthal face is large and, unlike the modern human face, is located more in front of the skull (anterior) than under it. Indeed, the entire dental anatomy is more anteriorly placed. Neanderthal front teeth are generally very well worn, indicating heavy usage. By contrast, modern humans tend to wear front and rear teeth about equally. Neanderthal rear teeth are often taurodont, which means they have an enlarged pulp cavity and fused roots. And their rear teeth are located farther forward than ours.

Our third molars, or wisdom teeth, often have difficulty erupting because of the crowding in our jaws. The modern human jaw has been pushed back and has shrunk—but it has regressed *faster* than it has shrunk—so that our third molars now often become impacted. Neanderthals had no such problem. They not only had plenty of room for their wisdom teeth, but extra room as well—a **retromolar space** behind the third molar. On the other hand, Neanderthals also had much larger sinuses than we do—so any perverse amusement they might have received from seeing their cousins with impacted wisdom teeth was probably offset during the pollen season!

Neanderthals are also very well known postcranially and fall outside the range of modern human variation in several features. Most of these features are associated simply with being short, stocky, and very muscular. They had heavy spines on the cervical vertebrae, where the neck muscles attach; and massive shoulder and upper-arm muscles, which appear as morphological differences in the scapula. Likewise, their ribs were thick and defined a barrel-shaped thorax, and their femurs were thick and bowed.

The Neanderthal pelvis has been of considerable interest. The pubic bones are very long, creating a larger pelvic outlet than modern humans have. Is this due, perhaps, to differences in length of gestation, or in locomotion? None of the above, argues Karen Rosenberg of the University of Delaware. Neanderthals were short, stocky, heavy people, and such people have longer pubic bones, give birth to bigger babies, and have larger pelvic outlets than do populations that have other body builds. While Neanderthals are outside the range of variation in modern human populations, the trends are present in modern humans; and one need only extrapolate the data to the Neanderthal body build. There seems to be no need to invoke different adaptations to explain the pubis and birth canal of Neanderthals, although it still is a diagnostic morphological feature.

retromolar space

A gap behind the third molar and ascending ramus of the jaw that is absent in modern humans.

MATERIAL CULTURE AND SOCIETY

The stone tools manufactured by early *Homo sapiens* were not very different from those of *Homo erectus*, consisting of similar-looking hand-axes and other bifaces. Neither is it thought that early *Homo sapiens* society was very different. Gradually, however, a new lithic technology and a new set of life-styles emerged.

Tools and Tool Manufacturing   The tool industry associated with the Neanderthals, during a period of time known as the Middle Paleolithic and dating from about 300,000 to about 35,000 years B.P., is called the **Mousterian** (Figure 12–13). It is named after the Neanderthal site of Le Moustier, in France. In several ways, the industry appears to be an "improvement" over the preceding Acheulean—traditional techniques were refined, and new ones were added.

First, a greater variety of tools was being made by Neanderthal times, reflecting an increased specialization of tool manufacture and use. Increased specialization, in turn, implies increased effectiveness at accomplishing any particular task. As many as sixty Mousterian tool types have been recognized by archaeologists, led by François Bordes, the leading figure in Middle Paleolithic prehistory in this century. All-purpose tools were no longer the rule.

Second, Mousterian tool-manufacturing techniques led to a more efficient use of stone, in that a greater length of useful sharp edge was produced per unit of raw material. This trend emerged with the Acheulean (which was more efficient than the Oldowan) and continued into the Upper Paleolithic.

Third, Neanderthals were becoming even more selective in the stones chosen for tool manufacture, a selectivity demanded by the diver-

Mousterian

The tool industry associated with the Neanderthals, primarily of western Europe and dating to the Middle Paleolithic.

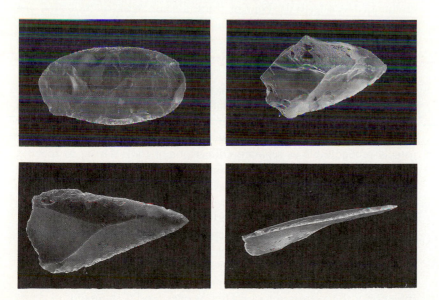

Figure 12–13.

Characteristic Mousterian stone tools.

sity in tool types. For the earliest hominid tool makers, the process was a spontaneous activity brought about by immediate need. By the time of the Neanderthals, it was a fully planned exercise with well-established rules and procedures and freed from the constraints of the specific materials present in the immediate area—raw materials and prepared cores could be taken and used anywhere.

The development of tool making as a foresighted procedure, and not merely a spontaneous one, is an important development in human cultural evolution. Many Neanderthal stone tools (and those of their contemporaries outside Europe) were made from a prepared core—a stone that was shaped beforehand and from which the characteristic high-quality tools were struck as needed. This multiphase process of tool manufacture reflects that Neanderthals were capable of forethought, abstract thought, and a certain degree of patience.

The best-known prepared core and flake tools were produced by the **Levallois** technique, which consisted of the following steps (Figure 12–14): (1) choosing an oval-shaped stone and chipping away its perimeter, (2) creating the striking platform by striking chips off the face of the stone, and (3) repeatedly striking flakes off the core, at the base of the striking platform. The flakes thus created are thinner, sharper, and more regular than those from earlier technologies and need no subsequent modifications.

Other means of tool manufacture were refined by Neanderthals, many of which involved subsequent modifications to the edges of particular tools, a process known as retouch. Not only were a greater number of tool types being made—different combinations of these types were being used at different locales, at different times, and possibly by different groups of Neanderthals. Four of these assemblages, or tool-kits, are presently recognized: (1) *Mousterian of Acheulean Tradition*, which contains up to 40 percent hand-axes; (2) *Quina Mousterian*, which contains few hand-axes but a preponderance of another tool, called the side scraper, and which has a distinctive form of retouch; (3) *Typical Mousterian*, which generally contains about the same number of each tool type; and (4) *Denticulate Mousterian*, named for a notched or toothed manner of retouch on up to 80 percent of its tools. These four assemblages appear in many sites throughout western Europe, although they are usually recognizable as separate collections of tools dating to specific times. Individual strata often contain a single, recognizable tool assemblage, although all four assemblages often occur (at different times) throughout the strata of a single site.

These observations—or properly, their interpretation—have led to one of the best-known (and most creative) debates in archaeology. On one hand, the late François Bordes argued that these different assemblages represent different ethnic or cultural groups in western Europe, quite isolated from one another and thus capable of maintaining the integrity of their separate tool traditions over tens of thousands of years.

Levallois

A technique of stone tool manufacture dating to the Middle Paleolithic and involving the preparation of a core from which numerous and uniformly shaped flake tools could be struck.

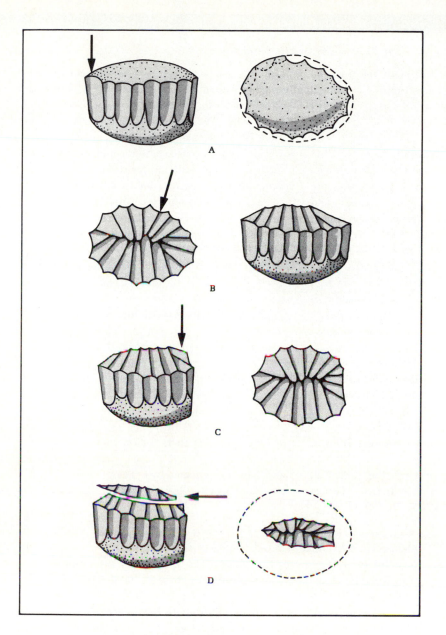

A

B

C

D

Figure 12-14.
The Levallois technique.
(a) Chipping away the perimeter
of the stone. (b) Creating the
striking platform. (c) Finishing
the striking platform. (d) Striking a flake tool off the core
(after Haviland, 1989).

On the other hand, Lewis Binford has argued that these assemblages represent different activities performed by the same basic groups of people,
although carried out at either different sites or different times. As you
might expect, it has proven to be a difficult question to resolve, and currently, it appears that the answer is more complex than either side once

Issues in Anthropology 12–1

Neanderthals in Fact and Fantasy.

The Neanderthal Man had plenty of brains but somehow they did him no good.

Will Cuppy

We have all seen the cartoons, the movies, and the paperback books that depict primitive people, especially our biologial ancestors. We all recognize the ubiquitous "cave man"—dumb, brutish, and carrying a club in one hand while pulling an unconscious woman by the hair with the other. Sometimes these "cave men" are shown fighting dinosaurs—their creators having misplaced about 60 million years of prehistory for the sake of high drama. Even when dinosaurs are acknowledged to have been long extinct, the Neanderthals exercise a fascination for the dramatic and literary imagination.

Some of these fictional depictions are more sophisticated than others. William Golding's moving novel *The Inheritors* depicts the chance meeting between a group of Neanderthals and a group of *Homo sapiens sapiens*. Told from the perspective of the Neanderthals, we encounter two *very* different creatures.

The Neanderthals are described as somewhat intelligent apes. Fur covers their bodies. They do not walk completely upright and are comfortable for long periods of time in the trees. They eat plants primarily, occasionally scavenge meat, and do not hunt. Their language is simple, consisting of short, direct statements. It is difficult for them to express complex concepts, to themselves and to one another. It is also difficult for them to think ahead farther than tomorrow. They are afraid of water.

Yet they display some recognizably human qualities. They grieve when one of their members dies and bury their dead with offerings and ritual. They practice a simple religion that stresses females and fertility. They are sensitive and caring animals and have much concern for group members who are in trouble or ill.

The biologically modern humans, *Homo sapiens sapiens*, are very different in Golding's depiction. They have hair, not fur, and much of their skin is visible. They are not as large or strong as the Neanderthals but are fully bipedal. Their sense of smell is less developed, although their use of language is advanced. They wear clothing and jewelry, have many artifacts (including spears and the bow and arrow), paint their bodies, construct shelters, and dance in elaborate rituals. They drink alcohol and fight among themselves. They construct canoes and fearlessly move upon the water.

claimed. For example, Harold Dibble of the University of Pennsylvania has shown that some of the differences among the assemblages may reflect simply the extent and manner of reuse (Chapter 10) of certain tool types.

One constructive result of this debate has been the subsequent work in ethnoarchaeology that Binford and his colleagues have conducted among the Inuit (Eskimo). Binford reasoned that the best resolution to the issue would be found by studying people who were having to adapt culturally to the same sort of environment as did the Neanderthals of glaciated Europe. And who better than the Inuit, gatherer-hunters (mostly hunters) coping with the Arctic? As you will see in Chapter 16, efforts such as Binford's have given archaeologists some new perspectives on site formation and the nature of the archaeological record.

The meeting between Neanderthals and moderns is tragic. The latter, depicted as fierce fighters when threatened, kill the former, who are gentle, though confused. Thus, in Golding's view, the Neanderthals were replaced through violence, which is dramatic, if not documentable. Likewise, it is not supported scientifically that modern humans had lighter skin than Neanderthals, as Golding describes it. This is, unfortunately, not the only novel that carries this distinction.

The far more popular *Clan of the Cave Bear* by Jean Auel (along with three sequels and a movie adaptation) tells a similar story of Neanderthals and *Homo sapiens sapiens* becoming aware of each other. Ayla, the modern human protagonist, is orphaned as a young girl by an earthquake, wanders alone awhile, and is found and raised by others—Neanderthals. They have memories stored in their occipital buns and do not practice ventral–ventral sex (similar to the Neanderthals in the film "Quest For Fire"). Throughout the story, she teaches them better ways to live and introduces them to Paleolithic feminism. Many of the Neanderthals, especially the males, resent and resist her, but her superior brains win out in the end. Indeed, she manages to collapse millennia of cultural history into her own lifetime.

Further, Ayla is tall, svelte, has light skin, blond hair, and blue eyes, and she is obviously very intelligent. The Neanderthals, in contrast, are swarthy—and stupid.

Novels about prehistory are often pleasant diversions—but they are contemporary fiction, not contemporary anthropology. More importantly, we may observe that early modern humans are often depicted as biologically looking like the stereotyped northwestern European of today, while Neanderthals are closer to non-European people. They are dehumanized in several ways, so that skin color and intelligence often appear to be correlated in this genre.

Another novel, Bjorn Kurtén's *Dance of the Tiger*, describes Neanderthals as lighter-skinned than the modern humans they encounter. Actually, this might be a more accurate depiction, given that the Neanderthals evolved in Europe, while modern humans appear to have emerged from Africa, nearer the equator. Yet, unfortunately, Kurtén's novel is not well known. Perhaps if it became better known, it would help to weaken popular cultural prejudices about any link between pigmentation and intelligence.

Rituals and Spiritual Beliefs   Of course, the Neanderthals did more than make stone tools. Indeed, these hominids—this variety of *Homo sapiens*—were not the dumb brutes that they are often made out to be in popular fiction and film (Box 12–1). They were fully dependent upon culture and upon their intellectual abilities to survive for the many tens of thousands of years that they did. As a result, we see in the archaeological record suggestions of some remarkable achievements and abilities beyond the carefully planned manufacture of stone tools. There is possibly evidence for the practice of rituals and a belief in the afterlife, and certainly evidence of group concern for individual welfare.

Evidence of ritual has been suggested at many sites, and this takes various forms. Several Neanderthal sites have turned up caches of red and black powder (used frequently by later modern human cave artists),

Figure 12-15

Evidence for ritual practices among Neanderthal. Here, at Drachenloch, Switzerland, bear skulls were stacked in a stone-lined "chest."

which suggests that Neanderthals were coloring something, although we do not know what. There are also circles of animal bones and horns, which could very well have served an unknown ritual function. Still, the best-known evidence for ritual practices is that centering around cave bears. A number of sites, including Regourdou in France, contain the remains of many of these bears, often arranged in patterns or piles that suggest special handling. At Drachenloch, in Switzerland, for example, bear skulls were found stacked in a stone-lined chest in the ground (Figure 12–15).

Ritual is more evident in another practice, the purposeful burial of the dead. Neanderthals often buried their dead, and for the first time in the fossil record, we find many fully articulated skeletons, in pits, with knees and elbows flexed. The inference is that the deceased had apparently been buried in a characteristic pose by surviving individuals. Grave goods, however, are poorly documented among Neanderthal burials. At La Ferrassie in France, an adult male and female were buried head to head, and nearby pits contained the remains of a ten-year-old, a three-year-old, a newborn, and a fetus. It seems Neanderthals were (for the first time in any species) consciously treating their dead in special ways, with associated special thoughts. One of these thoughts might have been a belief in the afterlife.

One of the most dramatic sites involving Neanderthal burial is Shanidar Cave, in present-day Iraq. Archaeologist Ralph Solecki uncovered the remains of nine individuals there, whose remains have been studied by Erik Trinkaus of the University of New Mexico. Two were children. Some had been crushed and killed by a rockfall, and others had been deliberately buried together. One was an adult male who apparently had been lain on a bed of wildflowers at the time of burial—concentrations of pollen suggested that this man had been surrounded with flowers. Might this indicate that care and respect for the dead were important to Neanderthals? Is this clear evidence for ritual among Neanderthals? Many archaeologists think so; and even if this is an over-interpretation, it is a story that attractively humanizes the Neanderthals.

Others, however, feel that the evidence for symbolic thought and ritual among Neanderthals has been overstated. Adopting this more skeptical attitude, Philip Chase and Harold Dibble of the University of Pennsylvania point to the site of Teshik-Tash in Uzbekistan, where a Neanderthal is reported to have been surrounded by goat horns. Not terribly surprising, they argue, when one considers that of the 768 non-rodent mammal bones excavated at the site, 760 were those of goats. Similarly, the concentrations of pollen at Shanidar could have been an artifact of the numerous rodent burrows, the presence of a beehive, or merely carried there on the bottom of the feet of the workmen at the site, who regularly adorned themselves with wildflowers. Although the archaeological evidence for burial at many sites is compelling, Chase and

Figure 12-16

Artist's rendition of Neanderthal life. Given that they had tools for skinning animals, and lived in cold climates, might they not have worn clothing?

Dibble urge a more cautious reading of the record, close examination of the original reports (many of which date from the nineteenth century), and a consideration of archaeological formation processes before accepting the idea of widespread ritual behavior among Neanderthals.

Possibly more intriguing, however, is the evidence about Neanderthal behavior afforded by the skeletons themselves. The same Shanidar Neanderthal found with the pollen had sustained major injuries to his right side, which had healed, and probably had had his right arm amputated. The bones of other Neanderthals suggest severe cases of arthritis and other illnesses or trauma, including fossils from La-Chappelle-aux-Saints, La Ferrassie, and La Quina in France, Sala in Czechoslovakia, and Krapina in Yugoslavia. What this shows is that individuals not well able to care for themselves were being kept alive and cared for by others. This apparent communal concern for individuals who cannot fend easily for themselves is a remarkable and very human characteristic, widespread among Neanderthals (Figure 12–16).

Hunting Patterns   Neanderthal hunting patterns have been the subject of much recent research in Paleolithic archaeology. Although Lewis Binford has maintained that Neanderthals were principally scavengers and small-game hunters, there is now good evidence to suggest that they regularly and efficiently hunted large game. At Mauran in the French Pyrenees, 90 percent of the faunal assemblage is large bovids (cows and bison), making it hard to argue for scavenging or small-game hunting. At La Quina in France, a dense accumulation of horse, bison, and reindeer bones, many with butchery marks, was found at the base of a large cliff—the animals must have been driven off the cliff as part of a hunting strategy. This is actually reminiscent of bison-kill sites formed tens of thousands of years later in the New World by modern humans. Wooden spears are found at Middle Paleolithic sites in England and Germany, and there is some evidence of hafting of Levallois points to spears.

At Combe Grenal in France, Philip Chase found that horses and bison remains were most often represented by meaty upper-limb bones than by the less-meaty distal extremities. And on these bones there were clear cut-marks (from a fresh kill) rather than signs of hacking (from the butchering of a partially dried-out carcass)—these were hunted, not merely scavenged.

Language Patterns   Finally, what of that quintessential mode of human symbolic behavior—language? Did Neanderthals have it? Because the vocal apparatus does not fossilize, it is impossible to say. Philip Lieberman of Brown University maintains that by virtue of the shape of their bony jaws and palates, the Neanderthals were more limited in the range of sounds they were capable of producing than are modern humans. This idea, however, failed to be supported when a Neanderthal burial at Kebara in Israel (nicknamed 'Moshe') turned up a fossil hyoid bone—a small bone in the throat virtually never found in the fossil record. If the sound production of Neanderthals was different from that of modern humans, the hyoid bone's shape might be expected to reflect that difference. In the case of Moshe the Neanderthal, the hyoid bone was slightly larger, but not differently shaped. Any differences that may have existed in their vocal tract are not preserved in the morphology of the hyoid bone.

HOMO SAPIENS SAPIENS

What happened to the Neanderthals of Europe and the Near East about 35,000 years ago? Did they "evolve into" modern humans, or were they replaced—eliminated—by modern people from elsewhere in the Old World (Figure 12–17)?

THEORIES OF ORIGIN

One theory holds that the ancestors of modern humans originated in Africa and then began to replace the populations of Europe and Asia some 100,000–200,000 years ago. In this view, called the **replacement hypothesis** and championed by Gunter Brauer of the University of Hamburg and Chris Stringer of the British Museum (Natural History), Asian *Homo erectus* would have had little or no genetic continuity to modern Asians, who would be the direct descendants of Africans. Likewise, the Neanderthals of western Europe were not themselves the ancestors of modern western Europeans, but were instead replaced by the African ancestors of the Europeans.

replacement hypothesis

The idea that the Middle and Upper Paleolithic peoples of Europe were not ancestors and descendants, respectively, but rather that Middle Paleolithic peoples of Africa were the ancestors of the Upper Paleolithic peoples of the entire world.

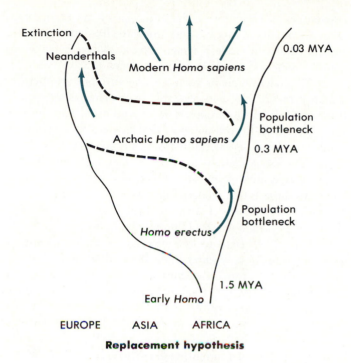

(a)

Replacement hypothesis

Figure 12–17. Two hypotheses.

(a) The replacement hypothesis involves small founding populations and the substitution of one population for another through time. (b) The regional continuity hypothesis emphasizes local anagenesis and limited gene flow.

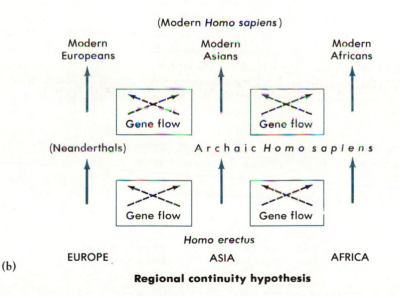

(b)

Regional continuity hypothesis

An alternative view, proposed by Milford Wolpoff of the University of Michigan, sees local evolution occurring on each continent. This is called the **regional continuity hypothesis**. The *Homo erectus* populations of China were the ancestors of the modern Chinese, and the Neanderthal

regional continuity hypothesis

The idea that on each continent of the Old World, peoples of the Middle Paleolithic were the ancestors of the people of the Upper Paleolithic in the same area.

populations of Europe were the ancestors of the Europeans. There was certainly, argues Wolpoff, some interbreeding among populations, but the transition to modern *Homo sapiens sapiens* occurred over a long period of time and largely in different places.

All modern humans are more similar to one another than any is to a human of 100,000 years ago; this immediately suggests a fairly recent divergence of human groups from one another. Further, proponents of the replacement hypothesis show that modern European skulls are more similar to *Homo sapiens* skulls from Africa and the Near East, such as those from Skhul, Qafzeh, and the Omo, and all more than 80,000 years old, than they are to the fossil populations in Europe of only 40,000 years ago. This suggests that modern Europeans are more likely descended from the earlier populations of Africa and the Near East, who simply replaced the prehistoric inhabitants of Europe, the Neanderthals.

Further, it begins to look as if the Neanderthal sites in the Near East may actually be *younger* than the modern human sites in the same area. Kebara, a Neanderthal burial, is dated to about 60,000 years B.P., but Skhul and Qafzeh, both of which have yielded modern human remains, are now dated to more than 90,000 years B.P. Did Neanderthals and modern humans coexist for tens of thousands of years in that area, only to have the moderns expand westward? Perhaps so, but the archaeological record cannot currently tell us for certain.

Yet another line of evidence can be invoked in support of the replacement hypothesis over the regional continuity hypothesis. If the latter were true, we would expect to find that the populations of Asia and of Europe have been accumulating genetic diversity for a very long time, and further, that the extent of genetic diversity for each continental population is roughly similar. That is, there should be nearly as much genetic diversity among modern Asians and Europeans as among modern Africans.

By contrast, the implications of the replacement hypothesis would be that only modern Africans have been accumulating genetic diversity for a long time. Why? Because modern humans would have existed in Europe and Asia for only a subset of the time that modern people have existed in Africa. Therefore, only modern *Africans* should have an exten-

Figure 12-18

Analysis of mitochondrial DNA shows that Africa has the most diversity and the most extreme variants. Therefore, it is reasoned that mtDNA has been evolving the longest in Africa.

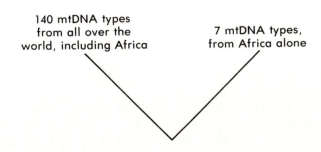

140 mtDNA types from all over the world, including Africa

7 mtDNA types, from Africa alone

sive genetic link to the past—and should have more genetic diversity than any other continental group because they have had more time to accumulate it. Further, the replacement hypothesis predicts that this genetic diversity has been accumulating for only a relatively short time, 100,000–200,000 years, since the first emergence of anatomically modern *Homo sapiens* in Africa—not over the many hundreds of thousands of years that *Homo erectus* lived in the Old World.

Rebecca Cann and her colleagues at Berkeley studied the genetic diversity in the human species for a small bit of genetic material known as mitochondrial DNA (**mtDNA**). Their studies yielded two major conclusions. First, there is far more diversity among living Africans than among other human groups (Figure 12–18). Second, having measured the extent of mtDNA diversity in modern New Guinea (which was first inhabited by humans 50,000–30,000 years ago), Australia (first inhabited 40,000 years ago), and the New World (first inhabited 12,000–20,000 years ago), Cann and colleagues extrapolated backward from the worldwide diversity they had found and asked, "How long has mtDNA diversity been accumulating in our species?" Their answer was about 150,000–300,000 years, again in substantial agreement with the predictions of the replacement hypothesis.

Other studies of genetic diversity have supported the conclusions that (1) Africans are more genetically diverse than are the populations of other continents, which implies the accumulation of genetic diversity over a longer period of time, and (2) this genetic variation has only been accumulating for perhaps 100,000–200,000 years. This conclusion effectively precludes local populations of 400,000 years ago from having been the ancestors of the modern people in the same regions. Rather, it appears that all humans are descended from a relatively small population of *Homo sapiens* which evolved 100,000–200,000 years ago in Africa.

CULTURAL TRANSITIONS

And yet, the transition between Neanderthal and modern *Homo sapiens sapiens* had some elements of continuity, one of which was cultural. The anatomically modern humans at Qafzeh 90,000 years ago are associated with typically Neanderthal (Mousterian) tools, while at Saint-Cesaire in France, 35,000-year-old Neanderthals are associated with Chatelperronian (Upper Paleolithic) tools. Other sites, such as Tönchesbeg in Germany and Seclin in France, have blade tools usually characteristic of modern humans, but a few tens of thousands of years earlier than modern humans are known to have inhabited the area—they were presumably made by Neanderthals. Another element is biological—regardless of the distinctiveness of the Neanderthal skeleton, the differences between it and a modern human are indeed rather subtle, turning on a bump here and a groove there. Many remains share some distinctive qualities of both Neanderthals and moderns—after all, this distinction is being made at

mtDNA

16,500 base-pairs of hereditary material, located in cellular structures known as mitochondria, outside the nucleus. It is relatively easy to isolate and inherited clonally from the mother, rather than being subject to ordinary Mendelian inheritance.

the *subspecies* level. Like contemporary human variation, it is likely that prehistoric human variation was largely continuous, not discrete.

These two subspecies coexisted extensively. Did they interbreed? Did they share ideas? Did they look upon each other as being as different as we perceive them to be? Were the Neanderthals conquered and exterminated, or were they genetically assimilated, that is, did they go out by violence or by sex? Whatever the answers to these questions may be, after 35,000 years ago, there are no more recognizable Neanderthal remains.

The Upper Paleolithic of the Old World

Shortly after the start of the Upper Paleolithic (about 40,000 years ago), biological diversity among the Hominidae had decreased to such an extent that there was now only one genus, one species, and one subspecies remaining (Figure 12–19). Skeletally, an Upper Paleolithic person could not be easily distinguished from any of us. Behaviorally, however, over the small span of time, compared with the hundreds of thousands of years of the Middle Paleolithic or millions of years of the Lower Paleolithic we find that this began a period of rapid cultural change.

While other, earlier groups of hominids had material culture that showed considerable stability over tens of thousands of years, people of the Upper Paleolithic displayed another hallmark of modern humans—the rapid adoption and diffusion of behavioral novelties. Tools became exceedingly more diversified, specialized, and efficient, in terms of both their manufacture and use. Hunting technologies were developed to such an extent that some animal species may have been driven to extinction. Social and economic networks appear to have been growing in size and

Figure 12-19

All measures of biological diversity show relatively little of it in contemporary humans. For example, chimpanzees and gorillas are each estimated to have 5 to 10 times as much genetic diversity as humans. We can see that taxonomic diversity has been steadily diminishing in the hominids since the lower Pleistocene. This also tends to suggest a fairly recent population contraction in the origin of modern humans, as the replacement hypothesis predicts.

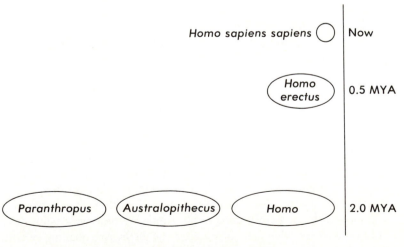

Hominid taxonomic/biological diversity
in the Pleistocene

complexity, along with the amount of trade and exchange. These aspects of culture appear to have worked because, from their skeletal remains, anatomically modern people seem to have lived longer and healthier lives than Neanderthals.

THE BEGINNINGS OF ART

The innovation that appears to differentiate human groups of the Upper Paleolithic from earlier ones, however, was not particularly useful in the procurement or preparation of food or any other material necessity of life. Modern humans of the European Upper Paleolithic created art—lots of art—something not discernible in the material culture of previous times. Items of personal decoration, such as beads and pendants, are found in the modern human burials of Upper Paleolithic Europe by 40,000 years ago. By 30,000 years ago, bone, antler, and ivory carvings are abundant. And slightly later, the famous cave paintings appear.

These aesthetic, symbolic displays provide the most radical departure in the behavior and life-style of *Homo sapiens sapiens* from all its relatives and ancestors. While we may be inclined to think of culture as technology, as the human adaptation for surviving and thriving in a material sense, it is important to remember that culture is also strongly symbolic. Symbols create feelings that motivate people, and art is an effective way of generating these feelings, whether they be feelings of belonging, feelings of power and bravery, feelings of love, or feelings of remorse. What in large part makes us humans and not Neanderthals is our ability to create and appreciate art—to have our thoughts and actions influenced by images.

Finally, during the Upper Paleolithic, the colonization of the entire earth (except Antarctica) by *Homo sapiens sapiens* was achieved. Humans reached a stage of technological competence that allowed them to move into the continent of Australia, and ultimately, throughout the New World.

TOOL ASSEMBLAGES

Archaeologists interested in the Upper Paleolithic in Europe, the Old World continent studied most intensively, recognize four major tool assemblages that partially followed one another as a chronological sequence. Earliest were the Perigordian and Aurignacian (c. 40,000–23,000 years B.P.), which at some sites occur repeatedly and in complex sequences. They were followed by the Solutrean (c. 20,000–17,000 years B.P.), which occurred at a time of environmental stress (a glacial maximum) and is characterized by thin, leaf-shaped points. Overlying these is the Magdalenian (c. 17,000–11,000 years B.P.), which represents an enormous increase in cultural variety and complexity, notably in the extensive use of fine bone and antler tools, rare in earlier Upper Paleolithic industries. These are also the people generally credited with cave paintings.

Figure 12-20. Characteristic Upper Paleolithic tools.

(a) Perigordian. (b) Aurignacian. (c) Solutrean. (d) Magdalenian.

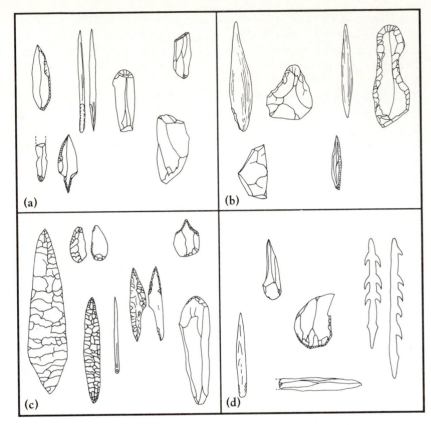

A major difference between Upper and Middle Paleolithic tool assemblages was the general development (certainly the refinement) of a blade technology. Blades are thinner and sharper than those in flaked tool assemblages and show a more economical use of the raw material. A second technological innovation was the extensive shaping of bones as tools. Hominids had probably used bones since the beginning of tool manufacturing, but with rare exceptions, such as a bone harpoon reported from the Middle Paleolithic of Zaire, only in the Upper Paleolithic do we find them. Third, and finally, there is much greater evidence for the hafting of sharp stone points onto spears during the Upper Paleolithic than in the Middle Paleolithic (Figure 12–20).

Specialization in the manufacture of tools continued, and nearly 150 Upper Paleolithic stone tool types have now been recognized. A greater variety of raw materials was being used as well, with specific raw materials chosen for particular purposes. The emergence of the punched blade technique, similar to the earlier Levallois prepared core but often involving the use of a softer striking tool (such as bone or antler), allowed the "mass production" of standardized, though highly specialized, implements.

FOOD PROCUREMENT

All Upper Paleolithic people got their food by gathering wild plants and hunting wild animals. They were thus gatherer-hunters, economically similar to several groups of people we can observe living today. They probably placed a greater emphasis on hunting over gathering, however, relative to living groups—for most of the Upper Paleolithic, the world's climate was colder than it is today, and modern gatherer-hunters in cold environments depend on animals to a great extent. These Upper Paleolithic people probably had an easier life than living gatherer-hunters, as well. The entire planet was available to Upper Paleolithic people—they had no competition from more technologically complex societies. Thus, prehistoric foragers exploited the world's richest territories.

They exploited these territories effectively. Indeed, by the Magdalenian period especially, they had become such skillful hunters that many animals (reindeer in particular) were being killed in great numbers. Many archaeologists believe that the heavy reliance on reindeer represented a breakthrough in hunting strategies—the foresight to anticipate the seasonal migrations of these animals. This may well have been the case for the people who hunted and killed horses in great numbers at the Upper Paleolithic site of Solutré, concludes archaeologist Sandra Olsen. The introduction of modern humans into areas that previously had few large predatory species, such as the New World about 12,000 years ago and Madagascar about 2,000 years ago, often coincide with the disappearance of large game. Some anthropologists believe that humans have been the cause of many extinctions of **megafauna** throughout their history.

NEWER WEAPONS

During the Upper Paleolithic, a new weapon, the spear thrower, or atl-atl, was developed (Figure 12–21). This acts mechanically as an artifical extension of the arm and adds greater velocity to the spear upon its release. Somewhat later, the bow and arrow became widely used.

OTHER ASPECTS OF CULTURE

Modern people of the Upper Paleolithic experienced considerable differences in other aspects of culture when compared with earlier hominid groups. Three major differences were: 1) increased population density, 2) more formal relationships between neighboring groups, and 3) more extensive and important trade networks.

Occupation sites of the Upper Paleolithic are more numerous and are considerably larger than those of the Middle Paleolithic. At many sites, such as Dolni Vestonice in Czechoslovakia, the remains of circular occupation structures, containing central hearths, are evident. These are suggestive of denser and more prolonged occupation.

While evidence exists of some Middle Paleolithic people's transporting raw materials over great distances, during the Upper Paleolithic, a

megafauna

Relatively large animals. The Pleistocene megafauna of the New World were an abundant food resource to Upper Paleolithic hunters.

Figure 12-21

Some examples of Atl-atls
(after Thomas, 1989).

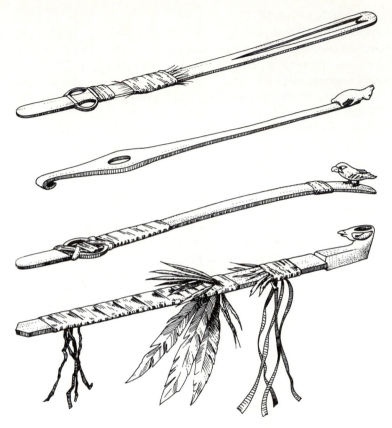

much higher proportion of materials was being transported as far as 50 km and more. As a result, people of the Upper Paleolithic had more regular access to imported materials, in many cases flint, chert, ivory, and shells. Many of these trade items were used for ornamentation—as necklaces, for instance. Often, they were left with the deceased as grave goods, something found only rarely and equivocally at Neanderthal sites. Some archaeologists feel that the existence of these grave goods and ornaments reflects a new symbolic power: the representation of status.

Among modern humans, decorations are used often to distinguish groups from one another. In the Upper Paleolithic, we find much more complex and regionally defined variations than at any previous time. Might this represent the earliest existence of ethnic traditions? Archaeologists feel that much of the complexity in Upper Paleolithic material culture, compared with earlier material culture, involves the differentiation of groups from one another. Thus were tribal boundaries established, and social relations among groups became a necessity. It was no longer each person for himself or herself, nor even each group for itself. Rather each group, asserting its individuality symbolically in its unique traditions, dealt, traded, and socially interacted with others like it.

Upper Paleolithic Art

The hallmark of these people, nevertheless, remains the fantastic art they created. Artistic expression appears virtually full blown in various forms during the Upper Paleolithic. One of the earliest is an anthropomorphic figure with the head of a lion from an Aurignacian site (about 32,000 years old) called Hohlenstein-Stadel in Germany. Later are the famous "Venus" figurines thought to have played a role in fertility rituals (Figure 12–22). Most spectacular, however, are the dramatic paintings that are found on the ceilings and walls of certain caves in western Europe, such as Lascaux in southern-central France and Altamira in northern Spain.

The story is that in 1879, a young girl named Maria de Sautuola was helping her father, Don Marcelino de Sautuola, conduct amateur archaeology in a cave at Altamira. While he was busy collecting artifacts, she wandered off into a different chamber using only a candle for light. She gazed around her and suddenly noticed on all sides a great herd of painted bison. That chamber is today called the Great Hall, and whether or not the story of Maria's discovery is accurate does not detract from the extraordinary paintings to be found there (Figure 12–23). Many other such sites are now known, the vast majority in southern France and northern Spain, called Franco-Cantabria.

Figure 12-22
A female Venus figurine of yellow steatite.

MEANING AND PURPOSE

Research by archaeologists such as Abbé Henri Breuil, André Leroi-Gourhan, and (more recently) Alexander Marshak of Harvard and Randall White of New York University, has revealed certain common characteristics of this art, and our understanding of its meaning and purpose is growing. For instance, the majority of the paintings depict animals, although there are also human stick figures, handprints, and geometric patterns. The animals, in contrast to the other subjects, are more realistic than abstract—often strikingly realistic in anatomy and pose. A number of the animals depicted are pregnant females or young individuals, and it is not uncommon to see them with spears stuck in their flanks, that is, in the act of being hunted. Many of the figures are located in difficult-to-reach places in the caves, and it is often not easy to see them. This raises the question of the purposes they might have served.

Successful Hunting   One suggestion is that the paintings were done to ensure successful hunting, or at least to ensure a continued abundance of game. The scenes of animals apparently being hunted support this view. Also, many of the animal figures, both carved and painted, have a series of spots or marks that appear to have been made at different times with different colors, perhaps symbolic wounds. The fact that the paintings are difficult to reach suggests that ritual was involved, that the paintings had a power that only special people could observe or interact with. This power was probably sympathetic magic, a common belief that

Figure 12-23

A fine example of Upper Paleolithic cave art.

the image of an object may affect or control the object itself by substituting for it symbolically (not unlike voodoo dolls, hanging someone in effigy, or even *The Picture of Dorian Gray*). The paintings might have also served as vehicles for self-expression, as art often does, or as ways of educating and indoctrinating the young, as symbolic forms of communication often do—in this case, into the knowledge and mysteries of hunting.

Geometric Pattern   The geometric patterns found on many cave walls are more difficult to explain. Leroi-Gourhan has argued that some geometric shapes represent males and others, females, and Alexander Marshack has argued that some geometric shapes represent the earliest astronomy—charting the phases of the moon. There is no way of confirming these interpretations at present, however, and they must be considered tentative.

Venus Figurines   The "Venus" figurines exaggerate the breasts, bellies, and hips of their subjects greatly. The extremities were of little interest to the artist (although occasionally, the hair was delineated). Most of these figurines date from 20,000–25,000 years ago, and the figures from the site of Dolni Vestonice (which also include animal figures) are some of the earliest ceramics known. There seems to be little doubt that the artist was attempting to represent a pregnant woman, with swollen breasts and belly. Perhaps the artist was trying to ensure a safe delivery with more ritual magic?

Prehistoric art abounds in the caves and open-air sites of the Upper Paleolithic, and the more that is discovered, the greater the chance of reaching a confident, comparative understanding of its meaning. But at the same time as Upper Paleolithic people were making these figurines and paintings, they were also embarking on a journey into unknown lands—the New World—many millennia before Columbus, and from the other direction.

The Final Frontiers

The last geographic expansion of the hominids occurred during the Upper Paleolithic, when people entered Australia and the Americas for the first time. These two colonizations conclude the migration and settlement of humans onto every continent, save Antarctica.

The earliest stone tool artifacts from Australia and New Guinea are dated to about 40,000–45,000 years B.P. From the site of Lake Mungo, about 26,000 years old, are evidences of complex funerary practices and possibly even cremation. The human remains from this site are characterized by fairly thin skull bones, small teeth, and small brow ridges. Somewhat later, about 10,000 years ago, remains from Kow Swamp show very different features—while still anatomically modern humans, the skulls are thicker and the teeth and brows larger.

Does this mean that Australia was settled by two (or more) biologically different human populations at different times? Or that the single group of founders evolved into diverse populations? Anthropologists are not in agreement, but because Australian aborigines are biologically very diverse, most anthropologists follow the hypothesis of Joseph Birdsell, that prehistoric Australia was colonized more than once by biologically different populations. The Kow Swamp cranial sample, it should be noted, had been affected by the cultural processes of cranial deformation, and the extent to which this may have created the robust appearance is unknown.

ENTERING THE NEW WORLD

Humans entered the New World by crossing from present-day Siberia into Alaska, across a land bridge known as **Beringia** (Figure 12–24). Today, this land bridge is submerged by the Bering Strait, but it was above sea level several times during the Paleolithic, when a significant portion of the earth's water was in the form of ice. A similar land bridge connected Australia, Tasmania, and New Guinea at various times.

Beringia

The land bridge between Siberia and Alaska that has periodically existed during glacials because of the lower sea level.

TIME OF COLONIZATION

Archaeologists agree that Beringia was indeed the route taken by *Homo sapiens sapiens* into the New World. Physical anthropology, demonstrating the biological similarity of native Americans to northern Asians, strongly attests to this conclusion as well. Still, there is some disagreement about the actual date of migration. Some, including the eminent Louis Leakey, have claimed that humans were present in the New World as long ago as 100,000 years ago, when there were not even modern humans in Europe. To prove an ancient occupation would require clear

Figure 12-24

The Bering Strait region, showing the extent of Beringia during the final phase of the most recent glacial (after Cantrell, 1989).

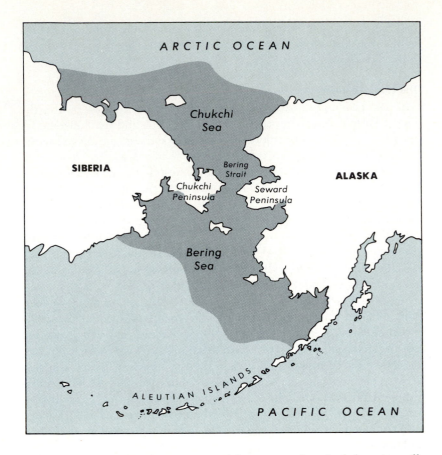

artifacts or human remains recovered from an undisturbed deposit, well-established dates, and a clear association between the dates and the artifacts. Most archaeologists feel that there is no evidence earlier than about 40,000 years ago and nothing of a convincing nature before 15,000–20,000 years ago. Several lines of evidence support the colonization of the New World at such a late date.

Archaeological Evidence   First, there is little archaeological evidence in Siberia or northern China—from where the immigrants came—that dates any earlier than 30,000 years B.P. While the archaeological record is admittedly poor and work is difficult because of climate and the political environment, it currently appears that these areas were largely uninhabited until well into the Upper Paleolithic. And if there were no people there, they could hardly have moved into the New World.

Second, the archaeological record in the New World itself contains little evidence predating about 20,000 years ago—10,000 years after the earliest occupation of Siberia—and what there is has been very controversial. There are, in fact, only a handful of sites that can be seriously regarded as possibly over 15,000 years old. One is the Meadowcroft

Rockshelter in Pennsylvania, carefully excavated by James Adavasio. Even here, questions remain about the earliest date of occupation (Box 12–2). Another anomalously ancient site is Pikimachay Cave in Peru, excavated by Richard MacNeish. Animal bones there have been ^{14}C dated to 22,000 B.P., although it is uncertain whether these are actually associated with the human occupation. Radiocarbon dating has also suggested some hearths associated with stone tools in South America to be more than 30,000 years old. Whether these are real indications of ancient occupation awaits more conclusive evidence. Recent excavations at Monte Verde, Chile, by Tom Dillehay of the University of Kentucky, have yielded many kinds of artifacts, and an extensive series of ^{14}C dates point to occupation 13,000 years ago. This is now one of the oldest well-accepted sites in the New World, but still far younger than some of the claims for other sites.

Tools   Third, the earliest strong evidence usually consists of stone tools, and these exhibit a rather uniform appearance throughout the New World until quite late, despite having a wide geographic distribution. Many artifacts recovered from sites stretching from Alaska to South America have a similar form, until nearly 12,000 years ago. Since regional and local traditions often develop after several centuries, the cultural near-uniformity at such a late date suggests the rapid spread of people from a common point of origin fairly late. If there were people in the Americas earlier, there do not seem to have been many of them, and they probably did not leave modern descendants.

About 12,000 years ago, strikingly abrupt and abundant evidence of extensive human occupation of the New World appears. This has generally been interpreted as reflecting the immigration and expansion of a group of people, known principally by their distinctive fluted projectile points. These stone tools are called **Clovis points** because the first one recognized was found near Clovis, New Mexico (Figure 12–25). Thus, these early immigrants are often associated with a "Clovis culture." Clovis points occur from east to west across North America and from Alaska to Guatemala, dating consistently from 12,000–11,000 B.P. They are usually associated with mammoth kills (at least in the west) and have little, if anything, in the way of evident cultural antecedents in the New World. At many Clovis sites, there is direct succession by widespread **Folsom points** and then by considerable geographical diversity in point styles and forms. The general observation remains that projectile points were most similar to one another when they first appeared in the archaeological record in different locations and environments. It seems reasonable to infer that the cultural diversity so characteristic of *Homo sapiens sapiens* came with time. The lack of diversity, therefore, may suggest a lack of time depth for human occupation of the New World.

Past Climates   The fourth line of evidence, again suggesting a relatively recent immigration to the New World, derives from studies of past

Figure 12-25
A typical Clovis projectile point, 11.47 mm in length (after Thomas, 1989).

Clovis point

A projectile point manufactured in the New World c. 12,000–11,000 years ago.

Folsom point

A projectile point manufactured in the New World c. 11,000–9,000 years ago.

Meadowcroft Rockshelter

Archaeologist C. Vance Haynes has suggested that the Paleoindian Period in the New World be divided into three subperiods: 1) The Early Period, dating to before 30,000 years ago, 2) The Middle Period, dating from 30,000 to 12,000 years ago, and 3) The Late Period, dating from 12,000 years ago to that time when the Paleoindian came to an end—this occurred at various times at various places (see Chapter 13). Most archaeologists agree with Haynes that there is no reliable evidence for human occupation in the New World during the Early Period—it was created to accomodate any archaeological remains that might be recovered in the future. And few archaeologists see very good evidence for significant human occupation during the Middle Period. Most claims for human occupation predating about 12,000 years ago have been shown to be based on ambiguous or misinterpreted evidence. There are a handful of exceptions, however, including the Meadowcroft Rockshelter.

Located in southwestern Pennsylvania, the Meadowcroft Rockshelter has been carefully excavated by archaeologist James Adavasio over several years. The rockshelter is a remarkably informative site, consisting of many stratigraphic layers accumulated over thousands of years and presently forming a deep record of past environments and human occupations. Apparently, the site was used by people intermittently throughout much of New World prehistory as they hunted wild animals, gathered wild plants, and processed various food items.

The most intriguing stratum at the site is the lowest one containing evidence for human occupation. Called Stratum IIa, it was found to contain artifacts that are, as a result of Adavasio's work,

climates. We have already mentioned that the route of entry into the Americas was across Beringia, and that this land bridge existed only periodically, when a substantial portion of the earth's water was taken up in glaciers, causing a drop in sea level. Indeed, the climate was cold enough for a sufficient drop in sea level at least four times over the past 60,000 years, but these periods were of varying durations.

The most recent time that the land bridge was passable began about 22,000 years ago, and sea level remained sufficiently low for approximately the next 10,000 years. Before this cold period, there were two intervals during which the bridge existed—one about 30,000 years ago, and one about 42,000 years ago—but these were of very brief duration. The previous extended period of cold dates from about 60,000 to about 50,000 years B.P., too early for credible immigration of hominids into the New World if the other evidence discussed here is accepted. The most likely conclusion is that people began to enter the New World in a significant way beginning about 22,000 years ago.

The study of past environments of the New World has shown that many large Pleistocene mammals (or megafauna) became extinct at precisely the same time as archaeological evidence suggests that the first large numbers of people were arriving. Paul Martin of the University of Arizona suggested that these Upper Paleolithic people rapidly over-the most carefully excavated and dated evidence for pre-Clovis occupation available. There are several reasons why Adavasio has several reasons to believe that these stone tools are clear evidence of a human presence during the Middle Period.

First, the stratigraphy of the rockshelter has been carefully observed and recorded. Second, numerous samples of organic material have been ^{14}C dated, and the stone artifacts were observed to be in clear association with the samples. Third, there is little question that the artifacts were manufactured by humans and are not the results of natural formation processes. Flakes and a number of biface tools are represented in the assemblage, although there are no fluted points. Indeed, the evidence suggests the presence of a pre-projectile point occupation dating to about 16,000 to 20,000 B.P.

Not everyone accepts these data. Some question the accuracy of the ^{14}C dates and raise the possibility that some of the dated charcoal samples were contaminated by bituminous coal, resulting in older-than-actual age determinations. Others have pointed out that only modern fauna and flora are represented and remind us that the environment was quite different during pre-Clovis times. Still others simply reject Adavasio's conclusions because of the early dates suggested—the conservative element in archaeology is not easily persuaded and is usually right.

Perhaps, however, this is a case in which that element is wrong. Meadowcroft Rockshelter is one of those key sites which may cause us to rethink long-held ideas.

hunted these animals, contributing to their extinction. Over-exploitation would have been possible in an environment free from competition, that is, in which no other humans or major predators were present. A recent and rapid expansion is indicated again.

However, not everyone agrees with this line of argument. The climate was changing rapidly at the end of the Pleistocene (the same time as the Clovis tradition), as the last glaciation was drawing to a close. It is likely, then, that many animals would have become extinct regardless of human intervention. Indeed, many species apparently not hunted by humans did become extinct, including many birds. Modern humans may not have helped matters, but the degree of their ecological impact remains the subject of debate.

Biological and Genetic Evidence   The final line of evidence for the late arrival of humans to the New World comes from studying the biology of the descendants of the first New World inhabitants—modern Native Americans. It has been shown that these people, living throughout the New World, are genetically less varied than are other continental populations. Morphologically, they also show a high degree of similarity. Dental variation, for instance, is less among Native Americans than among Asians. These observations again suggest relatively recent immigration.

Some speculations have centered on whether there was only one, or as many as three colonization events in the New World during the Pleistocene. One interpretation of the relationships of native American languages is that they cluster into three groups, reflecting three primeval migrations. Anatomical studies of skeletal remains tend to support this, although genetic analyses on living populations have been equivocal.

We may never know exactly when significant numbers of people reached the New World, how many waves of immigration occurred, how long they lasted, or where in Asia these colonists originated. However, it is well established that they arrived here as Upper Paleolithic gatherer-hunters, similar in life-style to the Magdalenian people of Europe, and in some ways to gatherer-hunters living today. The only animal species these people had domesticated was the dog (Chapter 13).

TRADE BECOMES MORE COMMON

The classical Upper Paleolithic subsistence pattern started to change shortly after the New World had been occupied, however. It did so also in the Old World at nearly the same time, during the late Magdalenian. Trade became an even more important economic activity, and more items were exchanged over longer distances. People increasingly exploited wild plant resources and placed less reliance on hunting, especially in eastern North America. Groups settled down for longer stretches and ceased to be completely nomadic. And population sizes and densities, apparently, were growing. The end of the Pleistocene was marked by the retreat of the glaciers about 10,000 years ago, which begins the present era, or Holocene.

Summary

The reliance on material culture for survival is one of the critical differences between humans and other living species. Although we cannot pinpoint when this gradually increasing reliance on technology for survival became irreversible, it can be traced to some extent in the development of the earliest surviving material culture, stone tools.

Where in the lower Pleistocene there had coexisted three genera of hominids (*Homo, Australopithecus,* and *Paranthropus*), by about 1 million years ago, there was but one genus. The transition of *Homo erectus* to *Homo sapiens* is not well documented, but probably about 400,000 years ago, *Homo erectus* populations were being supplanted by archaic *Homo sapiens* populations. Starting about 200,000 years ago, these, in turn, were supplanted by anatomically modern *Homo sapiens* populations, a process that was completed with the extinction of the Neanderthals, about 35,000 years ago. Then as now, hominids were continually striving to maintain or improve their quality of life by technological means. As a result, through time we find general improvement or refinement of the stone tools used by those people.

All humans are parts not only of the same species, but also of the same subspecies, *Homo sapiens sapiens*. Thus, as our cultural complexity has increased, apparently the biological diversity within our clade has decreased.

Hardly 10,000 years after the extinction of the Neanderthals, the remaining populations of humans began producing a greater variety of material items, such as bone and antler tools. They also began expressing themselves artistically and migrated into previously unoccupied lands (including Australia and the New World). Curiously, though Neanderthals buried their dead, the earliest remains of art, including clay figurines and cave paintings, are unique properties of the humans who have inhabited the earth since the extinction of the Neanderthals.

Questions for Review

1. What do you think are the possible causes and meaning of the apparent decline in diversity of the hominids between the Pliocene and the present?

2. What were the Neanderthals? Why are they no longer with us? Why do you think we classify them in the same species as ourselves?

3. Why are anthropologists reluctant to accept the sporadic reports of early (pre-20,000-years-ago) human occupation of the New World?

4. At what point in our history do you think humans began to change from having a relatively insignificant place in the ecosystem to having the kind of impact we do today? Do you think it is related to the geographic expansion of our species, or to the lack of diversity in contemporary hominids, or to other factors?

For Further Reading

Fagan, Brian M. (1987). *The great journey*. London: Thames and Hudson.

Klein, R. G. (1988). *The human career*. Chicago: University of Chicago Press.

Marchack, A. (1989). "Evolution of the human capacity: The symbolic evidence." *Yearbook of Physical Anthropology*, 32:1–34.

Mellars, P., & Stringer, C. (Eds.). (1989). *The human revolution*. Princeton: Princeton University Press.

Pfeiffer, John E. (1982). *The creative explosion*. New York: Harper and Row.

Cultural Evolution: Diachronic Studies

The Origins of Domestication

The Origins of Domestication

Subsistence Patterns

The species *Homo sapiens* has existed for at least 250,000 years, and for over 95 percent of that time, all humans have derived their sustenance by gathering wild plants and hunting wild animals. When you consider the millions of years that the Hominidae have existed, it should be clear that we evolved in the context of a stable gathering and hunting way of life. It is intriguing, then, to find so few people pursuing this mode of subsistence at the present time. Nevertheless, only small groups of gatherer-hunters survive, and these are now restricted to some of the least productive land areas in the world (Figure 13–1). They have been pushed into these areas by technologically more complex agriculturalists who continue to expand their territories. Two important questions for anthropologists are how and why this expansion has occurred.

Important changes in subsistence patterns emerged between 10,000 and 15,000 years ago independently among certain Upper Paleolithic people. These changes, or trends, occurred from the Paleolithic through the next recognized stage of cultural history—the Archaic, which is frequently called the Mesolithic (Middle Stone Age) or Epipaleolithic by archaeologists working in the Old World. **Domestication** succeeded the Archaic. In this chapter we consider these various developments, keeping in mind that our concern is for evolutionary processes and not arbitrary developmental stages.

domestication

The process of bringing plant and animal species under human control to a significant degree.

Archaic Trends

The Archaic should not be viewed as a time when there was a distinctive subsistence strategy or way of life being practiced. It should instead be seen as a series of cultural evolutionary trends which induced various human groups from gathering-hunting to adopting domestication. These trends emerged as early as 10,000 to 15,000 years ago in certain regions, including the Greater Southwest of the New World and the Near East in the Old World (Figure 13–2). In other areas, the Archaic did not get underway until nearly 7,000 years before now—about the same time this way of life was ending in the Near East. In some places, including the Great Basin of the American West, the Archaic did not end until modern times, and then only because of contact with industrial society.

Despite the various dates and durations of the Archaic, it can everywhere be recognized as having consisted of a number of cultural evolutionary developments, which on various independent occasions made the emergence of domestication possible.

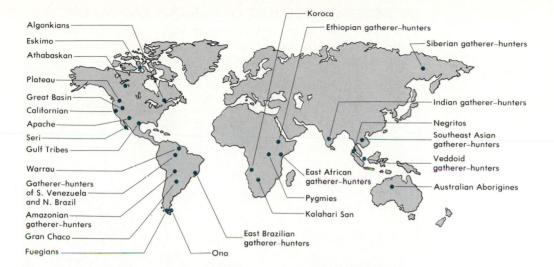

Figure 13-1

Distribution of present and
recent gatherer-hunters
throughout the world (after
Lee and DeVore, 1968).

INCREASING REGIONAL DIFFERENCES IN ARTIFACTS

Tool kits became more diversified in terms of both tool types and materials of manufacture during the entire Paleolithic, and particularly during the Upper Paleolithic. This trend continues through the Archaic. It acquires a distinctive spatial component as well, with the emergence of obvious regional variability. Furthermore, regional styles and forms become more distinctive, and recognizable regions become more numerous.

The Greater Southwest serves as a good example of the trend. This region was as culturally homogeneous as the rest of the New World during those times when Clovis and Folsom projectile points were being used. By the Plano subperiod, however, some regional differentiation was becoming evident with the emergence of the Cody Complex, restricted to the eastern portion of the southwest region and apparently reflecting a culture better adapted to a plains environment than to a desert environment. Then, from about 10,000 to 8,500 years ago, much of the southwest region west of the plains reflected an adaptive pattern known as the San Dieguito Tradition. The San Dieguito adaptation is poorly known, though it appears to have become more regionally varied through time. Much of what we know about this tradition comes from excavations at the site of Ventana Cave in southern-central Arizona, excavated in the 1940s by Emil Haury of the University of Arizona.

Near the end of the San Dieguito, increasing regional differentiation is seen with the appearance of the Amargosa Tradition in California. Then, following the San Dieguito and Amargosa, additional regional traditions emerged, such as the Cochise and the Oshara. Clearly, in the Greater Southwest (and elsewhere), the Archaic was a time when regional traditions were becoming more numerous and distinctive. This development was related to a second Archaic trend.

INCREASING MOVEMENT OF VARIOUS RAW MATERIALS
This trend reflects an increase during the Archaic in both the amount of raw material being moved and the distance that it was moved.

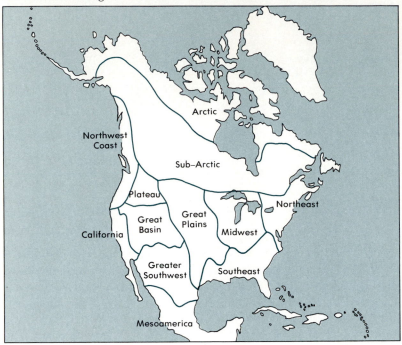

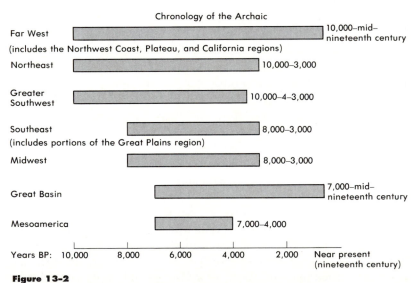

Figure 13-2

Archaic archaeological regions in North America, along with a general chronology of the Archaic in these regions (after Jennings, 1983).

Archaeological methods for measuring the movement of materials are straightforward. Different raw materials—and different specimens of a given raw material—have different points of origin, or places where they occur naturally. Archaeologists can find the source of certain types of material by looking for the presence or absence, or relative amounts, of particular elements that occur in the raw materials. They can do this because the relative amounts of these **trace elements** in the natural material will differ, depending on the precise point of origin of the material.

Trace element analysis has been done with a number of materials, including **obsidian**, a glassy volcanic rock. Many sources of obsidian have been located, helping archaeologists reconstruct past routes of exchange.

It is easy to see why this trend was closely related to the increasing regional differentiation of artifact styles and forms. When regional styles and forms become more numerous and distinctive, an increased incentive to trade develops, along with the incentive to move raw materials and products. The increased movement of raw materials might also be related to the changing patterns of movement among actual people as well.

INCREASINGLY REGULAR SEASONAL HABITATION OF SITES

Groups of people—more often and more regularly—could be found in distinctive locations at particular times or seasons of the year. In many places around the world, the full-scale nomadism of foraging bands was being replaced by a pattern of movement known as **transhumance**, which consisted of an alternating pattern of settled life and seasonal migration.

Some of the best-studied examples of this trend are found in the central highlands of Mexico, particularly in the *Tehuacan Valley* and the *Valley of Oaxaca* (Figure 13–3). Archaeology in these valleys has been conducted by Richard ("Scotty") MacNeish, Kent Flannery, and several others. The general environment of these highland valleys consists of a number of environmental zones, distinguishable on the basis of elevation and geography, the resulting climate, and the nature of the resources contained within them. The distribution of food resources is critical when discussing past settlement patterns.

Kent Flannery of the University of Michigan has been especially instructive in his assessments of changing settlement patterns and increasing transhumance during the Archaic. He has suggested the following general model of group movement through a typical year, based on the results of his fieldwork in the Valley of Oaxaca.

During the dry season, from October to March, human groups were generally (and logically) located near dense strands of those plants supplying food during the fall and winter (acorns, for example). People were also eating plant foods that were available year-round, especially when conditions were very dry and many resources were scarce. The hunting of white-tailed deer was also common during the dry season.

trace element

A chemical element that occurs in small quantities within a natural material (commonly rock) that is often geographically distinctive and can be used to locate the place of origin of the material.

obsidian

A glassy volcanic rock that can be made into sharp stone tools.

transhumance

A pattern of human settlement that involves alternating periods of settling down and migrating; often sensitive to seasonal and related environmental changes.

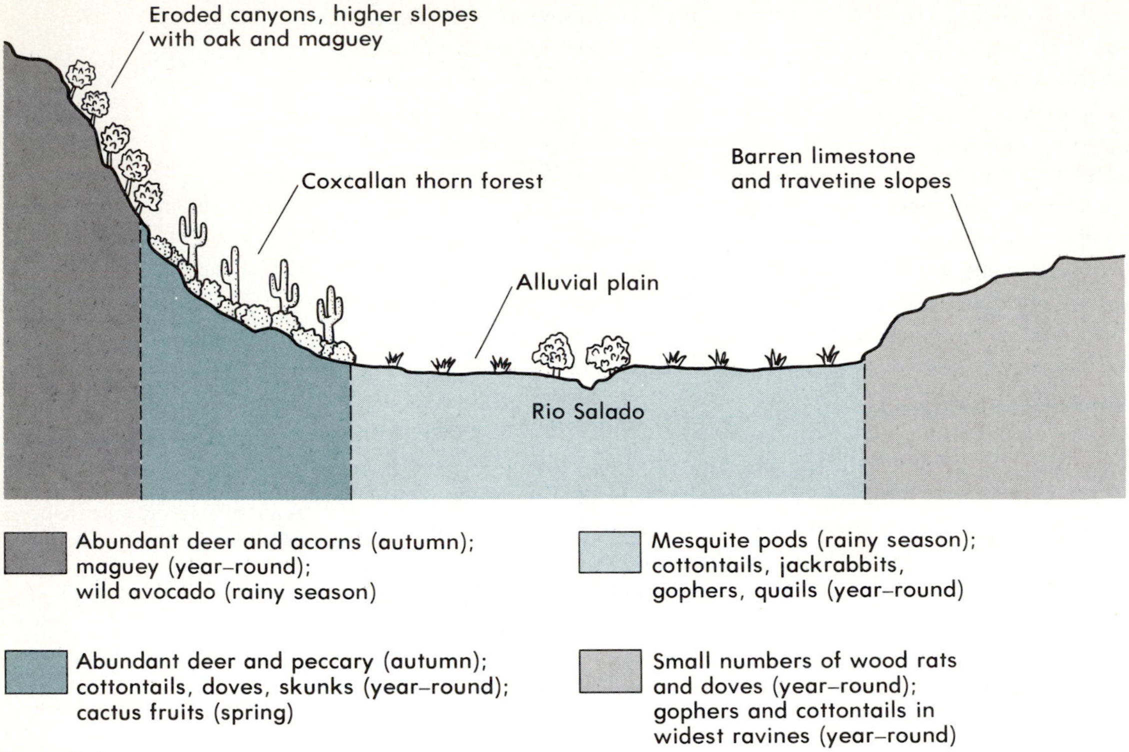

Figure 13-3

An idealized east-west transection of the central part of the Tehuacan Valley. East is to the left, and the width of the valley is about 20 km (after Coe and Flannery, 1971).

During the rainy season, from May to September, groups located themselves to efficiently exploit the many summer plants that were available, including mesquite beans, amaranth, wild avocado, and more. Hunted at this time were cottontail, opossum, skunk, raccoon, and gopher.

The important point is that these people became more sensitive to the changing availability of different food sources as the yearly cycles progressed, and as a result, their seasonal movements became more regular and pronounced. Flannery asserts that this trend is closely related to the fourth Archaic trend.

MORE EFFICIENT EXPLOITATION OF THE ENVIRONMENT

Subsistence strategies became more appropriate, given the nature of the physical environment, as the Archaic progressed. This increasing efficiency appears to have been in large measure a result of the fact that people were exploiting more secure food sources, such as plants. A great deal of this growing efficiency resulted merely from people making better choices, however, regarding which food resource to exploit at a given time. To document this point, it is useful to return to Flannery's work from Mesoamerica.

Flannery explains the increasingly regular seasonal habitation of sites through the Archaic by reference to the inferred increasing subsistence efficiency, and he does so by introducing two very important and powerful concepts—seasonality and scheduling.

Seasonality is simply the fact that specific food resources are in abundance and available for exploitation at specific times during the year. For example, in certain highland valleys of Mexico, wild mesquite beans were available in the summer, while white-tailed deer were most available in the winter. *Scheduling*, in contrast, consists of rational decisions regarding which resource to exploit at any particular time. Members of Archaic human groups found it necessary to make these decisions, given that more than one resource was available at one time but that each was to be found at a different location. Decisions regarding which resource to exploit depended on conditions that fluctuated year by year.

Archaic people became more knowledgeable about seasonality through time, and thus could make better scheduling decisions. This knowledge may also have been a necessary condition for domestication to occur later in prehistory.

INCREASING DEPENDENCE ON WILD PLANT FOOD RESOURCES

The necessary inverse trend is that there was a decrease in the dependence on wild *animal* food resources. These developments were mentioned before—people were using more secure resources as the Archaic continued because they were becoming more efficient exploiters. Plants are more secure, or reliable, simply because they cannot run away. In addition, plants cannot bite or otherwise injure a person, making their exploitation an easier and often more rewarding endeavor.

Archaeological evidence for this shift in subsistence patterns can come directly from the analysis of Archaic diets—from analyzing human **coprolites** for seeds and other plant food remains. Much more of our evidence is indirect, however, resulting in large part from the analysis of the relative quantities of various artifact types found at Archaic sites. As we have seen, during the Paleolithic and early Archaic, the majority of stone tools were of the *chipped-stone* type. They were manufactured by striking or pushing off various flakes in order to create a sharp edge or a desired shape. It is clear that many of these tools were used for stabbing, slicing, cutting, and other behaviors associated with hunting and the preparation of animal foodstuff.

By middle to late Archaic times, more and more of the tool assemblage consisted of *ground stone* tools (Figure 13–4). These tools were shaped by pecking and grinding and included the mano and metate. These tools were used primarily for processing plant foods—grinding wild

coprolite
Ancient fecal remains that can yield information on past diets and other behaviors.

Figure 13-4

Common implements for preparing plant foods—a ceramic husking tray and ground-stone querns and pestles.

grasses into flour, for example. The more of them present in the archaeological record, the greater the inferred emphasis on plant resources.

INCREASING DEPENDENCE ON AQUATIC FOOD RESOURCES

For the most part, aquatic food resources were close to land, small in size, occurring in abundance, and fairly motionless in their behavior. People did not hunt large ocean fish, but rather gathered items such as shellfish. Thus, we can say that as with land resources, Archaic people concentrated on those food sources that were reliable and easy to acquire.

Archaeological evidence for this trend comes in various forms. First, it appears that more and more sites dating to the middle and late Archaic were located near bodies of water. As we discuss shortly, this growing concentration of people, near the coasts especially, may be seen as a significant development in the rise of domestication.

Second, through time, the Archaic tool-kit in many locales consisted of an increasing number of implements useful in aquatic resource procurement. These items included harpoons, nets, and sinkers.

Finally, and possibly most direct, is the evidence that through time, increasing proportions of the refuse Archaic people left behind consisted of the remains of aquatic diets. This evidence is most striking when it comes to the remains of seashells, which often form immense mounds as evidence of Archaic occupation. Shell **middens** attained large sizes

midden

An archaeological deposit consisting of human refuse, often containing dietary refuse (bone and shell).

because people would deposit the remains of meals in the same places over extended periods of time and because the number of people alive at one time was increasing.

INCREASING POPULATION SIZES AND DENSITIES

This might very well have been the most significant of all the Archaic trends, because it had dramatic impacts on subsequent developments such as the rise of domestication and complex society (Chapter 14). Unfortunately, studying it requires the consideration of variables that are very difficult, if not impossible, to measure archaeologically. Indeed, accurately measuring the sizes and **densities** of prehistoric populations has been a vexing problem, despite the diverse efforts and contributions of a large number of archaeologists—for it is a key variable in models of cultural evolution.

Attempts have been made to estimate population sizes and densities by reference to and measurement of: 1) number of burials, 2) amount of floor space, 3) amount of sleeping space, 4) numbers of dwellings, 5) site acreage, 6) numbers of hearths, 7) relative and absolute amounts of different artifact types, and other criteria. All these approaches have faced problems because they are lacking, to some degree or another, at least one piece of information needed to reconstruct past population characteristics accurately.

One of these pieces of information is the **use-life** of the chosen archaeological item, whether burials, floor space, sleeping space, dwellings, or any other. The use-life is the average time that a particular type of artifact or feature remains in use, and knowing it is critical. If, for instance, dwellings lasted fifty years, each person might have only one or two in a lifetime. If they lasted a mere ten years, however, each person might be eventually represented by five or more. Archaeologists have no easy method of establishing use-life, especially since the range of times that individual artifacts in a type might remain useful is potentially large.

A second necessary piece of information is the total number of archaeological items present within the site or region for which past population size and density are being reconstructed. If there are fifty dwellings at an archaeological site, for example, but the archaeologist recognizes the presence of only ten, then estimates of past population will be too low.

A third necessary measure is the length of time the site or region was occupied. Whether ten or 100 generations of people occupied a site or region will influence the relationship between observed number of dwellings (to continue our example) and estimated population size at any one time. Knowing how population sizes and densities changed through time is an even greater challenge.

There are other obstacles as well, and it is difficult to know how a chosen archaeological item relates to number of people. This is reflected

population density
The number of people in relation to the available land.

use-life
The average length of time that a type of archaeological resource remains in use.

in the number of diverse suggestions regarding what item(s) to study and how to relate them to population. At the present time, it is impossible to suggest accurate absolute numbers of Archaic people—or absolute rates of population increase—for any region or area. Still, it is clear that later Archaic population sizes and densities were at least larger than those of the earlier Archaic. The trend is real, although we are not capable of measuring it with precision.

INCREASING SOCIAL DIFFERENTIATION IN TERMS OF SOCIAL ROLES AND ECONOMIC POSITIONS

This trend entailed a breakdown of the egalitarian nature of gatherer-hunter society. Status differences between individuals and small groups of people became significant. Perhaps these status differences were recognized as heritable and were thus **ascribed** rather than **achieved**. It is even possible that certain goods and services were available only to those of special status. Although social role differentiation became much greater after the rise of domestication, and especially in the context of complex society (Chapter 14), this trend was well enough underway during the Archaic to be visible in the archaeological record.

The best archaeological evidence for this trend is found through the analysis of burials. This is possible because the social roles an individual held in life are often expressed symbolically, including materially, at death through the practice of burial rituals. Archaeologists have known about these practices for many years, although only recently have they appreciated the complexity of the relationships between social roles, status positions, and the nature of burials. They have learned that it is not simply a matter of counting grave goods to estimate status.

During the Archaic, a growing number of individuals were buried in ways that suggest special roles and possibly high status. These burials, always a very small number of the total burials at a site, are often unique in orientation, position of skeleton, or nature and amount of grave goods. Sometimes the grave goods originated from a distant land, and sometimes they are not commonly found in other archaeological contexts. Often, these special burials are spatially segregated from the majority of interments. The archaeologist can almost always recognize something special about these burials and thus infer that there was something special about the buried individuals. Deciding what specifically was special about them is the challenge.

It is easy to see that the various Archaic trends were closely related to one another and served to take many human groups away from traditional gathering-hunting economic and social patterns. Increasing regional differentiation of artifact styles and forms accompanied the increasing movement of materials. This greater movement was in turn related to developing transhumance, itself closely tied to increased subsistence efficiency, a greater emphasis on plant and aquatic resources, rising population sizes and densities, and growing social differentiation.

ascribed status

Social position over which the individual in question has no control; for example, class (in societies with little opportunity for economic advancement), age, sex, and caste.

achieved status

Social position over which the individual in question can exercise control; for example, class (in societies with significant opportunity for economic advancement) and elected office.

The entire process might have been set into motion by external forces—environmental alterations developing at the end of the Pleistocene (Chapter 12). No matter what the cause, however, these various intertwined trends set the stage for a major transformation in cultural history—the rise of domestication.

The Rise of Domestication: Theories

Domestication means bringing various floral and faunal species—those important for subsistence or other technologically related human activities—under human control to some significant degree. This is a fairly straightforward definition, and a number of implications follow from it.

First, domestication was not an invention, but rather a gradual, long-term process that was consequently beyond the conscious grasp of any individual or group of individuals. This is a characteristic of most human phenomena, at least on the broad, cultural evolutionary scale. At first, it might not seem logical to view domestication in this way, inasmuch as most modern societies (including our own, very complex society) are dependent on this form of subsistence. It is easy to conclude that after some genius invented domestication, people naturally chose it over gathering and hunting. But there was probably little or nothing in the way of genius involved: People used knowledge that existed and took small but irreversible steps in order to maintain their quality of life, just as we do today.

Domestication exhibited certain general and regular patterns of development every time and in every place it emerged, and it emerged on every continent except Antarctica (where there are no indigenous people). For instance, broadly similar environments were the settings for some of the earliest instances of domestication.

Second, and somewhat in contrast to the first point, it can be shown that certain aspects of the initial domestication process were particular to certain specific areas of the world as well as to specific, relatively short periods of time. The occurrence of these historical developments, combined with the lack of good evidence for contact between the various areas where domestication emerged, indicates that the domestication process transpired independently several times on earth. Thus, domestication was an outgrowth of the *local* Archaic subsistence adaptations which preceded it.

We are addressing here, therefore, a major, significant evolutionary change experienced by different human groups in the course of cultural history. Domestication in the Near East was a critical process in our own cultural history. The importance of understanding this development has obviously been appreciated by archaeologists, and many theories have been proposed that try to explain why domestication occurred in the first place and why it has been adopted by so many people in the ensuing several thousand years. We consider a number of the better-known and influential of these.

V. GORDON CHILDE

Childe was an Australian-English Marxist archaeologist who was interested in the process of domestication as early as the 1920s. Today, his views are considered to be out of date, although they have had a profound influence on the ways archaeologists approach the topic of domestication. Particularly influential was Childe's adherence to a materialist perspective, making his theory scientifically testable by referring to the archaeological record (Chapter 2).

Childe suggested what is most commonly known as the *Oasis Theory* for the rise of domestication. It is also referred to as the Propinquity Theory and the Desiccation Theory, for reasons that will become obvious.

Childe argued that climatic changes after the Pleistocene resulted in a general drying of regions south of the farthest glacial advance. This drying (desiccation) forced all living things—plants, animals, and people—into smaller and smaller areas in which moisture could still be found (oases). The closeness (propinquity) of these life forms to one another led to increased contact among them, and thus, according to Childe, increased exploitation of the plants and animals by the more intelligent species—*Homo sapiens*. This increased exploitation eventually led to the practice of full-scale domestication.

Childe focused his study of early domestication on Egypt. Here, domestication has for thousands of years been limited to a thin strip of fertile land on each side of the Nile River, in the midst of inhospitable desert. Thus, it is easy to see why Childe would have constructed his theory in the manner in which he did, and there is still some merit in thinking that the Oasis Theory is applicable in the Egyptian case. However, similar oases are not evident, and were not present, in many areas of the world where domestication arose early and independently, such as the Tehuacan Valley in Mexico. The theory is thus quite narrow in its appropriate application.

The theory is also too general in regards to the terms and concepts it depends on, at least to be of much use for the modern archaeological community. For instance, it is not at all clear that the equatorial post-Pleistocene climate experienced drying over broad expanses of territory. Chances are better that small microenvironments changed in different ways to form a very complex (and not yet totally understood) global picture.

Childe died by jumping off a cliff in Australia in 1957; and his suicide note observed, tragically if insightfully, that "[t]o end his life deliberately is in fact something that distinguishes *Homo sapiens* from other animals even better than ceremonial burial of the dead." His role in maturing archaeological theory was considerable, in particular because of his scientific approach to cultural processes. The strength of Childe's theory remains in its testability.

ROBERT J. BRAIDWOOD

Braidwood, of the University of Chicago, attempted an archaeological test of Childe's Oasis Theory toward the middle of this century. He did so in the foothill region of the Zagros Mountains—near the famous *Fertile Crescent* of Mesopotamia, where domestication and complex society arose very early (Figure 13–5; Chapter 14). Braidwood soon became frustrated with the difficulty of determining whether or not Childe was right, however, and he also noted some flaws in Childe's reasoning. As a consequence, he developed his own theory for the rise of domestication, called the *Nuclear Zone Theory*.

Braidwood rejected Childe's views based on the fact that the Pleistocene was a time of cyclical climatic change (Chapter 12). The world has experienced a series of similar environmental changes and conditions, he reasoned—such as the proposed equatorial drying—before domestication finally arose. Childe gave no good explanation for its development at the particular time it emerged.

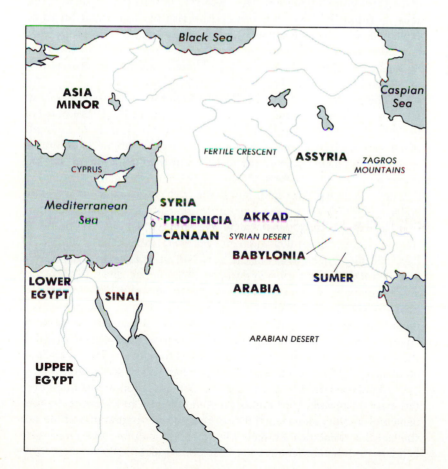

Figure 13–5

Southwest Asia, showing the Fertile Crescent (after Haviland, 1989).

To explain why the process of domestication occurred during only one of the hypothesized drying phases—the last—and not during any of the earlier ones, Braidwood found it necessary to invoke the concept of cultural readiness. He saw Upper Paleolithic and subsequent technological advances as permitting human experimentation with wild plants and animals across the earth. In those areas where the wild progenitors of easily domesticable species occurred in large quantities—the so-called Nuclear Zones—this experimentation eventually led to full-scale domestication and settled village life. Braidwood's excavations at the site of *Jarmo,* in the Zagros foothills, led him to believe that it was an example of such an early community.

As with Childe's theory, one weakness of Braidwood's views is that he relied on a simplistic view of Pleistocene and post-Pleistocene climatic conditions. Worse, Braidwood's theory is weakened because it is impossible to test it archaeologically. In the first place, the theory relies on vague, unmeasureable concepts such as cultural readiness. In the second place (and more damaging), the theory is inherently circular. If one accepts Braidwood's views, how is the rise of domestication to be explained? By recognizing that people became ready to practice it. And how does one determine whether people were ready for domestication? By seeing whether they practiced it. There is no independent testing involved; thus, it is not a very useful scientific theory.

The greatest problem with Braidwood's theory, however, lies in its teleological nature, criticized heavily by Lewis Binford (below). For Braidwood, the explanation for the occurrence of agriculture is simply that it was inevitable. But if it was inevitable, then there is nothing to explain; it happened because it had to, given the circumstances and the starting point. In Braidwood's theory, we have an explanation that assumes human behavior to be automatic over vast expanses of the globe and across thousands of years. Domestication is thus viewed as something that naturally occurred, given the proper environment and the necessary stage of technological development. But were there people who could have become agriculturists but did not? Not in Braidwood's theory. We may well regard an *invention or discovery* as automatic, given local history and circumstances: Somebody's discovery of something does not really need explaining as a cultural process, any more than the occurrence of a mutation requires an explanation in biology. But the *adoption or spread* of an innovation *does* require explanation: how some people come to utilize the new technique, item, or idea, and others to reject it. That is far from automatic, and Braidwood's teleological theory fails to address it.

Braidwood did not really interpret domestication in a cultural evolutionary framework. Furthermore, he did not take into account the fundamental stability and adaptability of the gatherer-hunter way of life nor the fact that domestication makes life more difficult for most people (see below)—and thereby requires a good reason to adopt it.

LEWIS R. BINFORD

Binford, of the University of New Mexico, sees global environmental changes during the immediate post-Pleistocene as instrumental in the development of domestication, like Childe. The environmental change used by Binford is not the undocumented and uncertain climatic drying, however, but the very definite rise in sea levels brought about by the melting of land-covering ice masses. He sees rising coastlines as shortening the length and amount of land area that comprised coastal zones. This, in turn, increased the population density of Archaic gatherer-hunter groups exploiting sea resources.

Note that no actual rise in population size was necessary for this kind of increasing population density to have occurred. This is an important point—one that does not escape Binford—because gatherer-hunter groups probably did everything possible to keep population sizes stable. According to Binford's theory, the population size stayed the same, while the amount of available *land* decreased.

Rising population densities are seen by Binford as leading to increasing population pressure. Coastal populations were approaching the **carrying capacity** of their environment. Because gatherer-hunter groups in general do not adapt well to conditions of population stress, this pressure resulted in the out-migration of portions of the population to other regions away from the coast. The people who emigrated—accustomed to exploiting sea resources—found these new areas to be **marginal environments** because there were no wild sea resources in abundance. Because of the population pressure at the coast, however, they had no other choice but to adapt.

Binford believes that the stress felt in the marginal areas led to the selection of different subsistence techniques that increased the unit output of the land, that is, the amount of food that could be extracted from a given parcel of territory. One result of these necessary and innovative techniques was domestication—taking control over various exploitable species—which does allow the acquistion of more food per area of ground surface.

Binford's theory has a number of strengths not found in the theories of Childe or Braidwood. First, he does take into account the **demographic** structure and stability of gatherer-hunter groups. This theory does not require any increase in population sizes, but instead holds post-Pleistocene environmental changes responsible for increasing population densities and pressure through the decrease of land area. Childe's theory is similar, although our current knowledge of gatherer-hunter demographics was not available in his day.

Binford also correctly recognizes that the development of domestication was not necessarily an advance or improvement, but rather a required response to deteriorating conditions. Although domestication does result in more food per unit area, it necessitates more work per per-

carrying capacity

The population size and density that a local environment can support, given the group's subsistence technology.

marginal environment

A natural setting or region that cannot support the population size and density of a human group without changes in the humans' subsistence technology.

demography

The statistical study of the characteristics of a population, such as birth rates, death rates, and life-spans.

son as well. It also causes other problems for many people, as we will see below.

Binford's theory is not without its problems, however, not the least of which lies in the comparison of expected to observed arachaeological data pertaining to sites of early domestication. In other words, Binford's model is testable, but not necessarily correct.

THE INFLUENCE OF ESTER BOSERUP

In the late 1960s and early 1970s, other scholars developed theories for the rise of domestication that also depended greatly on demographic theory and data. Seeing population pressure as an important independent variable (a cause, rather than an effect) in the rise of domestication was thus incorporated into a number of archaeological theories. The ideas of Danish economist Ester Boserup were instrumental in their development.

Boserup's major contribution to studies of the rise of domestication—and to all studies regarding cultural change, in fact—is that she argues that Malthus, the conservative social theorist who influenced Darwin, got things backwards. Malthus had argued in the late eighteenth century that food production could never keep up with population demands because people are reproducing far faster than their food supply can be increased (Chapter 3). In contrast, Boserup suggests that increasing population pressure itself has repeatedly required technological innovations that relieve the pressure, that is, allow a greater number and density of people to be fed. Necessity being the mother of invention, an increase in population leads to creative, technological solutions. Thus, demography becomes the independent variable in the equation, reversing Malthus, who failed to appreciate the ingenuity of human beings. Does population pressure lead to starvation or to innovation? Malthus argued the former, Boserup argues the latter.

Several archaeologists have incorporated Boserup's ideas into their theories, notably P. E. L. Smith and T. C. Young, who see some sort of environmental change in the post-Pleistocene as instrumental in the development of domestication. Thus, their views are similar to those of Childe and Binford. In their theories, however, no particular change is spelled out or emphasized, which is appropriate, given that past environmental conditions are yet to be understood in detail. Rather, they argue that general environmental trends allowed gatherer-hunters to adopt a **broad spectrum** type of subsistence system in an increasingly permissive environment.

The broad spectrum subsistence system was one in which the gathering of wild plants was emphasized over the hunting of wild animals and in which a wider range of plant resources was exploited. The system allowed or required a number of cultural adaptations, including transhumance and, in some cases, increasing *sedentism,* the habit of staying settled in one place over significant lengths of time. These cultural

broad spectrum

A subsistence technology in which the gathering of a wide range of plant species is emphasized.

adaptations—for which good empirical support exists in the archaeological record, and which were trends in the Archaic—are seen by Smith and Young as having led to increased population sizes.

Why would broad spectrum subsistence, along with increasing transhumance and sedentism, lead gatherer-hunters to increase their populations? The answer is found by considering demographic trends in light of the changing economic value of having children, given developing technologies.

While the theorists see population increasing in many places, they go on to point out that certain population growth occurred in **circumscribed** areas, that is, areas from which out-migration is very difficult or impossible. Hindrances to out-migration might be physical (water surrounding an island, mountains surrounding a valley) or social (neighboring people who do not want anyone moving through their territory). In either case, population increases in these places of fixed area will clearly lead to increasing population density and pressure—an impending deterioration in the quality of life because of too many people in too little space. Enter the ideas of Boserup—in circumscribed areas, where population pressure increased, creative behavioral solutions that allow the carrying capacity of the land to rise are necessary for a population to survive. One such behavior was domestication.

These theories might seem quite similar to that offered by Binford, and indeed, they are. Note, however, that Smith and Young see cultural adaptations as causing an increase in population size, while Binford emphasizes that gatherer-hunter cultural patterns keep populations in equilibrium.

circumscribed
Constrained, bounded.

KENT V. FLANNERY

During the 1960s and 1970s, Flannery developed a broad and innovative theory for the rise of domestication. We have already discussed Flannery's research in the Oaxaca Valley of Mexico.

Flannery has conducted fieldwork not only in Oaxaca, but also in the Near East, most notably at the site of *Ali Kosh*, a very early village on the Deh Luran Plain (Figure 13–6). First settled about 9,000 years ago, Ali Kosh was inhabited by domesticators as early as 8,500 B.P. One thousand years after this, the entire Near East was settled by agriculturalists specializing in intensive grain cultivation or animal husbandry.

Because Flannery has conducted investigations in both Oaxaca and the Deh Luran Plain, and has considered both the similarities and differences of New World and Old World domestication, his ideas have relatively broad applicability.

Like several of the theorists we have already considered, Flannery sees an environmental change during the post-Pleistocene as critical. Without specifying what this environmental shift was, he argues, as do Smith and Young, that it led to a permissive environmental situation and

Figure 13-6

The Deh Luran Plain and surrounding regions (after Hole, Flannery, and Neely, 1971).

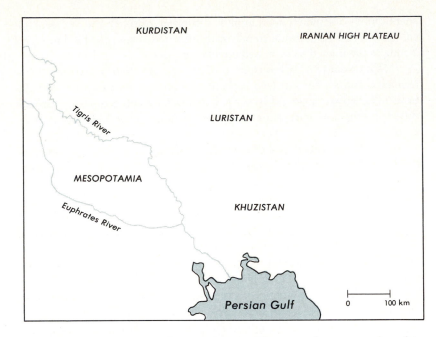

the practice of broad spectrum gathering. Flannery also argues that this subsistence system led to regular patterns of transhumance that became more sensitive to seasonal environmental variation through time.

Particular transhumant settlement systems—the actual patterns of movement undertaken by groups of people during the annual round—were determined by local conditions and factors of seasonality and scheduling. Regular patterns of transhumance lead to insignificant amounts of domestication, so insignificant that they might not always be recognized in the archaeological record. An example might have been the purposeful planting of certain plant species—perhaps making up as little as 5 percent of the diet—to ensure relatively easy harvesting the following year. Modern gatherer-hunters know about planting seeds, and there seems no reason to think our Archaic ancestors lacked that knowledge. They did not do much planting, though, because (contrary to popular belief) the work involved was not rewarded by a high return of food, but rather by a *predictable* return. As scheduling became a more significant part of life, however, people might have planted more extensively because it made life more secure. In the face of seasonal fluctuations, a little security may be quite valuable.

The major cultigens in both the Old and New Worlds—barley and wheat in the former, and maize (corn) in the latter—were not domesticated until hundreds of years after the first domestication was practiced (the earliest domesticated plants included various forms of squash and beans). These cultigens were not domesticated early most likely because they could not be controlled without a relatively great amount of work.

Why did they then become so important in the diet? First, because the wild forms could be found in abundance across large geographic areas and, once domesticated, were used widely. Second (and more important), because of the genetic effects within the species that domestication brought about.

Flannery's theory is powerful because he recognizes that domestication—human control—affects not only the people involved but also the resources themselves. Genetic traits in all species exhibit a certain amount of expressed or phenotypic variability. Populations of wild maize, wheat, and barley plants were no exception. Maize serves as a good example.

It is thought that, unlike its modern, domesticated form, wild maize had a very small number of seeds encased in hard, individual cases (called *glumes*) on stalks (called *rachis*) that were quite brittle. Phenotypic variability was expressed in the degree of hardness of the cases as well as in the degree of brittleness of the stalks. Natural selection seems to have favored the harder glumes and more brittle rachis, because of the increased protection and easier distribution of seeds that these conditions offered. A wild relative of corn, called **teosinte**, preserves many of the characteristics of the precursor of modern domestic corn.

As human groups began exploiting these wild plants more and more, and as they started to control them somewhat by planting the seeds to increase the efficiency of the scheduling system, something remarkable seems to have occurred to the nature of the selection involved. It appears that selection shifted in the opposite direction—toward smaller, softer glumes and tougher rachis. This is the condition of modern maize, and it is logical to expect the shift, given human intervention. Softer glumes made the seeds easier to process, and tougher rachis caused them to cling to the plant and thus be more easily gathered. Thus, humans more often collected, distributed, and possibly planted those individual specimens that would have had the *least* chance of propagating themselves in the wild. The result was that maize plants became genetically dependent on human interaction.

We can see, then, that human exploitation of these plants dramatically altered the evolutionary forces affecting them, and did so by making them more attractive food resources. We can say that a positive feedback relationship was put into action—human exploitation and control resulted in altered phenotypic variability and changing frequencies of phenotypes, which in turn resulted in even more human exploitation, and so on. Gradually, according to Flannery, this positive feedback relationship encouraged humans to schedule more and more time to the planting and harvesting of the major plant species. They did so because the plants were returning a greater quantity of food with increasing reliability. The plants in time began to look more modern, and eventually, the plants needed human intervention to survive at all (Figure 13–7).

teosinte

Wild plesiomorphic relative of corn, probably similar to its ancestor.

Figure 13-7

The evolution of Tehuacan maize. With years of hybridization and cultivation, the plant became larger and sturdier. Cobs became longer, the number of rows of kernels increased, and a single soft husk came to cover the entire cob.

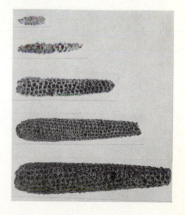

By this time, humans were getting many of their needed calories from the major plant species and were living in nearly permanent settlements in areas where these plants grew well.

RECENT APPROACHES

David Rindos has noted that one element lacking in many explanations of the rise of agriculture is knowledge of the genetic evolution of the cultigen itself and has argued for domestication as a coevolutionary process between humans and their food, each adapting to the other. While this is certainly another part of the equation, it still fails to answer the question of why a certain group of people at a certain time in a certain place adopted agriculture and abandoned the gathering-hunting way of life that had been so successful for so long.

A comprehensive model for the rise of plant food production in the Near East has been offered by Joy McCorriston and Frank Hole, integrating many of the theories we have discussed and relating these to the growing archaeological database.

There were four necessary preconditions for the origin of food production in the Near East: 1) climatic change, resulting in greater seasonality; 2) change to the environment wrought by humans; 3) new technologies; and 4) social changes. Apparently, the climate in the Jordan Valley was considerably irregular, with greater differences between summer and winter than at present. This selected for plants that could form new species and colonize new areas rapidly, annual plants as opposed to perennials; and the selection would have been intensified by human disturbance in the area. Further, the drier times probably forced people into larger congregations, stressing the local environment further and requiring creative solutions to the problem of feeding everyone.

Early annual plants are known from the burnt remains of wild cereals, about 12,000 to 11,000 B.P. (during the Epipaleolithic) at the sites of Abu Hureyra, Mureybat, and Wadi Hammeh. This was a necessity for domestication in the area, for these plants had to evolve before people could use them. McCorriston and Hole argue that they evolved as adaptive responses to the unstable climate and to colonized areas being increasingly concentrated with humans.

Social prerequisites to agriculture are important to consider as well, they argue. One needs the means to gather and process the plants in sufficient quantity at the right time, the means to store them, and the means to protect and distribute them. Agricultural economics is based on delaying gratification—working hard this month so that you can eat next December—very different from the here-and-now of gatherer-hunters.

The *Natufian* period in the Jordan Valley (12,500–10,500 B.P.) shows archaeological evidence, such as sickles, of harvesting wild plants. Increased sedentism is indicated by larger sites (villages) in addition to the smaller sites (camps) that were also present during the earlier Geometric Kebaran period. These village sites have large storage facilities and grinding tools and the first cemeteries in the area. Grinding cereals to prepare them for eating introduces fine bits of stone from the grinding surface into the food and produces greater tooth wear, also found in the Natufian.

In the pre-pottery Neolithic A (or PPNA, 10,000 to 9,500 B.P.), early domesticated wheat, barley, peas, and lentils appear in the archaeological record at the sites of Jericho, Nativ Hagdud, and Tell Aswad. Later, in the pre-pottery Neolithic B (PPNB, 9,500 to 8,000 B.P.), the plant domesticators adopted sheep and goat herding, as it diffused from the northern and eastern highlands and as they expanded outward. By 8,000 B.P., the basic structure of fully sedentary societies based on mixed farming economies was in place.

The Rise of Domestication: Evidence

Domestication arose initially and independently in several places on earth over the course of several thousand years, including southwest Asia (the Near and Middle East), southeast Asia, China, South America, and the central highlands of Mexico (Figure 13–8; Box 13–1). While there are several important similarities among all cases of the initial rise of domestication, a comparison of the Old and New Worlds points out some interesting differences.

RELIANCE ON DOMESTICATED ANIMALS

One of the most obvious differences was that people in the New World relied much less on domesticated *animals* than did people in the Old World. Many New World groups domesticated only the dog. A few groups kept turkeys and a number of other small species. Only in the highlands of the Andes did animals play a significant role in the subsistence economy, with llamas serving as beasts of burden.

In contrast, much of Old World domestication, from its first emergence, consisted of control over sheep, goats, and later cattle and pigs. Ali Kosh, for instance, became a settlement highly specialized in animal husbandry, as did a number of other Near Eastern villages, and imported much of its grain. The best explanation for this striking contrast between New and Old Worlds is that easily domesticable and useful animals did not occur in abundance over much of the former. As a result, New World residents never developed a host of technological items associated with animal domestication, including the plow. In addition, products such as leather and wool were not available to New World people as readily as they were to those in the Old World.

PLANT DOMESTICATION

A second difference between New World and Old World domestication was that very distinctive plant species were domesticated in each hemisphere. As mentioned, the staple crop of New World domesticators was maize. It still is. In contrast, many Old World cultivators concentrated on

Exception to the Rule: The Domestication of the Dog

The domestication of the dog from various species of wild wolves was in certain respects unique when compared with the domestication of other animals and plants. First, the process of dog domestication began well before any other species came under human control, at least 12,000 years ago. Second, many gatherer-hunter groups domesticated dogs and nothing else, maintaining a gathering and hunting way of life in all other respects. Gatherer-hunters living today have domesticated dogs. Finally, domesticated dogs can be found throughout the world. Various groups of people have come to rely on different combinations of domesticants; maize dominated in the New World, while wheat and barley became staples in many regions of the Old World, for instance. And domesticated animals in general were relatively rare in the former while economically significant in the latter. Domesticated dogs, in contrast, appear everywhere.

Why is the dog unique, the exception to the rule? There are several good reasons.

For one thing, dogs are useful companions to hunters. Dogs have a much better sense of smell than people and could locate prey in this manner while humans depended on eyesight. The two well-developed senses working together increased the chance for a successful hunt. Dogs could also run faster than people, at least over relatively short distances, and could overtake many wild animals that might otherwise escape. Humans contributed better endurance and perseverance. In addition, dogs could kill or at least injure many animals with their powerful jaws and large canines. Humans added diverse weapons to the arsenal. All in all, dogs and human hunters in combination made an effective hunting team with well-developed hunting skills. This undoubtedly benefited those Paleolithic groups who depended on wild animals for much of

wheat and barley. In China and southeast Asia, the staples were millet and, later, rice. In addition to these staples, New and Old World people domesticated very different collections of plants. Out of hundreds of species, only a handful are found in common, thus making it very unlikely that domestication in either hemisphere was in any way the result of contact with the other.

SETTLEMENTS

A third difference between the New and Old Worlds was that domestication occurred before settled, sedentary life in the former—at least in Central Mexico—while full-scale sedentism preceded domestication in many regions of the Old World. Keep in mind that this is a very general contrast. Not all New World residents were practicing domestication before settling down, and not all Old World people found it necessary to inhabit permanent settlements before relying on domesticated foods. Also, it must be noted that there is not full agreement among archaeologists about this contrast.

A number of important similarities are seen among all cases of initial, independently developed domestication. In almost all cases, it was a gradual process taking place over hundreds, if not thousands, of years. It

their food—a condition that was probably more common during and just after the Pleistocene.

Dogs also offered protection to humans, with their propensity to bark an alarm at any foreign presence. Many wild animals were a threat to Upper Paleolithic people, and it must have been reassuring to know the dogs would give a warning well before attack or even help defend the camp themselves.

But dogs offered other benefits as well. Wolves and dogs are pack animals, and thus highly social. Humans are highly social as well, as we know, and dogs might have easily adjusted to human groups. Different species, more accustomed to an isolated existence, did not make this adjustment without a lot of human encouragement.

By accepting a human group as the pack, with the humans clearly at the top of the hierarchy, a dog offered companionship and emotional warmth, qualities we appreciate to this day. And dogs from quite early might have offered literal warmth as well. Australian aborigines sleep with their dogs on cooler nights, and the number of dogs permitted to sleep with the people is determined by how cold it is. The phrase "three-dog night" is indeed Aborigine, meaning very cold weather. It was later taken for the name of a popular rock-and-roll band.

Today, there are hundreds of dog breeds, the result of continuous artificial selection for varied, favored traits. Dogs range greatly in overall size, length of hair, length of tail, color, temperament, and natural abilities. Still, all dogs remain our "best friends" (apologies to those who prefer cats), as they must have been during the later part of the Ice Ages.

Reference:

Clutton-Brock, J. (1987). *A history of domesticated animals.* Austin: University of Texas Press.

---

follows that domestication was an unconscious endeavor, not under the control of any individuals or small groups of individuals, much less the work of a single genius.

In spite of these general similarities, it is difficult to sort through the complete archaeological record and develop a simple model for the development of domestication. Many sites have contributed to the development of our present understanding of the processes that were involved. It is, however, possible to evaluate the various theories by looking at archaeological evidence for the rise of domestication in specific areas. One area, the Tehuacan Valley in the Mexican highlands, has been studied intensively and specifically for evidence of early domestication.

THE TEHUACAN VALLEY

Richard MacNeish chose to investigate this area for two reasons: 1) It appeared to be centrally located in respect to the geographical region in which the wild progenitors of maize could be found, and 2) the valley contained many dry caves, good settings for the preservation of perishable materials such as plant remains.

The valley is in the physiographic zone of Mexico known as the central highlands, though the valley floor elevation of 1,500 meters above

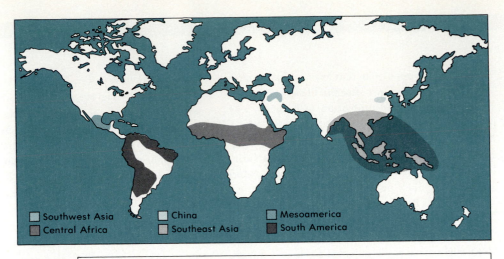

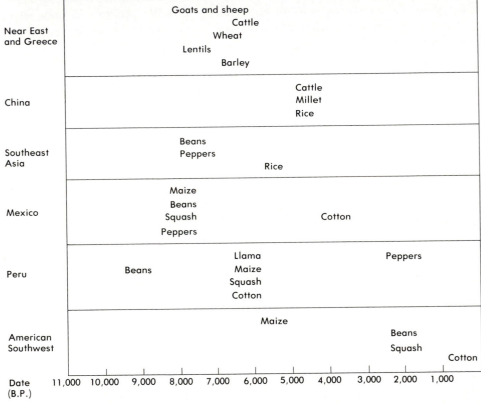

Figure 13-8

Areas of initial domestication, along with a chronology of the
domestication of various plants and animals (after Jolly and Plog, 1979).

sea level is relatively low for the region. The climate is quite dry, with most rainfall occurring during a two-month period in the summer. Indeed, the area can be considered marginal in many respects. It can also be thought of as circumscribed, being roughly surrounded by high mountains.

There are four major environmental zones in the valley, making it similar to other central highland locales (see above). These are: 1) the **alluvial plain** on either side of a small river, 2) the **limestone-travertine** slopes to the west, 3) the Coxcatlan thorn forest to the east, and 4) the surrounding higher mountains, once covered with oak forest. MacNeish excavated a number of dry caves and open-air sites in the valley. From the results of these excavations he has suggested the following phases and sequence of events.

The Ajuereado Phase, starting with the earliest evidence of people, dates from c. 12,000 to 9,200 B.P. Paleoindian and early Archaic adaptations were being practiced with small, seasonally wandering bands of gatherer-hunters concentrating on small game (such as rabbit) and a certain number of wild plants. The majority of the tools were made of chipped flint, evidence that subsistence activities were in large measure concerned with hunting.

The climate was only slightly cooler and wetter than it is today, and the vegetation was *xerophytic*—adapted for growth where there is a limited water supply. By the end of this phase, all fauna were of modern type.

The El Riego Phase dates from 9,200 to 7,200 years ago. During this phase, there continued to be small, seasonally wandering bands in the valley, although a population increase is apparent. In addition, plant collecting appears to have been taking on more importance than animal hunting—there is the first evidence of ground stone and pecked stone tools, including mortars, pestles, manos, and metates. There is also some evidence for emerging social stratification in the form of elaborate burials.

Sites become equally divided between what are called *microband* and *macroband* encampments, probably containing individual families and groups of related families, respectively. This pattern demonstrates the coalescing of groups at particular times of the year, in this case during the spring and wet seasons.

The Coxcatlan Phase dates from 7,200 to 5,400 years ago. During this time, there was still a division betwen microband and macroband settlements, although the latter seem to have been somewhat larger and in existence longer during the year. There is also evidence that domestication emerged for the first time during this phase, with certain varieties of squash and beans coming under human control. Plant collecting remained the primary method of acquiring food, however.

alluvial plain

A level or gently sloping land surface formed by extensive deposition of materials carried by flowing water.

limestone travertine

Two minerals formed by the deposition of geological materials in water.

Issues in Anthropology 13–2

Maize Domestication in the Southwest

The study of maize (corn) domestication in the southwestern United States is important, as it has played a major role among local populations for centuries. Maize played a crucial role in subsequent sociocultural development throughout the southwest and neighboring regions, particularly in the rise of sociocultural complexity (Chapter 14). It is important to know when and how domesticated maize emerged in the region, and some recent research suggests that certain long-held conclusions need to be rethought.

Maize probably arrived in the southwest nearly 4,000 years ago. A member of the so-called "Chapalote Series," this maize rapidly introgressed with a small, wild relative of modern corn, called teosinte, and spread among numerous societies. Yet it was not the only type of maize to impact on the region. A different type, called Maiz de Ocho, may

have had a profound effect on southwestern prehistory during early agricultural times. Maiz de Ocho became well adapted biologically to arid regions (as much of the southwest is), had large, floury kernels that produced high yields, and was easily milled. Thus, it is thought to have played an important role in subsequent southwestern sociocultural development. The traditional view, however, is that it arrived in the southwest well after the first maize, sometime near A.D. 700. This is the view that has now been challenged.

Archaeologists from New Mexico State University (including Steadman Upham and Richard MacNeish) and elsewhere have been excavating and analyzing materials from several rockshelters in southern New Mexico. Included are more than 350 maize specimens that currently provide the clearest evidence for the antiquity of Maiz

---

MacNeish's fourth phase—the Abejas Phase—dates from 5,400 to 4,300 years B.P. It was a critical time in regard to the development of domestication. A rapid and significant shift occurred in the settlement pattern of the people inhabiting the valley, with macroband settlements—some possibly inhabited year-round—moving from the thorn forest to the alluvial plain. Significantly, it was also during the Abejas Phase that maize was domesticated for the first time. It must be remembered, however, that about 70 percent of the food was still coming from the gathering of wild plants.

The Purron Phase dates from 4,300 to 3,500 years ago. It was a time of little change except for the introduction of pottery. The Ajalpan Phase dates from 3,500 to 2,900 years ago. It was during this time that full-scale sedentary maize domestication emerged. People were living in small, permanently occupied agricultural villages of 100 to 300 residents on the valley floor.

MacNeish's phases for the Tehuacan Valley continue, tracing the development of intensive agriculture and complex society. We need not consider these subsequent phases, however (Box 13–2).

tell

Earthen and rubble mound, usually covering the remains of a long-term settlement in the Near East.

ABU HUREYRA

Andrew Moore has investigated the rise of domestication in the Old World at the village site of **Tell** Abu Hureyra, in Syria. The site is

de Ocho in the southwest. Obsidian hydration and ^{14}C dates of these specimens (Chapter 2) have shown that the earliest form of Maiz de Ocho—called Proto-Maiz de Ocho—was in the region by the late second or early first millennium B.C. This is not much later than when the first Chapalote Maize arrived. Further, evidence from the rockshelters suggests that Maiz de Ocho itself was present shortly thereafter, many centuries before the previously assumed date of A.D. 700.

Upham points out that these dates are some of the most reliable that are available. The ^{14}C dates were taken on the maize specimens themselves, not on associated wood or charcoal pieces that could be from much earlier. In addition, many of the specimens come from well-documented stratigraphic contexts or from within rockshelters and were excavated with great care and precision.

These new, earlier dates support the idea that Maiz de Ocho evolved within the southwest and did not diffuse from a location to the south, in Central or South America. Previously, archaeologists assumed that it had (see Chapter 3 on diffusion). The dates also demonstrate that domesticated maize has had a long tenure in North America and (more significantly) a wide range of phenotypic expression. This most likely played a part in the rise of sociocultural complexity. Research by Upham and MacNeish may lead us to alter our thinking about prehistoric agriculture and society in the New World.

Reference:

Upham, S., MacNeish, R. S., Galinat, W. C., & Stevenson C. M. (1987). Evidence concerning the origin of Maiz de Ocho. *American Anthropologist* 89(2):410–419.

notable for its great size and because it was occupied throughout the period during which domestication was developed in the area—from about 11,500 to 7,000 B.P., with only a brief period of abandonment. The archaeological research is significant because it resulted in the recovery of very large numbers of artifacts, animal bones, and plant remains all collected under rigorous controls. It has been possible to study the rise of domestication there in great detail.

The village was constructed in a location good for both gathering-hunting and the practice of domestication. It was placed at the boundaries of several environmental zones, with abundant wild grains nearby, at one end of a migratory route for Persian gazelle. There was also good, cultivable soil close at hand near the Euphrates River (which, with the Tigris, formed the arms of the "Fertile Crescent").

During the phase known as Abu Hureyra I (11,500 to 10,000 B.P.), no domestication was practiced, and intensive gathering and hunting was the rule. More than 150 species of plants were systematically gathered, while large numbers of gazelle were killed each late April or May (which can be determined if one knows the breeding pattern of gazelle). The inhabitants were sedentary throughout the year during this phase, and population appears to have been rising during this occupation, to about 300 or 400 inhabitants at any time.

After a brief (400-year) period of abandonment, the site was resettled about 9,600 years ago. The occupants of the site during the Abu Hureyra II phase were domesticators, cultivating eight kinds of plants, especially wheat and barley. They also had domesticated sheep and goat, although they continued hunting gazelle on a large scale for at least another 600 years because it was such an abundant and easily obtained source of meat. By 9,000 years B.P., herding of sheep and goat was replacing gazelle hunting, most likely because of overkill of the wild animals.

Inhabitants of Abu Hureyra II lived in permanent, mudbrick, multiroomed dwellings. They appear to have practiced craft specialization and long-distance trade (Chapter 14). As evident by skeletons, life was not easy for these agricultural people. A few seem to have spent many hours kneeling to grind wheat with manos and metates, and this chore undoubtedly caused them great pain, for it resulted in permanent damage to their toes, legs, and backs. Others appear to have spent much time carrying heavy, grain-filled baskets on the heads, an arduous and painful task. The practice of domestication did allow the population of the site to increase approximately tenfold, yet their bones indicate that living conditions for many of these people deteriorated.

The transformation from gathering-hunting to domesticating was quite rapid and complete at Abu Hureyra, at least relative to other locations where it has been studied archaeologically. Because of the rapidity of the change and because of several other factors, including the presence of a sedentary village there during Abu Hureyra I, the site is in striking contrast to what occurred in the Tehuacan Valley of Mexico. These two cases underscore the difficulty of forming a single theory for the rise of domestication that is applicable in all places where it occurred.

The Impacts of Domestication

Domestication had profound effects on many aspects of human life, including patterns of settlement, nature of technology, social structure and organization, the economy, ideology, diet itself, demography, overall health, and ecology. In the following general discussion, we consider each in turn.

SETTLEMENT

Paleolithic gatherer-hunters lived in bands that were very fluid in terms of size, individual membership, and geographic location. We have noted that settlement patterns changed during the Archaic, as groups of people more regularly practiced transhumance through time. In many instances, domestication made it necessary for people to become more sedentary, although this was not so everywhere.

With the practice of domestication, people no longer found it necessary to travel to the locations of naturally occurring wild food resources. Domesticators can, to some degree, determine where they will grow crops and tend animals once they have gained control over those crops and animals. After a decision has been reached about location, however, it is almost always necessary for the people to remain there much of the time because the plants and animals become genetically dependent on human interaction. Such is the case for the majority of the staple domesticants, at least. Further, if one chooses to localize one's resources, one may be obliged to defend them.

These factors resulted in a settlement pattern that was not so clearly in a directly dependent relationship with the natural environment, but that was more difficult to change once it had been established. In general, then, people became more sedentary with the rise of domestication.

TECHNOLOGY

Domestication required the development of a new assemblage of tool types and technological aids. Chipped stone tools, for instance, were gradually replaced by greater quantities of ground stone artifacts used primarily for grinding plant products. Recall that this was one of the Archaic trends, which continued as domestication became more important and intensive among people who practiced it.

In addition to these changes in tools, domestication led to the emergence of various features and structures, such as game pens, kraals, and storage facilities. The requirements of sedentism itself led to the construction of more permanent living quarters, in fact. In many places, permanent habitations replaced the tenuous shelters of wandering people.

Perhaps the best known technological change associated with the rise of domestication was the emergence of pottery. Yet neither pottery nor domestication were necessary requirements for each other. They merely occurred together in many locales because they functioned well together.

SOCIAL STRUCTURE AND ORGANIZATION

For numerous reasons, domestication led to the development of more complex political and social systems among the people practicing it. For one thing, population sizes and densities generally rise dramatically with the emergence of domestication, and the very presence of more people requires more complex and effective means of organization and control. Also, increased sedentism means that some appropriate system of leadership and control is required—it can be considered as the need for effective crowd control in a setting where individuals cannot simply walk away from conflict. Finally, the very act of controlling food resources requires better organization and cooperation among workers if everyone is to be fed.

Increasing political and social complexity seems to be invariably accompanied by increasing economic inequality. Indeed, the egalitarian nature of gatherer-hunter groups apparently disappeared quite rapidly with the emergence of domestication, if not earlier, during the late Archaic. In contrast to gatherer-hunters, status among agriculturalists is no longer achieved, but more and more often ascribed by birth. A political and social elite appeared shortly after the rise of domestication. Authority and force were concentrated in the hands of a smaller group of people, and the majority of the population found it increasingly difficult to obtain luxury and (eventually) necessary goods. These trends could not be predicted as they were happening, but the fact that they occurred almost everywhere that domestication arose—on all continents independently—suggests that the changes were contingent upon the adoption of this new mode of subsistence.

The fundamental and meaningful social groups of the people also changed as a result of domestication. The primacy of the band and nuclear family were taken over by the village and extended family, respectively. The former transition occurred because of the emergence of sedentism and the settled community. The latter took place for the same reason and because people found it necessary to cooperate in groups larger than the nuclear family in order to accomplish the tasks of subsistence. Later, *lineages* emerged—collections of people held together by ancestor-descendant relationships, of larger size than the extended family. People identifed and grouped themselves with larger and larger groups as a result of domestication.

ECONOMY

The fundamental shift in economic systems that occurred with the emergence of domestication was a change from a situation in which **reciprocity** was primary to a situation in which **redistribution** was dominant. Reciprocity, the primary system of exchange among gatherer-hunters, is the principal mode of exchange practiced among social equals. When someone gives you something, you have an obligation to return something of equal worth—to reciprocate—because you originate within the system from positions of equality.

Redistribution, which did not entirely replace reciprocity but did become the dominant form of exchange, is quite different. With redistribution, all people centralize their contributions to the economy in one place. Then, a recognized official (sometimes called a big man or head man) redistributes these goods to everyone according to a complex set of rules and relationships. Social equality is no longer present or reflected in the system of exchange.

Redistribution is more effective than reciprocity among fairly large groups of people. By centralizing their resources, people can undertake projects and activities that a lone gatherer-hunter family cannot accomplish. Such undertakings involve initial accumulations of **capital,** by which people can be fed and supported by the group at large, or a segment of it, rather than by their own direct procurement activities. This was one of the most critical shifts ultimately brought about by domestication, for it led directly to an increasing **division of labor**.

reciprocity

Economic system based on equality of status and the possibility and fulfillment of equal-value exchanges.

redistribution

Economic system in which a central agent has control over the movement of resources contributed by other members of the group.

capital

Accumulated goods and wealth.

division of labor

A multiplication of ways of obtaining sustenance; domestication brings about a greater division of labor.

But redistribution does reflect and encourage social and economic inequality, both of which increased as domestication intensified and societies became more complex.

IDEOLOGY

At first, it might not seem reasonable to consider that the way people think and view the world has been affected by the type of subsistence they practiced, yet there is good evidence for this relationship, with the subsistence technology in large measure shaping the ideology.

The concept of private property and private ownership of land and materials seems to have been the result of domestication. When people do not live in one place for extended periods of time, it is impossible for them to accumulate material goods. Sedentism, which often accompanied domestication, made possible the accumulation of goods. Material goods could be acquired through trading surplus food for them, for example, and so agriculturalists would be encouraged to grow surpluses. People would thus work harder, gather more and more material around them, and believe they were better off because of it. The result, however, was an increase in social and economic inequality; less work for some, but more work for most.

The status positions of men and women also seem to have become significantly different with the rise of domestication as a result of an increasing division of labor. As families became larger and increased sedentism required greater attention to housekeeping, males became relatively more involved with subsistence (or economic) and females with domestic matters. This is particularly true with the intensification of agriculture.

The reasons are unclear, but the relative social statuses of men and women vary in proportion to their economic power. As women were removed from subsistence activities, they had less status because subsistence is the source of economy.

Religious systems also changed with the emergence of domestication. Many gatherer-hunter groups believe in amorphous forces that permeate the universe, are either good or evil, and rarely represent recognizable individual souls or deities. Agriculturalists, on the other hand, are usually devoted to recognizable spirit beings—commonly ancestors or other accepted personages. The forces are often personified and the spirit beings more powerful, and gods are the result. The type of religious beliefs a group of people holds is thus somewhat related to the type of subsistence they practice.

DIET

As we have discussed, domestication did allow higher population densities because it was one very important means of getting more energy—more food—out of a given area of land. Surprisingly, however, the shift to domestication also required more individual and group effort—more work—to get an adequate food supply. Thus, domestication can be viewed as an intensification of subsistence in terms of both labor and return.

There is an alternative way to view domestication, however: in terms of the quality of the diet rather than the quantity of input and output. In general, when domestication, is adopted a decrease occurs in the variety of food sources being exploited. The diet becomes more monotonous, with an increasing concentration on fewer food types.

Monotony, however, was the least of the problems faced by domesticators. Fewer different foods means better chances of not getting a balanced diet. Moreover, the greater danger of concentrating on a limited number of foods lies in a general evolutionary principle—the less variability, the less adaptability. With domestication, human existence became more precarious because the dietary variability was decreased.

If you rely on 100 species and one goes bad, you still have 99. But if you rely heavily on one, such as Irish farmers relied on the potato in the nineteenth century, then a problem with that one species can result in widespread disaster, as it did. Thus, the chances for widespread famine and death increased with domestication, where before, with gathering-hunting, large portions of the overall population were not threatened all at the same time.

Unfortunately, this trend of increasing dietary monotony and precariousness continues in the modern world, where the motivations of agribusiness have encouraged the production of very limited numbers of highly productive (and inexpensively grown) plant strains. The tendency to depend on fewer and fewer species has been taken to a new and different extreme by the recent trend to decrease genetic variability within species. Modern Western society is thus producing more food than ever, but the variation expressed by this food is minimal. One bad crop can be economically catastrophic.

There is still another reason why the diets of domesticators are poorer than the diets of gatherer-hunters. With domestication, it appears that the nutritional value of the diet decreases because of the types of food resources controlled and the methods of food preparation. Mark Nathan Cohen, for instance, has been collecting data suggesting that increasingly poor nutritional status was coincident with the rise of domestication. He interprets this as more evidence that population pressure and stress played important roles in encouraging subsistence intensification.

Finally, it can be argued that the growing social and economic inequality brought about by domestication led to a situation in which more and more people were being denied access to the best and greatest variety of available foods. Not only was everyone's diet diminishing in value, many people's diets were diminishing significantly more than others.

DEMOGRAPHY

What were the demographic changes that occurred in response to the practice of domestication? In a nutshell, domestication led to rapid and remarkable growth in population size, population density, and eventually population pressure. A good way of understanding why it had this general effect is to refer to the cultural adaptations suggested by Smith, Young, and other theorists concerned with the initial emergence of domestication.

First, increased sedentism had profound effects on demographic structure, primarily by removing the discouraging influence high mobility had on having many children. Paleolithic gatherer-hunters, being extremely mobile geographically, would not want many young children at the same time because these children would have been difficult to carry and manage as the people moved over the terrain. With settled village life, this important discouragement was removed.

Second, the practice of domestication required a more intensive labor effort. One cannot explain growing population sizes merely by recognizing that domestication raises the carrying capacity—that still does not tell you *why*. But the increasing labor requirements do offer an explanation. Where a child has neither the knowledge to be an effective gatherer nor the skill to be an effective hunter and is thus an economic liability in such a system, domestication requires as many hands as possible at the appropriate times. In short, the nature of the agricultural system favors large families, which in turn affects the role of women in the economic and social systems.

OVERALL HEALTH

A good example of the general decline in health brought by agriculture is afforded by the gatherer-hunters who inhabited present-day Illinois in A. D. 950. About a century later, hoes and other agricultural artifacts appear in the archaeological record, as well as a lot of corn. There appears to be genetic continuity between the populations, as there is no evidence of the later agriculturalists being immigrants. Excavations of pre- and postagricultural populations were carefully done and the skeletal materials analyzed by a group of physical anthropologists, led by Alan Goodman and George Armelagos.

They found that persistent bacterial infections, which leave traces on the outer surface (periosteum) of the long bones, tripled after agriculture. Nutritional anemia, which is detectable as expansion of the inner (cortical) part of long bones, increased, which suggested iron deficiency, particularly in women and children. Rates of arthritis increased, and broken bones increased (which may be related to a dietary zinc deficiency—corn is notoriously low in zinc). More generally, life expectancy, as judged from the demographic composition of the skeletal populations, decreased dramatically; and mortality within the first year of life increased sharply.

Patterns of disease are strongly related to demography. Among people with low population densities, the diseases to which they are most subject are *endemic*—always present in the environment. With a rise in population density, however, *epidemic* diseases become more of a threat. Infectious diseases cannot propagate themselves efficiently when there are relatively few hosts available; consequently, they are not generally a major threat to the health of such populations. Agriculture brings a change in patterns of disease.

ECOLOGY

Food production radically changed the interaction between society and environment. Where as foragers, people had rarely exploited any single resource too intensively, as agriculturists, overexploitation became apparently commonplace. Food production encouraged and permitted population growth, which in turn promoted more intensive exploitation of the earth.

At a Neolithic site called *'Ain Ghazal,* north of Amman, Jordan, the inhabitants of 9,000 years ago raised goats, grew cereals and legumes, supplemented these with wild foodstuffs, and developed a prosperous, complex village life. Yet the inhabitants of the same site 7,000 years ago were fairly poor, pastoral herders. What happened? The pattern is common at other sites in the Levant: People slowly destroyed their environment by continuously exploiting it. In the case of 'Ain Ghazal, 2,000 years of unrestrained food production in a once rich environment resulted in its permanent abandonment at the end of the Neolithic.

The Intensification and Spread of Domestication

Political and social trends, as well as the demographic conditions, are difficult to reconstruct from the archaeological record. Nevertheless, reconstructing cultural evolutionary patterns is a fundamental goal of archaeology. The ecological and biological patterns relating to those cultural evolutionary trends are somewhat less ambiguous.

It is important to realize that all the various changes described above—changes in settlement, technology, social structure and organization, economy, ideology, diet, demography, overall health, and ecology—worked together in response to the rise of domestication. Yet certain changes had more significance than others because they, in turn, had great impacts on subsequent cultural evolutionary developments. Demographic changes appear to have had profound effects and exerted a positive feedback on food production. There are, in fact, two general responses to a growing population: 1) *intensifying domesticating practices*—to get even more food out of a given piece of land and thus support more people; and 2) *expanding the territory* over which domestication is the primary subsistence practice—to take it into new areas, among people who did not previously practice it, either by changing their lifeways directly or by altering their environment to such an extent that a foraging lifeway is no longer possible.

More complex societies practicing domestication have had great success in either absorbing, conquering, or transforming less complex societies. This process is still going on today, with the last few gatherer-hunters being absorbed or destroyed by the agricultural and industrialized societies around them (Box 13–3).

INTENSIFICATION

One means of intensification involved decreasing the fallow time, or the period during which a field was left unplanted so that soil nutrients could be restored. Plots of land cannot support crops continuously, and it was recognized early in the history of domestication that lands had to be periodically rested if they were to produce a good harvest. Societies with growing populations tended to push the system to its limits, however, by shortening this rest period. These actions put a number of stresses on the overall subsistence system that might have furthered its precariousness.

Certain groups went further by planting individual crops closer together, attempting to obtain more food from a given area of land. This practice made the soil lose its nutrients at a faster pace than before and, combined with shortened fallow periods, might have made matters even more precarious.

People did try to counteract these dangers, and one way they did so involved experimentation with hybrid species that were quickly recognized as both hardier and capable of producing greater yields. These people were fully knowledgeable and skilled at domestication—they simply could not foresee the long-term ramifications of these practices.

Another response involved the introduction and increasingly common use of various fertilizers, such as human and animal waste products. Finally, though only after agriculture had been practiced for some time, human groups began experimenting with water control devices, or *irrigation*. What had been an exclusive reliance on *dry farming*—practicing domestication without the benefit of water control—shifted to various types of irrigation agriculture, which clearly allowed greater yields and thus the support of greater, more dense, populations.

With intensification often comes soil depletion. Another way to get more out of the land, either because of more people or poorer yields, is to farm more land. This entails expanding outward, onto land on which somebody else may be doing other things.

DIFFUSION

The characteristics of the environments where domestication spread determined in large part the nature of the subsistence practices. As farming spread, farmers could not always use the same techniques if the

Another Revolution in Food Production

Plant domestication radically transformed prehistoric societies, and in the Near East, it certainly set in motion the social forces that ultimately resulted in our present-day civilization.

It would be a mistake, however, to think that the story of the introduction of domesticated plants ended in the Neolithic. Indeed, anthropologist Sidney Mintz of Johns Hopkins has shown how the introduction of sugar radically affected western European diets only a few centuries ago. Associated with industrialism, sugar continues to have a strong impact upon other societies as they become industrialized. Is it possible that we could shed some new light on the economic and social changes that accompanied the large-scale production of wheat and barley in the Neolithic from a knowledge of what happened because of sugar in the Industrial Revolution?

Mintz begins by noting that although it is natural to like sweet foods, no nonindustrialized society consumes it to nearly the extent that industrialized societies do. Between 1650 and 1750, in fact, consumption of sugar in England rose about a hundredfold. Certainly, they liked sugar; but why did they suddenly start liking it so much? Food preferences are cultural; for example, the English even sugar their tea, a thought that is repulsive to most Chinese tea drinkers. This is not explicable by recourse to nature—it is a social fact that requires explanation by recourse to other social facts.

Sugar, which was a rare item through medieval times, has had five different culturally defined uses. It was recommended as a medicine by early herbalists, like tobacco and later heroin, which is a use that is generally foreign to us. It was used widely as a spice, still generally unfamiliar, but preserved in some of our ancient holiday traditions such as glazed ham and spice cookies. Third, it was used as a decoration, particularly when mixed with almond paste, and elaborate artistic works were often made, such as the "four-and-twenty blackbirds baked in a pie" of the old nursery rhyme. It is still used in this way, though to a much less elaborate extent, in ancient holiday rituals, on birthday and wedding cakes.

In the mid-seventeenth century, however, sugar began to change from a prestige item to a fairly inexpensive and accessible commodity. This was associated economically with hard and forced labor for many, notably slaves on the New World plantations on which it was being grown. It was also, however, associated with local social changes: the emergence of an industrial force of wage-earning laborers who were consumers, not producers, of

---

tropical forest

A mature and stable environment in which the diversity of species is great but the carrying capacity is relatively low and often approached.

environment differed. In some cases, such as in the Greater Southwest, the environment was not remarkably different from that in areas of initial development, and so the practice of domestication was not substantially altered. In other areas, by contrast, the environment was radically different, and subsistence (and other aspects of life) changed dramatically.

The particular type of environment we want to focus on has been called the **tropical forest**. These forests once covered a vast amount of the world's land surface, and domestication spread into many of these areas over the past several thousand years (Figure 13–9). Today, however, tropical forests are rapidly being destroyed by the insurgence of more complex societies. The Amazon basin is probably the best example of this kind of destruction, with thousands and thousands of acres of forest land

sugar. Sugar was also attractive to them because there was a strong tendency to emulate the wealthy, and as sugar dropped in price, it became attractive to those who were, or who wanted to feel, upwardly mobile.

By the mid-eighteenth century, radical social changes were occurring as the Industrial Revolution gained impetus. In part, the urban laborers found that tea with sugar and bread with jam made a minimal meal seem more warm and hearty than what would otherwise have been the quintessentially minimal meal, bread and water. The sugar and the jam, however, radically increased the caloric value of the meal, and to an impoverished population that was nutritionally marginal, the sugar was healthy. It filled a calorie gap that existed among the working poor.

Additionally, women began to enter the industrial work force, which gave them less time to put into their traditional domestic work. The reduced emphasis on cooking the nutritious, traditional diet of broth and porridge increased the demand for prepared, or easily preparable, foods—such as tea, jam, and bread. These were substitutes, but not nearly as nutritious; thus, as income rose, balanced nutrition suffered, even as calories increased.

Further, urban labor required that an increasing number of meals be taken outside the home. This required that the schedule of eating be rearranged to fit the schedule of working; the prepared, sugar-filled foods helped accomplish this as well. Workers became accustomed to social sugar-filled breaks in their day, for example.

Where in 1650 sugar was a rarity item in England, by 1750 it was a luxury item that middle-class people could enjoy to a great extent, and by 1850 it was a necessity. A century and a half later, our pattern of consumption is similar: sugar, and sugared prepared foods, form the basis of much of our dietary calories. Our lives and diets in urban industrialized society have been reshaped by the impact of the large-scale production of sugar only a few hundred years ago. Mintz emphasizes that this is an historical documentation of how a culture becomes different by consuming differently.

One may well wonder about the comparable transformative effects that regular, abundant supplies of wheat and barley may have had on the early agricultural societies of the Near East.

Reference:

Mintz, S. (1985). *Sweetness and power*. New York: Viking.

already lost. We should remember that the significance and extent of the diffusion of domestication into this type of environment were probably much greater than the present world map would lead us to believe.

It is also necessary to remember that domesticators living in tropical forests today are probably very different culturally and behaviorally from those who first accepted domestication centuries ago. Like present-day gatherer-hunters, these people have felt the impacts of culture contact and modernization and have been forced into smaller parcels of land as more complex technologies have taken over. We must be careful when making analogies with modern societies as we attempt to reconstruct what took place in the past.

The general term applied to domestication practiced in tropical

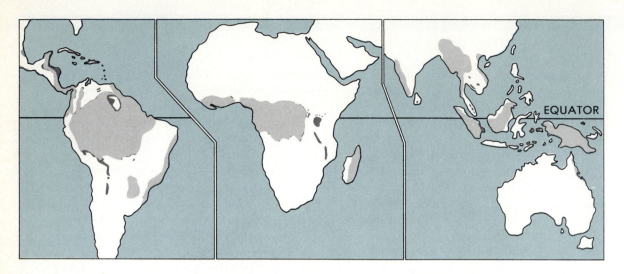

Figure 13-9

Worldwide distribution of tropical forests, past and present.

horticulture

Nonintensive agriculture, usually and necessarily practiced in tropical forests.

forests is **horticulture**. Other names given to this type of domestication (specific to certain areas) include *slash and burn*, *swidden*, and *milpa* agriculture.

Because of the nature of tropical forests, it was (and is today) necessary for people to adopt a less intensive subsistence technology than they might have elsewhere. As they brought agriculture into tropical forest regions, they were forced to do it somewhat differently and with attendant differences in aspects of their society.

First, villages were fairly small, and village inhabitants often found it necessary to split from the group in times of perceived environmental or social stress. In other words, group geographical fluidity was relatively high, similar to that of gatherer-hunter groups.

Second, the technology and tools of horticulturalists were relatively simple, compared with those of more intensive agricultural societies located in different environments. No irrigation was present, for the most part, and in those rare instances where irrigation was practiced, it was relatively simple. Tools were limited to digging sticks and other implements that are not associated with intensive cultivation.

A third similarity between gatherer-hunter and early horticultural societies is found in the realm of political, social, and economic practices. One does not commonly encounter complex governmental structures in horticultural societies, for instance, nor even the entrenched village hierarchies found in some of the earlier agricultural groups. Neither does one encounter any fixed economic classes, a significantly unequal distribution of necessary goods, or many bureaucratic social positions. These are absent primarily because horticulture allows many individual households to be self-sufficient and independent of larger village or societal organizations.

Because of the nature of the tropical forest environment, and because of the less intensive type of domestication necessary there, population densities cannot be very high. As a result, some demographic characteristics of horticulturists are similar to those of gatherer-hunter groups.

Finally, and obviously, the host of intensification practices put in use in other environments were generally absent among horticulturalists. Fallow periods were relatively long. Crops were not planted very close to one another. Irrigation, as mentioned, was simple if present at all.

Consideration of these several similarities between gatherer-hunters and horticulturalists makes it seem that the diffusion of domestication into tropical forests resulted in an almost complete return to or retention of a gatherer-hunter way of life. But in at least one important respect, horticultural societies were unique and did not resemble gatherer-hunter groups at all. This difference is important because it had significant impacts on subsequent cultural history.

The difference is that conflict and warfare appear to have been fairly common among horticultural societies, while quite rare among gatherer-hunters. Apparently, this difference emerged because horticulturalists lived very close to the carrying capacity of the environment. Gatherer-hunters generally did not. The former thus found it necessary to avoid any measureable fluctuations in the degree to which they exploited their environment and to carefully and systematically regulate their interactions with this environment. One of the ways they seem to have successfully met this need was to conduct raids against neighbors whom they perceived as enemies.

Continuous warfare and raiding among some horticulturalists promoted greater social complexity, with many of the characteristics of complex society and very different from either gatherer-hunters or other horticultural groups.

Indeed, the rarity of social complexity in tropical forests in general has recently been questioned. Through the use of modern remote sensing techniques, archaeologist Anna Roosevelt has discovered evidence for complex society in the Amazon basin, including numerous and densely spaced foundations, large refuse mounds, early, elaborate pottery, and some monumental architecture. Our knowledge of Amazon prehistory is changing rapidly (see Box 14–3 in the next chapter). The general rise of cultural complexity is taken up in the next chapter.

Summary

Humans have practiced gathering and hunting for most of their history, yet important changes began in several places around the world some 10,000 to 15,000 years ago. Artifact styles and forms became more regionally differentiated. An increasing amount and variety of raw materials were moved over greater distances. Habitation sites were occupied more regularly through the year, the environment was exploited more efficiently, and people came to depend more on plant and aquatic resources rather than on wild animals. Population sizes and densities were growing, and there was increasing social and economic differentiation within groups.

All these Archaic trends made domestication both possible and necessary. Indeed, there is no natural reason for domestication to emerge. It was not an invention or an advancement, but rather a cultural evolutionary process. Several theories attempt to explain its occurrence. Archaeological evidence shows that no single theory can explain it in all its original manifestations, though the theories that are testable have helped archaeologists focus on likely explanations for the adoption of agriculture in specific places.

The cultural results of domestication have been extensive. People often became more sedentary with domestication. Their technology changed in response to the shift in subsistence and settlement, with ground stone tools, permanent architecture, and pottery often coming into existence. Social structure and organization became generally more complex, the economy witnessed a shift from reciprocity to redistribution, and institutionalized inequality intensified. The belief in the importance of private property and ownership emerged, and new types of religion evolved. And diet changed, mostly for the worse, while population sizes and densities expanded. As the means for extracting food from the earth became more efficient, people often began to take their environment for granted and, in many cases, depleted or destroyed it.

Questions for Review

1. **Given the various disadvantages associated with domestication, why would people ever adopt it? Do you think the earliest domesticators had a free choice?**

2. What effects has the adoption of a subsistence pattern based on food production had upon other aspects of life? Why, for instance, do you suppose the religions of agricultualists tend to have more personalized gods than those of gatherer-hunters?

3. In science, correlation does not imply causation. For example, we find an increase in population associated with the origins of food production. Do you think populations increase because food production permits it, or do you think an increase in population forces a society to adopt domestication? How would you distinguish between these using archaeological data?

4. How can the nature of the environment affect the type of subsistence practiced?

For Further Reading

Green, S. W. (1980). Toward a general model of agricultural systems. In M. B. Schiffer (Ed.), *Advances in Archaeological Method and Theory* 3:311–355.

McCorriston, J., & Hole, F. (1991). The ecology of seasonal stress and the origins of agriculture in the Near East. *American Anthropologist*, 93:46–69.

Stark, B. L. (1986). Origins of food production in the New World. In D. J. Meltzer, D. D. Fowler, & J. A. Sabloff (Eds.), *American Archaeology, past and future: A celebration of the Society for American Archaeology.* Washington, D.C.: Smithsonian Institution Press.

Streuver, S. (Ed.). (1971). *Prehistoric agriculture.* Garden City, NY: The Natural History Press.

Wright, G. A. (1971). Origins of food production in Southeast Asia: A survey of ideas. *Current Anthropology*, 12:447–477.

The Rise of Complex Society

The Rise of Complex Society

pristine

Not significantly influenced by other cultures; in a general sense, pure and uncorrupted.

At the present time, all people everywhere either live in a complex society themselves or are profoundly influenced by the policies and politics of complex societies. Despite occasional news flashes concerning "**pristine**" isolated groups of gatherer-hunters who have no knowledge of twentieth-century technology, economy, or social systems, it is unlikely that any such groups exist now. While a high degree of cultural variation survives, the impacts of complex society on the world's people have been pervasive and widespread.

Yet the relatively recent rise of complex societies remains one of the most baffling watersheds in culture history, defying clear explanation. It is puzzling for a number of important reasons, not the least of which is the difficulty of defining precisely what constitutes a complex society. Other challenges that must be faced involve how to recognize degrees of social complexity (a particularly difficult task for archaeologists) and to explain why complexity should have ever evolved at all, and have done so independently in Central America, South America, the Near East, the Far East, south-central Asia, and both Egypt and sub-Saharan Africa. In this chapter, we consider these methodological and theoretical problems and discuss the nature of the archaeological record in relation to these issues.

The Nature of Complex Societies

Most of us have an implicit understanding of what a complex society is. We may even know something about when and where complex societies initially arose and later spread. Popular knowledge and interest is high when it comes to the ancient Egyptians, Sumerians, Greeks, and Romans of the Old World, and who among literate people has not been fascinated by the rise and fall of such impressive New World civilizations of the *Aztec, Inca,* and *Maya?*

Most of our images of early complex societies come from movies, novels, and expensive "coffee-table" books (Figure 14–1). Some of us are fortunate to visit large museums, where our notions can be refined and broadened. The images presented by all these sources—some accurate and some not so accurate—often include monumental temples and palaces of marble, towering pyramids and tombs, vast cities teeming with diverse people, large armies composed of violent men, poorly treated slaves, manipulative politicians, and so on.

These popular perceptions are widespread in our culture, and many people believe that most of what is to be known about complex societies is known. Yet a continuing and fundamental challenge to students of complex society is simply determining what defines one society as complex

Figure 14–1
Complex society, according to
Hollywood. While many of the
characteristics of complexity
are easily recognized, no simple
or clear definition is available.

and another as not complex (or *primitive*, a term that can have negative and disparaging connotations but that does not necessarily have to, as in biological comparisons, if used in a narrow sense). A related challenge, and possibly the more appropriate question to be addressed by anthropologists because of their interest in comparative research, involves determining or measuring degrees of complexity.

As a means of addressing the problem, we can make certain generalizations concerning the proper manner of viewing sociocultural complexity, and the first of these underscores the scope of the challenge.

LACK OF A CRITERION

No single criterion, or even a single set of criteria, appears to distinguish all occurrences of complex society from all occurrences of noncomplex society. In other words, complexity has exhibited and continues to exhibit many different characteristics, and scholars have yet to agree on any finite list of defining qualities. Indeed, we shall see that complex societies are exactly that—complex—and by their very nature must defy simple definitions. This is a situation similar to the one that physical anthropologists face when trying to define primates by a set of criteria that all primates meet and all non-primates lack (Chapter 5). Both complex societies and primates have been, and are, evolving systems, and this makes defining them exhaustively virtually impossible. However, with much effort, it is possible to devise lists of characters to help you identify a complex society or a primate when you encounter one.

It was not very long ago that archaeologists sought simple sets of criteria to recognize and define complex societies. One of the most influential of these sets was proposed by V. Gordon Childe, who, as we have already seen, was influential in studies regarding the rise of domestication (Chapter 13). Childe called the early rise of social complexity the *Urban Revolution* and recognized that it followed what he called the *Neolithic Revolution* (i.e., domestication) in several places around the Old World. He further claimed that a number of conditions were present in the first complex societies, including:

1. Relatively large and populous cities.
2. Labor specialization, particularly in the cities and most notably involving the movement of certain people away from subsistence activities.
3. The concentration of capital within cities and among certain people.
4. The presence of monumental public architecture in cities.
5. The presence of an elite class of nobles or priests—the same people possessing the majority of the economic capital.
6. Systems for recording information, that is, writing or numerical notation.
7. The development of certain abstract ways of thinking, or sciences, such as arithmetic and astronomy.
8. Sophisticated artistic expression.
9. Significant amounts of long-distance trade and exchange.
10. Some sort of urban solidarity at a scale not experienced previously and made necessary by the diversity of activities and occupations to be found.

Despite Childe's insights, it is currently agreed that none of these criteria is either necessary or sufficient for the occurrence of complex society. For instance, fairly large and populous cities seem to have arisen quite early in the Near East but were not present when complex society first arose in Mesoamerica. Yet the degree of urbanism present in later civilizations of the New World far exceeded anything to be found in the Old World until the time of Rome.

Furthermore, Childe never explained why these various things would appear together and thus could not address the question of why sociocultural complexity should have arisen. We recognize today that making lists of descriptive criteria is inappropriate for either defining or explaining complex entities in general. However, these criteria do help us identify a complex society when we see one.

THE SIMPLE-TO-COMPLEX CONTINUUM

The simple-to-complex society continuum is real. To put it another way, we know that some societies are more complex than others, despite our inability to determine systematically how, why, or by how much. France today is more complex than many societies in highland New Guinea. All societies at the present time are at a higher level of complexity than any that existed during the Paleolithic. Industrial nations since the eighteenth century are more complex than nonindustrial nations. How? In their population sizes, social relationships, degrees and distribution of political and economic power, and technologies. For example, people enter into more and diverse social relationships in a complex society. In relatively simpler societies, one interacts with family and with non-family differently, and with certain family members differently than with others. In our society, however, you have definite ways of interacting with your family, with people who sell you things, with people who want to buy things from you, with people who serve you lunch, with celebrities, with the police, with your teachers, and with a host of other people in your day-to-day existence.

Note, however, that these indicators are not measurements of sociocultural complexity—and certainly not universal—and their relative influences and evolutionary roles cannot be spelled out with confidence. A continuum of complexity exists, yet we do not know exactly how it is structured.

In a similar sense, we have no objective criteria on which to base the conclusion that prosimians, monkeys, apes, and humans are a group exhibiting increasing complexity. What we encounter instead are different specific strategies of adapting by the different groups of animals. Yet the evolution of something like a prosimian preceded, and was necessary for, the evolution of monkeys—and not vice-versa.

COMPLEXITY OF SOCIETIES VERSUS INDIVIDUAL COMPLEXITY

Although societies exhibit different degrees of complexity, the complexity is a property of the society and a product of its cultural history—the individual people in one society are no more or less complex than individuals in any other.

An appreciation of this fact will eliminate a long-standing and unfortunately still widespread myth, that people living in simple societies are themselves intellectually primitive. As Charles Darwin knew (Chapter 3), it requires skill, knowledge, and ingenuity to live in a simple society. And in a single generation, members of a simple society can become fully integrated into a complex society—if they so desire—indistinguishable from those members whose ancestors grew up in the complex society. This is because the complexity of a society is the result of its history, not of the innate properties or capabilities of its members.

Consider yourself trying to survive without the help and support of a vast number of other people living within your own society. You might own a personal computer, but you could never construct one by yourself from raw materials. You might own and operate a car and even repair certain parts of it, but again, it would be impossible for you to build and run one completely on your own from raw materials, not to mention refining your own oil! Even the simplest task is impossible without societal support, that complex network of social roles, positions, and history.

Yet conversely, the members of any simple society can feed, clothe, and care for themselves and thrive in their environment. They can cope because of their society's history. A great deal of knowledge and cleverness are properties of all humans in all societies, yet the specific society in which we are raised determines the kind of knowledge we get and the way we apply the cleverness we acquire.

INACCURATE CLASSIFICATIONS

heuristic

Useful in demonstrating a point, understanding a situation, or solving a problem, but not necessarily accurate or valid.

Taxonomic classifications of societies, depicting stages of complexity, are useful but not accurate. Here we can make the valuable distinction between **heuristic** devices and meaningful categorizations, so often required in physical anthropology and archaeology. Taxonomic classifications of sociocultural complexity are heuristic in that they help us organize vast amounts of diverse available data. In no way, however, should these schemes be viewed as accurately depicting the evolution of complexity as it actually occurred in any one place. Not only are complex societies complex, but the specific way in which each became complex is itself complex.

Different taxonomic schemes emphasize different aspects of society. We have organized data on cultural evolution by focusing on differences between technological and subsistence systems—foragers, horticulturalists, agriculturalists, complex societies, and industrial societies. Other analyses focus on economic exchange systems, observing that the prominent forms of exchange evolve from reciprocity, to redistribution, to (in some cases) the operations of a market. Still others give most of their attention to social-organizational systems, while yet another group has its greatest interest in evolving modes of ideology. We consider, at least briefly, all these various aspects of life. The point to remember here, however, is that all classifications are primarily heuristic devices—useful ways of organizing data—and not depictions of entire cultural systems or cultural evolutionary processes.

Two influential anthropologists who have suggested classifications of sociocultural complexity are Morton Fried and Elman Service. We consider their schemes later in this chapter, when we discuss the theoretical school each has helped shape in an attempt to explain the rise of sociocultural complexity.

MATCHING DEFINITIONS AND DATA

Definitions of complex society must match well with the available data for studying complex society, including archaeological data. There are numerous formal definitions of what constitutes a complex society. We limit our discussion to some of the more influential anthropological views, and in anthropology the data and definitions of complexity do not match well. This poor match can be seen most clearly when we attempt to describe the empirical correlates for the definitions.

Elman Service sees the legitimate **monopolization of force** by a recognized bureaucracy as a defining criterion of the **state**, itself the type of government necessary for the existence of a true complex society. *Force* is defined by anthropologists as the ability to influence people regardless of their opinions, in contrast to *authority*, which requires a degree of consent. And having a monopoly means simply that you have exclusive control or ownership over a commodity. But what exactly does monopolization of force mean in the empirical world?

1. Does it mean that parents, living in a complex society such as the United States, cannot order their children to bed at a certain time of night but must instead depend on representatives of the state to do so? Of course not. When children do not want to go to sleep at their bedtimes, it is the parents who rightfully have the ability to force them.

2. Does it mean that employers, living and operating a business in a similar complex society, cannot force their employees to work certain hours for certain wages, but must instead rely on representatives of the state to regulate matters? Sometimes, in some places and in certain cases, but not always.

3. Does it mean that a person cannot force a neighbor by any means possible to stop playing a stereo too loud, but must instead rely on representatives of the state (in this case, the police) when the neighbor refuses to turn down the music? In this case, the answer is yes, for that is the law, and relying on means other than the police could get you into a lot of trouble with the state.

These three examples point out the difficulty of defining monopolization of force empirically. Indeed, the state might have the recognized right to a monopoly of the force—governments certainly try to acquire it—but what we are really talking about are degrees of reasonableness. The exclusive right over force is expressed in the state's insistence that reasonable behavior (according to state definitions) be adhered to. Certainly, a parent can compel a child to go to bed, but not to stay there for, say, three weeks, and not by means of unreasonable physical abuse. Representatives of the state (government social workers) would separate the parent and child if this were to occur. Certainly employers can determine the work hours and wages of their employees, but these cannot be unreasonably long or low. Representatives of the state (perhaps from the Department of Labor) try to guard against it. And while the state would rather neighbors work out their noise problems on their own, in a reasonable manner, if things do get out of hand, the police will take over.

monopoly of force

Control of all the available, legitimate means of influencing people, regardless of their opinions.

state

The type of government found in complex societies, distinctive in having a monopoly of the available, legitimate force.

Defining monopolization of force within modern societies is hard enough—the task is enormous for the archaeologist interested in extinct complex societies.

A second influential definition of complex society has been offered by Leslie White (Figure 14–2). White believed that levels of sociocultural complexity should be measured with reference to the amount of energy a society can extract from the environment and the degree of efficiency by which it can be utilized. The more energy harnessed and the more efficiently, the more complex the society.

On the global scale, and in a very general sense, this definition is valid. Additionally, at first glance it might seem that energy procurement would be a relatively easy activity to measure empirically. Anthropologists such as Roy A. Rappaport, however, who studied the Tsembaga Maring horticulturalists in highland New Guinea, have found that measuring the use of energy even within simple societies is extremely complicated. White's definition has as much difficulty as Service's in matching the available data.

SERIES OF TRANSFORMATIONS

The rise of complex society was one of a series of transformations in cultural evolution. As such, it should exhibit certain general similarities to domestication and industrialism, the other most significant transformations in the evolution of culture. Before considering such similarities, however, let us consider the general temporal and spatial framework for the rise and spread of complex society around the world.

Figure 14–2
Leslie A. White

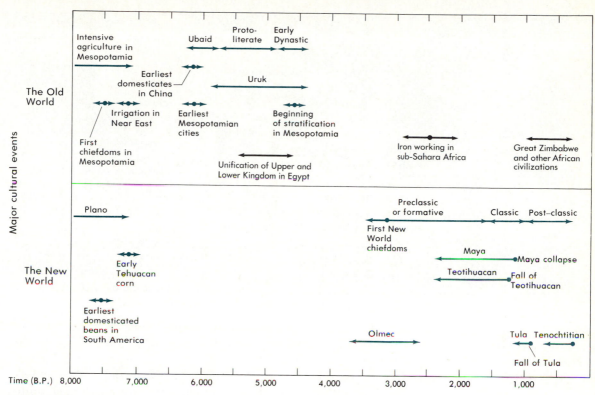

Figure 14-3

A chronology of the rise of complex society in various places around the world (after Jolly and Plog, 1979).

Descriptive Background

By employing these various guidelines, archaeologists see the first signs of complex society emerging in the Near East about 7,000 years ago (Figure 14–3). It is impossible to give a precise date for the rise of complexity because, like other evolutionary processes, it was a fairly gradual transformation, at least when it came to the calendar and the life-spans of individuals. Nevertheless, by 7,500 years ago, certain pottery styles were being widely distributed across northern Mesopotamia, and by 6,500 years ago, small cities with monumental architecture appeared across the southern Mesopotamian Alluvium (see below).

Similar archaeological evidence indicates that complexity arose later, though independently, in at least six or seven other places around the world (Figure 14–4)—Egypt, the Indus Valley of India, sub-Saharan Africa, and China in the Old World, as well as Mesoamerica and both eastern and western South America in the New World. It should be noted that western Europe did not evolve an indigenous complex society until the eleventh or twelfth century—after most of the rest of the world.

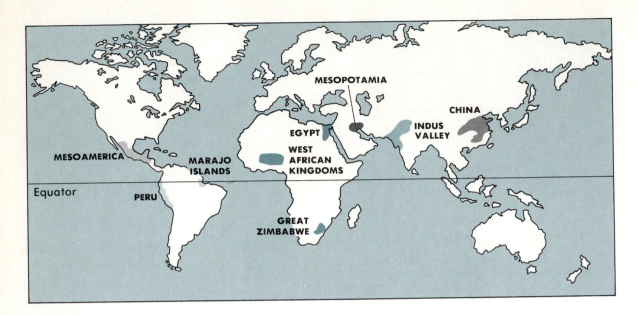

Figure 14-4

Locations of initial sociocultural complexity around the world.

In Egypt, the earliest signs of complexity appeared about 5,000 B.P., when the Upper and Lower Kingdoms were first united. There, as elsewhere, evidence of complex society consists of monumental architecture (suggesting the unequal distribution of goods and status) and the widespread distribution of architectural and pottery styles (suggesting economic and social interaction over a large region). Along the Indus River Valley, this transformation to complex society began about 4,500 years ago with the growing influence of the *Harappan* civilization. Indicators of complexity take the form of large, planned cities and uniform styles of art and architecture over a great area. And in China, particularly within the middle Wei and Hsiang-ho river valleys, complexity is first apparent possibly as early as 4,400 years ago and definitely by 3,800 years ago, with the appearance of large defensive structures, unequal distribution of wealth and status in burials and housing, and (once more) the widespread distribution of stylistic forms of art. Similarly, sub-Saharan Africa is recognized to have evolved centers of social complexity independently, perhaps 1,000 years ago.

The first complex societies in the New World developed later than the earliest ones of the Old World, though there is no evidence that New World people were influenced by Old World examples. In Mesoamerica, along the gulf coast of present-day Vera Cruz, initial complexity is associated with the rise of the Olmec c. 3,350 B.P. In South America, emerging social complexity is seen with the rapid spread of *Chavin* stylistic elements just after 3,000 years ago. The "Chavin Horizon" is recognized by the very widespread distribution of similar architectural and ceramic styles, most commonly depicting part-human and part-animal beasts.

It can thus be concluded that the trappings of complex society evolved from simpler social forms at least six or seven times independently, over the space of about 5,000 or 6,000 years. This period of time might appear lengthy until we recall that *Homo sapiens* had been present some 200,000 years or so up to that time, spending most of it foraging. Put in this temporal perspective, the initial rise of complexity can be seen as a radical, rapid evolutionary transformation. It was truly a "revolution" as named by Childe.

Differing forms and degrees of complex society subsequently spread over other areas outside these primary centers, including southern Europe, northern Africa, southeastern Asia, and the greater southwest of the United States. The extent to which complexity was independently invented or borrowed by these secondary centers is unclear and a matter of scholarly debate. Yet there is no question that such societies found complexity necessary, or adaptive, and so must have exhibited characteristics similar to those of the primary centers. Why else would complexity have been adopted? Indeed, in this sense it appears that developing sociocultural complexity mirrored some of the general characteristics of the rise of domestication, including the fact that it was neither inevitable nor progress. Complexity, despite its success in spreading around the world, has never been a better way of organizing people. In fact, like domestication, it seems to have led to a more precarious, less fair, less comfortable, and more disturbing way of life for more people. Thus, as is true with the rise of domestication, explaining the emergence of sociocultural complexity is a great challenge to archaeologists.

Conflicts Theories

One school, having roots in the scholarly writings of Karl Marx, sees social and class conflict as fundamentally responsible for the development of complex society. Perhaps best summarized by anthropologist Morton Fried, such **conflicts theories** view complexity as the outcome of a number of chronologically and functionally related developmental stages.

According to conflicts theorists, the first move away from the simple *egalitarian* social order found among gatherer-hunters involved the emergence of a situation in which luxury goods (items unnecessary for basic survival, such as jewelry) were distributed unequally. Individuals having greater status would have access to jewelry, while those having less status would not. If the trend continued, the unequal distribution of necessary goods (for example, food and shelter) followed, and true complexity as measured by inequality came into being. A few elite individuals would then have control over these **inelastic resources**, with the majority of the population clearly being treated unfairly.

Such unfair treatment inevitably led to conflict between emerging economic classes, and the elite erected the many other aspects of complex society as a means of maintaining the unfair status quo. Without

conflicts theory

Philosophy subsuming several theories that assume social and class antagonism as primarily responsible for the rise of complex society.

inelastic resources

Items that people cannot forego in a given quantity without facing dire consequences, regardless of their economic or social condition (food, for example). Elastic resources are those that people can more easily do without (luxuries).

such supporting mechanisms as standing armies, special systems of knowledge and communication, and religions that justified the inequalities, the small number of elite citizens would not have been able to keep the system operating. Thus, the rise of complex society was a necessary consequence of social and economic inequality.

MORTON FRIED

Morton Fried systematically outlined this school of thought in his 1967 book *The Evolution of Political Society*. He saw this sociocultural and political evolution as consisting of four stages. The first is the easily recognizable gatherer-hunter stage, in which society is egalitarian and status differences are temporary and determined only by age, sex, and ability. All status is achieved, and all people have equal access to all goods and social positions.

The second stage, according to Fried, involves the development of what he calls *ranked societies*. In these systems, only exotic or luxury items are distributed unequally. The third stage in Fried's model involves the development of what he calls *stratified societies,* and it is here that he sees basic and necessary goods, like food, being unequally distributed for the first time. This stage represents the initial development of true socioeconomic inequality. Notice also how this model is an example of a conflicts theory—none of the other characteristics of complexity have developed yet, only inequality—a conflict between classes.

This stage of stratified society is obviously the critical one in Fried's model. It is also a rather difficult one to accept because no examples of stratified societies can be clearly observed in either the archaeological or ethnographic records. The stratified society, according to Fried, is by its nature a very temporary and unstable one and is thus difficult to locate. True complex society develops rapidly out of the stratified condition, or the stratified society reverts rapidly back to a ranked society.

Fried's fourth step, when it does occur, involves the development of state governments and all the other characteristics of true complex societies in response to the growing unrest and conflict in a setting where a few people control the majority of the inelastic resources. As with other conflicts theories, complexity is seen as one necessary outcome of inequality.

ROBERT CARNEIRO

Another example of a conflicts theory is that developed by Robert Carneiro. Carneiro's model is quite similar to some of the theories we considered for the rise of domestication (Chapter 13). He sees population pressure having increased when population sizes grew in circumscribed areas, the result of the establishment of agriculture. Such population pressure, he argues, eventually led groups of people to take over other groups and their land through the mechanism of warfare and conquest. They needed to conquer these people, he argues, because they could no longer feed their own growing populations. The conquered people became the lower classes and were given fewer of the necessities of life, relative to what was available to the conquerors. And the socioeconomic level of any group of people was determined by the relative amount of time elapsing since their conquest. Such a process could be naturally reinforcing (Figure 14–5).

The other manifestations of complexity, such as a bureaucracy to administer the system and police to enforce it, are seen as developing naturally as the ever-enlarging militarily successful group took over more and more land and people.

Carneiro claims that similar scenarios occurred in many places where sociocultural complexity arose or later spread. He concentrates, however, on the rise of complex society in Peru, where clear evidence for environmental circumscription (fertile river valleys surrounded by desert) makes his theory applicable. There are, nevertheless, certain assumptions upon which his theory relies—assumptions that may be questioned.

Carneiro relies on Malthus, to whom increasing populations need greater quantities of food than the given land area can supply. He further assumes that warfare and conquest are the natural responses to increasing population pressure. Yet as we have seen, non-Malthusian economists emphasize alternative reactions to growing population sizes, such as the intensification of subsistence activities. People are not necessarily ravaged by overpopulation—they may devise the technological means of coping. In short, it has not been shown that warfare is a necessary response to a growing population in a circumscribed area.

KARL WITTFOGEL

A third conflicts theory was developed by Karl Wittfogel, who argued that complexity arose primarily out of the unequal access to the control

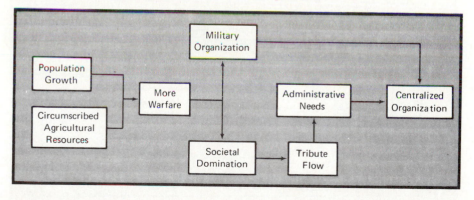

Figure 14–5

Schematic diagram of Carneiro's theory for the rise of complexity (after Thomas, 1989).

of large irrigation systems present in a number of developing agricultural societies. This *irrigation hypothesis*, discussed in great detail in Wittfogel's book *Oriental Despotism* (1957), argues that a small number of people—the emerging upper class or elite—might easily have gained control over the irrigation system because water control was critical to survival and because certain locations lent themselves to effective irrigation management and operation (Figure 14–6). If you live upriver, for example, you can manipulate the water supply for those living downstream. Through control of the irrigation system, the emerging elite persuaded the others to do their bidding, or to put it another way, acquired control over other people's lives. Other aspects of complex society evolved shortly thereafter, including writing and the calendar, which were mechanisms by which the elite maintained their control.

The fact that great irrigation systems are known to have been associated with several early complex societies makes Wittfogel's theory attractive. Yet the weakness of this theory lies in the fact that not all great civilizations relied on massive irrigation networks. One of the best examples can be found in the Valley of Oaxaca, in the central highlands of Mexico, where a high water table allowed simple pot irrigation at the household level to coexist with the recognizably complex society of *Monte Alban*, established 2,200 B.P. Thus, in Oaxaca it was possible for complex society to develop without intensive irrigation.

It is also true that very large irrigation systems were constructed and maintained by societies that never reached the state level of complexity. A good example of this situation is found in the greater southwest, primarily in the deserts of Arizona and particularly under what is now the modern city of Phoenix. There, the *Hohokam* flourished from c. 300 B.C.

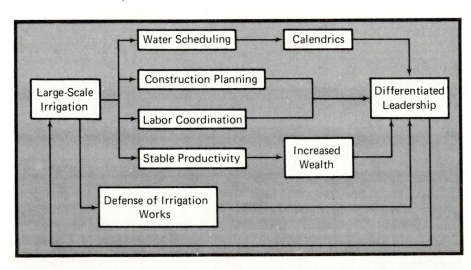

Figure 14–6

Schematic diagram of Wittfogel's theory for the rise of complexity (after Thomas 1989).

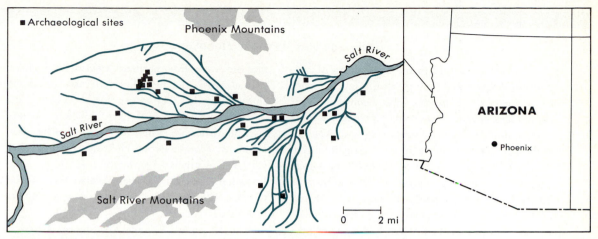

Figure 14-7

The system of Hohokam canals near modern Phoenix, Arizona (after Shorer and Ashmore, 1987).

(2,300 years ago) to A.D. 1200, largely because of their ability to control and channel water from the Salt and Gila Rivers in an otherwise inhospitable, arid environment. The scope of their irrigation practices was phenomenal, stretching mile after mile through barren desert landscape (Figure 14–7). So effective was their system of water control that European settlers in the nineteenth century found it useful to reopen and reuse some of the old prehistoric canals. Yet most archaeologists agree that the Hohokam never developed a state government nor established a true complex society (Box 14–1).

Massive irrigation is thus neither a sufficient nor a necessary condition for sociocultural complexity. Wittfogel's theory does not have general applicability. Still, in certain instances, irrigation did play an important role in cultural history. Wittfogel's contribution may help explain the rise of complex society in some areas, but not in all.

Benefits Theories

The second major school of thought concerning why complex society evolved is in a general way the opposite of conflicts theories. Again, a series of chronologically and functionally related steps are recognized by benefits theorists, but the overall process moves in a completely different direction.

Benefits theories depend on the notion that the members of any society as a group will perceive the utility of developing a more integrated and more highly differentiated social order, that is, imprecisely, a more complex society. The actual members of the society perceive the benefits to some degree and act rationally to bring the society into existence. It is not that their existence is threatened if they fail to do it, but rather, that it stands to be improved if they do it.

benefits theory

Philosophy subsuming several theories that assume groups of people perceive some utility in developing sociocultural complexity.

How Complex Were the Hohokam?

The Hohokam lived in the desert areas of present-day Arizona and Sonora, clearly not the most hospitable of environments. Most significant is the general lack of rain, only about a dozen inches each year at best, and less towards the west. Yet the Hohokam constructed impressive irrigation systems—miles of canals and related features—that supported intensive agriculture and allowed them to live in large, densely populated settlements. Some of their architecture was truly monumental, including the four-storied *Casa Grande* outside of present-day Florence, Arizona. Their system of trade and exchange was highly developed—they maintained contacts with neighboring groups over long periods of time, as reflected by the movement of many objects over relatively long distances. But was Hohokam society identifiably complex?

To answer this question, it helps to trace Hohokam prehistory from the time of its beginning. The Hohokam are recognized archaeologically with the beginning of the Pioneer Period, which some archaeologists claim started c. 300 B.C. Others, however, suggest as late as A.D. 500 for the beginning of the Hohokam—this lack of agreement on the fundamental issue of chronology reflects how little we know about Hohokam origins. Similarly, archaeologists do not agree on where the Hohokam came from. The two competing dominant views are

that they came from northern Mexico, from where, it is claimed, the Hohokam migrated north, or alternatively that they arose autochthonously in the Salt-Gila River Basin, where Hohokam society later flourished. In either case, and no matter when originally, Pioneer-Period Hohokam lived in small villages and practiced agriculture to some extent. Irrigation features were small, relative to what was to come. Clearly, theirs was *not* a complex society at the time.

The subsequent Colonial Period, lasting from c. A.D. 550/800 until c. A.D. 900/1000 (depending on whom you listen to), witnessed some dramatic developments. Hohokam influence spread throughout southern and central Arizona. Trade systems expanded as well, with the Hohokam exchanging shells from the Gulf of California for other goods with neighboring groups to the north and east. And ballcourts made their appearance at several Hohokam settlements. The purpose of these is thought to have been similar to that of Mesoamerican ballcourts, where ritual games remotely resembling soccer were played.

The Sedentary Period began c. A.D. 900/1000 and ended c. A.D. 1150. Trends of the previous two periods intensified, with Hohokam population sizes rising, dependence on agriculture growing, irrigation systems expanding, and trade networks enlarg-

---

As a first step, the people recognize that there is some sort of potential problem that must be coped with. Such a problem might be the acquisition of more food in times of environmental stress and shortage, gaining access to greater quantities of raw materials for tool manufacture, or even the need for social leadership itself.

Second, the most capable person, or group of people, is chosen to meet the perceived challenge. This response has been common among noncomplex gatherer-hunter groups for a very long time and in no way implies that complexity is inevitable. In some cases, however, a third step can occur, according to benefits theories.

This next step involves the establishment of certain leadership positions as permanent offices, rather than on an **ad-hoc basis,** and usually occurs when it is deemed a more efficient way of meeting recurring

ad-hoc basis
A decision made for a specific instance.

ing. Many exotic trade items could be found in the Hohokam area at this time, including copper bells, shells carved into pieces of jewelry, parrots, and pyrite mirrors. Sociocultural complexity was reaching unprecedented levels.

The Hohokam then entered the so-called Classic Period, dating from c. A.D. 1150 until sometime before the arrival of the Spanish. Several significant changes occurred during the Classic.

Until this time, most Hohokam structures were pit-houses, semisubterranean dwellings having an oval or circular shape. In the Classic, above-ground adobe compounds of rectangular rooms and plazas were constructed. Pottery styles changed as well, along with the preferred method of dealing with the dead—cremations were replaced by burials.

At the same time, the earlier trends continued. Population continued to rise in certain areas (while other areas were abandoned), and locations around present-day Pheonix became clearly urban. Irrigation systems, particularly canals, reached their greatest development. Was *this* a truly complex society?

Archaeologists tend to think not. There was indeed intensive agriculture, urbanism, extensive trade, craft specialization, and significant socioeconomic stratification as reflected in architectural differences. Housing for the Hohokam elite is easily distinguishable from housing for the commoners. And it was not the case that foreign intruders, the Salado people from the north, were responsible for the changes and innovations of the Classic Period. Hohokam cultural evolution was an internal phenomenon, and Hohokam cultural complexity reached impressive levels. But there is yet to be found any convincing archaeological evidence for a Hohokam state, a government having the legitimate monopoly of force.

No one knows for certain exactly when and how Hohokam society came to an end. When the Spanish entered the southwest, they found the Pima and Tohono O'odham (formally the Papago), agriculturalists who did *not* live in large settlements, depend on massive irrigation systems, participate in much long-distance trade, or exhibit much socioeconomic inequality. The archaeological ruins of the Hohokam were, even for the local people, the stuff of legends.

References:

Haury, Emil W. (1976). *The Hohokam*. Tucson: The University of Arizona Press.

McGuire, Randall H., & Schiffer, Michael B. (Eds.). (1982). *Hohokam and Patayan: Prehistory of southwestern Arizona*. New York: Academic Press.

needs. Finally, only after such leadership positions are established do the other manifestations of complex society develop. Included among these other manifestations is the unequal distribution and access to basic, necessary goods, or what we have been defining as true social and economic inequality.

ELMAN SERVICE

Service summarizes the general notions of benefits theories. To him, many groups of people recognized the need for leadership and organization itself and thus placed in charge those individuals considered most competent in general affairs. Only later, according to Service, did these leaders begin to take advantage of their influential and powerful positions.

Similar to Fried, Service sees four stages through which a society passes in evolving sociocultural complexity. The first of these is the egalitarian *band*, present among most gatherer-hunters and the only type of society to be found anywhere on earth until at least the Upper Paleolithic. Status differences between individuals in these relatively small, highly fluid groups are only based on sex, age, and performance, although the latter is only temporary. Economic differences are also temporary, in that every individual in the band shares in such a manner so that all individuals have an equal access to all goods. Most important to Service, however, is the fact that no individual in an egalitarian band holds institutionalized power over any other individual—there is no political power or force.

The second stage in Service's scheme is that of the *tribe*. Tribes are often found among early agriculturalists and are larger in size than bands. A recognized leader might be responsible for the redistribution of certain necessary goods (such a leader is often called a head man or a big man), but as with the band, there is no institutionalized unequal access to either power or wealth. The head man leads his people by setting a good example, not through the application of force.

The third stage is the *chiefdom*, found among fairly large agricultural groups and distinguishable from both the band and the tribe by the presence of institutionalized, hereditary inequality. At this point, status is ascribed and permanent—not achieved and temporary—and is no longer based on performance. In other words, appointed leaders are at this stage beginning to take advantage of their positions. True inequality is present, though the governing body does not have the legitimate right of complete force over the population.

The final stage in Service's scheme is, of course, the *state*. We have previously defined the most distinctive quality of this form of government, that being its legitimate claim over a monopoly of the force present within the society. We can add that many true complex societies with state governments have urban centers, control over large territories, economic classes based on occupation, standing armies, and a host of other characteristics. Recall, however, that no single list of criteria will adequately describe every instance of state formation, nor will it eliminate every example of noncomplex society.

WILLIAM RATHJE

Archaeologist William L. Rathje suggested another benefits theory for the rise of complexity among the Maya (Figure 14–8). The initial need arose in what Rathje recognizes as the core area of the central Mayan lowlands, in portions of Guatamala, Honduras, Belize, and the southern Yucatan of Mexico. The need was for greater quantities of three basic resources among the increasingly populous early agricultural villages located there: 1) salt, for the diet, which is often low in quantity if you

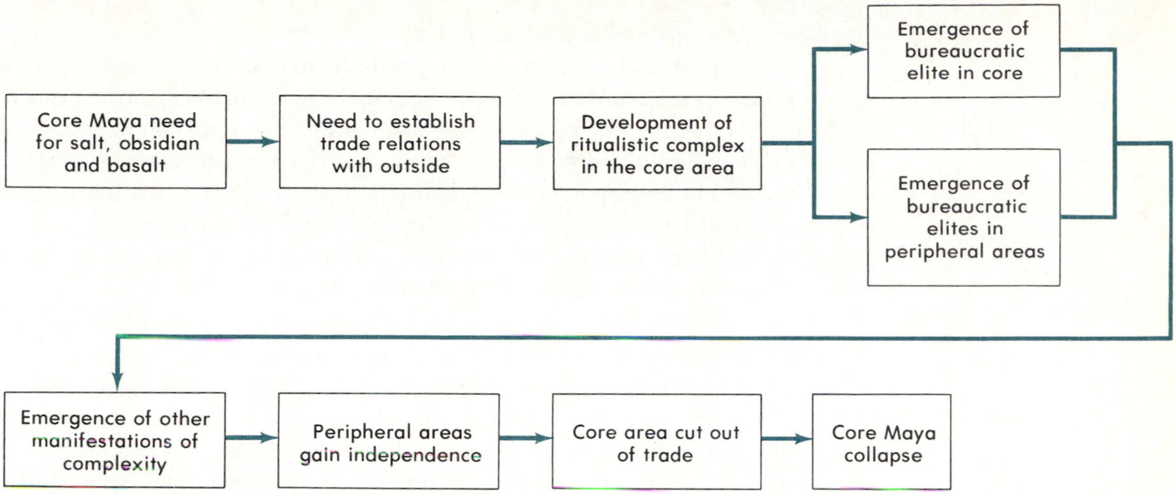

```
┌─────────────────┐   ┌─────────────────┐   ┌─────────────────┐                      ┌─────────────────┐
│ Core Maya need  │   │ Need to establish│   │ Development of  │                      │ Emergence of    │
│ for salt, obsidian│→│ trade relations  │→ │ ritualistic complex│ ─┬──────────────→ │ bureaucratic    │
│ and basalt      │   │ with outside     │   │ in the core area│   │                  │ elite in core   │
└─────────────────┘   └─────────────────┘   └─────────────────┘   │                  └─────────────────┘
                                                                    │                  ┌─────────────────┐
                                                                    │                  │ Emergence of    │
                                                                    └────────────────→ │ bureaucratic    │
                                                                                       │ elites in       │
                                                                                       │ peripheral areas│
                                                                                       └─────────────────┘

┌─────────────────┐   ┌─────────────────┐   ┌─────────────────┐   ┌─────────────────┐
│ Emergence of other│ │ Peripheral areas│   │ Core area cut out│  │ Core Maya       │
│ manifestations of │←│ gain independence│← │ of trade        │ ← │ collapse        │
│ complexity      │   │                 │   │                 │   │                 │
└─────────────────┘   └─────────────────┘   └─────────────────┘   └─────────────────┘
```

Figure 14-8

Schematic diagram of Rathje's theory for the rise (and collapse) of complexity.

depend on maize for a good part of your caloric intake; 2) obsidian, a volcanic glass that can be effectively made into necessary cutting tools; and 3) basalt, another volcanic rock easily manufactured into efficient grinding implements, such as metates.

None of these three resources occurred in abundance in the central lowland area. Thus, there was a need to acquire them from outside to maintain a comfortable and stable existence, and fortunately, just beyond the central area, these resources occurred in relative plenty. According to Rathje, people living in the central area recognized the benefits of establishing trade relations with people living just outside.

But a classic economic dilemma developed. What did they have that the surrounding people would want? According to Rathje, what they had were ideas, organization, and ways of motivating people, what can be called a *ritualistic complex*, that were perceived as useful and necessary in the surrounding communities. Part of this ritualistic complex might have been the very notion of leadership itself and the leaders as well. Thus, an important and valuable commodity could have been recognized ties to powerful central lowland families, established through marriage.

The point is that people in the central lowlands discovered that they had a commodity. For this trade system to continue operation, however, two things had to happen. First, a **bureaucratic elite** had to develop in the central area. Second, spin-off bureaucratic elites had to be established in those peripheral areas containing the needed raw materials. Both were necessary steps to keep the exchange operating efficiently and occurred at or slightly before the beginning of the *Mayan Classic* period, about 2,000 years ago.

bureaucratic elite

Small group of individuals who establish social policy and enjoy a preponderance of the social wealth; found in complex societies.

Other manifestations of complex society followed rapidly, first in the central lowlands, and subsequently in the peripheral areas, and all necessary to maintain the trade. An important strength of Rathje's theory is that there is a relatively good match between concepts and the empirical, material world of archaeological data. The record actually suggests that each development in complexity initially occurred in the central area and later spread out along lines of trade. Particular developments included the large-scale production of distinctive pottery and the construction of monumental forms of architecture.

Rathje's theory is also powerful because it can account for the *collapse* of sociocultural complexity, an apparently universal process that has, unfortunately, received little attention from archaeologists. In this model, the central elite trade with the periphery until the peripheral elite discover they can maintain sociocultural complexity on their own, that is, without any more reliance on the central lowlands. Because the peripheral leaders feel they no longer need additional knowledge and organization, and because they have in their own areas the natural resources (salt, obsidian, and basalt) so critical for survival, they can cut the central area out of the trade system and limit exchange among themselves. This is precisely what appears to have occurred slightly before the Mayan *Postclassic* period (c. A.D. 900).

What was happening in the central lowlands at that time? Remarkably, a massive building and manufacturing program was undertaken, only to be rapidly followed by sociocultural collapse. This great expenditure of labor and resources appears to have been an attempt on the part of the elite to maintain some sort of stability in the face of economic disaster. Since trade had come to a virtual standstill, the organization and production that the ritualistic complex generated could no longer be directed outward but instead had to be absorbed inward. Without the incoming goods to sustain it, however, the project could not last long, and the central area experienced a rapid and precipitous decline. Massive development was thus, in this case, a symptom of impending collapse, not a reflection of cultural flowering, as many archaeologists had believed.

ROBERT NETTING

A third benefits theory has been proposed by Robert Netting. Netting focuses on research issues of cultural ecology, which broadly speaking is the study of how groups of people interact adaptively with their environments (Chapter 4). He has used this background to formulate a theory for the rise of sociocultural complexity that incorporates the non-Malthusian views of Boserup. In some respects, Netting's arguments are in opposition to Carneiro's conflicts theory.

According to Netting, people experiencing increasing population pressure in a circumscribed area might recognize the benefits of broadening and reorienting political relationships. The particular problems that arise in the face of growing population include increasingly severe disputes over land; psychological problems centering around insecurity, powerlessness, and fear; and difficulties in maintaining established trade relations. Netting argues that the solutions, as recognized by the people involved, can be found by placing more people under the control of fewer people with greater power. These would tend to be religious leaders, according to Netting, who, like most benefits theorists, recognizes the important role of the **theocracy** (see below). The result is that people tend to benefit by the arrangement, and only in certain cases do the unfair and coercive aspects of complex society develop as consequences.

theocracy
A complex society in which the state (government) is run by religious leaders; often a precursor of later states.

Netting explicitly states that warfare and conquest are not the necessary outcomes of population growth in circumscribed areas, thus clearly distinguishing his theory from Carneiro's. He cites ethnographic examples of his theory in action, at various stages of operation, among a number of African societies.

Conflicts versus Benefits Theory

As with conflicts theories, there are both strengths and weaknesses to the benefits school of thought. Neither can thus be generally considered more accurate or appropriate. At the present time, this issue remains one of perspective, not of match to data. There is, however, no reason that a single theory should explain all the complex societies that have developed. It is conceivable that there are cases in which complex societies emerged for their benefits and other cases in which they emerged from conflicts.

Multicausal Theories

Several theories for the rise of complex society do not fall within either the conflicts or the benefits schools. These so-called multicausal explanations cannot be easily categorized as either (although each is inclined more in one direction than the other) because they do not recognize causality as limited to any particular situation or even general set of circumstances. Hence, the name we give them—multicausal. We consider one of these theories in some detail.

KENT FLANNERY

As discussed in Chapter 13, Flannery has made important contributions to our understanding of the rise of domestication. He has also proposed innovative models regarding the emergence of sociocultural complexity, based in large measure on the precepts of **General Systems Theory** (GST). General Systems theorists argue that all organizations consist of integrated parts, the nature and condition of which significantly affect one another. All such systems can be studied in similar manners and compared because they all operate according to general processes. Some archaeologists, like Flannery, view the institutions in society as forming large, very complicated systems that exhibit these same processes (Figure 14–9).

general systems theory
Perspective that views all organizations (physical, biological, social, and cultural) as consisting of integrated parts; the nature of any one part has a significant impact on the nature of the other parts.

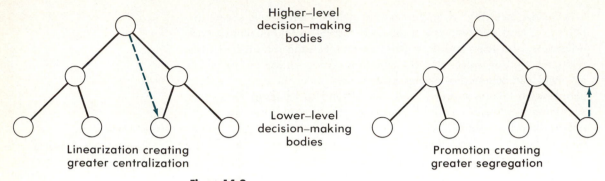

Figure 14-9

Schematic diagram of Flannery's theory for the rise of complexity.

Flannery's theory requires that we conceptualize society as a hierarchy consisting of decision-making bodies. *Centralization* is the degree of control higher-level decision-making bodies have over lower-level bodies. A major evolutionary process in hierarchies is *linearization*, the bypassing of mid-level bodies, so that higher-level bodies can control lower-level bodies more directly, thus leading to greater centralization. Another process is *promotion*, the raising of a body to a higher level in the hierarchy. This leads to greater *segregation*, the degree of autonomy possessed by each decision-making body. Centralization and segregation complement each other, and through the interplay of central control and lower-level autonomy, the overall sociocultural system becomes more complex.

According to Flannery, sociocultural complexity should be measured by reference to the degree of centralization (generated by linearization) and the degree of segregation (generated by promotion) exhibited by the society under study.

A concrete example of these abstract concepts will clarify their meanings. In very general terms, we can say that the United States government is composed of decision-making bodies on the federal, state, and local levels. The federal is the most inclusive and thus is at the highest level, with the state next highest, and the local level lowest. Every time the federal government bypasses state authority to influence local policy directly (the federal speed limit is one example), linearization has occurred. Such action results in more centralization and, according to Flannery, possibly greater sociocultural complexity.

Now, suppose one of the fifty states decides to declare its independence from federal control when it comes to some important policy matter. By doing so, it would essentially raise itself one notch higher on the hierarchy, at least as far as the particular policy issue was concerned. For example, an individual state might decide to ignore the federal speed limit, despite possible financial sanctions from Washington. This would be an example of promotion and again, possibly, greater complexity.

The greatest weakness with Flannery's views is that his abstract concepts are difficult to find in the archaeological record. How is one supposed to excavate, much less measure, such abstractions as centralization or segregation? The task appears impossible, and those who have attempted anything like it have faced grave methodological difficulties. Yet his ideas remain intriguing and should encourage future scholars to develop the proper empirical correlates. Furthermore, his theory, like Rathje's, can account for the *collapse* of sociocultural complexity by introducing the concept of **hypercoherence**.

Hypercoherence is a situation in which centralized decision making is too far removed from the relevant situations. It is brought about by excessive linearization, and it results in poor decisions being made because of a lack of knowledge or understanding of local conditions. It can lead to the rapid collapse of a complex society because it allows mistakes to escalate into major disasters through positive feedback. In an extensive bureaucracy, decisions have to be made in order for things to get done, but if the bureaucratic apparatus becomes too centralized and the people at the bottom are either unable or afraid to make and implement decisions, then the bureaucracy can, in essence, collapse under its own weight. This may have been occurring recently in eastern Europe's Soviet bloc.

hypercoherence
A situation in which social and bureaucratic institutions are so deeply intertwined with each other that the system is simply unable to make adaptive responses to threatening situations.

The Rise of Complex Society: Evidence

Like the rise of domestication, complex society emerged independently in the Old World and the New World. In all its manifestations, it exhibited broadly similar characteristics. Yet a comparison of the Old World and the New World also brings out some significant differences.

First, sociocultural complexity in the New World often involved intensive urbanization. Very large cities were integral parts of some of the most complex societies there, including *Teotihuacan* in the Valley of Mexico and the Aztec capital of *Tenochtitlan*, under present-day Mexico City. At the height of its occupation—c. 2,100 years ago (100 B.C.) until A.D. 700—the population of Teotihuacan reached 150,000 or more, and that of Tenochtitlan (c. A.D. 1325–1519) was probably even greater.

Urbanism did not reach the same level of development in the Old World, though it often appeared quite early. Some impressive examples of urban settlement, such as those within the Harappan civilization of the Indus Valley, exhibited signs of massive and effective municipal organization in the form of clear street plans and well-designed sewer systems. Still, none of the Old World settlements grew in size or density to be comparable with the New World examples.

A second difference was that metallurgy was a significant aspect of Old World complex societies. Copper, bronze, and eventually iron became important in the manufacture of tools and weapons. In contrast, metal did not play an important technological or economic role in either Mesoamerica or South America, although gold and silver were important in art and decoration.

Figure 14-10

The Near East, showing major geographical features and archaeological sites related to the rise of sociocultural complexity (after Wenke, 1984).

Finally, the continuing importance of domesticated animals in the Old World allowed certain nomadic groups to play important roles there while still maintaining a degree of sociocultural integrity. Although a number of nomadic people were in contact with New World civilizations, they were not capable of maintaining the pastoralist way of life. Even today, however, nomadic pastoralists remain an important element in certain regions of the Old World.

AN OLD WORLD CASE: EARLY COMPLEX SOCIETY IN THE NEAR EAST

As we saw in the previous chapter, the Near East (or southwest Asia) was the scene of some of the earliest domestication. Thus, it may not be surprising to learn that complex society emerged there first, hundreds and (in some cases) thousands of years before it did in Egypt, India, China, the central highlands of Mexico, or South America.

The Near East covers a large and environmentally diverse geographic region and includes parts of several modern-day countries, including Iran, Iraq, Turkey, Syria, Jordan, Lebanon, and Israel (Figure 14–10). Within the region are the mountainous highlands formed by the Zagros and Taurus chains, curving down from southern Anatolia to the east coast of the Persian Gulf. South and west of these mountains are the foothills, containing so much evidence for early domestication (Chapter 13). Beyond the foothills lies the famous Fertile Crescent, formed by the valley of the Tigris and Euphrates Rivers, and still farther lies the alluvium of southern *Mesopotamia*. To the far west of the region can be found the smaller Judean mountains and foothills, bordering the east coast of the Mediterranean Sea.

The earliest signs of growing sociocultural complexity in this region emerged nearly 9,000 years ago. For example, early monumental architecture appears at the site of *Jericho*, in the Levant, in the form of a massive stone wall. Shortly thereafter, the settlement of *Çatal Huyuk* was established in Anatolia. This community was one of the more impressive, early centers of sociocultural complexity—it was the largest settlement of its time in the Near East—though it probably was not the scene of true complex society as discussed here. Indeed, Çatal Huyuk was a community in which all members practiced simple irrigation agriculture or the breeding of cattle—no bureaucratic elite was present.

Çatal Huyuk was occupied from c. 8,500 years ago until c. 6,400 years ago. This agricultural community is thought to have had a population of as many as 6,000 people, making it unquestionably the largest of the time. The settlement consisted of mudbrick, multiroomed (and multistoried) dwellings, similar to Abu Hureyra II (Chapter 13) but on a much grander scale. In addition, there were about forty buildings at Çatal Huyuk that were larger and more elaborately designed than any of the others (Figure 14–11). These are called "shrines" by the site's excavator, James Mellaart. Little is really known about the function of these special dwellings, although they might be evidence for emerging social and economic stratification in the community or for an influential belief system spanning much of Anatolia. Archaeologists are currently debating these interpretations.

What is clear is that Çatal Huyuk was located at a strategic point in the Taurus Mountains, from where it was possible to control access to several obsidian sources. As Rathje pointed out when discussing the Maya, obsidian was a very important resource because it could be made easily into efficient cutting tools. And Çatal Huyuk was apparently trading obsidian (and other commodities such as food supplies and textiles) to settlements across much of Anatolia and the Levant. In addition, the occupants were manufacturing some of the finest obsidian tools of the time. Perhaps it was this central role in trade and manufacture that made the community so large and important.

Still, we do not recognize it as a true complex society. The craftsmen and traders of Çatal Huyuk were not full-time specialists, and everyone contributed to subsistence activities. Thus, all residents were dependent, to

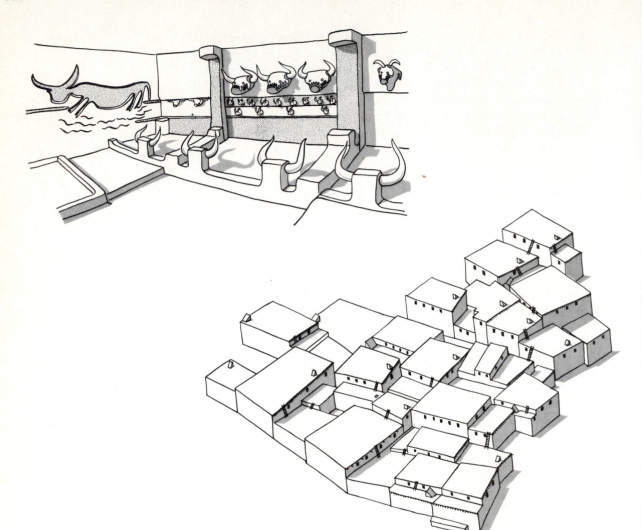

Figure 14-11

A reconstruction of a shrine, along with an artist's impression of the community of Çatal Huyuk.

one degree or another, on their own agricultural production. It is highly unlikely that any elite group could acquire an inordinate quantity of necessary resources under these circumstances. Nor could any governing body have the legitimate right over a monopoly of the force. We conclude, then, that Çatal Huyuk represents a transitional form in the evolution of complex society in the Near East.

The earliest clear evidence for true sociocultural complexity is recognized with the wide distribution of certain pottery styles across the region, beginning about 7,500 years ago. These ceramic forms are notable because of their wide distributions and distinctive, uniform appearances (Figures 14–12 and 14–13).

Earliest were the *Hassuna* ceramics, named after the archaeological site of Tell Hassuna. This ceramic style is most often found in rather small agricultural villages across northern Mesopotamia and Anatolia. Next (though overlapping in time) came *Samarra* ceramics, named after the site of Tell es-Sawwan on the Tigris River and distributed slightly to the south of the Hassuna forms. Many archaeological sites containing Samarran-style pottery exhibit evidence that suggests sociocultural complexity in the form of monumental architecture, irrigation systems, and defensive structures. There is also evidence for greater social differentiation within sites.

Finally (though also overlapping temporally) emerged the *Halafian* ceramic horizon, which was more widely distributed than either Hassuna or Samarra and has been found at many archaeological sites, such as Arpachiyah. Halafian ceramics, which were in use by 6,500 B.P., are associated with additional signs of emerging sociocultural complexity, includ-

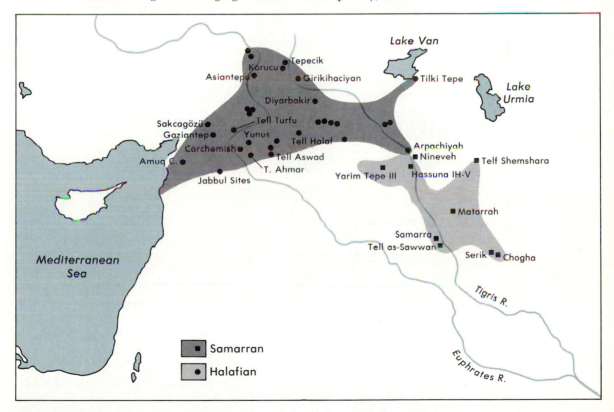

Figure 14-12

The distribution of Samarran and Halafian pottery, an early sign of the rise of complex society (after Wenke, 1984).

Hassunan pottery

Samarran pottery

Halafian pottery

Late Halafian pottery

Early Ubaid pottery

Figure 14-13

Some examples of pottery used in the emerging complex societies of the Near East (after Mellaart, 1975).

ing great degrees of intrasite variability, indicative of social and economic inequality. By this time, it appears, true complex society had arisen in the Near East.

The following major period, known as the *Ubaid* and dating to c. 7,300–5,600 years ago (note the temporal overlap again), was a time of extensive cultural change. For the first time, as far as we know, settlement occurred in the southern Mesopotamian alluvium with the establishment of communities like *Eridu*. More significant, true cities emerged for the first time throughout the Near East. Later, Ubaid-style ceramics are found beyond the boundaries of the region, suggesting very widespread trade and possible influence. Intrasite evidence suggests that social and economic inequality were common, and monumental architecture became enormous. Impressive temples were common, some situated on top of acropoli. Some evidence occurs of massive palaces late in the period, that is, monumental structures not directly associated with religious activities.

Toward the end of the Ubaid period, c. 5,800 years ago, the settlement of *Uruk* (alternatively called Warka, its Arabic name) grew impressively in both size and importance (Figure 14–14). By 5,000 years ago,

Figure 14-14
Uruk, or Warka.

polity

A political organization or a group of people and institutions under the control of a political organization.

city-state

An autonomous polity consisting of an urban center and its surrounding territory.

during the Uruk period proper (also called the Protoliterate period), the city was populated by more than 10,000 people and formed the nucleus of a large, influential **polity**. Indeed, Uruk may have been the first **city-state**, a complex urban society stretching over a large territory, yet highly centralized and administered from a single city. Other city-states emerged shortly thereafter, and between 5,000 and 4,350 years ago, the *Sumerian* civilization flourished. Although each of the approximately ten or twelve Sumerian city-states were politically independent most of the time, they all shared a common Mesopotamian culture, elements of which influenced many subsequent developments in Old World complex society.

From Sumerian times onward, Near Eastern prehistory and history are filled with significant and interesting events, people, and processes. Many of these are well known because they form the basis for many stories in the Bible. Yet the initial rise of complex society in the Near East was completed with the Sumerians, and it is there that we leave this tale.

A NEW WORLD CASE: THE OLMEC

Until about 3,500 years ago, no complex societies existed in the New World. All people lived by either gathering and hunting or by practicing simple agriculture. There were no cities, no impressive monumental architecture, no armies, no institutionalized inequality, nothing that we associate with sociocultural complexity. Yet conditions soon changed along the coast of the Gulf of Mexico, in the Mexican lowland areas of present-day Veracruz and Tabasco. In this Olmec heartland (Figure 14–15), the first signs of complex society survived until about 2,400 years ago, about 1,000 years after their emergence, and although the Olmec were not the most complex social order indigenous to the New World

Figure 14-15

The Olmec heartland.

Figure 14–16
A colossal Olmec head from
La Venta.

(there is some debate regarding the degree of complexity they maintained), theirs was unquestionably the earliest (Box 14–2). As with our Old World case, we will explore the earliest example of complex society in the New World.

The Olmec remain mysterious and poorly known. Archaeological investigations have concentrated on the large ceremonial centers of the society (not populous cities as could be found in the Near East), such as *San Lorenzo* and *La Venta*, and we do not clearly understand the nature and extent of diversity of Olmec settlement or society. Yet a number of material indications of their growth and influence in Mesoamerica leave little doubt that they were a powerful social force.

For one thing, the nature and very existence of the ceremonial centers themselves suggest a degree of sociocultural complexity completely unknown to earlier New World people. The several sites that make up San Lorenzo, for instance, occupied from about 3,500 to 2,900 years ago, are associated with a massive earthen platform mound—several acres in breadth—that some archaeologists believe was designed in the shape of a bird. It is thought that there were many structures built atop the mound, as well as plazas and other forms of monumental architecture. Within the mound was located a very sophisticated aqueduct system, consisting of numerous buried drains. Also found buried within the mound were a number of the most distinctive sculptural forms to be created by the Olmec—the giant, basalt stone heads.

These massive carved heads (Figure 14–16), which have been found at other locations in addition to San Lorenzo, are very impressive.

Issues in Anthropology 14–2

African Origins of the Olmec?

Because the Olmec was the first complex society to emerge in the New World, it has sometimes been ethnocentrically suggested that the roots of Olmec complexity were located in the Old World. There is no archaeological evidence for *any* contact with or influence from the Old to the New at this time. Still, the suggestions persist—some are even promoted by scholars.

Anthropologist Ivan Van Sertima has argued that black Africans made contact with New World natives well before the emergence of the Olmec, colonized portions of the New World, and contributed significantly to the evolution of complex society there. In his book *They Came Before Columbus*, Van Sertima offers several pieces of evidence supporting this claim:

1. Columbus wrote about the presence of "black indians" in the New World.
2. Certain skeletons, from pre-Colombian contexts, exhibit black African characteristics.
3. Olmec art, in particular the facial features of the giant heads, reflect a black African presence.

Each of these pieces of evidence is flawed. First, Columbus never reported *seeing* "black Indians." He only reported a story told to him by other native Americans. This is hearsay evidence in the extreme and cannot be accepted uncritically.

Second, Van Sertima refers to only a small number of skeletons from Mesoamerica, of questionable age (they could postdate the time of contact with Europeans) and questionable racial characteristics. As we have already noted, racial categories are not biological realities, and while different populations do exhibit average morphological differences, there is a great deal of overlap of measurements. The study of small samples is inadequate for making such a determination.

Third, as discussed in this chapter, the giant basalt heads are thought by archaeologists to be depictions of *infants*, not Africans. Besides, some of them do have clear *Asiatic* characteristics, including relatively flat faces and epicanthic folds on the eyes, which makes sense, given the Asian origin of native American people. The Olmec probably had epicanthic folds, and the heads are beyond reasonable doubt representations of Olmec people.

Some stand more than 3 meters high and weigh more than 50 tons. The basalt they were made from was often carried as far as 80 or 100 miles from its source. The absence of metal tools among the Olmec suggests they were carved with other stone implements, a considerable task requiring great skill. An important question, then, is why did the Olmec purposefully bury so many of these sculptures, as was the case at San Lorenzo? No one really knows.

Mysteriously, the site of San Lorenzo was rapidly deserted 2,900 years ago. The desertion was accompanied by the defacing of many early Olmec art forms and their rapid replacement by new art forms. Was this some sort of revolution or military invasion? Possibly, though we are not certain. What is known is that a second major ceremonial center was established at about the same time.

The site of La Venta, which was located on a small island along the Gulf coast and which is presently under an oil-drilling complex, was occupied from about 2,900 to about 2,400 years ago. Similar to San Lorenzo, it was a ceremonial center, highlighted in this case by a 110-meter-high

Van Sertima is wrong, but there is nothing terrible about that—all scholars misinterpret or misuse data on occasion. What makes this issue particularly difficult is the acceptance of his and similar conclusions because of *ethnic* and *political* associations. A black African role in New World prehistory is sometimes taught as historical fact not because there is any empirical evidence for it, but because it encourages pride in group membership. While ethnic pride is important, especially for people who have faced generations of prejudice and discrimination, it should not be instilled at the expense of historical accuracy. The peoples of sub-Sahara Africa were indeed responsible for many impressive cultural developments, which have often been ignored or downplayed by earlier generations of Europeans. But colonizing the New World was just not among their achievements.

Similar stories of Old World contact with the New World, similarly not supported by any archaeological evidence, have been touted by other ethnic groups for the same reason. Thus, we hear stories of pre-Colombian settlements by the Egyptians, Phoenicians, Greeks, Portuguese, Spanish, Welsh, Chinese, and Celtic peoples! Only *one* of these claims appears to have any validity at all—that regarding the Vikings, who probably maintained a minor settlement on Newfoundland during the eleventh century. Still, any contact between Vikings and native Americans did not affect New World society. Sociocultural complexity, initially among the Olmec, apparently arose in the New World completely independently of the Old World.

References:

Feder, Kenneth L. (1990). *Frauds, myths, and mysteries*. Mountain View, CA: Mayfield Publishing Co.

Bernal, I. (1969). *The Olmec world*. Berkeley, CA: University of California Press.

pyramid. A number of elaborate burials were located at La Venta, as well as more of the colossal stone heads.

La Venta was also abandoned quite rapidly, and materials there were similarly destroyed at that time. We do not clearly understand the reasons for this event either, nor do we know the people responsible. However, we can offer a few reasonable inferences about Olmec society in general.

Foremost, we can reiterate that the Olmec were living in a complex society, the first to develop in the New World. We can infer that certain institutions and conditions were present—some social and economic inequality, fairly large populations under the rule of a small elite (note, however, that the Olmec were not urban), monumental building activities, and so on. We concentrate on three aspects of Olmec complex society that archaeologists know the most about—trade and exchange, art and iconography, and religion.

Olmec influence appears throughout Mesoamerica, except for the basin of Mexico and the Mayan lowlands. Most, if not all, of this influence was expressed and maintained in the form of trade relations, or so the archaeological record leads us to believe. Small, portable trade objects of Olmec manufacture, primarily figurines and ceramic items, are found across Mesoamerica. It is thought that these objects signify trade relations between the Olmec elite and other, emerging elite groups throughout the region, the Olmec being in control of the system. If this was the case, the Olmec elite had great power and status across a very large area.

Olmec art, including the massive stone heads discussed previously, remains very distinctive. It had great influence on the religious and artistic themes of later New World civilizations. Three themes dominate Olmec **iconography**: 1) the Ware-Jaguar motif, with bizarre combinations of human and animal characteristics in single beings, 2) human babies, with infant characteristics appearing in everything from small, portable objects to the colossal stone heads, and 3) crocodiles (Figure 14–17). No one can explain these themes with certainty, although they appear to have had a tremendous influence over subsequent art forms.

Olmec religion appears to have played a very important role in the society. Indeed, the Olmec are thought to have lived in a very powerful theocracy, that is, a society in which church and state were combined and in which religious leaders also took the role of government leaders. Through time, there appears to have been a gradual growth in secularism and militarism, indicating a growing separation between the religious and governmental elite. But for most of Olmec time, the two were indivisible.

This pattern was very common in all early, emerging complex societies. We can see a similar theocratic structure followed by growing secularism in the Near East, for instance. It can also be seen among the Maya of the New World—secular and military power seem to have grown as the Post-Classic period was approached. It is difficult to explain this general process in complex societies, although it might have something to do with their growing size and the increasing bureaucratic specialization that becomes necessary. Or more cynically, it may simply be a reflection of the bureaucracy challenging the religious justification for the power wielded by the theocrats.

After the Olmec arose a series of complex societies in the New World, including Teotihuacan, the Maya, the Aztec of central Mexico, and the Inca of western South America. The Aztec and Inca, both Post-Classic civilizations, were destroyed by Spanish military and political might and European diseases in the sixteenth century.

The Impacts of Complex Society

The impacts of complex society have been global in their scope. Indeed, the policies and politics of sociocultural complexity have been so profound that many noncomplex social forms have been destroyed. Rapid changes to the sociocultural fabric of other societies began very soon after complex societies initially arose, and they continue to the present—

iconography

Illustration of a subject or idea by visual representation, such as pictures.

Figure 14–17

Olmec portable art.

one of the darker characteristics of complexity is the absorption or elimination of neighboring societies.

We can explore the impacts of complex society by focusing on several aspects of human life, as we did when considering the impacts of domestication in the previous chapter.

SETTLEMENT

Complex societies are often urban societies—in a general way, Childe was correct in recognizing the importance of cities when defining the criteria of complexity. Furthermore, the cities of complex societies attract people from noncomplex societies because they appear to offer the opportunity of economic and social gain and (in some cases) safety and freedom from tyranny. The relationship is one of positive feedback—cities multiply in size and influence and thus attract even more people.

The result has been that the earth's people have become increasingly urban, and the rate of global urbanization is rising rapidly. In 1950, for instance, only 16 percent of the world's population lived in cities of 100,000 or more. By 1975, this figure had risen to 26 percent. It is projected to reach 40 percent by the end of this century. This is a remarkable development, considering that cities are sociocultural phenomena of only the past several thousand years.

TECHNOLOGY

Complex societies allow technological development to occur at unprecedented rates because they contain a great amount of labor specialization. Every member of a complex society does not have to contribute to all the society's concerns—no individual could. More significantly, everyone does not have to be directly concerned with subsistence activities. People can derive their sustenance in diverse ways, the result being that many individuals contribute small parts to a complex, final product. This is not necessarily a more efficient way of getting the job done. As we saw with domestication, growing sociocultural complexity demands greater, more intensive labor input. The result is also more energy intensive, and this is what technological development is all about.

Thus, Leslie White was partially correct in a very general sense. Complex societies do exploit more energy than primitive societies. They can extract greater quantities of energy from the environment. The impacts of this ability include the disappearance of the noncomplex and the danger of environmental degradation on a global scale, both concerns of the modern world.

SOCIAL STRUCTURE AND ORGANIZATION

Complex societies are more socially heterogeneous and differentiated than are noncomplex societies. In addition, the rise of complex societies can be associated with a continued movement away from the egalitarian socioeconomic structure of gatherer-hunters. As we have noted, the ini-

Issues in Anthropology 14–3

Other Examples of Social Complexity

The fact that our own civilization is ultimately descended from those of Europe and the Near East should not blind us to the indigenous development of complex societies elsewhere. Often the cultures of contemporary peoples are not representative of cultures that existed in the same area hundreds or thousands of years ago; for complex societies fall as well as rise. Not only did sociocultural complexity evolve in Asia and Mesoamerica, but as well in the Amazonian basin in Brazil and in sub-Saharan Africa.

Marajo Island, at the mouth of the Amazon, was excavated in the 1940s by Betty Meggers of the Smithsonian, who concluded that while complexity was present, it was probably brought there by the complex societies of the Andes in Peru. The inhabitants of the island constructed large dwellings and engaged in widespread trade and warfare. In the 1980s, however, more extensive excavations by Anna Roosevelt of the American Museum of Natural History have suggested strongly that Marajo complexity was not brought from elsewhere but developed during its continuous 1,000-year

occupation. Other sites from Amazonia have yielded very early pottery—which indicates that however spectacular later complex societies of the Peruvian highlands may have been, they were not the only origin or source of complexity in South America.

In sub-Saharan Africa, complex societies have been recognized for considerably longer. For example, the site of Great Zimbabwe in the present-day country of Zimbabwe in southern Africa was sufficiently impressive to the sixteenth-century Portuguese that they denied humans were even capable of such work. Even at that time, Great Zimbabwe was a ruin, having gone into decline about a century earlier.

The site appears to have been occupied since the eleventh century and fairly rapidly became a preeminent trade center. The stone walls surrounding the site were constructed between the thirteenth and fifteenth centuries; and though the construction is not elaborate (lacking domes and arches), it is grand in scope. Its inhabitants included metallurgists and artisans, and the masonry at the site is dis-

---

tial emergence of sociocultural complexity led to the rise and growth of social and economic inequality. The situation became even more unfair as complex societies expanded and intensified, with more power and wealth being concentrated among fewer citizens. And, as complex societies came to control people from noncomplex social settings, the degree of inequity became staggering, to the point that members of noncomplex societies have been degraded, enslaved, and exterminated. Entire societies have been destroyed by the economic and military impacts of sociocultural complexity.

There might have been a change in this process, a reversal of sorts, when some societies evolved industrialization. In other words, individuals living in industrial and postindustrial societies might experience less socioeconomic inequality than those living in preindustrial states. We address this issue in the next chapter.

ECONOMY

Both reciprocity and redistribution continued to operate as systems of exchange after the rise of complex society. They still operate today in the

tinctive. Unfortunately, little more of them is known as the site was quite thoroughly looted by European treasure hunters in the nineteenth century.

In western Africa, kingdoms flourished at the same time western Europe was in the Dark Ages (Chapter 15). The kingdom of Ghana (northwest of present-day Ghana) was described by an Islamic traveler called al-Bakri in the eleventh century. Its capital is now identified as Kumbi Saleh in Mauritania, a large site that once contained two-story stone buildings and once harbored a trade in precious metals.

In the central African forest, sites are known with bronzework also dating to the European Dark Ages. Many of these sites are in Nigeria, including the palace of Benin and the village of Igbo Ukwu, where elaborate bronze sculptures and architecture have been found. In particular, the latter site is an ornate burial, representing a considerable concentration of wealth in a single family. At Ife, also in Nigeria, dried-mud buildings lined pavements made from pottery fragments; and altars containing terra-cotta and bronze figures had prominent places in the dwellings.

Iron working has a long history in Africa. Because it appears to have been smelted in Africa before softer metals were used, the technology is generally believed to have diffused from the north during the first millennium B.C. A few sites are known to have smelted copper at an early period, however. Iron was worked in eastern Africa with furnaces made of plaster and clay over a pit capable of generating temperatures of more than 1400° C, and their operations have been the subject of ethnoarchaeological investigation (Chapter 16).

References:

Gibbons, A. (1990). New view of early Amazonia. *Science* 248:1488–1490.

Phillipson, D. W. (1985). *African archaeology.* Cambridge, England: Cambridge University Press.

Van Noten, F., & Raymaekers, J. (1988). Early iron smelting in Central Africa. *Scientific American* 258(6):104–111.

United States and other highly complex social settings, although they are no longer dominant. Instead, other economic entities have become preeminent, such as the marketplace (as an institution, not a location). A market economy is defined by the existence of *autonomous price-fixing*. Here, unlike reciprocal and redistributive interactions, economic activities are largely separate from social activities. Supply and demand and the desire for profit are, very simply, what determine prices.

Economies in complex societies are multifaceted institutions that have profound impacts on all people throughout the world. The greatest single effect of complexity on economy, in fact, has been its growth into a single global phenomenon.

IDEOLOGY

As mentioned earlier, the bureaucracy of a complex society tends to become more secular through time, from an early theocracy to a situation in which church and state are recognizably separated institutions. This trend does not preclude the possibility that there can be a state-sanctioned religion or that church officials might have great power and influence over state affairs. The separation of church and state recognized in the United States Constitution and the official absence of religion in the Soviet Union are very recent developments in cultural evolution. But religious and secular matters were handled somewhat separately early in the development of sociocultural complexity.

The types of religion commonly practiced in complex societies are distinctive as well. Polytheism, the belief in a pantheon of well-defined deities (not simply abstract forces of nature), and monotheism, the belief in only one, are predominant. These religious forms, in which the controlling forces are somewhat humanlike and relatively distant (in time, space, and certain attributes) from the populace, might well reflect symbolically the increasing concentration of power among an economically distant elite. By mirroring in the religious belief system this growing social inequality, perhaps society created a means by which the people could more easily accept it.

WRITING

While noncomplex people have much to remember and much to know, sociocultural complexity places even greater demands on the accurate retention of information. With more people entering into more diverse social relationships, the possibility of widespread chaos exists without a way of establishing definitively who did what, where, when, and to whom.

The development of new economic systems necessitated an efficient and widely applicable record-keeping system; the centralization of political authority necessitated a means of recording laws; and the emergence of a political and religious elite made the details of certain people's lives important for all. These needs were met by the development, again independently throughout the world, of systems of writing. Though Childe was wrong in identifying writing as a key feature of sociocultural complexity, writing and complexity have often been intimately connected.

Summary

Like domestication, the emergence of complex society was a cultural evolutionary process that occurred several times independently around the world. While some societies are clearly more complex than others, there is no universally agreed-upon way of defining or measuring complexity. In addition, sociocultural complexity is not in any way related to individual capability—the members of simple societies are equally as complex as the members of complex societies.

Definitions of complex society do not match well with the available data for studying complex society, including the available archaeological data. Theories can be placed into two opposing schools of thought—conflicts theories and benefits theories. The former, derived from the writings of Karl Marx, views complexity as the outcome of the conflict of self-interest between social and economic classes. The latter school sees complexity emerging as a result of people trying to meet their various social and economic needs. A third group of theories, multicausal theories, combines aspects of both the conflicts and benefits schools.

The changes in settlement, technology, social structure and organization, economy, and ideology brought about by the emergence of complex society operated together to alter human existence in a revolutionary way. No matter how one envisions the proper condition and life-style of *Homo sapiens*, no matter how one measures the advantages and disadvantages of living under the influence of sociocultural complexity, one thing is certain: The past several thousand years of cultural history have witnessed monumental changes in the ways most humans carry on their affairs. These changes are irreversible: There is no turning back, only solving problems in new and creative ways.

Questions for Review

1. What do archaeologists mean by social or cultural "complexity"? Is it all relative, or is there a discrete threshold which can be crossed? According to Childe's criteria, could a simple society be partly complex or a complex society be partly simple?

2. For archaeologists, complexity must be reflected in material culture. Why is that? Could a society be complex without leaving material traces of that complexity?

3. How can we speak of complexity being adopted by noncomplex or simple societies? How would this happen? Is complexity something discrete enough to diffuse?

4. Which do you feel are generally more persuasive, conflicts or benefits theories? Why?

For Further Reading

Flannery, K. W. (1972). The cultural evolution of civilizations. *Annual Review of Ecology and Systematics*, 3:399–426.

Lamberg-Karlovsky, C. C., & Sabloff, J. A. (1987). *Ancient civilizations: The Near East and Mesoamerica*. Prospect Heights, IL: Waveland Press.

White, L. A. (1959). *The evolution of culture*. New York: McGraw-Hill.

Yoffee, N., & Cowgill, G. (Eds.). (1988). *The collapse of ancient states and civilizations*. Tucson: University of Arizona Press.

Recent Cultural History

Recent Cultural History

T he third major sociocultural transformation, after domestication and complexity, was industrialization. Unlike the first two, which occurred independently in several areas of the world, the Industrial Revolution occurred once, and was largely due to **colonialism**. We can never know whether societies other than urban eighteenth-century western Europe would independently have evolved industrialization. Nevertheless, as a specific result of the cultural history of western Europe and North America in the eighteenth and nineteenth centuries, a series of pervasive global changes occurred. We trace the history of these changes in this chapter.

Medieval archaeology is the archaeological study of the Middle Ages, primarily in Europe, dating from about A.D. 500 to about A.D. 1500. *Historical archaeology* is simply the archaeology of all times and places for which we have useful documentary (written) materials. Because there are documents from medieval times that we can study, medieval archaeology is a special type of historical archaeology, receiving attention here because of the crucial role the Middle Ages played in the rise of industrialism. Historical archaeology, though capable of covering a vast number of topics, emphasizes the impacts of European expansion—in large part made possible by the Industrial Revolution—on the people of the entire world.

Medieval and Historical Archaeology: A Background

Most medieval archaeology is conducted by Europeans, trained at European universities. This is significant because most historical archaeologists in the United States view method and theory in a very different way from their European colleagues.

For most European-trained archaeologists, their studies are a part of the discipline of history. Archaeology is viewed as one of several data-gathering techniques (along with archival, documentary research) to be employed by historians in their attempts to answer research questions. The archaeologist, as technician, supplies descriptive information about what happened in the past, when it happened, who did it, and sometimes how it was done. The historian then faces the task of interpreting why. Of course, the archaeologist and historian are often the same person, but it is as historian that this individual addresses the problem of explaining the past.

For archaeologists in the United States, the situation is strikingly different. Here, archaeology is a part of anthropology, not history—academically, more of a social science than a humanity. American archaeology has its own body of theory and method, rather than being simply a fact-gathering technique, and American archaeologists *as anthropologists* address both descriptive and explanatory questions. As is true for most anthropology, American archaeology is concerned with the general study of human behavior.

European archaeology is a branch of history because archaeologists there have a long tradition of studying their own ancestors—during the European past, prehistory merged with history along continuous lines. American archaeology is a part of anthropology because archaeologists here have traditionally studied the ancestors of native Americans—common foci of anthropology. Prehistory did not merge with history here, but instead was displaced by it. But what of American historical archaeologists, who primarily study the products of the descendants of Europeans? Should they be trained as historians or as anthropologists? There has never been total agreement among the archaeologists.

From the beginning of this century until 1967, most practitioners agreed that history was the parent discipline. Indeed, we can trace one of the roots of historical archaeology in the United States to the early twentieth century, when American historians began recognizing the importance of studying material culture. Archaeology was being viewed as a *technique* that might be of some use to historians. It was not considered an independent scientific field of study.

From the 1920s through the 1950s, sporadic attempts to bring together historians and archaeologists as intellectual equals yielded little, but growing, interest. Then, coincident with major theoretical changes in archaeology in the 1960s, a viewpoint emerged that historical archaeology should be a separate field of inquiry, no longer subordinate to history. This view was symbolized by the founding of the *Society for Historical Archaeology* (SHA) in 1967. Ironically, 1967 also witnessed the creation of the *Society for Post-Medieval Archaeology* in England, a group concerned with similar topics as the SHA although still incorporated within the disciplinary boundaries of history.

The debate regarding whether anthropology or history should serve as a parent discipline did not die easily. Still, in 1977, Stanley South published a very influential work titled *Method and Theory in Historical Archaeology,* the first book-length treatment taking an explicitly anthropological perspective. South argued that historical archaeologists should concentrate on reconstructing and explaining patterns in the archaeological record that reflect patterns in past societies—patterns of activities, social groups, and even geographic regions. The volume exhibits the very strong influence that Lewis Binford and the new archaeology have had on recent historical archaeology, placing it squarely within anthropology and independent of the discipline of history. South's work remains one of the most important sources in American historical archaeology.

It is inappropriate to judge whether American or European historical archaeology is better. It is far more constructive to devote our efforts to bridging the gap that remains between these two approaches so that more information and research conclusions can be exchanged and a better understanding of how to interpret the historical past can be reached by all.

Medieval Europe: Cultural History

It would be inappropriate, in fact impossible, to present a detailed discussion of medieval Europe here. Many histories are available to the interested student, some of great length and detail. Rather, we will show how medieval archaeology has contributed to our understanding of the origins of our modern society by briefly considering the cultural history of the Middle Ages as many archaeologists view it.

The European Middle Ages began c. A.D. 500, after the fall of the Roman Empire, and continued for a thousand years to c. A.D. 1500. During this time, Europe witnessed a complex chain of events and changing conditions, including the infamous Dark Ages and the devastation of the Bubonic Plague—otherwise known as the Black Death. Yet only the worst events are commonly remembered by name: Certain Europeans enjoyed periods of relative economic prosperity and technological innovation. The eleventh- and twelfth-century economic and social revival is an example (see below).

THE EARLY MIDDLE AGES AND THE MEROVINGIANS

During the first few centuries of the Middle Ages, medieval Europe was formed by a unique cultural synthesis, brought about by the blending of three important elements: 1) remnants of Roman institutions and traditions, themselves derived from Greek and even earlier societies; 2) what has been called the Germanic component (in the West) and the Oriental component (in the East); and 3) emerging (Catholic) Christianity.

Roman Influences   Rome, of course, was a complex society—an empire—similar to those considered in the previous chapter (Figure 15–1) and in large measure historically derived from earlier complex societies of Greece and the Near East. Several competing views try to explain why Roman society collapsed during the fifth century A.D., evoking such disparate forces as invasion, widespread sickness, and internal corruption. Perhaps Flannery's notion of hypercoherence could play a useful role in our understanding the fall of Rome. Regardless, the empire's demise left much of Europe in disarray, with Roman institutions and customs barely surviving in much-diminished form. Still, certain Roman traditions did survive and influence the development of medieval society.

It was in the political and legal spheres that Rome persisted. For example, Roman law was relatively tolerant of the cultural and economic differences to be found among the diverse subjects of the empire, at least when compared with the legal systems of other preindustrial complex societies. A belief in individual diversity and liberty re-emerged in the

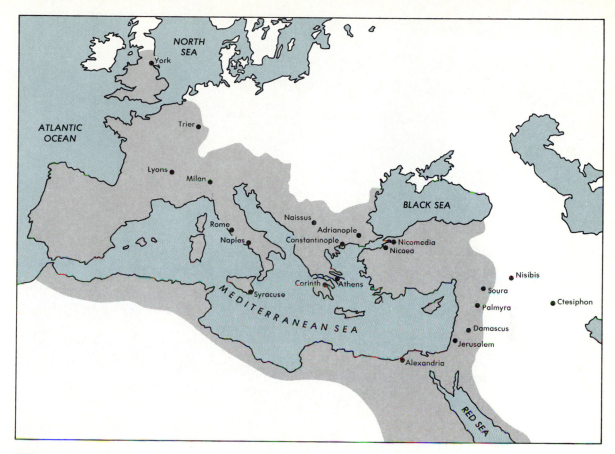

Figure 15-1

The extent of the Roman Empire, c. A.D. 400.

Middle Ages and persists to this day. Politically, in contrast, the Roman state was viewed as an omnipotent power to which all subjects must answer directly. This notion of state sovereignty was also to reappear in later medieval times, based on the Roman model, as complex society evolved in western Europe.

Germanic and Oriental Components   The Germanic and Oriental traditions of the people of Europe continued alongside these shadows of Roman rule, as they had survived Roman occupation during the height of the empire's existence. In the West, upon which we concentrate, Germanic society consisted of a collection of linguistically and culturally related groups (Figure 15–2). Some of these chiefdoms probably practiced what anthropologists recognize as a **segmentary lineage** system—a fluid way of grouping kin that is highly adaptive when the group is expanding into new territory. If true, this practice might help explain the success the Germanic people had in overrunning Roman society.

segmentary lineage

A fluid form of social and political organization based on descent, comprising a hierarchy of more and more inclusive relations and functioning primarily in situations of conflict.

Figure 15-2

Germanic groups in the sixth century A.D.

Emergence of Christianity   Finally, Christianity became a major social and religious force during the first several centuries of the Middle Ages. During Roman times, it spread primarily among slaves and the lower classes, assimilating many aspects of **pagan** theology and ritual. During the reign of Constantine the Great (A.D. 306–337), however, Christianity became the state religion. By the time of Theodosius (379–395), all non-Christian rituals were banned in the empire, and many non-Christian places of worship were destroyed. Since then, Christianity in its manifold forms has remained the dominant religious ideology of the Western world.

The Franks   Along with early Christians, many of the Germanic groups present in western Europe subsequent to the fall of Rome—the

pagan
Broad label covering a diverse set of non-Jewish and non-Christian religions, generally in the ancient world.

Visigoths, Ostrogoths, Vandals, Huns, Angles, Saxons, and others—had profound impacts on early medieval history. Yet the most significant founders and shapers of medieval society were the *Franks*. Members of a relatively populous society (but like the Hohokam, not regarded as a complex society), the Franks emerged in present-day France just as Rome was losing its grip over the territory.

The Franks claimed that their first ruler was Merovech—thus his dynasty is called *Merovingian*—but it appears that he was a mythical character, not unlike King Arthur. There is no question that his supposed grandson Clovis was a real person, however, ruling from A.D. 481 to A.D. 511. Clovis was a powerful leader, and after his death, the Merovingian dynasty rapidly collapsed in the face of internal strife (Figure 15–3). Indeed, one can see in medieval Europe episodes of alternating centralization and decentralization of power. The Merovingians represent probably the earliest steps toward indigenous social complexity in western Europe.

THE DARK AGES AND THE CAROLINGIANS

The Dark Ages in medieval Europe lasted from the early sixth century until c. 1000. There was a brief hiatus during this 500-year period, dating from the rise of Charlemagne in the late eighth century until shortly after his death (see below). Some scholars see an additional Dark Age occurring

Figure 15-3

The Merovingian family tree (after Holmes, 1988).

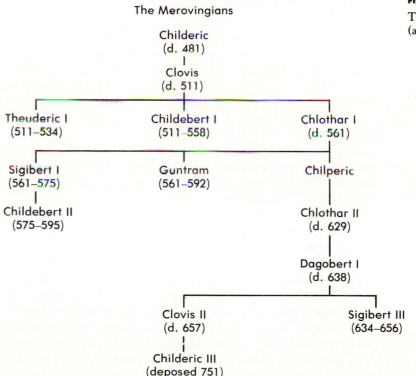

during the fourteenth century, when the Black Death swept through Europe (Chapter 17). All these "Dark Ages" have some common, general characteristics.

Invasions from Outside   First, they were often times of invasion from outside. This was particularly true for the Dark Ages after Charlemagne, when Arabs, Vikings, and various people from the East incessantly caused great destruction and despair. Still, there was another, brighter side to these invasions—they brought with them greater incidents of cultural contact, the knowledge of trade routes stretching great distances, and the increased possibility of acquiring new goods and knowledge.

Minimal Academic and Scientific Developments   Second, the Dark Ages were times when learning and scientific development were at a minimum. It appears that superstition and religious intolerance had great influence over people's lives—many criminals were tried by ordeal, and original thinking was repressed through fear and ignorance. Yet certain small enclaves in western Europe remained centers of learning, including those in Ireland and a few monastic sanctuaries on the continent. The writings of the Venerable Bede during the seventh century stand out as some of the greatest European scholarship of the period. Contemporary Arab scholarship was far in advance of European, particularly in math and astronomy.

Static or Declining Populations   Third, it is most likely that the Dark Ages were times when population sizes and densities were simply maintained or even declined, although such trends are difficult to measure with certainty (see Chapter 13). It appears that western Europe's population did not begin to climb significantly until the last few centuries of the Middle Ages (see below). And finally, it can be concluded that the Dark Ages were times when sociocultural complexity remained the same, or even unraveled to some extent. This was probably due to several factors: a static or declining population, and a de-emphasis on learning included. Regardless, degrees of sociocultural integration were low, trade and exchange were minimal, and subsistence practices were not at all intensive. Europe during the Dark Ages did not include anything we would identify as complex societies.

Geographical Factors   These Dark Ages were restricted to the west and had little effect on parts of eastern Europe, Byzantium, the Arabic world, and Scandinavia (not to mention other, more distant parts of the world). In addition, not all parts of western Europe were affected equally by the Dark Ages—different parts of Europe were "darker" than others. As mentioned, Ireland remained a center of learning during some of the earlier periods, and certain people there were largely responsible for the survival of European scholarship. Finally, many of the most well-known customs and institutions of the Middle Ages—in particular, Feudalism and the Manorial System—had their origins during the Dark Ages.

Revival of the Roman Empire in the West   During the Dark Ages, there was a rather short and ultimately unsuccessful attempt to reintegrate western European society. This attempt had its roots in the collapse of the Merovingian dynasty, in fact, which among other things resulted in an increase of power among the **independent nobility**. Thus, power was no longer concentrated in the hands of the few, as is found in any complex society, but rather was spread among individual mayors—otherwise known as lords.

One of the more successful of these mayors was Pepin of Heristal, who made the first serious attempt to reunite the various nobles in the realm. Pepin's son was Charles Martel, best known for defeating the Moors at the Battle of Tours and thus preventing the conquest of Europe from the west by North African Arabs. Charles's son was Pepin the Short, and Pepin's son was Charles the Great, or Charlemagne.

Charlemagne did reunite the nobility—and the society was reintegrated to the degree that in A.D. 800, there was an attempt to crown him the new Emperor of Rome. Some historians refer to this episode as the revival of the Roman Empire in the West. Others, however, recognize that the event was in large measure only a political agreement between Charlemagne and the Pope, designed to weaken the power of each individual noble. No matter how it is viewed, the Carolingian dynasty (named after Carolus, Latin for Charles) did not last long after Charlemagne's death, and Europe was thereafter plunged back into the Dark Ages for more than a century.

FEUDALISM AND MANORIALISM

As mentioned, a number of important medieval customs and institutions arose during the Dark Ages. Two of the more significant—feudalism and manorialism—were to have great impacts on subsequent cultural history.

Feudalism   *Feudalism* can be defined as governmental regulation by means of formal agreements between individuals, not between any recognized government and its subjects. It can be viewed as a social and political response to widespread sociocultural disintegration and chaos—it was a means of maintaining some semblance of order, some network of relationships, when no centralized leadership structure was present.

The feudal system came into being because there was no strong central government anywhere in western Europe during the Dark Ages. The system also came into existence because of widespread warfare, chaos, and fear—based both on reality and superstition—among the people. This fear encouraged individuals to place themselves in dependent relationships with those having more political power in order to gain protection. The relationship thus established is called **vassalage**, with the weaker person known as the vassal and the more powerful person, the lord.

The vassal would pledge certain services to the lord, primarily of a military nature. In return, the lord would sustain the vassal by providing

independent nobility

Small group of individuals who enjoyed a preponderance of the social wealth in medieval Europe, often independent of and opposed to various political powers, such as emerging kings.

vassal

A person given sustenance and protection by a lord, to whom various services were pledged in return.

Figure 15-4

A typical feudal pyramid.

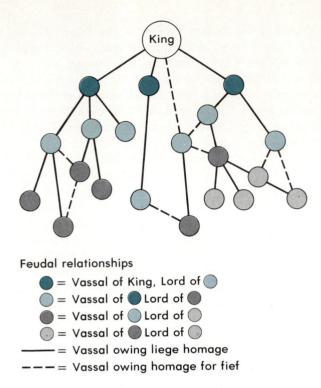

Feudal relationships

King

= Vassal of King, Lord of ◯
= Vassal of ⬤ Lord of ◯
= Vassal of ◯ Lord of ◯
= Vassal of ◯ Lord of ◯
——— = Vassal owing liege homage
– – – = Vassal owing homage for fief

him and his family with land, food, and protection. He would also guarantee the vassal justice in the feudal courts, important in an age lacking recognizable government authority. Soon, a complex hierarchy of vassal-lord relationships developed, a complex *feudal pyramid* that included many levels and degrees of relationship but that nevertheless was founded on agreements between individuals only (Figure 15–4).

It must be understood that the vassal-lord relationship was not really one of inferior to superior. Both members of the agreement were equally obligated to fulfill certain well-defined responsibilities. Each paid homage to the other, that is, offered ceremonial recognition of the importance of the relationship they had established. Indeed, certain vassals were very influential and wealthy individuals.

In addition, it must be remembered that the feudal system never involved more than a small percentage of the total population—those who were relatively wealthy and powerful to begin with. The vast majority of the population were not participants. These people were more directly associated with the manorial system, which we discuss shortly.

Finally, the practice of feudalism was instrumental in the evolution of certain architectural forms and strategies of war. The primary obligation of the vassals was fighting, and that of the lords was protection. At first, housing was unfortified, but as conflict grew, secure wooden structures were erected. These were often protected by earthen mounds, trenches, and moats. By the tenth century, some of the more powerful and wealthy lords were constructing true castles of stone, and these rapidly became larger and more impregnable (Figure 15–5).

Manorialism   In response to the increasing security offered by castles, tactics of warfare evolved increasingly to emphasize sieges and crop burnings over overt military attacks. As a result, conflict had a greater direct impact on the general, noncombative population through the inability to harvest crops. Carrying capacity (the amount of food the land could provide) remained low during the Dark Ages, as did population, in large measure because of the nature of warfare. This situation was counterbalanced and eventually reversed, however, by technological developments occurring in the economic context of *manorialism*.

The manorial system was the most pervasive economic order that emerged in response to the conditions of the Dark Ages. The lack of sociocultural integration of the times resulted in the existence of many independent manors ruled by lords and containing agricultural fields, for-

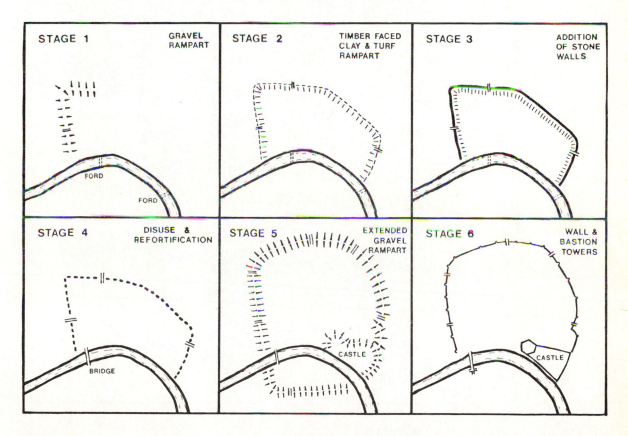

Figure 15-5

Sequence of construction of the defenses at Hereford, England.

peasant

A member of a class who work the land and who are forced to pay rent, taxes, or labor tribute to a ruling class.

est lands, at least one village, a manor house, and other fixtures (Figure 15–6). Individuals within the manor included the lord himself, his administrative staff (including a steward and a bailiff), and primarily **peasants**. The vast majority of people in Europe at the time were members of the peasantry, which is why the manorial system had a much more significant impact on daily life and history than did the feudal system.

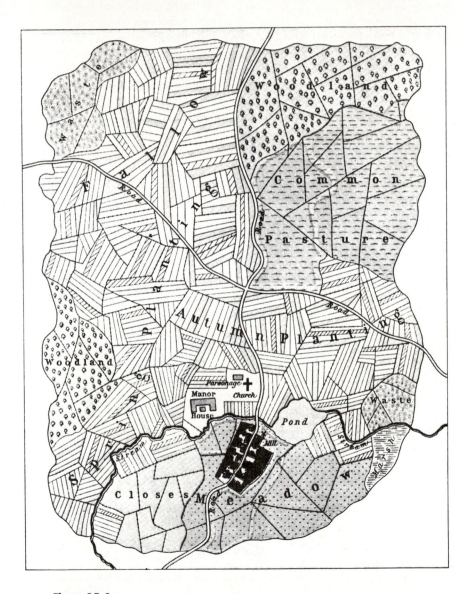

Figure 15-6

A plan of a typical medieval manor, showing land belonging to the peasants, the lord, and the parish church.

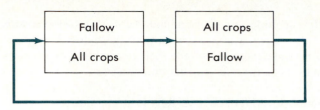

Schematic diagram of two–field system.

Figure 15-7
The two-field system versus
the three-field system of
agricultural production.

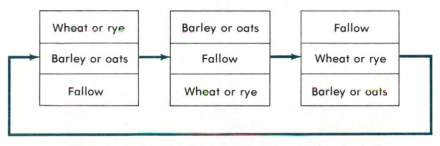

Schematic diagram of three–field system—each individual
field was further subdivided into strips of land owned
and worked by different people.

A major subsistence development occurred in the context of manorialism—the emergence and widespread acceptance of the *three-field system.* It replaced the earlier *two-field system* of Roman times, in which a
typical farm was divided into two areas—each year one area was planted
while the other lay fallow (Figure 15–7).

First introduced in German monasteries, the new system of crop
rotation called for farms to be divided into three areas. Each was subject
to autumn planting, spring planting, and fallow periods. Thus, double-
cropping was possible while still maintaining an adequate time for soil
rejuvenation. As a result, carrying capacity was dramatically increased—
now only one-third of the land was left fallow at any particular time,
where before, one-half was not being used.

Other technological advances took place at the same time, further
increasing the carrying capacity of the land and eventually offsetting the
effects of feudal warfare. The heavy wheeled plow was adopted, which
more effectively tilled the unwieldy wet soils found in western Europe.
The horse collar was developed and the iron horseshoe invented,
enabling farmers to exploit better the great power of this animal and thus
replace the traditional, inefficient ox. And water power was put to more
and more uses throughout Europe, supplementing human and animal
resources in the quest for greater amounts of harnessed energy.

These various technological and subsistence changes began during
Carolingian times or earlier and gradually improved and spread over the

next few centuries. In addition, and due to its growing economic importance, the manorial system encouraged sociocultural complexity as measured by the degree of social inequality—different classes of peasant emerged, including serfs, villeins, and freemen.

ECONOMIC AND SOCIAL REVIVAL

By the eleventh and early twelfth centuries there were noticeable increases in both 1) the overall population size and population densities in western Europe and 2) the amount of food being grown, and thus available, throughout western Europe. These two trends, originating in the Dark Age institutions of feudalism and (more especially) manorialism, were subsequently responsible for a host of other developments in succeeding centuries—developments that ultimately brought Europe out of the Middle Ages altogether.

Historians do not agree whether population growth preceded (and thus made necessary) the expansion and intensification of agriculture or whether agricultural development preceded (and thus allowed) population growth. Archaeologists, who often consider a much larger slice of cultural history, might contribute insights into this issue by comparing the European Middle Ages with other times and places. As we have seen in Chapter 13, many anthropologists feel that population change is a significant cause for other changes in subsistence technology, and it could have been that way during medieval times as well. Despite the greater historical detail provided by documents, the issue remains unresolved. Regardless of the chicken-or-egg nature of the argument, clearly the archaeological record indicates that subsistence intensified and population grew. Other, related trends followed.

First, an increasing number of people began migrating to and colonizing places where few people had lived previously. The majority of this migration was from west to east, though not as far east as Byzantium or the Russian steppes. The technological developments allowed more forest land to be cleared for agriculture, and the increasing population required that more land be farmed.

Second, and closely related, a dramatic increase occurred in the impact people were having on the environment, particularly in the amount of deforestation occurring throughout Europe. Until that time, the continent was in large part covered by forest. By the end of the Middle Ages, much of the land had been transformed into agricultural fields. (Even more deforestation occurred during subsequent, industrial times, and the modern landscape of Europe has little resemblance to its medieval counterpart.)

Third, political and social stability increased through the period. The amount of warfare decreased dramatically, particularly that caused by outside invasions. There was less internal conflict as well, in large measure because of the centralizing efforts of Catholicism.

In addition, there was increasing sociocultural differentiation across regions in Europe. Also related were increasing rates of trade and exchange, both in terms of number of goods and distance travelled. Trade could expand because of the increased stability and was encouraged by the increased regional differentiation. This trade was manifest in the growing number of **trade fairs** and the emergence of a number of trading centers, many of which later evolved into towns and cities.

There appears to have been an increasing potential for upward social mobility, particularly among the peasantry. It seems that the technological developments and economic growth of the time created a worker's market in many areas. Labor was in great and growing demand, and competition was increasing between lords and other landowners for this labor. As a result, the grip of the manorial system on peasants weakened, individual freedoms emerged, and the possibility for economic self-improvement increased.

Scholars debate whether and to what degree this late medieval recovery created a better way of life for the general population. (Some historians call it a renaissance, but it should not be confused with the better-known European Renaissance of the fifteenth to seventeenth centuries.) If it actually happened, this development was unique in cultural history—earlier times of increasing sociocultural complexity brought with them a less comfortable existence (Chapters 13 and 14). Still, there is good reason to believe that the economic and social revival of the eleventh and twelfth centuries was the beginning of a new trend that would intensify during industrial times and result in human groups reverting to some gatherer-hunter behavioral patterns. We discuss this remarkable series of developments below.

Finally, there was an overall increase in the amount of western European urbanization beginning in the eleventh and early twelfth centuries. Many older urban centers, such as London and Lyons and some dating back to Roman times, were repopulated or grew larger. And many new towns sprang up where none were before. A handful of them soon became major urban centers. This urban expansion, in turn, led to 1) an increase in the division of labor, and 2) an increase in the number and incidence of contagious diseases. Both had significant impacts on subsequent cultural history.

Urbanization in two areas, originating during this early period of European revival, culminated in the earliest expressions of the industrial age. One of these locales included the Italian trade cities (Pisa, Venice, and Genoa), and the other included the manufacturing centers of Flanders (Bruges, Ghent, and Liege).

This economic and social revival was so successful that it was soon possible for the western Europeans themselves to conquer foreign lands rather than be conquered by outsiders. Starting in the late eleventh century and continuing some 200 years, many Europeans participated in the famous *Crusades*—holy wars with the stated purpose of placing the Holy Lands under Christian control. In fact, the Crusades were reflections of

trade fair
Periodic gathering of merchants, artisans, and others to facilitate trade and exchange.

The Crusades

One of the outcomes of Europe's economic and social revival during the eleventh and twelfth centuries was the Crusades, a series of eight or nine invasions of non-European lands (depending on how you count them) that span two centuries from A.D. 1095 to A.D. 1290. The Crusades reflected western Europe's growing ability to invade, conquer, and to some degree hold foreign lands, accomplishments that were impossible previously. They did so on a scale not seen in a thousand years, unparalleled in its barbarity, and directed largely at "infidels" and Jews.

The Crusades are often called holy wars. The stated purpose of the Crusades was to take the Holy Land from non-Christians in order to give it to Christians. But there was more to it than that. As mentioned, the Crusades were reflections of economic and social growth within western Europe; they were demonstrations of western Europe's increasing capabilities to invade and conquer.

They were also economic tools used to increase the power of western European trade centers within the growing global economy. The Holy Land, clearly, was located in a strategic place when it came to long-distance trade with the Far East, an activity western Europe was developing. Merchants in the Italian trading ports, such as Venice and Genoa, recognized this strategic importance and thus supplied much-needed financial and military support to the Crusades.

Third, the Crusades were in large measure attempts by the western Catholic church to absorb the Eastern, Byzantine church, the ultimate goal of the popes being the ascendance of Rome to the

Europe's growing influence over non-European peoples, made possible by technological and economic developments (Box 15–1).

Indeed, the Crusades can most accurately be viewed as aspects of European economic policy, not religious actions. By invading settlements on the eastern Mediterranean, European rulers hoped to gain control over trade routes to the Orient and thus begin to dominate the known world. They did not always succeed, although it is clear that the balance of power was rapidly shifting to the West—the Crusades are clear evidence for this shift in power.

Ultimately, the revival also allowed the first true European monarchies to emerge during the twelfth and thirteenth centuries, evidence for the first true complex society in western Europe since Roman times. In France, the Capetian house gradually grew in strength from Carolingian times onward, until the reigns of Louis IX (1226–1270) and Phillip IV (1285–1314), during which the king and his administration had total control over policy (a monopoly of the force). In England, from the time of the Norman Conquest in 1066, the state emerged also, but in this case, the administration consisted of a number of decision-making bodies that were often in conflict. Precursors to the English Parliament (and the U. S. Congress) were in conflict with the king as early as the eleventh century. King John's signing of the Magna Carta in 1215 was evidence that an absolute monarchical dictatorship would not be tolerated.

Finally, we can see that the European revival first started in the supreme center and focus of all Christianity. The Church also gave support to the Crusades.

Finally, the Crusades were a social mechanism to displace some of the endemic warfare so intimately related to feudalism and so destructive in western Europe. By displacing this aggression to areas *outside* western Europe, and thus by increasing the degree of sociocultural stability *within* western Europe, the wealthy and powerful kept their wealth and power intact and unthreatened by the masses.

In terms of these various functions, the Crusades can be viewed at least partially as a success. Many scholars consider them a failure because the foreign occupations were not permanent and because they had few lasting sociocultural effects. If looked at in this different, functional way, however, the end of the Crusades in the late thirteenth cen-

tury can be seen as a reflection of changing conditions and needs in western Europe.

We can also see the Crusades as the beginning of the imperialism and colonialism that characterized European interaction with other cultures a few centuries later. It is certainly no wonder that many nations of the Third World, particularly in the Middle East, are very wary of the descendants of the Crusaders in the twentieth century.

References:

Runciman, S. (1951–54). *A History of the Crusades* (3 vols.). Cambridge, England: Cambridge University Press.

Setton, K. M. (1955). (Ed.). *A History of the Crusades*. Philadelphia: Univ. of Pennsylvania Press.

eleventh century culminated in the domination of European society and culture across the world—with the age of exploration and empire building through the industrialization of the planet.

Medieval Europe: Archaeological Evidence

Clearly, it is impossible to write a detailed cultural history of medieval Europe, even when restricting it to western Europe, in a single chapter. Instead, what we have presented are some of the highlights of this history, that most directly reflect social patterns and anthropological research interests. Some of these major topics of interest are: 1) the fall of Rome and beginning of the Dark Ages, 2) the way of life for most people during the Dark Ages, especially the nature of the manorial system, and 3) the economic and social revival after the Dark Ages, particularly the urbanization that resulted.

THE BEGINNING OF THE DARK AGES

The early Middle Ages are not well known, relative to later periods. With the fall of Rome, the amount of written material falls to nearly zero. Archaeological studies stand almost in isolation as a means to understanding this past time.

Even the physical remains of early medieval times are less informative than their Roman precursors. Most Roman structures were made of relatively durable materials, notably stone. Structures of the early Middle

Figure 15-8

Excavation of the Vicars Choral at the Bedern in York, England.

Ages were made of earth and wood and, for the most part, were smaller than those that came before or followed. Many have disappeared entirely.

Often, all that can be observed of this time is a layer of darkened earth between the Roman and subsequent horizons indicating that some activities were occurring but rarely containing enough evidence to indicate specifically what the activities were. This dark earth has suggested the presence of fires and the practice of cultivation, although no one is certain. What is clear is that the early Middle Ages was a time of societal disintegration, the abandonment of Roman towns and the dispersal of the population across the countryside, the curtailment of both trade and manufacturing activities, and a general lowering of sociocultural complexity. It is thought that there was even a significant shift in subsistence practices in some locations, with a substantial part of the diet coming once more from gathering and hunting rather than from agriculture or pastoralism.

Nevertheless, some archaeological evidence for the early Dark Ages has survived over the centuries. Examples have been found in the English city of York, for example, where extensive field research has been conducted over many years. In York, there is evidence that construction techniques were forgotten during the early Dark Ages, and as a result, many Roman-period structures were abandoned as they deteriorated—layers of earth formed over what were previously city streets and other activity areas (Figure 15–8). There is additional evidence for systematic and widespread looting of the abandoned city, an activity archaeologists recognize as one form of reuse in the face of economic hardship—entire buildings are thought to have been removed, piece by piece. Similar evidence can be found in other European cities.

LIFE IN THE DARK AGES

History paints a rather grim picture of the Dark Ages, and archaeology supports the contention that life was sometimes difficult. Yet we should not confuse living a difficult life with living in a relatively simple sociocultural setting—and the archaeological data suggest the latter more often than the former.

For instance, there is widespread evidence for a lack of social or political integration. As mentioned, urban life was rare, and most people lived dispersed across the countryside. Those few towns occupied during the time—parts of London comprise one example—exhibit hardly any planning, having little regularity in the layout of streets or activity areas. Manufacturing centers seem to have been few and far between, showing little in the way of craft specialization or special skills. These observations do not necessarily indicate a bad life, however—only a simpler one than that imposed earlier by the Romans.

The clearest evidence for hardship takes the form of defensive structures, increasingly common during the early Dark Ages. Roman

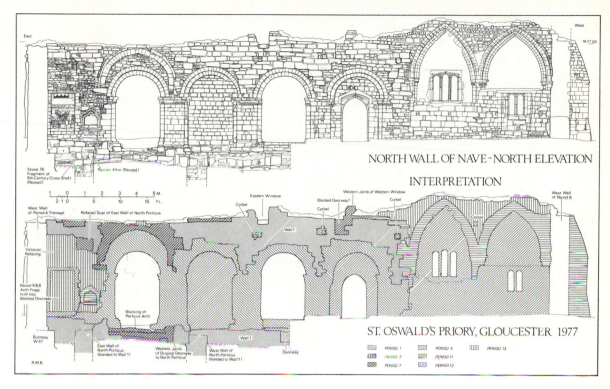

Figure 15-9

A profile of the medieval church of St. Oswald's in Gloucester, England.

walls and other defenses were refortified after years of neglect, and new ones were constructed, first of earth and later of stone. Surely, both invasion and internal conflict were significant aspects of life.

More evidence for the nature of life during the Dark Ages comes from the remains of churches (Figure 15–9). As Christianity replaced various Pagan religions, the Church became the most important integrating mechanism of the community. The size and mode of construction of a church can often suggest the ability of a community to cooperate and complete an expensive undertaking—many communities could not accomplish what they set out to do. In addition, a comparison of different churches in a single community, designed to serve different groups of people, can suggest the range of social classes and degree of inequality. While stratification survived in many settings, a return to a more egalitarian way of life seems to have taken place in certain instances. Finally, burials from church grounds give us some of our best information about health and life-style, though skeletal material can be difficult to interpret at times. Altogether, material remains from church grounds offer a wide variety of data.

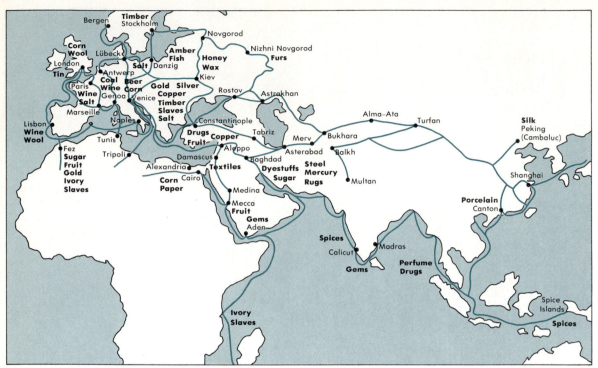

Figure 15-10

Trade routes between late medieval Europe and other Old World locations during the fourteenth century.

ECONOMIC AND SOCIAL REVIVAL AND URBANIZATION

The economic and social revival of the eleventh and early twelfth centuries is obvious in the archaeological record. Indeed, the overall amount of material evidence for the past increases rapidly when one moves from Dark Age to post-Dark Age contexts.

As discussed earlier, one aspect of this revival was an increase in urbanization—for various reasons, including increased population sizes and rates of migration, many new towns were founded across Europe. In addition, many of the older towns grew rapidly in size and population. Rates of construction climbed, and the use of durable materials such as stone became more common. Churches and other monumental structures grew in size, some reaching grand proportions.

The new urban areas exhibited greater planning in the form of grid street layouts and the separation of different activity centers. This planning reflects an increased level of sociocultural integration, the growing ability to organize large and diverse groups of people. Perhaps this ability is clearest to archaeologists in the orderly arrangements of the tenements they have excavated—combined working and living quarters for the emerging urban craftsmen arranged in parallel rows along numerous streets. There is little question but that life was becoming more regimented in concert with the increase in sociocultural complexity.

Finally, there is clear archaeological evidence that the number of crafts was increasing and that these craft specialties were thriving as a result of increased trade and exchange. Production levels reached all-time highs, and products moved from one end of Europe to the other and beyond (Figure 15–10). Trade was literally becoming a global endeavor primarily for the benefit of Europe, and manufacturing was requiring more specialization and skill. This was the beginning of the age of the apprentice and the **guild**.

Industrialism and the Colonization of North America: Cultural History

Once again, we are interested not so much in history as in the evolution of culture; consequently, our focus is not on the many people, places, and things that constitute the subjects of history, but rather on the rise and impact of industrialism, the most recent revolution in human society.

THE NATURE OF INDUSTRIALISM

In many respects, industrial societies are similar to nonindustrial complex societies. Both contain governments known as states, are highly integrated socially and politically, involve great numbers of people often living in dense concentrations, and are notable for a high level of labor specialization and trade. While avoiding the mistake of trying to define these societies by reference to a list of traits, we can see that industrial societies are supercomplex societies—having the same basic characteristics of complex societies but in exaggerated form.

In some respects, however, industrial societies are unique. For instance, it is likely that the quality of life in industrial societies is better for the majority, relative to nonindustrial complex societies—though it is also likely that the betterment of life for those in the industrial nations has come at the expense of those in other societies.

As mentioned, the potential for upward social mobility began to increase in western Europe during the eleventh century, a trend that might still be in progress. Further, the health of most people as measured by life expectancy and other parameters appears to have improved with the late Middle Ages and industrialism. Finally, the overall education level of the population rose with the industrial age, and education, as a road to upward mobility, is always a sign of a better way of life.

Disagreement exists as to whether life improves for the vast majority of people with industrialism. If it does, and if it has since the eighteenth century or earlier, then we are witness to a remarkable occurrence in cultural history—the first time that a major transformation in cultural evolution has led to a general improvement in the condition of those transformed. As we have seen, neither the rise of domestication nor the

guild

An association of merchants or craftsmen of similar interests and pursuits formed to regulate business practices and support fellow workers.

emergence of the first complex societies appears to have improved life for the people within the society that adopted it. How is it that industrialism might have done so?

The answer might lie in a comparison of industrial with gatherer-hunter societies. Remarkably, these two sociocultural forms, so different in levels of technological development, have a number of traits in common that distinguish them from agricultural and nonindustrial complex societies. In certain respects, then, the industrial world has been "reverting" to a gatherer-hunter social existence. A more comfortable life for the majority might be part of this trend.

For one thing, members of both gatherer-hunter and industrial societies are highly nomadic. The former are because of the need to travel to wild forms of food, while the latter are because of the need to relocate for employment. Industrial people, at least of the upper and middle classes, are also capable of moving frequently because of the transportation advances that have occurred over the past few hundred years. They can transport great numbers of material goods and thus can accumulate them without impeding movement. In this regard, the accumulation of goods, hunter-gatherer and industrial societies are very different, but in the extent to which one is not tied to the same piece of land for an entire lifetime, they are similar.

The mobility of these societies leads their members to stress the importance of the nuclear family while downplaying the extended family and placing much less importance on the descent group, or clan. Meaningful kin groups are generally relatively small because families and individuals are constantly on the move. Further, the composition of these groups is fluid—always changing—as individual members come and go. What might appear to be the extinction of the family in industrial societies, the breakdown of stable, permanent, and fixed relationships, might instead be the emergence of a more dynamic, more gatherer-hunter-like means of adaptation.

Finally, some evidence suggests that a more egalitarian way of life has emerged as societies have become more industrial. This process might have started as early as the eleventh and twelfth centuries, when Europe first experienced an economic and social revival (see above). At the present time, the rigid, nearly caste distinctions of aristocracy and peasantry are gone, and increasing numbers of people find they can achieve a certain amount of social and economic status during their own lifetimes. More and more often, one hears of the *meritocracy* of the modern, industrial West—a society in which one is (or at least should be) judged on personal achievement, not on inherited social position. Clearly, the modern world is not as egalitarian as any gatherer-hunter group. Many injustices and inequalities still exist. In these values, though, we appear to be heading in the direction of the gatherer-hunter condition as we continue to modernize.

The argument can be made that increasing equality *within* industrial nations has come about at the expense of people living *without,* that is, in the Third (or nonindustrial) World. Industrial societies have for centuries exploited nonindustrial societies, and the tradition continues unabated at the present time. Indeed, it might be worsening as international corporations flee the West for more inexpensive labor. In addition, the industrial world has polluted the environment extensively in order to raise the standard of living for its members. A high price has been paid so that *some* people can live richer lives.

EUROPE BEFORE INDUSTRIALISM

The Industrial Revolution had its roots in several places. The European Renaissance of the fifteenth to seventeenth centuries, although essentially a time for looking backward to the great achievements of the Mediterranean civilizations, nevertheless encouraged the consideration of technological development. The European exploration of the world, accelerating during the sixteenth century because of improvements in ship construction and navigation, introduced the West to vast stores of resources (including people) for exploitation and financial gain. The newly emerged strong nations of Portugal, Spain, England, and France had the ability to carry out this exploitation, and as a result, it was not long before Europe stood on the brink of world domination (Figure 15–11). For the prospects of trade, upward mobility, and great wealth, technological development in the form of industrialization was an adaptive and creative solution.

This industrial growth did not occur all at once. By 1700, many industries had already developed, while others were not yet in existence. In numerous places the iron, coal, and textile industries were established and expanding, and a number of support industries thrived in the shadows of these major endeavors. Long-distance trade and shipping were significant undertakings, and urbanization had reached remarkable heights, particularly in England. Europe was not a tranquil, rural backwater immediately prior to the Industrial Revolution, which emerged over the course of many years from medieval and post-medieval origins. The Industrial Revolution of the eighteenth century was outstanding only in that industrial growth accelerated during the period.

INDUSTRIAL EUROPE

Industrial Europe was a very different place from medieval or Renaissance Europe. Foremost, numerous technological innovations occurred over a short period of time, and that resulted in a very different way of life.

Some of the earliest and most important industrial developments occurred in transportation systems, which were necessary prerequisites for the expansion of trade. Sea transport advanced prior to industrialism, in

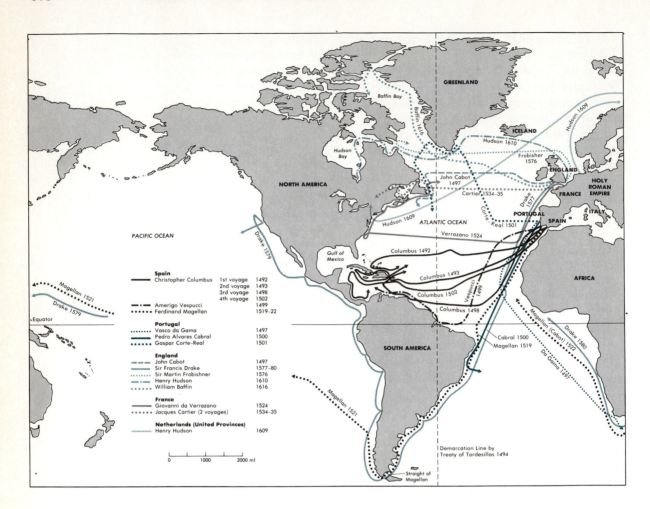

Figure 15-11

European exploration during the fifteenth to seventeenth centuries.

fact. Then, by the eighteenth century, early civil engineers began build-ing better roads, along which people could travel at faster speeds and with more comfort. Shortly thereafter, canals were constructed that were capa-ble of transporting large and heavy objects. By the early nineteenth cen-tury, the railroad was developed. Trains were capable of moving heavy objects rapidly, and so railroads quickly replaced both roads and canals as major transport systems.

All these developments affected the lives of the majority of people. Advances in transport facilitated the movement of both people and goods. As a result, numerous industries were in better contact with one another, prices tended to decline, and the overall industrial growth rate increased. In addition, there began a trend toward the separation of the work and living spaces, as workers could more efficiently commute to their jobs. Finally, the degree of contact between different segments of society increased, and therefore, so did the rate of cultural change.

Other necessary developments took place in the area of communication. Starting with the printing press before the Industrial Revolution and culminating with the telegraph of the 1830s (and even later with the telephone), advances in communication allowed more information to travel farther distances in less time. The social impact of this technology was no less significant than that of transportation and included the increased education of the populace, an overall increase in the public awareness of current events, and a growth in the importance of public opinion. Ultimately, these developments allowed a general strengthening of democratic institutions and practices and of other liberal ideals, such as equality and a diminishing tolerance for the abrogation of human rights. As with all technologies, however, advances in communication and transportation have been abused by those seeking to impose dictatorial rule.

Developments in both the transportation and communication industries allowed more territory and a greater number of people to fall within a single polity. Thus, advances in both these areas can be viewed as instrumental in leading to greater sociocultural complexity.

In a third way, the Industrial Revolution altered European society dramatically—new sources of power and methods of exploiting that power were discovered or developed. Besides the energy of people and animals, no other power sources existed in 1700 than water and wind. Yet within a single century, a number of additional sources were tapped and exploited, including steam, gas, oil, and electricity. New machines were built so that the available power could be used efficiently, and new industrial processes were developed so that the maximum number of products could be manufactured at the lowest cost. Efficiency and profit reached great heights, as capitalist Europeans indeed hoped they would.

The social implications of technological growth were enormous. Industrialism replaced the guild and domestic work organizations with the *factory system*, in which workers did not own the tools and machines they needed to do their jobs (Figure 15–12). The concentration of industries and their associated factories and jobs forced people into highly dense population concentrations, and the overall population sizes of industrial countries grew rapidly and dramatically.

As with the rise of domestication and complex society, demography played an important role in the emergence of industrialism. Populations rose as the Industrial Revolution progressed, primarily because of a decline in the death rate, especially the **perinatal** death rate. It is thought that this decline was itself brought about by medical advances, increased personal hygiene, and improvements in the average diet.

perinatal
Occurring around the time of birth.

Figure 15-12
A typical nineteenth-century factory scene.

Did population increases create the need for more intensive subsistence and technological practices? Or were population increases the result of a better way of life, brought about by subsistence and technological developments? If the former is correct, than the Industrial Revolution would appear to have been somewhat similar to the rise of domestication and complex society. If the latter is correct, however, then there were fundamental differences between the process of industrialism and the other major watersheds in cultural history we have considered.

To an industrial family, children are not the economic assets they are to agricultural families; thus, families tend to control their sizes more and are again like gatherer-hunters, although by different means. The net result is that the populations of industrial cultures are composed of more people than gatherer-hunters or agriculturists, but proportionally fewer of them are young, and many more of them are old.

Numerous explanations for why the Industrial Revolution occurred in Europe during the eighteenth century have been offered. Some are obviously outdated, claiming that European people or societies were somehow superior to others and thus more capable at bringing about industrialism. These views are not only racist and/or ethnocentric, but they also rest on the assumption that cultural history leads inexorably to industrialism, which is incorrect. It led to industrialism once, as far as we know; but that is hardly a compelling argument for industrialism as being another step on a path of history taken first by Europeans. No such path exists, and the emergence of industrialism in Europe was a product of local social conditions and history.

Another outdated theory claims that all complex societies had fallen by post-medieval times, leaving a competitive vacuum that Europeans easily filled. This theory is factually incorrect—there were a number of complex societies in existence during the time that Europeans were industrializing. Many came into conflict with expanding Europe. In addition, this theory is again conceptually faulty. It assumes that industrialism is an inevitable result of cultural history, naturally occurring when given the opportunity.

Other, more acceptable theories argue that European ideology at the end of the Middle Ages played a significant part in bringing about the industrial age. One influential argument is that the *Protestant ethic* in some European countries encouraged industrial growth because it resulted in behaviors useful in a capitalist environment. Originally outlined by religious leaders such as Martin Luther and John Calvin and analyzed in the works of Max Weber, the Protestant ethic held that God rewards those who live simple lives but who also prosper economically during the course of their lifetimes. Economic success was, in fact, viewed as a sign of divine blessing, in spite of the warning in Luke 18:25 about it being easier for a camel to pass through the eye of a needle than for a rich man to enter the kingdom of God. Nevertheless, people were encouraged by these socioreligious views to strive for more work, more profits, and more industry.

There is little question that the Protestant ethic has had profound effects on people's lives—it still does today. Yet it is difficult to accept an explanation for a major transformation in cultural history that limits itself to simply new ideas without asking where those ideas came from. Besides, non-Protestants have been equally as frugal and industrious as Protestants. As with the rise of domestication and complex society, the rise of industrialism might be better explained by reference to technological and subsistence conditions. Clearly, an industrial nation need not follow a Protestant form of religion, nor is it inevitable for a Protestant nation to adopt an industrial technology.

A group of theories that do take specific ideologies into account are related to the benefits theories we considered in the previous chapter on complex society. These theories argue that the Industrial Revolution took place when and where it did because of growing social needs for more industry. With European exploration and colonization came a dramatic expansion of the potential market. Concurrently, there was a decrease in available labor capable of manufacturing necessary goods. There was thus a need in Europe to intensify production. One creative, adaptive solution was to industrialize.

The growth of each industry required the growth of others, according to these theories, so that the entire technological realm expanded within a positive feedback system. The growing demand for iron required more fuel, and as the wood supply diminished, the demand for alternative fuels increased. Techniques for using coal were developed, and the need

Steam Power

Many scholars have recognized the harnessing and use of steam power as an important development of the Industrial Revolution. The availability of steam power dramatically increased the amount of energy humans could extract from the environment and control. Before steam, there was recourse to only people power and to that provided by domestic animals, wind, and water.

The history of how steam became a new source of power illustrates how the history of technology is a history of *process*, not a series of unrelated *inventions*.

During the second half of the seventeenth century, several scientists in England and on the continent, including Robert Boyle, Christian Huygens, and Denis Papin, were studying the nature of air pressure and vacuums. Their interests were largely theoretical, although it was not long before an inventor, Thomas Savory, applied their findings and constructed the first primitive steam engine. He did this in 1698, well before the Industrial Revolution gained momentum. His patent described his invention as "an engine to raise water by fire."

To serve its intended purpose, that is, to pump water out of mines, Savory's engine created a vacuum by raising steam through pipes and sluicing the outside of the boiler with cold water to produce condensation. Though rather inefficient (it could raise water only about 20 feet), this early use of steam power helped miners meet the rising demand for coal.

Then, in 1712, T. Thomas Newcomen introduced a new and much more efficient steam engine that operated in surprisingly modern fashion. The Newcomen Engine included a pump that sprayed cold water into a steam-filled cylinder, which created a vacuum and made atmospheric pressure force the piston down. Attached was an overhead rocking beam that was moved up and down by the piston. This use of steam power was a commercial success. It was inexpensive to manufacture and use, was reliable, and was widely used in mines and factories as the demand for more (and more efficient) energy continued to increase.

Inevitably, the Newcomen Engine was improved. James Watt, in partnership with the academician Joseph Black as well as the wealthy industrialist Matthew Boulton, was largely responsible for making it even more efficient, reliable, and versatile. He introduced a new model of steam engine in 1769, which required less energy to run (because it separated the heating and cooling processes) and which could be applied to many more operations (because of the use of wheels instead of only the up-and-down rocking beam).

More important than these mechanical improve-

for coal expanded. This growing demand for coal encouraged the digging of deeper mines, and these demanded more efficient methods of pumping out ground water so that the mines could continue to operate. The steam engine was developed to do that (Box 15–2). The system—obviously much more complicated than outlined here—ultimately resulted in the emergence of the industrial West.

COLONIAL AND INDUSTRIAL NORTH AMERICA

We need not review the general, historical outlines of how North America was colonized, eventually gained independence, and subsequently became a great industrial power. Rather, it will be stressed that the colonization of North America eventually led to its own industrial

ments was the fact that Watt and Boulton introduced high standards to assure that their engines were manufactured and operated with great precision. Earlier steam engines had not been made or used so carefully.

By the early nineteenth century, England was the leading industrial nation of the world, in no small part because of the high quality and great quantity of English steam engines. Indeed, by this time, steam engines had been placed on wheels, and the steam locomotive had become a reality thanks to the work of Richard Trevithick, irreversibly transforming the industrial world.

It is important to remember, however, that developments such as the steam engine and locomotive were not simply the products of individual great inventors. Rather, they were the products of cultural evolution. Theoretical developments allowed the more practical-minded to experiment with air pressure and vacuums. Sociocultural needs, like the growing need for coal from mines that filled with water, rewarded those who experimented with methods to remove that water. Improvements led the way to workable solutions, and subsequent innovations led to greater versatility and an increased number of applications and, in turn, greater demands.

The locomotive was not built without knowledge of the Watt Engine, the Newcomen Engine, or Savory's engine before that. Although we associate the engine with the name of the person who put it together, each inventor relied on a previous generation's knowledge and contemporary technology and was engaged in a competitive race to achieve the goal and be awarded the patent—a race that could easily have been lost to someone else, whose name would be attached to the engine instead.

Steam might have been the first new source of power to emerge during the Industrial Revolution, but it was not the last. Gas and electricity became alternatives during the nineteenth century. Even electromagnetism was explored as a possibility. The twentieth century has brought the use of fission power. In the near future, the remarkably powerful process of fusion might be harnessed. In a very general sense, Leslie White was right (Chapter 4) in that growing sociocultural complexity includes the use of greater and greater quantities of energy.

References:

Buchanan, R. A. (1965). *Technology and social progress.* Oxford, England: Pergamon Press.

Calder, R. (1968). *The evolution of the machine.* New York: American Heritage Publishing Company, The Smithsonian Library.

development and, thus, the emergence of similar sociocultural conditions as those in Europe.

Europeans began to colonize the New World in the late fifteenth century. In what was to become the United States, the colonial period continued for nearly 300 years, until the late eighteenth century, when, for various complex and related reasons, the colonies rebelled. Then, for the next 100 years or so, the newly born United States struggled to maintain its independence while expanding its physical territory (Figure 15–13). Despite successes in capturing land and in destroying many native American societies, the period was not an easy one for the country, suffering as it did a number of conflicts with foreign governments and, most threatening, the Civil War.

Indeed, it was not until the last few decades of the nineteenth century that the United States started to experience enough internal social stability and economic strength to approach the status of a world power. In large part, this strength came from a growing industrialism—the Industrial Revolution was being experienced for the first time in the New World. Certainly, experiments with industrial growth began in the United States as early as the revolutionary period, and by 1825 there were a number of industrial towns such as Lowell, Massachusetts, and Paterson, New Jersey, where manufacturing and regimented factory life were under the strict control of company owners. Still, industrialism did not have a significant impact on the country until decades later. As in Europe, much of these later impacts occurred because of developments in transportation, communication, and the use of energy.

It was possibly in the field of transportation, in particular the railroad, that industrialism had its greatest effect on the growth and development of the United States. There is archaeological evidence suggesting that the railroad caused major changes in American society.

Industrialism and the Colonization of North America: Archaeological Evidence

The archaeology of colonial and industrial North America is as diverse and complex as the cultural history. In the past few decades, a growing number of historical archaeologists have recovered materials and generated data from a wide range of site types, including rural homesteads, urban centers, trade centers, military outposts, religious missions, battlefields, cemeteries, and many others. Likewise, the people of interest to historical archaeologists working in North America were diverse, including all Europeans, African-Americans and Asian-Americans, and the numerous native Americans who came into contact with these groups. The research interests of the historical archaeologists cover the entire spectrum of history and cannot be reviewed here. Instead, we present two examples—one from the colonial east and the other from the emerging, industrial west.

FLOWERDEW HUNDRED

For the past several years, historical archaeologist James Deetz has been directing research at Flowerdew Hundred, Virginia, on the James River. Established in 1619, Flowerdew was a privately run plantation that continues operating as a farm. Thirty historical period sites on the property reflect continuous occupation since the early seventeenth century.

Using the changing diameters of smoking pipe stem bores as a guide, Deetz was able to date precisely the various sites at Flowerdew Hundred. He recognized that three distinct groups of sites were present, distinguishable by time and nature of occupation. Type One sites, evenly distributed across the bottomlands of the Hundred, dated to the c. 1620–1650 period. It appears they were abandoned quite rapidly, most

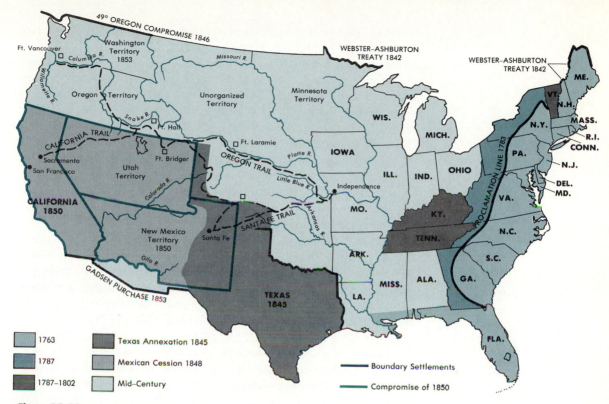

Figure 15-13

Territorial growth of the United States from pre-Revolutionary times to the mid-nineteenth century.

likely because of a drop in tobacco prices that occurred in the second half of the seventeenth century. Type Two sites, concentrated toward the northern and southern ends of the plantation, dated to c. 1640–1720. It appears the people once living at these sites had the strongest commitment to staying there and working the land. Finally, Type Three sites, again distributed across the bottomlands, dated from c. 1710 to 1750. These sites, probably occupied by small-time slave owners, were also abandoned rapidly, and the land was thereafter completely devoted to farming activities.

Type Three sites were notable because they were the only ones at which Colono Ware ceramics were recovered. It is thought by Deetz that the ceramics of this tradition were manufactured and used mainly by slaves in the American southeast, but it is known that African-Americans lived at Flowerdew Hundred since the early 1600s. Why should this distinctive type of pottery appear only in the early eighteenth century?

It seems that both African-American slaves and white servants often lived in the same house with planters and owners before the time of Type Three sites. Indeed, there was an overall greater degree of social and racial integration during this early period. As a result, all people had access to the same household goods, including ceramics—no one group had to manufacture its own. Afterward, however, slavery became a major institution, and race emerged as the most important criterion for slave status. African-Americans found themselves increasingly separated from other people—in social, economic, spatial, and material ways. They found it necessary to manufacture their own ceramic materials, and Colono Ware came into existence.

Deetz, therefore, has shown that changing social and economic relations have clear impacts on the material record. Archaeology can contribute much to our understanding of colonial conditions and trends.

CONSTRUCTION OF RAILROADS

The impacts of industrialism are perhaps clearest in the archaeological record of North America that pertains to the construction of railroads. This advance in transport had a remarkable impact on life-style and world view, as reflected in altered patterns of goods availability, resource distribution, systems of communication, and concepts regarding the nature of national expansion and the frontier. Changes in each of these aspects of life are visible in the archaeological record, an example being the results from a number of large projects in downtown El Paso, Texas.

Archaeology in El Paso has involved excavations at three sites: 1) the Kohlberg parking lot, where artifacts from both commercial and residential dwellings were recovered, 2) the Jacque's bar site in the very oldest part of town, where commercial activities were represented, and 3) the Cortez parking lot, where remains of El Paso's old Chinatown were recorded (Figure 15–14). These three excavated sites became scenes of intensive downtown redevelopment shortly after excavation, and the archaeology was conducted because the sites contained well-preserved materials representing people and events significant to El Paso's history.

The recovered material from all three sites represents the 1850–1920 period, from the first establishment of the El Paso community through its dramatic growth into an urban center during the early twentieth century. It has been possible for the archaeologists to address such issues as 1) the ecological history of the area, 2) changing patterns of refuse disposal in a growing city, 3) developing trade and economic conditions, and 4) the nature of interaction among the three largest ethnic populations in the area, namely Euro-Americans, Mexican-Americans, and overseas Chinese. Much of this research has involved detailed consideration of the impacts of the railroad on the city and its development.

Little of El Paso's history can be understood without reference to the railroads. The Southern Pacific was the first to arrive in May 1881, on its way to completing the second transcontinental line. Then, one month later, the Sante Fe arrived from the north. The Texas and Pacific, out of Texarkana, reached the city in December of that same year. The

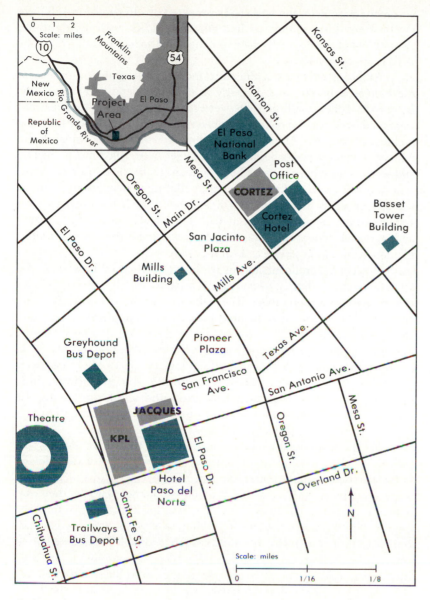

Figure 15–14
Downtown El Paso, Texas,
showing archaeological sites.

Galveston, Harrisburg and San Antonio moved in from Houston in January 1883. Finally, in March 1884, El Paso was connected by rail to the Mexican interior with the arrival of the Mexican Central. Within three years, the settlement was transformed from a sleepy hamlet to the commercial center of the greater southwest. Archaeological data reflect this transformation in a number of ways.

First, there is clear evidence in both the documentary and archaeological records for a rapid population increase. According to several documentary sources, the settlement consisted of 736 people in 1880, yet by the time the first railroad had appeared, 1,500 were living there. Several years later, in 1888, the population had soared to 11,069, and by 1910 it was nearly 40,000.

Archaeologically, this dramatic increase in population is seen in the increased amount and diversity of materials deposited in the city. Before the 1880s, trash deposits were small, manageable features that were used over a period of years—apparently, trash disposal was not a big problem in the city. After the 1880s, however—after the arrival of the railroads—trash deposits became much larger, were filled much quicker, and seem to have been more difficult to manage. In some instances, trash spilt out over the top of these features, polluting the streets and yards of the city. It seems that population was growing faster than management systems could respond, at least at first. Ultimately, growing population and increased amounts of refuse made it necessary for the city to initiate a municipal sanitation service to haul the trash away.

A second significant impact of the railroad could be seen in the increase in ethnic diversity—and ethnic separation—that this transportation revolution brought about. The railroads and the growth of El Paso's economic importance that resulted because of their presence increased the number of jobs available to unskilled workers. People from as far west as California and as far south as Mexico City converged on the city, looking for work. Among them were fairly diverse groups of Mexicans, overseas Chinese, and several others. Apparently, this increasing ethnic diversity resulted in increased separation and animosity among the groups, which might be a common outcome of intensified contact between any distinguishable populations.

To the archaeologists, however, it appears that this influx of peoples resulted in a blending of material cultural traditions, especially between the Mexican-American and Euro-American populations. Mexicans arriving in El Paso after the railroad did not abandon their own materials or their techniques of manufacture. Incoming Anglos from the eastern United States brought with them the goods they were accustomed to and continued to send for such goods. More important, it appears that both Mexicans and Anglos adopted material culture from each other, making it a significant part of their own lives. What resulted was one aspect of the distinctive *border culture*, to be found even today along the international boundary—a combination of material traditions and goods that, because of its hybrid nature, is unique.

The overseas Chinese present a slightly different picture, being more intent on maintaining their own traditions and not absorbing any from outside. Yet even these people could not help but be affected by their surroundings, and gradually they did adopt a more Western material tradition. The non-Chinese from the beginning appear to have freely adopted aspects of Oriental material culture and behavior, especially diet.

The railroads in El Paso had other impacts. We have discussed only two of the most important. And railroads elsewhere—merely one aspect of industrialism—profoundly changed the sociocultural landscape and history of North America. Clearly, the Industrial Revolution in the New World, as in the Old World, has had a remarkable impact on recent cultural history. This impact is still being felt today across the world, as all people are being brought, one way or another, into the modern age.

Summary

Complex societies today are in many ways different from the earlier complex societies described in Chapter 14. The Industrial Revolution, like the rise of domestication and the initial emergence of complexity, was a major watershed in cultural history that had profound impacts on societies around the world. The Industrial Revolution was initially a European phenomenon, having roots in the European Middle Ages.

Medieval archaeology is the study of the Middle Ages, primarily in Europe. It is a particular kind of historical archaeology, which is simply the archaeology of times and places for which we have useful documentary materials. The former is primarily a European endeavor and so is viewed as a subdiscipline of history. The latter has recently become explicitly anthropological, at least in the United States. Thus, the theoretical and methodological approaches of medieval and historical archaeology are significantly different.

Several important topics in medieval and subsequent cultural history are appropriate subjects of archaeological investigation. Included are the Dark Ages, the economic and social revival of the eleventh and twelfth centuries, medieval urbanization, ethnic relations in industrial communities, and the impacts of various technological developments on society.

Questions for Review

1. What makes the archaeology of historically documented societies different from history? How can archaeology provide a different perspective on historical times?

2. In the Middle Ages, Europe was technically backward compared to China. However, China was a large empire ruled by a single autocrat, and an emperor who wished to slow or stop the development of possibly threatening new technologies could do so. How was the political organization of Europe different, and how might that have affected the emergence of technology that ultimately led to Europe's political dominance?

3. The legal, political, and moral systems of Europe evolved along with technology, all being aspects of the evolving culture. For example, the undoing of hereditary aristocracy, the spread of wealth and possibility of upward mobility, the acceptance of change as part of life, and an emphasis on universal human rights are all industrial developments. When contemporary postindustrial technology (for example, missiles) diffuses to Third World nations with different legal, political, and moral systems, what major difficulties can you visualize? Can you relate this to the contemporary world situation? What solutions can you propose, bearing in mind the principles of cultural relativism?

4. Does cultural evolution seem to be gradual or saltational? How could you test this?

For Further Reading

Deegan, K. (1982). Avenues of inquiry in historical archaeology. In Schiffer, M. B. (Ed.). *Advances in archaeological method and theory.* New York: Academic Press 5:151–177.

Holmes, G. (Ed.). (1988). *The Oxford illustrated history of medieval Europe.* Oxford, England: Oxford University Press.

Schuyler, R. L. (Ed.). (1978). *Historical archaeology: A guide to substantive and theoretical contributions.* Farmingdale, NY: Baywood.

South, S. (1977). *Method and theory in historical archaeology.* New York: Academic Press.

White, L. T. (1962). *Medieval technology and social change.* Oxford, England: Clarendon.

Evolutionary Perspectives on Human Behavior

answer lies in the fact that most ethnographers—cultural anthropologists—have held little interest in the relationships between patterns of material culture and patterns of behavior. They have instead concentrated their efforts on understanding mostly nonmaterial phenomena—for example, kinship, religion, and ritual. In addition, most of this ethnographic information is not accessible in the rigorous quantitative fashion required of much archaeological research.

Qualitative investigations of the nonmaterial are not intrinsically less valuable than quantitative studies of the tangible. They simply focus on other aspects of culture. Thus, ethnoarchaeology has been a necessity. In this sense, ethnoarchaeology can be defined as ethnography from an archaeological perspective, conducted so that archaeological issues about the past can be more adequately addressed.

THE USE OF ANALOGY

The two recognized types of ethnoarchaeology have no clear boundary between them. First, and most traditional, is that type of ethnoarchaeology concerned with the past of a particular area or even group of people. The present is viewed as a current condition from which extrapolation into the past is possible by use of the *direct historical approach*. By this method, varying degrees of similarity are determined for artifacts in systemic context and from increasingly ancient archaeological contexts. The similarities are traced as far into the past as possible.

Second is the ethnoarchaeology of general issues, not limited to addressing research questions concerning any particular locale or society. Instead of the direct historical approach, archaeologists rely here on the use of general analogy in order to understand the past better by studying the present.

The use of analogy involves the reasoning that unknown relationships can be inferred with some confidence when associated, known relationships are available. In other words, it is assumed that if certain phenomena are known to be similar in some ways, the chances are improved that they are similar in other ways. The more ways in which the phenomena are known to be alike, the more confidence one can have in the inferred likenesses.

All archaeological interpretations depend on the use of analogy to one degree or another. The inferred relationships most often are from prehistoric contexts, while the known relationships derive from historical or modern (that is, ethnographic) settings. Unfortunately, archaeologists are not always aware that they are depending on analogy, which can sometimes result in faulty or weak interpretations.

When using analogy, archaeologists must be careful to avoid certain common pitfalls that lead to poor reasoning. They can do this by explicitly and repeatedly asking themselves a series of questions. First, how closely related—geographically and environmentally—are the two situations being compared? Second, how close are they in time? Third, what is the degree of historical continuity between them? And fourth, how generally similar are the two represented sociocultural systems?

The closer the two situations are geographically—in particular, the more similar their environments—the greater the chance that useful analogies will be found. For example, an archaeologist interested in studying the rise of domestication in tropical forests would find it most useful to study, as an ethnographer, present-day horticulturalists. This archaeologist would not find very many useful analogies by studying Eskimo culture. Someone interested in adaptation to an Ice Age environment, however, would undoubtedly find the Eskimo an appropriate subject of investigation. This is precisely what Lewis Binford did in his attempts to grapple with Mousterian tool assemblages from western Europe (Chapter 12).

The closer the two situations are in time, the greater the chance that useful analogies will be found. Because of evolution, the passing of time implies changes in environment and culture, and it is likely that greater passages of time reflect greater amounts of change. Of course, both the environment and culture can change very slowly under certain conditions, but in all cases, the best analogies will hold for situations not extremely removed from each other, temporally speaking. When studying the distant past, ethnoarchaeologists must be very cautious. Indeed, an archaeologist interested in conditions existing more than 35,000 years ago might find it necessary to consider biological evolutionary differences as well.

Greater historical continuity between the ethnographic and archaeological settings will also lead to a more useful application of analogy. Whenever possible, one should use the most direct historical link to the past or the closest possible approximation to it. We do not mean that general analogy, or the ethnoarchaeology of general issues, lacks merit. Indeed, this type of ethnoarchaeology has strengths that the more specific form does not, including a greater power to generate testable hypotheses about past ways of life. Rather, one must simply choose an ethnographic setting as close as possible to the past situation of interest. Of course, one must also consider at the same time the degree of similarity between sociocultural systems, both present and past. In fact, this might be the most important consideration.

The more generally similar the present and past sociocultural systems, the more useful and numerous will be the analogies. If one is interested in gatherer-hunters of the past, one should study gatherer-hunters. If one is interested in the emergence of complex societies, one should study living, nonindustrial complex groups. Ideally, in this example, one should study people whose societies are currently becoming more complex or whose societies have become complex in the recent past.

With these cautions in mind, it is easy to see the difficulties inherent in studies attempting analogies between living nonhuman primates and living people (Chapter 6). We must be careful when making analogies between two human groups, especially when these groups are largely separated in space, time, and history. Imagine the conceptual problems that must be overcome when separate biological *species* are being compared.

A problem that all ethnoarchaeologists must face is that no pristine groups of people exist on the earth—there are no societies, following traditions of the past, that have not felt the significant impact of the modern, industrial world. Thus, we must all be cautious with our use of analogy when comparing living people to those who lived at a time when there truly was no contact with any highly complex sociocultural order. Many changes have occurred as a result of this contact, although they might not appear very obvious at first (Box 16–1).

If the four questions regarding environmental, temporal, historical, and sociocultural similarities are not addressed, and if the archaeologist does not employ as many recognizable relationships as possible to support the suggested analogies, then the result is commonly flawed interpretation. If, on the other hand, the archaeologist carefully considers the range of possible similarities while maintaining an appreciation for the proper use of analogy, the interpretation can still be flawed, but at least the chances of success are improved, and a greater degree of confidence can be assigned to the inferences that emerge.

One of the best-known examples of the proper use of analogy in archaeology is Lewis Binford's analysis of **smudge pits** in prehistoric settlements along the Mississippi River valley. The actual use of these pits was unclear when Binford studied them. The only thing that the archaeological record indicated with certainty was that wood and corncobs had been burned within them, creating a lot of smoke. Binford, however, scoured the ethnographic and historical literature of the area and noted the common practice of animal hide smoking over small holes within which a smokey fire had been set.

Binford made a number of important observations. First, the physical characteristics of the hide-smoking holes, as described in the literature, were similar to the characteristics seen in the archaeological record. Second, the area described in the literature he searched—the Mississippi River Valley—was the same as the area in which the "smudge pits" occurred. These were geographic and environmental similarities. Third, the ethnographic-historical accounts (dating from the mid-eighteenth century) were recorded only a few centuries after the first occurrence of smudge pits in prehistory—sometime after A.D. 1000. There was also a fair amount of historical continuity and general sociocultural similarity between the prehistoric and ethnographic-historical settings. Binford concluded that an analogy could be suggested with confidence.

Appreciating the use of analogy, however, he phrased his conclusion as a hypothesis needing testing by reference to other data. If indeed these smudge pits were used for hide smoking, he reasoned, then additional evidence for that activity should be in the archaeological record. The evi-

smudge pits

Small holes found at certain sites along the middle and lower Mississippi River Valley and dating to after about A.D. 1000; called smudge pits because wood and corncobs were burned within them, creating smoke.

Issues in Anthropology 16–1

The "Gentle Tasaday"

No pristine, simple societies are left on earth. All people, everywhere have felt to one significant degree or another the impact of the modern world's economic and social systems. This is the result of a process started some 400 years ago with European expansion and colonialism, and while tremendous cultural variability remains, *all* societies are significantly different from those once existing in the distant past.

The Tasaday of the Philippines have often been described as a "stone-age" people, apparently unaffected by and unaware of the outside, modern world. Indeed, they were not discovered by outsiders until 1971, when a Philippine official stumbled upon them in the Mindanao rain forest. What he found was a group of gatherer-hunters—really only gatherers, as the Tasaday did not hunt—who knew the use of only simple tools and who freely shared their food and friendship. Indeed, it appeared he had found a pristine group untainted by sociocultural complexity.

Several anthropological studies of the Tasaday were undertaken, *National Geographic* wrote of them and produced a television documentary about them, and professional and popular interest grew. Then, in 1986, the Swiss journalist Oswald Iten visited the Tasaday area and discovered that they were gone! Since then, anthropologists have fiercely debated whether or not the Tasaday were a hoax.

There is good evidence to suggest they were. First, the caves and surrounding areas where the Tasaday were found are clean. There are no refuse dumps, no archaeological record of their ever having been there. Clearly, if a group of people, even with primitive technology, lived in an area for any significant length of time, there would be archaeological evidence of their existence. The claim that the Tasaday were a remarkably clean people does not explain the absence of all material culture.

Second, there is general agreement that the wild food resources in the Mindanao region are too scant

---

dence to be sought was described in the ethnographic-historical literature and included the fact that smoking occurred during the spring and summer, not during peak hunting times. Thus, if these were truly hide-smoking pits, they should occur at spring and summer camps and not at hunting camps.

The importance of Binford's work is in the realization that analogies are hypotheses, requiring repeated testing before being accepted. We cannot, as scientists, rely on commonsense comparisons between the present and the past, as these are very often based on assumptions that do not withstand careful scrutiny.

ETHNOARCHAEOLOGY AND THE STUDY OF GATHERER-HUNTERS

Much recent and innovative ethnoarchaeology has been conducted among the world's few remaining gatherer-hunter societies. Richard A. Gould has done extensive research among the Aborigines of central and western Australia. John Yellen has studied the !Kung San of the Kalahari to support gatherer-hunters without hunting and without assistance from horticulturalists. How did the Tasaday adequately feed themselves if they truly had no contact with the outside world? No one seems to know.

Third, the stone tools apparently used by the Tasaday are poorly made and extremely crude, even by Paleolithic standards. Anthropologists who have examined the tools say they are like nothing in use anywhere else and would have been of little functional value. Anyone could have made them, even someone unskilled and inexperienced in stone tool manufacture.

Fourth, demographers suggest that the Tasaday could not have survived in isolation, given the small number of them (about twenty-five when first discovered). Yet, related groups of people have never been found. How did the Tasaday replenish themselves generation after generation?

Finally, many linguists claim the language spoken by the Tasaday was not distinct, as first thought. Apparently, it was a dialect of Manobo, a well-known language spoken by neighboring groups, easily understood by native Manobo speakers. Apparently, the Tasaday were not as isolated as many first believed, and their language, lacking Spanish-derived words and agricultural terms, might have been created in a conscious fashion to make it *appear* distinct.

If the Tasaday were a hoax (and the issue has *not* been conclusively resolved), the question of why it was done still remains. While we cannot address this question here, we can point out again the important observation that pristine groups are nonexistent—ethnoarchaeologists and others who depend on the use of analogy must be cautious.

References:

Marshall, Eliot. (1989). Anthropologists debate Tasaday hoax evidence. *Science* 246:1113–1114.

Desert in southern Africa. Lewis Binford, discussed elsewhere, has spent time with the Nunamiut Eskimo in northern Alaska. And John Fisher and Helen Strickland have recently investigated the Efe Pygmies of Zaire. These are examples of studying living societies to better interpret the archaeological record of past gatherer-hunter groups, and all of them have focused on the structure and dynamics of gatherer-hunter campsite formation, occupation, and abandonment. Site structure has been investigated with an eye toward understanding the behavioral patterns that created it. Site formation and abandonment have been studied in order to understand the processes that have created the archaeological record.

Gatherer-hunter camps have a number of common, physical components. There is a central, open area. There are fireplaces outside of huts, around which many of the camp activities occur. There are, in addition, the huts of the various households that comprise the band. The fireplaces and huts are often spatially associated and surround the open area. Farther out are trash piles and other, small activity areas. Finally, there is the camp perimeter or boundary (Figure 16–1).

Figure 16–1

Schematic diagram of a typical gatherer-hunter camp.

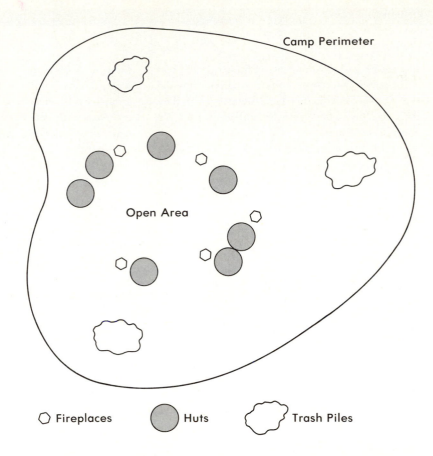

Camp Perimeter

Open Area

○ Fireplaces   ● Huts   ◯ Trash Piles

Despite these similarities, gatherer-hunter camps can differ in many significant ways. In a given environment and society, the size of the band and the length of time a camp is occupied will influence the number of huts present and the size and nature of trash piles. The relationship is not always straightfoward, however, and estimating measurements such as population size and density can be difficult. Gatherer-hunters often reoccupy old camps and reuse old huts. In addition, certain households occupy more than one hut during their stay at a single camp, while others do not. Hut membership also changes during the occupation of a camp. There is no clear formula relating number of huts to number of people in a band. And trash piles, while generally increasing in size as occupation time at a camp increases, can be spread out over a fairly large area and so are not easy to recognize archaeologically. In addition, although camps are generally kept clean, much of the trash produced just before a camp is abandoned is not redeposited in a trash pile.

The nature of the environment also affects the structure of gatherer-hunter camps. In tropical forests, such as the one occupied by the Efe

Pygmies of Zaire, camps are rather compact, and the camp perimeter is well defined. The jungle is difficult to clear and constantly encroaches on the living area. But in more arid regions, such as the Kalahari Desert of the !Kung San and especially the Australian outback of the Aborigines, camps can be very large and dispersed, with no obvious boundary, for there is little vegetation in the way. Complicating this picture further is the fact that social organization, interpersonal relationships, and simple personal preferences all affect internal camp layout.

The inescapable conclusion is that gatherer-hunter camps vary in many significant ways, for many reasons. Additionally, they do not last long in the archaeological record. Nomadic gatherer-hunters, quite logically, do not construct permanent structures or features. Ethnoarchaeology thus shows us that it is difficult to generalize about contemporary gatherer-hunter settings and that it is, therefore, a more formidable undertaking to arrive at confident statements regarding gatherer-hunter lifeways in the past.

HISTORICAL ARCHAEOLOGY AND EXPERIMENTAL ARCHAEOLOGY

Close ties exist among ethnoarchaeology, historical archaeology, and experimental archaeology. As defined in Chapter 15, historical archaeology is the archaeology of times and places for which we have useful documentary materials. *Experimental archaeology* is the present-day replication of past conditions (cultural and environmental) so that the circumstances leading to the formation of the archaeological record might be better understood.

The fundamental similarity among ethnoarchaeology, historical archaeology, and experimental archaeology is that all three are potential sources of analogies useful in interpreting the prehistoric past. In the case of ethnoarchaeology, the source is the ethnographic record. In the case of historical archaeology, the source is the documentary record, which contains much valuable information about behavior patterns and sociocultural conditions. Finally, in the case of experimental archaeology, the source is the outcome of the modern experiment, be it the manufacture of stone tools or the construction of traditional domestic structures.

François Bordes, the French Paleolithic archaeologist, was renowned for his skill at stone tool manufacture, a difficult (and sometimes dangerous) task to the beginner. So was Donald Crabtree, who took up stone tool making as a hobby while working as a mail carrier. He perfected various techniques over the subsequent several decades. Through the efforts of Bordes, Crabtree, and others, we now have learned more about stone tool making than we would have by only studying the artifacts (Figure 16–2).

Perhaps the most dramatic example of experimental archaeology is the *Overton Down* earthwork, in Wiltshire, England (Figure 16–3).

Overton Down is a large, artificial mound, shaped like a prism, several hundred feet long, 5 feet high, and 20 feet wide at its base. Running alongside it is an artificial ditch, 5 feet deep and 8 feet wide. This complex was constructed in 1960 by the British archaeologists P. A. Jewell and G. W. Dimbleby. Their goal was to record, at given time intervals, the effects of the environment on the form of the mound and ditch and on a sample of artifacts they had placed within the mound. By doing so, they hoped to distinguish environmental from cultural formation processes of the archaeological record (Chapter 10).

Within the first several years of experimentation, it was possible to observe certain changes to the mound, ditch, and artifacts. The height of the mound was slowly decreasing. Erosion was causing the ditch to fill up with dirt. Earthworms and moles were busy disturbing the locations of artifacts.

Jewell's and Dimbleby's original research design called for observations and some excavations at intervals of 2, 4, 8, 16, 32, 64, and 128

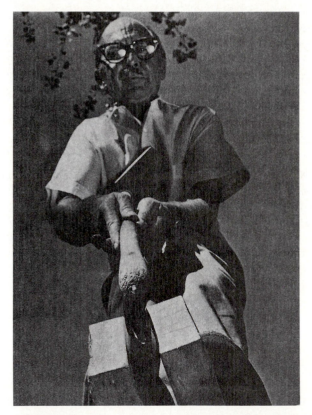

Figure 16-2

Don Crabtree using a "chest crutch" for extra force to produce long stone blades by pressure-flaking.

Figure 16-3
Overton Down in Wiltshire, England.

years, a very ambitious plan. If this study does continue well into the next century, we might learn a great deal about relatively long-term environmental impacts on archaeological sites.

Modern Material Culture Studies

Modern material culture studies consist of archaeological investigations of the present, conducted so that the present itself might be better understood. More than any other kind, this archaeology demonstrates the fact that the field of archaeology is not strictly the study of the past. The relationships between patterns of material culture and patterns of human behavior are interesting and significant in any temporal context, including that of today.

Archaeologists who study the present in order to better understand the present clearly appreciate that archaeology can contribute important anthropological knowledge. Sometimes, all archaeology appears limited in its ability to add to our understanding. Archaeologists are seen as studying material culture for the simple reason that nothing else is preserved, not because it is a valuable source of information. Modern

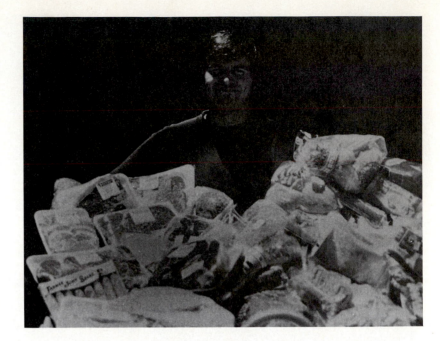

Figure 16-4

William L. Rathje surrounded by materials recovered by the Garbage Project, along with a Garbage Project data record.

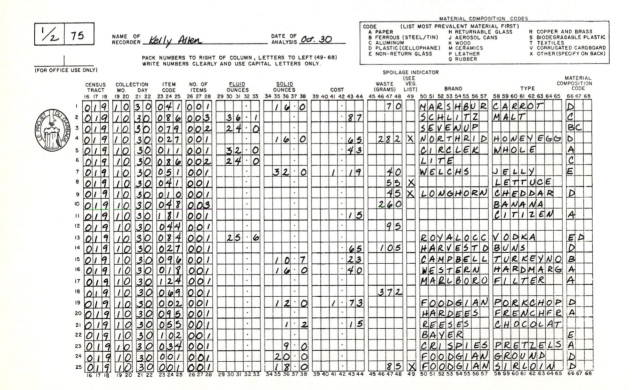

1/2	75

(FOR OFFICE USE ONLY)

NAME OF RECORDER *Kelly Allen*   DATE OF ANALYSIS *Oct. 30*

PACK NUMBERS TO RIGHT OF COLUMN, LETTERS TO LEFT (49-68)
WRITE NUMBERS CLEARLY AND USE CAPITAL LETTERS ONLY.

MATERIAL COMPOSITION CODES

CODE (LIST MOST PREVALENT MATERIAL FIRST)

A PAPER	H RETURNABLE GLASS
B FERROUS (STEEL/TIN)	J AEROSOL CANS
C ALUMINUM	K WOOD
D PLASTIC (CELLOPHANE)	M CERAMICS
E NON-RETURN GLASS	P LEATHER
	Q RUBBER
R COPPER AND BRASS	
S BIODEGRADABLE PLASTIC	
T TEXTILES	
V CORRUGATED CARDBOARD	
X OTHER (SPECIFY ON BACK)	

	CENSUS TRACT	COLL. MO	COLL. DAY	ITEM CODE	NO. OF ITEMS	FLUID OUNCES	SOLID OUNCES	COST	WASTE (GRAMS)	SPOILAGE IND.	BRAND	TYPE	MAT. COMP. CODE
1	019	10	30	041	001		16.0		70		MARSHBUR	CARROT	D
2	019	10	30	086	003	36.1		.87			SCHLITZ	MALT	C
3	019	10	30	079	002	24.0					SEVENUP		BC
4	019	10	30	027	001		16.0	.65	282	X	NORTHRID	HONEYEGG	DA
5	019	10	30	011	001	32.0		.43			CIRCLEK	WHOLE	AC
6	019	10	30	086	002	24.0					LITE		C
7	019	10	30	051	001		32.0	1.19	40		WELCHS	JELLY	E
8	019	10	30	041	001				55	X		LETTUCE	
9	019	10	30	010	001				45	X	LONGHORN	CHEDDAR	D
10	019	10	30	048	003				260			BANANA	
11	019	10	30	181	001			.15				CITIZEN	A
12	019	10	30	044	001				95				
13	019	10	30	084	001	25.6					ROYALOCC	VODKA	ED
14	019	10	30	027	001			.65	105		HARVESTD	BUNS	D
15	019	10	30	096	001		10.7	.23			CAMPBELL	TURKEYNO	B
16	019	10	30	018	001		16.0	.40			WESTERN	HARDMARGA	A
17	019	10	30	124	001						MARLBORO	FILTER	A
18	019	10	30	069	001				372				
19	019	10	30	002	001		12.0	1.73			FOODGIAN	PORKCHOP	D
20	019	10	30	095	001						HARDEES	FRENCHFR	A
21	019	10	30	055	001		1.2	.15			REESES	CHOCOLAT	
22	019	10	30	102	001						BAYER		E
23	019	10	30	034	001		9.0				CRISPIES	PRETZELS	A
24	019	10	30	001	001		20.0				FOODGIAN	GROUND	D
25	019	10	30	001	001		18.0		85	X	FOODGIAN	SIRLOIN	D

material culture studies are evidence that this is not so—studying material culture, even when other types of evidence are available, is still a useful undertaking.

Modern material culture studies are often referred to as "the archaeology of us." Most of these studies are conducted in Western industrial societies, and almost all the archaeologists involved are products of these societies. In contrast, most ethnoarchaeology is carried out in the nonindustrial world because of the need to find present-day groups of people who can provide the best analogies for those living in the past.

THE GARBAGE PROJECT

Examples of modern material culture studies include everything from the analysis of American ideology as reflected at museums to the study of the structure of urban supermarkets. At several universities, archaeology students are given the opportunity to conduct their own modern material culture studies, and more and more of this type of archaeology is being conducted all the time. Still, the most ambitious and best-known project of this kind is under the direction of William L. Rathje of the University of Arizona (we discussed some of Rathje's other work on the Maya in Chapter 14). Known as The Garbage Project (and sometimes "Le Projet du Garbage"), it has involved the systematic and detailed recording of trash coming directly from extant households and deposited in garbage cans (Figure 16–4—households are discussed in greater detail below). A number of sociocultural measures have been recorded as well by project personnel, including household members' attitudes and aspects of their social organization. This latter task has been accomplished through the use of questionnaires and interviews. The ultimate purpose of the project is to understand how attitudes and behaviors relate to patterns of material culture—patterns of refuse that can be observed in the modern archaeological record.

The Garbage Project started in 1973. The majority of investigations have taken place in Tucson, Arizona, although smaller projects have been conducted in cities such as Milwaukee, Wisconsin, and Sydney, Australia. Nearly 10,000 households have been studied. At the present time, Rathje and his colleagues have shifted their energies to excavating city refuse dumps in an attempt to grasp the problems of solid waste management.

Rathje's project and the others like it are serious archaeology. They are nothing like the various unethical (and many times illegal) searches that occur in the garbage of celebrities or suspected felons, by fans or feds. The Garbage Project has a number of built-in safeguards to ensure household anonymity. Individuals need not be identified, because the project is most interested in discovering patterns among groups of people. Thus, project personnel who collect the garbage off the curb never know what it contains, while those who sort the garbage never know precisely where it comes from.

THE GARBAGE PROJECT AND THE STUDY OF ALCOHOL CONSUMPTION

One study to emerge from Rathje's Garbage Project was a detailed investigation of how patterns of alcohol consumption relate to diverse sociocultural measures, including ethnic affiliation, socioeconomic status, and family structure. One goal of this study was to reach accurate measures of drinking behavior in modern, urban communities, such as Tucson, Arizona. An additional goal was to evaluate various solutions to the present-day problems of alcohol **abuse** constructively.

abuse

To use in a particular way or to a particular extent that injury or damage results.

The residents of 133 households were interviewed to obtain information regarding ethnic affiliation, income, wealth, occupation, amount of education, number and ages of children, and a host of other variables. In addition, refuse from these households' trash cans was collected, sorted, and measured for a period of at least five weeks. The type, brand, and size of all alcohol containers—for beer, wine, and spirits (hard liquor)—were routinely recorded.

As a first step in analysis, the amount of total alcohol intake suggested by household refuse was converted to rates of ethyl alcohol consumed. Much of the medical literature suggests that the incidence of **pathology** is highly correlated with the average intake of this drug, and so it was considered the best available measure of potential abuse. Beer is most often about 4.5 percent ethyl alcohol, while wine averages 12 percent. Hard liquors range from about 35 to more than 80 percent and average about 40 percent. Thus, by simply multiplying the suggested quantities of beer, wine, and hard liquor intake by 0.045, 0.12 and 0.4, respectively, combining these amounts for each household, and then dividing by five (for the number of weeks trash was collected), it was possible to arrive at an average per-week total ethyl alcohol consumption rate for each household.

pathology

Deviation from a normal or healthy state.

The range of drinking patterns found, irrespective of household sociology, was considerable. Some households had no evidence of alcohol consumption in their trash. Others exhibited more than 100 ounces of ethyl alcohol per week. A sample of households drank nothing but beer, others nothing but wine, and a larger sample drank a combination of beer, wine, and hard liquor. Clearly, the members of different households were drinking alcohol in different ways.

At this point in the study, however, it was necessary to consider whether anything might be distorting the data. Was it possible that the figures did not accurately reflect average or typical household alcohol consumption? Several possible distorting mechanisms could be envisioned. These included the varied number of people in households, the possible presence of seasonal drinking patterns, the occurrence of parties in households, the celebration of holidays in households, the possibility that trash was removed from households in alternative ways, and the possibility that alcohol containers (especially aluminum beer cans) were being recycled.

Fortunately, these and other potential distortions could be controlled for. The number of people in each household was known from questionnaires. Trash was collected at different times of the year, and no seasonal variation was apparent. Parties were recognized by the heavy consumption of a larger-than-average variety of alcohols and by the presence in trash of other party items such as chip wrappers and dip containers. Trash collected immediately following a number of holidays was evaluated so that holiday drinking patterns could be recognized. Alternative means of refuse disposal, such as trips to the municipal dump, were not considered to be significant distorting factors (although this conclusion remains uncertain). Finally, the possible recycling of aluminum beer cans was considered by comparing the number of cans with the amount of noncontainer evidence (cardboard cartons, plastic can holders, and so on) in the trash.

After performing these exercises, it was time to consider whether any of the available sociocultural measures correlated with rates of household ethyl alcohol consumption. Results were initially inconclusive. No individual measure correlated in a statistically significant sense with household consumption rates. Thus, no neighborhood or obvious group characteristic appeared to correspond with drinking behavior. Only after combining certain internal household measures—occupation type, age, and years of education of related household heads—were significant correlations observed. These three measures, combined, reflected the degree of *internal social heterogeneity* within households, the difference in social positions between the husband and the wife. Households in which husband and wife held similar social positions were scenes of very little or no drinking. Households in which the social positions of spouses were quite different all exhibited relatively heavy drinking behavior.

Individuals in households with great internal social heterogeneity might experience high degrees of stress because different social positions lead to different expectations and thus to conflicting views and opinions. Elevated alcohol consumption may be a response to stress. In contrast, heads of households with similar social positions might be under less stress and might demonstrate greater stability throughout their lives.

This suggested that rates of alcohol consumption, and thus the incidence of pathological drinking, were determined more by individual than social characteristics. This suggestion is supported by the majority of practitioners who treat problem drinking on a daily basis. Alcohol problems occur in all kinds of people. The most effective treatment plans consist of small group and one-on-one counseling. Educating the individual patient about the harm of excessive drinking, not trying to change the patient's social role, is most efficacious. In contrast, the various social responses to the use and abuse of alcohol, such as Prohibition, have met with failure.

While the results of this project support the clinical literature, they weaken the traditional views of most sociologists and anthropologists.

Archaeological data suggest that groups of people—ethnic, economic, and otherwise—do not consist of certain kinds of drinkers. The origin of drinking patterns and problems appears to be found neither in the nature of ethnic groups nor in economic conditions. Yet many social scientists have argued for years that economics, and particularly ethnicity, are powerful molders of drinking habits. Indeed, serious and legitimate research has given scientific support for such stereotypes as the drunken Irishman, and the Jew who, while drinking regularly, seldom drinks to excess. How can we reconcile these research conclusions with the results of the Garbage Project?

The answer seems to be found when we recognize the differences between expressed *attitudes* and actual *behaviors*. When people are asked how they feel about drinking alcohol—when is drinking appropriate, how much is too much, how should one act while drinking, and so on—very often, patterns of responses *do* correlate with ethnic identification and possibly with economic conditions as well. Thus, it is very possible that responses to the question "How much do you drink?" will be similarly patterned, but *not* because people are accurately reporting what they do. Consciously or unconsciously, people always distort their real behaviors for questionnaires because of the attitudes they hold.

Until the advent of modern material culture studies, investigators of alcohol consumption had available data from questionnaire and interview surveys, hospital records, police records, and other public sources. All of these data reported on the public display or revelation of alcohol use. All of them were thus reactive in nature, more clearly reflecting attitudes than actual behaviors. And those traditional sociological and anthropological views are based on a confusion between attitudes and acts.

THE GARBAGE PROJECT AND THE STUDY OF LANDFILLS

Rathje and his colleagues have recently expanded the Garbage Project to include the archaeological excavation of modern landfills. They have recovered materials from contemporary societies dating from several decades ago to the present and have thus made it necessary to address a definitional question—how long do material remains have to be in the archaeological record before they are no longer *modern* materials? Where is the temporal boundary between modern material culture studies and other archaeology? No one seems to know; at least, there is no widespread agreement.

More interesting are the results Rathje is obtaining regarding solid waste management in the modern, Western world. Many of us would agree that garbage presents a major problem. Much of it is toxic or otherwise dangerous, and the number of appropriate places to dispose of it are diminishing. Most critical, a lot of garbage does not decompose or revert to safe by-products very quickly. The amount of raw garbage is increasing at an alarming rate.

The nature of the problem, however, is not what many people would anticipate based on common experience. Archaeological excavations at **landfills** in Tucson, Phoenix, San Francisco, and Chicago show that the widely perceived major culprits of the garbage problem are not really responsible. Fast-food packaging makes up less than one-tenth of 1 percent of a landfill by weight. Disposable diapers, recently attacked by many as contributing substantially to landfill growth, actually comprise less than 1 percent. And all plastics, of all kinds, make up less than 5 percent.

The real culprit, according to Rathje's research, is paper. Somewhere between 40 and 50 percent of modern landfills consist of paper products (newspapers and telephone books, for example). Surprisingly, it is not degrading rapidly. In the late 1980s, Rathje unearthed newspapers from the early 1950s that are in good, readable condition. Ironically, this might be a blessing in disguise, for if the paper degraded rapidly, it would release tons of toxic paint and ink into the environment. Still, there is little question that a garbage problem, specifically the shrinking number of available landfills, has been caused primarily by the growing amount of paper waste that we discard.

What is the solution to this crisis? Many argue for increased recycling of paper products. Yet, as Rathje points out, the demand for recycleable materials is determined by the amount that can be used. The market at present appears flooded. If a significant number of additional people started recycling paper at once, the price for the raw material would plummet, threatening the entire recycling industry. What is needed along with any greater effort to recycle is the greater use of the product.

Thus, we face in landfills more of an economic problem than an ethical one—and the solution should, therefore, involve economic responses, quite independently of drives to educate or otherwise persuade people to be environmentally aware. Obviously, environmental concern is terribly important, but this problem and its solution are economic. This point is underscored by the observation that highly educated and concerned individuals do not recycle more than anyone else—in fact, the only reliable predictor of recycling effort is the amount of money people will receive for doing it.

Rathje not only makes these suggestions but also argues that the present garbage problem is not as bad as many would believe. Most estimates of pounds of garbage per person per day, which vary a great deal, are considered by Rathje to be exaggerations. In addition, he argues, per capita production of garbage is not rising but keeping steady. And we *are* managing our garbage in a much more efficient and aesthetic manner than we did 100 or 200 years ago. Residents of eighteenth or nineteenth century American cities would be astounded at the cleanliness of cities today, just as we would be revolted at the filth we would have found in urban centers of the past.

landfill

A low-lying area devoted to refuse disposal in which the waste is buried between layers of earth.

A Study of Infant Paraphernalia

A major *event* that occurs in many households is the arrival of a new baby. Then begins the *process* of rearing a child, which has a profound impact on household structure and function. What impact does the arrival of a baby have on household material culture?

This question initiated a student study of households and modern material culture at the University of Arizona. The goal was to see whether patterns of infant paraphernalia (all those things that come along with the baby) reflected sociocultural conditions such as household income, the ethnicity of household heads, the point along the developmental cycle of the household, and other variables.

A sample of thirty-four households that had recently witnessed the arrival of a baby were chosen. Household heads were interviewed for pertinent sociocultural information, and infant paraphernalia within each household was inventoried. A number of surprising observations were made.

Foremost, there was a clear impact on the households' material culture with the arrival of a baby. Literally *hundreds* of items entered the households, yet the nature of these materials did not correspond with sociocultural measures.

For instance, it was found that the quantity of infant paraphernalia was statistically the same in *all* households, even those of significantly different incomes. A household with an annual income of $58,000, for example, had the same amount of infant paraphernalia as a household with an income below $5,000!

In addition, the ethnic identity of household heads (in this study, either Euro-American or Hispanic) did not appear to influence the nature of infant paraphernalia, this in spite of the fact that

The Household

Many studies in ethnoarchaeology and modern material culture have focused on the household as both an analytical unit of study and a subject for investigation (Box 16–2). A *household* is defined as a group of people (household members) who eat and sleep together and conduct the work necessary to sustain the household through time. It is a social and economic unit of universal occurrence, common to all societies but differing from place to place in structure and composition. There is a very clear material element to households, that is, they can be recognized archaeologically. Furthermore, they have existed within human societies since well before the evolution of our species. Studying households cross-culturally from the perspectives of both ethnoarchaeology and modern material culture studies can thus contribute much information about how people have lived in the past, as well as about how they live today.

The evolutionary precursor to the household—often referred to as the home base—probably dates as far back as *Homo erectus*. Prehistoric sites hundreds of thousands of years old have afforded some compelling evidence that *Homo erectus* individuals were returning to a home base regularly and not wandering continuously across the landscape (Chapter

many of the parents wanted their children to grow up with their same identity. Material culture—infant paraphernalia—was apparently not playing an obvious role in patterns of enculturation.

All households acquired *most* of the infant paraphernalia from friends and relatives—about 80 percent as measured by number of items. This included large, expensive items, such as cribs and car seats. Likewise, all households gave away most outgrown infant paraphernalia to friends and relatives—again, about 80 percent. As many parents know, there is a vast underground economy in these goods, despite the best efforts of retail stores.

What are the ramifications of these results? It might be that patterns of infant paraphernalia are not sensitive indicators of sociocultural variability, at least those patterns that can be recorded through a simple inventory. It might be that income and ethnic differences do not appear in patterns of infant

paraphernalia until the baby is older—none was over two years of age. We do not know. A follow-up study, with a larger sample size, would have a good chance of either substantiating or refining the observations.

Still, it is intriguing to consider the possibility of infant paraphernalia having a uniform appearance in modern United States households, despite continuing sociocultural diversity. What might be the reasons for this uniform appearance?

References:

Rathje, William L. (1979). Modern material culture studies. In Schiffer, M.B. (Ed.), *Advances in archaeological method and theory, volume 2*, (pp. 1–37). New York: Academic Press.

Schlereth, Thomas J. (Ed.). (1982). *Material culture studies in America*. Nashville, TN: The American Association for State and Local History.

12). This type of behavior is in sharp contrast to what we find among the apes, who regularly build nests for sleeping but do not congregate at the same place at regular intervals (Chapter 6). The existence of the home base, or household, has probably had profound impacts on human cultural and psychological development through the ages.

What have ethnoarchaeologists and students of modern material culture learned about the various forms of households to be found around the world?

HOUSEHOLD TYPES

First, households come in a variety of forms. Most household members comprise a family, though even families differ in their composition. The most common type is the nuclear family, consisting of a parent or parents and economically dependent children. Another family type is the extended family, which contains additional relatives such as grandparents, aunts, and uncles.

Households can also consist of unrelated people or even a single person living alone. These are much more common in the modern world than in preindustrial societies. Finally, so-called special purpose households are made up of individuals who fill a shared social role, such as students or military personnel. Special-purpose households include dormitories, fraternity and sorority houses, barracks, and prisons.

Adding to the variety of household types is the fact that all households move through a *developmental cycle*. Initially, the household is established. Children are born. The children are reared until they can become economically independent and establish households of their own. Finally, the parent or parents find themselves alone in the household as it approaches its end. Not all households follow this cycle precisely, nor do any of them move from one stage to another after a set number of years. In addition, other household characteristics, such as the social and economic status of the household members, can change somewhat independently of these stages as the cycle progresses.

There are, in short, a large variety of household forms to be observed. Ethnoarchaeologists and students of modern material culture believe that each type has a recognizable assemblage of material culture associated with it and that unique patterns of material reflect the associated behaviors of household members. The material culture **correlates** of household types are complex and not yet fully understood, as subsequent discussions in this chapter illustrate. Still, there is little question that household form is reflected in the archaeological record.

HOUSEHOLD FUNCTIONS

All households serve a small number of similar functions. This is why the household, as a human phenomenon, is universal and why we can subsume so many apparently diverse forms under it.

The most common and important function of households is to have children and rear them properly. Of course, special-purpose households such as dorms and prisons do not serve this function, but they are in the minority. Most households, containing families, serve to extend the population into the next generation while (perhaps most importantly) training members of the next generation in proper behaviors and attitudes. This process, known as **enculturation**, assures that the culture will be perpetuated.

A second important function of households is to carry out certain economic activities necessary for the continuance of the society. These often include subsistence tasks and the manufacturing of basic tools and other commodities. While this function has lost importance in the industrial world, where other institutions such as corporations have taken over, it remains crucial among preindustrial people. Many ethnoarchaeologists have studied non-Western household production economy existing at the present time, and by so doing, better understand the nature of past economic systems. The household in all societies, however, is the most basic economic unit: It is the unit that eats the gathered or hunted food (or the grown and processed food) or that spends the paycheck.

The two functions of households discussed above are illustrated in

correlate

An associated occurrence, often a logical deduction.

enculturation

The incorporation of children into their society, learning proper behaviors and attitudes; different from acculturation, which is learning the behaviors of a different society, usually as an adult.

a series of related studies conducted by William A. Longacre of the University of Arizona. As discussed in Chapter 10, Longacre attempted to reconstruct aspects of prehistoric social organization by reference to the archaeological record. Specifically, he tried to establish the nature of residence and descent among inhabitants of the prehistoric Carter Ranch pueblo in eastern central Arizona by studying the distribution of ceramic designs in the ruin.

Longacre concluded that the prehistoric people were most likely matrilocal and possibly matrilineal. This conclusion was greatly dependent on the fact that living Hopi follow these organizational principles and on the observation that Hopi mothers teach daughters the art of pottery manufacture. But was this observation, in fact, true? Some anthropologists, including Michael Stanislawski, said no. Stanislawski claimed, in fact, that learning to make pottery is a complex undertaking among the Hopi, involving many individuals. The skills and knowledge do not necessarily pass directly from mother to daughter. Residence and descent rules may not be discernible in the distribution of pottery styles.

Longacre's work was criticized for other reasons as well, and he responded by conducting ethnoarchaeology among a group of people thought to be similar in significant ways to the prehistoric pueblo inhabitants. The Kalinga, living in northern Luzon in the Philippines, is one of only a handful of societies in which pottery is still produced at the household level. By studying the Kalinga as an ethnoarchaeologist, Longacre should learn a great deal about household production, structure, and the learning of ceramic traditions, and will be able to test hypotheses about the prehistoric Pueblo dwellers.

HOUSEHOLDS AND MATERIAL CULTURE

Households are associated with an array of material culture. Foremost is the dwelling, a recognizable area or (more commonly) structure within and around which most household activities take place. Dwellings vary in form depending on a number of factors, including the nature of available raw materials, social and technological characteristics of the society, social and economic status of household members, and stage within the developmental cycle. To appreciate the wide range of dwelling forms possible, consider the dwellings that you, your friends, and various relatives occupy. Most likely all are different and somewhat differently composed; yet all these reside in a single society, in a specific state of technological development.

Other dwellings from other parts of the world are at least as varied. Gatherer-hunters, such as the !Kung San of the Kalahari Desert, generally live in rather temporary structures because of their nomadic life-style (Figure 16–5). In contrast, the large extended families found among certain agriculturalists often live in sprawling, permanent compounds (Figure 16–6).

Households are also associated with a vast array of material objects

Figure 16-5

!Kung gatherer-hunter dwellings in Botswana.

Figure 16-6

Yoruba compounds in Africa.

that are concentrated within and around the dwelling itself. In a similar fashion, these artifacts and artifact patterns reflect the structure and form of the household—its social context, status, and developmental stage. Households in nonindustrial societies often contain the tools and results of independent household production (pottery-making tools such as paddles and scrapers, for example). Recently established households from all societies often have within them objects that symbolize their new emergence or that are necessary for their survival. Included might be wedding gifts and hand-me-downs (from other, older households). Households reaching a later stage, with older children, often contain the largest and most varied assemblage of material items to be found.

While the household may seem like something utterly mundane compared with the more glorified or idealized subjects of archaeology, they are of fundamental importance. Households are universal, sensitive indicators of the human condition. Again, we note that the household is a uniquely human institution, and thus, its investigation sheds light not only on who we are but also on how we differ from the other primates.

Our Lives Today

Both ethnoarchaeology and modern material culture studies are conducted in ongoing, living societies. Ethnoarchaeology is done in order to throw light on the past, while modern material culture studies are done in order to throw light on the present. Still, both increase our knowledge of human lives, today, in the modern Western world and in the rest of the world. Indeed, much of anthropology can be viewed as an attempt to understand and possibly improve the conditions of existence of *living* people. There are those who argue that without this goal, anthropology has little real value at all.

Summary

Archaeology *can* be the study of the past, but it is not *necessarily* the study of the past. Ethnoarchaeology and modern material culture studies both involve the investigation of patterns of behavior and patterns of material culture in contexts where both can be observed directly.

Ethnoarchaeology in particular is a source of analogies useful in interpreting the past. All archaeological interpretations depend on the use of analogy. Analogies should be thought of as hypotheses requiring testing, and commonsense comparisons of the present with the past should be avoided. Historical archaeology and experimental archaeology are additional sources of analogies.

The Garbage Project has been a long-term, ambitious investigation of modern material culture in several cities around the world. Garbage Project studies have focused on such issues as alcohol consumption and solid waste management, using the household as a unit of analysis. The household is a fundamental social and economic unit in human cultures.

Questions for Review

1. How might the use of analogy lead to circular reasoning when attempts are made to reconstruct past behavior? How could this be avoided? Can analogy be used when it is impossible to determine precisely how similar local histories, geographies, and environments were?

2. Studies of garbage have obvious utility for teaching us about things such as waste management and substance abuse. What makes modern material culture studies uniquely valuable as archaeology and as anthropology?

3. Why do archaeologists think that households in particular are so important to study? What might be some of the clearest indications of sociocultural complexity preserved in the household record of, for example, the Roman Empire, fifteenth-century Mesoamerica, or 1920s America?

For Further Reading

Binford, L. R. (1978). *Nunamiut ethnoarchaeology*. New York: Academic Press.

Gould, R. A. (Ed.). (1978). *Explorations in ethnoarchaeology*. Albuquerque: University of New Mexico Press.

Gould, R. A., & Schiffer, M. B. (Eds.). (1981). *Modern material culture: The archaeology of us*. New York: Academic Press.

Rathje, W. L. (1984). The garbage decade. *American Behavioral Scientist*, 28:9–29.

Rathje, W. L., & Schiffer, M. B. (1982). *Archaeology*. New York: Harcourt Brace Jovanovich.

Sorting Out Biology and Culture

Sorting Out Biology and Culture

The biological and cultural evolution of humans can be traced from their earliest primate ancestors to the present. What impact do biology and culture have on *Homo sapiens sapiens*? In other words, how do biology and culture affect our lives? Is it possible to separate the two? Which has the greater influence? Knowledge of whether and how biology or culture determine a given human condition can help shape opinions and policies.

The Naturalistic Fallacy

While human behavior is obviously different from nonhuman primate behavior, there are also clear similarities. Facial expressions of fear and happiness, for example, are remarkably easy to recognize across species (Figure 17–1). Why? Because of the common makeup of our facial musculature and nervous systems. The behavioral repertoires of ape babies and human babies are similar for the same reason.

But what about the behaviors of ape and human adults? Or adult societies? Here the comparisons are more difficult. After the acquisition of linguistic capabilities, the behavior of a human child becomes very different from the behavior of a young ape. The human begins to understand and react to sounds, words, and combinations of words—all symbols—in ways that the ape does not. This broad mental capability is at the root of the behavioral differences between humans and other primates, and language is so pervasive in structuring our behavior that it often obscures any similarities we might see between our own behavior and that of other primates.

There are, of course, many specific things that primates do and humans also do. One common misconception is that the behavior of nonhuman primates defines what is "natural" for humans, and therefore what is proper. This is incorrect, however, for two reasons. First, what other primates do is not necessarily natural for humans. Humans have autapomorphies, or uniquely derived characteristics, as all species do. Thus, a *difference* may simply be an evolutionary change, and therefore, natural. All our closest relatives are quadrupedal when on the ground, for example. Is it, therefore, natural for us to be quadrupedal as well? The answer is clearly no. Our bodies bear the evolutionary vestiges of ancestors who were quadrupedal, but the natural gait for us is bipedal—an autapomorphy of humans among living primates.

The second reason involves the equation of "natural" with "proper," a false equation that the eighteenth century philosopher David Hume called "the *naturalistic fallacy*." The problem is that what is proper is defined *culturally*, varying from place to place and time to time. What is

Figure 17-1

Harpo Marx and a cebus monkey demonstrate that facial expressions can be very similar across primate species.

proper for a member of one society is not necessarily proper for a member of another society—much less for a member of another species.

The existence of a behavior among nonhuman primates is not a justification for its existence among humans, where proper behavior—**morality**—has been constructed historically. Neither, however, is it a justification for condemning the behavior. Nonhuman primate behavior is simply irrelevant to the goodness or badness of human behavior. The failure to appreciate this is the naturalistic fallacy.

As an example, consider **homosexuality**, a controversial phenomenon in our society. It has long been known that homosexual behavior occurs among many nonhuman primates, but this knowledge is used in different ways by advocates of different moral stands. By those who are reluctant to tolerate it, homosexuality in primates can appear as part of the beastly nature in humans, which it is our duty to transcend. To those who wish it to be more widely accepted, homosexuality in primates can appear as part of the normal repertoire of primate behavior and, therefore, natural in humans. Both of these positions are unjustified, for what the birds and bees or the nonhuman primates do is irrelevant to what is considered acceptable behavior by the members of a human society. By the naturalistic fallacy, it is natural to be naked and sleep in trees, but no members of human societies do it.

The Nuclear Family: A Natural Unit?

A pervasive view in our society is that the nuclear family, as an economic and residential unit, is natural. Deviations from it are, therefore, considered undesirable. Yet the nuclear family (the "Leave It to Beaver"

morality

A set of principles determining behavior and thought deemed to be proper.

homosexuality

Sexual behavior directed toward a member of one's own sex; heterosexuality is directed toward a member of the opposite sex.

Figure 17-2

A "Leave It to Beaver" nuclear family.

family, consisting of father, mother, and dependent children—Figure 17–2) is not the only type found among humans. In many societies, family members reside with either the father's or mother's family of origin (respectively called patrilocal and matrilocal residence) and do not move away to their own private home at the time of marriage (anthropologists call this neolocal residence). Indeed, grandparents, cousins, uncles, aunts, and other relatives are important family members in nearly all but industrial societies. As we saw in the previous chapter, the household has many forms.

The nuclear family actually causes many modern social problems that most social systems are spared. For example, the elderly, who in many societies live with the family and help raise the children, are often very isolated and lonely in our society. Children, who in many societies are supervised by elder siblings and grandparents, now go to largely impersonal schools or daycare centers, are often supervised by peers, and generally do not participate in the economic activities of the household. Neither do women in this rosy view of the "natural" nuclear family, although in most societies, their economic contributions are critical. And in this nuclear family, it is the mother who rears the children almost singlehandedly, as the father is out earning a living—in many societies, rearing children is everyone's job.

Of course, this is not to say that any social system is better than any other, that the nuclear family is "bad"—we must retain our relativistic perspective. Still, it is important to emphasize that the social system of 1950s middle-class America was no more natural than any other (nor was it as widespread as many believe). To maintain that it was *more* natural is wrong, and to maintain that we must, therefore, revert to it is the naturalistic fallacy. It was the product of unique social and economic conditions, including postwar prosperity and American economic dominance. As always, culture has evolved since the 1950s, and we as humans living today must do the most natural thing for us—adjust our behavior to accommodate new social, political, and economic environments.

Nuclear families among nonhuman primates, of course, are very rare, as most primates do not even know who their fathers are.

The Problem of Homology across Species

If we try to extrapolate an understanding of human behavior from that of a nonhuman primate, it is essential that the behavior in question be homologous across taxa. "Aggression" among ants and "rape" among ducks, for example, do not mean the same thing in those species as they do in our culture—they are simply labels for the behavior given to them by ethologists.

One good example of a nonhomologous behavior is **infanticide**. In langur monkeys (colobines), and subsequently in other primate species, it was found that adults sometimes kill young. In humans, adults sometimes kill young—about 10 percent of human societies allow some form of infanticide. Are we seeing manifestations of the same phenomenon in these various species? Are the behaviors homologous? It turns out that in langurs, the infanticide is always committed by a new male invading a group. In humans, however, it is invariably the mother who kills the offspring, and the pattern of infanticide is based on social and (especially) economic criteria. Is infanticide the same thing in the two species? Probably not, although the same word is used to describe both phenomena. One should, therefore, be circumspect in reasoning from one to the other.

Often, however, it is not so easy to tell whether behaviors are homologous. Among chimpanzees, as noted in Chapter 6, females usually move out of the group into which they are born. Thus, the adults in a group are generally *related males* and *unrelated females* (since they came in from other groups). Among humans, similarly, it is more often the wife who leaves her family and moves in with her husband's family (*patrilocal residence*). Thus, the adult social group again consists of related males and unrelated females.

Is this similarity between chimpanzee society and human society significant? It is difficult to say. As noted, residence patterns in industrialized societies tend to be neolocal rather than patrilocal. And there are societies that practice matrilocal and other residence rules. Clearly, humans have considerable flexibility in this regard. In addition, the transfer of human females often involves strong reciprocal obligations between groups that do not seem to exist among chimpanzees. And finally, it appears that this behavioral trait is absent among other closely related species, such as gorillas. Perhaps this similarity between humans and chimps, then, is simply a coincidence. Unfortunately, there is no way to tell.

infanticide
Purposeful killing of an infant; among humans, it usually results from benign neglect and not from overt violence.

Learning and Instinct

We often form dichotomies between things that are learned and things that are instinctive, probably as a result of the biological controversies of the late nineteenth century (Chapter 3). Biologist August Weismann differentiated between the germ line and the soma—those cells that form the reproductive organs, and those cells that form the rest of the body. There is no transfer of information between them, which makes Lamarckian inheritance impossible. That is, things that occur to the soma cannot be transferred to the reproductive organs and passed on to offspring.

Behavior, on the other hand, has traditionally been more difficult to treat than Weismann's conceptual divorce between inherited characters and acquired characters would imply. Behaviors tend to be the products of genetic endowment and upbringing, which interact in complex ways to yield the adult behavioral repertoire. It is, consequently, highly misleading to ask whether a specific behavior is part of the genetic endowment *or* part of the acquired upbringing. A useful metaphor is to the art of M. C. Escher—one can often see two different things but finds it impossible to say where one begins and the other ends (Figure 17–3).

Consider as a more concrete example our quintessential biological adaptation, walking. As discussed in Chapter 11, there are numerous structural modifications within our bodies—of our toes, feet, knees, hips, pelvis, spine, and skull—that attest to our being biologically programmed to walk bipedally. Our bodies have been molded by millions of years of evolution not only to enable us to walk, but to *force* us to walk—as discussed in Chapter 6, humans have fewer locomotory options than other primates.

Figure 17-3

M. C. Escher's *Encounter,* in which the two figures blend with and emerge from each other.

And yet, we must *learn* to walk. We are not born doing it. A colt or baby gazelle can locomote in its fashion almost from birth. In contrast, we do not begin to walk until about a year after birth, and a human infant must observe and be actively taught to walk. Walking is *not a passive acquisition*. There are no modern experimental data, for obvious reasons, but reports of **feral** children (abandoned at birth and later found isolated from all human contact) indicate that they did not habitually walk—rather, they habitually moved on all fours. These unfortunates (such as Kamala, the Wolf-Child, found in India in the 1920s) are rare but instructive. They had not, apparently, learned the bipedal gait they were genetically programmed for. Later, after interacting with other humans, they adopted bipedalism.

Learned Behaviors in Primates

A reliance on learning characterizes the behavior of mammals in relation to other vertebrates and characterizes primates in relation to other mammals. Humans, of course, learn virtually all the things that enable them to survive—how to obtain and prepare food, how to skin an animal, how to build a fire, and so on. This is not to say there are no instinctive behaviors in humans. Such automatic behaviors might be present, but they are not significant parts of the adaptive complex by which humans survive.

Yet, while we can say with some degree of confidence that an isolated human being would have little chance for survival, we must say the same thing for an isolated chimpanzee or other primate. Learning is part of our primate biology—what is unique to humans is the symbolic and cumulative way in which we do it.

THE ROLE OF LEARNING IN NONHUMAN PRIMATES

Surprisingly little is known of the role of learning in other primate species. Some of the most interesting data have been collected by Japanese anthropologists studying the macaques of Koshima Island in Japan. These monkeys were being provisioned with sweet potatoes by humans, and in September 1953, a young female named Imo took her sweet potato and dipped it in a nearby brook before eating it. She apparently liked the result and continued to do it. Within a month, another young member of Imo's group began to do it as well. By January 1954, another young male and Imo's mother had followed suit. In the next two years, three more of Imo's relatives and four youngsters from other lineages were washing their sweet potatoes.

By 1958, few of the adults, but most of the monkeys under the age of seven were doing it. By 1960, however, the macaques of Imo's age were now having babies and teaching them the behavior as part of their ordinary feeding repertoire. Thus, in the 1960s, the new behavior became part of the normal existence of this macaque group (Figure 17–4).

feral

Once domesticated, but now wild; among humans, the term is used to describe children brought up without human social contact.

Figure 17-4

Japanese macaques washing sweet potatoes, a learned behavior.

Imo was not finished yet, though. In addition to sweet potatoes, the macaques were being provisioned with wheat. The monkeys, however, upon taking handfuls of wheat from the ground, found it difficult to separate the kernels from grains of sand. Imo, then four years old (1956), took her handful to the brook and dropped it on the water. As with the method of flotation in archaeology, the sand sank, the wheat floated, and Imo had a pure handful of wheat. This behavior spread more slowly (probably because the monkeys must release the food and then retrieve it, whereas in sweet potato washing, they can hold on to it) but also became widespread in the group.

The spread of the new behaviors was patterned. Juveniles and female relatives learned the behavior first. Adult males, apparently set in their ways, were most resistant to trying the innovation. It is also possible that the spread of the novelty was assisted by Imo's membership in a high-ranking lineage.

FOOD PREFERENCE AND ACQUISITION

Chimpanzees in different areas are known to have different social traditions. At Gombe and at Mahale, both in Tanzania, chimpanzee populations have different dietary preferences. For example, of three ant genera available (*Dorylus*, *Crematogaster*, and *Camponotus*), chimps at Gombe eat the first, infrequently eat the second, and reject the third. Chimps at Mahale reject the first and eat the second and third.

In addition to preferences, differences exist in acquisition strategies as well. Gombe chimps bang nuts against trees or rocks to open the shell and eat the fruit. At Mahale, they bite them open. Chimpanzees in West Africa use two stones ("hammer" and "anvil") to open palm nuts, but this has not been observed among Tanzanian chimps. Local variations also exist in termiting and in a similar behavior called "dipping for ants."

VARIATIONS IN SOCIAL SIGNALS

Most interesting, however, is the variation that exists in social signals. Chimpanzees studied at Mahale and Kibale (in Uganda) have a similar, stereotyped grooming behavior, which involves holding the hand of your partner upright and grooming the underarm with your free hand. The chimps of Gombe, however, do not clasp hands when they groom. This variation appears to be no more than a difference in social custom, or tradition—there is no other reason for it to exist. Clearly, nonhuman primates are not simply automata, working out hard-wired genetic instructions in their daily lives. They instead possess a complex array of learned behaviors whose spread and adoption are virtually unknown to us but which may serve to emphasize the complexity of their behavior.

Instinctive Behavior in Humans

The philosopher John Locke believed that the human mind at birth was a *tabula rasa*—a blank slate upon which experience alone inscribes (Chapter 3). When the field of psychology became an experimental science in the early part of this century, its practitioners adopted a position similar to the one Locke had two centuries earlier. To these **behaviorists**, human behavior consisted fundamentally of responses to diverse stimuli. Since, in this view, it is the environmental stimulus that determines how an individual will behave, these psychologists arrived at a view of human behavior that focused exclusively on the environment, the source of the stimuli, as the determinant of human behavior.

This view, however, is now widely appreciated as an exaggeration. Humans, as mammals and primates, have a number of instinctive behaviors not learned and not requiring stimulation. For example, human infants grasp instinctively. Primate infants must cling to their mother's fur in order not to be left behind (Figure 17–5), while human infants are carried. The latter nevertheless retain the instinctive grasping reflex of their primate heritage.

Humans also express fear and happiness in very stereotyped, and probably instinctive, ways. There are, however, very few known human instincts that can be divorced from the learning that is so much a feature of human behavior. Indeed, most of human behavior appears to involve the instinct to learn something—a language, for example—while the specific form that is learned—French, Kikuyu, or Hebrew—is a function of the cultural environment. That is, whatever language is being spoken around the developing child is the one acquired through its instinct to learn language.

Similarly, humans appear to be instinctively social, like most primates—but the specific social forms that a human adopts are those into which it is raised.

behaviorism

School of thought in psychology claiming that the consciousness or mind cannot be defined or studied; only observable and measurable behaviors can be.

Figure 17–5

An infant clinging to its mother's fur.

The Incest Taboo in Apes and Humans

A strong argument for the existence of a biologically based reduction in sexual affinity for a member of one's nuclear family comes from the study of nonhuman primates. The most intensive and long-term studies of cercopithecines have shown that matings between relatives who remain together as adults are rare.

Among the most closely studied chimpanzees of Gombe, neither Figan nor Faben ever tried to copulate with their mother, Flo, although they were present during her five estrus periods. Similarly, Evered never showed sexual interest in his mother, Olly. Yet, sometimes, a chimp male does try to copulate with his mother; and she invariably resists. Brother-sister matings are relatively rare and often actively discouraged by the sister.

Among humans, when incest occurs in the nuclear family, it is most often between father and daughter. Among chimpanzees, however, it is impossible for a daughter (or a researcher) to know who the father is, since females mate with several males during their estrus. Nevertheless, since females generally transfer out of their natal group, it seems that the opportunities for father-daughter sexual activity would be relatively diminished. Jane Goodall notes that older males tend to be less interested sexually in the younger females within their own community. Further, when a male and estrus female occasionally left together as a consort pair, in only 18 percent of the cases was the male even old enough to have been the female's father.

Similarly, the sparser data on gorillas suggests that a female transfers in preference to mating with a long-term silverback male (presumably her father).

Do these observations and inferences have relevance to our understanding of incest in humans? Obviously, it is difficult to say. It must, however, be pointed out that the incest taboo in human societies covers more people than simply the nuclear family. Perhaps these represent cultural extensions, to different groups of people, of a biologically based drive to engage in sexual activity preferentially outside the nuclear family.

Sigmund Freud had an explanation for the incest taboo that took into account some of the emotional conflicts a human must face when growing up. In particular, Freud was interested in the conflicts faced by small boys, who loved their mothers, wanted their mothers' total attention and devotion, and yet did not enjoy the same access to their mothers as did their fathers. And their fathers were powerful, frightening authorities, who could not be contested without great danger. How was a small child expected to cope with this situation, which Freud named the *Oedipus complex*? By virtue of the incest taboo, which made it improper for the boy to desire his mother in the same ways as his father did.

Does Freud's explanation have cross-cultural applicability? Can it explain all cases of the culturally universal incest taboo? Apparently not. Bronislaw Malinowski and other anthropologists have shown that there are certain situations in which the Oedipus complex is not significant. In cases of matrilineal descent, for instance, the male

How Can We Tell Whether a Behavior Is Instinctive?

cross-cultural universal

A human trait that occurs in similar form in all societies.

Usually the only signature of an instinctive trait in humans is its presence across cultures. If a behavior is present in all societies, then it is likely to be instinctive to the species. However, extremely few behaviors are **cross-cultural universals**. To establish that something is a cross-cultural universal requires extensive and reliable fieldwork in many, if not all, cultures of the world—in the words of Hamlet, "a consummation

adult having authority over a child is usually that child's mother's brother, or what we would call an "uncle"—he is the closest adult member born within the group. The child's father, in contrast, is considered a person with whom the child can joke and relax. But this is the person sleeping with the child's mother.

Indeed, the Oedipus complex seems to emerge only in those societies in which the two roles of male authority and mother's sexual partner can be found in the same individual. In matrilineal societies, where this does not occur, young boys need not face the conflict recognized by Freud. Still, incest taboos in one form or another are found in all societies.

There is a better explanation, and it is found by considering both prohibited and preferred marriage partners. In many societies in which the descent group has sociocultural importance, incest rules prohibit marriage with a *parallel cousin*—a person of your generation related to you through two same-sex siblings of the previous generation. Thus, your parallel cousins would be the children of your father's brother or your mother's sister. In contrast, a *preferred* marriage is with a *cross cousin*—a person of your generation related to you through two opposite-sex siblings of the previous generation. Your father's sister's children and your mother's brother's children are cross cousins. What is an explanation for these rules?

Parallel cousins might well be members of your descent group. But cross cousins are generally members of different groups, since in most societies, one spouse, usually the wife, joins the husband's group. This would put a brother and sister in different groups as adults. Their children, therefore, would be in different kin groups—in spite of being fairly close genetic relatives. Indeed, the closeness of the relation often makes them preferred as marriage partners—one's parents and other relatives have had opportunities to learn what they are like. Still, the most significant point is that a cross-cousin marriage would create a significant link between two groups—parallel-cousin marriage would not necessarily accomplish that. Incest taboos exist, it seems, to require groups of related people to form links, or alliances, with other groups through the institution of marriage.

As the anthropologist Edward Tylor said many years ago, groups of people face the choice between "marrying-out" or being "killed out." Alliances are critical for human group survival, and the complementary cultural universals of marriage and incest taboos help assure their survival.

Cross-cousin marriage is widespread, even found in historical western Europe. For example, Charles Darwin followed custom in marrying his cross-cousin, Emma Wedgwood. From a genetic standpoint, a rare recessive allele (good or bad) has a greater probability of becoming homozygous in the offspring of a cross-cousin marriage than in the offspring of the marriage of nonrelatives.

Reference:

Goodall, Jane. (1986). *The chimpanzees of Gombe*. Cambridge, MA: Harvard University Press.

devoutly to be wished." All ethnographic studies are not, obviously, equally reliable. Some universals have turned out to be artifacts of bad ethnography. For example, it was once believed that "belief in God" was universal and instinctive. Sometimes, however, a behavior that is alleged to be a cross-cultural universal turns out to be simply an artifact of terminology. Not only do all cultures not have an apparent "belief in God," but for those that can reasonably be considered to have it, it takes on

incest

Marriage or mating with someone who is defined as a relative, therefore taboo.

such a wide range of meanings that it cannot reasonably be considered a single phenomenon.

The **incest** taboo is often described as a cross-cultural universal and as an instinctive behavior in humans (Box 17–1). All cultures prohibit sexual relations with close relatives. This reflects, so one argument runs, an ingrained aversion to mating with those with whom we are kin. The aversion, again the argument runs, evolved in the human species as an adaptation to avoid inbreeding.

But, critics ask, if there is a natural aversion, then why do cultures bother to prohibit it? No one establishes rules to prohibit things that people do not want to do anyway. For example, humans are strongly programmed biologically not to walk on all fours. Yet no culture has rules against it. Why? Because it would be a meaningless rule. No one wants to do it, so what is the sense in banning it? Cultures do have rules, however, prohibiting murder. Why? Because people sometimes *want* to commit murder, and the rule is there to stop them. Presumably, therefore, the incest rule is there to prevent people from committing incest *because they might want to*—not because they have a biological predisposition *not* to want to.

The specifics of incest rules also vary from culture to culture and are exceedingly complex. In some societies, the incest taboo covers a ban on sexual relations with in-laws, even though they are not blood relatives. In some societies, one is encouraged to marry one type of cousin, while another type of cousin is prohibited. The existence of this pattern is particularly revealing when it comes to the inbreeding argument. Both types of cousins are equally distant genetically, yet one is covered by the incest taboo and the other is a preferred spouse. Instinct does not appear to play a large role here.

Furthermore, incest does occur. Statistics are hard to come by, but sexual abuse in the family is unfortunately more common than we care to admit. Usually, it involves father/daughter relationships as opposed to mother/son or brother/sister. Thus, whatever ingrained repulsion one may have to mating with close relatives must be rather weak if it can be so often suppressed.

On the other hand, some evidence exists suggesting that growing up with someone tends to reduce sexual desire toward that person. If true, this would be evidence for an aversion against *sibling* sexuality, primarily. Yet throughout history, some cultures have actually mandated brother-sister marriages, notably among the ancient Egyptian royalty. Thus, again, even such a narrowly-defined aversion would appear to be suppressible. But even if an ingrained aversion did exist, it would not be the same thing as the incest taboo. The incest taboo is a custom or law which culturally prohibits sexual activity with several different specifically defined relatives, some of whom may have grown up together, some of whom may not even be genetically close relatives or not even genetic relatives at all. Thus, as an explanation for the universality of taboos on incest, one that says merely that it is an inborn adaptation to reduce inbreeding is at best inadequate and incomplete. It is a reification—giving various things the same name and then arguing that they are the same phenomenon.

An adequate explanation of the incest taboo requires accounting for the variation that exists among the many forms it takes. The explanation of human variation, after all, is the primary concern of anthropology—variation in behavior, variation in biology, variation in modes of thought.

Language Universals and Variation

In the incredible diversity of the languages spoken over the face of the earth, very few regularities have been discovered. The sound production capabilities of human vocal tracts are apparently identical, yet each language uses certain sounds in its repertoire and not others. French, for example, uses nasal vowels, unlike English, but coincidentally like Hindi. Differences also exist at the level of grammar. In some languages, such as English, a normal declarative sentence has an order of words that goes subject-verb-object: John hit the ball. In others, such as Persian and Japanese, the proper order is subject-object-verb. In many Polynesian languages and some native American languages, the proper order is verb-subject-object. Some languages in South America have the object first. Are there patterns we can discern in the variety of human languages that might tell us something about the biology underlying it?

A very few striking regularities have been noted. These, however, may tell us something about the way the human mind translates mental processes into linguistic structures. One such regularity involves basic color terms. People in all cultures see the same colors, but often they differ according to which colors get specific names and which are considered to be simply shades of another color. English, for example, has eleven basic color terms: white, black, red, green, blue, yellow, brown, purple, pink, orange, and gray. Other colors, such as turquoise, magenta, peacock blue, or burnt sienna, are considered to be shades of the color terms already given.

There is, however, no logical or biological reason why there should be eleven basic color terms in a language and not twelve, thirteen, or any other number. In fact, most languages have a different number of basic color terms. But the variation is not random, for there are certain distinctions that all groups make and regularities that govern the others.

Among the Dugum Dani of New Guinea, there are only two basic color terms—one for all bright colors, and one for all dull colors. In essence, all other colors are considered to be shades of black and white. All known languages make this distinction. Some languages have three color terms, however, and the third basic color term always corresponds to red—never to blue, yellow, or another color. Languages with four basic color terms always distinguish terminologically among white, black, red, and either green, blue, or yellow. With five color terms, the colors white, black, red, yellow, and blue/green are named. A sixth color term in a language distinguishes blues from greens, and a seventh distinguishes brown. Languages that have more than seven basic color terms name any choice of purple, pink, orange, or gray.

There are thus many cultures, all of which give names to certain colors but not to others. There may be a weak relationship between technology and number of color terms—the cultures having the fewest color terms are among the technologically simplest. However, many technologically simple cultures have many color terms. Still, the pattern of *which* basic color terms are present in a society, given *how many* they have, is strong. No culture has three color terms for naming white, yellow, and green, for example; if it has three color terms they invariably are naming white, black, and red.

How do we explain the pattern? Physiologically, humans see brightness (light/dark) and hue (red/green and blue/yellow). Brightness is the most significant visual cue that is noted by humans, followed by the red/green hue. The variation in color terminology among human societies is, therefore, built on this fundamental physiological fact common to all people.

Linguists have noted other broad generalizations and universals among the languages spoken by the members of societies—fundamental aspects of sound and syntax. These appear to reflect basic ways in which the human mind imposes structure upon the information it needs to communicate. These are, however, regularities of human biology based on broad *similarities* of cultures that are otherwise very diverse. It is likely that they are effects of similarity in the general biology of the cognitive and linguistic faculties of humans. What about the *differences* among cultures? Can these be related to differences in their biology as well?

Nature and Nurture

Why does the behavior of one human differ from that of another? This is probably the central problem in the social sciences and, consequently, in anthropology.

Various schools of thought have arisen through the decades in support of the proposition that variation in human behavior is a result of (1) hereditary endowment or (2) circumstances of birth and development. In the early twentieth century, eugenicists tended to favor the former, behaviorists the latter. This tended to be framed in terms of a battle between extreme positions—those who favored "nature" and those who favored "nurture" as the cause of differences in behavior.

As we shall see, the question, as posed, is a false one, because it merges two very different things under a common name—yet another

Figure 17-6

(a) Monozygous twins share the same genotype and appear identical. (b) Dizygous twins do not share the same genotype, and while they may appear similar, this is not due to any special genetic affinity beyond ordinary siblings, and need not be the case.

reification. The question is, "Why do any two humans differ in their behavior from each other?" To answer it, we have to appreciate that two humans may come from the same society or from different societies. The reasons that two humans in the *same* society behave differently are not the same as the reasons that two humans from *different* societies behave differently.

Given the complex interaction between genotype and environment, resulting in a phenotype, it is difficult to imagine how one might be able to study the genetic or nongenetic basis for specific kinds of behaviors in the human species. After all, every human being has both a unique genetic endowment and a unique set of external circumstances.

THE CASE OF IDENTICAL TWINS

The exception to this generalization, of course, is the case of identical twins. About 4 births in 1,000 result in two children who are clones of each other. These are monozygous, or identical, twins—same sex, same genotype. About twice as frequent are *dizygous*, or fraternal, twins, who are no more similar than any other pair of siblings except that they happen to have been born at the same time (Figure 17–6).

Given that monozygous twins are genetically identical, could we simply tabulate their behavioral and mental similarities and infer that these similarities are because of their common heredity? Good science is never that easy. In fact, identical twins not only have the same genetic endowment but also share much of the same environment and upbringing. Often, their similarity is reinforced more strongly by parents dressing them and treating them alike. How, then, can we sort out genetic from environmental similarities, even in identical twins?

Figure 17-7

Identical twins in "psychic contact."

Adoption Studies   The answer seems to lie in adoption studies, where identical twins, separated at or near birth, are reared separately. Even here, though, most separated pairs of twins are reared by family members in the same socioeconomic class. However, a large enough sample of identical twins reared apart might suggest patterns in their behavior, patterns of behavioral concordance due to their common hereditary endowment and discordance due to their separate upbringing.

The largest sample of these identical twins raised apart was published by Cyril Burt and was discovered in the 1970s to have been falsified (Chapter 9). Such studies have consequently returned to the drawing board. Currently, while some data have been collected, it is not at all clear what the results show about the inheritance of intelligence or about behavior in general. Often, identical twins recorded as being reared apart turn out to have been reared by different members of the same family and, therefore, in quite similar environments.

Reliability of Information   One of the more fundamental problems involves the unreliability of anecdotal information. While the purpose of studying identical twins is to examine the effect of environmental variation on a common genetic background, this is sometimes confused in the popular literature with supposed psychic powers of identical twins. For example, *Newsweek* reported in 1987 on a pair of identical twins separated at birth and reunited after thirty-eight years. Both, according to this story, were named Jim, had married and divorced women named

Linda, married second wives named Betty, drove the same model of blue Chevrolet, had dogs named Toy, and had named their first sons James Al(l)an. Nobody thinks there are genes that lead people to women with certain names or determine the kind of car one drives, so the implication of this story is not about the scientific analysis of the heredity of behavior but about "psychic contact" between the two (Figure 17–7).

Greater light on these kinds of stories can be shed by a story that appeared at about the same time in *U.S. News and World Report*. Separated at birth, the identical twins shown in Figure 17–8 were reported to be 6'6" tall, 250-plus pounds, volunteer firemen, nonreligious Jews, Budweiser drinkers, and bachelors attracted to tall, slender, long-haired women. While none of these things is terribly extraordinary in and of itself, taken together they suggest incredible similarities. But look closely at the two men pictured. Though both were said to be 250-plus pounds, one has a much thicker neck and arms than the other—he is obviously 250 pounds plus a whole lot more! Although their body builds are different (and we know there is a strong hereditary component to body build), the information we were given led us to believe they were physically identical. So how trustworthy can we consider the rest of the anecdotal information to be?

The problem is that the media often confuse the issue of the genetic contribution to human behavior by presenting apparently extraordinary coincidences that cannot be attributable to genetics and implicitly inviting their readers to explain the apparent coincidence by reference to psychic forces. But these subjects are not being tested for psychic powers at all—they are being tested for concordance in behavior and personality traits, given the natural experiment of having identical genotypes and different upbringings. After all, if these twins are indeed communicating telepathically, then all the psychological tests they have been given are useless because they could be communicating the answers to each other! (No one has ever found psychic powers between monozygotic twins—such reports are probably contrived.)

It seems clear that there are some elements of personality and intelligence testing that are more concordant in identical twins than in fraternal twins. It is also clear, however, that there are many ways in which identical twins can be surprisingly different, such as in body build or handedness. The "natural experiment" has not been carefully enough controlled to say much more at present.

Figure 17–8

While described as physically identical twins, it is clear that these identical twins have some significant differences in body build.

COMPARISON OF ADOPTIVE CHILDREN WITH ADOPTIVE AND BIOLOGICAL PARENTS

Another way of studying the contribution of heredity to mental processes involves comparing adopted children with their biological parents and their adoptive parents. If, given a large sample of adoptees, the children are generally more similar to their biological parents than they are to their adoptive parents, then presumably, inheritance is playing a significant role in determining the children's' traits. This approach requires more sophisticated statistical analysis. Yet, as the analysis becomes more sophisticated, additional problems are detected.

For example, most studies find a higher correlation between the IQs of adopted children and their biological parents than between the IQs of adopted children and their adoptive parents. That is, the IQs of adopted children tend to track the IQs of their biological parents more closely than those of their adoptive parents. Yet a statistical problem underlies this conclusion. Adoptive parents tend to be carefully screened and tend to be similar to *each other*—economically, socially, demographically, and educationally. Biological parents are not screened for anything and tend to vary much more than adoptive parents. It is more difficult for a variable set of measurements (IQs of adopted children) to track a homogeneous set of measurements (IQs of adoptive parents) than to track another variable set of measurements (IQs of biological parents). Therefore, there is a built-in statistical bias—biological parents are "chosen" at random, but adoptive parents are not.

In spite of these analytical difficulties, the question of biological and environmental influences on IQs remains. A recent study from France indicates that adoptees into households of high socioeconomic status had significantly higher IQs than those adopted into households of low socioeconomic status. There is inferentially a strong nurture effect. But also, the biological offspring of high socioeconomic-status parents have higher IQ scores than the offspring of low socioeconomic-status parents, regardless of the *adoptive* environment. Does this reflect a genetic contribution to IQ or different circumstances of prenatal environment, such as nutrition, physical stress, and health care?

Variation within and among Groups

Studying the origin of variation—why two things are different from each other—is obviously a tricky undertaking. One important complicating factor emerges when the subjects of study are hierarchically organized. For example, a society is composed of humans, and a human is composed of cells. Humans in a society differ from one another, and cells in a human differ from one another. However, the explanation for why *cells* differ from one another is different from the explanation for why *humans* differ from one another. Specifically, even though humans are groups of genetically identical cells, one cell differs from another because it has different genes operating at different times. And one human differs from another because it possesses a different set of genes and has developed in a different environment.

Let us extend this hierarchy further. We have established that the explanation for cell diversity within a human is different from the explanation for human diversity within a society—even though each society is only a group of humans, and each human is only a group of cells. What about the explanation for the diversity of societies within the human species?

If we know that variation among humans in a single society is caused by a combination of genes and environments, do we now know the cause of variation among societies in the human species? Clearly not. The problem we have posed involves a different level in the hierarchy, and the components whose variation we are trying to explain are different. Cells compose humans, but humans have properties that cells lack. Similarly, humans compose societies, but societies have properties that individual humans lack. Indeed, the explanation for why one society is different from another is different than the explanation for why one human is different from another, which in turn is different from the explanation for why one cell is different from another.

The lesson here is a fundamental one in genetics. The cause of variation *among* groups is not the same as the cause of variation *within* a group. We have just seen that the cause of variation among humans (i.e., groups of cells) is different from the variation among cells within a single human. If we inquire, therefore, about the causes of differences in behavior, we must appreciate that an explanation for variation in behavior among humans is not an explanation for variation in behavior among *groups* of humans.

While humans behave differently from one another on account of their genetic compositions and circumstances, societies appear to differ from other societies by virtue of their surroundings and evolutionary histories, and not because of any differences that may exist among their gene pools. That is, even though a Frenchman and a Sherpa from Nepal differ from each other genetically (since they are different humans), the differences in the behavior of the French and the Sherpas—differences between the two societies—are attributable solely to their different histories and to the different circumstances to which the two societies have adapted.

We draw this conclusion principally from studies of assimilation and **acculturation**, the adoption of new lifeways by individuals of different societies. It appears that anybody from any culture can adopt the lifeways of another culture. How complete the adoption will be depends entirely upon how thoroughly the person is immersed in the new culture. Thus, the classroom in which you are studying anthropology is most likely filled with people whose recent ancestors spoke different languages, lived under different economic and political systems, and perceived the world and reacted to it in fundamentally different ways from you.

Regardless of the diversity in cultural ancestry, modern Korean-Americans, African-Americans, Italian-Americans, and others are all capable of functioning equally efficiently in this society, which is different from that of their ancestors. Although social prejudices may retard upward social mobility and ethnic traditions are often retained and reinforced at home, descendants of members of these various cultures have

acculturation
The process of adopting the behaviors and material culture of another society, usually as an adult; one aspect of assimilation.

all shown themselves capable of participating fully in American culture (Figure 17–9).

Consequently, there appears to be no evidence that differences in the gene pools of different populations have a significant impact on the lifeways the individuals adopt or the facility with which those people can adopt any particular lifeway. Different cultures represent differences among societies and are nonbiological in their origins. On the other hand, differences among individuals in the *same* society may sometimes have a significant genetic basis.

This conclusion is harmonious as well with a conclusion about genetic variation discussed in Chapter 9—in the human species, the great majority of genetic diversity exists within groups, and relatively little genetic variation is between groups. In addition, we can add that of the between-group genetic variation, little or none of it causes differences in behaviors among groups.

The Effect of Biological Differences on Cultural Patterns

Many schools of thought have proposed a biological basis for differences in behavior among cultures. However, there is little or no evidence to suggest that biological differences among groups play a significant role in explaining the differences in their behaviors. If anything, it appears that the opposite is true. Behavioral differences, as we shall see, tend to play a much greater role in making cultures biologically different.

One interesting speculation, however, was put forth by anthropologist Alice Brues in the 1950s. One of the adaptive microevolutionary features of populations is body build. One tends to find stocky people in

Figure 17-9

These students, while having different cultural backgrounds, share the ability to function efficiently in American society.

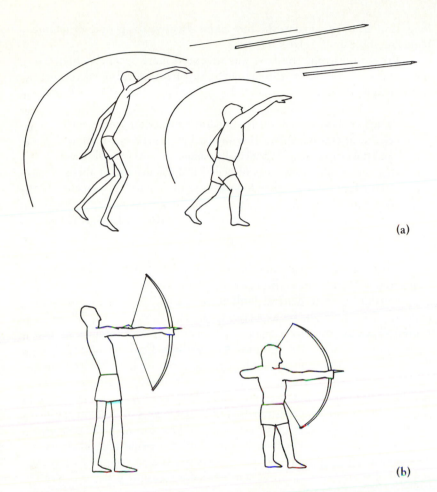

(a)

(b)

Figure 17-10.

Use of the spear versus use of the bow—the effect of body build. (a) Spear throwing is much more effective if you have a long, thin arm because the hand moves faster through a larger arc. (b) The bowstring can be drawn back farther by a person with a short, stout arm because of greater strength.

cold climates, presumably because stockiness enables greater retention of heat, and linear people in hot climates, because a lean body build permits greater dissipation of heat. Given this biological baseline, reasoned Brues, might the acceptance or rejection of a new technology be influenced by how efficient the technology was, given the body composition of the people that were deciding whether to adopt it?

In particular, she focused on two technologies, spears and bows, and the areas in which they were and were not adopted. The principles of physics dictate that the efficient use of a spear depends on how fast the hand is moving when it is released. This, in turn, depends on the length of the arm hurling it, all other things being equal. Thus, a person with a long, thin arm should be able to throw a spear with greater force than a person of the same body weight and a short, stout arm (Figure 17–10a).

On the other hand, the strength of a muscle is determined by its cross-sectional area, and therefore, the person with the short, stout arm can draw a bowstring back with greater strength than the person with the long, thin arm. This makes the bow more effective for people of lateral build and short limbs (Figure 17–10b).

Brues notes that the bow was invented more recently than the spear and yet was known throughout most of the world until recently supplanted by the gun. But in sub-Saharan Africa,

> **though the bow was known as a children's toy, or for special purposes such as fishing, these [long-limbed] people still clung to the hand-thrown spear as a principal weapon. . . . Apparently the efficiency of different types of body build for the use of these essential cultural artifacts has affected the choice of weapon when both were known.**
>
> **(Brues, 1977:171)**

Unfortunately, no attempt has been made to follow up this suggestion and see whether or not Brues's explanation is valid.

Certainly, more general biological factors, such as the stress of endemic disease, might be expected to affect cultural forms. The relationship between the environment and specific cultural forms is studied by cultural ecology (see Chapter 4). William Durham of Stanford University has argued, for example, that an interesting regularity joined many of the cultures of west Africa, who celebrate the beginning of the harvest of their main dietary staple, yams. The dry season, for harvesting, starts earlier as one proceeds north. The date of the yam festival initiating the yam harvest is set each year, after deliberation with the gods and ancestors, and one cannot harvest yam until the ritual festival is over. The rituals thus begin later as one proceeds south, in conjunction with the end of the rainy season and start of the dry season. What is the reason for prohibiting the harvesting of yams even though they may be ripe? Durham argues that this is a cultural response to the endemic stress of malaria—it prevents people from going out into the fields when the mosquitoes are thickest.

Cultural Analogs to Biological Strategies

Another way in which cultural and biological differences may relate to each other is also based upon the recognition that culture is an adaptive mechanism for human societies. Natural selection has adapted other species to their surroundings in such a way that the species exploit the environment in the most efficient manner possible. Human cultural behavior is directed toward exploiting the environment as well, and if there is a most efficient way, then perhaps cultures have independently hit on it—and perhaps we can generate hypotheses about human decision-making strategies for subsistence from the ways in which other animals exploit their resources.

This is the utility of *optimal foraging theory*, which seeks to predict the foraging behavior of animals from the quality, abundance, and distribution of the resources they exploit. In a situation where different strategies for behavior would produce different outcomes, we may be able to study adaptive behaviors favored by natural selection as biological adaptations in other species, to predict the most adaptive decisions the members of a society could make under similar circumstances. Presumably, people exploiting the same resources or in an analogous situation might choose to exploit them in a similar fashion.

To date, there has been little application of this approach in anthropology (most have been in archaeology) because it is highly theoretical and requires the quantification of a large number of variables. In principle, however, it could generate a series of hypotheses against which to test the actual behavior of human groups.

Another kind of modeling involves strategies of reproduction. For example, Trivers and Willard showed in 1972 that there are specific circumstances under which it would be most adaptive for a parent to favor male or female offspring. In particular, they showed that if females tend to reproduce more predictably than males (that is, males either reproduce very much or hardly at all, while females are all about equally prolific), then a parent in "good condition" should invest more heavily in male offspring, and a parent in "poor condition" should invest more heavily in female offspring (Figure 17–11). In essence, this is about genetic gambling—if you have a lot of capital ("good condition"), you can take risks with it (that is, invest your genes in male offspring in the hopes of hitting a longshot), but if you do not have a lot of capital, you have to play it safe with your genes and invest in daughters.

Given:

(1) Greater variation in male fitness (health, or status, or wealth, etc.) than in female fitness, and
(2) Variation in parental fitness

Then:

(1) A parent in *good* condition (healthy, or high-ranking, or wealthy, etc.) should tend to favor male offspring
(2) A parent in *poor* condition (sick, or low-ranking, or destitute, etc.) should tend to favor female offspring

---

Figure 17-11

A model of reproductive strategies introduced by Trivers and Willard.

Figure 17-12

The demographic transition of industrialization.
Stage 1: Both the Crude Birth Rate (CBR) and Crude Death Rate (CDR) are relatively high. Stage 2: The CDR drops, while the CBR stays about the same, leading to rapid population growth. Stage 3: The CBR starts to drop as well, though population continues to grow rapidly. Stage 4: Both the CBR and CDR are relatively low (after Light and Keller, 1975).

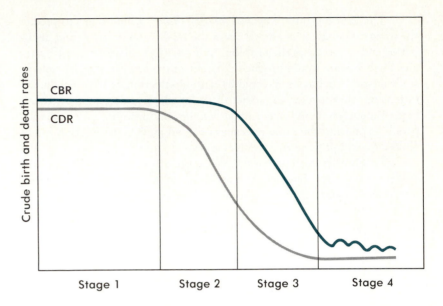

This represents a strategy that under the conditions specified would be favored by natural selection in a species. What about analogs in human societies? Have cultures hit on this strategy, where the investment capital is not genetic but economic? Indeed, in a detailed study of the demographic, economic, and social history of sixteenth century Portugal, James L. Boone has shown that (1) the requisite difference in male-female reproduction did exist and that (2) the highest economic strata of society tended to pass their wealth on through sons, while lower strata tended to invest in their daughters, who inherited from their parents in the form of dowries.

Perhaps this helps to explain the common social practice of *hypergamy*, or "marrying up"—having your daughter marry someone of higher status. It may simply be the optimal cultural solution to a problem faced by all organisms, that of how to invest time, energy, and resources most efficiently in the next generation, under a certain set of circumstances.

The Effect of Cultural Differences on Biological Patterns

In general, the effects of culture on biology are much more apparent than those of biology on culture. These effects fall into two broad categories: 1) the effects of cultural change on reproduction and survival and 2) the effects of cultural practices and attitudes on the spread of disease.

DEMOGRAPHIC PATTERNS AND CULTURAL CHANGE

Cultural change, especially technological change, can have profound effects on the demographic patterns in populations. The classic examples of this are the rise of domestication, complexity, and industrial society that occurred at various times and places (Chapters 13, 14, and 15). The first of these enabled more people to be fed from a given area of land, leading to increased population densities. These, in turn, led to a different pattern of diseases—epidemics of contagious diseases, which were not possible under conditions of low population density, now become a major stress.

Classically, the demography of gatherer-hunters involves a balance between fertility and mortality (that is, births and deaths) that was disrupted by the evolution of domestication. Economically, agriculture places a premium on the number of people—the amount of labor—available to exploit the land, and children are no exception. Where among gatherer-hunters a large number of children become an economic handicap if anything, among agrarian societies having many children is a major economic advantage. The result, of course, is that people decide to have more children when they start practicing domestication, and a population explosion ensues. This **demographic transition** is characteristic of the cultural change from gathering-hunting to agriculture. Another, more famous demographic transition is characteristic of the cultural change from agriculture to industrialism, as happened in Europe and the United States in the eighteenth and nineteenth centuries, and continues in other nations as they industrialize (Figure 17–12). Here, children eventually become economic liabilities again. Thus, people start having fewer of them. It appears that a major predictor of family size in most parts of the industrialized world today is educational level—meaning that the least educated have the most children, while many women in the middle and upper classes (the most educated) have careers or other interests that preclude having many children.

Thus, while we regard demographic variables, such as birth and death rates, as biological in nature, they change dramatically in response to cultural stimuli. Similarly, health, also biological in nature, is highly responsive to cultural variations.

demographic transition

Profound changes in population life-history measures, such as rates of fertility and mortality; apparently a response to cultural changes such as domestication and industrialism.

THE ROLE OF CULTURE IN THE SPREAD OF DISEASE

Epidemiology, the study of diseases in human populations, has shown that culture is a powerful determinant of the course a disease may take. One famous example involves a disease known as *Kuru*, which killed more than 400 people in 1957 and 1958. Interestingly, all of them were in a small group of villages in New Guinea. The disease, discovered by epidemiologist D. Carleton Gajdusek, was caused by a virus that takes decades to act after infecting its victim. The virus spread to new victims at funerals, where mourners would pass around (and possibly eat) the brains of the deceased. (The brain is where the virus is most prolific.) The eradication of Kuru involved the suppression of these funeral rites.

The relation of disease and culture is not limited to remote people and regions. The deadly bubonic plague, which swept across Europe in the fourteenth century (Figure 17–13), killing an estimated 20 million

Figure 17-13

The spread of the Black Death across Europe in the fourteenth century.

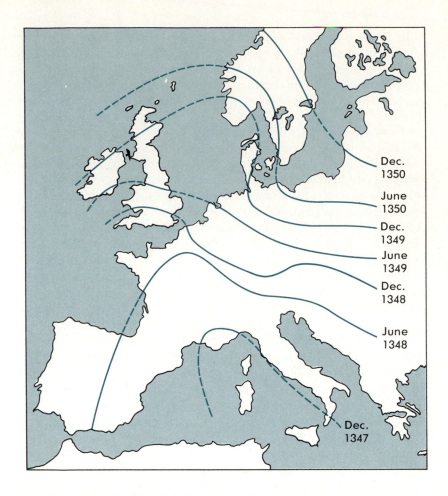

Dec. 1350

June 1350

Dec. 1349

June 1349

Dec. 1348

June 1348

Dec. 1347

people between 1349 and 1352, was in large measure culturally rooted. The disease is caused by a microorganism inside a flea, whose preferred host is a rat, but which will jump on and bite a human if it has a good opportunity. The disease gets its name from the related large boils, or buboes, and severe hemorrhaging causing black splotches—hence, the "Black Death."

Medically, the disease is caused by a bacterium, *Yersinia pestis*. But the epidemic was caused as much by social as biological factors. The Black Death entered Europe through commerce from Asia and spread by several means. First, urbanism and poor sanitary conditions gave the opportunity for extensive coexistence between rats and humans on a large scale. Second, the extensive shipping industry in the Mediterranean spread the disease to new urban centers. And third, official measures for dealing with outbreaks often centered on restricted quarantines and general fleeing. This ensured minimal treatment for patients and a very low recovery rate. Because the rats were unaffected by the quarantines, the disease was largely unchecked and continued to spread, and virtually all people in the quarantine area were condemned to contract it. Further, the two-week incubation period meant that those fleeing could often bring the disease to a new population of fleas, rats, and people.

Thus, the bubonic plague epidemic, while caused in one sense by biology, was caused in another sense by sociocultural factors—hygiene, ships, urbanism, and lack of a germ theory of disease for treatment. The result was an epidemic, a health problem of staggering proportions.

Other diseases also have close cultural ties. Tuberculosis, for example, is a disease virtually exclusive to urban areas, again medically caused by a bacterial agent but spread by the close proximity of people to one another. Polio is even more culturally bound, as it is a disease of *good* sanitation. Where sanitation is poor, children apparently develop immunities to many diseases (among them polio) by long-term exposure to excrement. Improved sanitary conditions led to a higher standard of general health but also removed the opportunity for immunization, which in turn led to polio's rise to dubious eminence as a major crippling disease. It has now been dealt with, also by cultural means—vaccination programs.

Human Rhythms

Humans live with rhythms, both biological and cultural. For example, the human brain keeps a daily rhythm, apparently involved in the consolidation of sleep into a long, regular period. Without alternating environmental cues of light and darkness, it keeps a twenty-five-hour rhythm; with such cues, it resets an hour each day. Thus, subjects kept in a windowless room with no time cues lose a day after three weeks.

BIOLOGICAL CYCLES

The pineal gland secretes a hormone called *melatonin* primarily at night, which appears to sensitize the brain for the induction of sleep. Melatonin appears to increase drowsiness, slow reaction time, and decrease alertness. The length of dark period appears to affect the secretion of melatonin such that when the days are short and dim (such as in northern winters), more melatonin is secreted. In some people, a heightened sensitivity to the daily photoperiod can result in depression, a *Seasonal Affective Disorder*, or SAD, which can be treated by exposure to bright light.

CULTURAL CYCLES

At the opposite end of the spectrum is a purely cultural rhythm, the week. The clustering of cycles of the earth's rotation (days) into groups of seven is simply a holdover from Babylonian, and later Hebrew, astrology. Ancient Italy used an eight-day week, and various peoples in ancient Mesoamerica used thirteen-day or twenty-day weeks. Yet this purely arbitrary cultural rhythm is so pervasive and ingrained in our religious and economic systems that it is almost impossible to disrupt.

Two major attempts to form a "scientific" society (paradoxically, "scientific" here meant to ignore the role of culture in human behavior) followed the French and Russian Revolutions. The French attempted to install a ten-day week, the Soviets a five-day week; both failed miserably. They should have taken a cue from Pope Gregory XIII, who reformed the calendar in 1582 by removing ten days. The change necessitated altering the monthly period, but Gregory was wise enough not to try and change the people's weekly period. Thus, he ruled that Thursday, October 4, should be followed by October 15—but that would not be a Monday (as the calendar indicated), but a Friday, as people expected to follow a Thursday.

Other rhythms are more biological (the environmental changes associated with the year) or a combination of biological and cultural (the month, whose length is close to the lunar cycle). The generalization appears to be that whatever the origin of the cycle, humans are reluctant to change it. The fact that a cycle is biological in origin does not at all mean that it is stronger than a nonbiological one; indeed, the common change of time zones and day length (spring forward, fall back for Daylight Savings) suggest that these may be more malleable than the cultural routines that structure our behavior.

Birth

Humans even have unique biological and cultural overlays to something as fundamentally ancient as birth (Figure 17–14), as anthropologist Wenda Trevathan has shown. One interesting biological change in humans has been the reorientation of the fetal position at birth, such that a human baby ordinarily rotates to face away from its mother while emerging. In other primates the newborn usually faces the mother. This is probably attributable to a difference in the human pelvic inlet, which was

Figure 17-14

Human birth

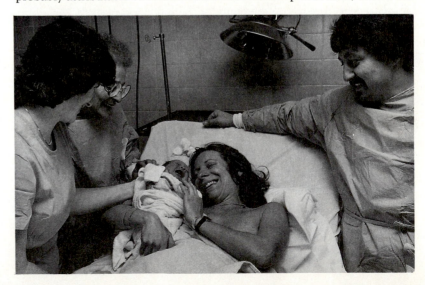

a byproduct of the assumption of an upright bipedal posture and might have encouraged hominid mothers to enlist the help of other group members during birth. For similar reasons, human labor and delivery are often long and painful experiences; they are relatively easy among the apes. Further, humans do not lick their newborns as other species do.

Humans are the only primates that do not consume the placenta after giving birth and the only primates in which giving birth is usually a social activity (with doctors, nurses, family, or midwives in attendance), not a solitary one. Humans are also unique among their catarrhine relatives in the extent to which a special bond exists between the child and its father.

The ultimate result of all these unique aspects of human birth is that there is an immediate bond created between the baby and the social group, not simply the mother. Having a baby is a significant moment for families and clans, not only for individuals.

Thus, understanding the ancestral biological characteristics of the human species is important, but one cannot understand the human condition without coming to grips with the unique biological or cultural aspects of humans.

Sexual Behavior

Because of its unique cultural overlay, sexual behavior in humans is among the most misunderstood behaviors in the species. Sexual behavior in nonhumans is almost exclusively biological, directed toward reproduction. Some non-reproductive sexual behavior is known, such as "g–g rubbing" in pygmy chimpanzees, genital contact between two females.

Sexual behavior in humans is more often directed at nonreproduction and, thus, is in apparent opposition to primate biology. Singles activities, birth control, homosexual behavior, postmenopausal sexuality, and sex during pregnancy are all sexual behaviors in which reproduction is either not desired or is impossible. Yet the situations listed represent the vast majority of sexual activity in our culture and in most of the world. Therefore, in humans, sexual activity is not principally directed at reproduction, as it is in other primates.

Why, then, do humans have sex if not for reproduction? One of the major biological uniquenesses in humans is the capacity in both sexes for intensely pleasurable and emotional *orgasm* as a result of sexual activity. This seems to serve a strong social and emotional function: to form or reinforce strong affective (sometimes even irrational) ties to another person—in other words, for pair bonding. That is, humans have bio-culturally divorced sexual activity from its primary role in reproduction and made it instead a pleasurable and emotional experience whose function is now principally to form bonds with another member of the species. Marriage is a cross-cultural universal whose function is to make sexual activity and reproduction legitimate. Thus, sex within the boundaries of marriage is strongly encouraged culturally.

Humans, in rending sexual activity from reproduction, have created a new set of possible goals toward which they can strive. A nonhuman can have no goal other than *parenthood*—and of course, that is not a conscious goal, but a drive that has evolved by natural selection. In human society, however, humans can seek *emotional intimacy or pair bonding* without reproduction; this can potentially be with a member of the opposite or the same sex. Rather than reproduce their genes, humans can instead strive to *promote ideas*. In the history of our culture, the Catholic clergy and many ascetics in other religions are examples of people who promote ideas rather than genes. Or, humans can strive for *economic goals*, with which reproduction might conflict. In our society, this is widespread among "yuppies," a married subset of whom are known to economists as "DINKs"—double income, no kids.

Thus, culture gives humans not only far more behavioral options than other animals, but new goals as well—intellectual, emotional, and economic—in addition to the reproductive goals we share with other species. Sometimes these goals conflict, and this contributes to giving the behavior of specific humans its unpredictable quality.

Biology and Culture: Sorting Them Out

There is no sorting of biological from cultural factors in human behavior because, as we have seen, culture is part of our biology. Humans are complex bio-cultural animals, and their behaviors as individuals and as members of groups are rooted in their evolutionary synapomorphies, autapomorphies, and the structure that culture has given to human lives. The differences in behaviors of humans within a single group is attributable to their different biologies (polymorphism), their different upbringings, and the decisions they are forced to make in the face of conflicting goals and opportunities to meet them. The differences in behaviors of *groups* of humans is due virtually entirely to their different histories and circumstances.

Summary

Humans are the products of both biological and cultural evolution, which operate by different mechanisms and can be compared only analogously. It is difficult to separate or sort out the different impacts of biology and culture—they are thoroughly intertwined.

It is important to avoid the naturalistic fallacy, which states that nonhuman (mostly nonhuman primate) animal behavior is more natural and thus proper or improper, depending on your view, for humans. We must also avoid using similar though nonhomologous behaviors across species as evidence for the presence or absence of natural behaviors.

Humans are neither totally biological nor totally cultural; neither are any individual human traits, and the question of whether it is either nature or nurture is invalid. Indeed, the question is invalid also when considering the other higher primates, who depend on both biology and learning to adapt.

When studying the role of biology, emphasis is given to cultural universals, traits that appear in all societies despite vast differences in other areas of life. When studying the role of culture, emphasis is given to the cultural diversity itself.

Biology does have an impact on culture, although culture has a greater impact on biology.

Questions for Review

1. How has the naturalistic fallacy been invoked for gender roles? Why do you think this area is so prone to this kind of fallacy?

2. The twins pictured in Figure 17–8 were also reported possibly to "share a gene for risk-taking." Given what you have learned about pleiotropy, epistasis, and the relation of phenotype to genotype, evaluate that statement. Why do you suppose those kinds of statements continue to be made?

3. What do you think about the possibility that dispersal in nonhuman primates (leaving one's group of birth) has evolved as a means of avoiding inbreeding? In posing the argument that this behavior has evolved under positive selection as a discrete trait, what assumptions must be made?

For Further Reading

Blaffer Hrdy, S. (1978). *The woman that never evolved*. Cambridge, MA: Harvard University Press.

Nishida, T. (1986). Local traditions and cultural transmission. In B. Smuts, D. Cheney, R. Seyfarth, R. Wrangham, & T. Struhsaker (Eds.), *Primate societies*. Chicago: University of Chicago Press (pp. 462–474).

Travathan, W. (1987). *Human birth*. Hawthorne, NY: Aldine de Gruyter.

The Importance of Anthropological Knowledge

The Importance of Anthropological Knowledge

culture bound

Significantly shaped by the culture in which it occurs, usually unwittingly; a characteristic of most human phenomena.

What Can Anthropology Reveal?

We deal with other people every day. We wonder why they behave as they do, how we came to be as we are, what our ancestors were like, and what our descendants may be and may do. That is why understanding evolutionary theory is relevant to modern times. While it has not been our intention to answer definitively all those questions (scientific endeavors, being **culture bound**, cannot answer questions definitively), the principles of biological and cultural evolution have permitted us to discern where the answers will lie or what they may look like when we find them.

First, anthropological knowledge tells us where we came from. We are products of biological and cultural evolution. Our ancestors 5 million years ago were apes, not any apes alive today but recognizable as apes. Our ancestors 20,000 years ago were gatherer-hunters, not any gatherer-hunters alive today but with an economic system more similar to those of modern gatherer-hunters than to our own. The biological processes that made us into *Homo sapiens sapiens* and the cultural evolutionary processes that made us participants in a large industrialized state are knowable, are mostly known, and continue to operate upon us.

Second, anthropological knowledge provides us all with a common heritage. While it is important to recognize and explain human variation, it is nevertheless clear that all *Homo sapiens sapiens* are biologically unified. It is important to appreciate the solidarity of humankind when so many social and political forces divide us into factions. While those factions are important cultural realities, they correlate very little with the distribution of biological diversity in the species.

Third, there are many ways of being human. This is the other unifying aspect of anthropological knowledge, the fact that all human societies are cultural. The specific rites, beliefs, and symbols vary greatly over space and time, but they are all simply manifestations of the unique way that humans function in groups. The values we hold now are different from those held by other peoples at other times but are also different from those held by *our own ancestors*. Since our lifeways and values have changed from those of our ancestors, we know that those of our descendants will be different from ours. With the same ethnocentrism that leads us to condemn the values of others or pride ourselves at having risen above our ancestors, our descendants may ethnocentrically lay claim to have risen above us. But no one culture will ever be better than any other, for *all* will have descendants with different values and attitudes. All are the descendants of some cultures and the ancestors of others.

Fourth, anthropological knowledge has the potential to improve and enrich the lives of people. Our knowledge of the human body, its function and history, and our knowledge of the material remains of culture can have practical benefit. This is known as *applied anthropology*.

Applied Anthropology

Applied anthropology is the use of anthropological knowledge to reach practical goals in international affairs and humanitarian efforts. International affairs, in the political realm, can fairly transparently be enhanced by a knowledge of the different societies involved. In the business world as well, anthropological knowledge has practical value. Ethnographic information provided by anthropologists to international business can be as apparently trivial as the fact that a car called a "Nova" would translate to "doesn't run" in Latin America—or as surprising as the recognition that the soft-drink slogan "Come alive" was suggesting to some eastern Asians the sinister forces of the undead.

Applied anthropology also has more noble applications in improving the quality of life for people around the world—feeding the hungry, housing the homeless, curing the sick, bringing resolution to conflict, and so on. The goals are held by various organizations—governments, public agencies, and private institutions—that employ anthropologists so that helpful policies and practices can be implemented.

Yet herein lies one of the potential problems with applied anthropology—the possibility of conflicting opinions between the organization and the social scientist. The former often has a particular goal or aim, while the latter has a certain expertise that might allow the aim to be achieved. The aim, however, might be considered unethical by the anthropologist, given the applied anthropologist's goal of improving the standard of living for a people while maintaining their way of life. The anthropologist may feel a professional obligation to place the population and its lifeways above the organizational policy if the two are in conflict.

A second and related potential problem is that applied anthropologists are often relatively powerless when it comes to actually implementing policies and practices. It is not often the case that anthropologists have the authority to act on their recommendations, especially if these are in conflict with the opinions of the organization. Indeed, it is not uncommon for anthropologists to be taken lightly. This is a problem faced by many social scientists when they attempt to become involved in policy decisions.

A third potential problem is that the anthropologist might not have the expertise to solve every problem. Indeed, anthropologists often disagree among themselves about the solutions to human problems. The results can be disastrous when the wrong policies and practices are applied.

Figure 18-1

A chimpanzee maintained in a laboratory setting. While some laboratory procedures on animals have been tragic and unnecessary, many are needed to improve the lives of people.

Applied Physical Anthropology

The recent emergence of applied physical anthropology has involved in part the application of anthropological knowledge to resolving medical problems, particularly in non-Western societies. As seen in Chapter 17, Kuru was eradicated after its cause was related to the funerary rites of the New Guinea Fore. But that was merely the first step in the research that ultimately led to the Nobel Prize for Carleton Gajdusek. Another important part of the work involved the determination that the disease was infectious and not hereditary. This was achieved by infecting a chimpanzee with the disease, which enabled the course of the disease to be tracked without the sacrifice of another human life.

Two points need to be made here. First, infection of a chimpanzee was possible because of the close biological and genetic relationship of chimpanzees to humans. Disease-causing microorganisms are usually highly specific to their host species, and therefore, only very close relatives of the host species can be cross-infected. While this undoubtedly saved human lives, it took chimpanzee lives. There is an obvious moral dilemma here, for it is impossible to weigh human lives against those of other species, especially of endangered species. When a cure or preventative for AIDS is discovered, it will have in part been based on information gathered from the study of **simian AIDS**, and the infection of chimpanzees with human AIDS. It is a tragedy to infect these primates with a deadly disease, but the humane attitude holds that the gain in human lives is worth the cost in nonhuman lives (Figure 18–1).

Second, while these sorts of biomedical studies are tragic for the dilemma of having to trade nonhuman primate lives for human lives, the tragedy is even greater when the evolutionary relationships are ignored

simian AIDS

Acquired immune deficiency syndrome found in some cercopithecine monkeys.

in biomedical research. One recent example involved the transplant of a baboon heart into a human patient (nicknamed Baby Fae) in 1984. While the intentions were humanitarian, the transplant was doomed from the start by virtue of the evolutionary difference between the hominoid body and cercopithecoid organ (Figure 18–2). The physicians did not use a chimp or gorilla heart—which would have been immunologically more compatible and, therefore, less likely to be rejected—because they were creationists and thought all species were equally distantly related from humans. Their ignorance did little for either the patient (who lived twenty days) or for the advancement of medicine.

MEDICAL ANTHROPOLOGY

More often, however, **medical anthropology** is involved in the interface between health care and non-Western cultures. Medical treatment is most effective when it is harmonized as much as possible with local views of the world. While we take certain views for granted, such as disease being caused by germs rather than by evil spirits; or hospitals being places to convalesce rather than to die, it is often difficult to apply modern medical techniques to people who do not share those beliefs (Figure 18–3). To impose modern medical beliefs forcibly on other people, when implementing those beliefs may or may not cure a particular illness, leads only to (justifiable) charges of imperialism and ethnocentrism and a greater distrust of Westerners and their culture.

A classic example involves the humanitarian efforts to feed malnourished Third World populations in the 1960s by giving them a healthy American dietary staple, milk. As noted in Chapter 9, most people in the world are unable to metabolize the sugar in milk effectively, which results in their becoming ill from it. This, of course, was unknown

medical anthropology

The study and application of health-care practices in relation to culture.

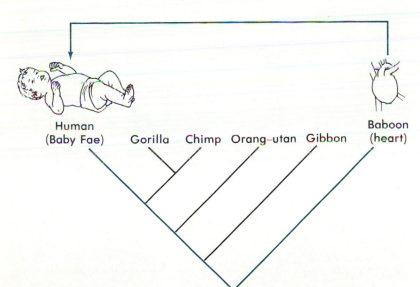

Human
(Baby Fae)   Gorilla   Chimp   Orang–utan   Gibbon   Baboon
(heart)

Figure 18-2

Using a baboon heart for a transplant into a human ignored the reality of evolutionary relationships and thus was not in the best interest of Baby Fae.

at the time the efforts were undertaken but resulted in Navajos throwing away the milk distributed to them, villagers in Colombia using it to whitewash their homes, and West Africans attributing evil spirits to the milk.

Medical anthropology is taking on even greater importance in the scientific community now that it is recognized that cultural behaviors can help to spread (and consequently, to help *prevent* the spread of) certain diseases. In our own time, AIDS can be taken as a paradigmatic example of a disease whose spread worldwide is intimately tied to behaviors and attitudes and whose eventual decline will have to be allied to understanding those behaviors and attitudes and modifying them.

In the United States (aside from intravenous drug users), the spread of AIDS began in the homosexual male community and consequently was restricted in large measure to that group during the early years of its spread. In Africa, however, AIDS was being principally spread not by male homosexuals, but by female prostitutes. Thus, in America it came largely to be regarded as a "gay plague," which was actually a historical accident stemming from the sexual orientation of its first American victims. In Africa it has been a predominantly heterosexually transmitted disease. The use of condoms is effective in retarding the spread of such venereally transmitted diseases, but in many communities, venereal diseases cannot be discussed openly, homosexuality is taboo, and condoms cannot be openly advertised. Indeed, in many ways, the attitudes and myths surrounding AIDS parallel strongly those that surrounded syphilis during World War I (Figure 18–4). Coping with the disease is a task not only for physicians but for medical anthropologists as well.

Figure 18-3

How would you convince someone who did not share your faith in our medical system that a hospital is where you are taken to be cured, and not to die?

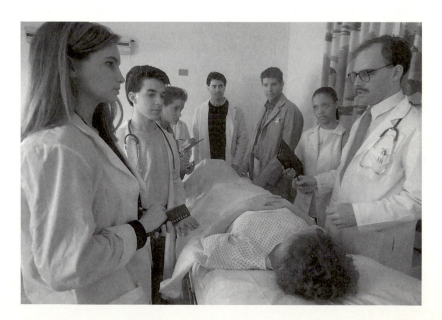

NUTRITIONAL ANTHROPOLOGY

Closely allied to, or even within, medical anthropology is the applied subdiscipline of *nutritional anthropology*. Here, anthropologists study the variation in diet from population to population, usually in conjunction with a humanitarian medical goal of improving health. They study the causes and consequences of malnutrition but also the links between specific dietary components and disease.

For example, among the Pima and Tohono O'odham (formally Papago) of Arizona, the incidence of diabetes (non-insulin-dependent diabetes, to be precise) is nearly twenty times as high in other (non-native American) populations. Correlated with this high risk of diabetes is extreme obesity, gallstones, and elevated cancer risk in the middle digestive area. This syndrome appeared following a radical change in diet that followed World War II and brought much higher proportions of carbohydrates into the diet. Anthropologist Kenneth Weiss has suggested that this *New World Syndrome* is the result of an evolutionary adaptation for storing nutrients as frugally as possible. The introduction of high-carbohydrate diets characteristic of industrialized societies would have a slight effect on the physiology of people without such an adaptation, but on people whose physiology may be genetically adapted to getting the most out of their diets, a flood of carbohydrates might overload the system. The result might well be the obesity and diabetes most diagnostic of this syndrome.

Figure 18-4

(a) During the first few decades of this century, people feared syphilis for irrational reasons and wrongly condemned those who had the condition. (b) Similar feelings are found today concerning AIDS and people who have AIDS.

(a)

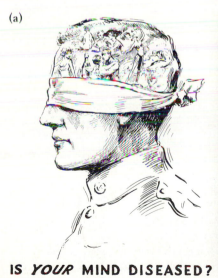

IS *YOUR* MIND DISEASED?

Figure 18-5

A forensic anthropologist, Dr. Walter H. Birkby of the Arizona State Museum.

Nutritional anthropologists also study the ways in which local diets are environmental adaptations, for one of the extraordinary things about humans is how flexible they appear to be in what they will ingest for their normal sustenance. The study of dietary variation in modern !Kung San (mainly vegetables), Eskimos (mainly meat), and industrialized Americans (mainly carbohydrates) is an integral part of the investigation of their adaptive behavior; diet is related to overall health, causes of disease, and death.

FORENSIC ANTHROPOLOGY

Another area of applied physical anthropology is in the knowledge of the skeleton and the application of that knowledge to legal issues. *Forensic anthropology*, therefore, studies skeletal trauma to determine the cause of death of crime victims as well as their age and sex (Figure 18–5). Sometimes it is also possible to make a positive identification of unknown skeletal remains. Thus, physical anthropologists can apply their knowledge to assist law enforcement organizations. Forensic anthropologists have applied their knowledge of the human skeleton to help identify, for example, the remains of Nazi war criminal Josef Mengele, and the bodies of Argentinian "desaparecidos" who were killed by the military regime in the 1970s.

Applied Archaeology

Many archaeologists in the United States practice applied archaeology, the use of archaeological knowledge to help conserve sites, artifacts, and other cultural materials, and thus the information they contain. This type of archaeology, often called *cultural resources management* or CRM, is not exclusive to academic settings and employs more professionals than universities and museums combined. It emerged in the United States during the 1960s and has grown rapidly since, in response to the expanding environmental awareness within the country and the resulting conservation legislation that has been passed.

PRACTICING CRM

Cultural resources—artifacts, sites, and other cultural materials—are nonrenewable, and the majority of them are threatened by treasure hunters and developers. Conservation legislation helps protect these resources when they are located on public lands or when they face possible disturbance from activities supported by public funds.

Treasure hunting, the unauthorized and unscientific removal of cultural resources from either the surface or subsurface, is always illegal when carried out on public lands. Penalties can be harsh. Treasure hunting remains a major problem, however, primarily because it can be a very profitable undertaking (Figure 18–6). Certain artifacts, if in good condition, can be worth tens of thousands of dollars on the black market. In

Figure 18-6
The results of treasure hunting. The archaeological site of Oldtown in south-western New Mexico appears totally covered by craters left from the search for Mimbres Pottery.

addition to this inducement is the simple curiosity of small-time, local collectors who desire a collection of their own. It is impossible to guard all resources, and many continue to be destroyed by the unscrupulous and ignorant.

Treasure hunting hurts all of us. It destroys archaeological context and thus the data necessary to reconstruct and understand past lifeways (Box 18–1). Without information on context, individual artifacts have little scientific or historical value. This is not only a loss to the professional archaeologist but to anyone who wishes to know his or her heritage more fully, or the heritage of all humankind. Everyone desires a connection to the past, and the treasure hunter denies this for us all.

Any endeavor that is publicly supported and that has the potential of destroying cultural resources is obligated by law to finance an archaeological investigation to ensure that important remains are not disturbed nor data lost. These investigations are carried out by professional archaeologists.

First, when the potentially disturbing project is still in the planning stages, the archaeologist conducts an assessment of the property under consideration. In fact, what the archaeologist performs is a reconnaissance of the property (Chapter 2) to gain a general understanding of the archaeological record. Relevant documents and available archaeological reports are consulted, the property is visited and sometimes surveyed, and recommendations are made concerning how the project should be carried out. Often, it is possible to suggest alternative procedures at this time since actual work has not started, so that the least damage will be done.

Next, the archaeologist will conduct subsurface testing of those locations still under consideration for the project. Testing consists of limited excavation in sample areas, and while it is somewhat more time con-

---

Issues in Anthropology 18–1

Treasure Hunting and the Destruction of Archaeological Data

In many parts of the world, including many parts of the United States, people collect archaeological resources for fun or profit. When they do not follow proper archaeological method, that is, when they do not record proper information and are interested only in the objects they discover, they are nothing more than treasure hunters. Many times, what they are doing is illegal, and it is always wrong. As a result of their activities, which are considerable, a substantial portion of the archaeological record has been destroyed.

Professional archaeologists have little interest in collecting objects because objects alone can tell them very little about prehistory or history. Ironically, treasure hunters who have a genuine interest in archaeology are hurting themselves (along with everyone else) because, without contextual information, they will not be able to learn very much about what they have found.

And those who treasure hunt merely for profit, without any interest in learning about the past or present, are simply treating us all unfairly by destroying information that rightly belongs to everyone. Sadly, the United States is generally behind other countries in aggressively discouraging profiteering in archaeological remains. In many

---

mitigate

To lessen or make less severe; in archaeology, to lessen the adverse impacts of any activity on the archaeological record.

suming and expensive than an assessment, it leads to a clearer understanding of the nature and extent of the archaeological record. Often, heavy machinery will be used during this stage (a backhoe, for example) since the goal is not so much the careful recording of data as it is the rapid documentation of cultural resources.

Testing allows the archaeologist to determine whether significant cultural resources are present in the project location. It is also decided whether the project (as envisioned) will have adverse impacts on these resources, and, if it will, what can be done to **mitigate** those impacts.

Significant cultural resources are defined legally as having at least one of the following characteristics:

1. That are associated with events that have made a significant contribution to the broad patterns of our history; or

2. That are associated with the lives of persons significant in our past; or

3. That embody the distinctive characteristics of a type, period, method of construction, or that represent the work of a master, or that possess high artistic values, or that represent a significant and distinguishable entity whose components may lack individual distinction; or

4. That have yielded, or may be likely to yield, information important in prehistory or history.

(Federal Register 1974:3369)

other countries, the sale of antiquities, no matter whether found on public or private land, is severely penalized because the artifacts are considered to be part of that country's national heritage.

Fortunately, there are laws that protect archaeological resources in the United States under certain circumstances. But these laws are difficult to enforce, particularly in isolated areas where many archaeological sites have been repeatedly disturbed. Increased public education about the value of proper archaeological fieldwork, a greater appreciation for the (nonmaterial) value of artifacts and context, and a more global perspective of ancient peoples as ancestors, are the core of a solution to this tragedy.

References:

Bassett, C. A. (1986). The culture thieves. *Science 86* 7(6):22–29.

Meyer, K. E. (1977). *The plundered past.* New York: Atheneum.

Robertson, M. G. (1972). Monument thievery in Mesoamerica. *American Antiquity* 37:147–155.

Shelton, D. (1986). Law and looting. *Archaeology* 39(4):80.

It should be clear that these criteria, particularly the last, allow *any* cultural resource to be judged significant. Thus, the determination of significance is left solely to the archaeologist, as it should be. And archaeologists consider a number of other criteria, based on their knowledge and expertise, when making the determination. Historically significant resources are those that reflect important historical trends, people, or events. Scientifically significant resources are those that contribute information of value to archaeologists. Cultural resources with ethnic significance relate to the history and integrity of ethnic minorities. And those with public significance contribute to the society as a whole. All criteria must be considered together when judging whether cultural resources are significant or not.

Adverse impacts are those that lead to the destruction of cultural material or data. They can be direct (the immediate consequences of the project) or indirect (not resulting from the project itself but occurring because of the project—an example would be increased visitation at an archaeological site because of road construction). Archaeologists must consider all possible ramifications of a project when determining the nature of impacts.

Mitigation of adverse impacts can take several forms. First, and best, is avoidance—arranging it so that the significant cultural resources do not face adverse impacts. This might involve moving the location of a project slightly or altering some project activities. While not always possible, avoidance should be the first choice when mitigation becomes necessary.

Another form of mitigation is full-scale excavation, carried out when avoidance is impossible (Figure 18–7). Usually, the assessment and testing phases have led to a clear understanding of the archaeological record, and excavation can proceed smoothly. Still, it is always better to avoid than to excavate.

Cultural resources management employs the majority of professional archaeologists today. In addition, a large number of theoretical and methodological innovations have been made by CRM archaeologists, primarily due to the constraints and demands of working in tandem with others outside the discipline. The CRM archaeologist does not have the luxury of studying a site or research issue methodically and patiently, yet remains responsible for doing a good job. Yet it is also important to remember that applied archaeologists do not rush their work. The current legislation allows them to begin work while the potentially damaging activity is still in the planning stages. They contribute to the overall work plan, and do not simply react to circumstances.

Some Conclusions about Evolutionary Anthropology

We have considered a wide range of topics in this book—including the emergence of the primates, the behaviors of our close relatives, the origins of domestication, sociocultural complexity in its varied forms, the conditions of industrial people, and the evolutionary theories that bind them all together.

The explanatory framework of biological and cultural change is evolution. There are several fundamental and important conclusions that should be drawn. First, humans have evolved biologically by the same principles of evolution that have operated within all species. Humans are

Figure 18-7

A full-scale excavation project in downtown El Paso, Texas, to mitigate the impacts of downtown redevelopment on the archaeological record.

thus products of the same forces in operation throughout the history of life, and not unique in this sense. We are more closely related to certain animals than to other animals and fit into the nested hierarchy of living beings as slightly made-over apes.

It follows, secondly, that the human body is a mosaic of old and new biological characters that evolved at different times. This is how evolution operates, and *Homo sapiens* is no exception. Studying nonhuman primates, further, can help us understand the primitive (plesiomorphic) aspects of our bodies—the parts that evolved relatively long ago. In contrast, understanding the novelties (autapomorphies) of humans is largely inferential but can be approached by way of contrast with our close biological relatives.

Third, humans are biologically diverse. Most of the biological variation in our species, however, is within-population variation. Thus, although some biological variation can be found among the human "races," it is insignificant when taken as a proportion of the diversity that exists in the species. The concept of the biological race is not a valid one, the "races" in reality being primarily social categories. This does not mean that the question of race in human affairs is a small one—on the contrary, race is a question of major significance in current affairs—but that it is a social problem and can be resolved only socially, not biologically.

Fourth, human beings are biologically individuals—no two are identical, biologically, with rare obvious exceptions. Individuality is, therefore, a biological fact, but again, the typological concept of race is not. There does not appear to be a biological property shared by members of one race to the exclusion of the members of other races. The cluster of individuals that does have biological significance is the population—and even that becomes fuzzy when there is extensive interbreeding, as inevitably accompanies cultural complexity and probably has occurred in non-complex societies as well.

Populations differ from one another to varying degrees, and their relationships to one another can be studied. Nevertheless, this gives us no information on which entities to recognize as races. Further, whatever clusters of populations do emerge are inevitably composed of highly diverse groups of people.

There are political implications of the fact that individuality, and not racial difference, is the principal source of biological diversity in our species. If rights are to be accorded differently to people because they are biologically different, then *everyone* must be accorded different rights. There is no biological justification for judging people differently on account of group membership, which may in turn be determined by a relatively small genetic contribution.

Instead, we accept the tenet of the Declaration of Independence that "all [people] are created equal," and we therefore accept the stated equality as a *social* fact not related to any aspects of biological diversity or uniformity. All people are biologically different but entitled to equal rights conferred by our society.

A related conclusion, of generally underappreciated significance, is that human differences are primarily of a sociocultural nature, not of a biological nature. Almost everything human groups do is a product of cultural evolution and therefore of social history, not of biological history. Thus, although any population of humans differs from any other biologically to some extent, the most obvious ways in which human groups differ from one another is in their modes of life, beliefs, languages, rituals, and so on. In other words, cultural differences are much more pervasive, and much more apparent, than biological differences among populations.

These cultural differences are all simply different ways of being human. These ways have varied and continue to vary widely over time and space, with each different human society coming to fulfill its necessity to communicate, to subsist, to explain, to interact, and to legislate, in one of a variety of possible manners. This diversity of cultures exists because cultural evolution is divergent, not progressive. Cultures are becoming different, not better. Some aspects of some cultures may be becoming better, but this is balanced by something else becoming worse.

Major cultural changes, including domestication, social stratification, political integration, and the rise and fall of states, have occurred a number of different times in a number of different places. Often they have involved large-scale changes in parallel when they occurred in different societies, which suggests that certain kinds of cultural changes are simple consequences of other changes. Yet each culture is an autonomous evolving unit at any time, in any place. Cultures can, consequently, be compared but not judged. Each simply reflects a different manner for its participants to express their humanness.

Summary

The Future Evolution of Our Species

Science-fiction stories have routinely tried to project images of the humans of the future (Figure 18–8). Often, this is called the next stage of evolution, as if biological evolution were governed by the Great Chain of Being and destined to continue along the same path that led to *Homo sapiens,* only carried farther. Images of this next stage often emphasize enlarged brains—since, after all, our brains have gotten fairly large over the past 1.5 million years.

And yet, evolution is not like a line, on which one can only go farther—but rather, like a tree, within which one can go in dif-

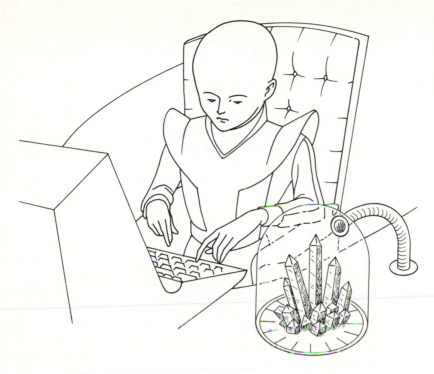

Figure 18-8

A popular image of a future human. More realistically, anthropologists predict that we will biologically appear much as we do today.

ferent directions. Remember that our cousins 1.5 million years ago, the bipedal *Paranthropus*, differed dentally from modern apes in a more extreme manner than modern humans do. That is, they had smaller canines and larger molars than we—they were dentally more human. Thus, if there is a line leading from ape to human, they were dentally farther along on it than we are.

Human adaptations are now principally cultural, not biological—a result of our taking a different evolutionary path, which involved an emphasis on the brain. A human poorly biologically adapted to the cold can nevertheless live comfortably in cold climates due to technology and can therefore thrive in an environment that would have reduced the chances of survival and reproduction of its ancestors. Further, the capacity of modern humans to adapt culturally seems not to be related to variation in the brain size of modern humans. Twentieth-century brains are not significantly larger than Paleolithic brains, nor the brains of people of other societies, nor even the brains of Neanderthals. Apparently, with *Homo sapiens*, cranial evolution reached a threshold at which cultural evolution took off on its own.

It seems fair to project, consequently, that since cultural evolution is the main form of our present adaptation, it will probably be the main way in which our descendants adapt as well. Because cultural evolution is not connected in any obvious way to modern brain variation, it follows that our descendants, however remote, need not have bigger brains than ours.

Most of the biological evolution of our species has been the result of the actions of genetic drift and natural selection. Genetic drift has produced nonadaptive differences among small populations, and natural selection has produced adaptive differences. Since most adaptation is now cultural, and it is a faster, more intensive, and more flexible means of adapting than adapting genetically, most of the selective pressures on human populations are being removed. Antimalarial drugs, for example, make genetic adaptations to malaria superfluous, as vitamin-D-supplemented milk helps ensure that children of light and dark skin color receive adequate amounts of vitamin D. Thus, whatever relative advantages certain genotypes may have afforded in particular environments at some time in the past are no longer relative advantages—if anyone of any genotype can adapt culturally to the same environment.

It seems as though the major evolutionary forces that have shaped our species are no longer operating strongly. Perhaps the next major episode in human evolution will occur when we colonize other planets and genetic drift again begins to play a role.

Cultural evolution is the major mode of human adaptation at present, and it is likely to be so in the future as well. Yet, as we have emphasized throughout this book, it is difficult to predict the specific course of cultural evolution. Modern problems, like nuclear waste and auto pollution, began as solutions to problems faced by an earlier generation. It seems fair to expect that as we solve the problems our generation faces, there will be unforeseen ones for the next generation.

While evolutionary anthropology can not directly solve these problems or predict the future, it is very likely that our ability to do both will be predicated in large measure upon what we learn about our past and about the processes in operation that will generate our future.

Questions for Review

1. Are we still evolving? If so, how?

2. Can you think of ways in which a knowledge of anthropology is relevant to understanding and perhaps solving current problems in America or in the world?

For Further Reading

Bodley, John H. (1976). *Anthropology and contemporary human problems.* Menlo Park, CA: Benjamin/Cummings.

Gould, S. J. (1988). The heart of terminology. *Natural History* 97(2):24–31.

Lipe, W. D. (1974). A conservation model for American archaeology. *The Kiva* 39(3/4):213–245.

McCracken, R. D. (1971). Lactase deficiency: An example of dietary evolution. *Current Anthropology* 12:479–518.

Schiffer, Michael B., & Gumerman, George J. (Eds.). (1977). *Conservation archaeology: A guide for cultural resource management studies.* New York: Academic Press.

Extant Primate Genera and Common Names
(after Martin, 1990)

Suborder Prosimii
    Superfamily Lemuroidea

Lemur	Lemur
Lepilemur	Sportive Lemur
Hapalemur	Gentle Lemur
Microcebus	Mouse Lemur
Cheirogaleus	Dwarf Lemur
Phaner	Fork-crowned Lemur
Allocebus	Hairy-eared Dwarf Lemur
Indri	Indri
Propithecus	Sifaka
Avahi	Avahi
Daubentonia	Aye-Aye
Varecia	Variegated Lemur

    Superfamily Lorisoidea

Galago	Bush Baby
Loris	Loris
Nycticebus	Slow Loris
Perodicticus	Potto
Arctocebus	Angwantibo

    Superfamily Tarsioidea

Tarsius	Tarsier

Suborder Anthropoidea
    Infraorder Platyrrhini
        Superfamily Ceboidea
            Family Cebidae

Cebus	Capuchin
Saimiri	Squirrel Monkey
Ateles	Spider Monkey
Brachyteles	Wooly Spider Monkey
Lagothrix	Wooly Monkey
Alouatta	Howler Monkey
Callicebus	Titi
Aotus	Night Monkey
Pithecia	Saki
Cacajao	Uakari
Chiropotes	Bearded saki

Family Callitrichidae
    Callithrix   Marmoset
    Callimico   Goeldi's monkey
    Cebuella   Pygmy marmoset
    Leontopithecus   Golden lion tamarin
    Saguinus   Tamarins

Infraorder Catarrhini
  Superfamily Cercopithecoidea
    Family Cercopithecidae
      Cercopithecus   Vervets, Guenons
      Allenopithecus   Allen's Swamp Monkey
      Miopithecus   Talapoin
      Erythrocebus   Patas
      Macaca   Macaques
      Papio   Baboon
      Mandrillus   Mandrill
      Theropithecus   Gelada
      Cercocebus   Terrestrial Mangabeys
      Lophocebus   Arboreal Mangabeys
      Pygathrix   Douc langur
      Rhinopithecus   Snub-nosed langurs
      Simias   Pagai Island Langur
      Colobus   Colobus
      Presbytis   Langurs
      Nasalis   Proboscis

  Superfamily Hominoidea
    Family Hylobatidae
      Hylobates   Gibbons

    Family Pongidae
      Pongo   Orang-utan
      Pan   Chimpanzee
      Gorilla   Gorilla

    Family Hominidae
      Homo   Humans

Major Bones of the Human Skeleton

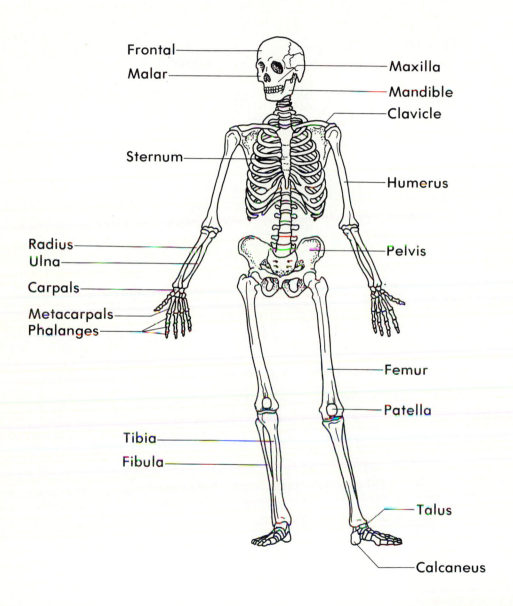

Frontal

Malar

Sternum

Radius

Ulna

Carpals

Metacarpals

Phalanges

Tibia

Fibula

Maxilla

Mandible

Clavicle

Humerus

Pelvis

Femur

Patella

Talus

Calcaneus

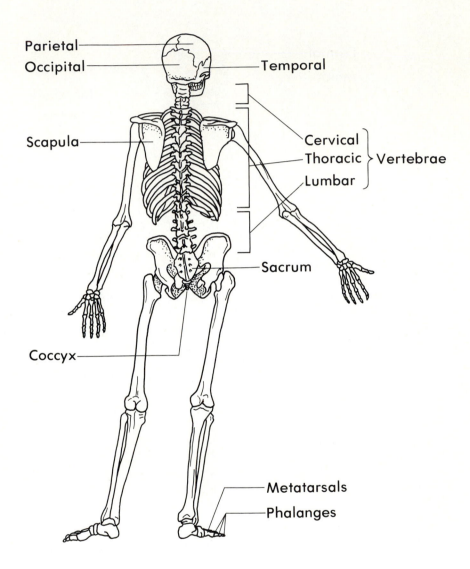

References

Chapter 1

Blount, B. G. (1974). *Language, culture, and society: A book of readings.* Cambridge, MA: Winthrop Publishers.

Buettner-Janusch, J. (1966). *Origins of man.* New York: Wiley.

Deetz, J. (1967). *Invitation to archaeology.* Garden City, NY: Natural History Press.

Finegan, E., & Besnier, N. (1989). *Language: Its structure and use.* San Diego: Harcourt, Brace, Jovanovich.

Geertz, C. (1973). *The interpretation of cultures.* New York: Basic Books.

Giglioli, P. P. (Ed.). (1972). *Language and social context: Selected readings.* New York: Penguin.

Hole, F., & Heizer, R. F. (1973). *An introduction to prehistoric archeology* (3d ed.). New York: Holt, Rinehart and Winston.

Kroeber, A. L. (1923). *Anthropology.* New York: Harcourt, Brace.

Montagu, M. F. A. (1960). *Introduction to physical anthropology* (3d ed.). Springfield, IL: Charles C. Thomas.

Chapter 2

Barker, P. A. (1977). *Techniques of archaeological excavation.* New York: Universe Books.

Clarke, D. L. (1978). *Analytical archaeology* (2d ed.). Rev. by Bob Chapman. New York: Columbia University Press.

Dunnell, R. C. (1971). *Systematics in prehistory.* New York: Free Press.

Feder, K. L. (1990). *Frauds, myths and mysteries: Science and pseudoscience in archaeology.* Mountain View, CA: Mayfield Publishing Company.

Gardner, M. (1957). *Fads & fallacies in the name of science.* New York: Dover Publications, Inc.

Gardner, M. (1981). *Science: Good, bad and bogus.* Buffalo, NY: Prometheus Books.

Harris, E. C. (1979). *Principles of archaeological stratigraphy.* New York: Academic Press.

Hull, D. L. (1988). *Science as a process.* Chicago: University of Chicago Press.

Joukowsky, M. (1980). *A complete manual of field archaeology: Tools and techniques of field work for archaeologists.* Englewood Cliffs, NJ: Prentice-Hall.

Kuhn, T. S. (1970). *The structure of scientific revolutions,* (2d ed.). Chicago: University of Chicago Press.

Lewin, R. (1987). *Bones of contention.* New York: Simon & Schuster.

Lyons, T. R. & Avery, T. E. (1977). *Remote sensing: A handbook for archeologists and cultural resource managers.* Washington, DC: Cultural Resources Management Division, National Park Service, U.S. Department of the Interior.

Marks, D. (Ed.) Investigating the paranormal. *Experientia,* 44:281–359.

Marquardt, W. H. (1978). Advances in archaeological seriation. In M. B. Schiffer (Ed.), *Advances in archaeological method and theory: Vol. 1* (pp. 266–314). New York: Academic Press.

Medawar, P. (1984). *Plato's republic.* New York: Oxford University Press.

Michels, J. W. (1973). *Dating methods in archaeology.* New York: Seminar Press.

Mueller, J. W. (Ed.) (1975). *Sampling in archaeology.* Tucson: University of Arizona Press.

Plog, S., Plog, F., & Wait, W. (1978). Decision making in modern surveys. In M. B. Schiffer (Ed.), *Advances in archaeological method and theory: Vol. 1* (pp. 384–421). New York: Academic Press.

Popper, K. R. (1968). *The logic of scientific discovery* (2d Harper Torchbook ed.). New York: Harper & Row.

Randi, J. (1982). *Flim-flam!* Buffalo, NY: Prometheus Books.

Staski, E. (1989). Surface and subsurface patterns of archaeological materials at Fort Fillmore, New Mexico. *North American Archaeologist* 10: 205–225.

Thomas, D. H. (1976). *Figuring anthropology*. New York: Holt, Rinehart and Winston.

Weiner, J. S. (1980). *The Piltdown forgery*. New York: Dover Publications.

Williams, S. (1991). *Fantastic archaeology: The wild side of North American prehistory*. Philadelphia: University of Pennsylvania Press.

Chapter 3

Bohannan, P. & Glazer, M. (Eds.). (1973). *High points in anthropology*. New York: Knopf.

Boorstin, D. J. (1983). *The discoverers*. New York: Random House.

Bowler, P. J. (1989). *Evolution: The history of an idea*. Berkeley: University of California Press.

Chetverikov, S. S. (1961). On certain aspects of the evolutionary process from the standpoint of modern genetics. *Proceedings of the American Philosophical Society* 105: 167–195. (Original work published 1926)

Clark, R. W. (1984). *The survival of Charles Darwin: A biography of a man and an idea*. New York: Random House.

Dobzhansky, T. (1937). *Genetics and the origin of species*. New York: Columbia University Press.

Fisher, R. A. (1958). *The genetical theory of natural selection*. New York: Dover Publications. (Original work published 1930)

Haldane, J. B. S. (1966). *The causes of evolution*. Ithaca, NY: Cornell University Press. (Original work published 1932)

Harris, M. (1979). *Cultural materialism: The struggle for a science of culture*. New York: Random House.

Hatch, E. (1973). *Theories of man and culture*. New York: Columbia University Press.

Kevles, D. (1985). *In the name of eugenics*. Berkeley, CA: University of California Press.

Kohn, D. (Ed.) (1985). *The Darwinian heritage*. Princeton, NJ: Princeton University Press.

Leaf, M. J. (1979). *Man, mind, and science: A history of anthropology*. New York: Columbia University Press.

Mayr, E. (1942). *Systematics and the origin of species*. New York: Columbia University Press.

Mayr, E. & Provine, W. (1980). *The evolutionary synthesis: Perspectives on the unification of biology*. Cambridge, MA: Harvard University Press.

Padover, S. K. (1978). *The essential Marx: The non-economic writings*. New York: New American Library.

Simpson, G. G. (1944). *Tempo and mode in evolution*. New York: Columbia University Press.

Stocking, G. W. (1987). *Victorian anthropology*. New York: Free Press.

Wright, S. (1931). Evolution in Mendelian populations. *Genetics* 16: 97–159.

Chapter 4

Barnett, H. G. (1942). Invention and cultural change. *American Anthropologist* 44: 14–30.

Basalla, G. (1988). *The evolution of technology*. New York: Cambridge University Press.

Bee, R. L. (1974). *Patterns and processes; an introduction to anthropological strategies for the study of sociocultural change*. New York: Free Press.

Benedict, R. (1956). The growth of culture. In H. L. Shapiro (Ed.). *Man, Culture, and Society* (pp. 182–195). New York: Oxford University Press.

Benton, M. (1990). Scientific methodologies in collision: The history of the study of the extinction of the dinosaurs. In M. Hecht, B. Wallace, & R. MacIntyre (Eds.). *Evolutionary biology*, Vol. 24 (pp. 371–401). New York: Plenum Press.

Burney, D. A., & MacPhee, R. (1988). Mysterious island. *Natural History*, 97(7):46–55.

Butzer, K. (1980). Civilizations: Organisms or systems? *American Scientist* 68:517–523.

Dunnell, R. C. (1980). Evolutionary theory and archaeology. In M. B. Schiffer (Ed.), *Advances in archaeological method and theory, Vol. 3* (pp. 38–99). New York: Academic Press.

Eldredge, N., & Gould, S. J. (1972). Punctuated equilibria: An alternative to phyletic gradualism. In T. J. Schopf (Ed.), *Models in paleobiology* (pp. 82–115). San Francisco: Freeman, Cooper & Co.

Elliot Smith, G. (1933). *The diffusion of culture*. London: Watts.

Ghiselin, M. (1975). A radical solution to the species problem. *Systematic Zoology* 23:536–554.

Gould, S. J., & Lewontin, R. C. (1979). The spandrels of San Marco and the Panglossian paradigm: A critique of the adaptationist programme. *Proceedings of the Royal Society of London*, Series B, 205:581–598.

Hull, D. L. (1976). Are species really individuals? *Systematic Zoology* 25:174–191.

Hill, J. N. (Ed.). (1977). *Explanation of prehistoric change*. Albuquerque: University of New Mexico Press.

Ingold, T. (1990). An anthropologist looks at biology. *Man* 25:208–229.

Marks, J., & Staski, E. (1988). Individuals and the evolution of biological and cultural systems. *Human Evolution* 3:147–161.

Mayr, E. (1988). *Toward a new philosophy of biology*. Cambridge, MA: Harvard University Press.

Murphy, R., & Steward, J. (1955). Tappers and trappers: Parallel processes in acculturation. *Economic Development and Culture Change* 4:335–355.

Plog, F. (1974). *The study of prehistoric change*. New York: Academic Press.

Raup, D. (1986). Biological extinction in earth history. *Science* 231:1528–1533.

Renfrew, C. (Ed.). (1973). *The explanation of culture change: Models in prehistory*. Pittsburgh, PA: University of Pittsburgh Press.

Renfrew, C. & Cooke, K. L. (Eds.). (1979). *Transformations: Math-ematical approaches to culture change*. New York: Academic Press.

Sharp, L. (1952). Steel axes for stone-age Australians. *Human Organization* 11:17–22.

Steward, J. (1955). *Theory of culture change*. Urbana: University of Illinois Press.

Wenke, R. J. (1981). Explaining the evolution of cultural complexity: A review. In M. B. Schiffer (Ed.), *Advances in archaeological method and theory: Vol. 4*. (pp. 79–127). New York: Academic Press.

White, L. A. (1949). *The science of culture, a study of man and civilization*. New York: Grove Press.

Yoffee, N. (1979). The decline and rise of Mesopotamian civilization: An ethnoarchaeological perspective on the evolution of social complexity. *American Antiquity* 44:5–35.

Chapter 5

Cartmill, M. (1974). Rethinking primate origins. *Science* 184:436–443.

Gregory, W. K. (1951). *Evolution emerging*. New York: Macmillan.

Hennig, W. (1965). Phylogenetic systematics. *Annual Review of Entomology* 10:97–116.

Hillis, D. M. (1987). Molecular versus morphological approaches to systematics. *Annual Review of Ecology and Systematics* 18:23–42.

Hooton, E. A. (1946). *Up from the ape* (2d ed.). New York: Macmillan.

Hull, D. L. (1970). Contemporary systematic philosophies. *Annual Review of Ecology and Systematics* 1:19–54.

Mayr, E. (1981). Biological classification: Towards a synthesis of opposing methodologies. *Science* 214:510–516.

Simpson, G. G. (1945). The principles of classification and a classification of mammals. *Bulletin of the American Museum of Natural History, Vol. 85*.

Washburn, S., & Patterson, B. (1951). Evolutionary importance of the South African 'man-apes'. *Nature* 167:650–651.

Chapter 6

Arens, W. (1979). *The man-eating myth*. New York: Oxford University Press.

Blaffer Hrdy, S. (1977). *The langurs of Abu*. Cambridge, MA: Harvard University Press.

Fossey, D. (1983). *Gorillas in the mist*. Boston: Houghton-Mifflin.

Gardner, R., & Gardner, B. (1969). Teaching sign language to a chimpanzee. *Science* 165:664–672.

Goodall, J. van Lawick. (1971). *In the shadow of man*. Boston: Houghton-Mifflin.

Kohler, W. (1925). *The mentality of apes*. London: Routledge and Kegan Paul.

Linden, E. (1974). *Apes, men, and language*. New York: Penguin.

Smuts, B. B. (1985). *Sex and friendship in baboons*. Hawthorne, NY: Aldine.

Strum, S. C. (1987). *Almost human: A journey into the world of baboons*. New York: Random House.

Washburn, S., & DeVore, I. (1961). The social life of baboons. *Scientific American* 204:62–71.

Yerkes, R. M. (1925). *Almost human*. New York: Century.

Zuckerman, S. (1932). *The social life of monkeys and apes*. London: Routledge and Kegan Paul.

Chapter 7

Bonne, B. (1966). Are there Hebrews left? *American Journal of Physical Anthropology* 24:135–146.

Bumpus, H. (1899). The elimination of the unfit as illustrated by the introduced sparrow, *Passer domesticus*. *Biological Lectures from the Marine Biology Laboratory, Wood's Holl [sic], 1898* (pp. 209–226).

Crow, J. F. (1986). *Basic concepts in population, quantitative, and evolutionary genetics*. New York: Freeman.

Hazelrigg, T. (1987). The *Drosophila white* gene: A molecular update. *Trends in Genetics*, 3:43–47.

Jacob, F. (1973). *The logic of life*. New York: Pantheon.

Karn, M. N., & Penrose, L. S. (1951). Birth weight and gestation time in relation to maternal age, parity, and infant survival. *Annals of Eugenics*, 15:206–233.

Livingstone, F. B. (1958). Anthropological implications of sickle cell gene distribution in West Africa. *American Anthropologist* 60:533–562.

McKusick, V. A. (1988). *Mendelian inheritance in man* (8th ed.). Baltimore: Johns Hopkins University Press.

Miller, C. (1961). Stature and build of Hawaiian-born youth of Japanese ancestry. *American Journal of Physical Anthropology* 19:159–172.

McKusick, V., Egeland, J., Eldridge, R., & Krusen, D. (1964). Dwarfism in the Amish. I: The Ellis Van Creveld syndrome. *Bulletin of Johns Hopkins Hospital* 115:306–336.

Provine, W. (1986). *Sewall Wright and evolutionary biology.* Chicago: University of Chicago Press.

Reed, T. E. (1969). Caucasian genes in American Negroes. *Science* 165:762–768.

Stern, C. (1943). The Hardy-Weinberg law. *Science* 97:137–138.

Stout, J. T., & Carey, C. T. (1988). The Lesch-Nyhan syndrome: Clinical, molecular and genetic aspects. *Trends in Genetics* 4:175–178.

Yamamoto, F., Clausen, H., White, T., Marken, J., & Hakomori, S. (1990). Molecular genetic basis of the histo-blood group ABO system. *Nature* 345:229–233.

Chapter 8

Goodman, M. (1963). Serological analyses of the systematics of recent hominoids. *Human Biology* 35:377–437.

Honig, G., and Adams, J. G., III. (1986). *Human hemoglobin genetics.* New York: Springer-Verlag.

Kimura, M. (1983). *The neutral theory of molecular evolution.* Cambridge, England: Cambridge University Press.

Li, W. H., & Graur, D. (1990). *Fundamentals of molecular evolution.* Sunderland, MA: Sinauer.

Myerowitz, R. (1988). Splice-junction mutation in some Ashkenazi Jews with Tay-Sachs disease: Evidence against a single deficit within this ethnic group. *Proceedings of the National Academy of Science* 85:3955–3959.

Myrianthopoulos, N., & Aronson, S. (1966). Population dynamics of Tay-Sachs disease. I: Reproductive fitness and selection. *American Journal of Human Genetics* 18:313–327.

Myrianthopoulos, N., & Aronson, S. (1972). Population dynamics of Tay-Sachs disease. II: What confers the selective advantage upon the Jewish heterozygote. In B. Volk & S. Aronson (Eds.), *Sphingolipids, sphingolipidoses and allied disorders* (pp. 561–570), New York: Plenum.

Sarich, V., & Wilson, A. (1967). Immunological time scale for hominid evolution. *Science* 158:1200–1203.

Chapter 9

Boas, F. (1912). Changes in the bodily form of descendants of immigrants. *American Anthropologist* 14:530–562.

Boyd, W. C. (1950). *Genetics and the races of man.* Boston: Little, Brown.

Chase, A. (1980). *The legacy of Malthus.* Urbana: University of Illinois Press.

Flatz, G. (1987). Genetics of lactose digestion in humans. In H. Harris and K. Hirschorn (Eds.), *Advances in Human Genetics,* (pp. 1–77) New York: Plenum.

Gould, S. J. (1978). Morton's ranking of races by cranial capacity. *Science* 200:503–509.

Grant, M. (1916). *The passing of the great race.* New York: Scribner's.

Hooton, E. A. (1939). *Twilight of man.* New York: G. P. Putnam's Sons.

Hulse, F. (1962). Race as an evolutionary episode. *American Anthropologist* 64:929–945.

Lewontin, R. C., Rose, S., and Kamin L. J. (1984). *Not in our genes.* New York: Pantheon.

Lewontin, R. C. (1972). The apportionment of human diversity. In T. Dobzhansky, M. Hecht, & W. Steere (Eds.), *Evolutionary biology, Vol. 6,* (pp. 381–398). New York: Appleton-Century-Crofts.

Michael, J. S. (1988). A new look at Morton's craniological research. *Current Anthropology* 29:349–354.

Mourant, A. E., Kopek, A. C., & Domaniewska-Sobczak, K. (1976). *The distribution of the human blood groups* (2d ed.). New York: Oxford University Press.

Stanton, J. (1960). *The leopard's spots.* Chicago: University of Chicago Press.

Chapter 10

Deetz, J. (1968). The inference of residence and descent rules from archeological data. In S. R. Binford & L. R. Binford (Eds.) *New perspectives in archeology.* (pp. 41–48) New York: Aldine.

Fleagle, J., Kay, R., & Simons, E. (1980). Sexual dimorphism in early anthropoids. *Nature* 287:328–330.

Hill, J. N. (1968). Broken K Pueblo: Patterns of form and function. In S. R. Binford & L. R. Binford. *New perspectives in archeology* (pp. 103–142) New York: Aldine.

Hill, J. N. & Evans, R. K. (1972). A model for classification and typology. In D. L. Clarke (Ed.), *Models in archaeology* (pp. 231–273). London: Methuen.

Landau, M. (1984). Human evolution as narrative. *American Scientist* 72:262–267.

Longacre, W. A. (1964). Archaeology as anthropology: A case study. *Science* 144:1454–1455.

Longacre, W. A., & Ayres, J. E. (1968). Archeological lessons from an Apache wickiup. In S. R. Binford & L. R. Binford (Eds.). *New perspectives in archeology* (pp. 151–159). New York: Aldine.

Schiffer, M. B. (1972). Archaeological context and systemic context. *American Antiquity* 37:156–165.

Tattersall, I., & Eldredge, N. (1977). Fact, theory, and fantasy in human paleontology. *American Scientist* 65:204–211.

Willey, G. R. (1974). The Viru Valley settlement pattern study. In G. R. Willey (Ed.). *Archaeological researches in retrospect* (pp. 149–176). Cambridge, MA: Winthrop Publishers.

Wood, W. R., & Johnson, D. L. (1978). A survey of disturbance processes in archaeological site formation. In M. B. Schiffer (Ed.). *Advances in archaeological method and theory: Vol. 1* (pp. 315–381). New York: Academic Press.

Chapter 11

Aiello, L., & Dean, C. (1990). *An introduction to human evolutionary anatomy.* San Diego: Academic Press.

Andrews, P., & Martin, L. (1987). Cladistic relationships of extant and fossil hominoids. *Journal of Human Evolution* 16:101–118.

Beard, K. C., Krishtalka, L., & Stucky, R. K. (1991). First skulls of the Early Eocene primate *Shoshonius cooperi* and the anthropoid-tarsier dichotomy. *Nature,* 349:64–66.

Dart, R. A. (1925). *Australopithecus africanus:* The man-ape of South Africa. *Nature* 115:195–199.

Delson, E. (1981). Paleoanthropology: Pliocene and Pleistocene human evolution. *Paleobiology* 7:298–305.

Falk, D., & Conroy, G. (1983). The cranial venous sinus system in *Australopithecus afarensis. Nature* 306:779–781.

Fedigan, L. M. (1986). The changing role of women in models of human evolution. *Annual Review of Anthropology* 15:25–66.

McHenry, H. (1975). Fossils and the mosaic nature of human evolution. *Science* 190:425–431.

Harrison, T. (1986). A reassessment of the phylogenetic relationships of *Oreopithecus bamboli* Gervais. *Journal of Human Evolution* 15:541–583.

Harrison, T. (1987). The phylogenetic relationships of the early catarrhine primates: A review of the current evidence. *Journal of Human Evolution* 16:41–80.

Hill, A. (1985). Early hominid from Baringo, Kenya. *Nature* 315:222–224.

Hill, A. & Ward, S. (1988). Origin of the Hominidae: The record of African large hominoid evolution between 14 my and 4 my. *Yearbook of Physical Anthropology* 31:49–83.

Holloway, R. (1983). Cerebral brain endocast pattern of *Australopithecus afarensis* hominid. *Nature* 303:420–422.

Howell, F. C. (1977). Hominidae. In V. Maglio & H. B. S. Cooke (Eds.), *Evolution of African mammals* (pp. 154–248). Cambridge, MA: Harvard University Press.

Johanson, D., & Taieb, M. (1976). Plio-Pleistocene hominid discoveries in Hadar, Ethiopia. *Nature* 260:293–297.

Johanson, D., & White, T. (1979). A systematic assessment of early African hominids. *Science* 203:321–330.

Kay, R., & Simons, E. (1980). The ecology of Oligocene African Anthropoidea. *International Journal of Primatology* 1:21–37.

Kay, R., Thorington, R., Jr., & Houde, P. (1990). Eocene plesiadapiform shows affinities with flying lemurs not primates. *Nature* 345:342–344.

Leakey, M., & Hay, R. (1979). Pliocene footprints in the Laetolil Beds at Laetoli, northern Tanzania. *Nature* 278:317–323.

Martin, L. (1985). Significance of enamel thickness in hominoid evolution. *Nature* 314:260–263.

Martin, R. D. (1990). Some relatives take a dive. *Nature,* 345:291–292.

Morgan, E. (1972). *The descent of woman.* New York: Stein & Day.

Olson, T. (1981). Basicranial morphology of the extant hominoids and Pliocene hominids: The new material from the Hadar Formation, Ethiopia, and its significance in early human evolution and taxonomy. In C.

Stringer (Ed.), *Aspects of human evolution* (pp. 99–128) London: Taylor and Francis.

Olson, T. (1985). Taxonomic affinities of the immature hominid crania from Hadar and Taung. *Nature* 316:539–540.

Pilbeam, D. (1968). The earliest hominids. *Nature* 219:1335–1338.

Pilbeam, D. (1982). New hominoid skull material from the miocene of Pakistan. *Nature* 295:232–234.

Potts, R. (1988). *Early hominid activities at Olduvai.* Hawthorne, NY: Aldine de Gruyter.

Reader, J. (1988). *Missing Links* (2d ed.). New York: Viking Penguin.

Shea, B. T. (1989). Heterochrony in human evolution: The case for neoteny reconsidered. *Yearbook of Physical Anthropology* 32:69–101.

Simons, E. (1989). Human origins. *Science* 245:1343–1350.

Simons, E., & Ettel, P. (1970). *Gigantopithecus. Scientific American* 222:76–85.

Skelton, R., McHenry, H., & Drawhorn, G. (1986). Phylogenetic analysis of early hominids. *Current Anthropology* 27:21–43.

Susman, R. L. (1988). Hand of *Paranthropus robustus* from Member 1, Swartkrans: Fossil evidence for tool behavior. *Science* 240:781–784.

Szalay, F., Rosenberger, A., & Dagosto, M. (1987). Diagnosis and differentiation of the order Primates. *Yearbook of Physical Anthropology* 30:75–105.

Tague, R., & Lovejoy, C. O. (1986). The obstetric pelvis of A. L. 288–1 (Lucy). *Journal of Human Evolution* 15:237–256.

Tuttle, R. H. (1988). What's new in African paleoanthropology? *Annual Review of Anthropology* 17:391–426.

Walker, A., & Andrews, P. (1973). Reconstruction of the dental arcades of *Ramapithecus wickeri. Nature* 244:313–314.

Walker, A., & Leakey, R. (1978). The hominids of East Turkana. *Scientific American* 239:54–66.

Walker, A., Leakey, R., Harris, J., & Brown, F. (1986). 2.5 myr *Australopithecus boisei* from west of Lake Turkana, Kenya. *Nature* 322:517–522.

Walker, A., & Teaford, M. (1989). The hunt for *Proconsul. Scientific American* 260:76–82.

Chapter 12

Adavasio, J. M., Donahue, J., & Stuckenrath, R. (1990). The Meadowcroft Rockshelter radiocarbon chronology 1975–1990. *American Antiquity* 55:348–354.

Arensburg, B., Tillier, A., Vandermeersch, B., Duday, H., Schepartz, L., & Rak, Y. (1989). A Middle Paleolithic human hyoid bone. *Nature* 338:758–760.

Binford, L. R. (1973). Interassemblage variability—the Mousterian and the "functional" argument. In C. Renfrew (Ed.), *The explanation of culture change: Models in prehistory* (pp. 227–254) Pittsburgh, PA: University of Pittsburgh Press.

Binford, L. R. (1981). *Bones: ancient men and modern myths.* New York: Academic Press.

Bordes, F. (1972). *A tale of two caves.* New York: Harper & Row.

Bordes, F. (1968). *The old stone age.* New York: McGraw-Hill.

Brain, C. K., & Sillen, A. (1988). Evidence from the Swartkrans cave for the earliest use of fire. *Nature* 336:464–466.

Bray, W. (1986). Finding the earliest Americans. *Nature* 321:726.

Bray, W. (1988). The Paleoindian debate. *Nature* 332:107.

Breuil, H. (1952). *Four hundred centuries of cave art.* Montignac, France: Centre d'études et de documentation préhistoriques.

Brown, F., Harris, J., Leakey, R., & Walker, A. (1985). Early *Homo erec-*

tus skeleton from west Lake Turkana, Kenya. *Nature* 316:788–792.

Bunn, H. (1981). Archaeological evidence for meat-eating by Plio-Pleistocene hominids from Koobi Fora and Olduvai Gorge. *Nature* 291:574–577.

Cann, R., Stoneking, M., & Wilson, A. (1987). Mitochondrial DNA and human evolution. *Nature* 325:31–36.

Chase, P., & Dibble, H. (1987). Middle Paleolithic symbolism: A review of current evidence and interpretations. *Journal of Anthropological Archaeology* 6:263–296.

Conkey, M. (1987). New approaches in the search for meaning: A review of research in "Paleolithic art". *Journal of Field Archaeology* 14:413–430.

Cuppy, W. (1931). *How to tell your friends from the apes.* New York: Horace Liveright.

Dibble, H. (1987). The interpretation of Middle Paleolithic scraper morphology. *American Antiquity* 52:109–117.

Fagan, B. M. (1987). *The great journey: The peopling of ancient America.* New York: Thames & Hudson.

Isaac, G. (1978). The food-sharing behaviour of protohuman hominids. *Scientific American* 238:90–108.

Jennings, J. D. (1989). *Prehistory of North America.* (3d edition) New York: McGraw-Hill.

Johansen, D., Masao, F., Eck, G., White, T., Walter, R., Kimbel, W., Asfaw, B., Manega, P., Ndessokia, P., & Suwa, G. (1987). New partial skeleton of *Homo habilis* from Olduvai Gorge, Tanzania. *Nature* 327:205–209.

Jones, R. (1987). Pleistocene life in the dead heart of Australia. *Nature* 328:666.

Leroi-Gourhan, A. (1968). The evolution of Paleolithic art. *Scientific American* 218:59–70.

de Lumley, H. (1969). A Paleolithic camp at Nice. *Scientific American* 220:42–50.

MacNeish, R. S. (1976). Early man in the New World. *American Scientist* 64:316–327.

Marshall, E. (1990). Clovis counterrevolution. *Science* 249:738–741.

Mead, J. I., & Meltzer, D. J. (Eds.). (1985). *Environments and extinctions: Man in late glacial North America.* Orono, ME: Center for the Study of Early Man, University of Maine at Orono.

Mellars, P. (1986). A new chronology for the French Mousterian period. *Nature* 322:410–411.

Mellars, P. (1989). Major issues in the emergence of modern humans. *Current Anthropology* 30:349–385.

McBrearty, S. (1990). The origin of modern humans. *Man* 25:129–143.

Morell, V. (1990). Confusion in earliest America. *Science* 248:439–441.

Pfeiffer, J. (1982). *The creative explosion: An inquiry into the origins of art and religion.* New York: Harper & Row.

Potts, R. (1984). Home bases and early hominids. *American Scientist* 72:338–347.

Rolland, N., & Dibble, H. (1990). A new synthesis of Middle Paleolithic variability. *American Antiquity,* 55:480–499.

Rosenberg, K. (1988). The functional significance of Neandertal pubic length. *Current Anthropology* 29:595–617.

Solecki, R. S. (1971). *Shanidar, the first flower people.* New York: Knopf.

Smith, F., & Spencer, F. (Eds.). (1984). *The origins of modern humans: A world survey of the fossil evidence.* New York: Alan R. Liss.

Straus, W., Jr., & Cave, A. (1957). Pathology and the posture of Neanderthal man. *Quarterly Review of Biology* 32:348–363.

Stringer, C., & Andrews, P. (1988). Genetic and fossil evidence for the origin of modern humans. *Science* 239:1263–1268.

Toth, N. (1987). The first technology. *Scientific American* 256:112–121.

Trinkaus, E., & Howells, W. (1979). The Neanderthals. *Scientific American* 241:118–134.

Vandiver, P., Soffer, O., Klima, B., & Svoboda, J. (1989). The origins of ceramic technology at Dolni Vestonice, Czechoslovakia. *Science* 246:1002–1008.

Vigilant, L., Pennington, R., Harpending, H., Kocher, T., & Wilson, A. (1989). Mitochondrial DNA sequences in single hairs from a southern African population. *Proceedings of the National Academy of Science* 86:9350–9354.

Walker, A., Zimmerman, M., & Leakey, R. (1982). A possible case of hypervitaminosis A in *Homo erectus*. *Nature* 296:248–250.

White, J., & O'Connell, J. (1979). Australian prehistory: New aspects of antiquity. *Science* 203:21–28.

White, R. (1989). Visual thinking in the Ice Age. *Scientific American* 261:92–99.

Chapter 13

Bender, B. (1975). *Farming in prehistory: From hunter-gatherer to food-producer*. New York: St. Martin's Press.

Binford, L. (1968). Post-Pleistocene adaptations. In S. R. Binford & L. R. Binford (Eds.), *New Perspectives in Archaeology* (pp. 313–341). Chicago: Aldine.

Boserup, E. (1965). *The conditions of agricultural growth; the economics of agrarian change under population pressure*. New York: Aldine.

Braidwood, R. J. (1960). The agricultural revolution. *Scientific American* 203:130–148.

Braidwood, R. J. (1971). The earliest village communities of southwestern Asia reconsidered. In S. Streuver (Ed.), *Prehistoric agriculture* (pp. 236–251). Garden City, NY: Natural History Press.

Braun, D. P., & Plog, S. J. (1982). Evolution of 'tribal' social networks: Theory and prehistoric North American evidence. *American Antiquity* 47:504–525.

Childe, V. G. (1939). *Man makes himself*. New York: Oxford University Press.

Cohen, M. N. (1977). *The food crisis in prehistory: Overpopulation and the origins of agriculture*. New Haven, CT: Yale University Press.

Cohen, M. N., & Armelagos, G. J. (1984). Paleopathology at the origins of agriculture: Editors' summation. In M. N. Cohen & G. J. Armelagos (Eds.), *Paleopathology at the origins of agriculture* (pp. 585–601). New York: Academic Press.

Flannery, K. V. (1965). The ecology of early food production in Mesopotamia. *Science* 147:1247–1256.

Flannery, K. V. (1971). Origins and ecological effects of early domestication in Iran and the Near East. In S. Streuver (Ed.), *Prehistoric agriculture* (pp. 50–79). Garden City, NY: Natural History Press.

Flannery, K. V. (1973). The origins of agriculture. *Annual Review of Anthropology* 2:271–310.

Goodman, A. H., Lallo, J., Armelagos, G. J., & Rose, J. C. (1984). Health changes at Dickson Mounds, Illinois (AD 950–1300). In M. N. Cohen & G. J. Armelagos (Eds.), *Paleopathology at the origins of agriculture* (pp. 271–305). New York: Academic Press.

Harris, D. R. (1972). The origins of agriculture in the tropics. *American Scientist* 60:180–193.

Hassan, F. A. (1974). Population growth and cultural evolution. *Reviews in Anthropology* 1:205–212.

Hassan, F. A. (1981). *Demographic archaeology*. New York: Academic Press.

Heiser, C. B. (1981). *Seed to civilization: The story of food* (2d ed.). San Francisco: W. H. Freeman.

Hole, F., & McCorriston, J. (in press). Seasonality, speciation and sedentism: The origins of agriculture in the Near East. *American Anthropologist* 93.

Jennings, J. D. (Ed.). (1983). *Ancient North Americans*. San Francisco: W. H. Freeman.

Legge, A. J., & Rowley-Conwy, P.A. (1986). Gazelle killing in Stone Age Syria. *Scientific American* 257:88–95.

MacNeish, R. S. (1971). Ancient Mesoamerican civilization. In S. Streuver (Ed.), *Prehistoric agriculture* (pp. 143–156). Garden City, NY: Natural History Press.

MacNeish, R. S., Fowler, M. L., Cook, A. G., Peterson, F. A., Nelken-Terner, A. & Neely, J. A. (Eds.). (1972). *The prehistory of the Tehuacan Valley. Vol. 5: Excava-tions and reconnaissance*. Austin: University of Texas Press.

Moore, A. M. (1979). A pre-Neolithic farmers' village on the Euphrates. *Scientific American* 241:62–70.

Rindos, D. (1984). *The origins of agriculture: An evolutionary perspective*. Orlando, FL: Academic Press.

Roosevelt, A. C. (1984). Population, health, and the evolution of subsistence: Conclusions from the conference. In M. N. Cohen & G. J. Armelagos (Eds.), *Paleopathology at the origins of agriculture* (pp. 559–583). New York: Academic Press.

Simmons, A. H., Kohler-Rollefson, I., Rollefson, G. O., Mandel, R., & Kafafi, Z. (1988). 'Ain Ghazal: A major Neolithic settlement in central Jordan. *Science* 240:35–39.

Young, T. C., & Smith, P. E. (1966). Research in the prehistory of central West Iran. *Science* 153:386–391.

Chapter 14

Adams, R. M. (1966). *The evolution of urban society: Early Mesopotamia and prehispanic Mexico*. Chicago: Aldine.

Cantrell, J. P. (1986). *Ancient Mexico: Cultural traditions in the land of the feathered serpent* (2nd ed.). Dubuque, IA: Kendall/Hunt Publishing.

Carneiro, R. L. (1970). A theory of the origin of the state. *Science* 169:733–738.

Carneiro, R. L. (1988). The circumscription theory: Challenge and response. *American Behavioral Scientist* 31(4):497–511.

Childe, V. G. (1950). The urban revolution. *Town Planning Review* 21:3–17.

Cohen, R. & Service, E. R. (Eds.). (1978). *Origins of the state: The anthropology of political evolution.* Philadelphia, PA: Institute for the Study of Human Issues.

Flannery, K. V. (1972). The cultural evolution of civilizations. *Annual Review of Ecology and Systematics* 3:399–426.

Flannery, K. V. (Ed.) (1976). *The early Mesoamerican village.* New York: Academic Press.

Fried, M. H. (1967). *The evolution of political society: an essay in political anthropology.* New York: Random House.

Mellaart, J. (1975). *The Neolithic of the Near East.* London: Thames and Hudson.

Netting, R. M. (1986). *Cultural ecology.* (2d ed.). Prospect Heights, Ill: Waveland Press.

Rathje, W. L. (1971). The origin and development of lowland Classic Maya civilization. *American Antiquity* 36:275–285.

Redman, C. L. (1978). *The rise of civilization: From early farmers to urban society in the ancient Near East.* San Francisco, CA: W. H. Freeman.

Roosevelt, A. C. (1991). *Moundbuilders of the Amazon.* San Diego: Academic Press.

Service, E. R. (1975). *Origins of the state and civilization: The process of cultural evolution.* New York: Norton.

Singh, P. (1974). *Neolithic cultures of western Asia.* New York: Seminar Press.

Weaver, M. P. (1981). *The Aztecs, Maya, and their predecessors: Archaeology of Mesoamerica.* (2d ed.). New York: Academic Press.

Wenke, R. J. (1990). *Patterns in prehistory: Humankind's first three million years* (3d ed.). New York: Oxford University Press.

Wittfogel, K. A. (1957). *Oriental despotism; a comparative study of total power.* New Haven, CT: Yale University Press.

Wright, H. T. (1977). Recent research on the origin of the state. *Annual Review of Anthropology* 6:379–397.

Chapter 15

Buchanon, R. A. (1965). *Technology and social progress.* Oxford, England: Pergamon.

Carver, M. (1987). *Underneath English towns: Interpreting urban archaeology.* London: D. T. Batsford.

Deetz, J. (1977). *In small things forgotten: The archaeology of early American life.* Garden City, NY: Anchor Press/Doubleday.

Deetz, J. (1988). American historical archeology: Methods and results. *Science* 239:362–367.

Hawke, D. F. (1988). *Everyday life in early America.* New York: Harper & Row.

Heer, F. (1962). *The medieval world.* London: Weidenfeld and Nicolson.

Hollister, C. W. (1982). *Medieval Europe: A short history.* (5th ed.). New York: Wiley.

Mathias, P. (1983). *The first industrial nation: An economic history of Britain, 1700–1914.* (2d ed.). New York: Methuen.

Noel Hume, I. (1969). *Historical archaeology.* New York: Knopf.

Noel Hume, I. (1982). *Martin's Hundred.* New York: Knopf.

Rowling, M. (1979). *Life in medieval times.* New York: Perigee.

Schuyler, R. (1970). Historical and historic sites archaeology as anthropology: Basic definitions and relationships. *Historical Archaeology* 4:83–89.

South, S. (Ed.). (1977). *Research strategies in historical archeology.* New York: Academic Press.

Staski, E. (1984). *Beneath the border city. Vol. 1: Urban archaeology in downtown El Paso.* Las Cruces, NM: New Mexico State University Museum Occasional Papers #12.

Staski, E. (1985). *Beneath the Border City. Vol. 2: The Chinese in El Paso.* Las Cruces, NM: New Mexico State University Museum Occasional Papers #13.

Wolf, E. R. (1982). *Europe and the people without history.* Berkeley: University of California Press.

Chapter 16

Binford, L. R. (1967). Smudge pits and hide smoking: The use of analogy in archaeological reasoning. *American Antiquity* 32:1–12.

Binford, L. R. (1978). Dimensional analysis of behavior and site structure: Learning from an Eskimo hunting stand. *American Antiquity* 43:330–361.

Binford, L. R. (1986). An Alyawara day: making men's knives and beyond. *American Antiquity* 51:547–562.

Coles, J. M. (1979). *Experimental archaeology.* New York: Academic Press.

Crabtree, D. E. (1968). Mesoamerican polyhedral cores and prismatic blades. *American Antiquity* 33:446–478.

Fisher, J. W., & Strickland, H.C. (1989). Ethnoarchaeology among the Efe pygmies, Zaire: Spatial organization of campsites. *American Journal of Physical Anthropology* 78:473–484.

Gould, R. A. (1978). The anthropology of human residues. *American Anthropologist* 80:815–835.

Gould, R. A. (1980). *Living archaeology.* New York: Cambridge University Press.

Jewell, P. A., & Dimbleby, G. W. (Eds.). (1966). The experimental earthwork on Overton Down, Wiltshire, England: The first four years. *Proceedings of the Prehistoric Society* 32:313–342.

Kramer, C. (Ed.). (1979). *Ethnoarchaeology: Implications of ethnography for archaeology*. New York: Columbia University Press.

Longacre, W. (1981). Kalinga pottery: An ethnoarchaeological study. In I. Hodder, G. Isaac, & N. Hammond (Eds.), *Pattern of the past* (pp. 49–66). New York: Cambridge University Press.

Netting, R. M., Wilk, R. R., & Arnold, E. J. (Eds.) (1984). *Households: Comparative and historical studies of the domestic group*. Berkeley: University of California Press.

Rathje, W. L. (1979). Modern material culture studies. In M. B. Schiffer (Ed.), *Advances in archaeological method and theory: Vol. 2* (pp. 1–37). New York: Academic Press.

Rathje, W. L. (1989). Rubbish! *The Atlantic Monthly* (Dec.): 99–109.

Staski, E. (1984). Just what can a 19th century bottle tell us? *Historical Archaeology* 18:38–51.

Yellen, J. (1977). *Archaeological approaches to the present: Models for reconstructing the past*. New York: Academic Press.

Chapter 17

Begley, S., et al. (1987). All about twins. *Newsweek* (23 Nov.):58–69.

Boone, J. L., III. (1986). Parental investment and elite family structure in preindustrial states: A case-study of late medieval–early modern Portuguese genealogies. *American Anthropologist* 88:859–878.

Brues, A. (1959). The spearman and the archer. *American Anthropologist* 61:457–469.

Brues, A. (1977). *People and races*. New York: Macmillan.

Capron, C., & Duyme, M. (1989). Assessment of effects of socio-economic status on IQ in a full cross-fostering study. *Nature* 340:552–554.

Durham, W. (1984). Testing the malaria hypothesis in West Africa. In J. E. Bowman (Ed.), *Distribution and evolution of hemoglobin and globin loci* (pp. 45–76). New York: Elsevier.

Gajdusek, D. C. (1977). Unconventional viruses and the origin and disappearance of kuru. *Science* 197:943–960.

Hausfater, G., & Blaffer Hrdy, S. (1985). *Infanticide*. Hawthorne, NY: Aldine.

Lang, J. S. (1987). How genes shape personality. *US News and World Report*, April 13:58–66.

McEvedy, C. (1988). The bubonic plague. *Scientific American* 258(2):118–123.

McNeill, W. H. (1976). *Plagues and peoples*. Garden City, NY: Anchor Press.

Trivers, R. L., & Willard, D. (1973). Natural selection of parental ability to vary the sex ratio of offspring. *Science* 179:90–92.

Wurtman, R. J., & Wurtman, J. J. (1989). Carbohydrates and depression. *Scientific American* 260(1):68–75.

Zerubavel, E. (1985). *The seven-day circle*. New York: Free Press.

Chapter 18

Bastide, R. (1971). *Anthropologie appliquée*. Paris: Payot.

Bodley, J. H. (1976). *Anthropology and contemporary human problems*. Menlo Park, CA: Cummings Publishing Co.

Bodley, J. H. (1982). *Victims of progress* (2d ed.). Palo Alto, CA: Mayfield Publishing Co.

Foster, G. M., & Anderson, B. G. (1978). *Medical anthropology*. New York: Wiley.

Goldschmidt, W. (Ed.). (1979). *The uses of anthropology*. Washington, DC: American Anthropological Association.

Harris, M. (1981). *America now: The anthropology of a changing culture*. New York: Simon and Schuster.

King, T. F., Hickman, P. P., & Berg, G. (1977). *Anthropology in historic preservation: Caring for culture's clutter*. New York: Academic Press.

Lipe, W. D. (1974). A conservation model for American archaeology. *The Kiva* 39(3–4):214–245.

Schiffer, M. B., & House, J. H. (1977). Cultural resource management and archaeological research: The cache project. *Current Anthropology* 18:43–68.

Schiffer, M. B., & Gumerman, G. J. (Eds.). (1977). *Conservation archaeology: A guide for cultural resource management studies*. New York: Academic Press.

Index

Page numbers in **boldface** indicate terms defined in the marginal glossary.

PHOTO CREDITS

Cover COMSTOCK/George Lepp.

Part Openers **p. 1**, Milton Mann/Cameramann International. **p. 151**, Dan McCoy/Rainbow. **p. 233**, Custom Medical Stock. **p. 361**, COMSTOCK/Michael Stuckey. **p. 489**, Eric Lessing/Photo Edit. **p. 609**, James Newberry, c/o East Texas State University Photography Dept., Commerce, Texas.

Chapter 1 **p. 6**, (upper left) Ed Staski/Jon Marks; (upper right) Angelique Hagerod; (center right) Meredith Small; (lower) Mexican National Tourist Council, Houston, Texas. **p. 7**, (upper left) Union Pacific Railroad; (lower left) Gary Stewart/Wide World Photos; (lower right) Gerard, *The Baptism of Christ*, Art Resources/Foto Marburg, Bruges, City Museum. **p. 9**, Original drawing by Sarah Landry. Reprinted by permission of the publishers from *The Insect Societies* by Edward O. Wilson, Cambridge, MA, The Belknap Press of Harvard University Press. Copyright © 1971 by the President and Fellows of Harvard College. **p. 13**, COMSTOCK/George Gerster. **p. 15**, Barry Iverson, Time, Inc. **p. 16**, Michael le Poer Trench/Time, Inc.

Chapter 2 **p. 32**, Joni Quenenmoen. **p. 36**, (upper left/[a]) Ninth-century B.C. Assyrian bas-relief, photo: Joseph Szaszfai/Yale University Art Gallery; (upper middle/[b]) Luca Signorelli, (Italian 1441–1523), *Adoration of the Magi*, egg tempera on panel, 13¾ × 17¼ inches, Yale University Art Gallery, James Jackson Jarves Collection; (upper right/[d]) 1961.18.34, Vincent van Gogh, (Dutch 1853–1890), *Night Cafe*, oil on canvas, 1883, 28½ × 36¼ inches, request of Stephen Carlton Clark, B.A. 1903, Yale University Art Gallery; (lower left/[e]) 1976.36, Winslow Homer (1836–1910), American XIX Century, *Deer Drinking*, watercolor, 14⅛ × 20⅛ inches, The Robert W. Carle Fund, Yale University Art Gallery; (lower middle/[c]) 1954.28.10, African: Senufo, Ivory Coast, Wooden Male Figure, h. 9⅞ inches, Yale University Art Gallery, gift of Mr. and Mrs. James M. Osborn for the Linton Collection of African Art; (lower right/[f]) 1958.27, Picasso, Pablo, (Spanish, 1881–1973), *First Steps*, oil on canvas, 1943, signed upper right corner, "Picasso", 51¼ × 38½ inches, (130.2 × 97.1 cm), Gift of Stephen C. Clark, BA 1903, Yale University Art Gallery. **p. 40**, "Ah, ha, just as I expected" from *Einstein Simplified* by Sidney Harris. Copyright © 1983 by Sidney Harris, New Haven, CT. **p. 41**, (upper) Ed Staski; (lower) York Archeological Trust, York, England. **p. 44**, Courtesy U.S. Department of the Interior/National Parks Service. **p. 45**, American Museum of Natural History. **p. 46**, (upper) Ed Staski; (lower) Fig. 3, Staski, "Surface and Subsurface Patterns of Archaeological Materials at Fort Fillmore, New Mexico," *North American Archaeologist*, (v. 10[3]:205:225, Surface survey and collection grids). Copyright © Baywood Publishing, Amityville, NY. **p. 48**, profile from Tepe Sabz, *Prehistory and Human Ecology of the Del Luran Plain*, by Hole, Flannery and Neely. Copyright © 1969 by Hole, Flannery and Neely. Reprinted by permission of Kent Flannery, Museum of Anthropology Publications, Ruthven Museums, University of Michigan, Ann Arbor. **p. 49**, David Hurst Thomas/American Museum of Natural History. **p. 49**, Ed Staski/Jon Marks. **p. 53**, Fig. 10–8, pp. 333, "Creating a frequency seriation by hand," courtesy Nicholas Amorosi, from *Archeology*, Second Edition, by David Thomas. Copyright © 1989 by Holt, Rinehart and Winston, Inc. Reprinted by permission of Harcourt Brace Jovanovich, Inc. **p. 54**, Courtesy the American Museum of Natural History. **p. 59**, (left and right) Ed Staski/Jon Marks. **p. 60**, AP/Wide World Photos.

Chapter 3 **p. 67**, (left and right) Yale University Library. **p. 68**, (lower left, upper right) Yale University Library. **p. 70**, Yale University Library. **p. 72**, Yale University Library. **p. 73**, Yale University Library. **p. 76**, Yale University Library. **p. 77**, (left and right) Yale University Library. **p. 79**, (upper) Yale University Library; (right) James P. Blair, *National Geographic*, April 1965, p. 520. Copyright © 1965 by The National Geographic Society. **p. 83**, Bettmann Archive. **p. 86**, Yale University Library. **p. 88**, Yale University Library. **p. 89**, Yale University Library. **p. 94**, Yale University Library. **p. 100**, Yale University Library. **p. 102**, Bettmann Archive.